Management and Cost Accounting

Instructor's Manual

COLIN DRURY

Management and Cost Accounting

SIXTH EDITION

Instructor's Manual

THOMSON

Australia • Canada • Mexico • Singapore • Spain • United Kingdom • United States

THOMSON

Management and Cost Accounting, 6th edition: Instructors Manual

Copyright © 2004 Colin Drury

The Thomson logo is a registered trademark used herein under licence.

For more information, contact Thomson Learning, High Holborn House,
50-51 Bedford Row, London WC1R 4LR or visit us on the World Wide Web at:
http://www.thomsonlearning.co.uk

British Library Cataloguing-in-Publication Data
A catalogue record for this book is available from the British Library

ISBN 1-84480-032-6

First edition published by Chapman & Hall 1985
Second edition published by Chapman & Hall 1988
Third edition published by Chapman & Hall 1992
Fourth edition published by International Thomson Business Press 1996
Fourth edition (revised) published by International Thomson Business Press 1999
Fifth edition published by Thomson Learning 2000
Sixth edition published by Thomson Learning 2004
Reprinted by Thomson Learning 2004

Typeset by Saxon Graphics Ltd, Derby
Printed by TJI Digital, Padstow, Cornwall

Contents

Preface   vii

Part I Questions   1

An introduction to cost terms and concepts   3
Cost assignment   6
Accounting entries for a job costing system   15
Process costing   22
Joint and by-product costing   30
Income effects of alternative cost accumulation systems   37
Cost-volume-profit analysis   45
Measuring relevant costs and revenues for decision-making   53
Activity-based costing   65
Pricing decisions and profitability analysis   71
Decision-making under conditions of risk and uncertainty   80
Capital investment decisions: 1   89
Capital investment decisions: 2   96
The budgeting process   108
Management control systems   116
Standard costing and variance analysis: 1   128
Standard costing and variance analysis: 2   139
Divisional financial performance measures   149
Transfer pricing in divisionalized companies   160
Cost management   169
Strategic management accounting   173
Cost estimation and cost behaviour   178
Quantitative models for the planning and control of inventories   185
The application of linear programming to management accounting   191

Part II Solutions   201

An introduction to cost terms and concepts   203
Cost assignment   205
Accounting entries for a job costing system   217
Process costing   227
Joint and by-product costing   245
Income effects of alternative cost accumulation systems   258
Cost-volume-profit analysis   267
Measuring relevant costs and revenues for decision-making   277
Activity-based costing   291
Pricing decisions and profitability analysis   299
Decision-making under conditions of risk and uncertainty   314
Capital investment decisions: 1   326
Capital investment decisions: 2   336
The budgeting process   354
Management control systems   362
Standard costing and variance analysis: 1   377
Standard costing and variance analysis: 2   392
Divisional financial performance measures   410
Transfer pricing in divisionalized companies   426
Cost management   440

Strategic management accounting   444
Cost estimation and cost behaviour   449
Quantitative models for the planning and control of inventories   458
The application of linear programming to management accounting   469

Part III Case study teaching note   485

Teaching Note: EVA at Ault Foods Limited   487

Preface

This manual is complementary to the main book, *Management and Cost Accounting*, and the *Student's Manual to Management and Cost Accounting*. The aim of the main text is to focus on the *application* of the principles to a wide range of problems.

It is essential that the student works through a wide range of problems to gain experience on the application of principles, but generally there is insufficient class-room time for tutorial guidance. The Students' Manual provides this guidance by enabling the student to work independently on problems and referring to the suggested solutions.

The Instructor's Manual provides solutions which are not generally available to students. The objective is to provide tutors with feedback information on the student's ability to solve problems independently. A short description of each question is given to enable tutors to select questions which are appropriate to specific courses.

Although the main text is conceived and developed as a unified whole, it can be tailored to the individual requirements of a course and to the preferences of the tutor concerned. If you wish to concentrate on management accounting rather than cost accounting then Chapters 4–7 in Part Two can be omitted as the remaining chapters do not rely heavily on this part of the book.

Alternatively the cost accounting Chapters 4–7 in Part Two can be delayed until Parts Three, Four and Five have been completed. If you wish a student to gain an insight into cost accounting but without an in-depth study then Chapters 3 and 7 should be assigned.

Chapters 24–26 examine the application of quantitative techniques to management accounting and have been delayed until Part Six. An alternative approach would be to assign Chapter 24 'Cost estimation and cost behaviour' immediately after Chapter 8 on 'Cost–Volume–Profit analysis' or after Chapter 16 which includes 'Flexible budgeting'. Chapter 25 'Quantitative models for planning and control of stocks' is self-contained and may be assigned to follow any of the Chapters in Part Three. Chapter 26 should be read after Chapter 19 has been completed. The following are suggested programmes for various courses.

A two year management accounting course for undergraduates
Part One, Chapter 3 (Part Two) and Parts Three to Six. If instructors wish to provide a short course on cost accounting then Chapters 4–7 from Part Two can also be assigned.

A one year degree or post-experience course in management accounting
Part One, Chapter 3 (Part Two), Part Three (the non-advanced reading sections within Chapters 8–13) and Part Four (non-advanced reading sections within Chapters 15, 16, 18, 20 and 21).

Foundation intermediate professional accountancy examination with a major emphasis on cost accounting
All of Parts One and Two, Chapters 8 and 9 of Part Three plus the non-advanced reading sections in Chapters 15, 16, 18 and 19 of Part Four.

Professional accounting examinations at the professional or advanced level
Revision of the prescribed reading for the intermediate/foundation level plus the remaining chapters of the book.

Part I

Questions

An introduction to cost terms and concepts

For the relevant cost data in items (1)–(7), indicate which of the following is the best classification.

Question IM 2.1 Intermediate: Cost classification

  (a) sunk cost   (d) fixed cost   (g) controllable cost
  (b) incremental cost   (e) semi-variable cost   (h) non-controllable cost
  (c) variable cost   (f) semi-fixed cost   (i) opportunity cost

  (1) A company is considering selling an old machine. The machine has a book value of £20 000. In evaluating the decision to sell the machine, the £20 000 is a ...
  (2) As an alternative to the old machine, the company can rent a new one. It will cost £3000 a year. In analysing the cost–volume behaviour the rental is a ...
  (3) To run the firm's machines, here are two alternative courses of action. One is to pay the operator a base salary plus a small amount per unit produced. This makes the total cost of the operators a ...
  (4) As an alternative, the firm can pay the operators a flat salary. It would then use one machine when volume is low, two when it expands, and three during peak periods. This means that the total operator cost would now be a ...
  (5) The machine mentioned in (1) could be sold for £8000. If the firm considers retaining and using it, the £8000 is a ...
  (6) If the firm wishes to use the machine any longer, it must be repaired. For the decision to retain the machine, the repair cost is a ...
  (7) The machine is charged to the foreman of each department at a rate of £3000 a year. In evaluating the foreman, the charge is a ...

A company manufactures and retails clothing. You are required to group the costs which are listed below and numbered (1)–(20) into the following classifications (each cost is intended to belong to only one classification):

Question IM 2.2 Intermediate: Cost classification

   (i) direct materials
  (ii) direct labour
 (iii) direct expenses
 (iv) indirect production overhead
  (v) research and development costs
 (vi) selling and distribution costs
 (vii) administration costs
(viii) finance costs

  (1) Lubricant for sewing machines
  (2) Floppy disks for general office computer
  (3) Maintenance contract for general office photocopying machine
  (4) Telephone rental plus metered calls
  (5) Interest on bank overdraft
  (6) Performing Rights Society charge for music broadcast throughout the factory
  (7) Market research undertaken prior to a new product launch
  (8) Wages of security guards for factory
  (9) Carriage on purchase of basic raw material
 (10) Royalty payable on number of units of product XY produced
 (11) Road fund licences for delivery vehicles
 (12) Parcels sent to customers
 (13) Cost of advertising products on television

(14) Audit fees
(15) Chief accountant's salary
(16) Wages of operatives in the cutting department
(17) Cost of painting advertising slogans on delivery vans
(18) Wages of storekeepers in materials store
(19) Wages of fork lift truck drivers who handle raw materials
(20) Developing a new product in the laboratory

(10 marks)
CIMA Cost Accounting 1

Question IM 2.3
Intermediate:
Analysis of costs
by behaviour for
decision-making

The Northshire Hospital Trust operates two types of specialist X-ray scanning machines, XR1 and XR50. Details for the next period are estimated as follows:

Machine	XR1	XR50
Running hours	1100	2000
	(£)	(£)
Variable running costs (excluding plates)	27 500	64 000
Fixed costs	20 000	97 500

A brain scan is normally carried out on machine type XR1: this task uses special X-ray plates costing £40 each and takes four hours of machine time. Because of the nature of the process, around 10% of the scans produce blurred and therefore useless results.

Required:
(a) Calculate the cost of a satisfactory brain scan on machine type XR1.   (7 marks)
(b) Brain scans can also be done on machine type XR50 and would take only 1.8 hours per scan with a reduced reject rate of 6%. However, the cost of the X-ray plates would be £55 per scan.

Required:
Advise which type should be used, assuming sufficient capacity is available on both types of machine.   (8 marks)
(Total marks 15)
CIMA Stage 1 Cost Accounting

Question IM 2.4
Intermediate:
Product cost
calculation

From the information given below you are required to:
(a) prepare a standard cost sheet for one unit and enter on the standard cost sheet the costs to show sub-totals for:
    (i)   prime cost
    (ii) variable production cost
    (iii) total production cost
    (iv) total cost
(b) calculate the selling price per unit allowing for a profit of 15% of the selling price.

The following data are given:

Budgeted output for the year   9800 units
Standard details for one unit:
Direct materials 40 square metres at £5.30 per square metre

Direct wages:
  Bonding department 48 hours at £2.50 per hour
  Finishing department 30 hours at £1.90 per hour
  Budgeted costs and hours per annum:

Variable overhead:	(£)	(hours)
Bonding department	375 000	500 000
Finishing department	150 000	300 000

AN INTRODUCTION TO COST TERMS AND CONCEPTS

Fixed overhead:	(£)	(hours)
Production	392 000	
Selling and distribution	196 000	
Administration	98 000	

(15 marks)
CIMA Cost Accounting 1

Cost assignment

Question IM 3.1
Intermediate

(a) Explain why predetermined overhead absorption rates are preferred to overhead absorption rates calculated from factual information after the end of a financial period.

(b) The production overhead absorption rates of factories X and Y are calculated using similar methods. However, the rate used by factory X is lower than that used by factory Y. Both factories produce the same type of product. You are required to discuss whether or not this can be taken to be a sign that factory X is more efficient than factory Y.

(20 marks)
CIMA Cost Accounting 1

Question IM 3.2
Intermediate

Critically consider the purpose of calculating production overhead absorption rates.

Question IM 3.3
Intermediate

(a) Specify and explain the factors to be considered in determining whether to utilize a single factory-wide recovery rate for all production overheads or a separate rate for each cost centre, production or service department. (12 marks)

(b) Describe three methods of determining fixed overhead recovery rates and specify the circumstances under which each method is superior to the other methods mentioned. (8 marks)

(Total 20 marks)
ACCA P2 Management Accounting

Question IM 3.4
Intermediate:
Overhead
analysis,
calculation of
overhead rate and
overhead charged
to a unit of output

A company makes a range of products with total budgeted manufacturing overheads of £973 560 incurred in three production departments (A, B and C) and one service department.

Department A has 10 direct employees, who each work 37 hours per week.

Department B has five machines, each or which is operated for 24 hours per week.

Department C is expected to produce 148 000 units of final product in the budget period.

The company will operate for 48 weeks in the budget period.

Budgeted overheads incurred directly by each department are:

Production department A	£261 745
Production department B	£226 120
Production department C	£93 890
Service department	£53 305

The balance of budgeted overheads are apportioned to departments as follows:

Production department A	40%
Production department B	35%
Production department C	20%
Service department	5%

Service department overheads are apportioned equally to each production department. You are required to:
(a) Calculate an appropriate predetermined overhead absorption rate in each production department. (9 marks)
(b) Calculate the manufacturing overhead cost per unit of finished product in a batch of 100 units which take 9 direct labour hours in department A and three machine hours in department B to produce. (3 marks)
(12 marks)
ACCA Foundation Paper 3

PTS Limited is a manufacturing company which uses three production departments to make its product. It has the following factory costs which are expected to be incurred in the year to 31 December:

Question IM 3.5 Intermediate: Overhead analysis sheet and calculation of overhead absorption rates

		(£)
Direct wages	Machining	234 980
	Assembly	345 900
	Finishing	134 525
		£
Indirect wages and salaries	Machining	120 354
	Assembly	238 970
	Finishing	89 700

	£
Factory rent	12 685 500
Business rates	3 450 900
Heat and lighting	985 350
Machinery power	2 890 600
Depreciation	600 000
Canteen subsidy	256 000

Other information is available as follows:

	Machining	Assembly	Finishing
Number of employees	50	60	18
Floor space occupied (m²)	1 800	1 400	800
Horse power of machinery	13 000	500	6 500
Value of machinery (£000)	250	30	120
Number of labour hours	100 000	140 000	35 000
Number of machine hours	200 000	36 000	90 000

You are required
(a) to prepare the company's overhead analysis sheet for the year to 31 December;
(9 marks)
(b) to calculate appropriate overhead absorption rates (to two decimal places) for each department. (6 marks)
(Total: 15 marks)
CIMA Stage 1 Accounting

**Question IM 3.6
Intermediate:
Overhead
analysis sheet
and calculation of
overhead rates**

Dunstan Ltd manufactures tents and sleeping bags in three separate production departments. The principal manufacturing processes consist of cutting material in the pattern cutting room, and sewing the material in either the tent or the sleeping bag departments. For the year to 31 July cost centre expenses and other relevant information are budgeted as follows:

	Total (£)	Cutting room (£)	Tents (£)	Sleeping bags (£)	Raw material stores (£)	Canteen (£)	Main-tenance (£)
Indirect wages	147 200	6 400	19 500	20 100	41 200	15 000	45 000
Consumable materials	54 600	5 300	4 100	2 300	—	18 700	24 200
Plant depreciation	84 200	31 200	17 500	24 600	2 500	3 400	5 000
Power	31 700						
Heat and light	13 800						
Rent and rates	14 400						
Building insurance	13 500						
Floor area (sq. ft)	30 000	8 000	10 000	7 000	1 500	2 500	1 000
Estimated power usage (%)	100	17	38	32	3	8	2
Direct labour (hours)	112 000	7 000	48 000	57 000	—	—	—
Machine usage (hours)	87 000	2 000	40 000	45 000	—	—	—
Value of raw material issues (%)	100	62.5	12.5	12.5	—	—	12.5

Requirements:
(a) Prepare in columnar form a statement calculating the overhead absorption rates for each machine hour and each direct labour hour for each of the three production units. You should use bases of apportionment and absorption which you consider most appropriate, and the bases used should be clearly indicated in your statement. (16 marks)
(b) 'The use of pre-determined overhead absorption rates based on budgets is preferable to the use of absorption rates calculated from historical data available after the end of a financial period.'
  Discuss this statement insofar as it relates to the financial management of a business. (5 marks)
(Total 21 marks)
ICAEW PI AC Techniques

**Question IM 3.7
Intermediate:
Computation of
three different
overhead
absorption rates
and a cost-plus
selling price**

A manufacturing company has prepared the following budgeted information for the forthcoming year:

	£
Direct material	800 000
Direct labour	200 000
Direct expenses	40 000
Production overhead	600 000
Administrative overhead	328 000
Budgeted activity levels include:	
Budgeted production units	600 000
Machine hours	50 000
Labour hours	40 000

It has recently spent heavily upon advanced technological machinery and reduced its workforce. As a consequence it is thinking about changing its basis for overhead absorption from a percentage of direct labour cost to either a machine hour or labour hour basis. The administrative overhead is to be absorbed as a percentage of factory cost.

Required:
(a) Prepare pre-determined overhead absorption rates for production overheads based upon the three different bases for absorption mentioned above.
(6 marks)
(b) Outline the reasons for calculating a pre-determined overhead absorption rate.
(2 marks)
(c) Select the overhead absorption rate that you think the organization should use giving reasons for your decision. (3 marks)
(d) The company has been asked to price job AX, this job requires the following:

Direct material	£3788
Direct labour	£1100
Direct expenses	£422
Machine hours	120
Labour hours	220

Compute the price for this job using the absorption rate selected in (c) above, given that the company profit margin is equal to 10% of the price.   (6 marks)
(e) The company previously paid its direct labour workers upon a time basis but is now contemplating moving over to an incentive scheme.
Required:
Draft a memo to the Chief Accountant outlining the general characteristics and advantages of employing a successful incentive scheme. (8 marks)
(Total 25 marks)
AAT Cost Accounting and Budgeting

BEC Limited operates an absorption costing system. Its budget for the year ended 31 December shows that it expects its production overhead expenditure to be as follows:

**Question IM 3.8
Intermediate:
Calculation of
overhead
absorption rates
and under/over-
recovery of
overheads**

	Fixed £	Variable £
Machining department	600 000	480 000
Hand finishing department	360 000	400 000

During the year it expects to make 200 000 units of its product. This is expected to take 80 000 machine hours in the machining department and 120 000 labour hours in the hand finishing department.
The costs and activity are expected to arise evenly throughout the year, and the budget has been used as the basis of calculating the company's absorption rates.
During March the monthly profit statement reported
(i) that the actual hours worked in each department were

Machining	6000 hours
Hand finishing	9600 hours

(ii) that the actual overhead costs incurred were

	Fixed £	Variable £
Machining	48 500	36 000
Hand finishing	33 600	33 500

(iii) that the actual production was 15 000 units.

Required:
(a) Calculate appropriate pre-determined absorption rates for the year ended 31 December
(4 marks)

(b) (i) Calculate the under/over absorption of overhead for each department of the company for March; (4 marks)

    (ii) Comment on the problems of using predetermined absorption rates based on the arbitrary apportionment of overhead costs, with regard to comparisons of actual/target performance; (4 marks)

(c) State the reasons why absorption costing is used by companies. (3 marks)

(Total 15 marks)

CIMA Stage 1 Accounting

Question IM 3.9
Intermediate:
Various overhead
absorption rates

AC Limited is a small company which undertakes a variety of jobs for its customers.

Budgeted profit and loss statement for the year ending 31 December

	(£)	(£)
Sales		750 000
Cost:		
Direct materials	100 000	
Direct wages	50 000	
Prime cost	150 000	
Fixed production overhead	300 000	
Production cost	450 000	
Selling, distribution and administration cost	160 000	
		610 000
Profit		£140 000
Budgeted data:		
Labour hours for the year	25 000	
Machine hours for the year	15 000	
Number of jobs for the year	300	

An enquiry has been received, and the production department has produced estimates of the prime cost involved and of the hours required to complete job A57.

	(£)
Direct materials	250
Direct wages	200
Prime cost	£450
Labour hours required	80
Machine hours required	50

You are required to:

(a) calculate by different methods *six* overhead absorption rates; (6 marks)

(b) comment briefly on the suitability of each method calculated in (a); (8 marks)

(c) calculate cost estimates for job A57 using in turn each of the six overhead absorption rates calculated in (a). (6 marks)

(Total 20 marks)

CIMA Foundation Cost Accounting 1

A company produces several products which pass through the two production departments in its factory. These two departments are concerned with filling and sealing operations. There are two service departments, maintenance and canteen, in the factory.

Predetermined overhead absorption rates, based on direct labour hours, are established for the two production departments. The budgeted expenditure for these departments for the period just ended, including the apportionment of service department overheads, was £110 040 for filling, and £53 300 for sealing. Budgeted direct labour hours were 13 100 for filling and 10 250 for sealing.

Service department overheads are apportioned as follows:

Maintenance	–	Filling	70%
Maintenance	–	Sealing	27%
Maintenance	–	Canteen	3%
Canteen	–	Filling	60%
	–	Sealing	32%
	–	Maintenance	8%

During the period just ended, actual overhead costs and activity were as follows:

	(£)	Direct labour hours
Filling	74 260	12 820
Sealing	38 115	10 075
Maintenance	25 050	
Canteen	24 375	

Required:
(a) Calculate the overheads absorbed in the period and the extent of the under/over absorption in each of the two production departments. (14 marks)
(b) State, and critically assess, the objectives of overhead apportionment and absorption. (11 marks)
(Total 25 marks)
ACCA Level 1 Cost and Management Accounting 1

A large firm of solicitors uses a job costing system to identify costs with individual clients. Hours worked by professional staff are used as the basis for charging overhead costs to client services. A predetermined rate is used, derived from budgets drawn up at the beginning of each year commencing on 1 April.

In the year to 31 March 2000 the overheads of the solicitors' practice, which were absorbed at a rate of £7.50 per hour of professional staff, were over-absorbed by £4760. Actual overheads incurred were £742 600. Professional hours worked were 1360 over budget.

The solicitors' practice has decided to refine its overhead charging system by differentiating between the hours of senior and junior professional staff, respectively. A premium of 40% is to be applied to the hourly overhead rate for senior staff compared with junior staff.

Budgets for the year to 31 March 2001 are as follows:

Senior professional staff hours	21 600
Junior professional staff hours	79 300
Practice overheads	£784 000

Required
(a) Calculate for the year ended 31 March 2000:
    (i) budgeted professional staff hours;
    (ii) budgeted overhead expenditure. (5 marks)

(b) Calculate, for the year ended 31 March 2001, the overhead absorption rates (to three decimal places of a £) to be applied to:
  (i) senior professional staff hours;
  (ii) junior professional staff hours. (4 marks)
(c) How is the change in method of charging overheads likely to improve the firm's job costing system? (3 marks)
(d) Explain briefly why overhead absorbed using predetermined rates may differ from actual overhead incurred for the same period. (2 marks)

(Total 14 marks)
ACCA Foundation Paper 3

Question IM 3.12 Intermediate: Reapportionment of service department costs

JR Co. Ltd's budgeted overheads for the forthcoming period applicable to its production departments, are as follows:

	(£000)
1	870
2	690

The budgeted total costs for the forthcoming period for the service departments, are as follows:

	(£000)
G	160
H	82

The use made of each of the services has been estimated as follows.

	Production department		Service department	
	1	2	G	H
G(%)	60	30	—	10
H(%)	50	30	20	—

Required:
Apportion the service department costs to production departments:
  (i) using the step-wise (elimination) method, starting with G;
  (ii) using the reciprocal (simultaneous equation) method;
  (iii) commenting briefly on your figures. (8 marks)

(Total 20 marks)
ACCA Paper 8 Managerial Finance

Question IM 3.13 Advanced: Reapportionment of service department costs and comments on apportionment and absorption calculation

The Isis Engineering Company operates a job order costing system which includes the use of predetermined overhead absorption rates. The company has two service cost centres and two production cost centres. The production cost centre overheads are charged to jobs via direct labour hour rates which are currently £3.10 per hour in production cost centre A and £11.00 per hour in production cost centre B. The calculations involved in determining these rates have excluded any consideration of the services that are provided by each service cost centre to the other.

The bases used to charge general factory overhead and service cost centre expenses to the production cost centres are as follows:
  (i) general factory overhead is apportioned on the basis of the floor area used by each of the production and service cost centres,
  (ii) the expenses of service cost centre 1 are charged out on the basis of the number of personnel in each production cost centre,
  (iii) the expenses of service cost centre 2 are charged out on the basis of the usage of its services by each production cost centre.

The company's overhead absorption rates are revised annually prior to the beginning of each year, using an analysis of the outcome of the current year and the draft plans and forecasts for the forthcoming year. The revised rates for next year are to be based on the following data:

	General factory overhead	Service cost centres 1	2	Product cost centres A	B
Budgeted overhead for next year (before any reallocation) (£)	210 000	93 800	38 600	182 800	124 800
% of factory floor area	—	5	10	15	70
% of factory personnel	—	10	18	63	9
Estimated usage of services of service cost centre 2 in forthcoming year (hours)	—	1 000	—	4 000	25 000
Budgeted direct labour hours for next year (to be used to calculate next year's absorption rates)	—	—	—	120 000	20 000
Budgeted direct labour hours for current year (these figures were used in the calculation of this year's absorption rates)	—	—	—	100 000	30 000

(a) Ignoring the question of reciprocal charges between the service cost centres, you are required to calculate the revised overhead absorption rates for the two production cost centres. Use the company's established procedures.   (6 marks)

(b) Comment on the extent of the differences between the current overhead absorption rates and those you have calculated in your answer to (a). Set out the likely reasons for these differences.   (4 marks)

(c) Each service cost centre provides services to the other. Recalculate next year's overhead absorption rates, recognizing the existence of such reciprocal services and assuming that they can be measured on the same bases as those used to allocate costs to the production cost centres.   (6 marks)

(d) Assume that:
   (i) General factory overhead is a fixed cost.
   (ii) Service cost centre 1 is concerned with inspection and quality control, with its budgeted expenses (before any reallocations) being 10% fixed and 90% variable.
   (iii) Service cost centre 2 is the company's plant maintenance section, with its budgeted expenses (before any reallocations) being 90% fixed and 10% variable.
   (iv) Production cost centre A is labour-intensive, with its budgeted overhead (before any reallocation) being 90% fixed and 10% variable.
   (v) Production cost centre B is highly mechanized, with its budgeted overhead (before any reallocations) being 20% fixed and 80% variable.
      In the light of these assumptions, comment on the cost apportionment and absorption calculations made in parts (a) and (c) and suggest any improvements that you would consider appropriate.   (6 marks)
      (Total 22 marks)
      ACCA Level 2 Management Accounting

Question IM 3.14 Advanced: Product cost calculation and costs for decision-making

Kaminsky Ltd manufactures belts and braces. The firm is organized into five departments. These are belt-making, braces-making, and three service departments (maintenance, warehousing, and administration).

Direct costs are accumulated for each department. Factory-wide indirect costs (which are fixed for all production levels within the present capacity limits) are apportioned to departments on the basis of the percentage of floorspace occupied. Service department costs are apportioned on the basis of estimated usage, measured as the percentage of the labour hours operated in the service department utilized by the user department.

Each service department also services at least one other service department.

Budgeted data for the forthcoming year are shown below:

	Belts	Braces	Admin-istration dept	Main-tenance dept	Ware-housing	Company total
(1) Output and sales (units):						
Output capacity	150 000	60 000				
Output budgeted	100 000	50 000				
Sales budgeted	100 000	50 000				
(2) Direct variable costs (£000):						
Materials	120	130	—	20	30	300
Labour	80	70	50	80	20	300
Total	200	200	50	100	50	600
(3) Factory-wide fixed indirect costs (£000)						1000
(4) Floor-space (%)	40	40	5	10	5	100
(5) Usage of service department labour hours (%)						
Administration	40	40	—	10	10	100
Warehousing	50	25	—	25	—	100
Maintenance	30	30	—	—	40	100

(a) You are required to calculate the total cost per unit of belts and braces respectively, in accordance with the system operated by Kaminsky Ltd.   (12 marks)

(b) In addition to the above data, it has been decided that the selling prices of the products are to be determined on a cost-plus basis, as the unit total cost plus 20%.

Two special orders have been received, outside the normal run of business, and not provided for in the budget.

They are as follows:

(i) an order for 1000 belts from Camfam, an international relief organization, offering to pay £5000 for them.

(ii) a contract to supply 2000 belts a week for 50 weeks to Mixon Spenders, a chainstore, at a price per belt of 'unit total cost plus 10%'.

You are required to set out the considerations which the management of Kaminsky Ltd should take into account in deciding whether to accept each of these orders, and to advise them as far as you are able on the basis of the information given.   (8 marks)

(c) 'Normalized overhead rates largely eliminate from inventories, from cost of goods sold, and from gross margin any unfavourable impact of having production out of balance with the long-run demand for a company's products.'

You are required to explain and comment upon the above statement.

(5 marks)

ICAEW Management Accounting

Accounting entries for a job costing system

XY Limited commenced trading on 1 February with fully paid issued share capital of £500 000, Fixed Assets of £275 000 and Cash at Bank of £225 000. By the end of April, the following transactions had taken place:

1. Purchases on credit from suppliers amounted to £572 500 of which £525 000 was raw materials and £47 500 was for items classified as production overhead.
2. Wages incurred for all staff were £675 000, represented by cash paid £500 000 and wage deductions of £175 000 in respect of income tax etc.
3. Payments were made by cheque for the following overhead costs:

	£
Production	20 000
Selling	40 000
Administration	25 000

4. Issues of raw materials were £180 000 to Department A, £192 500 to Department B and £65 000 for production overhead items.
5. Wages incurred were analysed to functions as follows:

	£
Work in progress – Department A	300 000
Work in progress – Department B	260 000
Production overhead	42 500
Selling overhead	47 500
Administration overhead	25 000
	675 000

6. Production overhead absorbed in the period by Department A was £110 000 and by Department B £120 000.
7. The production facilities, when not in use, were patrolled by guards from a security firm and £26 000 was owing for this service. £39 000 was also owed to a firm of management consultants which advises on production procedures; invoices for these two services are to be entered into the accounts.
8. The cost of finished goods completed was

	Department A £	Department B £
Direct labour	290 000	255 000
Direct materials	175 000	185 000
Production overhead	105 000	115 000
	570 000	555 000

9. Sales on credit were £870 000 and the cost of those sales was £700 000.
10. Depreciation of productive plant and equipment was £15 000.

Question IM 4.1
Intermediate:
Integrated cost accounting

11. Cash received from debtors totalled £520 000.
12. Payments to creditors were £150 000.

You are required
(a) to open the ledger accounts at the commencement of the trading period;
(b) using integrated accounting, to record the transactions for the three months ended 30 April;
(c) to prepare, in vertical format, for presentation to management,
  (i) a profit statement for the period;
  (ii) the balance sheet at 30 April.

(20 marks)
CIMA Stage 2 Cost Accounting

Question IM 4.2
Intermediate:
Interlocking
accounts

AZ Limited has separate cost and financial accounting systems interlocked by control accounts in the two ledgers. From the cost accounts, the following information was available for the period:

	(£)
Cost of finished goods produced	512 050
Cost of goods sold	493 460
Direct materials issued	197 750
Direct wages	85 480
Production overheads	
(as per the financial accounts)	208 220
Direct material purchases	216 590

In the cost accounts, additional depreciation of £12 500 per period is charged and production overheads are absorbed at 250% of wages.
  The various account balances at the beginning of the period were:

	(£)
Stores control	54 250
Work in progress control	89 100
Finished goods control	42 075

Required:
(a) Prepare the following control accounts in the cost ledger, showing clearly the double entries between the accounts, and the closing balances:
    Stores control
    Work in progress control
    Finished goods control
    Production overhead control   (10 marks)
(b) Explain the meaning of the balance on the production overhead control account.   (2 marks)
(c) When separate ledgers are maintained, the differing treatment of certain items may cause variations to arise between costing and financial profits. Examples of such items include stock valuations, notional expenses, and non-costing items charged in the financial accounts. Briefly explain the above *three* examples and state why they may give rise to profit differences.   (3 marks)
(Total 15 marks)
CIMA Stage 1 Cost Accounting

(a) Describe briefly *three* major differences between:
  (i) financial accounting, and
  (ii) cost and management accounting. (6 marks)
(b) Below are incomplete cost accounts for a period:

Question IM 4.3
Intermediate:
Preparation of
interlocking
accounts from
incomplete
information

	Stores ledger control account (£000)
Opening balance	176.0
Financial ledger control a/c	224.2

	Production wages control account (£000)
Financial ledger control a/c	196.0

	Production overhead control account (£000)
Financial ledger control a/c	119.3

	Job ledger control account (£000)
Opening balance	114.9

The balances at the end of the period were:

	(£000)
Stores ledger	169.5
Jobs ledger	153.0

During the period 64 500 kilos of direct material were issued from stores at a weighted average price of £3.20 per kilo. The balance of materials issued from stores represented indirect materials.

75% of the production wages are classified as 'direct'. Average gross wages of direct workers was £5.00 per hour. Production overheads are absorbed at a predetermined rate of £6.50 per direct labour hour.

Required:
Complete the cost accounts for the period. (8 marks)
(Total 14 marks)
ACCA Foundation Paper 3

On 30 October 2002 the following were among the balances in the cost ledger of a company manufacturing a single product (Product X) in a single process operation:

	Dr	Cr
Raw Material Control Account	£87 460	
Manufacturing Overhead Control Account		£5 123
Finished Goods Account	£148 352	

The raw material ledger comprised the following balances at 30 October 2002:

Direct materials:		
Material A:	18 760 kg	£52 715
Material B:	4 242 kg	£29 994
Indirect materials:		£4 751

12 160 kg of Product X were in finished goods stock on 30 October 2002.
   During November 1999 the following occurred:
 (i) Raw materials purchased on credit:
       Material A: 34 220 kg at £2.85/kg
       Material B: 34 520 kg at £7.10/kg
       Indirect: £7221
 (ii) Raw materials issued from stock:
       Material A: 35 176 kg
       Material B: 13 364 kg
       Indirect: £6917

Direct materials are issued at weighted average prices (calculated at the end of each month to three decimal places of £).
(iii) Wages incurred:
       Direct   £186 743 (23 900 hours)
       Indirect   £74 887
(iv) Other manufacturing overhead costs totalled £112 194. Manufacturing overheads are absorbed at a predetermined rate of £8.00 per direct labour hour. Any over/under absorbed overhead at the end of November should be left as a balance on the manufacturing overhead control account.
 (v) 45 937 kg of Product X were manufactured. There was no work-in-progress at the beginning or end of the period. A normal loss of 5% of input is expected.
(vi) 43 210 kg of Product X were sold. A monthly weighted average cost per kg (to three decimal places of £) is used to determine the production cost of sales.

Required:
(a) Prepare the following cost accounts for the month of November 2002.
    Raw Material Control Account
    Manufacturing Overhead Control Account
    Work-in-Progress Account
    Finished Goods Account
All entries to the accounts should be rounded to the nearest whole £. Clearly show any workings supporting your answer.   (16 marks)
(b) Explain the concept of equivalent units and its relevance in a process costing system.   (4 marks)
                                                                (Total 20 marks)
                                         ACCA Management Information Paper 3

**Question IM 4.5
Intermediate:
Labour cost
accounting and
recording of
journal entries**

(a) Identify the costs to a business arising from labour turnover.   (5 marks)
(b) A company operates a factory which employed 40 direct workers throughout the four-week period just ended. Direct employees were paid at a basic rate of £4.00 per hour for a 38-hour week. Total hours of the direct workers in the four-week period were 6528. Overtime, which is paid at a premium of 35%, is worked in order to meet general production requirements. Employee deductions total 30% of gross wages. 188 hours of direct workers' time were registered as idle.

Required:
Prepare journal entries to account for the labour costs of direct workers for the period.   (7 marks)
                                                                (Total 12 marks)
                                             ACCA Foundation Stage Paper 3

One of the production departments in A Ltd's factory employs 52 direct operatives and 9 indirect operatives. Basic hourly rates of pay are £4.80 and £3.90 respectively. Overtime, which is worked regularly to meet general production requirements, is paid at a premium of 30% over basic rate.

The following further information is provided for the period just ended:

Question IM 4.6
Intermediate:
Preparation of the
wages control
account plus an
evaluation of the
impact of a
proposed
piecework system

Hours worked:

Direct operatives:
Total hours worked	25 520 hours
Overtime hours worked	2 120 hours

Indirect operatives:
Total hours worked	4 430 hours
Overtime hours worked	380 hours

Production:
Product 1, 36 000 units in 7 200 hours
Product 2, 116 000 units in 11 600 hours
Product 3, 52 800 units in 4 400 hours

Non-productive time:	2 320 hours

Wages paid (net of tax and employees' National Insurance):
Direct operatives	£97 955
Indirect operatives	£13 859

The senior management of A Ltd are considering the introduction of a piecework payment scheme into the factory. Following work study analysis, expected productivities and proposed piecework rates for the direct operatives, in the production department referred to above, have been determined as follows:

	Productivity (output per hour)	Piecework rate (per unit)
Product 1	6 units	£1.00
Product 2	12 units	£0.50
Product 3	14.4 units	£0.40

Non-productive time is expected to remain at 10% of productive time, and would be paid at £3.50 per hour.

Required:
(a) Prepare the production department's wages control account for the period in A Ltd's integrated accounting system. (Ignore employers' National Insurance.)

(9 marks)

(b) Examine the effect of the proposed piecework payment scheme on direct labour and overhead costs.

(11 marks)
(Total 20 marks)
ACCA Cost and Management Accounting 1

Question IM 4.7
Intermediate:
Contract costing

Thornfield Ltd is a building contractor. During its financial year to 30 June 2000, it commenced three major contracts. Information relating to these contracts as at 30 June 2000 was as follows:

	Contract 1	Contract 2	Contract 3
Date contract commenced	1 July 1999	1 January 2000	1 April 2000
	(£)	(£)	(£)
Contract price	210 000	215 000	190 000
Expenditure to 30 June 2000:			
Materials and subcontract work	44 000	41 000	15 000
Direct wages	80 000	74 500	12 000
General expenses	3 000	1 800	700
Position at 30 June 2000			
Materials on hand at cost	3 000	3 000	1 500
Accrued expenses	700	600	600
Value of work certified	150 000	110 000	20 000
Estimated cost of work			
completed but not certified	4 000	6 000	9 000
Plant and machinery allocated			
to contracts	16 000	12 000	8 000

The plant and machinery allocated to the contracts was installed on the dates the contracts commenced. The plant and machinery is expected to have a working life of four years in the case of contracts 1 and 3 and three years in the case of contract 2, and is to be depreciated on a straight line basis assuming nil residual values.

Since the last certificate of work was certified on contract number 1, faulty work has been discovered which is expected to cost £10 000 to rectify. No rectification work has been commenced prior to 30 June 2000.

In addition to expending directly attributable to contracts, recoverable central overheads are estimated to amount to 2% of the cost of direct wages.

Thornfield Ltd has an accounting policy of taking two thirds of the profit attributable to the value of work certified on a contract, once the contract is one third completed. Anticipated losses on contracts are provided in full.

Progress claims equal to 80% of the value of work certified have been invoiced to customers.

You are required to:
(a) prepare contract accounts for each contract for the year to 30 June 2000, calculating any attributable profit or loss on each contract; (12 marks)
(b) calculate the amount to be included in the balance sheet of Thornfield Ltd as on 30 June 2000 in respect of these contracts. (4 marks)

(Total 16 marks)

ICAEW Accounting Techniques

(a) PZ plc undertakes work to repair, maintain and construct roads. When a customer requests the company to do work PZ plc supplies a fixed price to the customer and allocates a works order number to the customer's request. This works order number is used as a reference number on material requisitions and timesheets to enable the costs of doing the work to be collected.

PZ plc's financial year ends on 30 April. At the end of April 2000 the data shown against four of PZ plc's works orders were:

Works order number	488	517	518	519
Date started	1/3/99	1/2/00	14/3/00	18/3/00
Estimated completion date	31/5/00	30/7/00	31/5/00	15/5/00
	(£000)	(£000)	(£000)	(£000)
Direct labour costs	105	10	5	2
Direct material costs	86	7	4	2
Selling price	450	135	18	9
Estimated direct costs to complete orders:				
Direct labour	40	60	2	2
Direct materials	10	15	1	1
Independent valuation of work done up to 30 April 2000	350	30	15	5

Overhead costs are allocated to works orders at the rate of 40% of direct labour costs.

It is company policy not to recognize profit on long-term contracts until they are at least 50% complete.

Required:
  (i) State, with reasons, whether they above works orders should be accounted for using contract costing or job costing. (4 marks)
  (ii) Based on your classification at (i) above, prepare a statement showing *clearly* the profit to be recognized and balance sheet work in progress valuation of *each* of the above works orders in respect of the financial year ended 30 April 2000. (10 marks)
  (iii) Comment critically on the policy of attributing overhead costs to works orders on the basis of direct labour cost. (6 marks)
(b) Explain the main features of process costing. Describe what determines the choice between using process costing or specific order costing in a manufacturing organization. (10 marks)
(Total 30 marks)
CIMA Operational Cost Accounting Stage 2

Process costing

Question IM 5.1 Intermediate

(a) Describe the distinguishing characteristics of production systems where
   (i) job costing techniques would be used, and
   (ii) process costing techniques would be used.   (3 marks)

(b) Job costing produces more accurate product costs than process costing. Critically examine the above statement by contrasting the information requirements, procedures and problems associated with each costing method.
      (14 marks)
      (Total 17 marks)
      ACCA Level 1 Costing

Question IM 5.2 Intermediate: Preparation of process accounts with all output fully completed

A product is manufactured by passing through three processes: A, B and C. In process C a by-product is also produced which is then transferred to process D where it is completed. For the first week in October, actual data included:

	Process A	Process B	Process C	Process D
Normal loss of input (%)	5	10	5	10
Scrap value (£ per unit)	1.50	2.00	4.00	2.00
Estimated sales value of by-product (£ per unit)	—	—	8.00	—
Output (units)	5760	5100	4370	—
Output of by-product (units)	—	—	510	450
	(£)	(£)	(£)	(£)
Direct materials (6000 units)	12 000	—	—	—
Direct materials added in process	5 000	9000	4000	220
Direct wages	4 000	6000	2000	200
Direct expenses	800	1680	2260	151

Budgeted production overhead for the week is £30 500.
   Budgeted direct wages for the week are £12 200.
   You are required to prepare:
(a) accounts for process A, B, C and D.   (20 marks)
(b) abnormal loss account and abnormal gain account.   (5 marks)
      (Total 25 marks)
      CIMA P1 Cost Accounting 2

(a) 'Whilst the ascertainment of product costs could be said to be one of the objectives of cost accounting, where joint products are produced and joint costs incurred, the total cost computed for the product may depend upon the method selected for the apportionment of joint costs, thus making it difficult for management to make decisions about the future of products.'

You are required to discuss the above statement and to state *two* different methods of apportioning joint costs to joint products. (8 marks)

(b) A company using process costing manufactures a single product which passes through two processes, the output of process 1 becoming the input to process 2. Normal losses and abnormal losses are defective units having a scrap value and cash is received at the end of the period for all such units.

The following information relates to the four-week period of accounting period number 7.

Raw material issued to process 1 was 3000 units at a cost of £5 per unit.

There was no opening or closing work-in-progress but opening and closing stocks of finished goods were £20 000 and £23 000 respectively.

Question IM 5.3 Intermediate: Discussion question on methods of apportioning joint costs and the preparation of process accounts with all output fully completed

	Process 1	Process 2
Normal loss as a percentage of input	10%	5%
Output in units	2800	2600
Scrap value per unit	£2	£5
Additional components	£1000	£780
Direct wages incurred	£4000	£6000
Direct expenses incurred	£10 000	£14 000
Production overhead as a percentage of direct wages	75%	125%

You are required to present the accounts for
  Process 1
  Process 2
  Finished goods
  Normal loss
  Abnormal loss
  Abnormal gain
  Profit and loss (so far as it relates to any of the accounts listed above).
  (17 marks)
  (Total 25 marks)
  CIMA Stage 2 Cost Accounting

Industrial Solvents Limited mixes together three chemicals – A, B and C – in the ratio 3:2:1 to produce Allklean, a specialised anti-static fluid. The chemicals cost £8, £6 and £3.90 per litre respectively.

In a period, 12 000 litres in total were input to the mixing process. The normal process loss is 5% of input and in the period there was an abnormal loss of 100 litres whilst the completed production was 9500 litres.

There was no opening work-in-progress (WIP) and the closing WIP was 100% complete for materials and 40% complete for labour and overheads. Labour and overheads were £41 280 in total for the period. Materials lost in production are scrapped.

Question IM 5.4 Intermediate: Equivalent production and losses in process

Required:
(a) Calculate the volume of closing WIP. (3 marks)
(b) Prepare the mixing process account for the period, showing clearly volumes and values. (9 marks)
(c) Briefly explain what changes would be necessary in your account if an abnormal gain were achieved in a period. (3 marks)
  (Total 15 marks)
  CIMA Stage 1 Cost Accounting

Question 5.5
Intermediate:
Losses in process
(weighted
average)

(a) Outline the characteristics of industries in which a process costing system is used and give two examples of such industries. (5 marks)

(b) ATM Chemicals produces product XY by putting it through a single process. You are given the following details for November.

Input Costs

Materials costs	25 000 kilos at £2.48 per kilo
Labour costs	8 000 hours at £5.50 per hour
Overhead costs	£63 000

You are also told the following:
   (i) Normal loss is 4% of input.
   (ii) Scrap value of normal loss is £2.00 per kilo.
   (iii) Finished output amounted to 15 000 units.
   (iv) Closing work in progress amounted to 6000 units and was fully complete for material $\frac{2}{3}$ complete for labour and $\frac{1}{2}$ for overheads.
   (v) There was no opening work in progress.

Required:
   (i) Prepare the Process account for the month of November detailing the value of the finished units and the work in progress. (12 marks)
   (ii) Prepare an Abnormal Loss account. (2 marks)

(c) Distinguish between normal and abnormal losses, their costing treatment and how each loss may be controlled. (6 marks)
(Total 25 marks)
AAT Cost Accounting and Budgeting

Question IM 5.6
Intermediate:
Losses in process
(weighted
average)

A company manufactures a product that goes through two processes. You are given the following cost information about the processes for the month of November.

	Process 1	Process 2
Unit input	15 000	—
Finished unit input from Process 1	—	10 000
Finished unit output to Process 2	10 000	—
Finished unit output from Process 2	—	9 500
Opening WIP – Units	—	2 000
– Value	—	£26 200
Input – Materials	£26 740	
– Labour	£36 150	£40 000
– Overhead	£40 635	£59 700
Closing WIP – Units	4 400	1 800

You are told:
(1) The closing WIP in Process 1 was 80% complete for material, 50% complete for labour and 40% complete for overhead.
(2) The opening WIP in Process 2 was 40% complete for labour and 50% complete for overhead. It had a value of labour £3200, overheads £6000 for work done in Process 2.
(3) The closing WIP in Process 2 was two-thirds complete for labour and 75% complete for overhead.
(4) No further material needed to be added to the units transferred from Process 1.
(5) Normal loss is budgeted at 5% of total input in Process 1 and Process 2. Total input is to be inclusive of any opening WIP.
(6) Normal loss has no scrap value in Process 1 and can be sold for the input value from Process 1, in Process 2.

(7) Abnormal losses have no sales value.

(8) It is company policy to value opening WIP in a process by the weighted average method.

Required:

(a) Prepare accounts for:
   (i) Process 1.
   (ii) Process 2.
   (iii) Normal loss.
   (iv) Any abnormal loss/gain. (19 marks)

(b) Compare and contrast a joint product with a by-product. (6 marks)

(Total 25 marks)

AAT Cost Accounting and Budgeting

(a) A company uses a process costing system in which the following terms arise:
   conversion costs
   work-in-process
   equivalent units
   normal loss
   abnormal loss.

Required:

Provide a definition of each of these terms. (5 marks)

(b) Explain how you would treat normal and abnormal losses in process costs accounts. (4 marks)

(c) One of the products manufactured by the company passes through two separate processes. In each process losses, arising from rejected material, occur. In Process 1, normal losses are 20% of input. In Process 2, normal losses are 10% of input. The losses arise at the end of each of the processes. Reject material can be sold. Process 1 reject material can be sold for £1.20 per kilo, and Process 2 reject material for £1.42 per kilo.

Information for a period is as follows:

Process 1:
   Material input 9000 kilos, cost £14 964.
   Direct labour 2450 hours at £3.40 per hour.
   Production overhead £2.60 per direct labour hour.
   Material output 7300 kilos.

Process 2:
   Material input 7300 kilos.
   Direct labour 1000 hours at £3.40 per hour.
   Production overhead £2.90 per direct labour hour.
Material output 4700 kilos.

At the end of the period 2000 kilos of material were incomplete in Process 2. These were 50% complete as regards direct labour and production overhead. There was no opening work-in-process in either process, and no closing work-in-process in Process 1.

Required:

Prepare the relevant cost accounts for the period. (16 marks)

(Total 25 marks)

ACCA Level 1 Costing

ABC plc operates an integrated cost accounting system and has a financial year which ends on 30 September. It operates in a processing industry in which a single product is produced by passing inputs through two sequential processes. A normal loss of 10% of input is expected in each process.

The following account balances have been extracted from its ledger at 31 August:

	Debit (£)	Credit (£)
Process 1 (Materials £4400; Conversion costs £3744)	8144	
Process 2 (Process 1 £4431; Conversion costs £5250)	9681	
Abnormal loss	1400	
Abnormal gain		300
Overhead control account		250
Sales		585 000
Cost of sales	442 500	
Finished goods stock	65 000	

ABC plc uses the weighted average method of accounting for work in process.
During September the following transactions occurred:

Process 1

materials input	4000 kg costing £22 000
labour cost	£12 000
transfer to process 2	2400 kg

Process 2

transfer from process 1	2400 kg
labour cost	£15 000
transfer to finished goods	2500 kg

Overhead costs incurred amounted to	£54 000
Sales to customers were	£52 000

Overhead costs are absorbed into process costs on the basis of 150% of labour cost.

The losses which arise in process 1 have no scrap value: those arising in process 2 can be sold for £2 per kg.

Details of opening and closing work in process for the month of September are as follows:

	Opening	Closing
Process 1	3000 kg	3400 kg
Process 2	2250 kg	2600 kg

In both processes closing work in process is fully complete as to material cost and 40% complete as to conversion cost.

Stocks of finished goods at 30 September were valued at cost of £60 000.

Required:
Prepare the ledger accounts for September and the annual proft and loss account of ABC plc. (Commence with the balances given above, balance off and transfer any balances as appropriate.) (25 marks)

CIMA Stage 2 Operational Cost Accounting

The following information relates to a manufacturing process for a period:

Materials costs	£16 445
Labour and overhead costs	£28 596

10 000 units of output were produced by the process in the period, of which 420 failed testing and were scrapped. Scrapped units normally represent 5% of total production output. Testing takes place when production units are 60% complete in terms of labour and overheads. Materials are input at the beginning of the process. All scrapped units were sold in the period for £0.40 per unit.

Required:
Prepare the process accounts for the period, including those for process scrap and abnormal losses/gains.
(12 marks)
ACCA Foundation Stage Paper 3

Question IM 5.9
Intermediate:
Process accounts
involving an
abnormal gain
and equivalent
production

A company produces a single product from one of its manufacturing processes. The following information of process inputs, outputs and work in process relates to the most recently completed period:

	kg
Opening work in process	21 700
Materials input	105 600
Output completed	92 400
Closing work in process	28 200

Question IM 5.10
Intermediate:
Losses in process
(FIFO and
weighted average
methods)

The opening and closing work in process are respectively 60% and 50% complete as to conversion costs. Losses occur at the beginning of the process and have a scrap value of £0.45 per kg.

The opening work in process included raw material costs of £56 420 and conversion costs of £30 597. Costs incurred during the period were:

Materials input	£276 672
Conversion costs	£226 195

Required:
(a) Calculate the unit costs of production (£ per kg to four decimal places) using:
  (i) the weighted average method of valuation and assuming that all losses are treated as normal;
  (ii) the FIFO method of valuation and assuming that normal losses are 5% of materials input. (13 marks)
(b) Prepare the process account for situation (a) (ii) above. (6 marks)
(c) Distinguish between:
  (i) joint products, and
  (ii) by-products and contrast their treatment in process accounts. (6 marks)
(Total 25 marks)
ACCA Cost and Management Accounting 1

Question IM 5.11
Advanced: FIFO
method and
losses in process

(a) You are required to explain and discuss the alternative methods of accounting for normal and abnormal spoilage. (8 marks)

(b) Weston Harvey Ltd assembles and finishes trapfoils from bought-in components which are utilized at the beginning of the assembly process. The other assembly costs are incurred evenly throughout that process. When the assembly process is complete, the finishing process is undertaken. Overhead is absorbed into assembly, but not finishing, at the rate of 100% of direct assembly cost.

It is considered normal for some trapfoils to be spoiled during assembly and finishing. Quality control inspection is applied at the conclusion of the finishing process to determine whether units are spoiled.

It is accepted that the spoilage is normal if spoiled units are no more than one-eighteenth of the completed good units produced. Normal spoilage is treated as a product cost, and incorporated into the cost of good production. Any spoilage in excess of this limit is classed as abnormal, and written off as a loss of the period in which it occurs.

Trapfoils are valuable in relation to their weight and size. Despite vigilant security precautions it is common that some units are lost, probably by pilferage. The cost of lost units is written off as a loss of the period in which it occurs. This cost is measured as the cost of the bought-in components plus the assembly process, but no finishing cost is charged.

Weston Harvey uses a FIFO system of costing.

The following data summarize the firm's activities during November:

Opening work in process:

Bought-in components	£60 000
Direct assembly cost to 31 October	£25 000
No. of units (on average one-half assembled)	50 000

Direct costs incurred during November	
Bought-in components received	£120 000
Direct assembly cost	£40 000
Direct finishing cost	£30 000

Production data for November:	Trapfoils
Components received into assembly	112 000
Good units completed	90 000
Spoiled units	10 000
Lost units	2 000

None of the opening work in process had at that stage entered the finishing process. Similarly, nor had any of the closing work in process at the end of the month. The units in the closing work in process were, on average, one-third complete as to assembly; none had entered the finishing process.

You are required:
(i) to calculate the number of units in the closing work in process; (3 marks)
(ii) to calculate the number of equivalent units processed in November, distinguishing between bought-in components, assembly and finishing; (6 marks)
(iii) to calculate the number of equivalent units processed in November, subdivided into the amounts for good units produced, spoilage, lost units and closing work in process. (8 marks)

(Total 25 marks)
ICAEW Management Accounting

On 1 October Bland Ltd opened a plant for making verniers. Data for the first two months' operations are shown below:

Question IM 5.12
Advanced:
Comparison of
FIFO and
weighted average,
stock valuation
methods

	October (units)	November (units)
Units started in month	3900	2700
Units completed (all sold)	2400	2400
Closing work in progress	1500	1800
	(£)	(£)
Variable costs:		
Materials	58 500	48 600
Labour	36 000	21 000
Fixed costs	63 000	63 000
Sales revenue	112 800	120 000

At 31 October the units in closing work in progress were 100% complete for materials and 80% complete for labour. At 30 November the units in closing work in progress were 100% complete for materials and 50% complete for labour.

The company's policy for valuation of work in progress is under review. The board of directors decided that two alternative profit and loss statements should be prepared for October and November. One statement would value work in progress on a weighted average cost basis and the other would adopt a first-in, first-out basis. Fixed costs would be absorbed in proportion to actual labour costs in both cases.

For October both bases gave a closing work in progress valuation of £55 500 and a profit of £10 800. When the statements for November were presented to the board the following suggestions were made:

(1) 'We wouldn't have a problem over the valuation basis if we used standard costs.'

(2) 'Standard cost valuation could be misleading for an operation facing volatile costs; all data should be on a current cost basis for management purposes.'

(3) 'It would be simpler and more informative to go to a direct cost valuation basis for management use.'

(4) 'All that management needs is a cash flow report; leave the work in progress valuation to the year-end financial accounts.'

Requirements:

(a) Prepare profit and loss statements for November on the two alternative bases decided by the board of directors, showing workings. (9 marks)

(b) Explain, with supporting calculations, the differences between the results shown by each statement you have prepared. (6 marks)

(c) Assess the main strengths and weaknesses of each of the suggestions made by the directors, confining your assessment to matters relating to the effects of work in progress valuation on performance measurement. (10 marks)

(Total 25 marks)

ICAEW P2 Management Accounting

Joint and by-product costing

Question IM 6.1
Intermediate

(a) Explain briefly the term 'joint products' in the context of process costing.
(2 marks)

(b) Discuss whether, and if so how, joint process costs should be shared amongst joint products. (Assume that no further processing is required after the split-off point.)
(11 marks)

(c) Explain briefly the concept of 'equivalent units' in process costing.   (4 marks)
(Total 17 marks)
ACCA Level 1 Costing

Question IM 6.2
Intermediate

(a) Discuss the problems which joint products and by-products pose the management accountant, especially in his attempts to produce useful product profitability reports. Outline the usual accounting treatments of joint and by-products and indicate the extent to which these treatments are effective in overcoming the problems you have discussed. In your answer clearly describe the differences between joint and by-products and provide an example of each.
(14 marks)

(b) A common process produces several joint products. After the common process has been completed each product requires further specific, and directly attributable, expenditure in order to 'finish off' the product and put it in a saleable condition. Specify the conditions under which it is rational to undertake:
 (i) the common process, and
 (ii) the final 'finishing off' of each of the products which are the output from the common process.
Illustrate your answer with a single numerical example.   (6 marks)
(Total 20 marks)
ACCA P2 Management Accounting

Question IM 6.3
Intermediate

Explain how the apportionment of those costs incurred up to the separation point of two or more joint products could give information which is unacceptable for (i) stock valuation and (ii) decision-making. Use figures of your own choice to illustrate your answer.
(9 marks)
ACCA Level 2 Management Accounting

XYZ plc, a paint manufacturer, operates a process costing system. The following details related to process 2 for the month of October:

Question IM 6.4
Intermediate:
Preparation of
joint and by-
product process
account

Opening work in progress	5000 litres fully complete as to transfers from process 1 and 40% complete as to labour and overhead, valued at £60 000
Transfer from process 1	65 000 litres valued at cost of £578 500
Direct labour	£101 400
Variable overhead	£80 000
Fixed overhead	£40 000
Normal loss	5% of volume transferred from process 1, scrap value £2.00 per litre
Actual output	30 000 litres of paint X (a joint product) 25 000 litres of paint Y (a joint product) 7000 litres of by-product Z
Closing work in progress	6000 litres fully complete as to transfers from process 1 and 60% complete as to labour and overhead.

The final selling price of products X, Y and Z are:

Paint X	£15.00 per litre
Paint Y	£18.00 per litre
Product Z	£4.00 per litre

There are no further processing costs associated with either paint X or the by-product, but paint Y requires further processing at a cost of £1.50 per litre.
All three products incur packaging costs of £0.50 per litre before they can be sold.

Required:
(a) Prepare the process 2 account for the month of October, apportioning the common costs between the joint products, based upon their values at the point of separation
(20 marks)
(b) Prepare the abnormal loss/gain account, showing clearly the amount to be transferred to the profit and loss account. (4 marks)
(c) Describe one other method of apportioning the common costs between the joint products, *and* explain why it is necessary to make such apportionments, and their usefulness when measuring product profitability. (6 marks)
(Total 30 marks)
CIMA Stage 2 Operational Cost Accounting

QR Limited operates a chemical process which produces four different products Q, R, S and T from the input of one raw material plus water. Budget information for the forthcoming financial year is as follows:

Question IM 6.5
Intermediate:
Joint cost
apportionment
and a decision on
further
processing

	(£000)
Raw materials cost	268
Initial processing cost	464

Product	Output in litres	Sales (£1000)	Additional processing cost (£000
Q	400 000	768	160
R	90 000	232	128
S	5 000	32	—
T	9 000	240	8

The company policy is to apportion the costs prior to the split-off point on a method based on net sales value.

Currently, the intention is to sell product S without further processing but to process the other three products after the split-off point. However, it has been proposed that an alternative strategy would be to sell all four products at the split-off point without further processing. If this were done the selling prices obtainable would be as follows:

	Per litre (£)
Q	1.28
R	1.60
S	6.40
T	20.00

You are required:
(a) to prepare budgeted profit statement showing the profit or loss for each product, and in total, if the current intention is proceeded with;   (10 marks)
(b) to show the profit or loss by product, and in total, if the alternative strategy were to be adopted;   (6 marks)
(c) to recommend what should be done and why, assuming that there is no more profitable alternative use for the plant.   (4 marks)
(Total 20 marks)
CIMA Stage 2 Cost Accounting

Question IM 6.6
Intermediate:
Joint cost
apportionment
and decision on
further
processing

A company manufactures four products from an input of a raw material to process 1. Following this process, product A is processed in process 2, product B in process 3, product C in process 4 and product D in process 5.

The normal loss in process 1 is 10% of input, and there are no expected losses in the other processes. Scrap value in process 1 is £0.50 per litre. The costs incurred in process 1 are apportioned to each product according to the volume of output of each product. Production overhead is absorbed as a percentage of direct wages.

Data in respect of the month of October:

	Process					
	1	2	3	4	5	Total
	(£000)	(£000)	(£000)	(£000)	(£000)	(£000)
Direct materials at £1.25 per litre	100					100
Direct wages	48	12	8	4	16	88
Production overhead						66

	Product			
	A	B	C	D
Output (litres)	22 000	20 000	10 000	18 000
Selling price (£)	4.00	3.00	2.00	5.00
Estimated sales value at end of Process 1 (£)	2.50	2.80	1.20	3.00

You are required to:
(a) calculate the profit or loss for each product for the month, assuming all output is sold at the normal selling price;   (4 marks)
(b) suggest and evaluate an alternative production strategy which would optimize profit for the month. It should not be assumed that the output of process 1 can be changed;   (12 marks)
(c) suggest to what management should devote its attention, if it is to achieve the potential benefit indicated in (b).   (4 marks)
(Total 20 marks)
CIMA P1 Cost Accounting 2

Milo plc has a number of chemical processing plants in the UK. At one of these plants it takes an annual input of 400 000 gallons of raw material A and converts it into two liquid products, B and C.

Question IM 6.7
Advanced: Joint cost stock valuation and decision-making

The standard yield from one gallon of material A is 0.65 gallons of B and 0.3 gallons of C. Product B is processed further, without volume loss, and then sold as product D. Product C has hitherto been sold without further processing. In the year ended 31 July 2000, the cost of material A was £20 per gallon. The selling price of product C was £5 per gallon and transport costs from plant to customer were £74 000.

Negotiations are taking place with Takeup Ltd who would purchase the total production of product C for the years ending 31 July 2001 and 2002 provided it was converted to product E by further processing. It is unlikely that the contract would be renewed after 31 July 2002. New specialized transport costing £120 000 and special vats costing £80 000 will have to be acquired if the contract is to be undertaken. The vats will be installed in part of the existing factory that is presently unused and for which no use has been forecast for the next three years. Both transport and vats will have no residual value at the end of the contract. The company uses straight line depreciation.

Projected data for 2001 and 2002 are as follows:

	Liquid A	Liquid D	Liquid E
Amount processed (gallons)	400 000		
Processing costs (£):			
Cost of liquid A per gallon	20		
Wages to split-off	400 000 p.a.		
Overheads to split-off	250 000 p.a.		
Further processing			
Materials per gallon		3.50	3.30
Wages per gallon		2.50	1.70
Overheads		52 000 p.a.	37 000 p.a.
Selling costs (£):			
Total expenses	—	125 000 p.a.	—
Selling price per gallon (£)		40.00	15.50

Total plant administration costs are £95 000 p.a.

You are required to:
(a) Show whether or not Milo plc should accept the contract and produce liquid E in 2001 and 2002. (5 marks)
(b) Prepare a pro forma income statement which can be used to evaluate the performance of the individual products sold, assuming all liquid processed is sold, in the financial year to 31 July 2001,
    (i) assuming liquids D and C are sold,
    (ii) assuming liquids D and E are sold.
    Give reasons for the layout adopted and comment on the apportionment of pre-separation costs. (12 marks)
(c) Calculate, assuming that 10 000 gallons of liquid C remain unsold at 31 July 2000, and using the FIFO basis for inventory valuation, what would be the valuation of:
    (i) the stock of liquid C, and
    (ii) 10 000 gallons of liquid E after conversion from liquid C. (4 marks)
(d) Calculate an inventory valuation at replacement cost of 10 000 gallons of liquid E in stock at 31 July 2001, assuming that the cost of material A is to be increased by 25% from that date; and comment on the advisability of using replacement cost for inventory valuation purposes in the monthly management accounts. (4 marks)

Note: Ignore taxation. (Total 25 marks)
ICAEW P2 Management Accounting

Question IM 6.8
Advanced: Cost per unit calculation and decision-making

A chemical company has a contract to supply annually 3600 tonnes of product A at £24 a tonne and 4000 tonnes of product B at £14.50 a tonne. The basic components for these products are obtained from a joint initial distillation process. From this joint distillation a residue is produced which is processed to yield 380 tonnes of by-product Z. By-product Z is sold locally at £5 a tonne and the net income is credited to the joint distillation process.

The budget for the year ending 30 June 2001 includes the following data:

| | Joint Process | Separable cost | | |
		Product A	Product B	By-product Z
Variable cost per tonne of input (£)	5	11	2	1
Fixed costs for year (£)	5000	4000	8000	500
Evaporation loss in process (% of input)	6	10	20	5

Since the budget was compiled it has been decided that an extensive five-week overhaul of the joint distillation plant will be necessary during the year. This will cost an additional £17 000 in repair costs and reduce all production in the year by 10%. Supplies of the products can be imported to meet the contract commitment at a cost of £25 a tonne for A and £15 a tonne for B.

Experiments have also shown that the joint distillation plant operations could be changed during the year such that either:

 (i) The output of distillate for product A would increase by 200 tonnes with a corresponding reduction in product B distillate. This change would increase the joint distillation variable costs for the whole of that operation by 2%, or

(ii) The residue for by-product Z could be mixed with distillate for products A and B proportionate to the present output of these products. By intensifying the subsequent processing for products A and B acceptable quality could be obtained. The intensified operation would increase product A and B separable fixed costs by 5% and increase the evaporation loss for the whole operation to 11% and 21% respectively.

You are required to:
(a) calculate on the basis of the original budget:
  (i) the unit costs of products A and B; and
  (ii) the total profit for the year;
(b) calculate the change in the unit costs of products A and B based on the reduced production;
(c) calculate the profit for the year if the shortfall of production is made up by imported products;
(d) advise management whether either of the alternative distillation operations would improve the profitability calculated under (c) and whether you recommend the use of either.   (30 marks)
CIMA P3 Management Accounting

Question IM 6.9
Advanced: Calculation of cost per unit, break-even point and a recommended selling price

A chemical company produces amongst its product range two industrial cleaning fluids, A and B. These products are manufactured jointly. In 2001 total sales are expected to be restricted because home trade outlets for fluid B are limited to 54 000 gallons for the year. At this level plant capacity will be under-utilized by 25%.

From the information given below you are required to:
(a) draw a flow diagram of the operations;
(b) calculate separately for fluids A and B for the year:
  (i) total manufacturing cost;
  (ii) manufacturing cost per gallon;
  (iii) list price per gallon;
  (iv) profit for the year;

(c) calculate the break-even price per gallon to manufacture an extra 3000 gallons of fluid B for export and which would incur selling, distribution and administration costs of £1260;

(d) state the price you would recommend the company should quote per gallon for this export business, with a brief explanation for your decision.

The following data are given:

1. Description of processes

Process 1: Raw materials L and M are mixed together and filtered. There is an evaporation loss of 10%.

Process 2: The mixture from Process 1 is boiled and this reduces the volume by 20%. The remaining liquid distils into 50% extract A, 25% extract B, and 25% by-product C.

Process 3: Two parts of extract A are blended with one part of raw material N, and one part of extract B with one part of raw material N, to form respectively fluids A and B.

Process 4: Fluid A is filled into one-gallon labelled bottles and fluid B into six-gallon preprinted drums and they are then both ready for sale. One per-cent wastage in labels occurs in this process.

2. Costs

	Cost per gallon (£)
Raw material L	0.20
Raw material M	0.50
Raw material N	2.00
	Cost (£)
Containers: 1-gallon bottles	0.27 each
6-gallon drums	5.80 each
Bottle labels, per thousand	2.20

Direct wages:	Per gallon of input processed (£)
Process 1	0.11
Process 2	0.15
Process 3	0.20
Process 4	0.30

Manufacturing overhead:

Process	Fixed per annum (£)	Variable, per gallon of input processed (£)
1	6 000	0.04
2	20 250	0.20
3	19 500	0.10
4	14 250	0.10

By-product C is collected in bulk by a local company which pays £0.50 per gallon for it and the income is credited to process 2.

Process costs are apportioned entirely to the two main products on the basis of their output from each process.

No inventories of part-finished materials are held at any time.

Fluid A is sold through agents on the basis of list price less 20% and fluid B at list price less $33\frac{1}{3}\%$.

Of the net selling price, profit amounts to 8%, selling and distribution costs to 12% and administration costs to 5%.

Taxation should be ignored.

(30 marks)

CIMA P3 Management Accounting

Income effects of alternative cost accumulation systems

In product costing the costs attributed to each unit of production may be calculated by using either
(i) absorption costing, or
(ii) marginal (or direct or variable) costing.
Similarly, in departmental cost or profit reports the fixed costs of overhead or service departments may be allocated to production departments as an integral part of the production departments' costs or else segregated in some form.

Question IM 7.1
Intermediate

Required:
Describe absorption and marginal (or direct or variable) costing and outline the strengths and weaknesses of each method. (c. 11 marks)
ACCA P2 Management Accounting

Discuss the arguments for and against the inclusion of fixed overheads in stock valuation for the purpose of internal profit measurement.

Question IM 7.2
Intermediate

Solo Limited makes and sells a single product. The following data relate to periods 1 to 4.

Question IM 7.3
Intermediate:
Preparation of
variable and
absorption
costing
statements

	(£)
Variable cost per unit	30
Selling price per unit	55
Fixed costs per period	6000

Normal activity is 500 units and production and sales for the four periods are as follows:

	Period 1 units	Period 2 units	Period 3 units	Period 4 units
Sales	500	400	550	450
Production	500	500	450	500

There were no opening stocks at the start of period 1.

Required:
(a) Prepare operating statements for EACH of the periods 1 to 4, based on marginal costing principles. (4 marks)
(b) Prepare operating statements for EACH of the periods 1 to 4, based on absorption costing principles. (6 marks)
(c) Comment briefly on the results obtained in each period AND in total by the two systems. (5 marks)
(Total 15 marks)
CIMA Stage 1 Cost Accounting

Question IM 7.4
Intermediate:
Preparation of
variable and
absorption costing
systems and CVP
analysis

(a) PQ Limited makes and sells a single product, X, and has budgeted the following figures for a one-year period:

Sales, in units   160 000

	(£)	(£)
Sales		6 400 000
Production costs:		
Variable	2 560 000	
Fixed	800 000	
Selling, distribution and administration costs:		
Variable	1 280 000	
Fixed	1 200 000	
Total costs		5 840 000
Net profit		560 000

Fixed costs are assumed to be incurred evenly throughout the year. At the beginning of the year, there were no stocks of finished goods. In the first quarter of the year, 55 000 units were produced and 40 000 units were sold.

You are required to prepare profit statements for the first quarter, using
  (i) marginal costing, and
  (ii) absorption costing.   (6 marks)

(b) There is a difference in the profit reported when marginal costing is used compared with when absorption costing is used.

You are required to discuss the above statement and to indicate how each of the following conditions would affect the net profit reported
  (i) when sales and production are in balance at standard (or expected) volume,
  (ii) when sales exceed production,
  (iii) when production exceeds sales.
Use the figures from your answer to (a) above to support your discussion; you should also refer to SSAP 9.   (9 marks)

(c) WF Limited makes and sells a range of plastic garden furniture. These items are sold in sets of one table with four chairs for £80 per set.

The variable costs per set are £20 for manufacturing and £10 for variable selling, distribution and administration.

Direct labour is treated as a fixed cost and the total fixed costs of manufacturing, including depreciation of the plastic-moulding machinery, are £800 000 per annum. Budgeted profit for the forthcoming year is £400 000.

Increased competition has resulted in the management of WF Limited engaging market research consultants. The consultants have recommended three possible strategies, as follows:

	Reduce selling price per set by %	Expected increase in sales (sets) %
Strategy 1	5	10
Strategy 2	7.5	20
Strategy 3	10	25

You are required to assess the effect on profits of each of the three strategies, and to recommend which strategy, if any, ought to be adopted.   (10 marks)
(Total 25 marks)
CIMA Stage 2 Cost Accounting

A manufacturer of glass bottles has been affected by competition from plastic bottles and is currently operating at between 65 and 70 per cent of maximum capacity.

The company at present reports profits on an absorption costing basis but with the high fixed costs associated with the glass container industry and a substantial difference between sales volumes and production in some months, the accountant has been criticized for reporting widely different profits from month to month. To counteract this criticism, he is proposing in future to report profits based on marginal costing and in his proposal to management lists the following reasons for wishing to change:

1. Marginal costing provides for the complete segregation of fixed costs, thus facilitating closer control of production costs.
2. It eliminates the distortion of interim profit statements which occur when there are seasonal fluctuations in sales volume although production is at a fairly constant level.
3. It results in cost information which is more helpful in determining the sales policy necessary to maximise profits.

**Question IM 7.5
Intermediate:
Preparation of
variable and
absorption
costing profit
statements and
comments in
support of a
variable costing
system**

From the accounting records the following figures were extracted: Standard cost per gross (a gross is 144 bottles and is the cost unit used within the business):

	(£)
Direct materials	8.00
Direct labour	7.20
Variable production overhead	3.36
Total variable production cost	18.56
Fixed production overhead	7.52*
Total production standard cost	26.08

*The fixed production overhead rate was based on the following computations:

Total annual fixed production overhead was budgeted at £758 4000 or £632 000 per month.

Production volume was set at 1 008 000 gross bottles or 70 per cent of maximum capacity.

There is a slight difference in budgeted fixed production overhead at different levels of operating:

Activity level (per cent of maximum capacity)	Amount per month (£000)
50–75	632
76–90	648
91–100	656

You may assume that actual fixed production overhead incurred was as budgeted.

Additional information:

	September	October
Gross sold	87 000	101 000
Gross produced	115 000	78 000
Sales price, per gross	£32	£32
Fixed selling costs	£120 000	£120 000
Fixed administrative costs	£80 000	80 000

There were no finished goods in stock at 1 September.

You are required
(a) to prepare monthly profit statements for September and October using
    (i) absorption costing; and
    (ii) marginal costing;   (16 marks)
(b) to comment briefly on the accountant's three reasons which he listed to
    support his proposal.   (9 marks)
                                                                    (Total 25 marks)
                                                      CIMA Stage 2 Cost Accounting

Question IM 7.6 Intermediate: Calculation of overhead absorption rates and an explanation of the differences in profits

A company manufactures a single product with the following variable costs per unit

Direct materials	£7.00
Direct labour	£5.50
Manufacturing overhead	£2.00

The selling price of the product is £36.00 per unit. Fixed manufacturing costs are expected to be £1 340 000 for a period. Fixed non-manufacturing costs are expected to be £875 000. Fixed manufacturing costs can be analysed as follows:

Production 1	Department 2	Service Department	General Factory
£380 000	£465 000	£265 000	£230 000

'General Factory' costs represent space costs, for example rates, lighting and heating. Space utilization is as follows:

Production department 1	40%
Production department 2	50%
Service department	10%

60% of service department costs are labour related and the remaining 40% machine related.

Normal production department activity is:

	Direct labour hours	Machine hours	Production units
Department 1	80 000	2400	120 000
Department 2	100 000	2400	120 000

Fixed manufacturing overheads are absorbed at a predetermined rate per unit of production for each production department, based upon normal activity.

Required:
(a) Prepare a profit statement for a period using the full absorption costing system
    described above and showing each element of cost separately. Costs for the
    period were as per expectation, except for additional expenditure of £20 000 on
    fixed manufacturing overhead in Production Department 1. Production and
    sales were 116 000 and 114 000 units respectively for the period.   (14 marks)
(b) Prepare a profit statement for the period using marginal costing principles
    instead.   (5 marks)
(c) Contrast the general effect on profit of using absorption and marginal costing
    systems respectively. (Use the figures calculated in (a) and (b) above to
    illustrate your answer.)   (6 marks)
                                                                    (Total 25 marks)
                                           ACCA Cost and Management Accounting 1

Synchrodot Ltd manufactures two standard products, product 1 selling at £15 and product 2 selling at £18. A standard absorption costing system is in operation and summarised details of the unit cost standards are as follows:

Question IM 7.7
Advanced:
Preparation and
comments on
variable and
absorption
costing profit
statements

Standard Cost
Data – Summary

	Product 1 (£)	Product 2 (£)
Direct Material Cost	2	3
Direct Labour Cost	1	2
Overhead (Fixed and Variable)	7	9
	£10	£14

The budgeted fixed factory overhead for Synchrodot Ltd is £180 000 (per quarter) for product 1 and £480 000 (per quarter) for product 2. This apportionment to product lines is achieved by using a variety of 'appropriate' bases for individual expense categories, e.g. floor space for rates, number of workstaff for supervisory salaries etc. The fixed overhead is absorbed into production using practical capacity as the basis and any volume variance is written off (or credited) to the Profit and Loss Account in the quarter in which it occurs. Any planned volume variance in the quarterly budgets is dealt with similarly. The practical capacity per quarter is 30 000 units for product 1 and 60 000 units for product 2.

At the March board meeting the draft budgeted income statement for the April/May/June quarter is presented for consideration. This shows the following:

Budgeted Income Statement for April, May and June

		Product 1		Product 2
Budgeted Sales Quantity		30 000 units		57 000 units
Budgeted Production Quantity		24 000 units		60 000 units
Budgeted Sales Revenue		£450 000		£1 026 000
Budgeted Production Costs				
Direct Material		£48 000		£180 000
Direct Labour		24 000		120 000
Factory Overhead		204 000		540 000
		£276 000		£840 000
Add:				
Budgeted opening Finished Goods				
Stock at 1 April	(8000 units)	80 000	(3000 units)	42 000
		356 000		£882 000
Less:				
Budgeted closing Finished Goods				
Stock at 30 June	(2000 units)	20 000	(6000 units)	84 000
Budgeted Manufacuring Cost of Budgeted Sales		£336 000		£798 000
Budgeted Manufacturing Profit		£114 000		£228 000
Budgeted Administrative and Selling Costs (fixed)		30 000		48 000
Budgeted Profit		£84 000		£180 000

The statement causes consternation at the board meeting because it seems to show that product 2 contributes much more profit than product 1 and yet this has not previously been apparent.

The Sales Director is perplexed and he points out that the budgeted sales programme for the forthcoming quarter is identical with that accepted for the current quarter (January/February/March) and yet the budget for the current quarter shows a budgeted profit of £120 000 for each product line and the actual results seem to be in line with the budget.

The Production Director emphasises that identical assumptions, as to unit variable costs, selling prices and manufacturing efficiency, underlie both budgets but there has been a change in the budgeted production pattern. He produces the following table:

Budgeted Production	Product 1	Product 2
January/February/March	30 000 units	52 500 units
April/May/June	24 000 units	60 000 units

He urges that the company's budgeting procedures be overhauled as he can see no reason why the quarter's profit should be £24 000 up on the previous quarter and why the net profit for product 1 should fall from £4.00 to £2.80 per unit sold, whereas, for product 2 it should rise from £2.11 to £3.16.

You are required:
(a) To reconstruct the company's budget for the January/February/March quarter.

(6 marks)
(b) To restate the budgets (for both quarters) using standard marginal cost as the stock valuation basis.

(8 marks)
(c) To comment on the queries raised by the Sales Director and the Production Director and on the varying profit figures disclosed by the alternative budgets.

(8 marks)
(Total 22 marks)
ACCA Level 2 Management Accounting

**Question IM 7.8
Advanced:
Explanation of
difference
between
absorption and
variable costing
profit statements**

The accountant of Minerva Ltd, a small company manufacturing only one product, wishes to decide how to present the company's monthly management accounts. To date only actual information has been presented on an historic cost basis, with stocks valued at average cost. Standard costs have now been derived for the costs of production. The practical capacity (also known as full capacity) for annual production is 160 000 units, and this has been used as the basis for the allocation of production overheads. Selling and administration fixed overheads have been allocated assuming all 160 000 units are sold. The expected production capacity for 2001 is 140 000 units. It is anticipated now that, for the twelve months to 31 December 2001, production and sales volume will equal 120 000 units, compared to the forecast sales and production volumes of 140 000 units. The standard cost and standard profit per unit based on practical capacity is:

	(£ per unit)	(£ per unit)
Selling price		25.00
Production costs:		
Variable	8.00	
Fixed	6.00	
	14.00	
Variable selling costs	1.00	15.00
		10.00
Other fixed costs:		
Administration	2.10	
Selling	1.20	3.30
Standard profit per unit		6.70

The accountant has prepared the following three drafts (see below) of Minerva Ltd's profit and loss account for the month of November 2000 using three different accounting methods. The drafts are based on data relating to production, sales and stock for November 2000 which are given below.

Production and sales quantities November 2000

	(units)
Opening stock	20 000
Production	8 000
	28 000
Less Sales	10 000
Closing stock	18 000

The accountant is trying to choose the best method of presenting the financial information to the directors. The present method is shown under the Actual costs column; the two other methods are based on the standard costs derived above.

The following estimated figures for the month of December 2000 have just come to hand:

Sales 12 000 units at £25
Production costs:
  variable £116 000
  fixed £90 000

Production 14 000 units
Administration costs £24 500
Selling costs:
  variable £12 000
  fixed £15 000

Draft profit and loss accounts for the month ended 30 November 2000

	Actual costs (£000)	(£000)	Absorption cost method (£000)	(£000)	Variable cost method (£000)	(£000)
Sales (10 000 units at £25)		250		250		250
Opening stock	280		280		160	
Production costs:						
variable	60		112[a]		64	
fixed	66					
	406		392		224	
Closing stock	261	145	252	140	144	80
		105		110		170
Variable selling costs		—		—		10
Gross profit/contribution		105		110		160
Other expenses:						
Production – fixed	—		—		80	
Administration – fixed	23		21		28	
Selling:						
variable	11		10		—	
fixed	14	48	12	43	16	124
		57		67		36
Variances						
Production						
variable – expenditure			(4)		(4)	
fixed – volume			32		—	
– expenditure			(14)		(14)	
Administration – volume			7		—	
– expenditure			(5)		(5)	
Selling:						
variable – expenditure			1		1	
fixed – volume			4		—	
– expenditure		—	(2)	19	(2)	(24)
Net profit		57		48		60

Note
[a]Sum of variable and fixed costs.

Requirements

(a) Prepare a schedule explaining the *main* difference(s) between the net profit figures for November 2000 under the three different allocation methods.

(8 marks)

(b) Discuss the relative merits of the two suggested alternative methods as a means of providing useful information to the company's senior management.

(8 marks)

(c) Draw up a short report for senior management presenting your recommendations for the choice of method of preparing the monthly accounts, incorporating in your report the profit and loss account for November and the projected profit and loss account for December 2000 as examples of your recommendations.

(9 marks)

(Total 25 marks)

ICAEW P2 Management Accounting

Cost–volume–profit analysis

Shown below is a typical cost–volume–profit chart:

Required:

(a) Explain to a colleague who is not an accountant the reasons for the change in result on this cost–volume–profit chart from a loss at point (a) to a profit at point (b). (3 marks)

(b) Identify and critically examine the underlying assumptions of this type of cost–volume–profit analysis and consider whether such analyses are useful to the management of an organization. (14 marks)

(Total 17 marks)

ACCA Level 1 Costing

Question IM 8.1
Intermediate

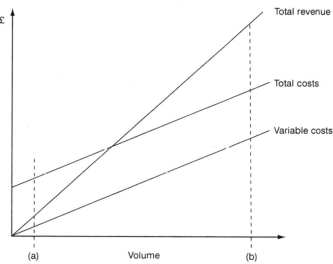

The graphs shown below show cost–volume–profit relationships as they are typically represented in (i) management accounting and (ii) economic theory. In each graph TR=total revenue, TC=total cost, and P=profit. You are required to compare these different representations of cost–volume–profit relationships, identifying, explaining and commenting on points of similarity and also differences. (15 marks)

ICAEW Management Accounting

Question IM 8.2
Intermediate

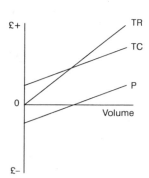
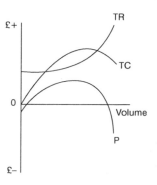

**Question IM 8.3
Intermediate**

'A break-even chart must be interpreted in the light of the limitations of its underlying assumptions...' (From *Cost Accounting: A Managerial Emphasis*, by C.T. Horngren.)

Required:
(a) Discuss the extent to which the above statement is valid and both describe and briefly appraise the reasons for five of the most important underlying assumptions of break-even analysis. (c. 14 marks)
(b) For any *three* of the underlying assumptions provided in answer to (a) above, give an example of circumstances in which that assumption is violated. Indicate the nature of the violation and the extent to which the break-even chart can be adapted to allow for this violation. (c. 6 marks)
(Total 20 marks)
ACCA P2 Management Accounting

**Question IM 8.4
Advanced**

The accountant's approach to cost–volume–profit analysis has been criticized in that, among other matters, it does not deal with the following:
(a) situations where sales volume differs radically from production volume;
(b) situations where the sales revenue and the total cost functions are markedly non-linear;
(c) changes in product mix;
(d) risk and uncertainty.

Explain these objections to the accountant's conventional cost–volume–profit model and suggest how they can be overcome or ameliorated. (17 marks)
ACCA Level 2 Management Accounting

**Question IM 8.5
Intermediate:
Multi-product
profit–volume
graph**

JK Limited has prepared a budget for the next twelve months when it intends to make and sell four products, details of which are shown below:

Product	Sales in units (thousands)	Selling price per unit (£)	Variable cost per unit (£)
J	10	20	14.00
K	10	40	8.00
L	50	4	4.20
M	20	10	7.00

Budgeted fixed costs are £240 000 per annum and total assets employed are £570 000.

You are required
(a) to calculate the total contribution earned by each product and their combined total contributions; (2 marks)
(b) to plot the data of your answer to (a) above in the form of a contribution to sales graph (sometimes referred to as a profit–volume graph) *on the graph paper provided*; (6 marks)
(c) to explain your graph to management, to comment on the results shown and to state the break-even point; (4 marks)
(d) to describe briefly three ways in which the overall contribution to sales ratio could be improved. (3 marks)
(Total 15 marks)
CIMA Stage 2 Cost Accounting

**Question IM 8.6
Intermediate:
Break-even chart
with increases in
fixed costs**

(a) Identify and discuss briefly *five* assumptions underlying cost–volume–profit analysis. (10 marks)
(b) A local authority, whose area includes a holiday resort situated on the east coast, operates, for 30 weeks each year, a holiday home which is let to visiting parties of children in care from other authorities. The children are accompanied by their own house mothers who supervise them throughout

their holiday. From six to fifteen guests are accepted on terms of £100 per person per week. No differential charges exist for adults and children.

Weekly costs incurred by the host authority are:

	(£ per guest)
Food	25
Electricity for heating and cooking	3
Domestic (laundry, cleaning etc.) expenses	5
Use of minibus	10

Seasonal staff supervise and carry out the necessary duties at the home at a cost of £11 000 for the 30-week period. This provides staffing sufficient for six to ten guests per week but if eleven or more guests are to be accommodated, additional staff at a total cost of £200 per week are engaged for the whole of the 30-week period.

Rent, including rates for the property, is £4000 per annum and the garden of the home is maintained by the council's recreation department which charges a nominal fee of £1000 per annum.

You are required to:
(i) tabulate the appropriate figures in such a way as to show the break-even point(s) and to comment on your figures; (8 marks)
(ii) draw, on the graph paper provided, a chart to illustrate your answer to (b)(i) above. (7 marks)
(Total 25 marks)
CIMA Cost Accounting Stage 2

(a) 'The analysis of total cost into its behavioural elements is essential for effective cost and management accounting.'

Required
Comment on the statement above, illustrating your answer with examples of cost behaviour patterns. (5 marks)
(b) The total costs incurred at various output levels, for a process operation in a factory, have been measured as follows:

Question IM 8.7 Intermediate: Analysis of costs into fixed and variable elements and break-even point calculation

Output (units)	Total cost (£)
11 500	102 476
12 000	104 730
12 500	106 263
13 000	108 021
13 500	110 727
14 000	113 201

Required:
Using the high–low method, analyse the costs of the process operation into fixed and variable components. (4 marks)
(c) Calculate, and comment upon, the break-even output level of the process operation in (b) above, based upon the fixed and variable costs identified and assuming a selling price of £10.60 per unit. (5 marks)
(Total 14 marks)
ACCA Foundation Paper 3

Question IM 8.8
Intermediate:
Non-graphical
CVP analysis and
the acceptance of
a special order

Video Technology Plc was established in 1987 to assemble video cassette recorders (VCRs). There is now increased competition in its markets and the company expects to find it difficult to make an acceptable profit next year. You have been appointed as an accounting technician at the company, and have been given a copy of the draft budget for the next financial year.

Draft budget for 12 months to 30 November 2001

	(£m)	(£m)
Sales income		960.0
Cost of sales:		
Variable assembly materials	374.4	
Variable labour	192.0	
Factory overheads – variable	172.8	
– fixed	43.0	(782.2)
		177.8
Gross profit		
Selling overheads – commission	38.4	
– fixed	108.0	
Administration overheads – fixed	20.0	(166.4)
Net profit		11.4

The following information is also supplied to you by the company's financial controller, Edward Davies:
1   planned sales for the draft budget in the year to 30 November 2001 are expected to be 25% less than the total of 3.2 million VCR units sold in the year to 30 November 2000;
2   the company operates a Just-In-Time stock control system, which means it holds no stocks of any kind;
3   if more than 3 million VCR units are made and sold, the unit cost of material falls by £4 per unit;
4   sales commission is based on the number of units sold and not on turnover;
5   the draft budget assumes that the factory will only be working at two-thirds of maximum capacity;
6   sales above maximum capacity are not possible.

Edward Davies explains that the Board is not happy with the profit projected in the draft budget, and that the sales director, Anne Williams, has produced three proposals to try and improve matters.
1   Proposal A involves launching an aggressive marketing campaign:
  (i)   this would involve a single additional fixed cost of £14 million for advertising;
  (ii)   there would be a revised commission payment of £18 per unit sold;
  (iii)   sales volume would be expected to increase by 10% above the level projected in the draft budget, with no change in the unit selling price.
2   Proposal B involves a 5% reduction in the unit selling price:
  (i)   this is estimated to bring the sales volume back to the level in the year to 30 November 2000.
3   Proposal C involves a 10% reduction in the unit selling price:
  (i)   fixed selling overheads would also be reduced by £45 million;
  (ii)   if proposal C is accepted, the sales director believes sales volume will be 3.8 million units.

Task 1
(a)   For each of the three proposals, calculate the:
  (i)   change in profits compared with the draft budget;
  (ii)   break-even point in units and turnover.
(b)   Recommend which proposal, if any, should be accepted on financial grounds.

(c) Identify *three* non-financial issues to be considered before a final decision is made.

Edward Davies now tells you that the company is considering a new export order with a proposed selling price of £3 million. He provides you with the following information:

1   The order will require two types of material:
   (i) material A is in regular use by the company. The amount in stock originally cost £0.85 million, but its standard cost is £0.9 million. The amount in stock is sufficient for the order. The current market price of material A to be used in the order is £0.8 million;
   (ii) material B is no longer used by the company and cannot be used elsewhere if not used on the order. The amount in stock originally cost £0.2 million although its current purchase price is £0.3 million. The amount of material B in stock is only half the amount required on the order. If not used on the order, the amount in stock could be sold for £0.1 million;
2   direct labour of £1.0 million will be charged to the order. This includes £0.2 million for idle time, as a result of insufficient orders to keep the workforce fully employed. The company has a policy of no redundancies, and spreads the resulting cost of idle time across all orders;
3   variable factory overheads are expected to be £0.9 million;
4   fixed factory overheads are apportioned against the order at the rate of 50% of variable factory overheads;
5   no sales commission will be paid.

Task 2
Prepare a memo for Edward Davies:
(a) showing whether or not the order should be accepted at the proposed selling price;
(b) identifying the technique(s) you have used in reaching this conclusion.

AAT Technicians Stage

PE Limited produces and sells two products, P and E. Budgets prepared for the next six months give the following information:

Question IM 8.9
Intermediate:
Calculation of
break-even points
based on different
product mix
assumptions

	Product P per unit £	Product E per unit £
Selling price	10.00	12.00
Variable costs: production and selling	5.00	10.00
Common fixed costs:		
production and selling		
for six months	£561 600	

(a) You are required, in respect of the forthcoming six months,
   (i) to state what the break-even point in £s will be and the number of each product this figure represents if the two products are sold in the ratio 4P to 3E;
        (3 marks)
   (ii) to state the break-even point in £s and the number of products this figure represents if the sales mix changes to 4P to 4E (ignore fractions of products);
        (3 marks)
   (iii) to advise the sales manager which product mix should be better, that in (a) (i) above or that in (a) (ii) above, and why;   (2 marks)
   (iv) to advise the sales manager which of the two products should be concentrated on and the reason(s) for your recommendation assume that whatever can be made can be sold, that both products go through a machining process and that there are only 32 000 machine hours available, with product P requiring 0.40 hour per unit and product E requiring 0.10 hour per unit.   (2 marks)

(b) You are required to compare and contrast the usefulness of a conventional break-even chart with a contribution break-even chart. Your explanation should include illustrative diagrams drawn within your answer book and not on graph paper.

(5 marks)
(Total 15 marks)
CIMA Stage 2 Cost Accounting

Question IM 8.10 Intermediate: Decision-making and non-graphical CVP analysis

York plc was formed three years ago by a group of research scientists to market a new medicine that they had invented. The technology involved in the medicine's manufacture is both complex and expensive. Because of this, the company is faced with a high level of fixed costs.

This is of particular concern to Dr Harper, the company's chief executive. She recently arranged a conference of all management staff to discuss company profitability. Dr Harper showed the managers how average unit cost fell as production volume increased and explained that this was due to the company's heavy fixed cost base. 'It is clear,' she said, 'that as we produce closer to the plant's maximum capacity of 70 000 packs the average cost per pack falls. Producing and selling as close to that limit as possible must be good for company profitability.' The data she used are reproduced below:

Production volume (packs)	40 000	50 000	60 000	70 000
Average cost per unit[a]	£430	£388	£360	£340
Current sales and production volume:	65 000 packs			
Selling price per pack:	£420			

[a]Defined as the total of fixed and variable costs, divided by the production volume

You are a member of York plc's management accounting team and shortly after the conference you are called to a meeting with Ben Cooper, the company's marketing director. He is interested in knowing how profitability changes with production.

Task 1
Ben Cooper asks you to calculate:
(a) the amount of York plc's fixed costs;
(b) the profit of the company at its current sales volume of 65 000 packs;
(c) the break-even point in units;
(d) the margin of safety expressed as a percentage.

Ben Cooper now tells you of a discussion he has recently had with Dr Harper. Dr Harper had once more emphasized the need to produce as close as possible to the maximum capacity of 70 000 packs. Ben Cooper has the possibility of obtaining an export order for an extra 5000 packs but, because the competition is strong, the selling price would only be £330. Dr Harper has suggested that this order should be rejected as it is below cost and so will reduce company profitability. However, she would be prepared, on this occasion, to sell the packs on a cost basis for £340 each, provided the order was increased to 15 000 packs.

Task 2
Write a memo to Ben Cooper. Your memo should:
(a) calculate the change in profits from accepting the order for 5000 packs at £330;
(b) calculate the change in profits from accepting an order for 15 000 packs at £340;
(c) briefly explain and justify which proposal, if either, should be accepted;
(d) identify *two* non-financial factors which should be taken into account before making a final decision.

AAT Technicians Stage

A company has two products with the following unit costs for a period:

	Product A (£/unit)	Product B (£/unit)
Direct materials	1.20	2.03
Direct labour	1.40	1.50
Variable production overheads	0.70	0.80
Fixed production overheads	1.10	1.10
Variable other overheads	0.15	0.20
Fixed other overheads	0.50	0.50

Production and sales of the two products for the period were:

	Product A (000 units)	Product B (000 units)
Production	250	100
Sales	225	110

Production was at normal levels. Unit costs in opening stock were the same as those for the period listed above.

Required:
(a) State whether, and why, absorption or marginal costing would show a higher company profit for the period, and calculate the difference in profit depending upon which method is used. (4 marks)
(b) Calculate the break-even sales revenue for the period (to the nearest £000) based on the above mix of sales. The selling prices of products A and B were £5.70 and £6.90 per unit, respectively. (7 marks)
(Total 11 marks)
ACCA Foundation Stage Paper 3

A local government authority owns and operates a leisure centre with numerous sporting facilities, residential accommodation, a cafeteria and a sports shop. The summer season lasts for 20 weeks including a peak period of 6 weeks corresponding to the school holidays. The following budgets have been prepared for the next summer season:

Accommodation
60 single rooms let on a daily basis.
35 double rooms let on a daily basis at 160% of the single room rate.
Fixed costs £29 900
Variable costs £4 per single room per day and £6.40 per double room per day.

Sports Centre
Residential guests each pay £2 per day and casual visitors £3 per day for the use of facilities.
Fixed costs £15 500

Sports Shop
Estimated contribution £1 per person per day.
Fixed costs £8250

Cafeteria
Estimated contribution £1.50 per person per day.
Fixed costs £12 750

During the summer season the centre is open 7 days a week and the following activity levels are anticipated:
Double rooms fully booked for the whole season.

Single rooms fully booked for the peak period but at only 80% of capacity during the rest of the season.

30 casual visitors per day on average.

You are required to

(a) calculate the charges for single and double rooms assuming that the authority wishes to make a £10 000 profit on accommodation;   (6 marks)

(b) calculate the anticipated total profit for the leisure centre as a whole for the season;   (10 marks)

(c) advise the authority whether an offer of £250 000 from a private leisure company to operate the centre for five years is worthwhile, assuming that the authority uses a 10% cost of capital and operations continue as outlined above.
                                                                                 (4 marks)
                                                                            (Total 20 marks)

CIMA Stage 3 Management Accounting Techniques

Measuring relevant costs and revenues for decision-making

'I remember being told about the useful decision-making technique of limiting factor analysis (also known as "contribution per unit of the key factor"). If an organisation is prepared to believe that, in the short run, all costs other than direct materials are fixed costs, is this not the same thing that throughput accounting is talking about? Why rename limiting factor analysis as throughput accounting?'

Question IM 9.1 Advanced

Requirements:
(a) Explain what a limiting (or 'key') factor is and what sort of things can become limiting factors in a business situation. Which of the factors in the scenario could become a limiting factor? (8 marks)
(b) Explain the techniques that have been developed to assist in business decision-making when single or multiple limiting factors are encountered. (7 marks)
(c) Explain the management idea known as throughput accounting. State and justify your opinion on whether or not throughput accounting and limiting factor analysis are the same thing. Briefly comment on whether throughput accounting is likely to be of relevance to SEL. (10 marks)

(Total 25 marks)

CIMA Stage 3 Management Accounting Applications

Company A expects to have 2000 direct labour hours of manufacturing capacity (in normal time) available over the next two months after completion of current regular orders. It is considering two options in order to utilize the spare capacity. If the available hours are not utilized direct labour costs would not be incurred.

Question IM 9.2 Intermediate: Determining minimum short-term acceptable selling price

The first option involves the early manufacture of a firm future order which would as a result reduce the currently anticipated need for overtime working in a few months time. The premium for overtime working is 30% of the basic rate of £4.00 per hour, and is charged to production as a direct labour cost. Overheads are charged at £6.00 per direct labour hour. 40% of overhead costs are variable with hours worked.

Alternatively, Company A has just been asked to quote for a one-off job to be completed over the next two months and which would require the following resources:
1. *Raw materials:*
   (i) 960 kg of Material X which has a current weighted average cost in stock of £3.02 per kg and a replacement cost of £3.10 per kg. Material X is used continuously by Company A.
   (ii) 570 kg of Material Y which is in stock at £5.26 per kg. It has a current replacement cost of £5.85 per kg. If used, Material Y would not be replaced. It has no other anticipated use, other than disposal for £2.30 per kg.
   (iii) Other materials costing £3360.

2. *Direct labour:* 2200 hours.

   Required:
   (a) Establish the minimum quote that could be tendered for the one-off job such that it would increase Company A's profit, compared with the alternative use of spare capacity. (Ignore the interest cost/benefit associated with the different timing of cash flows from the different options.)

(12 marks)

(b) Explain, and provide illustrations of, the following terms:
   (i)   sunk cost,   (3 marks)
   (ii) opportunity cost,   (3 marks)
   (iii) incremental cost.   (2 marks)
                                                        (Total 20 marks)
ACCA Level 1 Cost and Management Accounting 1

Question IM 9.3 Intermediate: Acceptance of a contract

JB Limited is a small specialist manufacturer of electronic components and much of its output is used by the makers of aircraft for both civil and military purposes. One of the few aircraft manufacturers has offered a contract to JB Limited for the supply, over the next twelve months, of 400 identical components.

The data relating to the production of each component is as follows:
(i)   Material requirements:
      3 kg material M1 – see note 1 below
      2 kg material P2 – see note 2 below
      1 Part No. 678 – see note 3 below
      Note 1. Material M1 is in continuous use by the company. 1000 kg are currently held in stock at a book value of £4.70 per kg but it is known that future purchases will cost £5.50 per kg.
      Note 2. 1200 kg of material P2 are held in stock. The original cost of this material was £4.30 per kg but as the material has not been required for the last two years it has been written down to £1.50 per kg scrap value. The only foreseeable alternative use is as a substitute for material P4 (in current use) but this would involve further processing costs of £1.60 per kg. The current cost of material P4 is £3.60 per kg.
      Note 3. It is estimated that the Part No. 678 could be bought for £50 each.
(ii) Labour requirements: Each component would require five hours of skilled labour and five hours of semi-skilled. An employee possessing the necessary skills is available and is currently paid £5 per hour. A replacement would, however, have to be obtained at a rate of £4 per hour for the work which would otherwise be done by the skilled employee. The current rate for semi-skilled work is £3 per hour and an additional employee could be appointed for this work.
(iii) Overhead: JB Limited absorbs overhead by a machine hour rate, currently £20 per hour of which £7 is for variable overhead and £13 for fixed overhead. If this contract is undertaken it is estimated that fixed costs will increase for the duration of the contract by £3200. Spare machine capacity is available and each component would require four machine hours.

      A price of £145 per component has been suggested by the large company which makes aircraft.

You are required to:
(a) State whether or not the contract should be accepted and support your conclusion with appropriate figures for presentation to management;
                                                            (16 marks)
(b) comment briefly on *three* factors which management ought to consider and which may influence their decision.   (9 marks)
                                                        (Total 25 marks)
CIMA Cost Accounting Stage 2

MEASURING RELEVANT COSTS AND REVENUES FOR DECISION-MAKING

You are the management accountant of a publishing and printing company which has been asked to quote for the production of a programme for the local village fair. The work would be carried out in addition to the normal work of the company. Because of existing commitments, some weekend working would be required to complete the printing of the programme. A trainee accountant has produced the following cost estimate based upon the resources as specified by the production manager:

Question IM 9.4
Intermediate:
Preparation of a
cost estimate
involving the
identification of
relevant costs

	(£)
Direct materials:	
paper (book value)	5 000
inks (purchase price)	2 400
Direct labour:	
skilled 250 hours at £4.00	1 000
unskilled 100 hours at £3.50	350
Variable overhead 350 hours at £4.00	1400
Printing press depreciation 200 hours at £2.50	500
Fixed production costs 350 hours at £6.00	2 100
Estimating department costs	400
	13 150

You are aware that considerable publicity could be obtained for the company if you are able to win this order and the price quoted must be very competitive.

The following are relevant to the cost estimate above:
1. The paper to be used is currently in stock at a value of £5000. It is of an unusual colour which has not been used for some time. The replacement price of the paper is £8000, while the scrap value of that in stock is £2500. The production manager does not foresee any alternative use for the paper if it is not used for the village fair programmes.
2. The inks required are not held in stock. They would have to be purchased in bulk at a cost of £3000. 80% of the ink purchased would be used in printing the programme. No other use is foreseen for the remainder.
3. Skilled direct labour is in short supply, and to accommodate the printing of the programmes, 50% of the time required would be worked at weekends, for which a premium of 25% above the normal hourly rate is paid. The normal hourly rate is £4.00 per hour.
4. Unskilled labour is presently under-utilized, and at present 200 hours per week are recorded as idle time. If the printing work is carried out at a weekend, 25 unskilled hours would have to occur at this time, but the employees concerned would be given two hours' time off (for which they would be paid) in lieu of each hour worked.
5. Variable overhead represents the cost of operating the printing press and binding machines.
6. When not being used by the company, the printing press is hired to outside companies for £6.00 per hour. This earns a contribution of £3.00 per hour. There is unlimited demand for this facility
7. Fixed production costs are those incurred by and absorbed into production, using an hourly rate based on budgeted activity.
8. The cost of the estimating department represents time spent in discussion with the village fair committee concerning the printing of its programme.

Required:
(a) Prepare a revised cost estimate using the opportunity cost approach, showing clearly the minimum price that the company should accept for the order. Give reasons for each resource valuation in your cost estimate. (16 marks)
(b) Explain why contribution theory is used as a basis for providing information relevant to decision-making. (4 marks)
(c) Explain the relevance of opportunity costs in decision-making. (5 marks)
(Total 25 marks)
CIMA Stage 2 Operational Costs Accounting

**Question IM 9.5
Intermediate:
Decision on
whether to launch
a new product**

A company is currently manufacturing at only 60% of full practical capacity, in each of its two production departments, due to a reduction in market share. The company is seeking to launch a new product which it is hoped will recover some lost sales.

The estimated direct costs of the new product, Product X, are to be established from the following information:

Direct materials:
Every 100 units of the product will require 30 kilos net of Material A. Losses of 10% of materials input are to be expected. Material A costs £5.40 per kilo before discount. A quantity discount of 5% is given on all purchases if the monthly purchase quantity exceeds 25 000 kilos. Other materials are expected to cost £1.34 per unit of Product X.

Direct labour (per hundred units):
Department 1: 40 hours at £4.00 per hour.
Department 2: 15 hours at £4.50 per hour.

Separate overhead absorption rates are established for each production department. Department 1 overheads are absorbed at 130% of direct wages, which is based upon the expected overhead costs and usage of capacity if Product X is launched. The rate in Department 2 is to be established as a rate per direct labour hour also based on expected usage of capacity. The following annual figures for Department 2 are based on full practical capacity:

Overhead, £5 424 000:
Direct labour hours, 2 200 000.

Variable overheads in Department 1 are assessed at 40% of direct wages and in Department 2 are £1 980 000 (at full practical capacity).
Non-production overheads are estimated as follows (per unit of Product X):

Variable,	£0.70
Fixed,	£1.95

The selling price for Product X is expected to be £9.95 per unit, with annual sales of 2 400 000 units.

Required:
(a) Determine the estimated cost per unit of Product X.   (13 marks)
(b) Comment on the viability of Product X.

(7 marks)
(c) Market research indicates that an alternative selling price for Product X could be £9.45 per unit, at which price annual sales would be expected to be 2 900 000 units. Determine, and comment briefly upon, the optimum selling price.

(5 marks)
(Total 25 marks)
ACCA Cost and Management Accounting 1

PDR plc manufactures four products using the same machinery. The following details relate to its products:

	Product A £ per unit	Product B £ per unit	Product C £ per unit	Product D £ per unit
Selling price	28	30	45	42
Direct material	5	6	8	6
Direct labour	4	4	8	8
Variable overhead	3	3	6	6
Fixed overhead*	8	8	16	16
Profit	8	9	7	6
Labour hours	1	1	2	2
Machine hours	4	3	4	5
	Units	Units	Units	Units
Maximum demand per week	200	180	250	100

*Absorbed based on budgeted labour hours of 1000 per week.

There is a maximum of 2000 machine hours available per week.

Requirement:
(a) Determine the production plan which will maximise the weekly profit of PDR plc and prepare a profit statement showing the profit your plan will yield.
(10 marks)
(b) The marketing director of PDR plc is concerned at the company's inability to meet the quantity demanded by its customers.
Two alternative strategies are being considered to overcome this:
(i) to increase the number of hours worked using the existing machinery by working overtime. Such overtime would be paid at a premium of 50% above normal labour rates, and variable overhead costs would be expected to increase in proportion to labour costs.
(ii) to buy product B from an overseas supplier at a cost of £19 per unit including carriage. This would need to be repackaged at a cost of £1 per unit before it could be sold.

Requirement:
Evaluate each of the two alternative strategies and, as management accountant, prepare a report to the marketing director, stating your reasons (quantitative and qualitative) as to which, if either, should be adopted. (15 marks)
(Total 25 marks)
CIMA Stage 2 Operational Cost Accounting

**Questions IM 9.7
Intermediate:
Allocation of
scarce capacity
and make or buy
decision where
scarce capacity
exists**

PQR Limited is an engineering company engaged in the manufacture of components and finished products.

The company is highly mechanised and each of the components and finished products requires the use of one or more types of machine in its machining department. The following costs and revenues (where appropriate) relate to a single component or unit of the finished product:

| | Components | | Finished products | |
| | A | B | C | D |
	£	£	£	£
Selling price			127	161
Direct materials	8	29	33	38
Direct wages	10	30	20	25
Variable overhead:				
Drilling	6	3	9	12
Grinding	8	16	4	12
Fixed overhead:				
Drilling	12	6	18	24
Grinding	10	20	5	15
Total cost	54	104	89	126

Notes
1. The labour hour rate is £5 per hour.
2. Overhead absorption rates per machine hour are as follows:

| | Variable | Fixed |
	£	£
Drilling (per hour)	3	6
Grinding (per hour)	4	5

3. Components A and B are NOT used in finished products C and D. They are used in the company's other products, none of which use the drilling or grinding machines. The company does not manufacture any other components.
4. The number of machine drilling hours available is limited to 1650 per week. There are 2500 machine grinding hours available per week. These numbers of hours have been used to calculate the absorption rates stated above.
5. The maximum demand in units per week for each of the finished products has been estimated by the marketing director as:

| Product C | 250 units |
| Product D | 500 units |

6. The internal demand for components A and B each week is as follows:

| Component A | 50 units |
| Component B | 100 units |

7. There is no external market for components A and B.
8. PQR Limited has a contract to supply 50 units of each of its finished products to a major customer each week. These quantities are included in the maximum units of demand given in note 5 above.

Requirement:
(a) Calculate the number of units of *each* finished product that PQR Limited should produce in order to maximise its profits, and the profit per week that this should yield. (12 marks)
(b) (i) The production director has now discovered that he can obtain unlimited quantities of components identical to A and B for £50 and £96 per unit respectively. State whether this information changes the production plan

of the company if it wishes to continue to maximise its profits per week. If appropriate, state the revised production plan and the net benefit per week caused by the change to the production plan. (7 marks)
(ii) The solution of problems involving more than one limiting factor requires the use of linear programming.
   Explain why this technique must be used in such circumstances, and the steps used to solve such a problem when using the graphical linear programming technique. (6 marks)
(Total 25 marks)
CIMA Stage 2 Operational Cost Accounting

B Ltd manufactures a range of products which are sold to a limited number of wholesale outlets. Four of these products are manufactured in a particular department on common equipment. No other facilities are available for the manufacture of these products.

Question IM 9.8 Intermediate: Limiting/key factors and a decision whether it is profitable to expand output by overtime

Owing to greater than expected increases in demand, normal single shift working is rapidly becoming insufficient to meet sales requirements. Overtime and, in the longer term, expansion of facilities are being considered.

Selling prices and product costs, based on single shift working utilizing practical capacity to the full, are as follows:

	Product (£/unit)			
	W	X	Y	Z
Selling price	3.650	3.900	2.250	2.950
Product costs:				
Direct materials	0.805	0.996	0.450	0.647
Direct labour	0.604	0.651	0.405	0.509
Variable manufacturing overhead	0.240	0.247	0.201	0.217
Fixed manufacturing overhead	0.855	0.950	0.475	0.760
Variable selling and admin overhead	0.216	0.216	0.216	0.216
Fixed selling and admin overhead	0.365	0.390	0.225	0.295

Fixed manufacturing overheads are absorbed on the basis of machine hours which, at practical capacity, are 2250 per period. Total fixed manufacturing overhead per period is £427 500. Fixed selling and administration overhead, which totals £190 000 per period, is shared amongst products at a rate of 10% of sales.

The sales forecast for the following period (in thousands of units) is:

Product W	190
Product X	125
Product Y	144
Product Z	142

Overtime could be worked to make up any production shortfall in normal time. Direct labour would be paid at a premium of 50% above basic rate. Other variable costs would be expected to remain unchanged per unit of output. Fixed costs would increase by £24 570 per period.

Required:
(a) If overtime is not worked in the following period, recommend the quantity of each product that should be manufactured in order to maximize profit. (12 marks)
(b) Calculate the expected profit in the following period if overtime is worked as necessary to meet sales requirements. (7 marks)
(c) Consider the factors which should influence the decision whether or not to work overtime in such a situation. (6 marks)
(Total 25 marks)
ACCA Cost and Management Accounting 1

**Question IM 9.9
Advanced: Key
factor and make
or buy decision**

A construction company has accepted a contract to lay underground pipework. The contract requires that 2500 m of 10″ pipe and 2000 m of 18″ pipe be laid each week.

The limiting factor is the availability of specialized equipment. The company owns 15 excavating machines (type A) and 13 lifting and jointing machines (type B). The normal operating time is 40 hours a week but up to 50% overtime is acceptable to the employees.

The time taken to handle each metre of pipe is:

Size of pipe	Minutes per metre	
	Machine A	Machine B
10″	6	12
18″	18	12

The costs of operating the machines are:

	Machine A (£)	Machine B (£)
Fixed costs, per week, each	450	160
Labour, per crew, per hour:		
up to 40 hours per week	10	12
over 40 hours per week	15	18

The costs of materials and supplies per metre are:

10″	£10
18″	£5

A subcontractor has offered to lay any quantity of the 10″ pipe at £18 per metre and of the 18″ pipe at £12 per metre.

You are required to:
(a) calculate the most economical way of undertaking the contract; (15 marks)
(b) state the weekly cost involved in your solution to (a) above; (5 marks)
(c) comment on the factors that management should consider in reaching a decision whether to adopt the minimum cost solution. (10 marks)

CIMA P3 Management Accounting

A South American farms 960 hectares of land on which he grows squash, kale, lettuce and beans. Of the total, 680 hectares are suitable for all four vegetables, but the remaining 280 hectares are suitable only for kale and lettuce. Labour for all kinds of farm work is plentiful.

The market requires that all four types of vegetable must be produced with a minimum of 10 000 boxes of any one line. The farmer has decided that the area devoted to any crop should be in terms of complete hectares and not in fractions of a hectare. The only other limitation is that not more than 227 500 boxes of any one crop should be produced.

Data concerning production, market prices and costs are as follows:

	Squash	Kale	Lettuce	Beans
Annual yield				
(boxes per hectare)	350	100	70	180
	(Pesos)	(Pesos)	(Pesos)	(Pesos)
Costs				
Direct:				
Materials per hectare	476	216	192	312
Labour:				
Growing, per hectare	896	608	372	528
Harvesting and packing, per box	3.60	3.28	4.40	5.20
Transport, per box	5.20	5.20	4.00	9.60
Market price, per box	15.38	15.87	18.38	22.27

Fixed overhead per annum:

	(Pesos)
Growing	122 000
Harvesting	74 000
Transport	74 000
General administration	100 000
Notional rent	74 000

It is possible to make the entire farm viable for all four vegetables if certain drainage work is undertaken. This would involve capital investment and it would have the following effects on direct harvesting costs of some of the vegetables:

	Capital cost	Change from normal harvesting costs	
		Squash	Beans
	(Pesos)	(Pesos per box)	
First lot of 10 hectares	19 000 total	+1.2	−1.2
Next lot of 10 hectares	17 500 total	+1.3	−1.3
Next lot of 10 hectares	15 000 total	+1.4	−1.4
Remaining land (per hectare)	1850	+1.5	−1.5

The farmer is willing to undertake such investment only if he can obtain a return of 15% DCF for a four-year period.

You are required to
(a) advise the farmer, within the given constraints,
   (i) the area to be cultivated with each crop if he is to achieve the largest total profit, (13 marks)
   (ii) the amount of this total profit, (3 marks)
   (iii) the number of hectares it is worth draining and the use to which they would be put; (10 marks)

(b) comment briefly on four of the financial dangers of going ahead with the drainage work. (4 marks)

Notes: Show all relevant calculations in arriving at your answer. Ignore tax and inflation. (Total 30 marks)

CIMA Stage 4 Management Accounting–Decision Making

Question IM 9.11
Advanced:
Relevant costs for
a pricing decision

Johnson trades as a chandler at the Savoy Marina. His profit in this business during the year to 30 June was £12 000. Johnson also undertakes occasional contracts to build pleasure cruisers, and is considering the price at which to bid for the contract to build the *Blue Blood* for Mr B.W. Dunn, delivery to be in one year's time. He has no other contract in hand, or under consideration, for at least the next few months.

Johnson expects that if he undertakes the contract he would devote one-quarter of his time to it. To facilitate this he would employ G. Harrison, an unqualified practitioner, to undertake his book-keeping and other paperwork, at a cost of £2000.

He would also have to employ on the contract one supervisor at a cost of £11 000 and two craftsmen at a cost of £8800 each; these costs include Johnson's normal apportionment of the fixed overheads of his business at the rate of 10% of labour cost.

During spells of bad weather one of the craftsmen could be employed for the equivalent of up to three months full-time during the winter in maintenance and painting work in the chandler's business. He would use materials costing £1000. Johnson already has two inclusive quotations from jobbing builders for this maintenance and painting work, one for £2500 and the other for £3500, the work to start immediately.

The equipment which would be used on the *Blue Blood* contract was bought nine years ago for £21 000. Depreciation has been written off on a straight-line basis, assuming a ten-year life and a scrap value of £1000. The current replacement cost of similar new equipment is £60 000, and is expected to be £66 000 in one year's time. Johnson has recently been offered £6000 for the equipment, and considers that in a year's time he would have little difficulty in obtaining £3000 for it. The plant is useful to Johnson only for contract work.

In order to build the *Blue Blood* Johnson will need six types of material, as follows:

| | No. of units | | Price per unit (£) | | |
| | | | Purchase price of stock items | Current purchase price | Current resale price |
Material code	In stock	Needed for contract			
A	100	1000	1.10	3.00	2.00
B	1 100	1000	2.00	0.90	1.00
C	—	100	—	6.00	—
D	100	200	4.00	3.00	2.00
E	50 000	5000	0.18	0.20	0.25
F	1 000	3000	0.90	2.00	1.00

Materials B and E are sold regularly in the chandler's business. Material A could be sold to a local sculptor, if not used for the contract. Materials A and E can be used for other purposes, such as property maintenance. Johnson has no other use for materials D and F, the stocks of which are obsolete.

The *Blue Blood* would be built in a yard held on a lease with four years remaining at a fixed annual rental of £5000. It would occupy half of this yard, which is useful to Johnson only for contract work.

Johnson anticipates that the direct expenses of the contract, other than those noted above, would be £6500.

Johnson has recently been offered a one-year appointment at a fee of £15 000 to manage a boat-building firm on the Isle of Wight. If he accepted the offer he would be unable to take on the contract to build *Blue Blood*, or any other contract. He would have to employ a manager to run the chandler's business at an annual cost (including fidelity insurance) of £10 000, and would incur additional personal living costs of £2000.

You are required:
(a) to calculate the price at which Johnson should be willing to take on the contract in order to break even, based exclusively on the information given above;

(15 marks)
(b) to set out any further considerations which you think that Johnson should take into account in setting the price at which he would tender for the contract.

(10 marks)
Ignore taxation.

ICAEW Management Accounting

Shortflower Ltd currently publish, print and distribute a range of catalogues and instruction manuals. The management have now decided to discontinue printing and distribution and concentrate solely on publishing. Longplant Ltd will print and distribute the range of catalogues and instruction manuals on behalf of Shortflower Ltd commencing either at 30 June or 30 November. Longplant Ltd will receive £65 000 per month for a contract which will commence either at 30 June or 30 November.

Question IM 9.12 Advanced: Decision on whether a department should be closed

The results of Shortflower Ltd for a typical month are as follows:

	Publishing (£000)	Printing (£000)	Distribution (£000)
Salaries and wages	28	18	4
Materials and supplies	5.5	31	1.1
Occupancy costs	7	8.5	1.2
Depreciation	0.8	4.2	0.7

Other information has been gathered relating to the possible closure proposals:
(i) Two specialist staff from printing will be retained at their present salary of £1500 each per month in order to fulfil a link function with Longplant Ltd. One further staff member will be transferred to publishing to fill a staff vacancy through staff turnover, anticipated in July. This staff member will be paid at his present salary of £1400 per month which is £100 more than that of the staff member who is expected to leave. On closure all other printing and distribution staff will be made redundant and paid an average of two months redundancy pay.
(ii) The printing department has a supply of materials (already paid for) which cost £18 000 and which will be sold to Longplant Ltd for £10 000 if closure takes place on 30 June. Otherwise the material will be used as part of the July printing requirements. The distribution department has a contract to purchase pallets at a cost of £500 per month for July and August. A cancellation clause allows for non-delivery of the pallets for July and August for a one-off payment of £300. Non-delivery for August only will require a payment of £100. If the pallets are taken from the supplier Longplant Ltd has agreed to purchase them at a price of £380 for each month's supply which is available. Pallet costs are included in the distribution material and supplies cost stated for a typical month.
(iii) Company expenditure on apportioned occupancy costs to printing and distribution will be reduced by 15% per month if printing and distribution departments are closed. At present, 30% of printing and 25% of distribution occupancy costs are directly attributable costs which are avoidable on closure, whilst the remainder are apportioned costs.
(iv) Closure of the printing and distribution departments will make it possible to sub-let part of the building for a monthly fee of £2500 when space is available.

(v) Printing plant and machinery has an estimated net book value of £48 000 at 30 June. It is anticipated that it will be sold at a loss of £21 000 on 30 June. If sold on 30 November the prospective buyer will pay £25 000.

(vi) The net book value of distribution vehicles at 30 June is estimated as £80 000. They could be sold to the original supplier at £48 000 on 30 June. The original supplier would purchase the vehicles on 30 November for a price of £44 000.

Required:

Using the above information, prepare a summary to show whether Shortflower Ltd should close the printing and distribution departments on financial grounds on 30 June or on 30 November. Explanatory notes and calculations should be shown. Ignore taxation. (22 marks)

ACCA Level 2 Cost and Management Accounting II

Activity-based costing

The traditional methods of cost allocation, cost apportionment and absorption into products are being challenged by some writers who claim that much information given to management is misleading when these methods of dealing with fixed overheads are used to determine product costs.

Question IM 10.1
Intermediate

You are required to explain what is meant by *cost allocation, cost apportionment* and *absorption* and to describe briefly the alternative approach of *activity-based costing* in order to ascertain total product costs. (15 marks)

CIMA Stage 2 Cost Accounting

'Attributing direct costs and absorbing overhead costs to the product/service through an activity-based costing approach will result in a better understanding of the true cost of the final output.'

Question IM 10.2
Intermediate

(*Source*: a recent CIMA publication on costing in a service environment.)

You are required to explain and comment on the above statement. (15 marks)

CIMA Stage 2 Cost Accounting

The basic ideas justifying the use of Activity Based Costing (ABC) and Activity Based Budgeting (ABB) are well publicised, and the number of applications has increased. However, there are apparently still significant problems in changing from existing systems.

Question IM 10.3
Advanced

Requirements:
(a) Explain which characteristics of an organisation, such as its structure, product range, or environment, may make the use of activity based techniques particularly useful. (5 marks)
(b) Explain the problems that may cause an organisation to decide not to use, or to abandon use of, activity based techniques. (8 marks)
(c) Some categorisations of cost drivers provide hierarchical models:
    (i) unit-level activities,
    (ii) batch activities,
    (iii) product sustaining activities,
    (iv) facility sustaining activities.
    Other analyses focus on 'value adding' and 'non-value adding' activities.

Requirement:
Explain what is meant by 'non-value adding activities', and discuss the usefulness of this form of analysis. (7 marks)
(Total 20 marks)
CIMA Stage 4 Management Accounting Control Systems

**Question IM 10.4
Intermediate:
Calculation of
ABC product
costs and a
discussion of the
usefulness of
ABC**

Trimake Limited makes three main products, using broadly the same production methods and equipment for each. A conventional product costing system is used at present, although an activity-based costing (ABC) system is being considered. Details of the three products for a typical period are:

	Hours per unit		Materials per unit	Volumes
	Labour hours	Machine unit	£	Units
Product X	½	1½	20	750
Product Y	1½	1	12	1250
Product Z	1	3	25	7000

Direct labour costs £6 per hour and production overheads are absorbed on a machine hour basis. The rate for the period is £28 per machine hour.
(a) You are required to calculate the cost per unit for each product using conventional methods. (4 marks)

Further analysis shows that the total of production overheads can be divided as follows:

	(%)
Costs relating to set-ups	35
Costs relating to machinery	20
Costs relating to materials handling	15
Costs relating to inspection	30
Total production overhead	100%

The following activity volumes are associated with the product line for the period as a whole.
Total activities for the period:

	Number of set-ups	Number of movements of materials	Number of inspections
Product X	75	12	150
Product Y	115	21	180
Product Z	480	87	670
	670	120	1000

You are required
(b) to calculate the cost per unit for each product using ABC principles; (15 marks)
(c) to comment on the reasons for any differences in the costs in your answers to (a) and (b). (3 marks)
(Total 22 marks)
CIMA Stage 3 Management Accounting Techniques

Duo plc produces two products A and B. Each has two components specified as sequentially numbered parts i.e. product A (parts 1 and 2) and product B (parts 3 and 4). Two production departments (machinery and fitting) are supported by five service activities (material procurement, material handling, maintenance, quality control and set up). Product A is a uniform product manufactured each year in 12 monthly high volume production runs. Product B is manufactured in low volume customised batches involving 25 separate production runs each month. Additional information is as follows:

	Product A	Product B
Production details:		
Components	Parts 1, 2	Parts 3, 4
Annual volume produced	300 000 units	300 000 units
Annual direct labour hours:		
Machinery department	500 000 DLH	600 000 DLH
Fitting department	150 000 DLH	200 000 DLH

Overhead Cost Analysis[a]

	(£000s)
Material handling	1 500
Material procurement	2 000
Set-up	1 500
Maintenance	2 500
Quality control	3 000
Machinery (machinery power, depreciation etc.)[b]	2 500
Fitting (machine, depreciation, power etc.)[b]	2 000
	15 000

[a] It may be assumed that these represent fairly homogeneous activity-based cost pools.

[b] It is assumed these costs (depreciation, power etc.) are primarily production volume driven and that direct labour hours are an appropriate surrogate measure of this.

Cost Driver Analysis

Cost Driver	Annual Cost Driver Volume per Component			
	Part 1	Part 2	Part 3	Part 4
Material movements	180	160	1 000	1 200
Number of orders	200	300	2 000	4 000
Number of set-ups	12	12	300	300
Maintenance hours	7 000	5 000	10 000	8 000
Number of inspections	360	360	2400	1 000
Direct labour hours	150 000	350 000	200 000	400 000
Direct labour hours	50 000	100 000	60 000	140 000

You are required to compute the unit costs for products A and B using (i) a traditional volume-based product costing system and (ii) an activity-based costing system.

(Adapted from Innes, J. and Mitchell, F., *Activity Based Costing: A Review with Case Studies*, Chartered Institute of Management Accountants, 1990)

Question IM 10.6 Advanced: Profitability analysis using ABC as traditional cost allocation bases

ABC plc, a group operating retail stores, is compiling its budget statements for the next year. In this exercise revenues and costs at each store A, B and C are predicted. Additionally, all central costs of warehousing and a head office are allocated across the three stores in order to arrive at a total cost and net profit of each store operation.

In earlier years the central costs were allocated in total based on the total sales value of each store. But as a result of dissatisfaction expressed by some store managers alternative methods are to be evaluated.

The predicted results before any re-allocation of central costs are as follows:

	A (£000)	B (£000)	C (000)
Sales	5000	4000	3000
Costs of sales	2800	2300	1900
Gross margin	2200	1700	1100
Local operating expenses			
Variable	660	730	310
Fixed	700	600	500
Operating profit	840	370	290

The central costs which are to be allocated are:

	(£000)
Warehouse costs:	
Depreciation	100
Storage	80
Operating and despatch	120
Delivery	300
Head office:	
Salaries	200
Advertising	80
Establishment	120
Total	1000

The management accountant has carried out discussions with staff at all locations in order to identify more suitable 'cost drivers' of some of the central costs. So far the following has been revealed.

	A	B	C
Number of despatches	550	450	520
Total delivery distances (thousand miles)	70	50	90
Storage space occupied (%)	40	30	30

1. An analysis of senior management time revealed that 10% of their time was devoted to warehouse issues with the remainder shared equally between the three stores.
2. It was agreed that the only basis on which to allocate the advertising costs was sales revenue.
3. Establishment costs were mainly occupancy costs of senior management.

This analysis has been carried out against a background of developments in the company, for example, automated warehousing and greater integration with suppliers.

Required:
(a) As the management accountant prepare a report for the management of the group which:
   (i) Computes the budgeted net profit of each store based on the *sales value* allocation base originally adopted and explains 'cost driver', 'volume' and

'complexity' issues in relation to cost allocation commenting on the possible implications of the dissatisfaction expressed. (6 marks)

(ii) Computes the budgeted net profit of each store using the additional information provided, discusses the extent to which an improvement has been achieved in the information on the costs and profitability of running the stores and comments on the results. (11 marks)

(b) Explain briefly how regression analysis and coefficient of determination (r^2) could be used in confirming the delivery mileage allocation method used in (a) above. (3 marks)

(Total 20 marks)

ACCA Paper 8 Managerial Finance

Excel Ltd make and sell two products, VG4U and VG2. Both products are manufactured through two consecutive processes – making and packing. Raw material is input at the commencement of the making process. The following estimated information is available for the period ending 31 March:

Question IM 10.7 Advanced: Unit cost computation based on traditional and ABC systems

(i)

	Making (£000)	Packing (£000)
Conversion costs:		
Variable	350	280
Fixed	210	140

40% of fixed costs are product specific, the remainder are company fixed costs. Fixed costs will remain unchanged throughout a wide activity range.

(ii) **Product information:**

	VG4	UVG2
Production time per unit:		
Making (minutes)	5.25	5.25
Packing (minutes)	6	4
Production sales (units)	5000	3000
Selling price per unit (£)	150	180
Direct material cost per unit (£)	30	30

(iii) Conversion costs are absorbed by products using estimated time based rates.

Required:
(a) Using the above information,
   (i) calculate unit costs for each product, analysed as relevant. (10 marks)
   (ii) comment on a management suggestion that the production and sale of one of the products should not proceed in the period ending 31 March. (4 marks)

(b) Additional information is gathered for the period ending 31 March as follows:
   (i) The making process consists of two consecutive activities, moulding and trimming. The moulding variable conversion costs are incurred in proportion to the temperature required in the moulds. The variable trimming conversion costs are incurred in proportion to the consistency of the material when it emerges from the moulds. The variable packing process conversion costs are incurred in proportion to the time required for each product. Packing materials (which are part of the variable packing cost) requirement depends on the complexity of packing specified for each product.
   (ii) The proportions of product specific conversion costs (variable and fixed) are analysed as follows:
   Making process: moulding (60%); trimming (40%)
   Packing process: conversion (70%); packing material (30%)

(iii) An investigation into the effect of the cost drivers on costs has indicated that the proportions in which the total product specific conversion costs are attributable to VG4U and VG2 are as follows:

	VG4U	VG2
Temperature (moulding)	2	1
Material consistency (trimming)	2	5
Time (packing)	3	2
Packing (complexity)	1	3

(iv) Company fixed costs are apportioned to products at an overall average rate per product unit based on the estimated figures.

Required:
Calculate amended unit costs for each product where activity based costing is used and company fixed costs are apportioned as detailed above. (12 marks)

(c) Comment on the relevance of the amended unit costs in evaluating the management suggestion that one of the products be discontinued in the period ending 31 March. (4 marks)

(d) Management wish to achieve an overall net profit margin of 15% on sales in the period ending 31 March in order to meet return on capital targets.

Required:
Explain how target costing may be used in achieving the required return and suggest specific areas of investigation. (5 marks)

(Total 35 marks)

ACCA Paper 9 Information for Control and Decision Making

Pricing decisions and profitability analysis

A company supplying capital equipment to the engineering industry is part of a large group of diverse companies. It determines its tender prices by adding a standard profit margin as a percentage of its prime cost.

Although it is working at full capacity the group managing director considers the company's annual return on capital employed as inadequate.

You are required, as the group assistant management accountant, to provide him with the following information:
(a) why the return-on-prime-cost (ROPC) approach to tendering would be likely to yield an inadequate return on capital employed; (7 marks)
(b) the steps involved in calculating a return on capital employed (ROCE) tendering rate for a particular contract; (7 marks)
(c) three problems likely to be encountered in meeting a pre-set profit target on a ROCE basis. (6 marks)
(Total 20 marks)
CIMA P3 Management Accounting

Question IM 11.1
Advanced

It has been stated that companies do not have profitable products, only profitable customers. Many companies have placed emphasis on the concept of Customer Account Profitability (CAP) analysis in order to increase their earnings and returns to shareholders. Much of the theory of CAP draws from the view that the main strategic thrust operated by many companies is to encourage the development and sale of new products to existing customers.

Requirements:
(a) Briefly explain the concept of CAP analysis. (5 marks)
(b) Critically appraise the value of CAP analysis as a means of increasing earnings per share and returns to shareholders. (15 marks)
(Total 20 marks)
CIMA Stage 4 Strategic Management Accounting and Marketing

Question IM 11.2
Advanced

A producer of high quality executive motor cars has developed a new model which it knows to be very advanced both technically and in style by comparison with the competition in its market segment.

The company's reputation for high quality is well-established and its servicing network in its major markets is excellent. However, its record in timely delivery has not been so good in previous years, though this has been improving considerably.

In the past few years it has introduced annual variations/improvements in its major models. When it launched a major new vehicle some six years ago the recommended retail price was so low in relation to the excellent specification of the car that a tremendous demand built up quickly and a two-year queue for the car developed within six months. Within three months a second-hand model had been sold at an auction for nearly 50% more than the list price and even after a year of production a sizeable premium above list price was being obtained.

The company considers that, in relation to the competition, the proposed new model will be as attractive as was its predecessor six years ago. Control of costs is very good so that accurate cost data for the new model are to hand. For the previous

Question IM 11.3
Advanced:
Discussion of
pricing strategies

model, the company assessed the long-term targeted annual production level and calculated its prices on that basis. In the first year, production was 30% of that total.

For the present model the company expects that the relationship between first-year production and longer-term annual production will also be about 30%, though the absolute levels in both cases are expected to be higher than previously.

The senior management committee, of which you are a member, has been asked to recommend the pricing approach that the company should adopt for the new model.

You are required
(a) to list the major pricing approaches available in this situation and discuss in some detail the relative merits and disadvantages to the company of each approach in the context of the new model;   (15 marks)
(b) to recommend which approach you would propose, giving your reasons;
                                                                              (5 marks)
(c) to outline briefly in which ways, if any, your answers to (a) and (b) above would differ if, instead of a high quality executive car, you were pricing a new family model of car with some unusual features that the company might introduce.
                                                                              (5 marks)
                                                                    (Total 25 marks)
CIMA Stage 4 Management Accounting Decision Making

**Question IM 11.4
Intermediate:
Computation of
minimum selling
price and
optimum price
from price–
demand
relationships**

In an attempt to win over key customers in the motor industry and to increase its market share, BIL Motor Components plc has decided to charge a price lower than its normal price for component TD463 when selling to the key customers who are being targeted. Details of component TD463's standard costs are as follows:

	Machine Group 1 (£)	Machine Group 7 (£)	Machine Group 29 (£)	Assembly (£)
Component TD463 Batch size 200 units				
Materials (per unit)	26.00	17.00	—	3.00
Labour (per unit)	2.00	1.60	0.75	1.20
Variable overheads (per unit)	0.65	0.72	0.80	0.36
Fixed overheads (per unit)	3.00	2.50	1.50	0.84
	31.65	21.82	3.05	5.40
Setting-up costs per batch of 200 units	£10.00	£6.00	£4.00	—

Required:
(a) Compute the lowest selling price at which one batch of 200 units could be offered, and critically evaluate the adoption of such a pricing policy.   (8 marks)
(b) The company is also considering the launch of a new product, component TDX489, and has provided you with the following information:

	Standard cost per box (£)
Variable cost	6.20
Fixed cost	1.60
	7.80

Market research forecast of demand:

Selling price (£)	13	12	11	10	9
Demand (boxes)	5000	6000	7200	11 200	13 400

The company only has enough production capacity to make 7000 boxes. However, it would be possible to purchase product TDX489 from a subcontractor at £7.75 per box for orders up to 5000 boxes and £7 per box if the orders exceed 5000 boxes.

Required:
Prepare and present a computation which illustrates which price should be selected in order to maximise profits. (8 marks)
(c) Where production capacity is the 'limiting factor', explain briefly the ways in which management can increase it without having to acquire more plant and machinery. (4 marks)
(Total 20 marks)
ACCA Paper 8 Managerial Finance

Josun plc manufactures cereal based foods, including various breakfast cereals under private brand labels. In March the company had been approached by Cohin plc, a large national supermarket chain, to tender for the manufacture and supply of a crunchy style breakfast cereal made from oats, nuts, raisins, etc. The tender required Josun to quote prices for a 1.5 kg packet at three different weekly volumes: 50 000, 60 000 and 70 000. Josun plc had, at present, excess capacity on some of its machines and could make a maximum of 80 000 packets of cereal a week.

Question IM 11.5 Advanced: Cost-plus and relevant cost information for pricing decisions

Josun's management accountant is asked to prepare a costing for the Cohin tender. The company prepares its tender prices on the basis of full cost plus 15% of cost as a profit margin. The full cost is made up of five elements: raw materials per packet of £0.30p; operating wages £0.12p per packet; manufacturing overheads costed at 200% of operating wages; administration and other corporate overheads at 100% of operating wages; and packaging and transport costing £0.10p per packet. The sales manager has suggested that as an incentive to Cohin, the profit margin be cut on the 60 000 and 70 000 tenders by ½% and 1% to 14½% and 14½% respectively. The manufacturing and administration overheads are forecast as fixed at £12 500 per week, unless output drops to 50 000 units or below per week, when a saving of £1000 per week can be made. If no contract is undertaken then all the manufacturing and administration overheads will be saved except for £600 per week. If the tender is accepted the volume produced and sold will be determined by the sales achieved by Cohin.

A week before the Cohin tender is to be presented for negotiation, Josun receives an enquiry from Stamford plc, a rival supermarket chain, to produce, weekly, 60 000 packets of a similar type of breakfast cereal of slightly superior quality at a price of £1.20 per 1.5 kg packet, the quality and mix of the cereal constituents being laid down by Stamford. This product will fill a gap in Stamford's private label range of cereals. The estimated variable costs for this contract would be: raw materials £0.40p per packet, operating labour £0.15p per packet and packaging and transport £0.12p per packet. None of the 80 000 weekly capacity could be used for another product if either of these contracts were taken up.

You are required to:
(a) compute the three selling prices per packet for the Cohin tender using Josun's normal pricing method; (3 marks)
(b) advise Josun, giving your financial reasons, on the relative merits of the two contracts; (6 marks)
(c) discuss the merits of full-cost pricing as a method of arriving at selling prices; (5 marks)
(d) make recommendations to Josun as to the method it might use to derive its selling prices in future; (3 marks)
(e) calculate the expected value of each tender given the following information and recommend which potential customer should receive the greater sales effort. It is estimated that there is a 70% chance of Stamford signing the contract for the weekly production of 60 000 packets, while there is a 20% chance of Cohin not accepting the tender. It is also estimated that the

probabilities of Cohin achieving weekly sales volumes of 50 000, 60 000 or 70 000 are 0.3, 0.5 and 0.2 respectively. The two sets of negotiations are completely independent of each other; (4 marks)

(f) provide, with reasons, for each of the two contracts under negotiation, a minimum and a recommended price that Josun could ask for the extra quantity that could be produced under each contract and which would ensure the full utilization of Josun's weekly capacity of 80 000 packets. (4 marks)

(Total 25 marks)

ICAEW P2 Management Accounting

Question IM 11.6 Advanced: Selection of optimal selling price based on demand and cost schedules

Sniwe plc intend to launch a commemorative product for the 2004 Olympic games onto the UK market commencing 1 August 2002. The product will have variable costs of £16 per unit.

Production capacity available for the product is sufficient for 2000 units per annum. Sniwe plc has made a policy decision to produce to the maximum available capacity during the year to 31 July 2003.

Demand for the product during the year to 31 July 2003 is expected to be price dependent, as follows:

Selling price per unit (£)	Annual sales (units)
20	2000
30	1600
40	1200
50	1100
60	1000
70	700
80	400

It is anticipated that in the year to 31 July 2004 the availability of similar competitor products will lead to a market price of £40 per unit for the product during that year.

During the year to 31 July 2004, Sniwe plc intend to produce only at the activity level required to enable them to satisfy demand, with stocks being run down to zero if possible. This policy is intended as a precaution against a sudden collapse of the market for the product by 31 July 2004.

Required:
(Ignoring tax and the time value of money.)

(a) Determine the launch price at 1 August 2002 which will maximize the net benefit to Sniwe plc during the two year period to 31 July 2004 where the demand potential for the year to 31 July 2004 is estimated as (i) 3600 units and (ii) 1000 units. (12 marks)

(b) Identify which of the launch strategies detailed in (a)(i) and (a)(ii) above will result in unsold stock remaining at 31 July 2004.

Advise management of the minimum price at which such unsold stock should be able to be sold in order to alter the initial launch price strategy which will maximize the net benefit to Sniwe plc over the life of the product. (6 marks)

(c) Comment on any other factors which might influence the initial launch price strategy where the demand in the year to 31 July 2004 is estimated at 1000 units. (4 marks)

(Total 22 marks)

ACCA Level 2 Management Accounting

XYZ is the only manufacturer of a product called the X. The variable cost of producing an X is £1.50 at all levels of output.

During recent months the X has been sold at a unit price of around £6.25. Various small adjustments (up and down) have been made to this price in an attempt to find a profit maximising selling price.

XYZ's Commercial Manager (an economics graduate) has recently commissioned a study by a firm of marketing consultants 'to investigate the demand structure for Xs and in particular to calculate the elasticity of demand for Xs produced by XYZ'. (*Note*: the elasticity of demand for a product is the proportion by which demand changes divided by the proportional price change which causes it.)

The consultants have reported back that at a unit price of £10 there is no demand for Xs but that demand increases by 40 Xs for each 1p (£0.01) that the unit price is reduced below £10. They have also reported that 'when demand is at around half its theoretical maximum the elasticity of demand is approximately 1.'

Upon receiving this report the Commercial Manager makes the following statement:

Recent experiences gained in adjusting the unit selling price of the X suggest that the product has quite an elastic demand structure. Small changes in the unit selling price produce far larger proportionate increases in demand. I find it difficult to accept that the elasticity of demand for the X is 1.

You are required:
(a) to write a memorandum to the Commercial Manager reconciling the consultants' report with his own observations on the elasticity of demand for the X;   (10 marks)
(b) to calculate the profit maximising unit selling price for the X (accurate to the nearest penny) and to calculate the elasticity of demand for the X at that selling price;   (10 marks)
(Total 20 marks)
CIMA Stage 4 Management Accounting Decision Making

**Question IM 11.7
Advanced:
Calculation of
elasticity of
demand, optimum
output and selling
price**

French Ltd is about to commence operations utilizing a simple production process to produce two products X and Y. It is the policy of French to operate the new factory at its maximum output in the first year of operations. Cost and production details estimated for the first year's operations are:

**Question 11.8
Advanced:
Calculation of unit
costs and
optimum selling
price**

Product	Production resources per unit		Variable cost per unit		Fixed production overheads directly attributable to product (£000)	Maximum production (000 units)
	Labour hours	Machine hours	Direct labour (£)	Direct materials (£)		
X	1	4	5	6	120	40
Y	8	2	28	16	280	10

There are also general fixed production overheads concerned in the manufacture of both products but which cannot be directly attributed to either. This general fixed production overhead is estimated at £720 000 for the first year of operations. It is thought that the cost structure of the first year will also be operative in the second year.

Both products are new and French is one of the first firms to produce them. Hence in the first year of operations the sales price can be set by French. In the second and subsequent years it is felt that the market for X and Y will have become more settled and French will largely conform to the competitive market prices that will become established. The sales manager has researched the first year's market potential and has estimated sales volumes for various ranges of selling price. The details are:

Product X		Product Y	
Range of per unit sales prices (£) (£)	Sales volume (000)	Range of per unit sales prices (£) (£)	Sales volume (000)
Up to 24.00	36	Up to 96.00	11
24.01 to 30.00	32	96.01 to 108.00	10
30.01 to 36.00	18	108.01 to 120.00	9
36.01 to 42.00*	8	120.01 to 132.00	8
		132.01 to 144.00	7
		144.01 to 156.00*	5

*Maximum price.

The managing director of French wishes to ascertain the total production cost of X and Y as, he says, 'Until we know the per unit cost of production we cannot properly determine the first year's sales price. Price must always ensure that total cost is covered and there is an element of profit – therefore I feel that the price should be total cost plus 20%. The determination of cost is fairly simple as most costs are clearly attributable to either X or Y. The general factory overhead will probably be allocated to the products in accordance with some measure of usage of factory resources such as labour or machine hours. The choice between labour and machine hours is the only problem in determining the cost of each product – but the problem is minor and so, therefore, is the problem of pricing.'

Required:
(a) Produce statements showing the effect the cost allocation and pricing methods mentioned by the managing director will have on
    (i) unit costs,
    (ii) closing stock values, and
    (iii) disclosed profit for the first year of operation.   (c. 8 marks)
(b) Briefly comment on the results in (a) above and advise the managing director on the validity of using the per unit cost figures produced for pricing decisions.
                                                                        (c. 4 marks)
(c) Provide appropriate statements to the management of French Ltd which will be of direct relevance in assisting the determination of the optimum prices of X and Y for the first year of operations. The statements should be designed to provide assistance in each of the following, separate, cases:
    (i) year II demand will be below productive capacity;
    (ii) year II demand will be substantially in excess of productive capacity.
    In both cases the competitive market sales prices per unit for year II are expected to be
        X – £30 per unit
        Y – £130 per unit
    Clearly specify, and explain, your advice to French for each of the cases described.
    (Ignore taxation and the time value of money.)   (c. 8 marks)
                                                                        (Total 20 marks)
                                                        ACCA P2 Management Accounting

AB p.l.c. makes two products, Alpha and Beta. The company made a £500 000 profit last year and proposes an identical plan for the coming year. The relevant data for last year are summarized in Table 1.

Table 1: Actuals for last year

	Product Alpha	Product Beta
Actual production and sales (units)	20 000	40 000
Total costs per unit	£20	£40
Selling prices per unit (25% on cost)	£25	£50
Machining time per unit (hours)	2	1
Potential demand at above selling prices (units)	30 000	50 000

Fixed costs were £480 000 for the year, absorbed on machining hours which were fully utilized for the production achieved.

A new Managing Director has been appointed and he is somewhat sceptical about the plan being proposed. Furthermore, he thinks that additional machining capacity should be installed to remove any production bottlenecks and wonders whether a more flexible pricing policy should be adopted.

Table 2 summarizes the changes in costs involved for the extra capacity and gives price/demand data, supplied by the Marketing Department, applicable to the conditions expected in the next period.

Table 2: Costs
Extra machining capacity would increase fixed costs by 10% in total. Variable costs and machining times per unit would remain unchanged.

	Product Alpha	Product Beta
Price/demand data		
Price range (per unit)	£20–30	£45–55
Expected demand (000 units)	45–15	70–30

You are required to
(a) calculate the plan to maximize profits for the coming year based on the data and selling prices in Table 1; (7 marks)
(b) comment on the pricing system for the existing plan used in Table 1; (3 marks)
(c) calculate the best selling prices and production plan based on the data in Table 2; (7 marks)
(d) comment on the methods you have used in part (c) to find the optimum prices and production levels. (3 marks)
Any assumptions made must be clearly stated. (Total 20 marks)
CIMA Stage 3 Management Accounting Techniques

Question 11.9
Advanced:
Calculation of optimal output level adopting a limiting factor approach and the computation of optimum selling prices using differential calculus

Question IM 11.10
Advanced:
Calculation of
optimum quantity
and prices for
joint products
using differential
calculus plus a
discussion of joint
cost allocations

Nuts plc produces alpha and beta in two stages. The separation process produces crude alpha and beta from a raw material costing £170 per tonne. The cost of the separation process is £100 per tonne of raw material. Each tonne of raw material generates 0.4 tonne of crude alpha and 0.6 tonne of crude beta. Neither product can be sold in its crude state.

The refining process costs £125 per tonne for alpha and £50 per tonne for beta; no weight is lost in refining. The demand functions for refined alpha and refined beta are independent of each other, and the corresponding price equations are:

$$P_A = 1250 - \frac{100Q_A}{32}$$

$$P_B = 666\tfrac{2}{3} - \frac{100Q_B}{18}$$

where P_A = price per tonne of refined alpha
P_B = price per tonne of refined beta
Q_A = quantity of refined alpha
Q_B = quantity of refined beta

The company is considering whether any part of the production of crude alpha or crude beta should be treated as a by-product. The by-product would be taken away free of charge by a large-scale pig farming enterprise.

Requirements
(a) If all the output of the separation process is refined and sold:
  (i) calculate the optimal quantity of raw material to be processed and the quantities and prices of the refined products, and
  (ii) determine the 'major' product which is worth refining and the 'minor' product which deserves consideration as a potential by-product, but do not attempt to calculate at this stage how much of the 'minor' product would be refined. (10 marks)
(b) Calculate:
  (i) the optimal quantity of the 'major' product which would be worth producing regardless of the value of the 'minor' product, and
  (ii) the quantity of the resulting 'minor' product that would be worth refining. (6 marks)
(c) Evaluate the principal methods and problems of joint-cost allocation for stock valuation, referring to Nuts plc where appropriate. (9 marks)
(Total 25 marks)
ICAEW P2 Management Accounting

Cassidy Computers plc sells one of its products, a plug-in card for personal computer systems, in both the UK and Ruritania. The relationship between price and demand is different in the two markets, and can be represented as follows:

| Home market: | Price (in £) $= 68 - 8Q1$ |
| Export market: | Price (in $) $= 110 - 10Q2$ |

where $Q1$ is the quantity demanded (in 000) in the home market and $Q2$ is the quantity demanded (in 000) in the export market. The current exchange rate is 2 Ruritanian dollars to the pound.

The variable cost of producing the cards is subject to economies of scale, and can be represented as:

$$\text{Unit variable cost (in £)} = 19 - Q \text{ (where } Q = Q1 + Q2).$$

Requirements
(a) Calculate the optimum selling price and total contribution made by the product if it can be sold
   (i) only in the home market
   (ii) only in the export market
   (iii) in both markets.   (10 marks)
(b) Calculate the optimum selling prices and total contribution made by the product if it can be sold in both markets, but subject to a constraint imposed by the Ruritanian government that the company can sell no more cards in Ruritania than it sells in its home market. How sensitive are the prices to be charged in each market and the total contribution, to changes in the exchange rate over the range $1=£0.25 to $1=£1.00?   (8 marks)
(c) How does the volatility of foreign exchange rates affect the ways in which export sales are priced in practice?   (7 marks)
                                                                (Total 25 marks)
                                            ICAEW P2 Management Accounting

Decision-making under conditions of risk and uncertainty

Question IM 12.1
Advanced:
Preparation of project statements for different demand levels and calculations of expected profit

Seeprint Limited is negotiating an initial one year contract with an important customer for the supply of a specialized printed colour catalogue at a fixed contract price of £16 per catalogue. Seeprint's normal capacity for producing such catalogues is 50 000 per annum.

Last year Seeprint Limited earned £11 000 profit per month from a number of small accounts requiring specialized colour catalogues. If the contract under negotiation is not undertaken, then a similar profit might be obtained from these customers next year, but, if it is undertaken, there will be no profit from such customers.

The estimated costs of producing colour catalogues of a specialized nature are given below.

The costs below are considered certain with the exception of the direct materials price.

Cost data:

	(£)
Variable costs per catalogue	
Direct materials	4.50
Direct wages	3.00
Direct expenses	1.30

	Output levels (capacity utilization)		
Semi-variable costs	**80%**	**100%**	**120%**
	(£)	**(£)**	**(£)**
Indirect materials	46 800	47 000	74 400
Indirect wages	51 200	55 000	72 000
Indirect expenses	6 000	8 000	9 600

Estimated fixed costs per annum:

Depreciation of specialist equipment	£8 000
Supervisory and management salaries	£20 000
Other fixed costs allocated to specialist colour catalogues production	£32 000

You are required to:
(a) Tabulate the costs and profits per unit and in total and the annual profits, assuming that the contract orders in the year are: (i) 40 000, (ii) 50 000 and (iii) 60 000 catalogues, at a direct material cost of £4.50 per catalogue. Comment on the tabulation you have prepared.   (10 marks)
(b) Calculate the expected profit for the year if it is assumed that the probability of the total order is:

0.4 for 40 000 catalogues
0.5 for 50 000 catalogues
0.1 for 60 000 catalogues

and that the probability of direct material cost is:

0.5 at £4.50 per catalogue
0.3 at £5.00 per catalogue
0.2 at £5.50 per catalogue. (6 marks)

(c) Discuss the implications for Seeprint Limited of the acceptance or otherwise of the contract with the important customer. (6 marks)

(Total 22 marks)

ACCA Level 2 Management Accounting

(a) The accountant of Laburnum Ltd is preparing documents for a forthcoming meeting of the budget committee. Currently, variable cost is 40% of selling price and total fixed costs are £40 000 per year.

Question IM 12.2 Advanced: CVP analysis and uncertainty

The company uses an historical cost accounting system. There is concern that the level of costs may rise during the ensuing year and the chairman of the budget committee has expressed interest in a probabilistic approach to an investigation of the effect that this will have on historic cost profits. The accountant is attempting to prepare the documents in a way which will be most helpful to the committee members. He has obtained the following estimates from his colleagues:

	Average inflation rate over ensuing year	Probability
Pessimistic	10%	0.4
Most likely	5%	0.5
Optimistic	1%	0.1
		1.0

	Demand at current selling prices	Probability
Pessimistic	£50 000	0.3
Most likely	£75 000	0.6
Optimistic	£100 000	0.1
		1.0

The demand figures are given in terms of sales value at the current level of selling prices but it is considered that the company could adjust its selling prices in line with the inflation rate without affecting customer demand in real terms.

Some of the company's fixed costs are contractually fixed and some are apportionments of past costs; of the total fixed costs, an estimated 85% will remain constant irrespective of the inflation rate.

You are required to analyse the foregoing information in a way which you consider will assist management with its budgeting problem. Although you should assume that the directors of Laburnum Ltd are solely interested in the effect of inflation on historic cost profits, you should comment on the validity of the accountant's intended approach. As part of your analysis you are required to calculate:
(i) the probability of at least breaking even, and
(ii) the probability of achieving a profit of at least £20 000. (16 marks)

(b) It can be argued that the use of point estimate probabilities (as above) is too unrealistic because it constrains the demand and cost variables to relatively few values. Briefly describe an alternative simulation approach which might meet this objection. (6 marks)

(Total 22 marks)

ACCA Level 2 Management Accounting

**Question IM 12.3
Advanced: Output
decision based on
expected values**

A ticket agent has an arrangement with a concert hall that holds pop concerts on 60 nights a year whereby he receives discounts as follows per concert:

For purchase of:	He receives a discount of:
200 tickets	20%
300 tickets	25%
400 tickets	30%
500 tickets or more	40%

Purchases must be in full hundreds. The average price per ticket is £3.

He must decide in advance each year the number of tickets he will purchase. If he has any tickets unsold by the afternoon of the concert he must return them to the box office. If the box office sells any of these he receives 60% of their price.

His sales records over a few years show that for a concert with extremely popular artistes he can be confident of selling 500 tickets, for one with lesser known artistes 350 tickets, and for one with relatively unknown artistes 200 tickets.

His records also show that 10% of tickets he returns are sold by the box office.

His administration costs incurred in selling tickets are the same per concert irrespective of the popularity of the artistes.

There are two possible scenarios in which his sales records can be viewed:

Scenario 1: that, on average, he can expect concerts with lesser known artistes
Scenario 2: that the frequency of concerts will be:

	(%)
with popular artistes	45
with lesser known artistes	30
with unknown artistes	25
	100

You are required to calculate:
A. separately for each of Scenarios 1 and 2:
    (a) the expected demand for tickets per concert;
    (b) (i) the level of his purchases of tickets per concert that will give him the largest profit over a long period of time;
        (ii) the profit per concert that this level of purchases of tickets will yield;
B. for Scenario 2 only: the maximum sum per annum that the ticket agent should pay to a pop concert specialist for 100% correct predictions as to the likely success of each concert.   (25 marks)
CIMA P3 Management Accounting

**Question 12.4
Advanced:
Contracting hotel
accommodation
based on
uncertain demand**

Crabbe, the owner of the Ocean Hotel, is concerned about the hotel's finances and has asked your advice. He gives you the following information:

We have rooms for 80 guests. When the hotel is open, whatever the level of business, we have to meet the following each month:

	(£)
Staff wages and benefits	12 500
General overheads (rates, electricity, etc)	8 000
Depreciation	2 200
Interest on mortgage and bank loan	1 800
Repayments on mortgage and bank loan	2 500
Drawings for my own needs	1 000
	28 000

'For our normal business we charge an average of £20 per night for each guest. Each guest-night involves variable costs of £4 for laundry and cleaning. Guests also spend money in the restaurant, which on average brings us another £5 per guest-night after meeting variable costs.

'I need advice on two problems; one concerns the month of September and the other relates to the winter.

(1) 'Normal business in September will depend on weather conditions, and the probabilities of occupancy from normal business are:

| | For month of September | | |
Weather condition	A	B	C
Probability	0.3	0.4	0.3
Occupancy (total guest-nights)	1440	1680	1920

'Airtravel Tours has enquired about a block booking at a discount in September. I intend to quote a discount of 40% on our normal guest-night charge. In the restaurant Airtravels package tourists will only bring us £3 per guest-night after variable costs. Airtravel could take all our capacity, but I have to decide how many guest-nights to offer. The contract will mean that I agree in advance to take the same number of Airtravel tourists every night throughout September. If they won't accept my price, I would be prepared to go as far as a 60% discount.

(2) 'When we come to the winter, trade is usually so bad that we close for three months. We retain only a skeleton staff, costing £1500 per month, and general overheads are reduced from £8000 to £2000. I am trying to find ways of keeping open this winter, but staying open will incur the full monthly outgoings.

'If we remained open for all three months I estimate our basic winter trade at reduced prices, together with income from conferences, would be as follows:

	Average number of guests per night	Charge per guest-night (£)	Restaurant revenue per guest-night net of variable costs (£)
Basic winter trade	12	14	5
Conferences, etc.	30	13	4

'Alternatively, I am considering offering a series of language courses. We could not take any other guests, and I estimate the total demand for the three months as follows:

Market condition	X	Y	Z
Probability	0.3	0.4	0.3
Occupancy (total guest-nights)	2160	4320	6480

'If the courses are offered we shall have to run them for the full three months irrespective of the take-up. The charge per night would be £24, and the revenue from the restaurant net of variable cost would only be £1 per guest-night.

We would have to spend about £5000 per month on tutors, and the courses would also have to be advertised beforehand at a cost of £1500.'

Assume 30-day months throughout.

Requirements:
(a) Calculate the number of guest-nights Crabbe should contract to Airtravel Tours at the quoted 40% discount.   (6 marks)

(b) Determine the minimum price per guest-night at which it would be worthwhile for Crabbe to do business with Airtravel, and the maximum number of guest-nights it would be worthwhile to contract at this price.

(4 marks)

(c) Assess which of the winter options Crabbe should undertake and state any reservation you may have about your assessment. (9 marks)

(d) Briefly explain the criteria on which you have identified costs to assess Crabbe's business options in requirements (a) to (c). (6 marks)

(Total 25 marks)

ICAEW P2 Management Accounting

Question IM 12.5 Advanced: Pricing and purchase contract decisions based on uncertain demand and calculation of maximum price to pay for perfect information

Z Ltd is considering various product pricing and material purchasing options with regard to a new product it has in development. Estimates of demand and costs are as follows:

If selling price per unit is		£15 per unit Sales volume	£20 per unit Sales volume
Forecasts	Probability	(000 units)	(000 units)
Optimistic	0.3	36	28
Most likely	0.5	28	23
Pessimistic	0.2	18	13
Variable manufacturing costs (excluding materials) per unit		£3	£3
Advertising and selling costs		£25 000	£96 000
General fixed costs		£40 000	£40 000

Each unit requires 3kg of material and because of storage problems any unused material must be sold at £1 per kg. The sole suppliers of the material offer three purchase options, which must be decided at the outset, as follows:

 (i) any quantity at £3 per kg, or

 (ii) a price of £2.75 per kg for a minimum quantity of 50 000 kg, or

(iii) a price of £2.50 per kg for a minimum quantity of 70 000 kg.

You are required, assuming that the company is risk neutral, to

(a) prepare calculations to show what pricing and purchasing decisions the company should make, clearly indicating the recommended decisions;

(15 marks)

(b) calculate the maximum price you would pay for perfect information as to whether the demand would be optimistic or most likely pessimistic. (5 marks)

(Total 20 marks)

CIMA Stage 3 Management Accounting Techniques

Warren Ltd is to produce a new product in a short-term venture which will utilize some obsolete materials and expected spare capacity. The new product will be advertised in quarter I with production and sales taking price in quarter II. No further production or sales are anticipated.

Sales volumes are uncertain but will, to some extent, be a function of sales price. The possible sales volumes and the advertising costs associated with each potential sales price are as follows:

Sales price £20 per unit		Sales price £25 per unit		Sales price £40 per unit	
Sales volume units (000)	Probability	Sales volume units (000)	Probability	Sales volume units (000)	Probability
4	0.1	2	0.1	0	0.2
6	0.4	5	0.2	3	0.5
8	0.5	6	0.2	10	0.2
		8	0.5	15	0.1
Advertising costs £20 000		£50 000		£100 000	

The resources used in the production of each unit of the product are:

Production labour:		grade 1	2 hours
		grade 2	1 hour
Materials:	X	1 unit	
	Y	2 units	

The normal cost per hour of labour is

	grade 1	£2
	grade 2	£3

However, before considering the effects of the current venture, there is expected to be 4000 hours of idle time for each grade of labour in quarter II. Idle time is paid at the normal rates.

Material X is in stock at a book value of £8 per unit, but is widely used within the firm and any usage for the purposes of this venture will require replacing. Replacement cost is £9 per unit.

Material Y is obsolete stock. There are 16 000 units in stock at a book value of £3.50 per unit and any stock not used will have to be disposed of at a cost, to Warren, of £2 per unit. Further quantities of Y can be purchased for £4 per unit.

Overhead recovery rates are

Variable overhead	£2 per direct labour hour worked
Fixed overhead	£3 per direct labour hour worked

Total fixed overheads will not alter as a result of the current venture.

Feedback from advertising will enable the exact demand to be determined at the end of quarter I and production in quarter II will be set to equal that demand. However, it is necessary to decide now on the sales price in order that it can be incorporated into the advertising campaign.

Required:
(a) Calculate the expected money value of the venture at each sales price and on the basis of this advise Warren of its best course of action. (12 marks)
(b) Briefly explain why the management of Warren might rationally reject the sales price leading to the highest expected money value and prefer one of the other sales prices. (4 marks)
(c) It will be possible, for the sales price of £40 per unit only, to ascertain which of the four levels of demand will eventuate. If the indications are that the demand

will be low then the advertising campaign can be cancelled at a cost of £10 000 but it would then not be possible to continue the venture at another sales price. This accurate information concerning demand will cost £5000 to obtain.

Indicate whether it is worthwhile obtaining the information and ascertain whether it would alter the advice given in (a) above.   (4 marks)
(Total 20 marks)
ACCA Level 2 Management Accounting

Question IM 12.7
Advanced: Hire of machine based on uncertain demand and value of perfect information

The Ruddle Co. Ltd had planned to install and, with effect from next April, commence operating sophisticated machinery for the production of a new product – product Zed. However, the supplier of the machinery has just announced that delivery of the machinery will be delayed by six months and this will mean that Ruddle will not now be able to undertake production using that machinery until October.

'The first six months of production' stated the commercial manager of Ruddle 'is particularly crucial as we have already contracted to supply several national supermarket groups with whatever quantities of Zed they require during that period at a price of £40 per unit. Their demand is, at this stage, uncertain but would have been well within the capacity of the permanent machinery we were to have installed. The best estimates of the total demand for the first period are thought to be:

Estimated demand – first 6 months

Quantity (000 units)	Probability
10	0.5
14	0.3
16	0.2

'Whatever the level of demand, we are going to meet it in full even if it means operating at a loss for the first half year. Therefore I suggest we consider the possibility of hiring equipment on which temporary production can take place'. Details of the only machines which could be hired are:

	Machine A	Machine B	Machine C
Productive capacity per six month period (units)	10 000	12 000	16 000
Variable production cost for each unit produced	£6.5	£6	£5
Other 'fixed' costs total for six months	£320 000	£350 000	£400 000

In addition to the above costs there will be a variable material cost of £5 per unit. For purchases greater than 10 000 units a discount of 20% per unit will be given, but this only applies to the excess over 10 000 units.

Should production capacity be less than demand then Ruddle could subcontract production of up to 6000 units but would be required to supply raw materials. Subcontracting costs are:

up to 4000 units subcontracted £30 per unit
any excess over 4000 units subcontracted £35 per unit.

These subcontracting costs relate only to the work carried out by the subcontractor and exclude the costs of raw materials.

The commercial manager makes the following further points, 'Due to the lead time required for setting up production, the choice of which machine to hire must be made before the precise demand is known. However, demand will be known in time for production to be scheduled so that an equal number of units can be produced each month. We will, of course, only produce sufficient to meet demand.'

DECISION-MAKING UNDER CONDITIONS OF RISK AND UNCERTAINTY

'We need to decide which machine to hire. However, I wonder whether it would be worthwhile seeking the assistance of a firm of market researchers? Their reputation suggests that they are very accurate and they may be able to inform us whether demand is to be 10, 14 or 16 thousand units.'

Required:
(a) For each of the three machines which could be hired show the possible monetary outcomes and, using expected values, advise Ruddle on its best course of action. (12 marks)
(b) (i) Calculate the maximum amount which it would be worthwhile to pay to the firm of market researchers to ascertain details of demand. (You are required to assume that the market researchers will produce an absolutely accurate forecast and that demand will be exactly equal to one of the three demand figures given.) (4 marks)
(ii) Comment on the view that as perfect information is never obtainable the calculation of the expected value of perfect information is not worthwhile. Briefly explain any uses such a calculation may have. (4 marks)
(Total 20 marks)

Ignore taxation and the time value of money.

ACCA P2 Management Accounting

Butterfield Ltd manufactures a single brand of dog-food called 'Lots O Grissle' (LOG). Sales have stabilized for several years at a level of £20 million per annum at current prices. This level is not expected to change in the foreseeable future (except as indicated below). It is well below the capacity of the plant. The managing director, Mr Rover, is considering how to stimulate growth in the company's turnover and profits. After rejecting all of the alternative possibilities that he can imagine, or that have been suggested to him, he is reviewing a proposal to introduce a new luxury dog-food product. It would be called 'Before Eight Mince' (BEM), and would have a recommended retail price of £0.50 per tin. It would require no new investment, and would incur no additional fixed costs.

Question IM 12.8 Advanced: Calculation of expected value of perfect and imperfect information

Mr Rover has decided that he will undertake this new development only if he can anticipate that it will at least break even in the first year of operation.
(a) Mr Rover estimates that BEM has a 75% chance of gaining acceptance in the marketplace. His best estimate is that if the product gains acceptance it will have sales in the forthcoming year of £3.2 million at retail prices, given a contribution of £1 million after meeting the variable costs of manufacture and distribution. If, on the other hand, the product fails to gain acceptance, sales for the year will, he thinks, be only £800 000 at retail prices, and for various reasons there would be a negative contribution of £400 000 in that year.

You are required to show whether, on the basis of these preliminary estimates, Mr Rover should give the BEM project further consideration.
(4 marks)
(b) Mr Rover discusses the new project informally with his sales director, Mr Khoo Chee Khoo, who suggests that some of the sales achieved for the new product would cause lost sales of LOG. In terms of retail values he estimates the likelihood of this as follows:

There is a 50% chance that sales of LOG will fall by half of the sales of BEM.

There is a 25% chance that sales of LOG will fall by one-quarter of the sales of BEM.

There is a 25% chance that sales of LOG will fall by three-quarters of the sales of BEM.

The contribution margin ratio of LOG is 25% at all relevant levels of sales and output. You are required to show whether, after accepting these further estimates, Mr Rover should give the BEM project further consideration.
(5 marks)
(c) Mr Rover wonders also whether, before attempting to proceed any further, he should have some market research undertaken. He approaches Delphi

Associates, a firm of market research consultants for whom he has a high regard. On previous occasions he has found them to be always right in their forecasts, and he considers that their advice will give him as near perfect information as it is possible to get. He decides to ask Delphi to advise him only on whether or not BEM will gain acceptance in the marketplace in the sense in which he has defined it; he will back Mr Khoo Chee Khoo's judgement about the effects of the introduction of BEM on the sales of LOG. If Delphi advise him that the product will not be accepted he will not proceed further. Delphi have told him that their fee for this work would be £100 000.

You are required to show whether Mr Rover should instruct Delphi Associates to carry out the market research proposals. (5 marks)

(d) Preliminary discussions with Delphi suggest that Delphi's forecast will not be entirely reliable. They believe that, if they indicate that BEM will gain acceptance, there is only a 90% chance that they will be right; and, if they indicate failure to gain acceptance, there is only a 70% chance that they will be right. This implies a 75% chance overall that Delphi will indicate acceptance, in line with Mr Rover's estimate.

You are required to show the maximum amount that Mr Rover should be prepared to pay Delphi to undertake the market research, given the new estimates of the reliability of their advice. (5 marks)

(e) You are required to outline briefly the strengths and limitations of your methods of analysis in (a)–(d) above. (6 marks)

ICAEW Management Accounting

Capital investment decisions: 1

The evidence of many recent studies suggests that there are major differences between current theories of investment appraisal and the methods which firms actually use in evaluating long-term investments.

You are required to:
(a) present theoretical arguments for the choice of net present value as the best method of investment appraisal;
(b) explain why in practice other methods of evaluating investment projects have proved to be more popular with decision-makers than the net present value method.

Question IM 13.1 Advanced

The following information relates to three possible capital expenditure projects. Because of capital rationing only one project can be accepted.

Question IM 13.2 Payback, accounting rate of return and NPV calculations plus a discussion of qualitative factors

| | Project | | |
	A	B	C
Initial Cost	£200 000	£230 000	£180 000
Expected Life	5 years	5 years	4 years
Scrap value expected	£10 000	£15 000	£8000
Expected Cash Inflows	(£)	(£)	(£)
End Year 1	80 000	100 000	55 000
2	70 000	70 000	65 000
3	65 000	50 000	95 000
4	60 000	50 000	100 000
5	55 000	50 000	

The company estimates its cost of capital is 18%.

Calculate
(a) The pay back period for each project. (4 marks)
(b) The Accounting Rate of Return for each project. (4 marks)
(c) The Net present value of each project. (8 marks)
(d) Which project should be accepted – give reasons. (5 marks)
(e) Explain the factors management would need to consider: in addition to the financial factors before making a final decision on a project. (4 marks)
(Total 25 marks)
AAT Stage 3 Cost Accounting and Budgeting

Question IM 13.3 Intermediate: Calculation of payback, NPV and ARR for mutually exclusive projects

Your company is considering investing in its own transport fleet. The present position is that carriage is contracted to an outside organization. The life of the transport fleet would be five years, after which time the vehicles would have to be disposed of.

The cost to your company of using the outside organization for its carriage needs is £250 000 for this year. This cost, it is projected, will rise 10% per annum over the life of the project. The initial cost of the transport fleet would be £750 000 and it is estimated that the following costs would be incurred over the next five years:

	Drivers' Costs (£)	Repairs & Maintenance (£)	Other Costs (£)
Year 1	33 000	8 000	130 000
Year 2	35 000	13 000	135 000
Year 3	36 000	15 000	140 000
Year 4	38 000	16 000	136 000
Year 5	40 000	18 000	142 000

Other costs include depreciation. It is projected that the fleet would be sold for £150 000 at the end of year 5. It has been agreed to depreciate the fleet on a straight line basis.

To raise funds for the project your company is proposing to raise a long-term loan at 12% interest rate per annum.

You are told that there is an alternative project that could be invested in using the funds raised, which has the following projected results:

> Payback=3 years
> Accounting rate of return=30%
> Net present value=£140 000.

As funds are limited, investment can only be made in one project.

Note: The transport fleet would be purchased at the beginning of the project and all other expenditure would be incurred at the end of each relevant year.

Required:
(a) Prepare a table showing the net cash savings to be made by the firm over the life of the transport fleet project. (5 marks)
(b) Calculate the following for the transport fleet project:
  (i) Payback period
  (ii) Accounting rate of return
  (iii) Net present value (13 marks)
(c) Write a short report to the Investment Manager in your company outlining whether investment should be committed to the transport fleet or the alternative project outlined. Clearly state the reasons for your decision.
(7 marks)
(Total 25 marks)
AAT Cost Accounting and Budgeting

You are employed as the assistant accountant in your company and you are currently working on an appraisal of a project to purchase a new machine. The machine will cost £55 000 and will have a useful life of three years. You have already estimated the cash flows from the project and their taxation effect, and the results of your estimates can be summarized as follows:

	Year 1	Year 2	Year 3
Post-tax cash inflow	£18 000	£29 000	£31 000

Your company uses a post-tax cost of capital of 8% to appraise all projects of this type.

Task 1
(a) Calculate the net present value of the proposal to purchase the machine. Ignore the effects of inflation and assume that all cash flows occur at the end of the year.
(b) Calculate the payback period for the investment in the machine.

Task 2
The marketing director has asked you to let her know as soon as you have completed your appraisal of the project. She has asked you to provide her with some explanation of your calculations and of how taxation affects the proposal.
  Prepare a memorandum to the marketing director which answers her queries. Your memorandum should contain the following:
(a) your recommendation concerning the proposal;
(b) an explanation of the meaning of the net present value and the payback period;
(c) an explanation of the effects of taxation on the cash flows arising from capital expenditure.

AAT Technicians Stage

The Portsmere Hospital operates its own laundry. Last year the laundry processed 120 000 kilograms of washing and this year the total is forecast to grow to 132 000 kilograms. This growth in laundry processed is forecast to continue at the same percentage rate for the next seven years. Because of this, the hospital must immediately replace its existing laundry equipment. Currently, it is considering two options, the purchase of machine A or the rental of machine B. Information on both options is given below:

Machine A – purchase

Annual capacity (kilograms)	£180 000
Material cost per kilogram	£2.00
Labour cost per kilogram	£3.00
Fixed costs per annum	£20 000
Life of machine	3 years
Capital cost	£60 000
Depreciation per annum	£20 000

Machine B – rent

Annual capacity (kilograms)	£170 000
Material cost per kilogram	£1.80
Labour cost per kilogram	£3.40
Fixed costs per annum	£18 000
Rental per annum	£20 000
Rental agreement	3 years
Depreciation per annum	nil

Other information:
1. The hospital is able to call on an outside laundry if there is either a breakdown or any other reason why the washing cannot be undertaken in-house. The charge would be £10 per kilogram of washing.
2. Machine A, if purchased, would have to be paid for immediately. All other cash flows can be assumed to occur at the end of the year.
3. Machine A will have no residual value at any time.
4. The existing laundry equipment could be sold for £10 000 cash.
5. The fixed costs are a direct cost of operating the laundry.
6. The hospital's discount rate for projects of this nature is 15%.

Task 1
You are an accounting technician employed by the Portsmere Hospital and you are asked to write a brief report to its chief executive. Your report should:
(a) evaluate the two options for operating the laundry, using discounted cash flow techniques;
(b) recommend the preferred option and identify *one* possible non-financial benefit;
(c) justify your treatment of the £10 000 cash value of the existing equipment;
(d) explain what is meant by discounted cashflow.

Note:
Inflation can be ignored.

AAT Technicians Stage

Question IM 13.6 Advanced: Comparison of NPV and IRR

Using the discounted cash flow yield (internal rate of return) for evaluating investment opportunities has the basic weakness that it does not give attention to the amount of the capital investment, in that a return of 20% on an investment of £1000 may be given a higher ranking than a return of 15% on an investment of £10 000.

Comment in general on the above statement and refer in particular to the problem of giving priorities to (ranking) investment proposals.

Your answers should make use of the following information.

	Project A cash flow (£)	Project B cash flow (£)
Year 0 (Capital investments)	1000	10 000
1 Cash flows	240	2 300
2 Cash flows	288	2 640
3 Cash flows	346	3 040
4 Cash flows	414	3 500
5 Cash flows	498	4 020
Cost of capital	10%	10%

Taxation can be ignored.

(20 marks)
ACCA P3 Financial Management

Losrock Housing Association is considering the implementation of a refurbishment programme on one of its housing estates which would reduce maintenance and heating costs and enable a rent increase to be made.

Relevant data are as follows:
  (i) Number of houses: 300.
  (ii) Annual maintenance cost per house: £300. This will be reduced by 25% on completion of the refurbishment of each house.
  (iii) Annual heating cost per house: £500. This will be reduced by 30% on completion of the refurbishment of each house.
  (iv) Annual rental income per house: £2100. This will be increased by 15% on completion of the refurbishment of each house.
  (v) Two contractors A and B have each quoted a price of £2000 per house to implement the refurbishment work.
  (vi) The quoted completion profiles for each contractor are as follows:

	Number of houses refurbished		
	Year 1	Year 2	Year 3
Contractor A	90	90	120
Contractor B	150	90	60

  (vii) Contractor A requires £100 000 at the commencement of the work and the balance of the contract price in proportion to the number of houses completed in each of years 1 to 3. Contractor B requires £300 000 at the commencement of the work and the balance of the contract price in proportion to the number of houses completed in each of years 1 to 3.
  (viii) An eight year period from the commencement of the work should be used as the time horizon for the evaluation of the viability of the refurbishment programme.

Assume that all events and cash flows arise at year end points. Savings and rent increases will commence in the year following refurbishment.
Ignore taxation.

Required:
(a) Prepare financial summaries and hence advise management whether to accept the quote from contractor A or contractor B in each of the following situations:
  (i) ignoring the discounting of cash flows; and
  (ii) where the cost of capital is determined as 14% and the discount factors given in appendix 1 are available. (14 marks)
(b) For contractor A only, calculate the maximum refurbishment price per house at which the work would be acceptable to Losrock Housing Association on financial grounds using discounted cash flows as the decision base, where the initial payment remains at £100 000 and the balance is paid in proportion to the houses completed in each of years 1 to 3. (5 marks)
(c) Suggest additional information relating to maintenance and heating costs which might affect the acceptability of the existing quotes per house where discounted cash flows are used as the decision base. (3 marks)
(Total 22 marks)
ACCA Level 2 Management Accounting

Question IM 13.8
Advanced: Replacement decision and the conflict between decision-making and performance evaluation models

Paragon Products plc has a factory which manufactures a wide range of plastic household utensils. One of these is a plastic brush which is made from a special raw material used only for this purpose. The brush is moulded on a purpose-built machine which was installed in January 1997 at a cost of £210 000 with an expected useful life of 7 years. This machine was assumed to have zero scrap value at the end of its life and was depreciated on the same straight line basis that the company used for all equipment.

Recently an improved machine has become available, at a price of £130 000, which requires two men to operate it rather than the five men required by the existing machine. It also uses a coarser grade of raw material costing £70 per tonne (1000 kg), compared with £75 per tonne for the present material. Further, it would use only 60% of the power consumed by the existing machine. However, it has an expected life of only three years and an expected scrap value of £10 000.

The factory manager is considering replacing the existing machine immediately with the new one as the suppliers have offered him £40 000 for the existing machine, which is substantially more than could be obtained on the second hand market, provided the new machine is installed by 1 January 2001. Unfortunately this would leave stocks of the old raw material sufficient to make 40 000 brushes which could not be used and which would fetch only £25 per tonne on resale.

The brush department is treated as a profit centre. Current production amounts to 200 000 brushes a year which are sold at a wholesale price of £1 each. The production of each brush uses 2 kg of the raw material, consumes 1 kW hour of electricity costing £0.05, and incurs direct labour costs amounting to £0.25 per brush. Overhead costs amount to £60 000 per annum and include £10 000 relating to supervision costs which vary according to the number of employees. The men no longer required to operate the new machine could be found employment elsewhere in the factory and would be paid their current wage although they would be performing less skilled work normally paid at 80% of their current rate.

Requirements:
(a) Evaluate the proposal to replace the existing machine with the new model, ignoring the time value of money in your analysis. (10 marks)
(b) Construct brush department profit and loss accounts for each alternative for 2001, 2002 and 2003. Indicate how the factory manager's decision might be influenced by these figures. (8 marks)
(c) Explain how your analysis would be affected if the new machine had a longer expected life and the time value of money was to be taken into account.
(7 marks)

Note: Ignore taxation. (Total 25 marks)
ICAEW P2 Management Accounting

Question IM 13.9
Advanced: Calculation of a contract price involving monthly discounting and compounding

Franzl is a contract engineer working for a division of a large construction company. He is responsible for the negotiation of contract prices and the subsequent collection of instalment monies from customers. It is company policy to achieve a mark-up of at least 10% on the direct production costs of a contract, but there is no company policy on the speed of customer payment. Franzl usually attempts to persuade customers to pay in six-monthly instalments in arrears.

Franzl is presently engaged in deciding upon the minimum acceptable price for contract K491, which will last for 24 months. He has estimated that the following direct production costs will be incurred:

	(£)
Raw material	168 000
Labour	120 000
Plant depreciation	18 400
Equipment rental	30 000
	336 400

On the basis of these costs Franzl estimates that the minimum contract price should be £370 000. The raw material and labour costs are expected to arise evenly over the period of the contract and to be paid monthly in arrears. Plant depreciation has been calculated as the difference between the cost of the new plant (£32 400) which will be purchased for the contract and its realizable value (£14 000) at the end of contract. Special equipment will be rented for the first year of the contract, the rent being paid in two six-monthly instalments in advance. The contract will be financed from head office funds, on which interest of 1% per month is charged or credited according to whether the construction division is a net borrower or net lender.

Requirements:

(a) Calculate the net present value of contract K491 assuming that Franzl's minimum price and normal payment terms are accepted. (5 marks)

(b) Assuming that the customer agrees to pay the instalments in advance rather than arrears, calculate the new contract price and mark-up that Franzl could accept so as to leave the net present value of the contract unchanged. (5 marks)

(c) Prepare two statements to show that the eventual cash surpluses generated in (a) and (b) are identical. The statements need show *only* the total cash received and paid for each category of revenue and expense. (6 marks)

(d) Discuss the factors that should influence the tender price for a long-term contract. (9 marks)

(Total 25 marks)

Note: Ignore taxation.

ICAEW Financial Management

Capital investment decisions: 2

**Question IM 14.1
Advanced**

You have been appointed as chief management accountant of a well-established company with a brief to improve the quality of information supplied for management decision-making. As a first task you have decided to examine the system used for providing information for capital investment decisions. You find that discounted cash flow techniques are used but in a mechanical fashion with no apparent understanding of the figures produced. The most recent example of an investment appraisal produced by the accounting department showed a positive net present value of £35 000 for a five-year life project when discounted at 14% which you are informed 'was the rate charged on the bank loan raised to finance the investment'. You note that the appraisal did not include any consideration of the effects of inflation nor was there any form of risk analysis.

You are required to:
(a) explain the meaning of a positive net present value of £35 000;   (4 marks)
(b) comment on the appropriateness or otherwise of the discounting rate used;
                                                                        (4 marks)
(c) state whether you agree with the treatment of inflation and, if not, explain how you would deal with inflation in investment appraisals;   (6 marks)
(d) explain what is meant by 'risk analysis' and describe ways this could be carried out in investment appraisals and what benefits (if any) this would bring.
                                                                        (6 marks)
                                                                (Total 20 marks)
CIMA Stage 3 Management Accounting Techniques Pilot Paper

**Question IM 14.2
Advanced**

In the context of capital budgeting, you are required to explain:
(a) the meaning of 'beta';   (4 marks)
(b) the function of 'beta' in the capital asset pricing model;   (4 marks)
(c) what one might do to overcome the difficulty that 'beta' for a proposed capital expenditure project is not necessarily the same as that for the company as a whole;   (8 marks)
(d) the major limitations to the use of the capital asset pricing model for the purposes of (c) above.   (4 marks)
                                                                (Total 20 marks)
CIMA Stage 4 Management Accounting – Decision-Making Pilot Paper

**Question IM 14.3
Advanced**

Describe and discuss the important stages that should be followed when a company wishes to develop and implement a new programme of capital investment.
    Do *not* confine your discussion to the nature and use of evaluation techniques in the appraisal of capital investments.   (25 marks)
ACCA Level 3 Financial Management

Data

Tilsley Ltd manufactures motor vehicle components. It is considering introducing a new product. Helen Foster, the production director, has already prepared the following projections for this proposal:

	Year			
	1	2	3	4
	(£000)	(£000)	(£000)	(£000)
Sales	8 750	12 250	13 300	14 350
Direct materials	1 340	1 875	2 250	2 625
Direct labour	2 675	3 750	4 500	5 250
Direct overheads	185	250	250	250
Depreciation	2 500	2 500	2 500	2 500
Interest	1 012	1 012	1 012	1 012
Profit before tax	1 038	2 863	2 788	2 713
Corporation tax @ 30%	311	859	836	814
Profit after tax	727	2 004	1 952	1 899

Helen Foster has recommended to the board that the project is not worthwhile because the cumulative after tax profit over the four years is less than the capital cost of the project.

As an assistant accountant at the company you have been asked by Philip Knowles, the chief accountant, to carry out a full financial appraisal of the proposal. He does not agree with Helen Foster's analysis, and provides you with the following information:

- the initial capital investment and working capital will be incurred at the beginning of the first year. All other receipts and payments will occur at the end of each year;
- the equipment will cost £10 million;
- additional working capital of £1 million;
- this additional working capital will be recovered in full as cash at the end of the four-year period;
- the equipment will qualify for a 25% per annum reducing balance writing down allowance;
- any outstanding capital allowances at the end of the project can be claimed as a balancing allowance;
- at the end of the four-year period the equipment will be scrapped, with no expected residual value;
- the additional working capital required does not qualify for capital allowances, nor is it an allowable expense in calculating taxable profit;
- Tilsley Ltd pays corporation tax at 30% of chargeable profits;
- there is a one-year delay in paying tax;
- the company's cost of capital is 17%.

Task

Write a report to Philip Knowles. Your report should:
(a) evaluate the project using net present value techniques;
(b) recommend whether the project is worthwhile;
(c) explain how you have treated taxation in your appraisal;
(d) give *three* reasons why your analysis is different from that produced by Helen Foster, the production director.

Notes:

Risk and inflation can be ignored.

AAT Technicians Stage

Question IM 14.5 Advanced: Calculation of IRR and incremental yield involving identification of relevant cash flows

LF Ltd wishes to manufacture a new product. The company is evaluating two mutually exclusive machines, the Reclo and the Bunger. Each machine is expected to have a working life of four years, and is capable of a maximum annual output of 150 000 units.

Cost estimates associated with the two machines include:

	Reclo £000	Bunger £000
Purchase price	175	90
Scrap value	10	9
Incremental working capital	40	40
Maintenance (per year)	40 (20 in year 1)	
Supervisor	20	
Allocated central overhead	35	
Labour costs (per unit)	£1.30	
Material costs (per unit)	£0.80	

The Reclo requires 120 square metres of operating space. LF Ltd currently pays £35 per square metre to rent a factory which has adequate spare space for the new product. There is no alternative use for this spare space. £5000 has been spent on a feasibility survey of the Reclo.

The marketing department will charge a fee of £75 000 per year for promoting the product, which will be incorporated into existing plans for catalogues and advertising. Two new salesmen will be employed by the marketing department solely for the new product, at a cost of £22 500 per year each. There are no other incremental marketing costs.

The selling price in year one is expected to be £3.50 per unit, with annual production and sales estimated at 130 000 units throughout the four year period. Prices and costs after the first year are expected to rise by 5% per year. Working capital will be increased by this amount from year one onwards.

Taxation is payable at 25% per year one year in arrears and a writing-down allowance of 25% per year is available on a reducing balance basis.

The company's accountant has already estimated the taxable operating cash flows (sales less relevant labour costs, materials costs etc., but before taking into account any writing-down allowances) of the second machine, the Bunger. These are:

	Bunger – £000			
Year	1	2	3	4
Taxable operating cash flows	50	53	55	59

Required:
(a) Calculate the expected internal rate of return (IRR) of each of the machines. State clearly any assumptions that you make. (14 marks)
(b) Evaluate, using the incremental yield method, which, if either, of the two machines should be selected. (6 marks)
(c) Explain briefly why the internal rate of return is regarded as a relatively poor method of investment appraisal. (5 marks)
(Total 25 marks)
ACCA Level 3 Financial Management

Eckard plc is a large, all-equity financed, divisionalized textile company whose shares are listed on the London Stock Exchange. It has a current cost of capital of 15%. The annual performance of its four divisions is assessed by their return on investment (ROI), i.e. net profit after tax divided by the closing level of capital employed. It is expected that the overall ROI for the company for the year ending 31 December 2000 will be 18%, with the towelling division having the highest ROI of 25%. The towelling division has a young, ambitious managing director who is anxious to maintain its ROI for the next two years, by which time he expects to be able to obtain a more prestigious job either within Eckard plc or elsewhere. He has recently turned down a proposal by his division's finance director to replace an old machine with a more modern one, on the grounds that the old one has an estimated useful life of four years and should be kept for that period. The finance director has appealed to the main board of directors of Eckard plc to reverse her managing director's decision.

The following estimates have been prepared by the finance director for the new machine:

Investment cost: £256 000, payable on 2 January 2001.

Expected life: four years to 31 December 2004.

Disposal value: equal to its tax written down value on 1 January 2004 and receivable on 31 December 2004.

Expected cash flow savings: £60 000 in 2001, rising by 10% in each of the next three years. These cash flows can be assumed to occur at the end of the year in which they arise.

Tax position: the company is expected to pay 35% corporation tax over the next four years. The machine is eligible for a 25% per annum writing down allowance. Corporation tax can be assumed to be paid 12 months after the accounting year-end on 31 December. No provision for deferred tax is considered to be necessary.

Old machine to be replaced: this would be sold on 2 January 2001 with an accounting net book value of £50 000 and a tax written down value of nil. Sale proceeds would be £40 000, which would give rise to a balancing charge. If retained for a further four years, the disposal value would be zero.

Relevant accounting policies: the company uses the straight-line depreciation method with a full year's depreciation being charged in both the year of acquisition and the year of disposal. The capital employed figure for the division comprises all assets excluding cash.

Requirements

(a) Calculate the net present value to Eckard plc of the proposed replacement of the old machine by the new one. (8 marks)

(b) Calculate, for the years 2001 and 2002 only, the effect of the decision to replace the old machine on the ROI of the towelling division. (7 marks)

(c) Prepare a report for the main board of directors recommending whether the new machine should be purchased. Your report should include a discussion of the effects that performance measurement systems can have on capital investment decisions. (10 marks)

(Total 25 marks)

ICAEW P2 Financial Management

**Question IM 14.6
Advanced: Net
present value
calculation for the
replacement of a
machine and a
discussion of the
conflict between
ROI and NPV**

Question IM 14.7
Advanced:
Determining the
optimum
replacement
period for a fleet
of taxis

Eltern plc is an unlisted company with a turnover of £6 million which runs a small fleet of taxis as part of its business. The managers of the company wish to estimate how regularly to replace the taxis. The fleet costs a total of £55 000 and the company has just purchased a new fleet. Operating costs and maintenance costs increase as the taxis get older. Estimates of these costs and the likely resale value of the fleet at the end of various years are presented below.

Year	1 (£)	2 (£)	3 (£)	4 (£)	5 (£)
Operating costs	23 000	24 500	26 000	28 000	44 000
Maintenance costs	6 800	9 200	13 000	17 000	28 000
Resale value	35 000	24 000	12 000	2 000	200

The company's cost of capital is 13% per year.

Required:
(a) Evaluate how regularly the company should replace its fleet of taxis. Assume all cash flows occur at the year end and are after taxation (where relevant). Inflation may be ignored. (10 marks)
(b) Briefly discuss the main problems of this type of evaluation. (4 marks)
ACCA Level 3 Financial Management

Question IM 14.8
Advanced:
Relevant cash
flows and taxation
plus unequal lives

Pavgrange plc is considering expanding its operations. The company accountant has produced *pro forma* profit and loss accounts for the next three years assuming that:

(a) The company undertakes no new investment.
(b) The company invests in Project 1.
(c) The company invests in Project 2.

Both projects have expected lives of three years, and the projects are mutually exclusive.
   The *pro forma* accounts are shown below:
(a) *No new investment*

Years	1 (£000)	2 (£000)	3 (£000)
Sales	6500	6950	7460
Operating costs	4300	4650	5070
Depreciation	960	720	540
Interest	780	800	800
Profit before tax	460	780	1050
Taxation	161	273	367
Profit after tax	299	507	683
Dividends	200	200	230
Retained earnings	99	307	453

(b) *Investment in Project 1*

Years	1 (£000)	2 (£000)	3 (£000)
Sales	7340	8790	9636
Operating costs	4869	5620	6385
Depreciation	1460	1095	821
Interest	1000	1030	1030
Profit before tax	11	1045	1400
Taxation	4	366	490
Profit after tax	7	679	910
Dividends	200	200	230
Retained earnings	(193)	479	680

(c) *Investment in Project 2*

Years	1 (£000)	2 (£000)	3 (£000)
Sales	8430	9826	11314
Operating costs	5680	6470	7230
Depreciation	1835	1376	1032
Interest	1165	1205	1205
Profit before tax	(250)	775	1847
Taxation	0	184	646
Profit after tax	(250)	591	1201
Dividends	200	200	230
Retained earnings	(450)	391	971

The initial outlay for Project 1 is £2 million and for Project 2 £3½ million.

Tax allowable depreciation is at the rate of 25% on a reducing balance basis. The company does not expect to acquire or dispose of any fixed assets during the next three years other than in connection with Projects 1 or 2. Any investment in Project 1 or 2 would commence at the start of the company's next financial year.

The expected salvage value associated with the investments at the end of three years is £750 000 for Project 1, and £150 0000 for Project 2.

Corporate taxes are levied at the rate of 35% and are payable one year in arrears.

Pavgrange would finance either investment with a three year term loan at a gross interest payment of 11% per year. The company's weighted average cost of capital is estimated to be 8% per annum.

Required:
(a) Advise the company which project (if either) it should undertake. Give the reasons for your choice and support it with calculations.

(12 marks)
(b) What further information might be helpful to the company accountant in the evaluation of these investments? (3 marks)
(c) If Project 1 had been for four years duration rather than three years, and the new net cash flows of the project (after tax and allowing for the scrap value) for years four and five were £77 000 and (£188 000) respectively, evaluate whether your advice to Pavgrange would change. (5 marks)
(d) Explain why the payback period and the internal rate of return might not lead to the correct decision when appraising mutually exclusive capital investments.
(5 marks)
(Total 25 marks)
ACCA Level 3 Financial Management

**Question IM 14.9
Advanced:
Adjusting cash
flows for inflation
and the
calculation of NPV
and ROI**

The general manager of the nationalized postal service of a small country, Zedland, wishes to introduce a new service. This service would offer same-day delivery of letters and parcels posted before 10am within a distance of 150 kilometres. The service would require 100 new vans costing $8000 each and 20 trucks costing $18 000 each. 180 new workers would be employed at an average annual wage of $13 000 and five managers at average annual salaries of $20 000 would be moved from their existing duties, where they would not be replaced.

Two postal rates are proposed. In the first year of operation letters will cost $0.525 and parcels $5.25. Market research undertaken at a cost of $50 000 forecasts that demand will average 15 000 letters per working day and 500 parcels per working day during the first year, and 20 000 letters per day and 750 parcels per day thereafter. There is a five day working week. Annual running and maintenance costs on similar new vans and trucks are currently estimated in the first year of operation to be $2000 per van and $4000 per truck respectively. These costs will increase by 20% per year (excluding the effects of inflation). Vehicles are depreciated over a five year period on a straight-line basis. Depreciation is tax allowable and the vehicles will have negligible scrap value at the end of five years. Advertising in year one will cost $500 000 and in year two $250 000. There will be no advertising after year two. Existing premises will be used for the new service but additional costs of $150 000 per year will be incurred.

All the above cost data are current estimates and exclude any inflation effects. Wage and salary costs and all other costs are expected to rise because of inflation by approximately 5% per year during the five year planning horizon of the postal service. The government of Zedland will not permit annual price increases within nationalized industries to exceed the level of inflation.

Nationalized industries are normally required by the government to earn at least an annual after tax return of 5% on average investment and to achieve, on average, at least zero net present value on their investments.

The new service would be financed half with internally generated funds and half by borrowing on the capital market at an interest rate of 12% per year. The opportunity cost of capital for the postal service is estimated to be 14% per year. Corporate taxes in Zedland, to which the postal service is subject, are at the rate of 30% for annual profits of up to $500 000 and 40% for the balance in excess of $500 000. Tax is payable one year in arrears. All transactions may be assumed to be on a cash basis and to occur at the end of the year with the exception of the initial investment which would be required almost immediately.

Required:
(a) Acting as an independent consultant prepare a report advising whether the new postal service should be introduced. Include in your report a discussion of other factors that might need to be taken into account before a final decision was made with respect to the introduction of the new postal service. State clearly any assumptions that you make. (18 marks)
(b) Monte Carlo simulation has been suggested as a possible method of estimating the net present value of a project. Briefly assess the advantages and disadvantages of using this technique in investment appraisal. (7 marks)
(Total 25 marks)
ACCA Level 3 Financial Management

The board of directors of Portand Ltd are considering two *mutually exclusive* investments each of which is expected to have a life of five years. The company does not have the physical capacity to undertake both investments. The first investment is relatively capital intensive whilst the second is relatively labour intensive.

Forecast profits of the two investments are:

Investment 1 (requires four new workers)

			(£000)			
Year	0	1	2	3	4	5
Initial cost	(500)					
Projected sales		400	450	500	550	600
Production costs		260	300	350	450	500
Finance charges		21	21	21	21	21
Depreciation[1]		125	94	70	53	40
Profit before tax		(6)	35	59	26	39
Average profit before tax £30 600.						

Investment 2 (requires nine new workers)

			(£000)			
Year	0	1	2	3	4	5
Initial cost	(175)					
Projected sales		500	600	640	640	700
Production costs		460	520	550	590	630
Depreciation[1]		44	33	25	18	14
Profit before tax		(4)	47	65	32	56
Average profit before tax £39 200.						

[1] Depreciation is a tax allowable expense and is at 25% per year on a reducing balance basis. Both investments are of similar risk to the company's existing operations.

Additional information
(i) Tax and depreciation allowances are payable/receivable one year in arrears. Tax is at 25% per year.
(ii) Investment 2 would be financed from internal funds, which the managing director states have no cost to the company. Investment 1 would be financed by internal funds plus a £150 000 14% fixed rate term loan.
(iii) The data contains no adjustments for price changes. These have been ignored by the board of directors as both sales and production costs are expected to increase by 9% per year, after year one.
(iv) The company's real overall cost of capital is 7% per year and the inflation rate is expected to be 8% per year for the foreseeable future.
(v) All cash flows may be assumed to occur at the end of the year unless otherwise stated.
(vi) The company currently receives interest of 10% per year on short-term money market deposits of £350 000.
(vii) Both investments are expected to have negligible scrap value at the end of five years.

Director A favours Investment 2 as it has a larger average profit.

Director B favours Investment 1 which she believes has a quicker discounted payback period, based upon cash flows.

Director C argues that the company can make £35 000 per year on its money market investments and that, when risk is taken into account, there is little point in investing in either project.

Required:
(a) Discuss the validity of the arguments of each of Directors A, B and C with respect to the decision to select Investment 1, Investment 2 or neither. (7 marks)
(b) Verify whether or not Director B is correct in stating that Investment 1 has the quicker discounted payback period.
  Evaluate which investment, if any, should be selected. All calculations must be shown. Marks will not be deducted for sensible rounding. State clearly any assumptions that you make. (14 marks)
(c) Discuss briefly what non-financial factors might influence the choice of investment. (4 marks)
(Total 25 marks)
ACCA Level 3 Financial Management

Question IM 14.11
Advanced: Sensitivity analysis and alternative methods of adjusting for risk

Parsifal Ltd is a private company whose ordinary shares are all held by its directors. The chairman has recently been impressed by the arguments advanced by a computer salesman, who has told him that Parsifal will be able to install a fully operational computer system for £161 500. This new system will provide all the data currently being prepared by a local data-processing service. This local service has a current annual cost of £46 000. According to the salesman, annual maintenance costs will be only £2000 and if properly maintained the equipment can be expected to last 'indefinitely'.

The chairman has asked the company accountant to evaluate whether purchase of the computer system is worthwhile. The accountant has spoken to a friend who works for a firm of management consultants. She has told him that Parsifal would probably have to employ two additional members of staff at a total cost of about £15 000 per annum and that there would be increased stationery and other related costs of approximately £4000 per annum if Parsifal purchased the computer system. She also estimates that the useful life of the system would be between 6 and 10 years, depending upon the rate of technological change and changes in the pattern of the business of Parsifal. The system would have no scrap or resale value at the end of its useful life.

The company accountant has prepared a net present value calculation by assuming that all the annual costs and savings were expressed in real terms and that the company had a real cost of capital of 5% per annum. He chose this course of action because he did not know either the expected rate of inflation of the cash flows or the cost of capital of Parsifal Ltd. All cash flows, except the initial cost of the system, will arise at the end of the year to which they relate.

You are required to:
(a) estimate, using the company accountant's assumptions, the life of the system which produces a zero net present value, (3 marks)
(b) estimate the internal real rate of return arising from purchase of the computer system, assuming that the system will last:
  (i) for 6 years, and
  (ii) indefinitely, (5 marks)
(c) estimate the value of the annual running costs (maintenance, extra staff, stationery and other related costs) that will produce a net present value of zero, assuming that the system will last for 10 years, (3 marks)
(d) discuss how the company accountant should incorporate the information from parts (a), (b) and (c) above in his recommendation to the directors of Parsifal Ltd as to whether the proposed computer system should be purchased, (7 marks)
(e) discuss how the company accountant could improve the quality of his advice. (7 marks)

Ignore taxation
(Total 25 marks)
ICAEW P2 Financial Management

Galuppi plc is considering whether to scrap some highly specialized old plant or to refurbish it for the production of drive mechanisms, sales of which will last for only three years. Scrapping the plant will yield £25 000 immediately, whereas refurbishment will require an immediate outlay of £375 000.

Each drive mechanism will sell for £50 and, if manufactured entirely by Galuppi plc, give a contribution at current prices of £10. All internal company costs and selling prices are predicted to increase from the start of each year by 5%. Refurbishment of the plant will also entail fixed costs of £10 000, £12 500 and £15 000 for the first, second and third years respectively.

Estimates of product demand depend on different economic conditions. Three have been identified as follows:

Economic condition	Probability of occurrence	Demand in the first year (units)
A	0.25	10 000
B	0.45	15 000
C	0.3	20 000

Demand in subsequent years is expected to increase at 20% per annum, regardless of the initial level demanded.

The plant can produce up to 20 000 drive mechanisms per year, but Galuppi plc can supply more by contracting to buy partially completed mechanisms from an overseas supplier at a fixed price of £20 per unit. To convert a partially completed mechanism into the finished product requires additional work amounting, at current prices, to £25 per unit. For a variety of reasons the supplier is only willing to negotiate contracts in batches of 2000 units.

All contracts to purchase the partially completed units must be signed one year in advance, and payment made by Galuppi plc at the start of the year in which they are to be used.

Galuppi plc has a cost of capital of 15% per annum, and you may assume that all cash flows arise at the end of the year, unless you are told otherwise.

Requirements:
(a) Determine whether refurbishment of the plant is worthwhile. (17 marks)
(b) Discuss whether the expected value method is an appropriate way of evaluating the different risks inherent in the refurbishment decision of Galuppi plc. (8 marks)

(Total 25 marks)
ICAEW P2 Financial Management

Question IM 14.13 Advanced: Calculation of NPV from incomplete data involving taxation, financing costs and identification of relevant cash flows and cost of capital

An unqualified colleague has recently been moved to another office whilst part way through a job. His working notes on a capital investment project have been given to you.

AXT project (working draft) (£000)

	Year 0	1	2	3	4
Sales			4500	5300	6000
Outflows					
Materials		200	850	1200	1320
Wages		180	960	1200	1360
Salaries		50	110	130	150
Head office overhead		85	90	95	100
Other fixed costs		20	400	420	440
Market research	110				
Warehouse rent		40	40	40	40
Opportunity costs:					
Labour		80	80		
Warehouse space		60	60	60	60
Exports		110	110	110	110
Interest		70	286	286	286
Tax allowable depreciation		135	391	293	220
Profit before tax	(110)	(1030)	1123	1466	1914
Tax	(36)	(340)	371	484	632
Other outflows					
Land	300				
Building	240	510			
Machinery		650			(80)
Total working capital		400	440	460	480
Net flows	(614)	(2250)	312	522	882

Working notes:

  (i) The investment will be financed by a 12% fixed rate term loan, £540 000 to be drawn down immediately, £156 0000 to be drawn down at the end of year one.

  (ii) Working capital of £480 000 is expected to be returned in full in year five.

  (iii) Highly skilled labour would need to be taken from other jobs losing £80 000 per year post-tax contributions for two years. These workers could not be replaced in the other jobs.

  (iv) The warehouse space could be rented to another company for £60 000 per year if not used for this investment.

  (v) The project will result in a reduction in existing exports of another product, causing pre-tax contributions to fall by £110 000 per year.

  (vi) One manager, at an initial year one salary of £25 000 per year (increasing by 5% per year) will be transferred from another division. If he had not been transferred he would have been made redundant at an immediate after tax cost to the company of £40 000. This manager is additional to the salaries shown in the working draft.

  (vii) Data includes the estimated effects of inflation on costs and prices wherever relevant.

  (viii) Head office cash flows for overhead will increase by £40 000 as a result of the project in year one, rising by £5000 per year after year one.

  (ix) Tax is at a rate of 33% per year payable one year in arrears. The company has other profitable projects.

  (x) Tax allowable depreciation is 2.5% per year straight line on buildings and 25% per year reducing balance on machinery.

  (xi) Land and buildings are expected to increase in value by 5% per year.

  (xii) The company's cost of capital is 16%.

(xiii) Company equity beta is 1.3

Company asset beta is 1.1

Average equity beta of companies in the same industry as the new AXT project is 1.5

Average asset beta of companies in the same industry as the new AXT project is 1.2

The market return is 15% per year and the risk free rate 6% per year.

(xiv) Company gearing:

Book value 60% equity, 40% debt

Market value 76% equity, 24% debt.

(xv) The market research survey was undertaken last month.

(xvi) The company has a time horizon of three years of sales for evaluating this investment.

Required:

(a) Using the working draft and any other relevant information, complete the appraisal of the AXT project.

There are no arithmetic errors in the working draft, but there might be errors of principle that result in incorrect data.

State clearly any assumptions that you make. (20 marks)

(b) Discuss possible limitations of net present value as the decision criterion for a capital investment. (5 marks)

(Total 25 marks)

ACCA Level 3 Financial Management

The budgeting process

**Question IM 15.1
Intermediate**

Outline:
(a) the objectives of budgetary planning and control systems; (7 marks)
(b) the organization required for the preparation of a master budget. (10 marks)
(Total 17 marks)
ACCA Level 1 Costing

**Question IM 15.2
Intermediate**

The preparation of budgets is a lengthy process which requires great care if the ultimate master budget is to be useful for the purposes of management control within an organization.

You are required:
(a) to identify and to explain briefly the stages involved in the preparation of budgets identifying separately the roles of managers and the budget committee; (8 marks)
(b) to explain how the use of spreadsheets may improve the efficiency of the budget preparation process. (7 marks)
(Total 15 marks)
CIMA Stage 1 Accounting

**Question IM 15.3
Advanced**

What is zero-base budgeting and how does it differ from other more traditional forms of budgeting? Discuss the applicability of zero-base budgeting to profit-orientated organizations.
ACCA Level 2 Management Accounting

**Question IM 15.4
Advanced**

The chief executive of your organization has recently seen a reference to zero-base budgeting. He has asked for more details of the technique.
    You are required to prepare a report for him explaining:
(a) what zero-base budgeting is and to which areas it can best be applied;
(b) what advantages the technique has over traditional type budgeting systems; and
(c) how the organization might introduce such a technique. (20 marks)
CIMA P3 Management Accounting

**Question IM 15.5
Advanced**

Prepare brief notes about zero-base budgeting covering the following topics:
(a) what zero-base budgeting means;
(b) how zero-base budgeting would operate;
(c) what problems might be met in introducing zero-base budgeting;
(d) what special advantages could be expected from zero-base budgeting, as compared with more traditional budgeting methods, for an organization operating in an economic recession. (20 marks)
CIMA P3 Management Accounting

A budgetary planning and control system may include many individual budgets which are integrated into a 'master budget'.

You are required to outline and briefly explain with reasons the steps which should normally be taken in the preparation of master budgets in a manufacturing company, indicating the main budgets which you think should normally be prepared.
(12 marks)
ICAEW Management Accounting

Question IM 15.6
Advanced

The managing director of your company believes that the existing annual budget system is costly to operate and produces unsatisfactory results due to: long preparation period; business decisions being made throughout the year; unpredictable changes in the rate of general inflation; sudden changes in the availability and price of raw materials. He has read about rolling budgets and wonders whether these might be more useful for his decision-making.

You are required, as the management accountant, to prepare a paper for him covering the following areas.
(a) a brief explanation of rolling budgets; (4 marks)
(b) how a rolling budget system would operate; (4 marks)
(c) *three* significant advantages of a rolling budget system; (6 marks)
(d) *three* problems likely to be encountered in using a rolling budget system
(6 marks)
CIMA P3 Management Accounting

Question IM 15.7
Advanced

Explain the specific roles of planning, motivation and evaluation in a system of budgetary control.
(7 marks)
ACCA Level 2 Management Accounting

Question IM 15.8
Advanced

X plc manufactures Product X using three different raw materials. The product details are as follows:

Question IM 15.9
Intermediate:
Preparation of
functional
budgets

Selling price per unit £250

Material A	3 kgs	material price £3.50 per kg
Material B	2 kgs	material price £5.00 per kg
Material C	4 kgs	material price £4.50 per kg
Direct labour	8 hours	labour rate £8.00 per hour

The company is considering its budgets for next year and has made the following estimates of sales demand for Product X for July to October:

July	August	September	October
400 units	300 units	600 units	450 units

It is company policy to hold stocks of finished goods at the end of each month equal to 50% of the following month's sales demand, and it is expected that the stock at the start of the budget period will meet this policy.

At the end of the production process the products are tested: it is usual for 10% of those tested to be faulty. It is not possible to rectify these faulty units.

Raw material stocks are expected to be as follows on 1 July:

Material A	1000 kgs
Material B	400 kgs
Material C	600 kgs

Stocks are to be increased by 20% in July, and then remain at their new level for the foreseeable future.

Labour is paid on an hourly rate based on attendance. In addition to the unit direct labour hours shown above, 20% of *attendance time* is spent on tasks which support production activity.

Requirements:

(a) Prepare the following budgets for the quarter from July to September inclusive:
    (i) sales budget in quantity and value;
    (ii) production budget in units;
    (iii) raw material usage budget in kgs;
    (iv) raw material purchases budget in kgs and value;
    (v) labour requirements budget in hours and value. (16 marks)

(b) Explain the term 'principal budget factor' and why its identification is an important part of the budget preparation process. (3 marks)

(c) Explain clearly, using data from part (a) above, how you would construct a spreadsheet to produce the labour requirements budget for August. Include a specimen cell layout diagram containing formulae which would illustrate the basis for the spreadsheet. (6 marks)

(Total 25 marks)

CIMA Stage 2 Operational Cost Accounting

Question IM 15.10
Intermediate:
Preparation of
functional
budgets

D Limited is preparing its annual budgets for the year to 31 December 2001. It manufactures and sells one product, which has a selling price of £150. The marketing director believes that the price can be increased to £160 with effect from 1 July 2001 and that at this price the sales volume for each quarter of 2001 will be as follows:

	Sales volume
Quarter 1	40 000
Quarter 2	50 000
Quarter 3	30 000
Quarter 4	45 000

Sales for each quarter of 2002 are expected to be 40 000 units.

Each unit of the finished product which is manufactured requires four units of component R and three units of component T, together with a body shell S. These items are purchased from an outside supplier. Currently prices are:

Component R	£8.00 each
Component T	5.00 each
Shell S	£30.00 each

The components are expected to increase in price by 10% with effect from 1 April 2001; no change is expected in the price of the shell.

Assembly of the shell and components into the finished product requires 6 labour hours: labour is currently paid £5.00 per hour. A 4% increase in wage costs is anticipated to take effect from 1 October 2001.

Variable overhead costs are expected to be £10 per unit for the whole of 2001; fixed production overhead costs are expected to be £240 000 for the year, and are absorbed on a per unit basis. Stocks on 31 December 2000 are expected to be as follows:

Finished units	9000 units
Component R	3000 units
Component T	5500 units
Shell S	500 units

Closing stocks at the end of each quarter are to be as follows:

Finished units	10% of next quarter's sales
Component R	20% of next quarter's production requirements
Component T	15% of next quarter's production requirements
Shell S	10% of next quarter's production requirements

Requirement:

(a) Prepare the following budgets of D Limited for the year ending 31 December 2001, showing values for each quarter and the year in total:
   (i) sales budget (in £s and units)
   (ii) production budget (in units)
   (iii) material usage budget (in units)
   (iv) production cost budget (in £s).   (15 marks)

(b) Sales are often considered to be the principal budget factor of an organisation.

Requirement:

Explain the meaning of the 'principal budget factor' and, assuming that it is sales, explain how sales may be forecast making appropriate reference to the use of statistical techniques and the use of microcomputers.   (10 marks)

(Total 25 marks)

CIMA Stage 2 Operational Cost Accounting

The following data and estimates are available for ABC Limited for June, July and August.

Question IM 15.11 Intermediate: Preparation of cash budgets

	June (£)	July (£)	August (£)
Sales	45 000	50 000	60 000
Wages	12 000	13 000	14 500
Overheads	8 500	9 500	9 000

The following information is available regarding direct materials:

	June (£)	July (£)	August (£)	September (£)
Opening stock	5000	3500	6 000	4000
Material usage	8000	9000	10 000	

Notes:

1. 10% of sales are for cash, the balance is received the following month. The amount received in June for May's sales is £29 500.
2. Wages are paid in the month they are incurred.
3. Overheads include £1500 per month for depreciation. Overheads are settled the month following. £6500 is to be paid in June for May's overheads.
4. Purchases of direct materials are paid for in the month purchased.
5. The opening cash balance in June is £11 750.
6. A tax bill of £25 000 is to be paid in July.

Required:

(a) Calculate the amount of direct material purchases in *each* of the months of June, July and August.   (3 marks)

(b) Prepare cash budgets for June, July and August.   (9 marks)

(c) Describe briefly the advantages of preparing cash budgets.   (3 marks)

(Total marks 15)

CIMA Stage 1 Cost Accounting

**Question IM 15.12
Intermediate:
Preparation of
cash budgets**

A company is to carry out a major modernization of its factory commencing in two weeks time. During the modernization, which is expected to take four weeks to complete, no production of the company's single product will be possible.

The following additional information is available:

(i) *Sales/Debtors:* Demand for the product at £100 per unit is expected to continue at 800 units per week, the level of sales achieved for the last four weeks, for one further week. It is then expected to reduce to 700 units per week for three weeks, before rising to a level of 900 units per week where it is expected to remain for several weeks. All sales are on credit, 50% being received in cash in the week following the week of sale and 50% in the week after that.

(ii) *Production/Finished goods stock:* Production will be at a level of 1200 units per week for the next two weeks. Finished goods stock is 2800 units at the beginning of week 1.

(iii) *Raw material stock:* Raw material stock is £36 000 at the beginning of week 1. This will be increased by the end of week 1 to £40 000 and reduced to £10 000 by the end of week 2.

(iv) *Costs*

	(£ per unit)
Variable:	
Raw material	35
Direct labour	20
Overhead	10
Fixed:	
Overhead	25

Fixed overheads have been apportioned to units on the basis of the normal output level of 800 units per week and include depreciation of £4000 per week.

In addition to the above unit costs, overtime premiums of £5000 per week will be incurred in weeks 1 and 2. During the modernization variable costs will be avoided, apart from direct labour which will be incurred at the level equivalent to 800 units production per week. Outlays on fixed overheads will be reduced by £4000 per week.

(v) *Payments:* Creditors for raw materials, which stand at £27 000 at the beginning of week 1, are paid in the week following purchase. All other payments are made in the week in which the liability is incurred.

(vi) *Liquidity:* The company has a bank overdraft balance of £39 000 at the beginning of week 1 and an overdraft limit of £50 000.

The company is anxious to establish the liquidity situation over the modernization period, excluding the requirements for finance for the modernization itself.

Required:
(a) Prepare a weekly cash budget covering the six-week period up to the planned completion of the modernization. (15 marks)
(b) Comment briefly upon any matters concerning the liquidity situation which you feel should be drawn to the attention of management. (7 marks)
(Total 22 marks)
ACCA Level 1 Costing

The Rosrock Housing Association has two types of housing estate in the Rosburgh area (A and B).

The following information is available:

(i) The association has its own squad of painters who carry out painting and decorating work on the housing estates. The estimated cost for each house in which the work will be done in 2001 is as follows: Painting

	(£)
(a) Direct material cost	75
(b) Direct labour cost	270

(c) In 2001 overhead cost is absorbed at 20% on direct material cost plus 100% on direct labour cost. Only 30% of material related overhead and $33\frac{1}{3}\%$ of labour related overhead is variable, the remainder is fixed overhead and the absorption rate is arrived at using the budgeted number of houses which require painting and decorating each year.

(d) Fixed overhead may be analysed into:

1. Items avoidable on cessation of the service	30%
2. Depreciation of equipment and premises	20%
3. Apportionment of head office costs	50%

(e) Direct material and direct labour cost are wholly variable.

(ii) The total number of houses of each type and the percentage requiring painting and decorating each year is as follows:

	Estate Type A	Estate Type B
Total number of houses	500	600
Percentage of houses requiring maintenance each year:	30%	20%

(iii) Where relevant, all future costs are expected to increase each year by a fixed percentage of the previous year's level due to changes in prices and wage rates as follows:

Direct material cost	5%
Direct labour cost	7%
Overhead cost	6%

(iv) Forecast balances at 31 December 2000 and other cash flow timing information is as follows:

(a) Creditors for materials: £2100. Credit purchases are 90% of purchases, the remainder being cash purchases. The credit purchases outstanding at a year end are estimated at 10% of the annual materials purchased on credit. There are no materials on hand on 31 December 2000.

(b) Labour costs accrued: £2800. Labour costs outstanding at a year end are estimated at 4% of the annual total earnings for the year.

(c) Creditors for variable overheads: £600. Variable overheads are paid 60% in the month of incidence and 40% in the month following. Variable overheads are deemed to accrue evenly each month throughout the year.

(d) Fixed overheads are paid in twelve equal amounts with no accruals or prepayments.

Required:

(a) Prepare a cash budget for the existing painting and decorating function for the period 1 January 2001 to 31 December 2003 which shows the cash flows for each of the years 2001, 2002 and 2003. (Calculations should be rounded to the nearest whole £.) (14 marks)

(b) An outside company has offered to undertake all painting and decorating work for a three year period 2001 to 2003 for a fixed fee of £135 000 per annum.

(i) Calculate whether the offer should be accepted on financial grounds using the information available in the question. (2 marks)

(ii) List and comment upon other factors which should be taken into account by Rosrock Housing Association management when considering this offer. (6 marks)

(Total 22 marks)

ACCA Level 2 Cost and Management Accounting

Question IM 15.14
Intermediate:
Direct labour
budget and labour
cost accounting

A company, which manufactures a range of consumer products, is preparing the direct labour budget for one of its factories. Three products are manufactured in the factory. Each product passes through two stages: filling and packing.

Direct labour efficiency standards are set for each stage. The standards are based upon the number of units expected to be manufactured per hour of direct labour. Current standards are:

	Product 1 (units/hour)	Product 2 (units/hour)	Product 3 (units/hour)
Filling	125	300	250
Packing	95	100	95

Budgeted sales of the three products are:

Product 1	850 000 units
Product 2	1 500 000 units
Product 3	510 000 units

Production will be at the same level each month, and will be sufficient to enable finished goods stocks at the end of the budget year to be:

Product 1	200 000 units
Product 2	255 000 units
Product 3	70 000 units

Stocks at the beginning of the budget year are expected to be:

Product 1	100 000 units
Product 2	210 000 units
Product 3	105 000 units

After completion of the filling stage, 5% of the output of Products 1 and 3 is expected to be rejected and destroyed. The cost of such rejects is treated as a normal loss.

A single direct labour hour rate is established for the factory as a whole. The total payroll cost of direct labour personnel is included in the direct labour rate. Hours of direct labour personnel are budgeted to be split as follows:

	% of Total time
Direct work	80
Holidays (other, than public holidays)	7
Sickness	3
Idle time	4
Cleaning	3
Training	3
	100%

All direct labour personnel are employed on a full-time basis to work a basic 35 hour, 5 day, week. Overtime is to be budgeted at an average of 3 hours per employee, per week. Overtime is paid at a premium of 25% over the basic hourly rate of £4 per hour. There will be 250 possible working days during the year. You are to assume that employees are paid for exactly 52 weeks in the year.

Required:
Calculate:
(a) The number of full-time direct employees required during the budget year.

(14 marks)

(b) The direct labour rate (£ per hour, to 2 decimal places).   (5 marks)
(c) The direct labour cost for each product (pence per unit to 2 decimal places).

(6 marks)

(Total 25 marks)

ACCA Level 1 Costing

Management control systems

**Question IM 16.1
Intermediate**

You have applied for the position of assistant accountant in a company manufacturing a range of products with a sales turnover of £12 million per annum and employing approximately 300 employees. As part of the selection process you are asked to spend half an hour preparing a report, to be addressed to the managing director, on the topic of 'cost control'.

You are required to write the report which should deal with what is meant by 'cost control', its purpose and the techniques which you believe would be useful within this particular company. (20 marks)

CIMA Foundation Cost Accounting 1

**Question IM 16.2
Intermediate**

Outline the main features of a responsibility accounting system. (6 marks)

ACCA Level 2 Management Accounting

**Question IM 16.3
Intermediate**

Explain the meaning of each of the undernoted terms, comment on their likely impact on cash budgeting and profit planning and suggest ways in which any adverse effects of each may be reduced.

(a) Budgetary slack. (7 marks)
(b) Incremental budgets. (7 marks)
(c) Fixed budgets. (6 marks)
(Total 20 marks)

ACCA Level 2 Cost and Management Accounting II

**Question IM 16.4
Advanced**

(a) Discuss the use of the following as aids to *each* of planning and control:
   (i) rolling budgets
   (ii) flexible budgets
   (iii) planning and operational variances. (9 marks)
(b) Discuss the extent to which the incidence of budgetary slack is likely to be affected by the use of each of the techniques listed in (a). (6 marks)
(Total 15 marks)

ACCA Paper 9 Information for Control and Decision Making

**Question IM 16.5
Advanced**

In the context of budgetary control, certain costs are not amenable to the use of flexible budgets. These include some costs which are often called 'discretionary' (or 'programmed').

You are required to explain:
(a) the nature of discretionary (or programmed) costs and give *two* examples;
(b) how the treatment of these costs differs from that of other types of cost in the process of preparing and using budgets for control purposes. (20 marks)

CIMA P3 Management Accounting

'Textbooks on accounting often describe management information and financial control systems as if they work in exactly the same way as machine control systems. Many accountants appear to assume that they do work in this way. The problem is that business operations do not function like machines. Unless a financial control system is very well designed and managed, then it can easily distort the functioning of a business operation.'

One comment on the design and use of financial control systems

Requirements
Having regard to this comment,
(a) • explain the concepts of management information system design, and the role that such systems play in the financial control of business operations;
   • explain the role that performance evaluation plays in a management information system;
   • compare and contrast output controls and input controls in the context of a management information system;   (11 marks)
(b) explain
   • the manner in which management information systems can distort the functioning of the business operations they are meant to serve;
   • he action that might be taken by the chartered management accountant in order to avoid such distortion;   (9 marks)
(c) explain how the use of PCs, spreadsheets and databases contributes to the cost-effectiveness of management information systems.   (5 marks)
                                                                   (Total 25 marks)
                            CIMA Stage 3 Management Accounting Applications

(a) In the context of budgeting, provide definitions for *four* of the following terms:
       aspiration level;
       budgetary slack;
       feedback;
       zero-base budgeting;
       responsibility accounting.   (8 marks)
(b) Discuss the motivational implications of the level of efficiency assumed in establishing a budget.   (9 marks)
                                                                   (Total 17 marks)
                            ACCA Level 2 Management Accounting

In the context of budgeting, describe the meaning of and write notes on *four* of the following terms:
       Feedback control;
       Feedforward control;
       Budgetary slack;
       Aspiration level;
       Control limits;
       Noise.   (17 marks)
                            ACCA Level 2 Management Accounting

'Budgeting is too often looked upon from a purely mechanistic viewpoint. The human factors in budgeting are more important than the accounting techniques. The success of a budgetary system depends upon its acceptance by the company members who are affected by the budgets.'

Discuss the validity of the above statement from the viewpoint of both the planning and the control aspects of budgeting. In the course of your discussion present at least one practical illustration to support your conclusions.   (20 marks)
                            ACCA P2 Management Accounting

Question IM 16.10
Advanced

'The major reason for introducing budgetary control and standard costing systems is to influence human behaviour and to motivate the managers to achieve the goals of the organization. However, the accounting literature provides many illustrations of accounting control systems that fail to give sufficient attention to influencing human behaviour towards the achievement of organization goals.'

You are required:
(a) To identify and discuss four situations where accounting control systems might not motivate desirable behaviour.
(b) To briefly discuss the improvements you would suggest in order to ensure that some of the dysfunctional behavioural consequences of accounting control systems are avoided.

Question IM 16.11
Advanced

'The final impact which any accounting system has on managerial and employee behaviour is dependent not only upon its design and technical characteristics but also in the precise manner in which the resulting information is used' (A. Hopwood, *Accounting and Human Behaviour*).
Discuss this statement in relation to budgeting and standard costing.

Question IM 16.12
Advanced

'Motivation is the over-riding consideration that should influence management in formulating and using performance measures, and in designing management control systems.'
Discuss this statement in relation to the design and implementation of budgetary control systems.

Question IM 16.13
Advanced

(a) Discuss the behavioural arguments for and against involving those members of management who are responsible for the implementation of the budget in the annual budget setting process. (10 marks)
(b) Explain how the methods by which annual budgets are formulated might help to overcome behavioural factors likely to limit the efficiency and effectiveness of the budget. (7 marks)
(Total 17 marks)

Question IM 16.14
Advanced

(a) An extensive literature on the behavioural aspects of budgeting discusses the propensity of managers to create budgetary slack.
You are required to explain three ways in which managers may attempt to create budgetary slack, and how senior managers can identify these attempts to distort the budgetary system. (6 marks)
(b) Managerial behaviour can be quite different from that discussed in (a).
You are required to explain circumstances in which managers may be motivated to set themselves very high, possibly unachievable budgets.
(6 marks)
(c) Sections (a) and (b) above are examples of differing managerial behaviour in disparate situations. There are theories which attempt to explain the consequences for the design of management accounting systems of disparate situations, one of which is contingency theory.

You are required to explain
• the contingency theory of management accounting
• the effects of environmental uncertainty on the choice of managerial control systems and on information systems for managerial control. (13 marks)
(Total 25 marks)
CIMA Stage 4 Management Accounting – Control and Audit

An article in *Management Accounting* concluded that there will always be some budgetary padding in any organisation.

Question IM 16.15 Advanced

Requirements:
(a) As Management Accountant, write a report to your Finance Director, explaining what steps can be taken by you, and by senior management when approving budgets, to minimise budgetary slack. (8 marks)
(b) The Finance Director, having read the report referred to in part (a), discussed the problem with the Managing Director and suggested that appropriate action be taken to reduce budgetary slack.

The Managing Director expressed doubts, stating that in his opinion removing all budget padding could cause considerable problems.

Requirement:
Explain the arguments that can be advanced for accepting some budgetary slack, and the advantages of this to the manager being appraised and to the organisation. Discuss whether the budget review and approval process should permit managers to build in some budgetary slack. (12 marks)
(Total 20 marks)
CIMA Stage 4 Management Accounting Control Systems

(a) The following report has been prepared, relating to one product for March. This has been sent to the appropriate product manager as part of PDC Limited's monitoring procedures.

Question IM 16.16 Intermediate: Criticism and redrafting of a performance report

Monthly variance report – March 1

	Actual	Budget	Variance	%
Production volume (units)	9 905	10 000	95 A	0.95 A
Sales volume (units)	9 500	10 000	500 A	5.00 A
Sales revenue (£)	27 700	30 000	2300 A	7.67 A
Direct material (kg)	9 800	10 000	200 F	2.00 F
Direct material (£)	9 600	10 000	400 F	4.00 F
Direct labour (hours)	2 500	2 400	100 A	4.17 A
Direct labour (£)	8 500	8 400	100 A	1.19 A
Contribution (£)	9 600	11 600	2000 A	17.24 A

The product manager has complained that the report ignores the principle of flexible budgeting and is unfair.

Required:
Prepare a report addressed to the management team which comments critically on the monthly variance report. Include as an appendix to your report the layout of a revised monthly variance report which will be more useful to the product manager. Include row and column headings, but do *not* calculate the contents of the report. (15 marks)
(b) Explain the differences between budgetary control and standard costing/variance analysis. In what circumstances would an organization find it beneficial to operate both of these cost control systems? (5 marks)
(Total 20 marks)
CIMA Operational Cost Accounting Stage 2

**Question IM 16.17
Intermediate:
Preparation of
flexible budgets
and an
explanation of
variances**

You have been provided with the following operating statement, which represents an attempt to compare the actual performance for the quarter which has just ended with the budget:

	Budget	Actual	Variance
Number of units sold (000s)	640	720	80
	£000	£000	£000
Sales	1024	1071	47
Cost of sales (all variable)			
Materials	168	144	
Labour	240	288	
Overheads	32	36	
	440	468	(28)
Fixed labour cost	100	94	6
Selling and distribution costs:			
Fixed	72	83	(11)
Variable	144	153	(9)
Administration costs:			
Fixed	184	176	8
Variable	48	54	(6)
	548	560	(12)
Net profit	36	43	7

Required:
(a) Using a flexible budgeting approach, re-draft the operating statement so as to provide a more realistic indication of the variances and comment briefly on the possible reasons (other than inflation) why they have occurred.   (12 marks)
(b) Explain why the original operating statement was of little use to management.
(2 marks)
(c) Discuss the problems associated with the forecasting of figures which are to be used in flexible budgeting.   (6 marks)
(Total 20 marks)
ACCA Paper 8 Managerial Finance

**Question IM 16.18
Intermediate:
Responsibility
centre
performance
reports**

Data
Jim Smith has recently been appointed as the Head Teacher of Mayfield School in Midshire. The age of the pupils ranges from 11 years to 18 years. For many years, Midshire County Council was responsible for preparing and reporting on the school budget. From June, however, these responsibilities passed to the Head Teacher of Mayfield School.

You have recently accepted a part-time appointment as the accountant to Mayfield School, although your previous accounting experience has been gained in commercial organisations. Jim Smith is hoping that you will be able to apply that experience to improving the financial reporting procedures at Mayfield School.

The last budget statement prepared by Midshire County Council is reproduced below. It covers the ten months to the end of May and all figures refer to cash *payments* made.

Midshire County Council Mayfield School
Statement of school expenditure against budget: 10 months ending May

	Expenditure to date	Budget to date	Under/ over spend	Total budget for year
Teachers full-time	1 680 250	1 682 500	2 250 Cr	2 019 000
Teachers part-time	35 238	34 600	638	41 520
Other employee expenses	5 792	15 000	9 208 Cr	18 000
Administrative staff	69 137	68 450	687	82 140
Caretaker and cleaning	49 267	57 205	7 938 Cr	68 646
Resources (books, etc.)	120 673	100 000	20 673	120 000
Repairs and maintenance	458	0	458	0
Lighting and heating	59 720	66 720	7 000 Cr	80 064
Rates	23 826	19 855	3 971	23 826
Fixed assets: furniture and equipment	84 721	100 000	15 279 Cr	120 000
Stationery, postage and phone	1 945	0	1 945	0
Miscellaneous expenses	9 450	6 750	2 700	8 100
Total	2 140 477	2 151 080	10 603 Cr	2 581 296

Task 1
Write a memo to Jim Smith. Your memo should:
(a) identify *four* weaknesses of the existing statement as a management report;
(b) include an improved *outline* statement format showing revised column headings and a more meaningful classification of costs which will help Jim Smith to manage his school effectively (figures are not required);
(c) give *two* advantages of your proposed format over the existing format.

Data
The income of Mayfield School is based on the number of pupils at the school. Jim Smith provides you with the following breakdown of student numbers.

Mayfield School:
Student numbers as at 31 May

School year	Age range	Current number of pupils
1	11–12	300
2	12–13	350
3	13–14	325
4	14–15	360
5	15–16	380
6	16–17	240
7	17–18	220
Total number of students		2175

Jim also provides you with the following information relating to existing pupils:
- pupils move up one school-year at the end of July;
- for those pupils entering year 6, there is an option to leave the school. As a result only 80% of the current school-year 5 pupils go on to enter school-year 6;
- of those currently in school-year 6 only 95% continue into school-year 7;
- pupils currently in school-year 7 leave to go on to higher education or employment;
- the annual income per pupil is £1200 in years 1 to 5 and £1500 in years 6 to 7.

The new year 1 pupils come from the final year at four junior schools. Not all pupils, however, elect to go to Mayfield School. Jim has investigated this matter and derived accurate estimates of the proportion of final year pupils at each of the four junior schools who go on to attend Mayfield School.

The number of pupils in the final year at each of the four junior schools is given below along with Jim's estimate of the proportion likely to choose Mayfield School.

Junior School	Number in final year at 31 May	Proportion choosing Mayfield School
Ranmoor	60	0.9
Hallamshire	120	0.8
Broomhill	140	0.9
Endcliffe	80	0.5

Task 2
(a) Forecast the number of pupils and the income of Mayfield School for the next year from August to July
(b) Assuming expenditure next year is 5% more than the current annual budgeted expenditure, calculate the budgeted surplus or deficit of Mayfield School for next year.

AAT Technicians Stage

Question IM 16.19 Advanced: Design of a management control system

Maxcafe Ltd sold its own brand of coffee throughout the UK. Sales policies, purchasing and the direction of the company was handled from head office in London. The company operated three roasting plants in Glasgow, Hull and Bristol. Each plant had profit and loss responsibility and the plant manager was paid a bonus on the basis of a percentage on gross margin. Monthly operating statements were prepared for each plant by head office and the following statement is a monthly report for the Glasgow plant:

**Operating statement
Glasgow plant
April**

		(£)
Net sales		1 489 240
Less: Cost of sales		
Special coffee – at contract cost		747 320
Roasting and grinding:		
Labour	76 440	
Fuel	49 560	
Manufacturing expenses	67 240	
		193 240
Packaging:		
Container	169 240	
Packing carton	18 280	
Labour	24 520	
Manufacturing expenses	50 880	262 920
Total manufacturing cost		1 203 480
Gross margin on sales		285 760

Each month the plant manager was given a production schedule for the current month and a tentative schedule for the next month. Credit collection and payment was done by Head Office. The procurement of special coffee for roasting operations was also handled by the purchasing department at Head Office. The objective of the purchasing department was to ensure that any one of forty grades of special coffee was available for the roasting plants.

Based on estimated sales budgets, purchase commitments were made that would provide for delivery in 3 to 15 months from the date that contracts for purchases were made. While it was possible to purchase from local brokers for immediate delivery, such purchases were more costly than purchases made for delivery in the country of origin and hence these 'spot' purchases were kept to a minimum. A most important factor was the market 'know-how' of the purchasing department, who must judge whether the market trend was up or down and make commitments accordingly.

The result was that the purchasing department was buying a range of coffees for advance delivery at special dates. At the time of actual delivery, the sales of the company's coffee might not be going as anticipated when the purchase commitment was made. The difference between actual deliveries and current requirements was handled through either 'spot' sales of surplus special grades or 'spot' purchases when actual sales demand of the completed coffee brands was greater than the estimated sales.

In accounting for coffee purchases a separate record was maintained for each purchase contract. This record was charged with coffee purchased and import and transport expenses, with the result that a net cost per bag was developed for each purchase. The established policy was to treat each contract on an individual basis. When special coffee was delivered to a plant, a charge was made for the cost represented by the contracts which covered that particular delivery of coffee, with no element of profit or loss. When special coffee was sold to outsiders, the sales were likewise costed on a specific contract basis with a resulting profit or loss on these transactions.

For the past several years there has been some dissatisfaction on the part of plant managers with the method of computing gross margins subject to bonuses. This had finally led to a request from the managing director to the accountant to study the whole method of reporting on results of *plant operations* and the *purchasing operation*.

Required:
(a) An explanation to the managing director indicating any weaknesses of the current control system, and
(b) an explanation of what changes you consider should be made in the present reporting and control system.

Question IM 16.20 Advanced: Comments on an existing performance measurement and bonus system and recommendations for improvement

1. You are the group management accountant of a large divisionalised group.

There has been extensive board discussion of the existing system of rewarding Divisional General Managers with substantial bonuses based on the comparison of the divisional profit with budget.

The scheme is simple: the divisional profit (PBIT) is compared with the budget for the year. If budget is not achieved no bonus is paid. If budget is achieved a bonus of 20% of salary is earned. If twice budgeted profit is achieved, a bonus of 100% of salary is paid, which is the upper limit of the bonus scheme. Intermediate achievements are calculated pro rata.

The Finance Director has been asked to prepare a number of reports on the issues involved, and has asked you to prepare some of these.

He has decided to use the results for Division X as an example on which the various discussions could be based. A schedule of summary available data is given below.

Division X
Summary of management accounting data

	Strategic plan 2001 Prepared Aug 2000	Budget 2001 Prepared Oct 2000	Latest estimate 2001 Prepared April 2001
Sales of units by Division X	35 000	36 000	35 800
Sales	28 000	28 800	28 100
Marginal costs	14 350	15 300	14 900
Fixed factory cost	6 500	6 800	7 200
Product development	2 000	2 000	1 400
Marketing	3 500	3 200	2 600
PBIT	1 650	1 500	2 000

Division X manufactures and sells branded consumer durables in competitive markets. High expenditure is required on product development and advertising, as the maintenance of market share depends on a flow of well-promoted new models.

Reliable statistics on market size are available annually. Based on the market size for 2000, where stronger than anticipated growth had occurred, a revised market estimate of 165 000 units for 2001 is agreed by group and divisional staff in May 2001. This is a significant increase on the estimate of 150 000 units made in May 2000 and used since.

The Divisional General Manager has commented that action now, almost half way through the year, is unlikely to produce significant results during this year. However, had he known last year, at the time of producing the budget, that the market was growing faster, he could have taken the necessary action to maintain the strategic plan market share. The actions would have been

- cutting prices by £10 per unit below the price at present charged and used in the latest estimate for 2001,
- increasing marketing expenditure by £300 000 compared with the strategic plan.

The Group Managing Director, commenting on the same data, said that the Divisional General Manager could have maintained both strategic plan market share and selling prices by an alternative approach.

The approach, he thought, should have been

- maintaining expenditure on product development and marketing at 20% of sales over the years,
- spending his time controlling production costs instead of worrying about annual bonuses.

You are required:

(a) to analyse and comment on the results of Division X, making appropriate comparisons with Budget, with Plan and with new available data. Present the results in such a form that the Board can easily understand the problems involved; (17 marks)

(b) to comment on the advantages and problems of the existing bonus system for the Divisional General Manager and the way in which the present bonus scheme may motivate the Divisional General Manager; (8 marks)

(c) to make specific proposals, showing calculations if appropriate, for an alternative bonus scheme, reflecting your analysis in (a).

(8 marks)

A non-executive director has commented that he can understand the case for linking executive directors' rewards to group results. He is not convinced that this should be extended to divisional managers, and certainly not to senior managers below this level in divisions and head office.

(d) Explain and discuss the case for extending bonus schemes widely throughout the organisation. (7 marks)

(Total 40 marks)

CIMA Stage 4 Management Accounting – Control and Audit

A new private hospital of 100 beds was opened to receive patients on 2 January though many senior staff members including the supervisor of the laundry department had been *in situ* for some time previously. The first three months were expected to be a settling-in period; the hospital facilities being used to full capacity only in the second and subsequent quarters.

In May the supervisor of the laundry department received her first quarterly performance report from the hospital administrator, together with an explanatory memorandum. Copies of both documents are set out below.

The supervisor had never seen the original budget, nor had she been informed that there would be a quarterly performance report. She knew she was responsible for her department and had made every endeavour to run it as efficiently as possible. It had been made clear to her that there would be a slow build up in the number of patients accepted by the hospital and so she would need only 3 members of staff, but she had had to take on a fourth during the quarter due to the extra work. This extra hiring had been anticipated for May, not late February.

Rockingham Private Patients Hospital Ltd

MEMORANDUM   30 April

To: All Department Heads/Supervisors

From: Hospital Administrator

Attached is the Quarterly Performance Report for your department. The hospital has adopted a responsibility accounting system so you will be receiving one of these reports quarterly. Responsibility accounting means that you are accountable for ensuring that the expenses of running your department are kept in line with the budget. Each report compares the actual expenses of running your department for the quarter with our budget for the same period. The difference between the actual and forecast will be highlighted so that you can identify the important variations from budget and take corrective action to get back on budget. Any variation in excess of 5% from budget should be investigated and an explanatory memo sent to me giving reasons for the variations and the proposed corrective actions.

Performance report – laundry department
3 months to 31 March

	Actual	Budget	Variation (Over) Under	% Variation
Patient days	8 000	6 500	(1 500)	(23)
Weight of laundry processed (kg)	101 170	81 250	(19 920)	(24.5)
	(£)	(£)	(£)	
Department expenses				
Wages	4 125	3 450	(675)	(19.5)
Supervisor salary	1 490	1 495	5	—
Washing materials	920	770	(150)	(19.5)
Heating and power	560	510	(50)	(10)
Equipment depreciation	250	250	—	—
Allocated administration costs	2 460	2 000	(460)	(23)
Equipment maintenance	10	45	35	78
	9 815	8 520	(1 295)	(15)

Comment: We need to have a discussion about the overexpenditure of the department.

You are required to:
(a) discuss in detail the various possible effects on the behaviour of the laundry supervisor of the way that her budget was prepared and the form and content of the performance report, having in mind the published research findings in this area, (15 marks)
(b) re-draft, giving explanations, the performance report and supporting memorandum in a way which, in your opinion, would make them more effective management tools. (10 marks)
(Total 25 marks)
ICAEW P2 Management Accounting

Question IM 16.22
Advanced:
Aspiration levels

Individual performance measurement is likely to be related to the aspiration level of the individual and the timing and level of the target set.

Discuss the above statement in the context of each of Tables 1 and 2. The tables provide illustrations expressed in terms of output, of the results of two separate studies linking targets, aspiration levels and achievement. (15 marks)

Table 1

		Actual achievement (units)		
Target	Target Units	Aspiration level set by individual before knowing target	Aspiration level set by individual after knowing target	Average
Implicit	not quoted	53	57	55
Explicit: low	35	45	44	44.5
Explicit medium	50	54	54	54
Explicit: high	70	40	60	50

Table 2

Target (units)	Aspiration level of individual (where target is known) (units)	Actual achieved (units)
70	80	80
90	90	90
110	100	100
130	120	112
150	110	90
180	nil	80

ACCA Paper 9 Information for Control and Decision Making

Incorporated Finance plc is a finance company having one hundred branch offices in major towns and cities throughout the UK. These offer a variety of hire purchase and loan facilities to personal customers both directly and through schemes operated on behalf of major retailers. The main function of the branches is to sell loans and to ensure that repayments are collected; the head office is responsible for raising the capital required, which it provides to branches at a current rate of interest.

Each year branch managers are invited to provide estimates of the following items for the forthcoming year, as the start of the budgetary process:

Value of new loans (by category e.g. direct, retail, motor)
Margin percentage (i.e. loan rate of interest less cost of capital provided by head office)
Gross margin (i.e. value of new loans × margin percentage)
Branch operating expenses
Net margin (i.e. gross margin less operating expenses)

The main branch expenses relate to the cost of sales and administrative staff, and to the cost of renting and maintaining branch premises, but also include the cost of bad debts on outstanding loans.

These estimates are then passed to headquarters by area and regional managers and are used, together with other information such as that relating to general economic conditions, to set an overall company budget. This is then broken down by headquarters into regional figures; regional managers then set the area budgets and area managers finally set branch budgets. However, a common complaint of branch managers is that the budgets they are set often bear little resemblance to the estimates they originally submitted.

Budget targets are set for the five items specified above, with managers receiving a bonus based on the average percentage achievement of all five targets, weighted equally.

Requirements
(a) Discuss the advantages and disadvantages of allowing managers to participate in budget-setting, and suggest how Incorporated Finance plc should operate its budgetary system. (15 marks)
(b) The managing director is considering changing the performance evaluation and bonus scheme so that branch managers are set only a net margin target. Prepare a report for him outlining the advantages and disadvantages of making such a change. (10 marks)
(Total 25 marks)
ICAEW P2 Management Accounting

Question IM 16.23 Advanced: Advantages and disadvantages of participation and comments on a new performance measurement and evaluation system

Standard costing and variance analysis: 1

Question IM 18.1 Intermediate: Flexible budgets and computation of labour and material variances

(a) JB plc operates a standard marginal cost accounting system. Information relating to product J, which is made in one of the company departments, is given below:

Product J	Standard marginal product cost Unit (£)
Direct material	
6 kilograms at £4 per kg	24
Direct labour	
1 hour at £7 per hour	7
Variable production overhead[a]	3
	34

[a] Variable production overhead varies with units produced

Budgeted fixed production overhead, per month: £100 000.
Budgeted production for product J: 20 000 units per month.
Actual production and costs for *month 6* were as follows:

Units of J produced	18 500 (£)
Direct materials purchased and used: 113 500kg	442 650
Direct labour: 17 800 hours	129 940
Variable production overhead incurred	58 800
Fixed production overhead incurred	104 000
	735 390

You are required to:
(i) prepare a columnar statement showing, by element of cost, the:
   (i) original budget;
   (ii) flexed budget;
   (iii) actual;
   (iv) total variances; (9 marks)
(ii) subdivide the variances for direct material and direct labour shown in your answer to (a) (i)–(iv) above to be more informative for managerial purposes.
(4 marks)
(b) Explain the meaning and use of a 'rolling forecast'. (2 marks)
(Total 15 marks)
CIMA State 2 Cost Accounting

Question IM 18.2
Intermediate:
Reconciliation of
standard and
actual cost for a
variable costing
system

Data

You are employed as the assistant management accountant in the group accountant's office of Hampstead plc. Hampstead recently acquired Finchley Ltd, a small company making a specialist product called the Alpha. Standard marginal costing is used by all the companies within the group and, from 1 August, Finchley Ltd will also be required to use standard marginal costing in its management reports. Part of your job is to manage the implementation of standard marginal costing at Finchley Ltd.

John Wade, the managing director of Finchley, is not clear how the change will help him as a manager. He has always found Finchley's existing absorption costing system sufficient. By way of example, he shows you a summary of its management accounts for the three months to 31 May. These are reproduced below.

Statement of budgeted and actual cost of Alpha Production –
3 months ended 31 May

Alpha production (units)	Actual		Budget		Variance
		10 000		12 000	
	Inputs	(£)	Inputs	(£)	(£)
Materials	32 000 metres	377 600	36 000 metres	432 000	54 400
Labour	70 000 hours	422 800	72 000 hours	450 000	27 200
Fixed overhead absorbed		330 000		396 000	66 000
Fixed overhead unabsorbed		75 000		0	(75 000)
		1 205 400		1 278 000	72 600

John Wade is not convinced that standard marginal costing will help him to manage Finchley. 'My current system tells me all I need to know,' he said. 'As you can see, we are £72 600 below budget which is really excellent given that we lost production as a result of a serious machine breakdown.'

To help John Wade understand the benefits of standard marginal costing, you agree to prepare a statement for the three months ended 31 May reconciling the standard cost of production to the actual cost of production.

Task 1

(a) Use the budget data to determine:
  (i) the standard marginal cost per Alpha; and
  (ii) the standard cost of actual Alpha production for the three months to 31 May.
(b) Calculate the following variances:
  (i) material price variance;
  (ii) material usage variance;
  (iii) labour rate variance;
  (iv) labour efficiency variance;
  (v) fixed overhead expenditure variance.
(c) Write a *short* memo to John Wade. Your memo should:
  (i) include a statement reconciling the actual cost of production to the standard cost of production;
  (ii) give *two* reasons why your variances might differ from those in his original management accounting statement despite using the same basic data;
  (iii) *briefly* discuss *one* further reason why your reconciliation statement provides improved management information.

Data

On receiving your memo, John Wade informs you that:

• the machine breakdown resulted in the workforce having to be paid for 12 000

hours even though no production took place;
- an index of material prices stood at 466.70 when the budget was prepared but at 420.03 when the material was purchased.

Task 2

Using this new information, prepare a revised statement reconciling the standard cost of production to the actual cost of production. Your statement should subdivide:
- both the labour variances into those parts arising from the machine breakdown and those parts arising from normal production; and
- the material price variance into that part due to the change in the index and that part arising for other reasons.

Data

Barnet Ltd is another small company owned by Hampstead plc. Barnet operates a job costing system making a specialist, expensive piece of hospital equipment.

Existing system

Currently, employees are assigned to individual jobs and materials are requisitioned from stores as needed. The standard and actual costs of labour and material are recorded for each job. These job costs are totalled to produce the marginal cost of production. Fixed production costs – including the cost of storekeeping and inspection of deliveries and finished equipment – are then added to determine the standard and actual cost of production. Any costs of remedial work are included in the materials and labour for each job.

Proposed system

Carol Johnson, the chief executive of Barnet, has recently been to a seminar on modern manufacturing techniques. As a result, she is considering introducing Just-in-Time stock deliveries and Total Quality Management. Barnet would offer suppliers a long-term contract at a fixed price but suppliers would have to guarantee the quality of their materials.

In addition, she proposes that the workforce is organised as a single team with flexible work practices. This would mean employees helping each other as necessary, with no employee being allocated a particular job. If a job was delayed, the workforce would work overtime without payment in order for the job to be completed on time. In exchange, employees would be guaranteed a fixed weekly wage and time off when production was slack to make up for any overtime incurred.

Cost of quality

Carol has asked to meet you to discuss the implications of her proposals on the existing accounting system. She is particularly concerned to monitor the cost of *quality*. This is defined as the total of all costs incurred in preventing defects plus those costs involved in remedying defects once they have occurred. It is a single figure measuring all the explicit costs of quality that is, those costs collected within the accounting system.

Task 3

In preparation for the meeting, produce *brief* notes. Your notes should:
- (a) identify *four* general headings (or classifications) which make up the *cost of quality*;
- (b) give one example of a type of cost likely to be found within each category;
- (c) assuming Carol Johnson's proposals are accepted, state, with reasons, whether or not:
  - (i) a standard marginal costing system would still be of help to the managers;
  - (ii) it would still be meaningful to collect costs by each individual job;
- (d) identify *one* cost saving in Carol Johnson's proposals which would not be recorded in the existing costing system.

AAT Technicians Stage

You are the management accountant of T plc. The following computer printout shows details relating to April:

Question IM 18.3
Intermediate:
Calculation of
labour, material
and overhead
variances and
reconciliation of
budgeted and
actual profit

	Actual	Budget
Sales volume	4900 units	5000 units
Selling price per unit	£11.00	£10.00
Production volume	5400 units	5000 units
Direct materials		
kgs	10 600	10 000
price per kg	£0.60	£0.50
Direct labour		
hours per unit	0.55	0.50
rate per hour	£3.80	£4.00
Fixed overhead:		
Production	£10 300	£10 000
Administration	£3 100	£3 000

T plc uses a standard absorption costing system.
There was no opening or closing work-in-progress.

Requirements:
(a) Prepare a statement which reconciles the budgeted profit with the actual profit for April, showing individual variances in as much detail as the above data permit   (20 marks)
(b) Explain briefly the possible causes of
    (i) the material usage variance;
    (ii) the labour rate variance; and
    (iii) the sales volume profit variance.   (6 marks)
(c) Explain the meaning and relevance of interdependence of variances when reporting to managers.   (4 marks)
(Total 30 marks)
CIMA Stage 2 Operational Cost Accounting

A manufacturing company has provided you with the following data, which relate to component RYX for the period which has just ended:

	Budget	Actual
Number of labour hours	8 400	7 980
Production units	1 200	1 100
Overhead cost (all fixed)	£22 260	£25 536

Overheads are absorbed at a rate per standard labour hour.

Required:
(a) (i) Calculate the fixed production overhead cost variance and the following subsidiary variances:
        expenditure
        efficiency
        capacity
    (ii) Provide a summary statement of these four variances.   (7 marks)
(b) Briefly discuss the possible reasons why adverse fixed production overhead expenditure, efficiency and capacity variances occur.   (10 marks)
(c) Briefly discuss two examples of interrelationships between the fixed production overhead efficiency variances and the material and labour variances.   (3 marks)
(Total 20 marks)
ACCA Paper 8 Managerial Finance

**Question IM 18.5
Intermediate:
Labour and
overhead
variances and
export wage rate
analysis**

Data

The Eastern Division of Countryside Communications plc assembles a single product, the Beta. The Eastern Division has a fixed price contract with the supplier of the materials used in the Beta. The contract also specifies that the materials should be free of any faults. Because of these clauses in the contract, the Eastern Division has no material variances when reporting any differences between standard and actual production.

You have recently accepted the position of assistant management accountant in the Eastern Division. One of your tasks is to report variances in production costs on a four-weekly basis. Fixed overheads are absorbed on the basis of standard labour hours. A colleague provides you with the following data:

Standard costs and budgeted production – four weeks ended 27 November

	Quantity	Unit price	Standard cost per Beta
Material	30 metres	£12.00	£360.00
Labour	10 hours	£5.25	£52.50
Fixed overhead	10 hours	£15.75	£157.50
Standard cost per Beta			£570.00
Budgeted production	1200 Betas	£570.00	£684 000

Actual production – four weeks ended 27 November

	Quantity	Total cost
Actual cost of material	31 200 metres	£374 400
Actual cost of labour	11 440 hours	£59 488
Actual fixed cost overheads		£207 000
Actual cost of actual production		£640 888
Actual production	1040 Betas	

Task 1

(a) Calculate the following variances:
   (i) the labour rate variance;
   (ii) the labour efficiency variance (sometimes called the utilisation variance);
   (iii) the fixed overhead expenditure variance (sometimes known as the price variance);
   (iv) the fixed overhead volume variance;
   (v) the fixed overhead capacity variance;
   (vi) the fixed overhead efficiency variance (sometimes known as the usage variance).
(b) Prepare a statement reconciling the standard cost of actual production with the actual cost of actual production.

Data

When the Eastern Division's budget for the four weeks ended 27 November was originally prepared, a national index of labour rates stood at 102.00. In preparing the budget, Eastern Division had allowed for a 5% increase in labour rates. For the actual four weeks ended 27 November, the index stood at 104.04.

Because of this, Ann Green, Eastern Division's production director, is having difficulty understanding the meaning of the labour rate variance calculated in task 1.

Task 2

Write a memo to Ann Green. Your memo should:
(a) identify the original labour rate before allowing for the 5% increase;
(b) calculate the revised standard hourly rate using the index of 104.04;

(c) subdivide the labour rate variance calculated in task 1(a) into that part due to the change in the index and that part arising for other reasons;
(d) *briefly* interpret the possible meaning of these two subdivisions of the labour rate variance;
(e) give *two* reasons why the index of labour rates might not be valid in explaining part of the labour rate variance;
(f) *briefly* explain the meaning of the following variances calculated in task 1 and for *each* variance suggest one reason why it may have occurred;
    (i) the fixed overhead expenditure (or price) variance;
    (ii) the fixed overhead capacity variance;
    (iii) the fixed overhead efficiency (or usage) variance.

AAT Technicians Stage

(a) Explain fully how the variances between actual and standard production overhead costs may be analysed, where overhead absorption is based upon separate direct labour hour rates for variable and fixed overheads. (12 marks)
(b) Calculate fixed production overhead variances in as much detail as possible, in the following situation:

Question IM 18.6 Intermediate: Discussion and calculation of overhead variances

	Budget	Actual
Fixed overhead (£)	246 000	259 000
Direct labour (hours)	123 000	141 000
Output (units)	615 000	(see below)

The company operates a process costing system. At the beginning of the period 42 000 half completed units were in stock. During the period 680 000 units were completed and 50 000 half completed units remained in stock at the end of the period. (13 marks)
(Total 25 marks)
ACCA Level 1 Costing

The following profit reconciliation statement has been prepared by the management accountant of ABC Limited for March:

Question IM 18.7 Calculation of actual input data working back from variances

			(£)
Budgeted profit			30 000
Sales volume profit variance			5 250A
Selling price variance			6 375F
			31 125

Cost variances:	A (£)	F (£)	
Material:			
price	1 985		
usage		400	
Labour:			
rate		9 800	
efficiency	4 000		
Variable overhead:			
expenditure		1 000	
efficiency	1 500		
Fixed overhead:			
expenditure		500	
volume	24 500		
	31 985	11 700	
			20 285A
Actual profit			10 840

The standard cost card for the company's only product is as follows:

		(£)
Materials	5 litres at £0.20	1.00
Labour	4 hours at £4.00	16.00
Variable overhead	4 hours at £1.50	6.00
Fixed overhead	4 hours at £3.50	14.00
		37.00
Standard profit		3.00
Standard selling price		40.00

The following information is also available:
1. There was no change in the level of finished goods stock during the month.
2. Budgeted production and sales volumes for March were equal.
3. Stocks of materials, which are valued at standard price, decreased by 800 litres during the month.
4. The actual labour rate was £0.28 lower than the standard hourly rate.

Required:
(a) Calculate the following:
    (i)   the actual production/sales volume;   (4 marks)
    (ii) the actual number of hours worked;   (4 marks)
    (iii) the actual quantity of materials purchased;   (4 marks)
    (iv) the actual variable overhead cost incurred;   (2 marks)
    (v) the actual fixed overhead cost incurred.   (2 marks)
(b) ABC Limited uses a standard costing system whereas other organizations use a system of budgetary control. Explain the reasons why a system of budgetary control is often preferred to the use of standard costing in non-manufacturing environments.
                              (9 marks)
                        (Total 25 marks)
CIMA Stage 2 Operational Cost Accounting

**Question IM 18.8
Intermediate:
Calculation of
inputs working
backwards from
variances**

The following data have been collected for the month of April by a company which operates a standard absorption costing system:

Actual production of product EM	600 units
Actual costs incurred:	(£)
Direct material E 660 metres	6 270
Direct material M 200 metres	650
Direct wages 3200 hours	23 200
Variable production overhead (which	
varied with hours worked)	6 720
Fixed production overhead	27 000
Variances	(£)
Direct material price:	
Material E	330 F
Material M	50 A
Direct material usage:	
Material E	600 A
Material M	nil
Direct labour rate	800 A
Direct labour efficiency	1400 A
Variable production overhead:	
expenditure	320 A
efficiency	400 A
Fixed production overhead:	
expenditure	500 F
volume	2500 F

Opening and closing work in progress figures were identical, so can be ignored.

You are required to:
(a) prepare for the month of April a statement of total standard costs for product EM; (3 marks)
(b) prepare a standard product cost sheet for one unit of product EM; (7 marks)
(c) calculate the number of units of product EM which were budgeted for April; (2 marks)
(d) state how the material and labour cost standards for product EM would originally have been determined. (3 marks)
(Total 15 marks)
CIMA Stage 2 Cost Accounting

(a) A factory is planning to produce and sell 8000 units of product P during the next 4-week operating period.
Its standard product unit and total costs are as follows:

Question IM18.9 Advanced: Preparation of an operating control statement and the computation of labour, material and overhead variances

	Costs per unit (£)	Total costs (£)
Direct material 1.111 units at £5.40/unit	6.00	48 000
Direct labour 0.6 hours at £5.00/hour	3.00	24 000
Variable overhead 0.6 hours at £0.50/hour	0.30	2 400
Fixed overhead	5.95	47 600

The product sells for £16.50/unit.
The following details relate to the actual results for the 4-week period:

Actual orders received for the 4-week period:	8200 units
Actual sales:	7500 units
Actual production:	7500 units
Units of direct material purchased and issued into production:	7750 units
Direct material price per unit:	5.60
Direct labour hours:	4700
Direct labour rate (per hour):	£5.25

Total overhead expenditure amounted to £49 000 of which variable overhead was £2150.

You are required to
(i) produce an Operating Control Statement which analyses the budget: actual comparisons for the four-week period; (7 marks)
(ii) arrange the results you have produced in a way which will improve management's understanding and interpretation of their meaning, explaining the basis of the presentation you have adopted. (8 marks)
(b) Some consider that the key to fair assessment of management performance is provided by the concept of controllability, i.e. measurements should be based on factors over which management has control. However, identifying controllability may raise complex issues.
You are required to discuss the management accounting problems which arise in attributing performance to managers in a manner which recognizes controllability. (10 marks)
(Total 25 marks)
CIMA Stage 4 Management Accounting Control and Audit

**Question IM 18.10
Advanced:
Variance
calculations and
reconciliation of
budgeted and
actual profit**

Bamfram plc is a well established manufacturer of a specialized product, a Wallop, which has the following specifications for production:

Components	Standard quantity	Standard price(£)
WALS	15	60
LOPS	8	75

The standard direct labour hours to produce a Wallop at the standard wage rate of £10.50 per hour has been established at 60 hours per Wallop.

The annual fixed overhead budget is divided into calendar months with equal production per month. The budgeted annual fixed overheads are £504 000 for the budgeted output of 2400 Wallops per annum.

Mr Jones, a marketing person, is now the managing director of Bamfram plc and must report to the board of directors later this day and he seeks your advice in respect of the following operating information for the month of May:

	(£)	(£)
Sales		504 000
Cost of sales:		
Direct materials	281 520	
Direct labour	112 320	
	393 840	
Fixed production overheads	42 600	436 440
Gross profit		67 560
Administration expenses		11 150
Selling and distribution expenses		17 290
Net profit		39 120

The sales manager informs Mr Jones that despite adverse trading conditions his sales staff have been able to sell 180 Wallops at the expected standard selling price.

The production manager along with the purchasing department manager are also pleased that prices for components have been stable for the whole of the current year and they are able to provide the following information:

Stocks for May are as follows:

	1 May	31 May
Component WALS	600	750
Component LOPS	920	450

The actual number of direct labour hours worked in May was 11 700, considerably less than the production manager had budgeted. Further, the purchasing manager advised that WALS had cost £171 000 at a price of £57 per unit in the month of May and 1000 LOPS had been acquired for £81 000.

Mr Jones, eager to please the board of directors, requests you, as the newly appointed management accountant, to prepare appropriate statements to highlight the following information which is to be presented to the board:

(a) The standard product cost of a Wallop.   (3 marks)
(b)   (i) The direct material variances for both price and usage for each component used in the month of May assuming that prices were stable throughout the relevant period.
       (ii) The direct labour efficiency and wage rate variances for the month of May.
      (iii) The fixed production overhead expenditure and volume variances.
            Note: You may assume that during the month of May there is no change in the level of finished goods stocks.   (10 marks)

(c) A detailed reconciliation statement of the standard gross profit with the actual gross profit for the month of May. (4 marks)
(d) Draft a brief report for Mr Jones that he could present to the board of directors on the usefulness, or otherwise, of the statement you have prepared in your answer to (c) above. (5 marks)
(Total 22 marks)
ACCA Level 2 Management Accounting

Tardy Taxis operates a fleet of taxis in a provincial town. In planning its operations for November it estimated that it would carry fare-paying passengers for 40 000 miles at an average price of £1 per mile. However, past experience suggested that the total miles run would amount to 250% of the fare-paid miles. At the beginning of November it employed ten drivers and decided that this number would be adequate for the month ahead.

Question IM 18.11 Advanced: Computation of variances and the reconciliation of budgeted and actual profits for a taxi firm

The following cost estimates were available:

Employment costs of a driver	£1000 per month
Fuel costs	£0.08 per mile run
Variable overhead costs	£0.05 per mile run
Fixed overhead costs	£9000 per month

In November revenue of £36 100 was generated by carrying passengers for 38 000 miles. The total actual mileage was 105 000 miles. Other costs amounted to:

Employment costs of drivers	£9600
Fuel costs	£8820
Variable overhead costs	£5040
Fixed overhead costs	£9300

The saving in the cost of drivers was due to one driver leaving during the month; she was not replaced until early December.

Requirements:
(a) Prepare a budgeted and actual profit and loss account for November, indicating the total profit variance. (6 marks)
(b) Using a flexible budget approach, construct a set of detailed variances to explain the total profit variance as effectively as possible. Present your analysis in a report to the owner of Tardy Taxis including suggested reasons for the variances. (14 marks)
(c) Outline any further variances you think would improve your explanation, indicating the additional information you would require to produce these. (5 marks)
(Total 25 marks)
ICAEW P2 Management Accounting

Question IM 18.12
Advanced:
Calculation of
sales variances
on an absorption
and variable
costing basis and
reconciliation of
actual with
budgeted margin

Claylock Ltd make and sell a single product. The company operates a standard cost system and the following information is available for period 5:

(i) Standard product cost per unit:

	(£)
Direct material 8 kilos at £5.40 per kilo	43.20
Direct labour 2.5 hours at £4.50 per hour	11.25
Fixed production overhead	17.00

(ii) The standard selling price per unit is £90.

(iii) Direct labour hours worked total 12 000 hours. Labour productivity in comparison to standard was 90%.

(iv) 42 000 kilos of direct material were purchased at £5.60 per kilo. Issues from stores to production totalled 36 000 kilos during the period.

(v) Stocks of finished goods rose from nil to 300 units during the period. It was budgeted that all units produced would be sold during the period.

(vi) Stocks of raw materials and finished goods are valued at standard cost.

(vii) Summary operating statement for period 5:

	(F) (£)	(A) (£)	(£)
Budgeted sales revenue			450 000
Sales volume variance			88 200 (A)
Standard sales revenue			361 800
Less: Standard cost of sales			287 229
Standard production margin			74 571
Variance analysis:			
Sales price	30 150		
Direct material cost		16 176	
Fixed overhead volume		11 560	
Fixed overhead expenditure	1 500		
	31 650	27 736	3 914 (F)
Actual production margin			78 485

Note: (F) = favourable   (A) = adverse.

Required:

(a) Determine the values of the sales volume variance when it is expressed alternatively in terms of: standard revenue; standard production margin; and standard contribution. Discuss which valuation, when combined with the sales price variance, provides a measure of whether the sales variance have resulted in a net cash benefit to the company. (9 marks)

(b) Analyse the direct material cost variance into relevant sub-variances and comment on the method by which material usage is valued by Claylock Ltd. (7 marks)

(c) Analyse the fixed overhead volume variance into two sub-variances and comment on the relevance of each sub-variance as perceived by adherents of absorption costing. (7 marks)

(d) Prepare an operating statement for period 5 which amends the statement given in the question into standard marginal cost format. Explain the reason for any difference in the actual production margin from that reported under the present system. Comment also on any changes in the variances reported in the amended statement. (7 marks)

(Total 30 marks)

ACCA Level 2 Cost and Management Accounting II

Standard costing and variance analysis: 2

Variance analysis involves the separation of individual cost variances into component parts. The benefit that may be derived from variance analysis depends on the interpretation and investigation of the component variances. A company has recently been carrying out a study on its use of variance analysis.

Question IM 19.1 Advanced

Requirement:
Explain, with the aid of simple numeric examples, for each of the following variance analysis exercises,
- their logic, purpose and limitation; and
- how the management accountant should go about investigating the component variances disclosed.
(a) The separation of the fixed overhead volume variance into capacity utilisation and efficiency components. (9 marks)
(b) The separation of the materials usage variance into materials mixture and materials yield components. (8 marks)
(c) The separation of the labour rate variance into planning and operational components. (8 marks)
(Total 25 marks)
CIMA Stage 3 Management Accounting Applications

In the new industrial environment, the usefulness of standard costing is being challenged, and new approaches sought.

Question IM 19.2 Advanced

One approach, pioneered by the Japanese, is to replace standard costs by target costs.

You are required
(a) to describe the problems associated with standard costing in the new industrial environment; (6 marks)
(b) to explain what target costs are, and how they are developed and used; (6 marks)
(c) to contrast standard and target costs. (5 marks)
(Total 17 marks)
CIMA Management Accounting Techniques

Variance investigation decisions are normally explained in textbooks by simple models, which assume the availability of a significant amount of information.
An example of this approach is:

Question IM19.3 Advanced

The managers estimate the probability of any variance being due to a controllable, and therefore correctable, cause at 25%. They estimate the cost of investigating a variance at £1400, and the cost of correcting the cause of a correctable variance at £400. The investigation process is regarded as 100% reliable in that a correctable cause of the variance will be found if it exists.

Managers estimate the loss due to not investigating, and hence not discovering, a correctable cause of the variance, averages 75% of the size of the variance. For example, the loss from the failure to discover a correctable £4000 variance would be £3000.

Requirement:
(a) Calculate the minimum size of variance that would justify investigation.

(8 marks)

In addition to the approach described above, alternative approaches exist to decide whether to investigate variances by using criteria related to the absolute size of the variance, and criteria based on the percentage from standard.

Requirement:
(b) (i) Explain why these approaches are taken rather than the approach described in (a) above.
    (ii) Comment on the appropriateness of the alternative approaches described above.

(12 marks)

(Total 20 marks)

CIMA Stage 4 Management Accounting Control Systems

Question IM 19.4 Advanced

(a) Specify and explain the factors to be considered in determining whether to investigate a variance which has been routinely reported as part of a standard costing system.

(12 marks)

(b) Describe how accumulated production variances should be treated at the end of an accounting period.

(8 marks)

(Total 20 marks)

ACCA P2 Management Accounting

Question IM 19.5 Intermediate: Calculation of variances and accounting entries for an interlocking standard costing system

B Ltd manufactures a single product in one of its factories. Information relating to the month just ended is as follows:

(i) Standard cost per hundred units:

	(£)
Raw materials: 15 kilos at £7 per kilo	105
Direct labour: 10 hours at £6 per hour	60
Variable production overhead: 10 hours at £5 per hour	50
	215

(ii) 226 000 units of the product were completed and transferred to finished goods stock.
(iii) 34 900 kilos of raw material were purchased in the month at a cost of £245 900.
(iv) Direct wages were £138 545 representing 22 900 hours' work.
(v) Variable production overheads of £113 800 were incurred.
(vi) Fixed production overheads of £196 800 were incurred.
(vii) Stocks at the beginning and end of the month were:

	Opening Stock	Closing Stock
Raw materials	16 200 kilos	16 800 kilos
Work in progress	—	4000 units (complete as to raw materials but only 50% complete as to direct labour and overhead)
Finished goods	278 000 units	286 000 units

Raw materials, work in progress, and finished goods stocks are maintained at standard cost. You should assume that no stock discrepancies or losses occurred during the month just ended.

Required:
(a) Prepare the cost ledger accounts relating to the above information in B Ltd's interlocking accounting system. Marginal costing principles are employed in the cost ledger.

(17 marks)

(b) Explain and contrast the different types of standards that may be set as a benchmark for performance measurement. (8 marks)
(Total 25 marks)
ACCA Cost and Management Accounting 1

Fischer Ltd manufactures a range of chess sets, and operates a standard costing system. Information relating to the Spassky design for the month of March is as follows:

(1) Standard costs per 100 sets

	(£)
Raw materials:	
Plaster of Paris, 20kg at £8 per kg	160
Paint, ½ litre at £30 per litre	15
Direct wages, 2½ hours at £10 per hour	25
Fixed production overheads, 400% of direct wages	100
	300

(2) Standard selling price per set £3.80
(3) Raw materials, work in progress and finished goods stock records are maintained at standard cost.
(4) Stock levels at the beginning and end of March were as follows:

	1 March	31 March
Plaster of Paris	2800 kg	2780 kg
Paint	140 litres	170 litres
Finished sets	900 sets	1100 sets

There was no work in progress at either date.

(5) Budgeted production and sales during the month were 30 000 sets. Actual sales, all made at standard selling price, and actual production were 28 400 and 28 600 sets respectively.
(6) Raw materials purchased during the month were 5400kg of plaster of Paris at a cost of £43 200 and 173 litres of paint at a cost of £5800.
(7) Direct wages were 730 hours at an average rate of £11 per hour.
(8) Fixed production overheads amounted to £34 120.

Requirement:
Prepare for the month of March:
(a) the cost ledger accounts for raw materials, work in progress and finished goods; (10 marks)
(b) (i) budget trading statement,
   (ii) standard cost trading statement,
   (iii) financial trading statement, and
   (iv) a reconciliation between these statements identifying all relevant variances. (14 marks)
(Total 24 marks)
ICAEW Accounting Techniques

Question IM 19.7
Intermediate:
Accounting
entries for a
standard process
costing system

A firm produces a plastic feedstock using a process form of manufacture. The firm operates in an industry where the market price fluctuates and the firm adjusts output levels, period by period, in an attempt to maximise profit which is its objective. Standard costing is used in the factory and the following information is available.

Process 2 receives input from process 1 and, after processing, transfers the output to finished goods. For a given period, the opening work-in-process for process 2 was 600 barrels which had the following values:

	Value (£)	Percentage complete
Input material (from process 1)	3 000	100
Process 2 material introduced	6 000	50
Process 2 labour	1 800	30
Process 2 overhead	2 700	30
	£13 500	

During the period, 3700 barrels were received from process 1 and at the end of the period, the closing work-in-progress was at the following stages of completion:

	Percentage completion
Input material	100
Process 2 material introduced	50
Process 2 labour	40
Process 2 overhead	40

The following standard variable costs have been established for process 2:

	Standard variable cost per barrel (£)
Input material (standard cost process 1)	5
Process 2 material	20
Labour	10
Overhead	15
	£50

During the period, actual costs for process 2 were

	(£)
Material	79 500
Labour	39 150
Overhead	60 200
	£178 850

In addition you are advised that the following theoretical functions have been derived:

Total cost (£) = 100 000 + 20Q + 0.005Q^2
Price per barrel (£) = 76 − 0.002Q

where Q represents the number of barrels.

You are required to
(a) determine the theoretical production level which will maximize profit;

(6 marks)

(b) prepare the process 2 account assuming that the calculated production level is achieved; (7 marks)
(c) prepare the accounts for process 2 material, labour and overhead showing clearly the variance in each account. (7 marks)
(Total 20 marks)
CIMA Stage 3 Management Accounting Techniques

A company operates a number of hairdressing establishments which are managed on a franchise arrangement. The franchisor offers support using a PC package which deals with profit budgeting and control information.

Question IM 19.8 Advanced: Mix variances and reconciliation as actual and budgeted profit

Budget extracts of one franchisee for November are shown below analysed by male and female clients. For the purposes of budget projections average revenue rates are used. At the month end these are compared with the average monthly rates actually achieved using variance analysis. Sales price, sales quantity, sales mix and cost variances are routinely produced in order to compare the budget and actual results.

Staff working in this business are paid on a commission basis in order to act as an incentive to attract and retain clients. The labour rate variance is based on the commission payments, any basic pay is part of the monthly fixed cost.

Budget

	Male	Female
Clients	4000	1000
	(£)	(£)
Average revenue (per client)	7.5	18.0
Average commission (per client)	3.0	10.0
Total monthly fixed cost	£20 000	

Actual results

	Male	Female
Clients	2000	2000
	(£)	(£)
Average revenue (per client)	8.0	20.0
Average commission (per client)	3.5	11.0
Total monthly fixed cost	£24 000	

Required:
(a) Reconcile the budgeted and actual profit for November by calculating appropriate price, quantity, mix and cost variances, presenting the information in good form. You should adopt a contribution style, with mix variances based on units (i.e. clients). (10 marks)
(b) Write a short memorandum to the manager of the business commenting on the result in (a) above. (4 marks)
(c) Comment on the limitations associated with generating sales variances as in (a) above. (6 marks)
(Total 20 marks)
ACCA Paper 8 Managerial Finance

Question IM 19.9 Advanced: Detailed variance analysis (including revision variances) plus an explanation of the meaning of operating statement variances

Tungach Ltd make and sell a single product. Demand for the product exceeds the expected production capacity of Tungach Ltd. The holding of stocks of the finished product is avoided if possible because the physical nature of the product is such that it deteriorates quickly and stocks may become unsaleable.

A standard marginal cost system is in operation. Feedback reporting takes planning and operational variances into consideration.

The management accountant has produced the following operating statement for period 9:

Tungach Ltd
Operating Statement – Period 9

	(£)	(£)
Original budgeted contribution		36 000
Revision variances:		
Material usage	9 600(A)	
Material price	3 600(F)	
Wage rate	1 600(F)	4 400(A)
Revised budgeted contribution		31 600
Sales volume variance:		
Causal factor		
Extra capacity	4 740(F)	
Productivity drop	987.5(A)	
Idle time	592.5(A)	
Stock increase	2 370(A)	790(F)
Revised standard contribution		
for sales achieved		32 390
Other variances:		
Material usage	900(F)	
Material price	3 120(A)	
Labour efficiency	1 075(A)	
Labour idle time	645(A)	
Wage rate	2 760(A)	
		6 700(A)
Actual contribution		25 690

(F) = favourable   (A) = adverse

Other data are available as follows:
(i) The original standard contribution per product unit as determined at period 1 was:

	(£)	(£)
Selling price		30
Less: Direct material 1.5 kilos at £8	12	
Direct labour 2 hours at £4.50	9	21
Contribution		9

(ii) A permanent change in the product specification was implemented from period 7 onwards. It was estimated that this change would require 20% additional material per product unit. The current efficient price of the material has settled at £7.50 per kilo.
(iii) Actual direct material used during period 9 was 7800 kilos at £7.90 per kilo. Any residual variances are due to operational problems.
(iv) The original standard wage rate overestimated the degree of trade union pressure during negotiations and was £0.20 higher than the rate subsequently agreed. Tungach Ltd made a short-term operational decision to pay the workforce at £4.60 per hour during periods 7 to 9 in an attempt to minimise the

drop in efficiency likely because of the product specification change. Management succeeded in extending the production capacity during period 9 and the total labour hours paid for were 9200 hours. These included 150 hours of idle time.

(v) Budgeted production and sales quantity (period 9)   4000 units
    Actual sales quantity (period 9)   4100 units
    Actual production quantity (period 9)   4400 units

(vi) Stocks of finished goods are valued at the current efficient standard cost.

Required:

(a) Prepare detailed figures showing how the material and labour variances in the operating statement have been calculated.   (8 marks)

(b) Prepare detailed figures showing how the sales volume variance has been calculated for each causal factor shown in the operating statement.   (6 marks)

(c) Prepare a report to the management of Tungach Ltd explaining the meaning and relevance of the figures given in the operating statement for period 9. The report should contain specific comments for any two of the sales volume variance causal factors and any two of the 'other variances'. The comments should suggest possible reasons for each variance, the management member likely to be answerable for each variance and possible corrective action.

              (8 marks)
              (Total 22 marks)
ACCA Level 2 Management Accounting

Casement Ltd makes windows with two types of frame: plastic and mahogany. Products using the two types of materials are made in separate premises under the supervision of separate production managers.

Data for the three months ended 30 November are shown below.

Question IM 19.10 Advanced: Reconciliation of budgeted and actual profit including operating and planning variances plus an interpretation of the reconciliation statement

	Plastic		Mahogany		Totals	
Sales units	Budget 3000 (£000)	Actual 2500 (£000)	Budget 1000 (£000)	Actual 1250 (000)	Budget 4000 (£000)	Actual 3750 (£000)
Sales revenue	660	520	340	460	1000	980
Materials	(147)	(120)	(131)	(160)	(278)	(280)
Labour	(108)	(105)	(84)	(85)	(192)	(190)
Fixed production overheads	(162)	(166)	(79)	(83)	(241)	(249)
Sales commissions	(33)	(26)	(17)	(23)	(50)	(49)
Other selling and administration costs					(128)	(133)
Net profit					111	79

Casement Ltd sells to a wide variety of users, so that window sizes and shapes vary widely; consequently a square metre of window is adopted as the standard unit for pricing and costing.

Sales budgets were based on the expectation that the company's share of the regional market in windows would be 12%. The Window Federation's quarterly report reveals that sales in the regional market totalled 25 000 units in the three months ended 30 November. The managing director of Casement Ltd is concerned that the company's sales and profit are below budget; she wants a full analysis of sales variances as well as an analysis of the cost variances which can be obtained from the data.

Labour costs comprise the wages of shop-floor employees who receive a fixed wage for a 40-hour week; no overtime is worked. Production managers receive a fixed monthly salary which is included in production overheads, plus an annual personal performance bonus (excluded from the above data) which is decided by the board of directors at the end of each year. Sales representatives are paid a monthly retainer plus commission of 5% on all sales.

The management of Casement Ltd is keen to improve performance and is reviewing the company's reward structure. One possibility which is under consideration is that the company should adopt a profit-related pay scheme. The scheme would replace all the existing arrangements and would give every employee a basic remuneration equal to 90% of his or her earnings last year. In addition every employee would receive a share in the company's profit; on the basis of the past year's trading this payment would amount to about 17% of basic remuneration for each employee.

Requirements
(a) Prepare a variance report for the managing director on the results for the quarter ended 30 November, providing market share and market volume (or size) variances, sales mix variance and basic cost variances, from the available information. (10 marks)
(b) Interpret your results in part (a) for the benefit of the managing director. (7 marks)
(c) Examine the issues (excluding taxation) which should be considered by the management of Casement Ltd in relation to the company's reward structure, with particular reference to the proposal to move to a profit-related pay scheme. (8 marks)
(Total 25 marks)
ICAEW P2 Management Accounting

Question IM 19.11 Advanced: Labour planning and operating variances

A standard costing and budgetary control system which provides management with a range of planning and operational variances for each four week accounting period should facilitate improved feedback control information which may then be used for improved feedforward control.
(a) Explain the meaning of the terms planning and operational variances, feedback control and feedforward control. (6 marks)
(b) Explain and illustrate with reference to direct labour cost variances, ways in which a planning and operational variance analysis could provide management with
 (i) additional feedback control information
 (ii) additional feedforward control information. (14 marks)

Use the following direct labour cost information for any illustrative content of your answer.
 Original standard per product unit: 0.4 hours
 Original wage rate per hour: £4
 Budget output per month: 1000 units
 Actual results for January:
 Output: 1000 units; direct labour hours incurred: 420 hours at £4.50 per hour.

At the end of January it has been established that the original standard time allowance per unit was understated by 10%. In addition, the completion of negotiations with the trade union has resulted in a wage rate of £4.25 being agreed from 1 January. (20 marks)
ACCA Level 2 Cost Accounting II

Blue Ltd manufactures a single product, the standards of which are as follows:

	(£)	(£)
Standards per unit:		
Standard selling price		268
Less Standard cost:		
Materials (16 units at £4)	64	
Labour (4 hours at £3)	12	
*Overheads (4 hours at £24)	96	172
Standard profit		96

*Total overhead costs are allocated on the basis of budgeted direct labour hours. The following information relates to last month's activities:

	Budgeted	Actual
Production and sales	600 units	500 units
Direct labour	2400 hours at £3	2300 hours at £3
Fixed overheads	£19 200	£20 000
Variable	38 400	£40 400
Materials	9600 units at £4 per unit	9600 units at £4 per unit

The actual selling price was identical to the budgeted selling price and there was no opening or closing stocks during the period.
(a) You are required to calculate the variances and reconcile the budgeted and actual profit for each of the following methods:
   (i) The traditional method.
   (ii) The opportunity cost method assuming materials are the limiting factor and materials are restricted to 9600 units for the period.
   (iii) The opportunity cost method assuming labour hours are the limiting factor and labour hours are restricted to 2400 hours for the period.
   (iv) The opportunity cost method assuming there are *no scarce inputs*.
(b) Briefly explain and comment on any differences between your answers to (a) (i) to (a) (iv) above.

Question IM 19.13
Advanced:
Performance
reports for sales
and product
managers

Zits Ltd makes two models for rotary lawn mowers, the Quicut and the Powacut. The company has a sales director and reporting to her, two product managers, each responsible for the profitability of one of the two models. The company's financial year ended on 31 March. The budgeted and actual results for the two models for the year ended on 31 March are given below:

	Quicut		Powacut		Total	
	Budget	Actual	Budget	Actual	Budget	Actual
Sales units	240	280	120	110	360	390
(000 units)	(£000)	(£000)	(£000)	(000)	(£000)	(£000)
Sales revenue	28 800	32 200	24 000	24 200	52 800	56 400
Costs:						
Variable	9 600	11 480	7 200	6 820	16 800	18 300
Traceable fixed						
manufacturing	8 200	7 600	6 800	6 800	15 000	14 400
Period costs:						
Manufacturing					5 700	6 000
Administration					4 300	4 500
and selling						
					41 800	43 200
Net Profit before Tax					£11 000	£13 200

The accountant had drawn up a series of flexed budgets at the beginning of the year should the actual volume differ from budget. The variable costs were unchanged, but the budgeted fixed costs, assuming a constant sales mix, for the different output ranges were as given below:

Output range (000 units)	300–360 (£000)	361–420 (£000)
Traceable fixed manufacturing costs	15 000	16 000
Period cost – manufacturing	5 700	6 000
– administration and selling	4 300	4 500
	£25 000	£26 500

The sales director has just received information from the trade association that industry rotary lawn mower sales for the twelve months ended on 31 March were 1.3 million units as against a forecast of 1.0 million.

Requirements:
(a) Prepare a schedule of variances which will be helpful to the sales director, and a schedule of more detailed variances which will be appropriate to the two product managers who are treated as profit centres. (16 marks)
(b) Discuss the results scheduled in (a) above identifying which of the variances are planning and which are operating variances. (9 marks)
(Total 25 marks)
ICAEW Management Accounting

Question IM 19.14
Advanced: Investigation of variances

(a) Describe and comment briefly on the basis and limitations of the control chart approach to variance investigation decisions. (6 marks)
(b) The following analysis is available for the month of April for Department A:

	(£)
Standard direct material	72 000
Material usage variance	4 500 unfavourable
Material mix variance	2 500 unfavourable

The following estimates have also been made for Department A:

	(£)
Estimated cost of investigating the total material variance	1 000
Estimated cost of correcting the total variance if investigated and found to be out of control	2 000
Estimated cost of permitting out-of-control material variances to continue	10 000

Maximum Probability of a given total variance:

Probability	0.99	0.98	0.96	0.93	0.89	0.85	0.8	0.75
Total Variance £000	1	2	3	4	5	6	7	8

You are required to determine, using a payoff table, whether the variance should be investigated. (6 marks)
(c) You are uncertain of the estimated probability in (b). Calculate the probability estimate at which you would be indifferent between investigating and not investigating the variance. (6 marks)
(d) Discuss the use of mathematical models for the variance investigation decision. (7 marks)
(Total 25 marks)
CIMA Stage 4 Management Accounting Control and Audit

Divisional financial performance measures

A large organisation, with a well-developed cost centre system, is considering the introduction of profit centres and/or investment centres throughout the organisation, where appropriate. As management accountant, you will be providing technical advice and assistance for the proposed scheme.

Question IM 20.1
Advanced

You are required:
(a) to describe the main characteristics and objectives of profit centres and investment centres; (4 marks)
(b) to explain what conditions are necessary for the successful introduction of such centres; (5 marks)
(c) to describe the main behavioural and control consequences which may arise if such centres are introduced; (4 marks)
(d) to compare two performance appraisal measures that might be used if investment centres are introduced. (4 marks)
CIMA Stage 3 Management Accounting Techniques

From an accounting perspective an organizational unit of an accounting entity may be a cost centre or a profit centre or an investment centre. Explain these categories, describe the strengths and weaknesses of each and conditions in which each would be most appropriate if the aim is to develop efficient planning and control procedures.

Question IM 20.2
Advanced

(7 marks)
ACCA Level 2 Management Accounting

Divisionalization is a common form of organizational arrangement but there is some diversity of opinion as to the best measure of divisional performance.
  Discuss this topic and describe and compare the main performance measures that have been suggested. (17 marks)
ACCA Level 2 Management Accounting

Question IM 20.3
Advanced

Critically discuss the methods of evaluating the performance of managers of divisionalized companies. What factors should be considered in designing control systems for evaluating divisional profit performances?

Question IM 20.4
Advanced

'In the control of divisional operations within a large company, conflicts often arise between the aims of the organization as a whole and the aspirations of the individual divisions.'
  What forms may these conflicts take, and how would you expect the finance function to assist in the resolution of such conflicts?

Question IM 20.5
Advanced

Question IM 20.6 Advanced

Divisionalised structures are normal in large firms, and occur even when centralised structures would be feasible.

Requirements:
(a) Explain and discuss the arguments for divisionalised structures in large firms.

(6 marks)
(b) Explain the costs and potential inefficiencies of a divisionalised structure.

(6 marks)
(c) Explain how adoption of a divisionalised structure changes the role of top management and their control of subordinates.   (8 marks)

(Total 20 marks)

CIMA Stage 4 Management Accounting Control Systems

Question IM 20.7 Advanced: Establishing a system of divisional performance measurement in a hospital

(a) Briefly explain how the measurement of divisional performance differs when assessing the achievement of strategic targets as distinct from operational targets.   (5 marks)

(b) J is a hospital which supplies a wide range of healthcare services. The government has created a competitive internal market for healthcare by separating the function of service delivery from purchasing. The government provides funds for local health organisations to identify healthcare needs and to purchase services from different organisations which actually supply the service. The service suppliers are mainly hospitals.

J is service supplier and has established contracts with some purchasing organisations. The healthcare purchasing organisations are free to contract with any supplier for the provision of their healthcare requirements.

Previously, J was organised and controlled on the basis of functional responsibility. This meant that each specialist patient function, such as medical, nursing and pharmacy services, was led by a manager who held operational and financial responsibility for its activities throughout the hospital. J now operates a system of control based on devolved financial accountability. Divisions comprising different functions have been established and are responsible for particular categories of patient care such as general medical or general surgical services. Each division is managed by a senior medical officer.

J's Board recognises that it exists in a competitive environment. It believes there is a need to introduce a system of divisional appraisal. This measures performance against strategic as well as operational targets, using both financial and non-financial criteria. The Board is concerned to develop a system which improves the motivation of divisional managers. This will encourage them to accept responsibility for achieving strategic as well as operational organisational targets. In particular, the Board wishes to encourage more contractual work to supply services to healthcare purchasing organisations from both within and outside its local geographical area. It is a clear aim of the Board that a cultural change in the management of the organisation will result from the implementation of such a system.

Requirement:
Discuss the issues which the Board of J should take into consideration in establishing a system of performance measurement for divisional managers in order to ensure the attainment of its strategic targets.   (15 marks)

(Total 20 marks)

CIMA Stage 4 Strategic Management Accounting and Marketing

XYZ plc operates a divisional organisation structure. The performance of each division is assessed on the basis of the Return on Capital Employed (ROCE) that it generates.

For this purpose the ROCE of a division is calculated by dividing its 'trading profit for the year by the 'book value of net assets that it is using at the end of the year. Trading profit is the profit earned excluding extraordinary items. Book value of net assets excludes any cash, bank account balance or overdraft because XYZ plc uses a common bank account (under the control of its head office) for all divisions.

At the start of every year each division is given a target ROCE. If the target is achieved or exceeded then the divisional executives are given a large salary bonus at the end of the year.

In 2000, XYZ plc's division A was given a target ROCE of 15%. On 15 December 2000 A's divisional manager receives a forecast that trading profit for 2000 would be £120 000 and net assets employed at the end of 2000 would be £820 000. This would give an ROCE of 14.6% which is slightly below A's target.

The divisional manager immediately circulates a memorandum to his fellow executives inviting proposals to deal with the problem. By the end of the day he has received the following proposals from those executives (all of whom will lose their salary bonus if the ROCE target is not achieved):

(i) *from the Works Manager:* that £100 000 should be invested in new equipment resulting in cost savings of £18 000 per year over the next fifteen years;

(ii) *from the Chief Accountant:* that payment of a £42 000 trade debt owed to a supplier due on 16 December 2000 be deferred until 1 January 2001. This would result in a £1000 default penalty becoming immediately due;

(iii) *from the Sales Manager:* that £1500 additional production expenses be incurred and paid in order to bring completion of an order forward to 29 December 2000 from its previous scheduled date of 3 January 2001. This would allow the customer to be invoiced in December, thereby boosting 2000 profits by £6000, but would not accelerate customer payment due on 1 February 2001;

(iv) *from the Head of Internal Audit:* that a regional plant producing a particular product be closed allowing immediate sale for £120 000 of premises having a book value of £90 000. This would result in £50 000 immediate redundancy payments and a reduction in profit of £12 600 per year over the next fifteen years;

(a) You are required to assess *each* of the above *four* proposals having regard to
   - their effect on divisional performance in 2000 and 2001 as measured by XYZ plc's existing criteria;
   - their intrinsic commercial merits;
   - any ethical matters that you consider relevant.
   You should ignore taxation and inflation. (20 marks)

(b) You are required to discuss what action XYZ plc's Finance Director should take when the situation at division A and the above four proposals are brought to his attention. (5 marks)
(Total 25 marks)
CIMA Stage 4 Management Accounting Decision Making

**Question IM 20.9
Advanced:
Calculation of
NPV and ROI and
a discussion as to
whether goal
congruence exists
plus a further
discussion
relating to
resolving the
conflict between
decision-making
and performance
evaluation models**

J plc's business is organized into divisions. For operating purposes, each division is regarded as an investment centre, with divisional managers enjoying substantial autonomy in their selection of investment projects. Divisional managers are rewarded via a remuneration package which is linked to a Return on Investment (ROI) performance measure. The ROI calculation is based on the net book value of assets at the beginning of the year. Although there is a high degree of autonomy in investment selection, approval to go ahead has to be obtained from group management at the head office in order to release the finance.

Division X is currently investigating three independent investment proposals. If they appear acceptable, it wishes to assign each a priority in the event that funds may not be available to cover all three. Group finance staff assess the cost of capital to the company at 15%.

The details of the three proposals are:

	Project A (000)	Project B (£000)	Project C (£000)
Initial cash outlay on fixed assets	60	60	60
Net cash inflow in year 1	21	25	10
Net cash inflow in year 2	21	20	20
Net cash inflow in year 3	21	20	30
Net cash inflow in year 4	21	15	40

Ignore tax and residual values.
Depreciation is straight-line over asset life, which is four years in each case.

You are required
(a) to give an appraisal of the *three* investment proposals from a divisional and from a company point of view;   (13 marks)
(b) to explain any divergence between these two points of view and to demonstrate techniques by which the views of both the division and the company can be brought into line.   (12 marks)
(Total 25 marks)
CIMA Stage 4 Management Accounting Control and Audit

**Question IM 20.10
Advanced: Merits
and problems
associated with
three proposed
divisional
performance
measures**

Sliced Bread plc is a divisionalized company. Among its divisions are Grain and Bakery. Grain's operations include granaries, milling and dealings in the grain markets; Bakery operates a number of bakeries.

The following data relate to the year ended 30 November:

	Grain (£000)	Bakery (£000)
Sales	44 000	25 900
Gain on sale of plant	—	900
	44 000	26 800
Direct labour	8 700	7 950
Direct materials	25 600	10 200
Depreciation	700	1 100
Divisional overheads	5 300	4 550
Head office costs (allocated)	440	268
	40 740	24 068

	Grain (£000)	Bakery (£000)
Fixed assets (at cost less accumulated depreciation)	7000	9000
Stocks	6350	1800
Trade debtors	4000	2100
Cash at bank	1500	—
Bank overdraft	—	750
Trade creditors	3000	2150

Divisional managements (DMs) are given authority to spend up to £20 000 on capital items as long as total spending remains within an amount provided for small projects in the annual budget. Larger projects, as well as sales of assets with book values in excess of £20 000, must be submitted to central management (CM). All day-to-day operations are delegated to DMs, whose performance is monitored with the aid of budgets and reports.

The basis for appraising DM performance is currently under review. At present divisions are treated as investment centres for DM performance appraisal, but there is disagreement as to whether return on capital employed or residual income is the better measure. An alternative suggestion has been made that DM performance should be appraised on the basis of controllable profit; this measure would exclude depreciation and gains or losses on sale of assets, treating investment in fixed assets as a CM responsibility.

The cost of capital of Sliced Bread plc is 15% per annum.

Requirements
(a) Calculate for both divisions the three measures (return on capital employed, residual income and controllable profit) which are being considered by Sliced Bread plc, and state any assumptions or reservations about the data you have used in your calculations. (5 marks)
(b) Examine the merits and problems of Sliced Bread plc's three contemplated approaches to DM performance appraisal, and briefly suggest how CM could determine the required level of performance in each case. (15 marks)
(c) Discuss briefly whether further measures are needed for the effective appraisal of DM performance. (5 marks)
(Total 25 marks)

Indico Ltd is a well established company which has operated in a sound but static market for many years where it has been the dominant supplier. Over the past three years it has diversified into three new product areas which are unrelated to each other and to the original business.

Indico Ltd has organised the operation of its four activities on a divisional basis with four divisional general managers having overall responsibility for all aspects of running each business except for finance. All finance is provided centrally with routine accounting and cash management, including invoicing, debt collection and bill payments, being handled by the Head Office. Head Office operating costs were £1 million in 2000. The total capital employed at mid-2000 amounted to £50 million, of which £20 million was debt capital financed at an average annual interest rate of 10%. Head Office assets comprise 50% fixed assets and 50% working capital. To date, the company has financed its expansion without raising additional equity capital, but it may soon require to do so if further expansion is undertaken. It has estimated that the cost of new equity capital would be 20% per annum. No new investment was undertaken in 2000 pending a review of the performance of each division.

Question IM 20.11 Advanced: Discussion of residual income and ROI and the problems with using these measures to evaluate a speculative new division operating in a high technology industry

The results for the divisions for the year to 31 December 2000 are as follows:

	Division			
	A (£m)	B (£m)	C (£m)	D (£m)
Sales	110.0	31.0	18.0	13.0
Trading profit	2.0	1.1	1.2	0.5
Exchange gain (1)	2.0	—	—	—
Profit after currency movement	4.0	1.1	1.2	0.5
Exceptional charge (2)	—	—	(1.8)	—
Profit(loss) after exceptional charges	4.0	1.1	(0.6)	0.5
Group interest charge (3)	(1.1)	(0.3)	(0.2)	(0.1)
Net divisional profit(loss)	2.9	0.8	(0.8)	0.4
Depreciation charged above	3.0	1.0	2.0	0.4
Net assets (at year end)	23.5	9.5	4.0	1.8

(1) The exchange gain represents the difference between the original sterling value of an overseas contract and the eventual receipts in sterling.
(2) The exceptional charge relates to the closure of a factory in January 2000.
(3) Group interest is purely a notional charge from Head Office based on a percentage of sales.

Requirements
(a) Calculate the return on investment and residual income for each division, ignoring the Head Office costs and stating any assumptions you consider appropriate. Explain how this information is useful in evaluating divisional performance, and outline the main standards of comparison you would use.

(13 marks)
(b) Explain how you would deal with the Head Office costs in measuring divisional performance within Indico Ltd. (4 marks)
(c) Discuss the problems arising from using return on investment and residual income to evaluate a speculative new division operating in a high technology industry. State how you could improve these measures to enable better divisional comparisons to be made. (8 marks)
(Total 25 marks)
ICAEW P2 *Management Accounting*

Question IM 20.12
Advanced:
Performance
reporting and a
discussion of key
measurement
issues for a
divisionalized
company

A recently incorporated power company, set up after the privatisation of the electricity and coal industries, owns the following assets:

An electricity generating station, capable of being fuelled either by coal or by oil.
Three coal mines, located some ten to twenty miles from the generating station, connected to a coal preparation plant.
A coal preparation plant, which takes the coal from the three mines and cleans it into a form suitable for use in the generating plant. As a by-product, a quantity of high quality coal is produced which can be sold on the industrial market. The plant has a rail link to the generating station.

The electricity generated is distributed via power lines owned by a separate company, which has an obligation to provide the distribution service on pre-set terms. The market for electricity is highly competitive with demand varying both by the time of day (in the short-term) and by season of the year (in the medium-term).

The power company is in the process of developing a management accounting system which will be used to provide information to assist in setting electricity tariffs for customers and to hold managers within the company accountable for their performance. Initially there are five main operating units, with a manager responsible for each, namely the generating station, the three coal mines and the coal preparation plant.

Requirements
(a) Outline, using pro-forma (i.e. without figures) reports where necessary, the accounting statements you would recommend as a basis for the evaluation of the performance of each of the unit managers. (10 marks)
(b) Discuss the key measurement issues that need to be resolved in designing such a responsibility accounting system. (8 marks)
(c) Explain how the information required for tariff-setting purposes might differ from that used for performance evaluation. (7 marks)

(Total 25 marks)
ICAEW P2 Management Accounting

A group of companies has hitherto used historical costing in the performance evaluation of its investment centres.

Whilst a few of those investment centres (class A) have replaced their fixed assets fairly regularly, the majority (class B) have, amongst their fixed assets, plant and equipment bought at a fairly even rate over the past 25 years. During that time their manufacturing technologies have changed very little, but these technologies are expected to change much more rapidly in the near future.

The group now wishes to evaluate its investment centres on a current cost basis.

You are required to prepare notes for a paper for the executive management committee to show
(a) the impact for performance evaluation of the difference between class A and class B investment centres that are likely to result from the change to a current cost basis in respect of
  (i) their depreciation charges, (7 marks)
  (ii) their relative standing as measured by their return on capital employed; (7 marks)
(b) what steps would be needed to revalue the plant and equipment. (6 marks)

(Total 20 marks)
CIMA Stage 4 Management Accounting Decision Making

Question IM 20.13 Advanced: Discussion relating to historical and current cost asset valuations for performance evaluation

(a) Meldo Division is part of a vertically integrated group where all divisions sell externally and transfer goods to other divisions within the group. Meldo Division management performance is measured using controllable profit before tax as the performance measurement criterion.
  (i) Show the cost and revenue elements which should be included in the calculation of controllable divisional profit before tax. (3 marks)
  (ii) Discuss ways in which the degree of autonomy allowed to Meldo Division may affect the absolute value of controllable profit reported. (9 marks)
(b) Kitbul Division management performance is measured using controllable residual income as the performance criterion.

  Explain why the management of Kitbul Division may make a different decision about an additional investment opportunity where residual income is measured using:
  (i) straight-line depreciation or
  (ii) annuity depreciation based on the cost of capital rate of the division.

  Use the following investment information to illustrate your answer:

Investment of £900 000 with a three year life and nil residual value.
Net cash inflow each year of £380 000.
Cost of capital is 10%. Imputed interest is calculated on the written-down value of the investment at the start of each year.
Present value of an annuity of £1 for three years at 10% interest is £2.487. (8 marks)

(Total 20 marks)
ACCA Level 2 Cost Accounting II

Question IM 20.14 Advanced: Calculations of residual income using straight line and annuity depreciation

Question IM 20.15 Advanced: Divisional performance measurement using different methods of asset valuation plus non-financial measures

(a) When a previously centralized organization decides to decentralize a major part of its planning and control functions to a series of independent divisional operating units, the nature of and flow of accounting and other information will require redefinition.

You are required to

(i) identify the main problems faced at the level of both central and divisional management in carrying out their planning and control functions which arise from the changes in the flow of information resulting from decentralization;
(5 marks)

(ii) explain the purposes which performance measures serve in the context of the problems identified in (i). (5 marks)

(b) The new managing director of the ABC Hotels group intends to conduct a survey of financial performance in each region of the country in which the group operates. Initially, a pilot study is to be carried out in the Midshires region.

He discovers that the available accounting information is based on historical cost, with management performance in each hotel measured as a return on investment (ROI). However, the practice has been that the group finance director requires requests for additional investment funds to be evaluated using the discounted cash flow (DCF) criterion.

The managing director has asked you, as the group's financial advisor, to see whether the existing information provides an adequate basis for the evaluation of the group's investments and its divisional performance. As part of the investigation, you have produced the following information, using the company's existing accounting information and your own estimates, relating to the year ended June 2000:

| | Midshire region | | |
	Hotel X	Hotel Y	Hotel Z
Value of investment:	(£m)	(£m)	(£m)
Historical cost	2.0	2.3	3.5
Current cost	4.5	3.5	4.6
Disposal value	7.2	3.8	4.5
Operating income	0.8	0.4	0.5
Year in which hotel opened	1987	1995	1997

The 'investment' includes land, buildings and the hotel fixtures and fittings.

The historical cost valuation is net of accumulated depreciation.

The current cost valuation is the current cost of replacing the buildings and facilities to their present standard at current prices. It includes an indexation of the cost of land for the general increase in prices.

You are also informed that the group recently asked hotel managers to put forward proposals to improve and modernise their facilities.

A minimum 12% DCF rate of return was to be used to evaluate each proposal, a rate which the company's brokers affirm would be seen as a satisfactory return.

Details of the proposals from the Midshire region hotels were:

	Hotel X (£000)	Hotel Y (000)	Hotel Z (£000)
Investment cost	500	730	800
Annual cash operating income	67	90	155

You are required to advise on:

(i) the current and prospective future financial position of the Midshire region hotels; (10 marks)

(ii) additional information which may be used to supplement the general rate of return measures in the evaluation of the hotels' managements. (5 marks)

(Total 25 marks)

CIMA Stage 4 Management Accounting – Control and Audit

Scenario

Frantisek Precision Engineering plc (FPE) is an engineering company which makes tools and equipment for a wide range of applications. FPE has twelve operating divisions, each of which is responsible for a particular product group. In the past, divisional performance has been assessed on the basis of Residual Income (RI). RI is calculated by making a finance charge (at bank base rate + 2%) on net assets (excluding cash) as at the end of the year to each division.

Rapier Management Consultants have recently been engaged to review the management accounting systems of FPE. In regard to the performance evaluation system, Rapier have reported as follows:

RI is a very partial and imperfect performance indicator. What you need is a more comprehensive system which reflects the mission, strategy and technology of each individual division. Further, executives should each be paid a performance bonus linked to an indicator which relates to their own personal effectiveness.

FPE's Directors provisionally accepted the Rapier recommendation and have carried out a pilot scheme in the diving equipment (DE) division. DE division manufactures assorted equipment used by sport and industrial divers. Safety is a critical factor in this sector. Customers will not readily accept new products, design features and technologies, and therefore many remain unexploited.

At the start of 2000, Rapier designed a performance evaluation system for DE division as follows:

Factor	Calculated
Return on Capital Employed (ROCE)	Operating profit for the year divided by book value of net assets (excluding cash) at the end of the year.
Cash conversion period (CCP)	Number of days' debtors plus days' stock minus days' creditors outstanding at the end of the year.
Strategy	Number of new products and major design features (innovations) successfully brought to market.

Under the terms of DEs new performance evaluation system, the bases of bonuses for individual divisional managers are:

ROCE over 10%	Chief Executive, Production Manager, Sales Manager
CCP less than 40 days	Accountant, Office Manager
More than 4 innovations	Chief Executive, Design Manager

DE divisions accounting office currently consists of four employees. The division does not have its own bank account. All main accounting systems are operated by FPE's Head Office. DE's accounting staff draw information from the main accounting system in order to prepare weekly budgetary control reports which are submitted to Head Office. The reports prompt regular visits by Head Office accountants to investigate reported cost variances.

Part One

In November 2000, DE's Accountant predicts that DE's results for 2000 will be as follows:

	2000		End 2000
Sales	£6 900 000	Stock	£530 000
Purchases	£2 920 000	Debtors	£1 035 000
Operating profit	£450 000	Creditors	£320 000
Number of innovations	4	Net assets	£4 800 000

The Accountant further forecasts that in the absence of some change in policy or new investment, the corresponding figures for 2001 and end-2001 will be similar to those shown above for 2000. Upon receiving this forecast, DE division's Chief Executive convenes a meeting of his managers to discuss strategy for the rest of 2000 and for 2001. Several proposals are made, including:

From the Office Manager:

I propose that we immediately dispose of £160 000 of stock at cost and defer a creditor payment of £180 000 due 16 December 2000 until 2 January 2001. The first measure will reduce profit by £16 500 a year from 2001 onwards. The second measure will incur an immediate £2000 penalty.

From the Production Manager:

I recommend we invest £400 000 in new equipment, either immediately or in early 2001. This will increase operation profit by £25 000 per year for eight years and the equipment will have a residual value of £40 000 at the end of its life.

From the Design Manager:

I propose we introduce a new electronic digital depth gauge to the market. This will involve an initial investment of £100 000 in new equipment, either immediately or in early 2001, which will have a life of at least ten years. Sales will have to be on 6 months 'buy or return' credit in order to overcome market resistance. I forecast that the new depth gauge will generate £20 000 extra operating profit per year with purchases, sales, stock and creditors all increasing in proportion.

Requirements:
(a) Explain the impact of each proposal on the reported performance of DE division in 2000 and 2001, having regard to the new performance evaluation criteria stated in the Scenario.
State whether or not each proposal is likely to be acceptable to members of DE management. (15 marks)
(b) State your views (supported by financial evaluation) on the inherent merits of each proposal, having regard to factors you consider relevant. (10 marks)
Note: Where relevant, you may assume that depreciation is on a straight-line basis and DCF evaluation is carried out using an 8% discount rate and 10-year time horizon.

Part Two

A great deal of management accounting practice (including divisional performance evaluation) can be carried out with varying degrees of sophistication. Many new techniques have been developed in recent years. The degree of sophistication adopted in any case is partly influenced by the imagination and knowledge of the management accountant, and partly by the availability of management information technology.

Requirements:
(a) In the light of this quotation, state your views on the advantages and disadvantages to FPE of using a firm of consultants to advise on the design of management accounting systems.

Explain your opinion on the merits of the statement quoted above. (10 marks)

(b) Explain the main purpose of divisional organisation and the main features of the management accounting systems that are used to support it. (5 marks)

(c) Explain the changes that might be required in the management accounting operation of DE division if that division became an independent business.

(10 marks)

Part Three

There is nothing inherently wrong with the factors used in DE's new performance evaluation system. The problem is what those factors are used for – in particular, their use as a basis for management remuneration. For one thing, almost any factor is highly vulnerable to manipulation: for another thing, they can seriously distort business decision making.

Requirements:

Having regard to this statement,

(a) explain the strengths and weaknesses of RI and ROCE as divisional business performance indicators as far as FPE is concerned; (5 marks)

(b) comment critically on the statement made by Rapier (quoted in the Scenario). In particular, explain the problems connected with linking management pay to performance, and the measures that management accountants might take to deal with these problems; (7 marks)

(c) explain what JIT philosophy is, in the light of a proposal to adopt just-in-time (JIT) practices in the DE division. Write a report for FPE management on whether or not DE division's Production Manager should be paid a bonus linked to CCP instead of one linked to ROCE (see Scenario), in the light of the proposal to adopt JIT practices in the DE division. (13 marks)

CIMA State 3 Management Accounting Applications

Transfer pricing in divisionalized companies

Question IM 21.1
Advanced

(a) Outline and discuss the main objectives of a transfer pricing system. (5 marks)
(b) Consider the advantages and disadvantages of
   (i) market price-based transfer prices; and
   (ii) cost-based transfer prices.
   Outline the main variants that exist under each heading. (9 marks)
(c) Discuss the relevance of linear programming to the setting of transfer prices.
   (3 marks)
   (Total 17 marks)
   ACCA Level 2 Management Accounting

Question IM 21.2
Advanced

Exel Division is part of the Supeer Group. It produces a basic fabric which is then converted in other divisions within the group. The fabric is also produced in other divisions within the Supeer Group and a limited quantity can be purchased from outside the group. The fabric is currently charged out by Exel Division at total actual cost plus 20% profit mark-up.
(a) Explain why the current transfer pricing method used by Exel Division is unlikely to lead to:
   (i) maximization of group profit and
   (ii) effective divisional performance measurement. (6 marks)
(b) If the supply of basic fabric is insufficient to meet the needs of the divisions who convert it for sale outside the group, explain a procedure which should lead to a transfer pricing and deployment policy for the basic fabric for group profit maximization. (6 marks)
(c) Show how the procedure explained in (b) may be in conflict with other objectives of transfer pricing and suggest how this conflict may be overcome.
   (5 marks)
   (Total 17 marks)
   ACCA Level 2 – Cost and Management Accounting II

Question IM 21.3
Advanced:
Discussion of
transfer price
where there is an
external market
for the
intermediate
product

Fabri Division is part of the Multo Group. Fabri Division produces a single product for which it has an external market which utilizes 70% of its production capacity. Gini Division, which is also part of the Multo Group requires units of the product available from Fabri Division which it will then convert and sell to an external customer. Gini Division's requirements are equal to 50% of Fabri Division's production capacity. Gini Division has a potential source of supply from outside the Multo Group. It is not yet known if this source is willing to supply on the basis of (i) only supplying *all* of Gini Division's requirements or (ii) supplying any part of Gini Division's requirements as requested.
(a) Discuss the transfer pricing method by which Fabri Division should offer to transfer its product to Gini Division in order that group profit maximization is likely to follow.
   You may illustrate your answer with figures of your choice. (14 marks)
(b) Explain ways in which (i) the degree of divisional autonomy allowed and (ii) the divisional performance measure in use by Multo Group may affect the transfer pricing policy of Fabri Division. (6 marks)
   (Total 20 marks)
   ACCA Level 2 Cost and Management Accounting II

(a) Spiro Division is part of a vertically integrated group of divisions allocated in one country. All divisions sell externally and also transfer goods to other divisions within the group. Spiro Division performance is measured using profit before tax as a performance measure.
  (i) Prepare an outline statement which shows the costs and revenue elements which should be included in the calculation of divisional profit before tax.
  (4 marks)
  (ii) The degree of autonomy which is allowed to divisions may affect the absolute value of profit reported.
    Discuss the statement in relation to Spiro Division. (6 marks)
(b) Discuss the pricing basis on which divisions should offer to transfer goods in order that corporate profit maximising decisions should take place. (5 marks)
(Total 15 marks)
ACCA Paper 9 Information for Control and Decision Making

**Question IM 21.4
Advanced**

(a) The transfer pricing method used for the transfer of an intermediate product between two divisions in a group has been agreed at standard cost plus 30% profit markup. The transfer price may be altered after taking into consideration the planning and operational variance analysis at the transferor division.
  Discuss the acceptability of this transfer pricing method to the transferor and transferee divisions. (5 marks)
(b) Division A has an external market for product X which fully utilises its production capacity.
  Explain the circumstances in which division A should be willing to transfer product X to division B of the same group at a price which is less than the existing market price. (5 marks)
(c) An intermediate product which is converted in divisions L, M and N of a group is available in limited quantities from other divisions within the group and from an external source. The total available quantity of the intermediate product is insufficient to satisfy demand.
  Explain the procedure which should lead to a transfer pricing and deployment policy resulting in group profit maximisation. (5 marks)
(Total 15 marks)
ACCA Paper 9 Information for Control and Decision Making

**Question IM 21.5
Advanced**

Alton division (A) and Birmingham division (B) are two manufacturing divisions of Conglom plc. Both of these divisions make a single standardized product; A makes product I and B makes product J. Every unit of J requires one unit of I. The required input of I is normally purchased from division A but sometimes it is purchased from an outside source.
The following table gives details of selling price and cost for each product:

**Question IM 21.6
Advanced:
Resolving a
transfer price
conflict**

	Product I (£)	Product J (£)
Established selling price	30	50
Variable costs		
Direct material	8	5
Transfers from A	—	30
Direct labour	5	3
Variable overhead	2	2
	15	40
Divisional fixed cost (per annum)	£500 000	£225 000
Annual outside demand with current selling prices (units)	100 000	25 000
Capacity of plant (units)	130 000	30 000
Investment in division	£6 625 000	£1 250 000

Division B is currently achieving a rate of return well below the target set by the central office. Its manager blames this situation on the high transfer price of product I. Division A charges division B for the transfers of I at the outside supply price of £30. The manager of division A claims that this is appropriate since this is the price 'determined by market forces'. The manager of B has consistently argued that intra group transfers should be charged at a lower price based on the costs of the producing division plus a 'reasonable' mark-up.

The board of Conglom plc is concerned about B's low rate of return and the divisional manager has been asked to submit proposals for improving the situation. The board has now received a report from B's manager in which he asks the board to intervene to reduce the transfer price charged for product I. The manager of B also informs the board that he is considering the possibility of opening a branch office in rented premises in a nearby town, which should enlarge the market for product J by 5000 units per year at the existing price. He estimates that the branch office establishment costs would be £50 000 per annum.

You have been asked to write a report advising the board on the response that it should make to the plans and proposals put forward by the manager of division B. Incorporate in your report a calculation of the rates of return currently being earned on the capital employed by each division and the changes to these that should follow from an implementation of any proposals that you would recommend.

(22 marks)

ACCA Level 2 Management Accounting

Question IM 21.7 Advanced: Apportionment of company profit to various departments

AB Limited which buys and sells machinery has three departments:

New machines (manager, Newman)
Second-hand machines (manager, Handley)
Repair workshops (manager, Walker)

In selling new machines Newman is often asked to accept an old machine in part exchange. In such cases the old machine is disposed of by Handley.

The workshops do work both for outside customers and also for the other two departments. Walker charges his outside customers for materials at cost and for labour time at £8 per hour. This £8 is made up as follows:

Per hour (£)		
Fixed costs	2.00	(10 000 budgeted hours per annum)
Variable costs	4.50	
Profit	1.50	
	£8.00	

AB Limited wishes to go over to a profit centre basis of calculations so as to be able to reward its three managers according to their results. It wishes to assess the situation in the context of the following transaction:

Newman sold to PQ Limited a new machine at list price of £16 000, the cost of which to AB Limited was £12 000.

To make the sale, however, Newman had to allow PQ Limited £5000 for its old machine in part exchange.

PQ Limiteds old machine was in need of repair before it could be re-sold and Newman and Handley were agreed in their estimate of those repairs as £50 in materials and 100 hours of workshop's labour time. That estimate was proved to be correct when the workshops undertook the repair.

At the time of taking PQ Limited's machine in part exchange Handley would have been able to buy a similar machine from other dealers for £3700 without the need for any repair. When the machine had been repaired he sold it to ST Limited for £4200.

You are required to:

(a) show how you would calculate the profit contribution for each of the three departments from the above transaction.

(b) re-calculate the profit contribution for each department if there were the following alternative changes of circumstances:

   (i) When the workshops came to repair the old machine they found that they required an extra 50 hours of labour time because of a fault not previously noticed.

   (ii) Before deciding on the figure he would allow PQ Limited for their old machine, Newman asks Walker to estimate the cost of repairs. This estimate is £50 in materials and 100 hours of workshops labour time. When, however, workshops came to repair the old machine, it took them 50% longer than estimated.

(c) recommend briefly how to deal with the following situations in the context of profit centre calculation:

   (i) The manufacturer of the new machines allows AB Limited £200 per machine for which AB Limited undertakes to do all warranty repairs. Over the year the total cost of repairs under warranty exceeds the amount allowed by the supplier.

   (ii) Although 4000 hours of workshop time were budgeted to be reserved for the other two departments, their load increases over the year by 20% (at standard efficiency). The load from outside customers, however, stays as budgeted.

(25 marks)

CIMA P3 Management Accounting

English Allied Traders plc has a wide range of manufacturing activities, principally within the UK. The company operates on the divisionalized basis with each division being responsible for its own manufacturing, sales and marketing, and working capital management. Divisional chief executives are expected to achieve a target 20% return on sales.

A disagreement has arisen between two divisions which operate on adjacent sites. The Office Products Division (OPD) has the opportunity to manufacture a printer using a new linear motor which has recently been developed by the Electric Motor Division (EMD). Currently there is no other source of supply for an equivalent motor in the required quantity of 30 000 units a year, although a foreign manufacturer has offered to supply up to 10 000 units in the coming year at a price of £9 each. EMD's current selling price for the motor is £12. Although EMD's production line for this motor is currently operating at only 50% of its capacity, sales are encouraging and EMD confidently expects to sell 100 000 units in 2001, and its maximum output of 120 000 units in 2002.

EMD has offered to supply OPD's requirements for 2001 at a transfer price equal to the normal selling price, less the variable selling and distribution costs that it would not incur on this internal order. OPD responded by offering an alternative transfer price of the standard variable manufacturing cost plus a 20% profit margin. The two divisions have been unable to agree, so the corporate operations director has suggested a third transfer price equal to the standard full manufacturing cost plus 15%. However, neither divisional chief executive regards such a price as fair.

Question IM 21.8
Advanced: Computation of three different transfer prices and the extent to which each price encourages goal congruence

EMD's 2001 budget for the production and sale of motors, based on its standard costs for the forecast 100 000 units sales, but excluding the possible sales to OPD, is as follows:

	(£000)
Sales Revenue (100 000 units at £12.00 each)	1200
Direct Manufacturing Costs	
Bought-in materials	360
Labour	230
Packaging	40
Indirect Manufacturing Costs	
Variable overheads	10
Line production managers	30
Depreciation	
Capital equipment	150
Capitalized development costs	60
Total manufacturing costs	880
Sales and Distribution Costs	
Salaries of sales force	50
Carriage	20
General Overhead	50
Total costs	1000
Profit	200

Notes
(1) The costs of the sales force and indirect production staff are not expected to increase up to the current production capacity.
(2) General overhead includes allocations of divisional administrative expenses and corporate charges of £20 000 specifically related to this product.
(3) Depreciation for all assets is charged on a straight line basis using a five year life and no residual value.
(4) Carriage is provided by an outside contractor.

Requirements
(a) Calculate each of the three proposed transfer prices and comment on how each might affect the willingness of EMD's chief executive to engage in inter-divisional trade. (10 marks)
(b) Outline an alternative method of setting transfer prices which you consider to be appropriate for this situation, and explain why it is an improvement on the other proposals. (5 marks)
(Total 15 marks)
ICAEW P2 Management Accounting and Financial Management 2

Question IM 21.9 Advanced: Optimal output and transfer price where the market for the intermediate product is imperfect

Engcorp and Flotilla are UK divisions of Griffin plc, a multinational company. Both divisions have a wide range of activities. You are an accountant employed by Griffin plc and the Finance Director has asked you to investigate a transfer pricing problem.

Engcorp makes an engine, the Z80, which it has been selling to external customers at £1350 per unit. Flotilla wanted to buy Z80 engines to use in its own production of dories; each dory requires one engine. Engcorp would only sell if Flotilla paid £1350 per unit. The managing director of Engcorp commented:

'We have developed a good market for this engine and £1350 is the current market price. Just because Flotilla is not efficient enough to make a profit is no reason for us to give a subsidy.'

Flotilla has now found that engines suitable for its purpose can be bought for £1300 per unit from another manufacturer. Flotilla is preparing to buy engines from this source.

From information supplied by the divisions you have derived the following production and revenue schedules which are applicable over the capacity range of the two divisions:

| | Engcorp's data for Z80 engines | | Flotilla's data for dories | |
Annual number of units	Total manufacturing cost (£000)	Total revenue from outside sales (£000)	Total cost of producing dories excluding engine costs (£000)	Total revenue from sales of dories (£000)
100	115	204	570	703
200	185	362	1120	1375
300	261	486	1670	2036
400	344	598	2220	2676
500	435	703	2770	3305
600	535	803	3320	3923
700	645	898	3870	4530
800	766	988	4420	5126

Requirements
(a) Ignoring the possibility that Flotilla could buy engines from another manufacturer, calculate to the nearest 100 units:
  (i) the quantity of Z80 production that would maximize profits for Griffin plc, and
  (ii) the consequent quantity of Z80 units that would be sold to external customers and the quantity that would be transferred to Flotilla. (8 marks)
(b) Explain the issues raised by the problems of transfer pricing between Engcorp and Flotilla, and discuss the advantages and disadvantages of the courses of action which could be taken. (10 marks)
(c) Discuss the major considerations in setting transfer prices for a profit-maximizing international group. (7 marks)
(Total 25 marks)
ICAEW P2 Management Accounting

Question IM 21.10 Advanced: Calculation of optimum selling price using calculus as the effect of using the imperfect market price as the transfer price

HKI plc has an Engineering Division and a Motorcycle Division. The Engineering Division produces engines which it sells to 'outside' customers and transfers to the Motorcycle Division. The Motorcycle Division produces a powerful motorbike called the 'Beast' which incorporates an HKI engine in its design.

The Divisional Managers have full control over the commercial policy of their respective Divisions and are each paid 1% of the profit that is earned by their Divisions as an incentive bonus.

Details of the Engineering Division's production operation for the next year are expected to be as follows:

Annual fixed costs   £3 000 000
Variable cost per engine   £350

Details of the Motorcycle Division's production operation for the next year are expected to be as follows:

Annual fixed costs   £50 000
Variable cost per Beast   £700*

*Note: this figure excludes transfer costs

Both Divisions have significant surplus capacity.

Market research has indicated that demand from 'outside' customers for HKI plcs products is as follows:

- 9000 engines are sold at a unit selling price of £700; sales change by an average of 10 engines for each £1 change in the selling price per engine;
- 1000 Beasts are sold at a unit selling price of £2200; sales change by an average of 125 Beasts for each £100 change in the selling price per Beast.

It is established practice for the Engineering Division to transfer engines to the Motorcycle Division at 'market selling price'.

You are required
(a) to calculate the unit selling price of the Beast (accurate to the nearest penny) that should be set in order to maximize HKI plc's profit;   (7 marks)
(b) to calculate the selling price of the Beast (accurate to the nearest penny) that is likely to emerge if the Engineering Division Manager sets a market selling price for the engine which is calculated to maximize profit from engine sales to outside customers. You may assume that both Divisional Managers are aware of the information given above. Explain your reasoning and show your workings;   (8 marks)
(c) to explain why you agree or disagree with the following statement made by the Financial Director of HKI plc:

'Pricing policy is a difficult area which offers considerable scope for dysfunctional behaviour. Decisions about selling prices should be removed from the control of Divisional Managers and made the responsibility of a Head Office department.'

(12 marks)
(Total 27 marks)
CIMA Stage 4 Management Accounting – Decision Making

Question IM 21.11 Advanced: Various aspects of divisional performance evaluation and transfer pricing involving the algebraic manipulation of figures to identify likely outcomes

Scenario

Chambers plc produces motor components and a vehicle called the *Rambler*. The company is split into three operating divisions – Engines, Transmissions and Assembly. The Rambler is produced in the Assembly division. Each Rambler incorporates an engine produced in the Engines division and a transmission system produced in the Transmissions division.

Each operating division is both a profit and an investment centre, with the performance of divisional managers assessed on return on capital employed (ROCE) achieved. In addition to their salary, each manager is paid a bonus each year linked to ROCE achieved in the current year. Chambers plc is financed by various means and has an average cost of capital of 7% per annum.

Relevant details concerning the three operating divisions in the coming year are as follows:

Engines division:

- The variable cost of engine production is £600 per unit.
- Annual demand from outside customers for engines varies with price: it is 5000 units at unit price £1000 and changes by 5 units with each £1 change in unit price.
- Fixed costs are £5 000 000 per year, and capital employed is £5 200 000.

Transmissions division:

- The variable cost of transmission unit production is £350 per unit.
- Annual demand from outside customers for transmission units varies with price: it is 2500 units at unit price £1200 and changes by 5 units with each £2 change in unit price.
- Fixed costs are £5 200 000 per year, and capital employed is £8 100 000.

Assembly division:

- The variable cost (excluding transfer charges) of Rambler production is £1500 per unit.
- Annual demand for ramblers varies with price: it is 4000 units at a unit price of £6000 and changes by 2 units with each £1 change in unit price.
- Fixed costs are £5 800 000 per year, and capital employed is £10 200 000.

There are no capacity constraints in any of the divisions.

Chambers plc's transfer pricing policy is that goods transferred between divisions should be at the price charged to outside customers for the relevant units. In setting selling prices to outside customers, the Engines and Transmissions divisions must ignore the effect of transfers to the Assembly division. The manager of the Assembly division treats transfer prices for units received as variable costs.

An investment in new equipment (having a life of 5 years and a residual value of nil) is being considered by the management of the Transmissions division. The equipment would cost £850 000 and would reduce the variable cost per transmission unit by £30.

Part One

Requirements:
(a) Calculate for each division the output, product price, profit and ROCE that is likely to emerge, given the existing transfer pricing system and assuming that each divisional manager will act to maximise the ROCE of his/her own division.
    Ignore the investment in new equipment.   (7 marks)
(b) Determine and state the optimum output level and selling price for each division from the point of view of Chambers plc as a whole.
    Prepare a statement showing the resultant profit and ROCE of each division, assuming that the existing transfer policy system remains in place.
    Ignore the investment in new equipment.   (7 marks)
(c) Prepare a financial analysis to show the impact of the investment in new equipment on the profit and ROCE of the three divisions, given the existing transfer pricing and performance appraisal systems. State whether or not the management of the Transmissions division is likely to adopt the proposed new investment.   (6 marks)
(d) State whether or not the proposed new investment is to the advantage of Chambers plc as a whole, assuming that decisions concerning output, etc. continue to be determined by the existing transfer pricing and performance appraisal systems.
    Support your answer with a discounted cash flow analysis.   (5 marks)

Note: The following information is given to illustrate a methodology that might be used to solve the requirements of the question:

- The demand function for sales by the Engines division to outside customers may be represented by the following equation, where y = unit selling price and x = demand:

$$y = 2000 - \frac{x}{5}$$

- The corresponding marginal revenue function may be represented by:

$$y = 2000 - \frac{x}{2.5}$$

(Total 25 marks)

Part Two

The concept of divisional organisation is to place divisional managers in the same risk/reward position as independent entrepreneurs. In theory, this induces divisional managers to act in a manner calculated to maximise the wealth of the company's shareholders. This may or may not work in practice but you may be sure of one thing – divisional organisation creates a lot of employment for chartered management accountants.

Requirements:

Having regard to the above statement,

(a) explain how the divisional performance appraisal and transfer pricing systems at Chambers plc might contribute to maximising the wealth of shareholders;

(7 marks)

(b) explain the limitations of ROCE as a divisional performance indicator, and suggest alternative measures that might be more effective; (7 marks)

(c) explain why and how the concept behind divisional organisation might be extended into many areas of government/public service; (5 marks)

(d) explain why divisional organisation generates work for management accountants, and suggest actions which might be taken to make such work cost-effective. (6 marks)

(Total 25 marks)

Part Three

An effective transfer pricing system in the context of a divisional organisation has to satisfy several basic criteria. The problem is that nobody has yet invented a system of transfer pricing that is capable of doing this with perfection.

Requirements:

Having regard to the above statement,

(a) explain what criteria an effective system of transfer pricing has to satisfy;

(7 marks)

(b) state how far the system used by Chambers plc meets the criteria you have identified in your answer to (a); advise Chambers plc on how it might modify its transfer pricing system in order to make it more effective. (9 marks)

(c) explain the features of transfer pricing systems based on
    (i) marginal cost,
   (ii) opportunity cost, and·
  (iii) cost plus;
state how far each of these systems meets the criteria you have identified in your answer to requirement (a). (9 marks)

(Total 25 marks)

CIMA Stage 3 Management Accounting Applications

Cost management

(a) Overtime premiums and shift allowances can be traced to specific batches, jobs or products and should be considered to be direct labour rather than indirect labour.

    You are required to discuss the above statement.   (12 marks)

(b) Your managing director, after hearing a talk at a branch meeting on just-in-time (JIT) manufacturing would like the management to consider introducing JIT at your unit which manufactures typewriters and also keyboards for computing systems.

    You are required as the assistant management accountant, to prepare a discussion paper for circulation to the directors and senior management, describing just-in-time manufacturing, the likely benefits which would follow its introduction and the effect its introduction would probably have on the cost accounting system.   (13 marks)

(Total 25 marks)
CIMA Stage 2 Cost Accounting

Question IM 22.1
Advanced

(a) Life Cycle Costing normally refers to costs incurred by the user of major capital equipment over the whole of the useful equipment life. Explain the determination and calculation of these costs and the problems in their calculation.

    (8 marks)

(b) In the strategy and marketing literature there is continual discussion of the product life cycle.

    You are required to explain, for *each* of the *four* stages of the product life cycle,

- start-up
- growth
- maturity
- harvest,

which system of product costing would be most useful for decision making and control, and why.

    Explain briefly in your answer possible alternative organizational structures at each stage in the life cycle.   (12 marks)

(Total 20 marks)
CIMA Stage 4 Management Accounting – Control and Audit

Question IM 22.2
Advanced

**Question IM 22.3
Advanced**

Kaplan ('Relevance Regained', *Management Accounting*, September 1988) states the view that the 'time-honoured traditions of cost accounting' are 'irrelevant, misleading and wrong'. Variance analysis, product costing and operational control are cited as examples of areas where information provided by management accountants along traditional lines could well fail to meet today's needs of management in industry.

You are required to
(a) state what you consider to be the main requirements for effective operational control and product costing in modern industry;   (10 marks)
(b) identify which 'traditional cost accounting' methods in the areas quoted in (a) *may be considered* to be failing to supply the appropriate information to management, and explain why;   (9 marks)
(c) recommend changes to the 'traditional cost accounting' methods and information which would serve to meet the problems identified in (b). (6 marks)
                    (Total 25 marks)
CIMA Stage 4 Management Accounting – Control and Audit

**Question IM 22.4
Advanced**

A company is proposing the introduction of an activity-based costing (ABC) system as a basis for much of its management accounting information.
(a) Briefly describe how ABC is different from a traditional absorption approach to costing and explain why it was developed.   (8 marks)
(b) Discuss the advantages and limitations of this 'approach based on activities' for management accounting information in the context of:
    (i) preparing plans and budgets
    (ii) monitoring and controlling operations
    (iii) decision-making, for example, product deletion decisions.   (12 marks)
                    (Total 20 marks)
ACCA Paper 8 Managerial Finance

**Question IM 22.5
Advanced**

'Japanese companies that have used just-in-time (JIT) for five or more years are reporting close to a 30% increase in labour productivity, a 60% reduction in inventories, a 90% reduction in quality rejection rates, and a 15% reduction in necessary plant space. However, implementing a just-in-time system does not occur overnight. It took Toyota over twenty years to develop its system and realize significant benefits from it.' *Source:* Sumer C. Aggrawal, *Harvard Business Review* (9/85)

Requirements:
(a) Explain how the benefits claimed for JIT in the above quotation are achieved and why it takes so long to achieve those benefits.   (15 marks)
(b) Explain how management information systems in general (and management accounting systems in particular) should be developed in order to facilitate and make best use of JIT.   (10 marks)
                    (Total 25 marks)
CIMA Stage 3 Management Accounting Applications

**Question IM 22.6
Advanced:
Feedback control
theory and
product quality
measurement**

(a) In control theory, a 'feedback control' mechanism is one which supplies information to determine whether corrective action should be taken to re-establish control of a system.

You are required to:
(i) illustrate by means of a diagram how the feedback mechanism operates within a control system, adding a commentary describing how the system functions;   (9 marks)
(ii) distinguish 'feedforward' from 'feedback' control, giving *two* examples of *each* from within management accounting.   (4 marks)
(b) Achievement of a high standard of product quality has become a major issue in modern manufacturing industry.

In support of programmes aimed at achieving acceptable quality standards, some companies have introduced detailed 'quality cost' measurement schemes.

In others, the philosophy has been that no measurement procedures should be devoted especially to the measurement of quality costs: quality cost schemes designed to measure performance in this area are considered to add to administrative burdens; in reality 'quality' should be the expected achievement of the required product specification.

  (i) set out a classification of quality costs which would be useful for reporting purposes. Give examples of actual costs which would be represented in each classification; (7 marks)

 (ii) discuss the reality of the differences of philosophy expressed in the opening statement. Do they represent fundamental differences or may they be reconciled? (5 marks)

(Total 25 marks)
CIMA Stage 4 Management Accounting – Control and Audit

Bushworks Ltd convert synthetic slabs into components AX and BX for use in the car industry. Bushworks Ltd is planning a quality management programme at a cost of £250 000. The following information relates to the costs incurred by Bushworks Ltd both before and after the implementation of the quality management programme:

Question IM 22.7
Advanced: Financial evaluation of implementing a quality management programme

1. *Synthetic slabs*
   Synthetic slabs cost £40 per hundred. On average 2.5% of synthetic slabs received are returned to the supplier as scrap because of deterioration in stores. The supplier allows a credit of £1 per hundred slabs for such returns. In addition, on receipt in stores, checks to ensure that the slabs received conform to specification costs £14 000 per annum.

   A move to a just-in-time purchasing system will eliminate the holding of stocks of synthetic slabs. This has been negotiated with the supplier who will deliver slabs of guaranteed design specification for £44 per hundred units, eliminating all stockholding costs.

2. *Curing/moulding process*
   The synthetic slabs are issued to a curing/holding process which has variable conversion costs of £20 per hundred slabs input. This process produces sub-components A and B which have the same cost structure. Losses of 10% of input to the process because of incorrect temperature control during the process are sold as scrap at £5 per hundred units. The quality programme will rectify the temperature control problem thus reducing losses to 1% of input to the process.

3. *Finishing process*
   The finishing process has a bank of machines which perform additional operations on type A and B sub-components as required and converts them into final components AX and BX respectively. The variable conversion costs in the finishing process for AX and BX are £15 and £25 per hundred units respectively. At the end of the finishing process 15% of units are found to be defective. Defective units are sold for scrap at £10 per hundred units. The quality programme will convert the finishing process into two dedicated cells, one for each of component types AX and BX. The dedicated cell variable costs per hundred sub-components A and B processed will be £12 and £20 respectively. Defective units of components AX and BX are expected to fall to 2.5% of the input to each cell. Defective components will be sold as scrap as at present.

4. *Finished goods*
   A finished goods stock of components AX and BX of 15 000 and 30 000 units respectively is held throughout the year in order to allow for customer demand fluctuations and free replacement of units returned by customers due to

specification faults. Customer returns are currently 2.5% of components delivered to customers. Variable stock holding costs are £15 per thousand component units.

The proposed dedicated cell layout of the finishing process will eliminate the need to hold stocks of finished components, other than sufficient to allow for the free replacement of those found to be defective in customer hands. This stock level will be set at one month's free replacement to customers which is estimated at 500 and 1000 units for types AX and BX respectively. Variable stockholding costs will remain at £15 per thousand component units.

5. *Quantitative data*

Some preliminary work has already been carried out in calculating the number of units of synthetic slabs, sub-components A and B and components AX and BX which will be required both before and after the implementation of the quality management programme, making use of the information in the question. Table 1 summarises the relevant figures.

Table 1

	Existing situation		Amended situation	
	Type A/AX (units)	Type B/BX (units)	Type A/AX (units)	Type B/BX (units)
Sales	800 000	1 200 000	800 000	1 200 000
Customer returns	20 000	30 000	6 000	12 000
Finished goods delivered	820 000	1 230 000	806 000	1 212 000
Finished process losses	144 706	217 059	20 667	31 077
Input to finishing process	964 706	1 447 059	826 667	1 243 077
	2 411 765		2 069 744	
Curing/moulding losses	267 974		20 907	
Input to curing/moulding	2 679 739		2 090 651	
Stores losses	68 711		—	
Purchase of synthetic slabs	2 748 450		2 090 651	

Required:

(a) Evaluate and present a statement showing the net financial benefit or loss per annum of implementing the quality management programme, using the information in the question and the data in Table 1.

(*All relevant workings must be shown*) (27 marks)

(b) Explain the meaning of the terms internal failure costs, external failure costs, appraisal costs and prevention costs giving examples of each. (8 marks)

Strategic management accounting

Management accounting practice has traditionally focused on techniques to assist organisational decision-making and cost control. In concentrating on the internal environment, the management accounting function has been criticised for not addressing the needs of senior management to enable effective strategic planning. In particular, the criticism has focused on inadequate provision of information which analyses the organisation's exposure to environmental change and its progress towards the achievement of corporate objectives.

Question IM 23.1
Advanced

Requirement:
Explain how Strategic Management Accounting can provide information which meets the requirements of senior managers in seeking to realise corporate objectives.

(20 marks)
CIMA Stage 4 Strategic Management Accountancy and Marketing

The new manufacturing environment is characterised by more flexibility, a readiness to meet customers' requirements, smaller batches, continuous improvements and an emphasis on quality.

In such circumstances, traditional management accounting performance measures are, at best, irrelevant and, at worst, misleading.

Question IM 23.2
Advanced

You are required:
(a) to discuss the above statement, citing specific examples to support or refute the views expressed; (10 marks)
(b) to explain in what ways management accountants can adapt the services they provide to the new environment. (7 marks)
(Total 17 marks)
CIMA Stage 3 Management Accounting Techniques

Research on Performance Measurement in Service Businesses, reported in *Management Accounting*, found that 'performance measurement often focuses on easily quantifiable aspects such as cost and productivity whilst neglecting other dimensions which are important to competitive success'.

Question IM 23.3
Advanced

You are required:
(a) to explain what 'other dimensions' you think are important measures of performance; (8 marks)
(b) to describe what changes would be required to traditional information systems to deal with these 'other dimensions'. (9 marks)
(Total 17 marks)
CIMA Stage 3 Management Accounting

**Question IM 23.4
Advanced**

The 'Balanced Scorecard' approach aims to provide information to management to assist strategic policy formulation and achievement. It emphasises the need to provide the user with a set of information which addresses all relevant areas of performance in an objective and unbiased fashion.

Requirements
    (i) Discuss in general terms the main types of information which would be required by a manager to implement this approach to measuring performance;
    and
    (ii) comment on three specific examples of per-formance measures which could be used in a company in a service industry, for example a firm of consultants. (10 marks)

CIMA Stage 4 Strategic Financial Management

**Question IM 23.5
Advanced: Design
and discussion of
key performance
indicators for DIY
outlets and
regional
companies**

Duit plc has recently acquired Ucando Ltd which is a regional builders' merchants/DIY company with three outlets all within a radius of 40 miles. Duit plc is building up its national coverage of outlets. Duit plc has set up regional companies each with its own board of directors responsible to the main board situated in London.

It is expected that eventually each regional company will have between 10 and 20 outlets under its control. A regional company will take over control of the three Ucando Ltd outlets. Each outlet will have its own manager, and new ones have just been appointed to the three Ucando Ltd outlets.

The outlets' managers will be allowed to hire and fire whatever staff they need and the introduction of a head count budget is being considered by Head Office. Each outlet manager is responsible for his own sales policy, pricing, store layout, advertising, the general running of the outlet and the purchasing of goods for resale, subject to the recommendations below. Duit plc's policy is that all outlet managers have to apply to the regional board for all items of capital expenditure greater than £500, while the regional board can sanction up to £100 000 per capital expenditure project.

The outlets will vary in size of operations, and this will determine the number of trade sales representatives employed per outlet. There will be a minimum of one trade sales representative per outlet under the direction of the outlet manager. Each manager and representative will be entitled to a company car.

Outlet sales are made to both retail and trade on either cash or credit terms. Debtor and cash control is the responsibility of regional office. Cash received is banked locally, and immediately credited to the Head Office account. Credit sales invoices are raised by the outlet with a copy sent to regional office. Within each outlet it is possible to identify the sales origin, e.g. timber yard, saw mill, building supplies, kitchen furniture, etc.

Timber for resale is supplied to an outlet on request from stocks held at regional office or direct from the ports where Duit (Timber Importers) Ltd has further stocks. Duit Kitchens Ltd provides kitchen furniture that the outlets sell. Duit plc also has a small factory making windows, doors and frames which are sold through the outlets. When purchasing other products for resale, the outlet is requested to use suppliers with which Head Office has negotiated discount buying arrangements. All invoices for outlet purchases and overheads are passed by the respective outlet manager before being paid by regional office. In existing Duit outlets a perpetual inventory system is used, with a complete physical check once a year.

Information concerning last year's actual results for one of Ucando Ltd's outlets situated at Birport is given below:

Birport DIY outlet
Trading and profit and loss accountfor year to 31 March

	(£)	(£)
Sales (1)		1 543 000
Less Cost of sales		1 095 530
Prime gross margin (29%)		447 470
Less:		
Wages (2)	87 400	
Salaries (3)	45 000	
Depreciation:		
equipment (4)	9 100	
buildings	3 500	
vehicles (3 cars)	6 500	
Vehicle running expenses	6 170	
Leasing of delivery lorry	6 510	
Lorry running expenses	3 100	
Energy costs	9 350	
Telephone/stationery	9 180	
Travel and entertaining	3 490	
Commission on sales	7 770	
Bad debts written off	9 440	
Advertising	25 160	
Repairs	6 000	
Rates, insurance	13 420	
Sundry expenses	10 580	
Delivery expenses	7 400	269 070
Net profit		£178 400
(11.56%)		

Position at 31 March

	(£)
Debtors	100 900
Stock	512 000

Notes:
(1) Sales can be identified by till code–cash/credit, trade/retail, timber, kitchen furniture, frames, heavy building supplies, light building supplies, sawmill etc.
(2) Workforce distributed as follows: timber yard (3), sawmill (1), sales (7), general duties (1), administration (3).
(3) Paid to sales representatives (2), assistant manager, manager.
(4) Equipment used in sales area, sawmill, yard.

Requirements:
(a) Describe a cost centre, a profit centre and an investment centre and discuss the problems of and benefits from using them for management accounting purposes. (7 marks)
(b) Suggest key performance indicators which can be used either individually or jointly by each member of the management team for the regional outlet network, i.e. those in the regional office, the outlets and their departments, in a responsibility reporting system for their evaluation purposes. (6 marks)
(c) Justify the key performance indicators that you have suggested in (b) incorporating, where appropriate, reference to whether the individuals or entities are being treated as cost, profit or investment centres. (6 marks)

(d) Design a pro forma monthly report without figures which can be used by both the outlet manager for his management and control needs and by the regional board to evaluate the outlet. The report can include two or more sections if you wish. Provide a brief explanation for the format chosen. (6 marks)

Note: The manufacturing companies and the importing company report direct to the main board. (Total 25 marks)

ICAEW Management Accounting

Question IM 23.6
Advanced:
Financial and
non-financial
performance
measures

Scotia Health Consultants Ltd provides advice to clients in medical, dietary and fitness matters by offering consultation with specialist staff.

The budget information for the year ended 31 May is as follows:

(i) Quantitative data as per Appendix.
(ii) Clients are charged a fee per consultation at the rate of: medical £75; dietary £50 and fitness £50.
(iii) Health foods are recommended and provided only to dietary clients at an average cost to the company of £10 per consultation. Clients are charged for such health foods at cost plus 100% mark-up.
(iv) Each customer enquiry incurs a variable cost of £3, whether or not it is converted into a consultation.
(v) Consultants are *each* paid a fixed annual salary as follows: medical £40 000; dietary £28 000; fitness £25 000.
(vi) Sundry other fixed cost: £300 000.

Actual results for the year to 31 May incorporate the following additional information:

(i) Quantitative data as per Appendix.
(ii) A reduction of 10% in health food costs to the company per consultation was achieved through a rationalisation of the range of foods made available.
(iii) Medical salary costs were altered through dispensing with the services of two full-time consultants and sub-contracting outside specialists as required. A total of 1900 consultations were sub-contracted to outside specialists who were paid £50 per consultation.
(iv) Fitness costs were increased by £80 000 through the hire of equipment to allow sophisticated cardio-vascular testing of clients.
(v) New computer software has been installed to provide detailed records and scheduling of all client enquiries and consultations. This software has an annual operating cost (including depreciation) of £50 000.

Required:
(a) Prepare a statement showing the financial results for the year to 31 May in tabular format. This should show:
   (i) the budget and actual gross margin for each type of consultation and for the company
   (ii) the actual net profit for the company
   (iii) the budget and actual margin (£) per consultation for each type of consultation. (Expenditure for each expense heading should be shown in (i) and (ii) as relevant.) (15 marks)
(b) Suggest ways in which each of the undernoted performance measures (1 to 5) could be used to supplement the financial results calculated in (a). You should include relevant quantitative analysis from the Appendix below for each performance measure:
1. Competitiveness; 2 Flexibility; 3. Resource utilisation; 4. Quality; 5. Innovation. (20 marks)
(Total 35 marks)

Appendix
Statistics relating to the year ended 31 May

	Budget	Actual
Total client enquiries:		
new business	50 000	80 000
repeat business	30 000	20 000
Number of client consultations:		
new business	15 000	20 000
repeat business	12 000	10 000
Mix of client consultations:		
medical	6 000	5 500
		(note 1)
dietary	12 000	10 000
fitness	9 000	14 500
Number of consultants employed:		
medical	6	4
		(note 1)
dietary	12	12
fitness	9	12
Number of client complaints:	270	600

Note 1: Client consultations *includes* those carried out by outside specialists. There are now 4 full-time consultants carrying out the remainder of client consultations.

ACCA Paper 9 Information for Control and Decision Making

Cost estimation and cost behaviour

Question IM 24.1
Advanced

Discuss the conditions that should apply if linear regression analysis is to be used to analyse cost behaviour.
(6 marks)
ACCA Level 2 Management Accounting

Question IM 24.2
Advanced

(a) Briefly discuss the problems that occur in constructing cost estimation equations for estimating costs at different output levels.
(7 marks)
(b) Describe four different cost estimation methods and for each method discuss the limitations and circumstances in which you would recommend their use.
(18 marks)

Question IM 24.3
Advanced

Explain the 'learning curve' and discuss its relevance to setting standards. (5 marks)
ACCA Level 2 Management Accounting

Question IM 24.4
Advanced

(a) Comment on factors likely to affect the accuracy of the analysis of costs into fixed and variable components.
(8 marks)
(b) Explain how the analysis of costs into fixed and variable components is of use in planning, control and decision-making techniques used by the management accountant.
(9 marks)
(Total 17 marks)
ACCA Level 2 Management Accounting

Question IM 24.5
Advanced:
Comparison of
independent
variables for cost
estimates

Abourne Ltd manufactures a microcomputer for the home use market. The management accountant is considering using regression analysis in the annual estimate of total costs. The following information has been produced for the twelve months ended 31 December:

Month	Total cost Y (£)	Output, X_1 (numbers)	Number of employees, X_2 (numbers)	Direct labour hours, X_3 (hours)
1	38 200	300	28	4 480
2	40 480	320	30	4 700
3	41 400	350	30	4 800
4	51 000	500	32	5 120
5	52 980	530	32	5 150
6	60 380	640	35	5 700
7	70 440	790	41	7 210
8	32 720	250	41	3 200
9	75 800	820	41	7 300
10	71 920	780	39	7 200
11	68 380	750	38	6 400
12	33 500	270	33	3 960
	$\Sigma Y =$ 637 200	$\Sigma X_1 =$ 6 300	$\Sigma X_2 =$ 420	$\Sigma X_3 =$ 65 220

Additionally:

$$\Sigma Y^2 \quad = \quad 36\ 614.05 \times 10^6$$
$$\Sigma X_1^2 \quad = \quad 3.8582 \times 10^6$$
$$\Sigma X_2^2 \quad = \quad 14\ 954$$
$$\Sigma X_3^2 \quad = \quad 374.423 \times 10^6$$
$$\Sigma X_1 Y \quad = \quad 373.537\ 4 \times 10^6$$
$$\Sigma X_2 Y \quad = \quad 22.812\ 84 \ \times 10^6$$
$$\Sigma X_3 Y \quad = \quad 3692.277\ 4 \times 10^6$$

The management accountant wants to select the best independent variable (X_1, X_2 or X_3) to help in future forecasts of total production costs using an ordinary least-squares regression equation. He is also considering the alternatives of using the Hi-Lo and multiple regression equations as the basis for future forecasts.

You are required to:
(a) Identify which one of the three independent variables (X_1, X_2 or X_3) given above is likely to be the least good estimator of total costs (Y). Give your reasons, but do not submit any calculations. (3 marks)
(b) Compute separately, for the remaining two independent variables, the values of the two parameters α and β for each regression line. Calculate the coefficient of determination (R^2) for each relationship. (6 marks)
(c) State, with reasons, which one of these independent variables should be used to estimate total costs in the future given the results of (b) above. (3 marks)
(d) Devise the two equations which could be used, using the Hi-Lo technique, instead of the two regression lines computed in (b) above and comment on the differences found between the two sets of equations. (5 marks)
(e) Comment critically on the use of Hi-Lo and ordinary least-squares regression as forecasting and estimating aids using the above results as a basis for discussion. In addition, comment on the advantages and problems of using multiple regression for forecasting and estimating; and state whether, in your opinion, the management accountant should consider using it in the present circumstances. (8 marks)

Note: The following formulae can be used to answer the above question.

$$\beta = \frac{\Sigma xy - n\bar{x}\bar{y}}{\Sigma x^2 - n\bar{x}^2}$$

$$\alpha = \bar{y} - \beta\bar{x}$$

$$R^2 = \frac{\alpha\Sigma y + \beta\Sigma xy - n\bar{y}^2}{\Sigma y^2 - n\bar{y}^2}$$

$$Se = \sqrt{\frac{\Sigma y^2 - \alpha\Sigma y - \beta\Sigma xy}{n-2}}$$

$$S\beta = \frac{Se}{\sqrt{\Sigma x^2 - nx^2}}$$

ICAEW P2 Management Accounting

**Question IM 24.6
Advanced:
Calculation of co-
efficient of
determination**

A management accountant is analysing data relating to retail sales on behalf of marketing colleagues. The marketing staff believe that the most important influence upon sales is local advertising undertaken by the retail store. The company also advertises by using regional television areas. The company owns more than 100 retail outlets, and the data below relate to a sample of 10 representative outlets.

Outlet number	Monthly sales (£000)	Local advertising by the retail store (£000 per month)	Regional advertising by the company (£000 per month)
	y	x_1	x_2
1	220	6	4
2	230	8	6
3	240	12	10
4	340	12	16
5	420	2	18
6	460	8	20
7	520	16	26
8	600	15	30
9	720	14	36
10	800	20	46

The data have been partly analysed and the intermediate results are available below.

Σy = 4550 Σy^2 = 2 451 300 $\Sigma x_1 y$ = 58 040
Σx_1 = 113 Σx_1^2 = 1 533 $\Sigma x_2 y$ = 121 100
Σx_2 = 212 Σx_2^2 = 6 120 $\Sigma x_1 x_2$ = 2 780

You are required to examine closely, using co-efficients of determination, the assertion that the level of sales varies more with movements in the level of local advertising than with changes in the level of regional company advertising. (8 marks)
Note that the co-efficient of determination for y and x_1 may be calculated from

$$r^2 = \frac{n \Sigma x_1 y - \Sigma x_1 \Sigma y}{\left(n \Sigma x_1^2 - (\Sigma x_1)^2 \right) \times \left(n \Sigma y^2 - (\Sigma y)^2 \right)}$$

CIMA Stage 3 Management Accounting Techniques

The Crispy Biscuit Company (CBC) has developed a new variety of biscuit which it has successfully test marketed in different parts of the country. It has, therefore, decided to go ahead with full-scale production and is in the process of commissioning a production line located in a hitherto unutilized part of the main factory building. The new line will be capable of producing up to 50 000 packets of new biscuit each week.

Question IM 24.7
Advanced:
Estimates of sales
volume and
revenues using
regression
analysis and
calculation of
optimum price
using differential
calculus

The factory accountant has produced the following schedule of the expected unit costs of production at various levels of output:

	Production level (packets per week)				
	(10 000)	(20 000)	(30 000)	(40 000)	(50 000)
Unit costs (pence)					
Labour (1)	20.0	15.0	13.3	12.5	12.0
Materials	8.0	8.0	8.0	8.0	8.0
Machine costs (2)	8.0	5.0	4.0	3.5	3.2
Total direct costs	36.0	28.0	25.3	24.0	23.2
Factory overhead (3)	9.0	7.0	6.3	6.0	5.8
Total costs	45.0	35.0	31.6	30.0	29.0

(1) The labour costs represent the cost of the additional labour that would require to be taken on to operate the new line.
(2) Machine costs include running costs, maintenance costs and depreciation.
(3) Factory overhead costs are fixed for the factory overall but are allocated to cost centres at 25% of total direct costs.

In addition to establishing product acceptability, the test marketing programme also examined the likely consumer response to various selling prices. It concluded that the weekly revenue likely to be generated at various prices was as follows:

Retail price	Revenue to CBC
£0.62	£15 190
£0.68	£14 960
£0.78	£11 310
£0.84	£10 500
£0.90	£10 350
£0.98	£4 900

The above prices represent the prices at which the product was test marketed, but any price between £0.60 and £0.99 is a possibility. The manufacturer receives 50% of the retail revenue.

Requirements
(a) Estimate the variable costs of producing the new biscuit, using any simple method (such as the high–low method). (3 marks)
(b) Using linear regression, estimate the relationship between the price charged by CBC and the expected demand. (6 marks)
(c) Using the above estimates, calculate the optimum price and evaluate how sensitive your solution is to changes in this price. (8 marks)
(d) Outline the practical problems faced in attempting to derive a unit cost for a new product. (8 marks)
(Total 25 marks)
ICAEW P2 Management Accounting

The question provided the following formula for answering this question:

$$b = \frac{\Sigma(x-\bar{x})(y-y)}{\Sigma(x-\bar{x})^2} \text{ or } \frac{n\Sigma xy - \Sigma x \Sigma y}{n\Sigma x^2 - (\Sigma x)^2}$$

and $a = \bar{y} - b\bar{x}$

**Question IM 24.8
Advanced:
Learning curves**

Present a table of production times showing the following columns for E. Condon Ltd, which produces up to 16 units while experiencing a 90% learning curve, the first unit requiring 1000 hours of production time:
(1) units produced,
(2) total production time (hours),
(3) average production time per unit in each successive lot (hours),
(4) cumulative average production time per unit (hours), and
(5) percentage decline in (4). (10 marks)

ICAEW Management Accounting

**Question IM 24.9
Advanced: The
application of the
learning curve to
determine target
cash flows**

Leano plc is investigating the financial viability of a new product X. Product X is a short life product for which a market has been identified at an agreed design specification. It is not yet clear whether the market life of the product will be six months or 12 months.

The following estimated information is available in respect of product X:
(i) Sales should be 10 000 units per month in batches of 100 units on a just-in-time production basis. An average selling price of £1200 per batch of 100 units is expected for a six month life cycle and £1050 per batch of 100 units for a 12 month life cycle.
(ii) An 80% learning curve will apply in months 1 to 7 (inclusive), after which a steady state production time requirement will apply, with labour time per batch stabilising at that of the final batch in month 7. Reductions in the labour requirement will be achieved through natural labour turnover. The labour requirement for the first batch in month 1 will be 500 hours at £5 per hour.
(iii) Variable overhead is estimated at £2 per labour hour.
(iv) Direct material input will be £500 per batch of product X for the first 200 batches. The next 200 batches are expected to cost 90% of the initial batch cost. All batches thereafter will cost 90% of the batch cost for each of the second 200 batches.
(v) Product X will incur directly attributable fixed costs of £15 000 per month.
(vi) The initial investment for the new product will be £75 000 with no residual value irrespective of the life of the product.

A target cash inflow required over the life of the product must be sufficient to provide for:
(a) the initial investment plus $33\frac{1}{3}\%$ thereof for a six month life cycle, or
(b) the initial investment plus 50% thereof for a 12 month life cycle.

Note: learning curve formula:

$$y=ax^b$$

where y = average cost per batch
a = cost of initial batch
x = total number of batches
b = learning factor (=−0.3219 for 80% learning rate)

Required:
(a) Prepare detailed calculations to show whether product X will provide the target cash inflow over six months and/or 12 months. (17 marks)
(b) Calculate the initial batch labour hours at which the cash inflow achieved will be exactly equal to the target figure where a six month life cycle applies. It has been determined that the maximum labour and variable overhead cost at which the target return will be achieved is £259 000. All other variables remain as in part (a). (6 marks)
(c) Prepare a report to management which:
  (i) explains why the product X proposal is an example of a target costing/pricing situation; (3 marks)
  (ii) suggests specific actions which may be considered to improve the return on investment where a six month product cycle is forecast; (6 marks)

(iii) comments on possible factors which could reduce the rate of return and which must, therefore, be avoided. (3 marks)

(Total 35 marks)

ACCA Paper 9 Information for Control and Decision Making

Question IM 24.10 Advanced: Application of learning curve to determine the incremental costs for different production batches

Limitation plc commenced the manufacture and sale of a new product in the fourth quarter of 2000. In order to facilitate the budgeting process for quarters 1 and 2 of 2001, the following information has been collected:

(i) Forecast production/sales (batches of product):

quarter 4,	2000	30 batches
quarter 1,	2001	45 batches
quarter 2,	2001	45 batches

(ii) It is estimated that direct labour is subject to a learning curve effect of 90%. The labour cost of batch 1 of quarter 4, 2000 was £600 (at £5 per hour). The labour output rates from the commencement of production of the product, after adjusting for learning effects, are as follows:

Total produced (batches)	Overall average time per batch (hours)
15	79.51
30	71.56
45	67.28
60	64.40
75	62.25
90	60.55
105	59.15
120	57.96

Labour hours worked and paid for will be adjusted to eliminate spare capacity during each quarter. All time will be paid for at £5 per hour.

(iii) Direct material is used at the rate of 200 units per batch of product for the first 20 batches of quarter 4, 2000. Units of material used per batch will fall by 2% of the original level for each 20 batches thereafter as the learning curve effect improves the efficiency with which the material is used. All material will be bought at £1.80 per unit during 2001. Delivery of the total material requirement for a quarter will be made on day one of the quarter. Stock will be held in storage capacity hired at a cost of £0.30 per quarter per unit held in stock. Material will be used at an even rate throughout each quarter.

(iv) Variable overhead is estimated at 150% of direct labour cost during 2001.

(v) All units produced will be sold in the quarter of production at £1200 per batch.

Required:

(a) Calculate the labour hours requirement for the second batch and the sum of the labour hours for the third and fourth batches produced in quarter 4, 2000. (3 marks)

(b) Prepare a budget for each of quarters 1 and 2, 2001 showing the contribution earned from the product. Show all relevant workings. (14 marks)

(c) The supplier of the raw material has offered to deliver on a 'just-in-time' basis in return for a price increase to £1.90 per unit in quarter 1, 2001 and £2 per unit thereafter.

(i) Use information for quarters 1 and 2, 2001 to determine whether the offer should be accepted on financial grounds.

(ii) Comment on other factors which should be considered before a final decision is reached. (8 marks)

(d) Limitation plc wish to prepare a quotation for 12 batches of the product to be produced at the start of quarter 3, 2001.

Explain how the learning curve formula $y=ax^b$ may be used in the calculation of the labour cost of the quotation. Your answer should identify each of the variables y, a, x and b. No calculations are required. (5 marks)

(Total 30 marks)

ACCA Level 2 Cost and Management Accounting II

Quantitative models for the planning and control of inventories

A company is planning to purchase 90 800 units of a particular item in the year ahead. The item is purchased in boxes, each containing 10 units of the item, at a price of £200 per box. A safety stock of 250 boxes is kept.

The cost of holding an item in stock for a year (including insurance, interest and space costs) is 15% of the purchase area. The cost of placing and receiving orders is to be estimated from cost data collected relating to similar orders, where costs of £5910 were incurred on 30 orders. It should be assumed that ordering costs change in proportion to the number of orders placed. 2% should be added to the above ordering costs to allow for inflation.

Required:
Calculate the order quantity that would minimize the cost of the above item, and determine the required frequency of placing orders, assuming that usage of the item will be even over the year.

(8 marks)

ACCA Foundation Stage Paper 3

**Question IM 25.1
Intermediate:
Calculation of
EOQ and
frequency at
ordering**

Most textbooks consider that the optimal re-order quantity for materials occurs when 'the cost of storage is equated with the cost of ordering'. If one assumes that this statement is acceptable and also, in attempting to construct a simple formula for an optimal re-order quantity, that a number of basic assumptions must be made, then a recognised formula can be produced using the following symbols:

C_o = cost of placing an order
C_h = cost of storage per annum, expressed as a percentage of stock value
D = demand in units for a material, per annum
Q = re-order quantity, in units
$Q/2$ = average stock level, in units
p = price per unit

You are required:
(a) to present formulae, using the symbols given above, representing:
    (i)   total cost of ordering,
    (ii) total cost of storage,
    (iii) total cost of ordering and storage,
    (iv) optimal re-order quantity; (4 marks)
(b) to state the limitations experienced in practice which affect the user of the formula for optimal re-order quantity as expressed in (a) (iv) above; (4 marks)
(c) to calculate the optimal re-order quantity from the following data:
    Cost of storage is 20% per annum of stock value
    Cost of placing an order is £30 each
    Demand for material is 2000 units per annum
    Price of material is £70 per unit; (3 marks)
(d) to explain a system of stock usage which renders economic order quantity re-ordering obsolete. (4 marks)
(Total 15 marks)
CIMA Stage 2 Cost Accounting

Question IM 25.3
Intermediate:
Calculation of
EOQ

Sandy Lands Ltd carries an item of inventory in respect of which the following data apply:

fixed cost of ordering per batch	£10
expected steady quarterly volume of sales	3125 units
cost of holding one unit in stock for one year	1

You are required to:

(i) calculate the minimum annual cost of ordering and stocking the item;

(4 marks)

(ii) calculate to the nearest whole number of units the optimal batch size if the expected steady quarterly volume of sales

first falls to 781 units and

second rises to 6250 units

and to state the relationship between the rates of change of sales and the optimal batch size;

(4 marks)

(iii) explain the basis of the derivation of the formula for the optimal batch size which is given in the table of formulae.

(4 marks)

ICAEW Management Accounting

Question IM 25.4
Intermediate:
Calculation of
EOQ and a make
or buy decision

A company is considering the possibility of purchasing from a supplier a component it now makes. The supplier will provide the components in the necessary quantities at a unit price of £9. Transportation and storage costs would be negligible.

The company produces the component from a single raw material in economic lots of 2000 units at a cost of £2 per unit. Average annual demand is 20 000 units. The annual holding cost is £0.25 per unit and the minimum stock level is set at 400 units. Direct labour costs for the component are £6 per unit, fixed manufacturing overhead is charged at a rate of £3 per unit based on a normal activity of 20 000 units. The company also hires the machine on which the components are produced at a rate of £200 per month.

Should the company make the component?

Question IM 25.5
Intermediate:
Calculation of
minimum
purchase cost
when cost per
unit is not
constant

A company is reviewing the purchasing policy for one of its raw materials as a result of a reduction in production requirement. The material, which is used evenly through-out the year, is used in only one of the company's products, the production of which is currently 12 000 units per annum. Each finished unit of the product contains 0.4kg of the material. 20% of the material is lost in the production process. Purchases can be made in multiples of 500kg, with a minimum purchase order quantity of 1000kg.

The cost of the raw material depends upon the purchase order quantity as follows:

Order quantity (kg)	Cost per kg (£)
1000	1.00
1500	0.98
2000	0.965
2500	0.95
3000 and above	0.94

Costs of placing and handling each order are £90, of which £40 is an apportionment of costs which are not expected to be affected in the short term by the number of orders placed. Annual holding costs of stock are £0.90 per unit of average stock, of which only £0.40 is expected to be affected in the short term by the amount of stock held.

The lead time for the raw materials is one month, and a safety stock of 250kg is required.

Required:

(a) Explain, and illustrate from the situation described above, the meaning of the terms 'variable', 'semivariable' and 'fixed' costs.

(8 marks)

(b) Calculate the annual cost of pursuing alternative purchase order policies and thus advise the company regarding the purchase order quantity for the material that will minimize cost.
(14 marks)
(Total 22 marks)
ACCA Level 1 Costing

Whirlygig plc manufactures and markets automatic dishwashing machines. Among the components which it purchases each year from external suppliers for assembly into the finished article are window units, of which it uses 20 000 units per annum.

Question IM 25.6 Advanced: Evaluation of an increase in order size incorporating quantity discounts

It is considering buying in larger amounts in order to claim quantity discounts. This will lower the number of orders placed but raise the administrative and other costs of placing and receiving orders. Details of actual and expected ordering and carrying costs are given in the table below:

	Actual	Proposed
O = Ordering cost per order	£31.25	£120
P = Purchase price per item	£6.25	£6.00
I = (annual) Inventory holding cost (as a percentage of the purchase price)	20%	20%

To implement the new arrangements will require reorganisation costs estimated at £10 000 which can be wholly claimed as a business expense for tax purposes in the tax year before the system comes into operation. The rate of corporate tax is 33%, payable with a one-year delay.

Required:
(a) Determine the change in the economic order quantity (EOQ) caused by the new system.
(4 marks)
(b) Calculate the payback period for the proposal and comment on your results.
(10 marks)
(c) Briefly discuss the suitability of the payback method for evaluating investments of this nature.
(6 marks)
(Total 20 marks)
ACCA Paper 8 Managerial Finance

Wagtail Ltd uses the 'optimal batch size' model (see below) to determine optimal levels of raw materials. Material B is consumed at a steady, known rate over the company's planning horizon of one year; the current usage is 4000 units per annum. The costs of ordering B are invariant with respect to order size; clerical costs of ordering have been calculated at £30 per order. Each order is checked by an employee engaged in using B in production who earns £5 per hour irrespective of his output. The employee generates a contribution of £4 per hour when not involved in materials checks and the stock check takes five hours. Holding costs amount to £15 per unit per annum.

Question IM 25.7 Advanced: Quantity discounts and calculation of EOQ

The supplier of material B has very recently offered Wagtail a quantity discount of £0.24 a unit on the current price of £24, for all orders of 400 or more units of B.

You are required to:
(a) calculate the optimal order level of material B, ignoring the quantity discount;
(3 marks)
(b) evaluate whether the quantity discount offered should be taken up by Wagtail;
(5 marks)
(c) explain how uncertainties in materials usage and lead time may be incorporated into the analysis.
(8 marks)

Note: Ignore taxation.

ICAEW P2 Financial Management

Question IM 25.8 Advanced: Calculation of EOQ and a comparison of relevant purchasing costs of different suppliers

Mr Evans is a wholesaler who buys and sells a wide range of products, one of which is the Laker. Mr Evans sells 24 000 units of the Laker each year at a unit price of £20. Sales of the Laker normally follow an even pattern throughout the year but to protect himself against possible deviations Mr Evans keeps a minimum stock of 1000 units. Further supplies of the Laker are ordered whenever the stock falls to this minimum level and the time lag between ordering and delivery is small enough to be ignored.

At present, Mr Evans buys all his supplies of Lakers from May Ltd, and usually purchases them in batches of 5000 units. His most recent invoice from May Ltd was as follows:

	(£)
Basic price: 5000 Lakers at £15 per unit	75 000
Delivery charge: Transport at £0.50 per unit	2 500
Fixed shipment charge per order	1 000
	78 500

In addition, Mr Evans estimates that each order he places costs him £500, comprising administrative costs and the cost of sample checks. This cost does not vary with the size of the order.

Mr Evans stores Lakers in a warehouse which he rents on a long lease for £5 per square foot per annum. Warehouse space available exceeds current requirements and, as the lease cannot be cancelled, spare capacity is sublet on annual contracts at £4 per square foot per annum. Each unit of Laker in stock requires 2 square feet of space. Mr Evans estimates that other holding costs amount to £10 per Laker per annum.

Mr Evans has recently learnt that another supplier of Lakers, Richardson Ltd, is willing, unlike May Ltd, to offer discounts on large orders. Richardson Ltd sells Lakers at the following prices:

Order size	Price per unit (£)
1–2999	15.25
3000–4999	14.50
5000 and over	14.25

In other respects (i.e. delivery charges and the time between ordering and delivery) Richardson Ltd's terms are identical to those of May Ltd.

You are required to:
(a) calculate the optimal re-order quantity for Lakers and the associated annual profit Mr Evans can expect from their purchase and sale, assuming that he continues to buy from May Ltd, (10 marks)
(b) prepare calculations to show whether Mr Evans should buy Lakers from Richardson Ltd rather than from May Ltd and, if so, in what batch sizes, (8 marks)
(c) explain the limitations of the methods of analysis you have used. (7 marks)
Ignore taxation.

(Total 25 marks)
ICAEW Elements of Financial Decisions

A company needs to hold a stock of item X for sale to customers.

Although the item is of relatively small value per unit, the customers quality control requirements and the need to obtain competitive supply tenders at frequent intervals result in high procurement costs.

Basic data about item X are as follows:

Annual sales demand (d) over 52 weeks	4095 units
Cost of placing and processing a purchase order (procurement costs, C_s)	£48.46
Cost of holding one unit for one year (C_h)	£4.00
Normal delay between placing purchase order and receiving goods	3 weeks

**Question IM 25.9
Advanced:
Calculation of
EOQ and
discussion of
safety stocks**

You are required to:
(a) calculate
   (i) the economic order quantity for item X,
   (ii) the frequency at which purchase orders would be placed, using that formula,
   (iii) the total annual procurement costs and the total annual holding costs when the EOQ is used; (6 marks)
(b) explain why it might be unsatisfactory to procure a fixed quantity of item X at regular intervals if it were company policy to satisfy all sales demands from stock and if
   (i) the rate of sales demand could vary between 250 and 350 units per four-week period or
   (ii) the delivery delay on purchases might vary between 3 and 5 weeks
   suggesting in each case what corrective actions might be taken; (6 marks)
(c) describe in detail a fully-developed stock control system for item X (or other fast-moving items), designed to ensure that stock holdings at all times are adequate but not excessive. Illustrate your answer with a freehand graph, not to scale. (8 marks)
(Total 20 marks)
CIMA Stage 4 Financial Management

The financial controller of Mexet plc is reviewing the company's stock management procedures. Stock has gradually increased to 25% of the company's total assets and, with finance costs at 14% per annum, currently costs the company £4.5 million per year, including all ordering and holding costs.

Demand for the company's major product is not subject to seasonal fluctuations. The product requires £6 million of standard semi-finished goods annually which are purchased in equal quantities from three separate suppliers at a cost of £20 per unit. Three suppliers are used to prevent problems that could result from industrial disputes in a single supplier.

**Question IM 25.10
Advanced:
Calculation of
EOQ, safety
stocks and
stockholding
costs where
demand is
uncertain**

Stock costs £2 per unit per year to hold, including insurance costs and financing costs, and each order made costs £100 fixed cost and £0.10 per unit variable cost. There is a lead time of one month between the placing of an order and delivery of the goods. Demand fluctuation for the company's finished products results in the following probability distribution of monthly stock usage.

Usage per month	19 400	23 000	25 000	27 000	30 000
Probability	0.10	0.22	0.36	0.20	0.12

The cost per unit of running out of stock is estimated to be £0.4.

Required:
(a) Calculate the economic order quantity for the semi-finished goods. (3 marks)
(b) Determine what level of safety stock should be kept for these goods. (8 marks)
(c) Calculate the change in annual stock management costs that would result if the goods were bought from only one supplier. Assume that no quantity discounts are available. (5 marks)

(d) The financial controller feels that JIT (just in time) stock management might be useful for the company, but the three suppliers will only agree to this in return for an increase in unit price.

Explain the possible advantages and disadvantages of JIT, and briefly discuss whether or not Mexet should introduce it. (9 marks)

(Total 25 marks)

ACCA Level 3 Financial Management

Question IM 25.11 Advanced: Calculation of stockholding costs, costs of stockouts when demand is uncertain and a discussion of JIT

Rainbow Ltd is a manufacturer which uses alkahest in many of its products. At present the company has an alkahest plant on a site close to the company's main factory. A summary of the alkahest plants budget for the next year is shown below.

Production	300 0000 litres of alkahest
Variable manufacturing costs	£840 000
Fixed manufacturing costs	£330 000

The budget covers costs up to and including the cost of piping finished alkahest to the main factory. At the main factory alkahest can be stored at a cost of £20 per annum per thousand litres, but additional costs arise in storage because alkahest evaporates at a rate of 5% per annum. Production of alkahest is adjusted to meet the demands of the main factory; in addition safety stocks of 60 000 litres are maintained in case of disruption of supplies.

The alkahest plant has a limited remaining life and has been fully depreciated. The management of Rainbow Ltd is considering whether the plant should be retained for the time being or should be closed immediately. On closure the equipment would be scrapped and the site sold for £400 000. Employees would be redeployed within the company and supplies of alkahest would be bought from an outside supplier.

Rainbow Ltd has found that Alchemy plc can supply all its alkahest requirements at £370 per thousand litres. Transport costs of £30 per thousand litres would be borne by Rainbow Ltd. There would be administration costs of £15 000 per year, in addition to order costs of £60 for each delivery. It has been decided that if purchases are made from Alchemy plc the safety stock will be increased to 100 000 litres.

Rainbow Ltd has 250 working days in each year and a cost of capital of 15% per annum. The company's current expectations for demand and costs apply for the foreseeable future.

Requirements:

(a) Calculate the total annual costs of the options available to Rainbow Ltd for its supply of alkahest and interpret the results for management. (10 marks)

(b) Calculate the expected annual stock-outs in litres implied by a safety stock of 100 000 litres and calculate the stock-out cost per litre at which it would be worthwhile to increase safety stock from 100 000 litres to 120 000 litres, under the following assumptions:

(i) for any delivery there is a 0.8 probability that lead time will be 5 days and a 0.2 probability that lead time will be 10 days, and

(ii) during the lead time for any delivery there is a 0.5 probability that Rainbow Ltd will use alkahest at the rate of 10 000 litres per day and a 0.5 probability that the company will use alkahest at the rate of 14 000 litres per day.

(6 marks)

(c) Explain the requirements for the successful adoption of a just-in-time inventory policy and discuss the relative costs and benefits of just-in-time policies compared with economic-order-quantity policies. (9 marks)

(Total 25 marks)

ICAEW P2 Management Accounting

The application of linear programming to management accounting

G Limited, manufacturers of superior garden ornaments, is preparing its production budget for the coming period. The company makes four types of ornament, the data for which are as follows:

Question IM 26.1
Intermediate:
Optimal output using the graphical approach

Product	Pixie (£ per unit)	Elf (£ per unit)	Queen (£ per unit)	King (£ per unit)
Direct materials	25	35	22	25
Variable overhead	17	18	15	16
Selling price	111	98	122	326

Direct labour hours:	Hours per unit	Hours per unit	Hours per unit	Hours per unit
Type 1	8	6	—	—
Type 2	—	—	10	10
Type 3	—	—	5	25

Fixed overhead amounts to £15 000 per period.

Each type of labour is paid £5 per hour but because of the skills involved, an employee of one type cannot be used for work normally done by another type.

The maximum hours available in each type are:

Type 1	8 000 hours
Type 2	20 000 hours
Type 3	25 000 hours

The marketing department judges that, at the present selling prices, the demand for the products is likely to be:

Pixie	Unlimited demand
Elf	Unlimited demand
Queen	1500 units
King	1000 units

You are required:
(a) to calculate the product mix that will maximize profit, and the amount of the profit; (14 marks)
(b) to determine whether it would be worthwhile paying Type 1 Labour for overtime working at time and a half and, if so, to calculate the extra profit for each 1000 hours of overtime; (2 marks)
(c) to comment on the principles used to find the optimum product mix in part (a), pointing out any possible limitations; (3 marks)
(d) to explain how a computer could assist in providing a solution for the data shown above. (3 marks)
(Total 22 marks)
CIMA Stage 3 Management Accounting Techniques

Question IM 26.2
Advanced:
Optimal output
using the
graphical
approach and the
impact of an
increase in
capacity

A company makes two products, X and Y. Product X has a contribution of £124 per unit and product Y £80 per unit. Both products pass through two departments for processing and the times in minutes per unit are:

	Product X	Product Y
Department 1	150	90
Department 2	100	120

Currently there is a maximum of 225 hours per week available in department 1 and 200 hours in department 2. The company can sell all it can produce of X but EEC quotas restrict the sale of Y to a maximum of 75 units per week.

The company, which wishes to maximize contribution, currently makes and sells 30 units of X and 75 units of Y per week.

The company is considering several possibilities including
(i) altering the production plan if it could be proved that there is a better plan than the current one;
(ii) increasing the availability of either department 1 or department 2 hours. The extra costs involved in increasing capacity are £0.5 per hour for each department;
(iii) transferring some of their allowed sales quota for Product Y to another company. Because of commitments the company would always retain a minimum sales level of 30 units.

You are required to
(a) calculate the optimum production plan using the existing capacities and state the extra contribution that would be achieved compared with the existing plan;
(8 marks)
(b) advise management whether they should increase the capacity of *either* department 1 *or* department 2 and, if so, by how many hours and what the resulting increase in contribution would be over that calculated in the improved production plan.
(7 marks)
(c) calculate the minimum price per unit for which they could sell the rights to their quota, down to the minimum level, given the plan in (a) as a starting point.
(5 marks)
(Total 20 marks)
CIMA Stage 3 Management Accounting Techniques

Question IM 26.3
Advanced:
Maximizing profit
and sales revenue
using the
graphical
approach

Goode, Billings and Prosper plc manufactures two products, Razzle and Dazzle. Unit selling prices and variable costs, and daily fixed costs are:

	Razzle (£)	Dazzle (£)
Selling price per unit	20	30
Variable costs per unit	8	20
Contribution margin per unit	12	10
Joint fixed costs per day	£60	

Production of the two products is restricted by limited supplies of three essential inputs: Raz, Ma, and Taz. All other inputs are available at prevailing prices without any restriction. The quantities of Raz, Ma, and Taz necessary to produce single units of Razzle and Dazzle, together with the total supplies available each day, are:

	kg per unit required		Total available
	Razzle	Dazzle	(kg per day)
Raz	5	12.5	75
Ma	8	10	80
Taz	2	0	15

William Billings, the sales director, advises that any combination of Razzle and/or Dazzle can be sold without affecting their market prices. He also argues very strongly that the company should seek to maximize its sales revenues subject to a minimum acceptable profit of £44 per day in total from these two products.

In contrast, the financial director, Silas Prosper, has told the managing director, Henry Goode, that he believes in a policy of profit maximization at all times.

You are required to:
(a) calculate:
   (i) the profit and total sales revenue per day, assuming a policy of profit maximization, (10 marks)
   (ii) the total sales revenue per day, assuming a policy of sales revenue maximization subject to a minimum acceptable profit of £44 per day, (10 marks)
(b) suggest why businessmen might choose to follow an objective of maximizing sales revenue subject to a minimum profit constraint. (5 marks)
(Total 25 marks)
ICAEW Management Accounting

Usine Ltd is a company whose objective is to maximize profits. It manufactures two speciality chemical powders, gamma and delta, using three processes: heating, refining and blending. The powders can be produced and sold in infinitely divisible quantities.

The following are the estimated production hours for each process per kilo of output for each of the two chemical powders during the period 1 June to 31 August:

Question IM 26.4 Advanced: Optimal output and shadow prices using the graphical approach

	Gamma (hours)	Delta (hours)
Heating	400	120
Refining	100	90
Blending	100	250

During the same period, revenues and costs per kilo of output are budgeted as

	Gamma (£ per kilo)	Delta (£ per kilo)
Selling price	16 000	25 000
Variable costs	12 000	17 000
Contribution	4 000	8 000

It is anticipated that the company will be able to sell all it can produce at the above prices, and that at any level of output fixed costs for the three month period will total £36 000.

The company's management accountant is under the impression that there will only be one scarce factor during the budget period, namely blending hours, which cannot exceed a total of 1050 hours during the period 1 June to 31 August. He therefore correctly draws up an optimum production plan on this basis.

However, when the factory manager sees the figures he points out that over the three month period there will not only be a restriction on blending hours, but in addition the heating and refining hours cannot exceed 1200 and 450 respectively during the three month period.

Requirements:
(a) Calculate the initial production plan for the period 1 June to 31 August as prepared by the management accountant, assuming blending hours are the only scarce factor. Indicate the budgeted profit or loss, and explain why the solution is the optimum. (4 marks)

(b) Calculate the optimum production plan for the period 1 June to 31 August, allowing for both the constraint on blending hours and the additional restrictions identified by the factory manager, and indicate the budgeted profit or loss. (8 marks)

(c) State the implications of your answer in (b) in terms of the decisions that will have to be made by Usine Ltd with respect to production during the period 1 June to 31 August after taking into account all relevant costs. (2 marks)

(d) Under the restrictions identified by the management accountant and the factory manager, the shadow (or dual) price of one extra hour of blending time on the optimum production plan is £27.50. Calculate the shadow (or dual) price of one extra hour of refining time. Explain how such information might be used by management, and in so doing indicate the limitations inherent in the figures. (6 marks)

Note: Ignore taxation.
Show all calculations clearly. (20 marks)
ICAEW Management Accounting and Financial Management I Part Two

Question IM 26.5
Advanced:
Formulation of initial tableau and interpretation of final tableau

The Alphab Group has five divisions A, B, C, D and E. Group management wish to increase overall group production capacity per year by up to 30 000 hours. Part of the strategy will be to require that the minimum increase at any one division must be equal to 5% of its current capacity. The maximum funds available for the expansion programme are £3 000 000.

Additional information relating to each division is as follows:

Division	Existing capacity (hours)	Investment cost per hour (£)	Average contribution per hour (£)
A	20 000	90	12.50
B	40 000	75	9.50
C	24 000	100	11
D	50 000	120	8
E	12 000	200	14

A linear programme of the plan has been prepared in order to determine the strategy which will maximise additional contribution per annum and to provide additional decision-making information. The Appendix to this question shows a print-out of the LP model of the situation.

Required:
(a) Formulate the mathematical model from which the input to the LP programme would be obtained. (6 marks)

(b) Use the linear programme solution in the Appendix in order to answer the following:
   (i) State the maximum additional contribution from the expansion strategy and the distribution of the extra capacity between the divisions. (3 marks)
   (ii) Explain the cost to the company of providing the minimum 5% increase in capacity at each division. (3 marks)
   (iii) Explain the effect on contribution of the limits placed on capacity and investment. (2 marks)
   (iv) Explain the sensitivity of the plan to changes in contribution per hour. (4 marks)
   (v) Group management decide to relax the 30 000 hours capacity constraint. All other parameters of the model remain unchanged. Determine the change in strategy which will then maximise the increase in group contribution. You should calculate the increase in contribution which this change in strategy will provide. (6 marks)

(vi) Group management wish to decrease the level of investment while leaving all other parameters of the model (as per the Appendix) unchanged. Determine and quantify the change in strategy which is required indicating the fall in contribution which will occur. (6 marks)

(c) Explain the limitations of the use of linear programming for planning purposes. (5 marks)

(Total 35 marks)

Appendix
Divisional investment evaluation
Optimal solution – detailed report

Variable	Value
1 DIV A	22 090.91
2 DIV B	2 000.00
3 DIV C	1 200.00
4 DIV D	2 500.00
5 DIV E	2 209.09

	Constraint	Type	RHS	Slack	Shadow price
1	Max. Hours	<=	30 000.00	0.00	11.2727
2	DIV A	>=	1 000.00	21 090.91	0.0000
3	DIV B	>=	2 000.00	0.00	−2.7955
4	DIV C	>=	1 200.00	0.00	−1.6364
5	DIV D	>=	2 500.00	0.00	−4.9091
6	DIV E	>=	600.00	1 609.09	0.0000
7	Max. Funds	<=	3 000 000.00	0.00	0.0136

Objective function value=359 263.6

Sensitivity Analysis of Objective Function Coefficients

Variable	Current coefficient	Allowable minimum	Allowable maximum
1 DIV A	12.50	10.7000	14.0000
2 DIV B	9.50	−Infinity	12.2955
3 DIV C	11.00	−Infinity	12.6364
4 DIV D	8.00	−Infinity	12.9091
5 DIV E	14.00	12.5000	27.7778

Sensitivity Analysis of Right-hand Side Values

	Constraint	Type	Current value	Allowable minimum	Allowable maximum
1	Max. Hours	<=	30 000.00	18 400.00	31 966.67
2	DIV A	>=	1 000.00	−Infinity	22 090.91
3	DIV B	>=	2 000.00	0.00	20 560.00
4	DIV C	>=	1 200.00	0.00	18 900.00
5	DIV D	>=	2 500.00	0.00	8 400.00
6	DIV E	>=	600.00	−Infinity	2 209.09
7	Max. Funds	<=	3 000 000.00	2 823 000.00	5 320 000.00

Note: RHS=Right-hand side

ACCA Paper 9 Information for Control and Decision Making

Question IM 26.6
Advanced: Formulation of an initial tableau and interpretation of a final tableau using the simplex method

Hint: Reverse the signs and ignore entries of 0 and 1.

The Kaolene Co. Ltd has six different products all made from fabricated steel. Each product passes through a combination of five production operations: cutting, forming, drilling, welding and coating.

Steel is cut to the length required, formed into the appropriate shapes, drilled if necessary, welded together if the product is made up of more than one part, and then passed through the coating machine. Each operation is separate and independent, except for the cutting and forming operations, when, if needed, forming follows continuously after cutting. Some products do not require every production operation.

The output rates from each production operations, based on a standard measure for each product, are set out in the tableau below, along with the total hours of work available for each operation. The contribution per unit of each product is also given. It is estimated that three of the products have sales ceilings and these are also given below:

Products	X_1	X_2	X_3	X_4	X_5	X_6
Contribution per unit (£)	5.7	10.1	12.3	9.8	17.2	14.0
Output rate per hour:						
Cutting	650	700	370	450	300	420
Forming	450	450	—	520	180	380
Drilling	—	200	380	—	300	—
Welding	—	—	380	670	400	720
Coating	500	—	540	480	600	450
Maximum sales units (000)	—	—	150	—	20	70

	Cutting	Forming	Drilling	Welding	Coating
Production hours available	12 000	16 000	4000	4000	16 000

The production and sales for the year were found using a linear programming algorithm. The final tableau is given below.

X_1	X_2	X_3	X_4	X_5	X_6	X_7	X_8	X_9	X_{10}	X_{11}	X_{12}	X_{13}	X_{14}	Variable in basic solution	Value of variable in basic solution
1	0	−1.6	−0.22	−0.99	0	10.8	0	−3.0	-18.5	0	0	0	0	X_1	43 287.0 units
0	0	−0.15	−0.02	0.12	0	−1.4	1	−0.3	0.58	0	0	0	0	X_8	15 747.81 hours
0	1	0.53	0	0.67	0	0	0	3.33	0	0	0	0	0	X_2	13 333.3 units
0	0	1.9	1.08	1.64	1	0	0	0	12	0	0	0	0	X_6	48 019.2 units
0	0	0.06	0.01	0	0	−1.3	0	0.37	0.63	1	0	0	0	X_{11}	150 806.72 hours
0	0	1	0	0	0	0	0	0	0	0	1	0	0	X_{12}	150 000.0 units
0	0	0	0	1	0	0	0	0	0	0	0	1	0	X_{13}	20 000.0 units
0	0	−1.9	−1.0	−1.6	0	0	0	0	−12	0	0	0	1	X_{14}	21 980.8 units
0	0	10.0	4	6.83	0	61.7	0	16.0	62.1	0	0	0	0	$(Z_j\!-\!C_j)$	£1 053 617.4

Variables X_7 to X_{11} are the slack variables relating to the production constraints, expressed in the order of production. Variables X_{12} to X_{14} are the slack variables relating to the sales ceilings of X_3, X_5 and X_6 respectively.

After analysis of the above results, the production manager believes that further mechanical work on the cutting and forming machines costing £200 can improve their hourly output rates as follows:

Products	X_1	X_2	X_3	X_4	X_5	X_6
Cutting	700	770	410	500	330	470
Forming	540	540	—	620	220	460

The optimal solution to the new situation indicates the shadow prices of the cutting, drilling and welding sections to be £59.3, £14.2 and £71.5 per hour respectively.

Requirements:
(a) Explain the meaning of the seven items ringed in the final tableau.   (9 marks)
(b) Show the range of values within which the following variables or resources can change without changing the optimal mix indicated in the final tableau
   (i) c_4: contribution of X4
   (ii) b_5: available coating time.   (4 marks)
(c) Formulate the revised linear programming problem taking note of the revised output rates for cutting and forming.   (5 marks)
(d) Determine whether the changes in the cutting and forming rates will increase profitability.   (3 marks)
(e) Using the above information discuss the usefulness of linear programming to managers in solving this type of problem.   (4 marks)
(Total 25 marks)
ICAEW P2 Management Accounting

(a) The Argonaut Company makes three products, Xylos, Yo-yos and Zicons. These are assembled from two components, Agrons and Bovons, which can be produced internally at a variable cost of £5 and £8 each respectively. A limited quantity of each of these components may be available for purchase from an external supplier at a quoted price which varies from week to week.

Question IM 26.7 Formulation of initial tableau and interpretation of final tableau using the simplex method

   The production of Agrons and Bovons is subject to several limitations. Both components require the same three production processes (L, M and N), the first two of which have limited availabilities of 9600 minutes per week and 7000 minutes per week respectively. The final process (N) has effectively unlimited availability but for technical reasons must produce at least one Agron for each Bovon produced. The processing times are as follows:

Process	L	M	N
Time (mins) required to produce			
1 Agron	6	5	7
1 Bovon	8	5	9

The component requirements of each of the three final products are:

Product	Xylo	Yo-yo	Zicon
Number of components required			
Agrons	1	1	3
Bovons	2	1	2

The ex-factory selling prices of the final products are given below, together with the standard direct labour hours involved in their assembly and details of other assembly costs incurred:

Product	Xylo	Yo-yo	Zicon
Selling price	£70	£60	£150
Direct labour hours used	6	7	16
Other assembly costs	£4	£5	£15

The standard direct labour rate is £5 per hour. Factory overhead costs amount to £4350 per week and are absorbed to products on the basis of the direct labour costs incurred in their assembly. The current production plan is to produce 100 units of each of the three products each week.

Requirements:
(i) Present a budgeted weekly profit and loss account, by product, for the factory.   (4 marks)
(ii) Formulate the production problem facing the factory manager as a linear program:
  (1) assuming there is no external availability of Agrons and Bovons;
                                                                                                    (5 marks)

  and

  (2) assuming that 200 Agrons and 300 Bovons are available at prices of £10 and £12 each respectively.   (4 marks)
(b) In a week when no external availability of Agrons and Bovons was expected, the optimal solution to the linear program and the shadow prices associated with each constraint were as follows:

Production of Xylos	50 units
Production of Yo-yos	0 units; shadow price £2.75
Production of Zicons	250 units

Shadow price associated with:
Process L	£ 0.375 per minute
Process M	£ 0.450 per minute
Process N	£ 0.000 per minute
Agron availability	£ 9.50 each
Bovon availability	£ 13.25 each

If sufficient Bovons were to become available on the external market at a price of £12 each, a revised linear programming solution indicated that only Xylos should be made.

Requirement:
Interpret this output from the linear program in a report to the factory manager. Include calculations of revised shadow prices in your report and indicate the actions the manager should take and the benefits that would accrue if the various constraints could be overcome.   (12 marks)
                                                                                       (Total 25 marks)
ICAEW P2 Management Accounting

Question IM 26.8 Advanced: Single and multi-period capital rationing

Raiders Ltd is a private limited company which is financed entirely by ordinary shares. Its effective cost of capital, net of tax, is 10% per annum. The directors of Raiders Ltd are considering the company's capital investment programme for the next two years, and have reduced their initial list of projects to four. Details of the projects are as follows:

Cash flows (net of tax)

	Immediately (£000)	After one year (£000)	After two years (£000)	After three years (£000)	Net present value (at 10%) (£000)	Internal rate of return (to nearest 1%)
Project						
A	−400	+50	+300	+350	+157.0	26%
B	−300	−200	+400	+400	+150.0	25%
C	−300	+150	+150	+150	+73.5	23%
D	0	−300	+250	+300	+159.5	50%

None of the projects can be delayed. All projects are divisible; outlays may be reduced by any proportion and net inflows will then be reduced in the same proportion. No project can be undertaken more than once. Raiders Ltd is able to invest surplus funds in a bank deposit account yielding a return of 7% per annum, net of tax.

You are required to:
(a) prepare calculations showing which projects Raiders Ltd should undertake if capital for immediate investment is limited to £500 000, but is expected to be available without limit at a cost of 10% per annum thereafter;   (5 marks)
(b) provide a mathematical programming formulation to assist the directors of Raiders Ltd in choosing investment projects if capital available immediately is limited to £500 000, capital available after one year is limited to £300 000, and capital is available thereafter without limit at a cost of 10% per annum;

(8 marks)
(c) outline the limitations of the formulation you have provided in (b);   (6 marks)
(d) comment briefly on the view that in practice capital is rarely limited absolutely, provided that the borrower is willing to pay a sufficiently high price, and in consequence a technique for selecting investment projects which assumes that capital is limited absolutely, is of no use.   (6 marks)
(Total 25 marks)
ICAEW Financial Management

The directors of Anhang plc are considering how best to invest in four projects, details of which are given below.

Question IM 26.9
Advanced: Capital rationing and beta analysis

	Project I	Project II	Project III	Project IV
Net present value (£000)	+80	+40	+120	+110
Beta factor of project	1.0	1.0	0.8	1.2
Initial payment (000)	50	40	90	55

The net present values of the projects have been calculated using specific, risk-adjusted discount rates. The directors choice is complicated because Anhang plc has only £90 000 currently available for investment in new projects. Each project must start on the same date and cannot be deferred. Acceptance of any one project would not affect acceptance of any other and all projects are divisible. The directors at a recent board meeting were unable to agree upon how best to invest the £90 000. A summary of the views expressed at the meeting follows:
 (i) Wendling argued that as the presumed objective of the company was to maximize shareholder wealth, project III should be undertaken as this project produced the highest net present value.
 (ii) Ramm argued that as funds were in short supply investment should be concentrated in those projects with the lowest initial outlay, that is in projects I and II.
(iii) Ritter suggested that project III should be accepted on the grounds of risk reduction. Project III has the lowest beta, and by its acceptance the risk of the company (the company's present beta is 1.0) would be reduced. Ritter also cautioned against acceptance of project IV as it was the most risky project; he pointed out that its high net present value was, in part, a reward for its higher level of associated risk.
(iv) Punto argued against accepting project III, stating that if the project were discounted at the company's cost of capital, its net present value would be greatly reduced.

Requirements:
(a) Write a report to the directors of Anhang plc advising them how best to invest the £90 000, assuming the restriction on capital to apply for one year only. Your report should address the issues raised by each of the *four* directors.   (17 marks)

(b) Explain why the criteria you have used in (a) above to determine the best allocation of capital may be inappropriate if funds are rationed for a period longer than one year. (4 marks)

(c) Describe the procedures available to a company for the selection of projects when capital is rationed in more than one period. (4 marks)

(Total 25 marks)

ICAEW Financial Management

Part II

Solutions

An introduction to cost terms and concepts

Solutions to Chapter 2 questions

(1) (a); (2) (d); (3) (e); (4) (f); (5) (i); (6) (b); (7) (h).

(i) Direct materials	(ii) Direct labour	(iii) Direct expenses
9	16	10

(iv) Indirect production overhead	(v) Research and development costs	(vi) Selling and distribution costs
1	20	7
6		11
8		12
18		13
19		17

(vii) Administration costs	(viii) Finance costs
2	5
3	
4	
14	
15	

(a) Variable cost per running hour of Machine XR1

	(£)
(£27 500/1100 hours)=	25
Fixed cost " " " " " " " " " (£20 000/1100 hours) =	18.182

Cost of brain scan on Machine XRI: (£)

	(£)
Variable machine cost (4 hours × £25)	100
X-ray plates	40
Total variable cost	140
Fixed machine cost (4 hours × £18.182)	72.73
Total cost of a scan	212.73
Total cost of a satisfactory scan (£212.73/0.9)	236.37

(b) It is assumed that fixed costs will remain unchanged and also that they are not relevant to the decision. The relevant costs are the incremental costs of an additional scan:

Machine XR1: (£)

	(£)
Variable cost per scan	140
Variable cost per satisfactory scan (£140/0.9)	155.56

Machine XR50: (£)

Variable machine cost per scan (£64 000/2000 hours × 1.8 hours)		57.60
X-ray plates		55.00
Variable cost per scan		112.60
Variable cost per satisfactory scan (£112.60/0.94)		119.79

The relevant costs per satisfactory scan are cheaper on Machine XR50 and therefore brain scans should be undertaken on this machine.

Solution IM 2.4

(a)
Standard cost sheet (per unit)

		(£)	(£)
Direct materials 40 m² at £5.30 per m²			212
Direct wages:			
Bonding dept 48 hours at £2.50 per hour		120	
Finishing dept 30 hours at £1.90 per hour		57	
			177
(i) Prime cost			389
Variable overhead:[a]			
Bonding dept 48 hours at £0.75 per hour		36	
Finishing dept 30 hours at £0.50 per hour		15	
			51
(ii) Variable production cost			440
Fixed production overhead[b]			40
(iii) Total production cost			480
Selling and distribution cost[c]		20	
Administration cost[c]		10	
			30
(iv) Total cost			510

Notes

[a] Variable overhead rates: $\text{Bonding} = \dfrac{£375\,000}{500\,000 \text{ hours}} = £0.75$

$$\text{Finishing} = \frac{£150\,000}{300\,000 \text{ hours}} = £0.50$$

[b] Fixed production overhead rate per unit of output $= \dfrac{£392\,000}{9800 \text{ units}} = £40$

The fixed production overhead rate per unit of output has been calculated because there appears to be only one product produced. Alternatively, a fixed production hourly overhead rate can be calculated and charged to the product on the basis of the number of hours which the product spends in each department.

[c] Selling and production cost per unit of output $= \dfrac{£196\,000}{9800 \text{ units}} = £20$

$$\text{Administration cost per unit of output} = \frac{£98\,000}{9800 \text{ units}} = £10$$

(b) Selling price per unit $£510 \times \dfrac{100}{85} = \underline{\underline{600}}$

Cost assignment

Solutions to Chapter 3 questions

Solution IM 3.1

(a) For the answer to this question see 'Budgeted overhead rates' in Chapter 3.
(b) A lower production overhead rate does not necessarily indicate that factory X is more efficient than factory Y. The reasons for this are:
   (i) Factory Y's operations might be highly mechanized, resulting in large depreciation costs, whereas factory X's operations might be labour-intensive. Consequently products produced in factory Y will incur higher overhead and lower labour costs, whereas products produced in factory X will incur lower overhead and higher labour costs.
  (ii) Factory Y may have invested in plant with a larger operating capacity in order to meet future output. This will result in larger fixed costs and a higher overhead rate.
 (iii) Both factories may use different denominators in calculating the overhead rates. For example, if factory Y uses normal capacity and factory X uses maximum practical capacity then factory Y will have a higher overhead rate.
 (iv) Current budgeted activity might be used by both firms to calculate the overhead rate. The level of budgeted sales will determine budgeted activity. The lower overhead rate of factory X might be due to a higher sales volume rather than efficient factory operations.
  (v) Different cost classification might result in different overhead rates. Factory X might treat all expenditure as a direct cost wherever possible. For example, employers' costs might be charged out by means of an inflated hourly wage rate. Factory Y may treat such items as overhead costs.

See answer to Question 3.27 in the text for the answer to this question.

Solution IM 3.2

(a) For the answer to this question see 'Blanket overhead rates' in Chapter 3.
(b) For the answer to this question see Appendix 3.2 to Chapter 3.

Solution IM 3.3

(a)

Solution IM 3.4

	Production department			Service department	Total
	A	B	C		
	(£)	(£)	(£)	(£)	(£)
Direct	261 745	226 120	93 890	53 305	635 060
Indirect	135 400 (40%)	118 475 (35%)	67 700 (20%)	16 925 (5%)	338 500
Service dept appointment	23 410 $(\frac{1}{3})$	23 410 $(\frac{1}{3})$	23 410 $(\frac{1}{3})$	(70 230)	
	420 555	368 005	185 000	—	973 560
Allocation base (1)	17 760 =£23.68 per direct labour hour	5 760 =£63.89 per m/c hour	148 000 =£1.25 per hour		

Note:

1. Dept. A direct labour hours
   = 10 × 37 × 48
   = 17 760
   Dept. B machine hours
   = 5 × 24 × 48
   = 5760
   Dept. C units
   = 148 000

(b)

Dept A	£
9 direct labour hours at £23.68	213.12
Dept B	
3 m/c hours at £63.89	191.67
Dept C	
100 units at £1.25	125.00
	529.79

Cost per unit = £5.30 (£529.79/100)

Solution IM 3.5

(a)

Overhead analysis sheet

Expense	Apportionment basis	Machining (£)	Assembly (£)	Finishing (£)	Total (£)
Indirect wages/salaries	Allocated	120 354	238 970	89 700	449 024
Rent	Area	5 708 475	4 439 925	2 537 100	12 685 500
Business rates	Area	1 552 905	1 207 815	690 180	3 450 900
Heat/light	Area	443 408	344 872	197 070	985 350
Machine power	Horsepower	1 878 890	72 265	939 445	2 890 600
Plant department	Value of plant	375 000	45 000	180 000	600 000
Canteen subsidy	No. of employees	100 000	120 000	36 000	256 000
Total		10 179 032	6 468 847	4 669 495	21 317 374

(b) Most of the overheads in the machine department are likely to be machine related and therefore it is appropriate to use a machine hour rate. The machine hour cost rate is also used for the finishing department, because machine hours are the predominant activity. Similar arguments can be used to justify the use of a direct labour hour overhead rate in the assembly department. The overhead rates are as follows:

$$\text{Machining} \quad \frac{£10\,179\,032}{200\,000} = £50.90 \text{ per machine hour}$$

$$\text{Assembly} \quad \frac{£6\,468\,847}{140\,000} = £46.21 \text{ per direct labour hour}$$

$$\text{Finishing} \quad \frac{£4\,669\,847}{90\,000} = £51.88 \text{ per machine hour}$$

(a)

Overhead analysis sheet

	Total (£)	Cutting (£)	Tents (£)	Bags (£)	Stores (£)	Canteen (£)	Maintenance (£)
		Production			Service		
Indirect wages	147 200	6 400	19 500	20 100	41 200	15 000	45 000
Consumable materials	54 600	5 300	4 100	2 300	—	18 700	24 200
Plant depreciation	84 200	31 200	17 500	24 600	2 500	3 400	5 000
Power^a	31 700	5 389	12 046	10 144	951	2 536	634
Heat and light^b	13 800						
Rent and rates^b	14 400	11 120	13 900	9 730	2 085	3 475	1 390
Building insurance^b	13 500						
	359 400	59 409	67 046	66 874	46 736	43 111	76 224
Reapportionment:							
Stores^c	–	29 210	5 842	5 842	(46 736)	—	5 842
Canteen^d	–	2 694	18 476	21 941		(43 111)	—
Maintenance^e	–	1 887	37 731	42 448			(82 066)
	359 400	93 200	129 095	137 105			
Machine hours	87 000	2 000	40 000	45 000			
Labour hours	112 000	7 000	48 000	57 000			
Machine hour rate		£46.60	£3.23	£3.05			
Overheads per labour hour		£13.31	£2.69	£2.41			

Notes

Bases of apportionment: ^{a} estimated power usage; ^{b} area; ^{c} value of issues; ^{d} direct labour hours; ^{e} machine hours. Actual basis for other costs.

(b) See section on budgeted overhead rates in Chapter 3 for the answer to this question. In addition the following points should be made:
   (i) It draws attention to the under/over recovery of overheads arising from changes in production levels.
   (ii) There is difficulty in determining estimated overheads and an appropriate level of activity when calculating predetermined overhead rates.

(a) Percentage of direct labour cost method = (£600 000/£200 000) × 100
                                          = 300% of direct labour cost
   Direct labour hour method = (£600 000/40 000 direct labour hours)
                             = £15 per direct labour hour
   Machine hour method   = (£600 000/50 000 machine hour)
                             = £12 per machine hour

(b) See 'Predetermined overhead rates' in Chapter 3 for the answer to this question.
(c) The question states that the company has become machine-intensive and implies that in the long term there is a closer association between overhead expenditure and machine hours than the other two methods. Therefore the best measure of overhead resources consumed by jobs or products is machine hours.

(d)

Job Ax	(£)
Direct material	3788
Direct labour	1100
Direct expenses	422
Prime cost	5310
Production overhead (120 machine hours × £12)	1440
Factory cost	6750
Administrative overheads (20% × £6750)	1350
Total cost	8100
Profit (£8100/0.90 − £8100)	900
Selling price	9000

Workings
Administration overhead absorption rate = Total admin. overheads/total factory cost
= £328 000/£1 640 000
= 20% of factory cost

(e) The general characteristics of incentive schemes should ensure that:
  (i) the scheme is simple to understand and administer;
  (ii) payment should be made as quickly as possible after production;
  (iii) there should be no limit on earnings and employees must be safe-guarded from earning lower wages than time rate wages arising from problems which are outside their control.

  The advantages of incentive schemes are:
  (i) increased production and lower average unit costs;
  (ii) increased morale of the workforce;
  (iii) attraction of more efficient workers to the company.

Solution IM 3.8

(a) Predetermined machine hour rate $= \dfrac{\text{machine department overheads (£1 080 000)}}{\text{machine hours (80 000)}}$

Machining department = £13.50 per machine hour
Hand finishing department = £760 000/120 000 labour hours
= £6.33 per labour hour

(b) (i)

	Machine department (£)	Hand finishing department (£)
Overhead incurred	84 500	67 100
Overhead absorbed	81 000 (6000 × £13.50)	60 800 (9600 × £6.33)
Under recovery of overheads	3 500	6 300

  (ii) Overheads that are apportioned to cost centres tend to be on an arbitrary basis and are unlikely to be controllable by the cost centre manager. Managers should be held accountable for only those overheads that they can control. See 'Guidelines for applying the controllability principle' in Chapter 18 for a more detailed discussion of controllable and non-controllable costs.

(c) Absorption costing is used by companies to ensure that all products/services bear an equitable share of company overheads. The Statement of Standard Accounting Practice (SSAP 9) requires that stocks should be valued at full production cost. Therefore absorption costing is required to allocate overheads to products in order to meet financial accounting requirements.

Solution IM 3.9

(a) (i) Percentage of direct materials $= \dfrac{\text{production overhead}}{\text{direct materials}} \times 100$

$= \dfrac{£300\ 000}{£100\ 000} \times 100 = 300\%$

(ii) Percentage of direct wages $= \dfrac{\text{production overhead}}{\text{direct wages}} \times 100$

$= \dfrac{£300\ 000}{£50\ 000} \times 100 = 600\%$

(iii) Percentage of prime cost $= \dfrac{\text{production overhead}}{\text{prime cost}} \times 100$

$= \dfrac{£300\ 000}{£150\ 000} \times 100 = 200\%$

(iv)

$$\text{Units of output} = \frac{\text{production overhead}}{\text{units}}$$

$$= \frac{\pounds300\,000}{300} = \pounds1000 \text{ per unit}$$

(v)

$$\text{Labour hour rate} = \frac{\text{production overhead}}{\text{labour hours}}$$

$$= \frac{\pounds300\,000}{25\,000} = \pounds12 \text{ per hour}$$

(vi)

$$\text{Machine hour rate} = \frac{\text{production overhead}}{\text{machine hours}}$$

$$= \frac{\pounds300\,000}{15\,000} = \pounds12 \text{ per hour}$$

(b) The answer to this question is explained in Appendix 3.2 to Chapter 3.

(c)

	(i) Percentage of direct materials (£)	(ii) Percentage of direct wages (£)	(iii) Percentage of prime cost (£)	(iv) Units of output (£)	(v) Labour hour rate (£)	(vi) Machine hour rate (£)
Direct materials	250	250	250	250	250	250
Direct wages	200	200	200	200	200	200
Prime cost	450	450	450	450	450	450
Production overhead	750^a	1200^b	900^c	1000^d	960^e	1000^f
Total cost	1200	1650	1350	1450	1410	1450

Notes
^{a}£250 × 300%
^{b}£200 × 600%
^{c}£450 × 200%
^{d}1 unit of output at £1000
^{e}80 direct labour hours at £12 per hour
^{f}50 machine hours at £20 per hour

(a) In order to ascertain the actual overhead traced to the production departments, it is necessary to allocate the service department overheads to the filling and sealing departments:

Solution IM 3.10

	Filling (£)		Sealing (£)		Maintenance (£)		Canteen (£)	
Allocated	74 260		38 115		25 050		24 375	
Reallocation of:								
Canteen	14 625	(60%)	7 800	(32%)	1 950	(8%)	(24 375)	
Maintenance	18 900	(70%)	7 290	(27%)	(27 000)		810	(3%)
Canteen	486	(60%)	259	(32%)	65	(8%)	(810)	
Maintenance	47	(70/97)	18	(27/97)	–		–	
	108 318		53 482					

Predetermined overhead rates:

	Filling (£)	Sealing (£)
Budgeted overheads	110 040	53 300
Budgeted direct labour hours	13 100	10 250
Direct labour hour overhead rate	8.40	5.20
Overhead incurred	108 318	53 482
Overhead allocated	107 688 (12 820 × £8.40)	52 390 (10 075 × £5.20)
(Under)/over recovery	(630)	(1 092)

(b) The objectives of overhead apportionment and absorption are:

(i) To meet the stock valuation and profit measurement requirements for financial accounting purposes. Financial accounting regulations in most countries require that all manufacturing overheads be traced to products for stock valuation purposes.

(ii) For various decisions, such as pricing decisions, management require estimates of the total product costs.

(iii) Overhead costs may be traced to different segments of the business, such as product groups or geographical regions, in order to assess the performance of each segment.

Overhead apportionment and absorption can be criticized on the following grounds:

(i) The process includes many arbitrary apportionments and does not provide an accurate indication of the resources consumed by each product. In tracing overheads to products, the allocation procedure assumes that all overheads are related to volume. This is inappropriate for many fixed overheads, since they are fixed in the short term, and tend to be caused by factors other than volume, such as the diversity of the product range, number of set-ups and range of component parts which the firm stocks.

(ii) Fixed overheads are sunk costs, and will tend not to change in the short term. Hence they are unaffected in the short term, irrespective of which decisions are taken. Arbitrary overhead allocations should not be used for decision-making purposes.

(iii) Overhead allocations are normally undertaken for stock valuation purposes. The procedures are not intended to meet other requirements, such as decision-making and performance evaluation.

(iv) Individuals should not be held accountable for costs which they cannot control. Arbitrary apportionment of overheads is therefore inappropriate for cost control and performance measurement purposes.

Solution IM 3.11

(a) (i) An over-absorption of overheads occurs because the actual overhead charged to products (or clients) exceeds the overheads incurred. Therefore £747 360 (£742 600 actual overheads + £4760 over-absorption were charged to clients during direct hours worked, the actual professional staff hours worked during the period were 99 648 (£747 360/£7.50 hourly overhead rate). Therefore budgeted professional staff hours = 98 288 (99 648 − 1360).

(ii) Budgeted overhead expenditure

= Budgeted hours (98 288) × Overhead rate (£7.50)

= £737 160

(b) To determine the overhead rate the senior staff hours should be weighted by a factor of 1.4 and the junior staff hours by a factor of 1.0:

Senior staff = 21 600 × 1.4 = 30 240
Junior staff = 79 300 × 1.0 = 79 300
109 540

Allocation of overheads:
Senior staff = 30 240/109 540 × £784 000 = £216 434
Junior staff = 79 300/109 540 × £784 000 = £567 566
$$\overline{£784\ 000}$$

Senior staff overhead allocation rate = £216 434/21 600
    = £10.020 per hour
Junior staff overhear allocation rate = £567 566/79 300 hours
    = £7.157 per hour

(c) Presumably the senior staff consume a greater proportion of the overhead costs than the junior staff and the revised method is an attempt to reflect this difference in resource consumption. For example, senior staff are likely to require more office space and make greater demands on secretarial time, telephones, etc. The revised method creates two separate cost centres and overhead rates whereas the previous the method used a single blanket rate for the whole organization.

(d) See the section on under- and over-recovery of overheads in Chapter 3 for the answer to this question. Differences between overhead incurred and overhead absorbed may be due to:
(1) differences between actual and budgeted expenditure;
(2) differences between actual and budgeted activity level.

(i) With the step-wise method the costs of the first service department (Department **Solution IM 3.12** G specified in the question) are reapportioned to the second department but return allocations are not made from the second department back to the first department.

	Production depts			Internal services	
	1	2		G	H
	(£000)	(£000)		(£000)	(£000)
Overheads	870	690	Costs	160	82
G apportioned	96 (60%)	48 (30%)		−160	16 (10%)
					98
H apportioned	61 ($^{50}/_{80}$)	37 ($^{30}/_{80}$)			−98
	1027	775			

(ii) Let G = Service Department G overheads
Let H = Service Department H overheads

$$G = 160 + 0.2H$$
$$H = 82 + 0.1G$$

Rearranging the above equations

$$-0.2H + G = 160 \qquad (1)$$
$$1H - 0.1\,G = 82 \qquad (2)$$

Multiply equation (1) by 1 and equation (2) by 10

$$-0.2H + G = 160$$
$$10H - G = 820$$

Add the above equations together:

$$9.8H = 980$$
$$H = 100$$

Substituting for the value of H in equation (1)

$$-0.2\,(100) + G = 160$$
$$G = 180$$

		Production depts		
Internal Services	Total (£000)		1 (£000)		2 (£000)
G (180 × 90%)	162	$(\frac{6}{9})$	108	$(\frac{3}{9})$	54
H (100 × 80%)	80	$(\frac{5}{8})$	50	$(\frac{3}{8})$	30
	242		158		84
Overheads (given)			870		690
			1028		774

(iii) The simultaneous equation method will yield more accurate allocations because it takes into account the fact that service departments serve each other whereas the step-wise method ignores such reciprocal usage. The step-wise method involves simpler computations and, in this question, does not give a significantly different answer. However, the step-wise method may yield inaccurate results where service costs are high and there are more than two service departments with significantly different usage ratios between the departments.

Solution IM 3.13

(a)

	General factory overhead (£)	Service cost centres		Production cost centres	
		1 (£)	2 (£)	A (£)	B (£)
Primary allocation	210 000	93 800	38 600	182 800	124 800
Apportionment of general factory overhead [a]	(210 000)	10 500	21 000	31 500	147 000
	—	104 300	59 600	214 300	271 800
Charges by service cost centre 1 [b]		(104 300)	—	91 262	13 038
		—	59 600	305 562	284 838
Charges by service cost centre 2 [c]			(59 600)	8 221	51 379
			—	£313 783	£336 217
Budgeted direct labour hours				120 000	20 000
Absorption rates				£2.61	£16.81

Notes
[a] General factory overhead is apportioned to service cost centres before reallocation to production centres as indicated in note (i) of the question.
[b] Because reciprocal allocations are not made, the costs allocated to service cost centre 1 are reallocated as follows:

£91 262 (63/72 × £104 300) to production cost centre A
£13 038 (9/72 × £104 300) to production cost centre B

[c] Reciprocal charges are not made. Therefore the allocation is as follows:

4 000/29 000 × £59 600 = £8 221 to production cost centre A
25 000/29 000 × £59 600 = £51 379 to production cost centre B

(b) The difference may be due to the following:
(i) Changes occurred in projected overhead expenditure compared with expenditure which was used to determine the current year's overhead rate.
(ii) Current overhead rates do not include a proportion of the service cost centres overhead.

(iii) Budgeted activity for the next year is greater than the current year for production cost centre A. If this is not matched by a corresponding increase in overhead expenditure then the hourly overhead rate will decline. Budgeted activity for production cost centre B is lower than the current year, resulting in an increase in the overhead rate. Because fixed overheads do not change in relation to activity, the hourly overhead rate will fluctuate whenever changes in activity occur. (See Example 3.2 in Chapter 3 for an illustration.)

(c) This question can be answered by using either the repeated distribution or simultaneous equation methods. Both methods are illustrated in Appendix 3.1 to Chapter 3. The simultaneous equation method is illustrated below:

Let X = total overhead of service cost centre 1
Y = total overhead of service cost centre 2

Then
$X = 104\,300 + \frac{1}{30}Y$ (i.e. 1000/30 000 hrs of service cost centre 2 overheads)
$Y = 59\,600 + \frac{1}{5}X$ (i.e. 18% out of total of 90% of service cost centre 1 overheads)

Rearranging the above equations:
$$X - \tfrac{1}{30}Y = 104\,300 \qquad (1)$$
$$-\tfrac{1}{5}X + Y = 59\,600 \qquad (2)$$

Multiply equation (1) by 1 and equation (2) by 5:
$$X - \tfrac{1}{30}Y = 104\,300$$
$$-X + 5Y = 298\,000$$

Adding the above equations together:
$$\frac{149}{30}Y = 402\,300$$
$$Y = \frac{402\,300 \times 30}{149}$$
$$Y = 81\,000$$

Substituting for Y in equation (1) results in the following equation:
$$X - \tfrac{1}{30} \times 81\,000 = 104\,300$$
$$X = 107\,000$$

The service cost centre overheads of £107 000 (service cost centre 1) and £81 000 (service cost centre 2) are now apportioned to the production cost centres as follows:

	General factory overhead (£)	Service cost centre 1 (£)	Service cost centre 2 (£)	Production cost centre A (£)	Production cost centre B (£)
Primary allocation	210 000	93 800	38 600	182 800	124 800
Apportionment of general factory overhead	(210 000)	10 500	21 000	31 500	147 000
	—	104 300	59 600	214 300	271 800
Charges by service cost centre 1 [a]		(107 000)	21 400	74 900	10 700
Charges by service cost centre 2 [b]		2 700	(81 000)	10 800	67 500
		—	—	£300 000	£350 000
Budgeted direct labour hours				120 000	20 000
Absorption rates				£2.50	£17.50

Notes
^{a} 18/90 × £107 000 = £21 400 to service cost centre 2 (18% out of 90%)
  63/90 × £107 000 = £74 900 to production cost centre A
   9/90 × £107 000 = £10 700 to production cost centre B
^{b} 1000/30 000 × £81 000 = £2700 to service cost centre 1
   4000/30 000 × £81 000 = £10 800 to production cost centre A
  25 000/30 000 × £81 000 = £67 500 to production cost centre B

(d) The answer should include the following points:
  (i) The overhead rate calculations do not distinguish between fixed and variable elements. Such an analysis is necessary for decision-making purposes.
  (ii) The majority of service cost centre 1 costs are variable. It is preferable to determine an activity measure which exerts most influence on the variable costs and apportion the costs on the basis of this measure. The present method of apportionment appears to be inappropriate.
  (iii) Service cost centre 2 is the maintenance department and the majority of costs are fixed, thus suggesting preventive maintenance be undertaken. The question does not make it clear which hourly base is used for allocating overheads (direct labour hours or machine hours). Machine hours should be used for allocating variable costs, since these costs are likely to vary with this activity base. Preventive maintenance should be apportioned on the basis of the planned hours which the maintenance staff intend to allocate to each department.
  (iv) Production cost centre B is highly mechanized, thus suggesting that a machine hour rate might be preferable to the present direct labour hour rate.

Solution IM 3.14   (a)   *Department cost statement*

	Belts (£000)	Braces (£000)	Administration (£000)	Maintenance (£000)	Warehousing (£000)	Total (£000)
Direct variable costs:						
Materials	120	130	—	20	30	300
Labour	80	70	50	80	20	300
	200	200	50	100	50	600
Factory-wide indirect cost per floorspace	400	400	50	100	50	1000
	600	600	100	200	100	1600
Service departments						
Administration ^{a}	40	40	(100)	10	10	—
	640	640	—	210	110	1600
Maintenance ^{b}	79	79	—	(264)	106	—
Warehousing ^{b}	108	54	—	54	(216)	—
	£827	£773	—	—	—	£1600

Cost per unit: Belts $\dfrac{£827\,000}{100\,000} = £8.27$

               Braces $\dfrac{£773\,000}{50\,000} = £15.46$

Notes
^{a} Administration does not receive any charges from the other service departments. Therefore the reciprocal basis does not apply.
^{b} The simultaneous equation method is used to allocate the maintenance and warehouse costs.

Let M = total cost of the maintenance department
          W = total cost of the warehousing department

Then $M = 210 + 0.25W$ (1)
          $W = 110 + 0.4M$ (2)

Multiplying equation (1) by 4 and equation (2) by 1, and rearranging the resulting equations:

$$4M - W = 840$$
$$-0.4M + W = 110$$
$$3.6M = 950$$
$$M = £263.89$$

Substituting the value of M into equation (2):

$$W = 110 + 0.4 \times 263.89$$
$$W = £215.56$$

(b) Kaminsky Ltd has spare capacity, and therefore any sales revenue in excess of variable costs will provide a contribution towards fixed costs and profit. Therefore it is necessary to calculate the variable cost per unit for belts and braces. The calculations of the unit variable cost are as follows:

	Belts (£000)	Braces (£000)	Administration (£000)	Maintenance (£000)	Warehousing (£000)	Total (£000)
Direct variable costs:						
Materials	120	130	—	20	30	300
Labour	80	70	50	80	20	300
	200	200	50	100	50	600
Service departments						
Administration	20	20	(50)	5	5	—
	220	220	—	105	55	600
Maintenance[a]	39.6	39.6	—	(132)	52.8	—
Warehousing[a]	53.9	26.9	—	26.95	(107.8)	—
	313.5	286.5	—	—	—	600

Variable cost per unit: Belts $\dfrac{£313\ 500}{100\ 000} = £3.135$

Braces $\dfrac{£286\ 500}{50\ 000} = £5.73$

Note
[a] The simultaneous equation method is used to allocate the service department costs as follows:

Let M = maintenance department variable costs
          W = warehousing department variable costs

Then $M = 105 + 0.25W$ (1)
          $W = 55 + 0.4M$ (2)

Multiplying equation (1) by 4 and equation (2) by 1:

$$4M - W = 420$$
$$-0.4M + W = 55$$
$$3.6M = 475$$
$$M = 131.94$$

Substituting in equation (2):

$$W = 55 + 0.4 \times 131.94$$
$$W = 107.8$$

Camfan order

	(£)
Contract price	5000
Variable costs (1000 belts at £3.135)	3135
Contribution	1865

If this order is accepted, profits will increase by £1865, provided that better opportunities are not available and the normal selling price will not be affected. It is unlikely that such a small order will affect the normal selling price.

Mixon Spenders contract

The normal unit cost based on a normal activity of 100 000 belts is £8.27. If this unit cost is used as the basis for determining the 'cost-plus' selling price then the agreed selling price will be £9.10 (£8.27 + 10%). The normal selling price will be £9.92 (£8.27 + 20%). The contribution from supplying 100 000 belts will be £596 500 [(£9.10 − £3.135 variable cost) × 100 000]. Total demand will now be 200 000 belts, but maximum output is 150 000 belts. Therefore existing sales will be reduced by 50 000 belts. The lost contribution is £339 250 [50 000 × (£9.92 − £3.135)]. Consequently total contribution will increase by £257 250.

Alternatively, Kaminsky might base selling price on unit costs at maximum capacity of 150 000 units. The revised unit cost will be as follows:

Fixed costs apportioned to belts	= £513 500 (£827 000 total cost − £313 500 variable cost)
Fixed costs per unit (£)	= 3.42 (£513 500/150 000 units)
Variable cost per unit (£)	= 3.135
Total cost per unit (£)	= 6.555
Selling price for contract	= £7.21 (£6.555 + 10%).

The total contribution from the contract will be £407 500, consisting of 100 000 units at a contribution per unit of £4.075 (£7.21 − £3.135). This will still cover the contribution sacrificed on existing business. On the basis of the above quantitative information, the contract should be accepted. However, before acceptance, the following qualitative factors should be considered:

(i) Will the long-term disadvantages from a loss of customer goodwill from depriving normal customers of 50 000 units outweigh the short-term advantage of taking on the contract?

(ii) An attractive feature of the contract is that it will result in certain sales of 2000 units per week, thus enabling production, cash flows etc. to be forecasted more accurately.

(c) For the answer to this question see 'alternative denominator level measures' in Chapter 7. In addition the answer should emphasize that normal overhead rates reflect a long-term planned activity base which is expected to satisfy demand levels over a series of years. Over this period, fluctuations in customer demand, seasonal and cyclical changes will be incorporated into an annual rate. A normalized overhead rate recognizes that the company's overhead cost commitment is related to the long-run demand for its products. A normalized overhead rate is preferable for pricing purposes, since the alternative of basing overhead rates on the activity for next year will result in higher selling prices when demand is low if cost-plus pricing is used. Prices should be lower when demand is depressed. A normalized overhead rate should avoid such inconsistencies.

Accounting entries for a job costing system

Solutions to Chapter 4 questions

(a) and (b)

Fixed assets

	(£000)
Balance b/f	275

Share capital

	(£000)
Balance b/f	500

Creditors control

	(£000)		(£000)
Bank	150	Stores control	525
Balance c/f	487.5	Production overhead control	47.5
		Production overhead control	26
		Production overhead control	39
	637.5		637.5
		Balance b/f	487.5

Provision for depreciation

	(£000)
Production overhead control	15

Bank

	(£000)		(£000)
Balance b/f	225	Wages control	500
Debtors	520	Production overhead control	20
		Sales overhead control	40
		Administration overhead control	25
		Creditors control	150
		Balance c/f	10
	745		745
Balance b/f	10		

Wages control

	(£000)		(£000)
Bank	500	WIP: Department A	300
Wage deductions	175	WIP: Department B	260
		Production overhead control	42.5
		Sales overhead control	47.5
		Administration overhead control	25
	675		675

Wage deductions

		(£000)
	Wages control	175

Stores control

	(£000)		(£000)
Creditors control	525	WIP: Department A	180
		WIP: Department B	192.5
		Production overhead control	65
		Balance c/f	87.5
	525		525
Balance b/f	87.5		

Production overhead control

	(£000)		(£000)
Creditors control	47.5	WIP control: Department A	110
Bank	20	WIP control: Department B	120
Stores control	65	Profit and loss	25
Wages control	42.5		
Creditors control	26		
Creditors control	39		
Provision for depreciation	15		
	255		255

WIP control: Department A

	(£000)		(£000)
Stores control	180	Finished goods control	570
Wages control	300	Balance c/f	20
Production overhead control	110		
	590		590
Balance b/f	20		

WIP control: Department B

	(£000)		(£000)
Stores control	192.5	Finished goods control	555
Wages control	260	Balance c/f	17.5
Production overhead control	120		
	572.5		572.5
Balance b/f	17.5		

Selling overhead control

	(£000)		(£000)
Bank	40	Profit and loss	87.5
Wages control	47.5		
	87.5		87.5

Administration overhead control

	(£000)		(£000)
Bank	25	Profit and loss	50
Wages control	25		
	50		50

Debtors control

	(£000)		(£000)
Sales	870	Bank	520
		Balance c/f	350
	870		870
Balance b/f	350		

Finished goods control

	(£000)		(£000)
WIP Control: Department A	570	Cost sales	700
WIP Control: Department B	555	Balance c/f	425
	1125		1125
Balance b/f	425		

Cost of sales

	(£000)		(£000)
Finished goods control	700	Profit and loss	700
	700		700

Sales

	(£000)		(£000)
Profit and loss	870	Debtors	870

(c) (i) *Profit statement for the period 1 February to 30 April*

	(£000)	(£000)
Sales		870
Cost of sales		700
Gross profit		170
Under-absorption of production overheads	25	
Selling overheads	87.5	
Administration overheads	50	162.5
Net profit		7.5

(ii) *Balance sheet as at 30 April*

	(£000)	(£000)	(£000)
Fixed assets at cost			275
Provision for depreciation			15
Written down value			260
Current assets			
Stock: Finished goods		425	
WIP: Department A	20		
WIP: Department B	17.5	37.5	
Raw materials		87.5	
		550	
Debtors		350	
Bank		10	
		910	
Current liabilities			
Creditors	487.5		
Wage deductions	175	662.5	247.5
			507.5
Financed:			
Capital			500
Profit			7.5
			507.5

Solution IM 4.2

(a)

Stores control

	(£)		(£)
Balance b/d	54 250		
Direct material purchases			
(Cost Control a/c)	216 590	Work-in-progress	197 750
		Balance c/d	73 090
	270 840		270 840
Balance b/d	73 090		

Work-in-progress control

	(£)		(£)
Balance b/d	89 100		
Stores control	197 750	Finished goods control	512 050
Direct wages	85 480		
Production overhead			
control	213 700		
		Balance c/d	73 980
	586 030		586 030
Balance b/d	73 980		

Finished goods control

	(£)		(£)
Balance b/d	42 075		
Work-in-progress	512 050	Cost of sales	493 460
		Balance c/d	60 665
	554 125		554 125
Balance b/d	60 665		

Production overhead control

	(£)		(£)
Cost Control a/c	208 220	Work-in-progress	213 700
Additional depreciation	12 500	(250% × £85 480)	
		Balance to profit and loss a/c	7020
		(Under-absorbed overhead)	
	220 720		220 720

(b) The balance on the production overhead control account represents the under-absorption of production overheads. The balance is transferred to the profit and loss account.

(c) Stocks may be valued on a variable costing basis for internal profit measurement whereas for external financial accounting stocks must be valued on an absorption costing basis. Because stocks are part of the cost of goods sold calculation, the profits will differ in the financial and cost accounts. Sometimes for decision-making it is appropriate to include imputed costs that do not involve cash outlays. Examples of imputed costs include notional costs such as the notional rent for the use of a building that is owned. The notional rent represents an opportunity cost of the rent from the alternative use of the buildings that ought to be taken into account for decision-making. Incorporating notional expenses in the cost accounts will result in the cost accounts reporting a smaller profit than the financial accounts. Items such as profit and losses on the sale of assets and debenture interest paid are not recorded in the cost accounts whereas these items are recorded in the financial accounts. Therefore the inclusion of these items in the financial accounts will result in a difference in profits between the financial and cost accounts.

(a) See the comparison between management accounting and financial accounting in **Solution IM 4.3** Chapter 1 for the answer to this question.

(b) Note that the job ledger control account shown in the question is equivalent to the work in progress control account described in Chapter 4.

Stores ledger control account

	(£000)		(£000)
Opening balance	176.0	Job ledger control A/c	
Financial ledger		(64 500 kg × £3.20)	206.4
control A/c	224.2	Production o'head control	
		A/c (Balancing figure)	24.3
		Closing blanace	169.5
	400.2		400.2

Production wages control account

	(£000)		(£000)
Financial ledger		Job ledger control A/c (75%)	147.0
control A/c	196.0	Production o'head control	
		A/c (25%)	49.0
	196.0		196.0

Production overhead control account

	(£000)		(£000)
Financial ledger		Job ledger control A/c (1)	191.1
control A/c	119.3	Under-absorbed overhead	
Stores ledger control A/c	24.3	(Balance to profit and loss	
Production wages contol		A/c)	1.5
A/c	49.0		
	192.6		192.6

Job ledger control account

	(£000)		(£000)
Opening balance	114.9	Cost of sales A/c (balancing	
Stores ledger control A/c	206.4	figure)	506.4
Production wages control		Closing balance	153.0
A/c	147.0		
Production o'head			
control A/c	191.1		
	659.4		659.4

Note:
(1) Direct labour hours $= \dfrac{\text{Direct labour wages (£147 000)}}{\text{Direct labour wage rate (£5)}} = 29\ 400$ hours

Overhead charged to production = 29 400 direct labour hours × direct labour rate (£6.50) = £191 100.

Solution IM 4.4   (a)

Raw material control account

	(£)		(£)
Opening balance	87 460	Work-in-progress (1)	194 550
Cost ledger control	200 740	Manufacturing overhead	
		control a/c (1)	6 917
		Closing balance	86 733
	288 200		288 200

Manufacturing overhead control account

	(£)		(£)
Raw material control	6 917	Opening balance	5 123
Wages control	74 887	Work-in-progress (2)	191 200
Cost ledger control	112 194		
Closing balance	2 325		
	196 323		196 323

Work-in-progress account

	(£)		(£)
Raw material control	194 550	Finished goods (3)	570 308
Wages control	186 743	Abnormal loss to profit and	
Manufacturing overhead		loss account (3)	2 185
control a/c	191 200		
	572 493		572 493

Finished goods account

	(£)		(£)
Opening balance	148 352	Production cost of sales	534 508
Work-in-progress (3)	570 308	Closing balance	184 152
	718 660		718 660

Workings
(1) Raw material:

	Material A		Material B		Indirect	Total
	(kg)	(£)	(kg)	(£)	(£)	(£)
Opening balance	18 760	52 715	4 242	29 994	4 751	87 460
Purchases	34 220	97 527	13 520	95 992	7 221	200 740
	52 980	150 242	17 762	125 986	11 972	288 200
Issues^a	35 176	99 759	13 364	94 791	6 917	201 467
Closing balance	17 804	50 483	4 398	31 195	5 055	86 733

Total direct materials issue cost = £194 550 (£99 759 + £94 791)
Total input of direct materials = 48 540 kg (35 176 + 13 364)

Notes
^aThe cost of the materials issues is calculated as follows:
 Material A = £2.836 per kg (£150 242/52 980 kg)
 Material B = £7.093 per kg (£125 986/17 762 kg)

Direct materials issued = 48 540 kg (35 176 + 13 364)
                   £194 550 (99 759 + 94 791)

(2) Overheads absorbed = 23 900 hrs at £8.00 = £191 200

(3) Calculation of cost of finished goods transfer and abnormal loss

Expected output (48 540 kg × 0.95) =   46 113 kg
Actual output   45 937 kg
                                     ─────────
Abnormal loss   176 kg
                                     ─────────

Cost per kg = £12.415 per kg (£572 493/46 113 kg)
Output = 45 937 kg at £12.415 = £570 308
Abnormal loss = 176 kg at £12.415 = £2 185

(4) Calculation of cost of sales

	(kg)	(Total £)
Opening balance	12 160	148 352
Production	45 937	570 308
	58 097	718 660
Cost of sales^a	43 210	534 508
Closing balance	14 887	184 152

Notes
^aIssue cost = £718 660/58 097 kg = £12.37
Cost of sales = 43 210 kg × £12.37 = £534 508

(b) See 'Equivalent production' in Chapter 6 for the answer to this question.

Solution IM 4.5

(a) The costs of labour turnover include:
  (i) leaving costs associated with completing the appropriate documentation and lost production if the employees cannot be immediately replaced;
  (ii) recruitment costs resulting from the advertising, selection and engagement of new staff;
  (iii) learning costs including training costs, the cost arising from lower productivity and defective work during the learning period.

(b) *Workings:*

Basic time = 40 workers × 38 hours per week for 4 weeks = 6080 hours
Overtime = Total hours (6528) − Basic time (6080) = 448 hours

		(£)
Total wages = Basic pay (6528 hours × £4)		=26 112
Overtime premium (448 hours × £1.40)		627.20
		26 739.20
Less deductions (30% × £26 739.20)		8 021.76
Net amount paid		18 717.44
Cost of productive time		
(6.528 hours − 188 hours idle time) × £4		25 360
Cost of idle time (188 hours × £4)		752

Journal entries:

	Dr	Cr
Wages control	£26 739.20	
Bank		£18 717.44
Employee deductions		8 021.76

Being analysis of gross wages for direct workers

Work in progress	£25 360.00	
Production overhead (1)	£1 379.20	
Wages control		£26 739.20

Being the allocation of gross wages for the period

Note:
(1) Production overhead = Idle time (£752) + Overtime premium (£627.20)

Solution IM 4.6

(a) *Workings*
Gross wages paid

	(£)
Direct (25 520 hours × £4.80)	122 496.00
(2120 overtime hours × £1.44)	3 052.80
	125 548.80
Indirect (4430 hours × £3.90)	17 277.00
(380 hours × £1.17)	444.60
	17 721.60

Tax and employees' national insurance

	(£)
Direct (£125 548.80 − £97 955)	27 593.80
Indirect (£17 721.60 − £13 859)	3 862.60
	31 456.40

Productive hours (7200 + 11 600 + 4400)	23 200 hours
Direct labour unproductive labour hours (25 520 − 23 200)	2 320 hours
Productive hours charged to WIP (23 200 × £4.80)	£111 360.00

Charge to production overhead

	(£)	(£)
Gross wages of indirect workers	17 721.60	
Overtime premium (direct workers)	3 052.80	
Unproductive time of direct workers (2320 × £4.80)	11 136.00	31 910.40

Wages control account

	(£)		(£)
Cash/bank (net wages):		WIP	111 360.00
Direct	97 955.00	Production overhead	31 910.40
Indirect	13 859.00		
Tax and national			
insurance	31 456.40		
	143 270.40		143 270.40

(b) The cost of the proposed piecework scheme based on the production for the current period is as follows:

	(£)
Product 1 (36 000 units × £1)	36 000.00
2 (116 000 units × £0.50)	58 000.00
3 (52 800 units × £0.40)	21 120.00
	115 120.00
Unproductive time (see note*)	6 766.67
	121 886.67

*Calculation of wages paid for unproductive time

Productive time is:

Product 1 (36 000 units/6 units per hour)	6 000 hours
2 (116 000 units/12 units per hour)	9 666.67 hours
3 (52 800 units/14.4 units per hour)	3 666.67 hours
	19 333.34 hours

Wages paid for unproductive time
(10% × 19 333.34 hours × £3.50)   £6 766.67

The direct labour cost per unit for the current scheme is:

Product 1 (7200 hours × £4.80)/36 000 units   = £0.96
2 (11 600 hours × £4.80)/116 000 units   = £0.48
3 (4400 hours × £4.80)/52 800 units   = £0.40

The current piecework rates exceed the above unit costs but the overall costs are lower with the piecework scheme because of less unproductive time and a saving in overtime. It is also likely that overhead costs will be reduced because of a reduction in overtime in respect of indirect labour.

(a)

Solution IM 4.7

Contract accounts

	1 (£)	2 (£)	3 (£)		1 (£)	2 (£)	3 (£)
Plant on site	16 000	12 000	8 000	Materials stock c/f	3 000	3 000	1 500
Materials	44 000	41 000	15 000	Cost of work not			
Wages	80 000	74 500	12 000	certified c/f	4 000	6 000	9 000
General expenses	3 000	1 800	700	Plant on site c/f	12 000	10 000	7 500
Central overheads	1 600	1 490	240	Cost of work certified			
Accrued				(balance)	136 300	112 390	18 540
expenses c/f	700	600	600				
Provision for							
faulty work c/f	10 000						
	155 300	131 390	36 540		155 300	131 390	36 540
Cost of work				Attributable sales			
certified b/f	136 300	112 390	18 540	revenue	145 433	110 000	18 540
Profit taken				Loss taken		2 390	
this period	9 133						
	145 433	112 390	18 540		145 433	112 390	18 540
Cost of work not				Accrued			
certified b/f	4 000	6 000	9 000	expenses b/f	700	600	600
Material stock b/f	3 000	3 000	1 500	Provision for			
Plant on site b/f	12 000	10 000	7 500	faulty work b/f	10 000		

Profit calculations

Contract 1: $\frac{2}{5}$ × £13 700 profit.

Contract 2: The loss to date (£112 390 − £110 000) is written off.

Contract 3: The contract is less than one-third complete. Therefore no profit is taken for the period.

(b) *Balance sheet (extracts)*

	(£)	(£)
Plant on site [a] (£12 000 + £10 000 + £7500)		29 500
Raw material stock (£3000 + £3000 + £1500)		7 500
Cost of work completed to date [b]		
(£140 300 + £118 390 + £27 540)	286 230	
Add profit taken (£9133 − £2390)	6 743	
	292 973	
Less progress payments received [c]		
(£120 000 + £88 000 + £16 000)	224 000	68 973
Accrued expenses (£10 000 + £1900)		11 900

Notes
[a] Closing value of plant on site is calculated as follows:

Contract 1 = £16 000 − (£16 000/4)
Contract 2 = £12 000 − (£4000 annual depreciation for 6 months)
Contract 3 = £ 8000 − (£2000 annual depreciation for 3 months)

[b] Note that completed work to date consists of the cost of uncertified work plus the cost of the certified work.

[c] It is assumed that cash has been received in respect of the invoiced value of work certified.

Solution IM 4.8

(a) (i) *Orders 488 and 517:*
Both orders span two accounting years and are of significant value. The should therefore be treated as long-term contracts.

Orders 518 and 519:
Both orders are of small value and short duration even though they span two accounting years. Because of the short duration it is inappropriate to apportion the profits between the accounting periods. Profit should be recognized when the orders are completed. However, if a loss is foreseen it should be charged to the first accounting period.

(ii)

Works order number	488	517	518	519	Total
	(£000)	(£000)	(£000)	(£000)	
Valuation of work done	350	30	15	5	
Total sales value	450	135	18	9	
Direct costs incurred to date	(191)	(17)	(9)	(4)	
Overhead at 40% on labour	(42)	(4)	(2)	(0.8)	
Total costs to date	(233)	(21)	(11)	(4.8)	
Costs to complete, inclusive of overheads	(66)	(99)	—	—	
Total costs to complete	(299)	(120)			
Estimated contract profit	151	15			
Recognized profit	117(1)	nil (2)	nil (3)	nil (3)	117
Total costs incurred to date	233	21	11	4.8	
Less: included in cost of sales	233	—	—	—	
WIP	nil	21	11	4.8	36.8

Notes:

(1) $\dfrac{\text{Value of work certified (£350)}}{\text{Contract price (£450)}} \times$ Estimated profit from the contract (£151).

(2) No profit is taken since the contract is at an early stage of completion.
(3) Profit to be recognized on completion.

(iii) Attributing overheads to products on the basis of direct labour is justified if the majority of overhead resources consumed by products is caused by direct labour. In today's environment direct labour has diminished in importance and it is claimed that many overhead costs are caused by factors other than direct labour (such as the number of deliveries, etc.). Using direct labour means that overheads allocated to orders will be reduced by reducing a diminishing labour content. However, the end result will be a minor reduction in direct labour costs. Those overheads that are not caused by direct labour will remain unchanged. Inaccurate product costs will also be reported.

(b) See the section on job and process costing in Chapter 2 and the introduction in Chapter 5 for the answer to this question.

Process costing

Solutions to Chapter 5 questions

(a) See section on job and process costing systems in Chapter 2 and the introduction to Chapter 5 for the answer to this problem.

Solution IM 5.1

(b) It would appear that a job costing system provides more accurate product costs because a separate cost is calculated for each job whereas with a process costing system the cost per unit is an average cost. On the other hand, a greater proportion of the costs are likely to be direct under process costing. With a job costing system, a large proportion of costs will be treated as overheads and the problem of apportioning and allocating overheads will result in inaccurate product costs. In this sense process costing might yield more accurate product costs. However, one problem with process costing is that there is a need to estimate the degree of completion of closing stocks of WIP in order to estimate equivalent units and cost per unit. If it is difficult to produce an accurate estimate of the degree of completion then the product costs will also be inaccurate. Therefore it depends on the circumstances – in some situations job costing product costs will be more accurate and in other situations process costing product costs may be more accurate.

(a) The question does not indicate the method of overhead recovery. It is assumed that overheads are to be absorbed using the direct wages percentage method.

Solution IM 5.2

Process A account

	Units	Price (£)	Amount (£)		Units	Price (£)	Amount (£)
Direct materials	6000		12 000	Normal loss (scrap			
Direct materials added			5 000	account)	300	1.5	450
Direct wages			4 000	Process B	5760	5.5	31 680
Direct expenses			800				
Production overhead			10 000				
(250% direct wages)			31 800				
Abnormal gain account	60	5.5	330				
	6060		32 130		6060		32 130

$$\text{Cost per unit} = \frac{\text{cost of production} - \text{scrap value of normal loss}}{\text{expected output}}$$

$$= \frac{£31\ 800 - £450}{5700\ \text{units}} = £5.50$$

Process B account

	Units	Price (£)	Amount (£)		Units	Price (£)	Amount (£)
Process A	5760	5.5	31 680	Normal loss (scrap			
Direct materials added			9 000	account)	576	2.0	1 152
Direct wages			6 000	Process C	5100	12.0	61 200
Direct expenses			1 680	Abnormal loss	84	12.0	1 008
Production overhead							
(250% direct wages)			15 000				
	5760		63 360		5760		63 360

$$\text{Cost per unit} = \frac{£63\,360 - £1152}{5760 - 576 \text{ units}} = £12$$

Process C account

	Units	Price (£)	Amount (£)		Units	Price (£)	Amount (£)
Process B	5100		61 200	Normal loss (scrap account)	255	4.0	1 020
Direct materials added			4 000				
Direct wages			2 000	Finished goods	4370	16.0	69 920
Direct expenses			2 260	Process D	510	8.0	4 080
Production overhead (250% direct wages)			5 000				
			74 460				
Abnormal gain	35	16.0	560				
	5135		75 020		5135		75 020

$$\text{Cost per unit} = \frac{£74\,460 - £1020 - £4080}{5100 - 255 - 510 \text{ units}} = £16$$

Process D account (by-product)

	Units	Price (£)	Amount (£)		Units	Price (£)	Amount (£)
Process C	510		4080	Normal loss (scrap account)	51	2.0	102
Direct materials added			220				
Direct wages			200	Finished goods	450	11.0	4950
Direct expenses			151	Abnormal loss	9	11.0	99
Production overhead (250% direct wages)			500				
	510		5151		510		5151

$$\text{Cost per unit} = \frac{£5151 - £102}{510 - 51 \text{ units}} = £11$$

(b)

Abnormal gain account

	Units	Price (£)	Amount (£)		Units	Price (£)	Amount (£)
Normal loss account	60	1.5	90	Process A	60		330
Normal loss account	35	4.0	140	Process C	35		560
Profit and loss account			660				
	95		890		95		890

Abnormal loss account

	Units	Price (£)	Amount (£)		Units	Price (£)	Amount (£)
Process B	84		1008	Normal loss account	84	2.0	168
Process D	9		99	Normal loss account	9	2.0	18
				Profit and loss account			921
	93		1107		93		1107

Normal loss account (income due)

	(£)		(£)
Process A normal loss	450	Abnormal gain account	90
Process B normal loss	1152	Abnormal gain account	140
Process C normal loss	1020		
Process D normal loss	102		
Abnormal loss account	168		
Abnormal loss account	18		

(a) See 'Methods of apportioning joint costs to products' and 'Limitations of joint cost allocations for decision-making' in Chapter 6 for the answer to this question. **Solution IM 5.3**

(b)

Process 1

	Units	(£)		Units	(£)
Stock – material	3000	15 000	Process 2	2800	33 600
Components stock		1 000	Normal loss	300	600
Wages		4 000			
Expenses		10 000			
Production overhead		3 000			
		33 000			
Abnormal gain	100	1 200			
	3100	34 200		3100	34 200

$$\text{Cost per unit} = \frac{£33\,000 - £600}{2700} = £12$$

Process 2

	Units	(£)		Units	(£)
Process 1	2800	33 600	Finished goods	2600	59 800
Components stock		780	Normal loss	140	700
Wages		6 000	Abnormal loss	60	1 380
Expenses		14 000			
Production overhead		7 500			
	2800	61 880		2800	61 880

$$\text{Cost per unit} = \frac{£61\,880 - £700}{2600 \text{ units}} = £23$$

Finished goods

	(£)		(£)
Balance b/f	20 000	Cost of sales	56 800
Process 2	59 800	Balance	23 000
	79 800		79 800

Normal loss/scrap

	(£)		(£)
Process 1	600	Abnormal gain (process 1)	200
Process 2	700	Cash	1100
	1300		1300

Abnormal loss

	(£)		(£)
Process 2	1380	Cash	300
		Profit and loss account	1080
	1380		1380

Abnormal gain

	(£)		(£)
Normal loss (100 × £2)	200	Process 1	1200
Profit and loss account	1000		
	1200		1200

Profit and loss account

	(£)		(£)
Abnormal loss	1080	Abnormal gain	1000

(a) Input – materials 12 000

Normal loss (5%)	600
Abnormal loss	100
Completed production	9 500
Balance (Closing WIP)	1 800

(b) *Statement of completed production and calculation of cost per unit [a]*

Cost element	Total cost (£)	Completed units	Closing WIP equiv. units	Abnormal loss[b]	Total equiv. units	Cost per unit (£)
Materials	79 800[c]	9 500	1 800	100	11 400	7.00
Labour and overhead	41 280	9 500	720	100	10 320	4.00
						11.00

Value of WIP

Materials (1800 units at £7)	12 600	
Labour and overhead (720 units at £4)	2 880	15 480
Abnormal loss (100 units at £11)		1 100
Completed units (9500 units at £11)		104 500
		121 080

Note
[a]The calculations are based on the short-cut method. For an alternative approach see Appendix to Chapter 5.
[b]It is assumed that losses are detected at the completion stage.
[c] See process account for calculation.

(c)

Mixing process account

Materials: A	6 000	48 000	Normal loss	600	—
B	4 000	24 000	Abnormal loss	100	1 100
C	2 000	7 800	Completed production	9 500	104 500
	12 000	79 800	Closing WIP	1 800	15 480
Labour and overheads		41 280			
	12 000	121 080		12 000	121 080

(d) See 'Abnormal gains' in Chapter 5 for the answer to this question

(a) See Chapter 5 for the answer to this question.

(b) The question does not specify at what point in the production process the losses are detected. It is assumed that the losses are detected at the end of the process when production is fully complete. Therefore normal losses are not charged to WIP. The input to the process is 25 000 units and the output consists of 15 000 completed units, 6000 WIP and a normal loss of 1000 units (4% × 25 000). The balance of 3000 units represents the abnormal loss.

Statement of equivalent production and calculation of cost per unit

	Cost (£)	Comp. units	Abnormal loss	Normal loss	Closing WIP	Total equiv. units	Cost per unit (£)	WIP (£)
Materials	62 000	15 000	3000	1000	6000	25 000	2.48	14 880
Labour	44 000	15 000	3000	1000	4000	23 000	1.913	7 652
Overhead	63 000	15 000	3000	1000	3000	22 000	2.8636	8 592
	169 000						7.2566	31 124

Cost of completed units (15 000 × £7.2566)	108 850	
Add normal loss (1000 ×£7.2566 − £2000 scrap value)	5 256	114 106
Abnormal loss (3000 × £7.2566)		21 770
		167 000

Process account

	Units	(£)		Units	(£)
Materials	25 000	62 000	Finished goods stock	15 000	114 106
Labour		44 000	Normal loss	1 000	2 000
Overhead		63 000	Abnormal loss	3 000	21 770
			WIP	6 000	31 124
	25 000	169 000		25 000	169 000

Abnormal loss account

	(£)		(£)
Process account	21 770	Profit and loss account	21 770

The question implies that there is no scrap value in respect of abnormal losses.

(c) See 'Normal and abnormal losses' in Chapter 5 for the answer to this question. Normal losses are assumed to be uncontrollable losses that are inherent in the production process. Abnormal losses are avoidable and controllable and the firm should investigate abnormal losses, ascertain the reason for their occurrence and take appropriate remedial action.

(a)

Production statement (units)

	Process 1	Process 2
Input:		
Opening WIP	—	2 000
Input	15 000	10 000
	15 000	12 000
Output:		
Completed units	10 000	9 500
Normal loss (5%)	750	600
Closing WIP	4 400	1 800
Abnormal (gain)/loss (balance)	(150)	100
	15 000	12 000

It is assumed that losses are detected at the completion stage. Therefore normal losses are not charged to WIP.

Process 1
Statement of equivalent production and calculation of cost per unit

	Cost (£)	Completed units	Normal loss	Abnormal gain	Closing WIP equiv. units	Total equiv. units	Cost per unit (£)
Materials	26 740	10 000	750	(150)	3520	14 120	1.8938
Labour	36 150	10 000	750	(150)	2200	12 800	2.8242
Overhead	40 635	10 000	750	(150)	1760	12 360	3.2876
	103 525						8.0056

	(£)	(£)
Value of closing WIP:		
Materials (3520 units at £1.8938)	6 666	
Labour (2200 units at £2.8242)	6 213	
Overhead (1760 units at £3.2876)	5 786	
		18 665
Cost of completed units (10 000 × £8.0056)	80 056	
Add cost of normal loss (750 × £8.0056)	6 004	
		86 060
Cost allocated to abnormal gain (150 × £8.0056)		(1 200)
		103 525

Process 2
Statement of equivalent production and calculation of cost per unit

	Opening WIP (£)	Current cost (£)	Total cost (£)	Comp. units	Normal loss	Abnormal loss	Closing WIP	Total equiv. units	Cost per unit (£)
Previous process cost	17 000[a]	86 060[b]	103 060	9500	600	100	1800	12 000	8.5883
Labour	3 200	40 000	43 200	9500	600	100	1200	11 400	3.7895
Overhead	6 000	59 700	65 700	9500	600	100	1350	11 550	5.6883
	26 200		211 960						18.0661

	(£)	(£)
Value of closing WIP:		
Previous process cost (1800 × £8.5883)	15 459	
Labour (1200 × £3.7895)	4 547	
Overhead (1350 × £5.6883)	7 679	
		27 685
Completed units (9500 × £18.0061)	171 628	
Add cost of normal loss (600 × £18.0661)	10 840	
Less sale proceeds of normal loss (600 × £8.0056)	4 803	6 037 177 665
Cost of abnormal loss (100 × £18.0661)		1 807
		207 157

Notes
[a] Total opening WIP (£26 200) − labour (£3200) − overheads (£6000).
[b] Cost of completed production transferred from Process 1.

(i)

Process 1

	Units	(£)		Units	(£)
Material	15 000	26 740	Transfer to Process 2	10 000	86 060
Labour		36 150	Closing WIP	4 400	18 665
Overheads		40 635	Normal loss	750	
Abnormal gain	150	1 200			
	15 150	104 725		15 150	104 725

(ii)

Process 2

	Units	(£)		Units	(f)
Opening WIP	2 000	26 200	Finished units	9 500	177 665
Transfer from Process 1	10 000	86 060	WIP	1 800	27 685
Labour		40 000	Normal loss	600	4 803
Overheads		59 700	Abnormal loss	100	1 807
	12 000	211 960		12 000	211 960

(iii)

Normal loss account

	Units	(£)		Units	(£)
Process 2 account	600	4803	Cash book	600	4803

(iv)

Abnormal gain/(loss) account

	(£)		(£)
Process 2 account	1807	Process 1 account	1200
		Profit and loss account	607
	1807		1807

(b) See the introduction to Chapter 6 and 'Accounting for by-products' in Chapter 6 for the answer to this question.

(a) See Chapter 5 for a description of each of the terms.
(b) See 'Normal and abnormal losses' in Chapter 5 for the answer to this question.

Solution IM 5.7

(c) *Workings*

Process 1 abnormal gain = input (9000) − (7300 completed units + 1800 normal loss)
= 100 units.
Process 2 abnormal loss = input (7300) − (4700 completed units + 2000 WIP + 530 normal loss)
= 70 units.

It is assumed that the intention of the question is that normal loss is 10% of the input which reached the final inspection stage where the inspection occurs. Therefore normal loss is 530 units [10% × (7300 input − 2000 WIP)]. The cost per unit of output for process 1 is:

$$\frac{\text{cost of production} - \text{scrap value of normal loss}}{\text{expected output}}$$

$$= \frac{£14\,964 + (2450 \times £6) - (1800 \times £1.20)}{(80\% \times 9000)}$$

$$= £3.82$$

Process 1

	Units	(£)		Units	(£)
Materials	9000	14 964	Completed units		
Conversion cost		14 700	(7300 × £3.82)	7300	27 886
Abnormal gain			Normal loss		
(100 × £3.82)	100	382	(1800 × £1.20)	1800	2 160
		30 046			30 046

Abnormal gain account

	(£)		(£)
Normal loss	120	Process 1	382
Profit and loss account	262		
	382		382

Normal loss (income due) account

	(£)		(£)
Process 1	2160	Abnormal gain (100 × £1.20)	120
Process 1	753	Cash (balance)	2793
	2913		2913

Process 2 account

	(£)		(£)
Process 1	27 886	Finished goods (W1)	24 456
Conversion cost	6 300	Normal loss (530 × £1.42)	753
		Abnormal loss (W1)	337
		Closing WIP (W1)	8 640
	34 186		34 186

Abnormal loss account

	(£)		(£)
Process 2	337	Cash (sale of £70 units at £1.42)	99
		Profit and loss account	238
	337		337

Working

(W1) The cost per unit calculation for Process 2 is as follows:

		Completed units	Normal loss	Abnormal loss	WIP equivalent units	Total equivalent units	Cost per unit	WIP value
	(£)						(£)	(£)
Previous process	27 886	4700	530	70	2000	7300	3.82	7640
Conversion cost	6 300	4700	530	70	1000	6300	1.00	1000
	34 186						4.82	8640

	(£)	(£)
Completed units (4700 × £4.82)		22 654
Share of normal loss (530 × £4.82)	2554.60	
Less sale proceeds (530 × £1.42)	752.60	1 802
Cost of completed units		24 456
Abnormal loss (70 × £4.82)		337
WIP		8 640
		33 433

Note that the cost of the input (£34 186) less the sale proceeds of the normal loss equals the cost of the output. The normal loss of £1802 ought to be apportioned between completed units and abnormal loss where this will have a significant impact on the value of completed units and abnormal loss. If this approach is adopted, the normal loss of £1802 could be apportioned as follows:

Completed units [4700/(4700 + 70)] × £1802 = £1776
Abnormal loss   [70/(4700 + 70)] × £1802 =   £26

Given that the above adjustment will only have a minor effect on the process costs, there is little point in reflecting this apportionment in the process accounts.

Statement of input and output (Kgs)

	Process 1	Process 2
Opening WIP	3000	2250
Input for the period	4000	2400
Total input	7000	4650
Transferred to next process/finished stock	2400	2500
Closing WIP	3400	2600
Normal loss (10%)	400	240
Balance – Abnormal loss/(gain)	800	(690)
	7000	4 650

Statement of completed production and calculation of cost per unit [a] *(Process 1)*

	Opening WIP	Current cost	Total cost	Completed units	Closing WIP	Abnormal loss [b]	Total equiv. units	Cost per unit
	(£)	(£)	(£)					(£)
Materials	4 400	22 000	26 400	2 400	3 400	800	6 600	4.00
Conversion cost	3 744	30 000[c]	33 744	2 400	1 360	800	4 560	7.40
			60 144					11.40

Completed production (2400 units at £11.40)		27 360
Closing WIP: Materials (3400 units at £4)	13 600	
Conversion cost (1360 units at £7.40)	10 064	23 664
Abnormal loss (800 units at £11.40)		9 120
		60 144

Statement of completed production and calculation of cost per unit[a] *(Process 2)*

	Opening WIP	Current cost	Total cost	Completed units	Closing WIP	Abnormal gain [b]	Total equiv. units	Cost per unit
	(£)	(£)	(£)					(£)
Previous process cost	4431	27 360	31 791					
Less normal loss			(480)					
(240 units at £2)			31 311	2500	2600	(690)	4410	7.10
Conversion cost	5250	37 500[c]	42 750	2500	1040	(690)	2850	15.00
			73 061					22.10

Completed production (2500 units at £22.10)		55 250
Closing WIP: Previous process cost (2600 units at £7.10)	18 460	
Conversion cost (1040 units at £15)	15 600	34 060
Abnormal gain (690 units at £22.10)		(15 249)
		74 061

Notes

[a] The calculations are based on the short-cut method. For an alternative approach see Appendix to Chapter 5.

[b] It is assumed that losses/gains are detected at the completion stage

[c] Labour cost plus overheads (150% of overhead cost)

Process 1

	(kgs)	(£)		(kgs)	(£)
WIP b/fwd	3000	8144	Normal loss	400	—
Stock control	4000	22 000	Process 2	2400	27 360
Wages control		12 000	Abnormal loss	800	9 120
Overhead control		18 000	WIP c/fwd	3400	23 664
	7000	60 144		7000	60 144

Process 2

	(kgs)	(£)		(kgs)	(£)
WIP b/fwd	2250	9 681	Normal loss	240	480
Process 1	2400	27 360	Finished goods	2500	55 250
Wages control		15 000	WIP c/fwd	2600	34 060
Overhead control		22 500			
Abnormal gain	690	15 249			
	5340	89 790		5340	89 790

Abnormal loss

	(£)	(£)	
B/fwd	1 400	Profit and loss a/c	10 520
Process 1	9 120		
	10 520		10 520

Abnormal gain

	(£)	(£)	
Normal loss	1 380	B/fwd	300
Profit and loss a/c	14 169	Process 2	15 249
	15 549		15 549

Overhead control

	(£)		(£)
Bank/expense creditors	54 000	B/fwd	250
		Process 1	18 000
		Process 2	22 500
		Profit and loss a/c	13 250
	54 000		54 000

Sales

	(£)	(£)	
Proft and loss a/c	637 000	B/fwd	585 000
		Debtors	52 000
	637 000		637 000

Finished goods

	(£)	(£)	
B/fwd	65 000	Cost of sales	60 250
Process 2	55 250	C/fwd	60 000
	120 250		120 250

Cost of sales

	(£)	(£)	
B/fwd	442 500	Profit and loss a/c	502 750
Finished goods	60 250		
	502 750		502 750

ABC plc – Profit and loss account for the year ended September

	(£)	(£)	
Cost of sales	502 750	Sales	637 000
Abnormal loss	10 520	Abnormal gain	14 169
Overhead control	13 250		
Profit	124 649		
	651 169		651 169

In the appendix to Chapter 5 it was stated that if the normal loss was of significant **Solution IM 5.9** value there are strong arguments for allocating this loss between the completed units and the abnormal loss (or abnormal gain). This is because the cost of the abnormal loss (gain) should be recorded at the cost per unit of normal output. The answer below adopts this approach but it is likely to be confusing for the student. For this question the students are likely to find the short-cut approach easier to understand. The answer using the short-cut approach is also shown below. Alternatively, lecturers may prefer to adopt the approach presented in the text and not allocate the normal loss between completed production and the abnormal gain.

Statement of cost per unit

	Completed units	Normal loss	Abnormal gain	Total equiv. units	Cost per unit
	(£)				(£)
Materials (1)	16 245	9580	500	(80)	10 000	1.6245
Labour and overheads	28 596	9580	300	(48)	9 832	2.9084
	44 841					4.5329

Note:
(1) Period cost (£16 445) less normal scrap (500 × £0.40) = £16 245

Cost of normal loss to allocate to completed production and abnormal gain:

	(£)
Materials (500 units × £1.6245)	812.25
Labour and overhead (300 units × £2.9084)	872.52

Cost of normal loss allocated to completed production:
Materials (9.580/(9.580 + (−80)) × £812.25	819.09
Labour and overhead (9.580/(9.580 + (−48)) × £872.52	876.91
	1696.00

Cost of completed production:
Completed units (9580 × £4.5329)	43 425.18
Add share of normal loss	1 696.00
	45 121.18

Valuation of abnormal gain:

	(£)
Materials (80 × £1.6245)	129.96
Labour and overhead (48 × £2.9084)	139.60
Share of normal loss:	
Materials (80/9580 + (−80)) × £812.25	6.84
Labour and overhead (48/9580 + (−48)) × £872.52	4.39
	280.79

Statement of cost per unit using the short-cut method:

	Completed units	Abnormal gain	Total equiv. units	Cost per unit
	(£)			(£)
Material	16 245	9580	(80)	9.500	1.71
Labour and overhead	28 596	9580	(48)	9.532	3.00
	44 841				4.71

		(£)
Cost of completed production (9850 × £4.71)		45 121.80
Abnormal gain:		
Materials (80 units × £1.71)		136.80
Labour and overhead (48 × £3)	144.00	280.80
Net cost		44 841.00

Process account

	(£)		(£)
Materials	16 445	Finished goods	45 121.80
Labour and overhead	28 596	Normal scrap	200.00
Abnormal gain	280.80		
	45 321.80		45 321.80

Normal loss (Income due)

	(£)		(£)
Process account	200	Abnormal gain (80 × 40p)	32
		Cash from scrap sold	
		(420 × 40p)	168
	200		200

Abnormal gain account

	(£)		(£)
Normal loss account	32	Process account	280.80
Profit and loss account	248.80		
	280.80		280.80

Solution IM 5.10   (a) (i)

Production statement

Input:	(£)
Opening WIP	21 700
Materials input	105 600
	127 300

Output:	
Completed units	92 400
Closing WIP	28 200
Normal loss (balance)	6 700
	127 300

Statement of equivalent production and calculation of cost per unit

	Opening WIP (£)	Current cost (£)	Total cost (£)	Comp. units	Closing WIP equiv. units	Normal loss	Total equiv. units	Cost per unit (£)
Materials	56 420	276 672	333 092	92 400	28 200	6 700	127 300	2.6166
Conversion cost	30 597	226 195	256 792	92 400	14 100	—	106 500	2.4112
								5.0278

Losses are detected at the start of the process and therefore should be allocated between completed units and closing WIP. No conversion costs will be incurred in respect of the units lost. The cost of the normal loss is calculated as follows:

	(£)
Materials (6700 units × £2.6166)	17 531
Less scrap value of normal loss (6700 × £0.45)	3 015
	14 516

The net cost of the normal loss relates to materials and the normal loss cost per unit of equivalent production is £0.1204 (£14 516/120 600). Therefore the cost per unit of equivalent production is:

	(£)
Materials (£2.6166 + £0.1204)	2.737
Conversion cost	2.4112
Total cost	5.1482

Alternatively, the short-cut method can be used when losses are apportioned between completed units and WIP. With this method normal losses are ignored in the calculation of equivalent units. The revised calculations are:

	Costs (£)	Completed units	WIP equiv. units	Total equiv. unit	Cost per unit (£)
Materials	330 077[a]	92 400	28 200	120 600	2.737
Conversion cost	256 792	92 400	14 100	106 500	2.4112
					5.1482

Note
[a] £333 092 total cost less scrap value of normal loss (£3015).

(a) (ii)

Production statement

Input:	(kg)
Opening WIP	21 700
Materials input	105 600
	127 300

Output:	
Completed units	92 400
Closing WIP	28 200
Normal loss (5% × 105 600)	5 280
Abnormal loss (balance)	1 420
	127 300

Statement of equivalent production and calculation of cost of completed production and WIP

	Current cost (£)	Completed units less opening WIP requirements	Normal loss equiv. units	Abnormal loss equiv. units	Closing WIP equiv. units	Total equiv. units	Cost per unit (£)
Materials	276 672	70 700	5280	1420	28 200	105 600	2.62
Conversion cost	226 195	79 380	—	—	14 100	93 480	2.4197
							5.0397

The cost of the normal loss is calculated as follows:

	(£)
Materials (5280 units × £2.62)	13 834
Less scrap value of normal loss (5 280 kg × £0.45)	2 376
	11 458

The cost of the normal loss is allocated in the ratio of equivalent production for materials between completed units, abnormal loss and closing WIP as follows:

	(£)
Completed units (70 700/100 320 × £11 458)	8 075
Abnormal loss (1 420/100 320 × £11 458)	162
Closing WIP (28 200/100 320 × £11 458)	3 221
	11 458

	(£)	(£)
Cost per equivalent unit of normal loss materials (£11 458/100 320)	0.1142	
Cost per equivalent unit of normal loss (excluding materials)	2.62	
Cost per unit (materials)	2.7342	
Cost per unit (conversion cost)	2.4197	
Total cost per unit	5.1539	
Cost of completed production:		
Opening WIP (£56 420 + £30 597)	87 017	
Materials (70 700 × £2.62)	185 234	
Conversion cost (79 380 × £2.4197)	192 076	
Share of normal loss	8 075	
		472 402
Abnormal loss:		
Materials (1 420 × £2.62)	3 720	
Share of normal loss	162	
		3 882
Closing WIP:		
Materials (28 200 × £2.62)	73 884	
Conversion cost (14 100 × £2.4197)	34 118	
Share of normal loss	3 222	111 224
		587 508

(b) *Process account*

Opening WIP:		Completed units	472 402
Materials	56 420	Abnormal loss	3 882
Conversion costs	30 597	Normal loss (sale	
		proceeds)	2 376
	87 017	Closing WIP	111 224
Input costs:			
Materials	276 672		
Conversion costs	226 195		
	589 884		589 884

(c) See introduction to Chapter 6 and 'Accounting for by-products' in Chapter 6 for the answer to this question.

(a) The answer should include an explanation of the accounting treatment of normal **Solution IM 5.11**
and abnormal losses as indicated in Chapter 5. A discussion of the alternative
treatment of losses might include the following:
   (i) The stage where the loss is assumed to occur will determine how much of
   the loss is allocated to completed production and closing WIP. If the loss is
   assumed to occur at the end of the process, it will be charged to completed
   production only.
   (ii) The normal loss may be charged to the good output only or apportioned
   between the good output and the abnormal loss.
   (iii) Losses may be valued at variable cost or absorption cost. If the loss has
   resulted in the consumption of scarce resources then a charge might be
   added to reflect the opportunity cost of the scarce capacity.

(b) (i) *Calculation of units in closing WIP*

	Units
Total input:	
Opening assembly WIP	50 000
Units added to assembly process	112 000
	162 000
Output to be accounted for (162 000 units):	
Good units completed	90 000
Spoiled units	10 000
Lost units	2 000
Closing WIP (difference)	60 000
	162 000

(ii) *Calculation of equivalent units processed*

	Total units	Components	Assembly	Finishing
Units started and finished [a]	40 000	40 000	40 000	40 000
Completion of opening WIP [a]	50 000	Nil	25 000	50 000
Spoilage [b]	10 000	10 000	10 000	10 000
Losses	2 000	2 000	2 000	Nil
Closing WIP	60 000	60 000	20 000	Nil
	162 000	112 000	97 000	100 000

Notes
[a] The opening WIP completed in this period is 50 000 units. Therefore 40 000
units out of the 90 000 completed units will be started and finished during
the period. The opening WIP will be fully completed as far as components
are concerned, so no additional equivalent units will be completed in this
period. The opening WIP for assembly is 50% complete. Therefore the
remaining 50% (i.e. 25 000 units) will be completed in this period. All the
opening work in progress will be completed in this period in the finishing
process.
[b] Spoilage is recognized at the end of the finishing process. Therefore the
10 000 spoilt units will be passed from the assembly to finishing process
and will not be considered to be spoilt until the end of the finishing
process.

(iii) *Calculation of cost per equivalent unit: assembly process*

Cost element	Current costs (£)	Completed units less opening WIP equivalent units	Spoiled units	Lost units	Closing WIP equivalent units	Total equivalent units	Cost per unit (£)
Bought in components	120 000	40 000	10 000	2000	60 000	112 000	1.071 43
Direct costs	40 000	65 000	10 000	2000	20 000	97 000	0.824 74
Overhead	40 000						1.896 17
	200 000						

		(£)
Closing WIP: Components (60 000 × £1.071 43)	64 286	
Direct costs and overheads (20 000 × £0.824 74)	16 495	80 781
Completed units plus spoiled units transferred:		
Components (50 000 × £1.071 43)	53 571	
Direct costs etc. (75 000 × £0.824 74)	61 856	
Add opening WIP (£60 000 + £25 000 + £25 000)	110 000	225 427
Lost units (2000 × £1.896 17) written off		3 792
Total assembly costs accounted for		310 000

Finishing process

Completed units transferred from assembly process: 90 000 + 10 000 = 100 000 units. Finishing process costs:

	(£)	(£)
Transferred from assembly	225 427	
Finishing costs	30 000	255 427

Completed cost per unit = £2.554 27 (£255 427/100 000 units).
  Of the 100 000 units transferred, 90 000 units are completed and 10 000 units are spoiled. Therefore

Normal loss   = 5000 units ($\frac{1}{18}$ × 90 000)
Abnormal loss = 5000 units (balance)

The costs of £255 427 can be analysed as follows:

Completed units = £242 656 (95 000 × £2.554 27)
Abnormal loss   = £12 771 (5000 × £2.554 27)

Note that the normal loss is charged to the completed units.

Solution IM 5.12

(a) The closing stock valuation for October which is given in the question does not distinguish between materials and conversion cost. It is therefore necessary to prepare the following statement for October:

October cost schedule (weighted average basis)

	Total cost (£)	Completed units	Closing WIP equivalent units	Total equivalent units	Cost per unit (£)	WIP value (£)
Materials	58 500	2400	1500	3900	15.00	22 500
Conversion cost	99 000	2400	1200	3600	27.50	33 000
					42.50	55 500

November cost schedule (weighted average basis)

	Opening WIP (£)	Current cost (£)	Total cost (£)	Completed units	Closing WIP equivalent units	Total equivalent units	Cost per unit (£)	WIP value (£)
Materials	22 500	48 600	71 100	2400	1800	4200	16.9286	30 471
Conversion cost	33 000	84 000	117 000	2400	900	3300	35.4545	31 909
							52.3831	62 380

November cost schedule (FIFO basis)

	Current cost (£)	Completed units less opening WIP equivalent units	Closing WIP equivalent units	Current total equivalent units	Cost per unit (£)	WIP value (£)
Materials	48 600	900	1800	2700	18	32 400
Conversion cost	84 000	1200	900	2100	40	36 000
					58	68 400

Profit statements

	Weighted average (£)	(£)	FIFO (£)	(£)
Sales revenue		120 000		120 000
Opening WIP	55 500		55 500	
Variable costs	69 600		69 600	
Fixed costs	63 000		63 000	
	188 100		188 100	
Closing WIP	62 380		68 400	
Cost of sales		125 720		119 700
Profit/(loss)		(5 720)		300

(b) The difference in profits is due entirely to the difference between the average cost and FIFO stock valuations. Unit costs increased from £42.50 in October to £58 in November. With the average cost method, the stock valuation is based on both October and November costs. This is because the opening WIP value for November is merged with the current costs to calculate the average cost per unit. With the FIFO method, the cost per unit is based entirely on November costs. The closing WIP is assumed to come from the new units which have been started during the period.

(c) 1. *Use of standard costs*: The statement is correct. Standard costs per equivalent unit produced would be used to value stocks, and costs per unit would be the same each period (except for where standards are periodically changed). Consequently standard cost per equivalent unit for the opening WIP would be identical to the standard cost per equivalent unit for the current period, and the two alternative methods of allocating opening WIP to the current period would result in the calculation of identical unit costs. The use of standard costs would also provide useful information for cost control purposes. Periodic comparisons of actual and standard performance could be made to determine whether the process was running efficiently. The standard costing system should pinpoint costs which may be out of control. It is necessary to ensure that standards set are attainable and that variances are not a result of unreasonable standards.

2. *Use of current costs*: If current costs are used for stock valuation purposes, it will be necessary to adjust this valuation for financial accounting purposes. Therefore using current costs is likely to involve additional work. In addition, profit will be affected by temporary price changes.

   The comparison of actual costs with standard costs can be inappropriate when costs change frequently throughout the year. The standard cost is likely to represent an average target cost for the year. If costs increase rapidly throughout the year then favourable variances will arise in the early part of the year and these variances will be compensated by adverse variances in the later part of the year. A possible solution is to change the standards each month or to separate the variances into their planning and operational elements (see 'Criticisms of standard costing variance analysis' in Chapter 19 for a discussion of planning and operating variances).

3. *Use of direct cost valuation*: Variable costing is preferable to absorption costing for managerial purposes. Monthly profit is a function of sales with a variable

costing system, whereas monthly profit will be a function of sales and production with an absorption costing system. Managers might also be motivated to increase stocks in order to reduce the amount of fixed overheads allocated to an accounting period. For a more detailed discussion of the advantages of variable costing see 'Some arguments in favour of variable costing' in Chapter 7. The disadvantage of variable costing is that the control of fixed costs might be ignored.

If a variable costing system is used, it will be necessary to convert the stock valuation to an absorption costing basis for financial accounting. Note that if a variable costing system is used, a decision will still have to be made whether to use the FIFO or the weighted average stock valuations.

4. *Use of cash flow reports*: It is important that profit statements be prepared at frequent intervals for control purposes. Annual profit statements are inadequate for control purposes. If stock levels change significantly during a period, cash flow statements will not provide an indication of profit and production performance for the period. Management should receive periodic profit statements and cash flow statements. It is important that both cash flows and profits be monitored at frequent intervals.

Joint and by-product costing

Solutions to Chapter 6 questions

(a) See Chapter 6 for the answer to this question.

(b) The answer should stress that joint cost apportionment should not be used for decision-making purposes. The sole purpose of joint cost apportionments is to value closing stock at the end of each accounting period in order to determine profit. If all production for the period were sold, the problem of joint cost apportionment would not exist. The two main methods of apportioning joint costs are the physical measures method and the sales value method. The sales value method is recommended. For an explanation of why this method is recommended see Chapter 6.

(c) See 'Opening and closing work in progress' in Chapter 5 for the answer to this question.

(a) See Chapter 6 for the answer to this question.

(b) (i) It is rational to undertake a common process if the total revenue from the sale of the products from the joint process exceeds the joint costs plus further processing costs of those products which are further processed. Consider the following example.

A joint process costs £600, and joint products A, B and C emerge. The further processing costs and sales revenue from the finished products are as follows:

Product	Additional finishing costs (£)	Sales revenue from finished product (£)
A	300	600
B	400	800
C	500	1000
	1200	2400

In the above example total revenue (£2400) is greater than joint costs (£600) plus the additional costs of processing (£1200). Therefore it is rational to undertake the joint process.

(ii) It is rational to 'finish off' each of the products from the joint process if the additional revenues from further processing exceed the additional costs of further processing. For an illustration of this statement see Example 6.3 in Chapter 6.

Solution IM 6.3 For the answer to this question see 'Methods of allocating joint costs to products' and 'Limitations of joint cost allocations for decision-making' in Chapter 6.

Solution IM 6.4 (a) *Statement of input and output (litres)*

Input		Output	
Opening WIP	5 000	Joint product X	30 000
Transferred from process 1	65 000	Joint product Y	25 000
		By-product Z	7 000
		Normal loss (5% × 65 000)	3 250
		Closing WIP	6 000
			71 250
		Difference = Abnormal gain	(1 250)
	70 000		70 000

In Chapter 6 it was pointed out the by-products should not be charged with any portion of the joint costs that are incurred before the split-off point. Therefore the completed production for calculating the cost per unit of the joint process consists of 55 000 litres for X and Y and excludes the output of the by-product. It was also pointed out in Chapter 6 that by-product net revenues (the sales revenue of the by-product less the additional further processing costs after split-off point) should be deducted from the cost of the joint production process.

In order to simplify the answer the short-cut method is used. Also note that the opening WIP value of £60 000 is not analysed by the elements of cost. The question can therefore only be answered using the FIFO method. It is assumed that losses and gains consist of fully complete units.

Statement of cost per unit:

Cost element	Current period cost (£)	Completed units less opening WIP equivalent units	Abnormal gain	Closing WIP equivalent units	Current total equivalent units	Cost per unit (£)
Previous process cost[1]	547 500	50 000	(1250)	6000	54 750	10.00
Conversion cost	221 400	53 000	(1250)	3600	55 350	4.00
	768 900					14.00

		(£)	(£)
Completed production:			
Opening WIP		60 000	
Previous process cost (50 000 × £10)		500 000	
Conversion cost (53 000 × £4)		212 000	772 000
Closing WIP			
Previous process cost (6000 × £10)		60 000	
Conversion cost (3600 × £4)		14 400	74 400
Abnormal gain (1250 × £14)			(17 500)
			828 900

Note:

(1) Previous process cost = £578 500 − by-product net revenue (7000 × £3.50) − Scrap value of normal loss (3250 × £2)

It is assumed that joint costs are to be allocated on the basis of net realizable value at split-off point:

	(£)
Paint X (30 000 × (£15 − £0.50) =	435 000
Paint Y (25 000 × (£18 − £2)) =	400 000
	835 000

Allocated to Paint X (£435/£835 × £772 000) = £402 180
Allocated to Paint Y (£400/£835 × £772 000) = £369 820

Process 2 account, October 1997

	(litres)	(£)		(litres)	(£)
Opening WIP	5 000	60 000	Normal loss	3 250	6 500
Process 1	65 000	578 500	Paint X	30 000	402 180
Direct labour		101 400	Paint Y	25 000	369 820
Variable overhead		80 000	By-product Z	7 000	24 500
Fixed overhead		40 000	Closing WIP	6 000	74 400
Abnormal gain	1 250	17 500			
	71 250	877 400		71 250	877 400

(b) To help you understand the answer the normal loss account is also shown below:

Normal loss (income due)

	(£)		(£)
Process 2 account	6500	Abnormal gain (1250 × £2)	2500
		Cash from scrap sold	
		(2000 × £2)	4000
	6500		6500

Abnormal gain account:

	(£)		(£)
Normal loss account	2 500	Process 2 Account	17 500
Profit and loss account	15 000		
	17 500		17 500

(c) See the section on methods of allocating joint costs to joint products for the answer to this question.

Solution IM 6.5

(a)

Product	Sales value (£000)	Costs beyond split-off point (£000)	Net sales value (£000)	Proportion of total (%)	Joint costs apportioned (£000)
Q	768	160	608	62.30	456
R	232	128	104	10.65	78
S	32	—	32	3.28	24
T	240	8	232	23.77	174
	1272	296	976		732

Budgeted product profitability statement

	Q (£000)	R (£000)	S (£000)	T (£000)	Total (£000)
Sales	768	232	32	240	1272
Joint process costs	(456)	(78)	(24)	(174)	(732)
Further processing costs	(160)	(128)		(8)	(296)
Profit	152	26	8	58	244

(b)	Q	R	S	T	Total
Sales	512	144	32	180	868
Joint process costs	(456)	(78)	(24)	(174)	(732)
Profit	56	66	8	6	136

(c)

	Q (£000)	R (£000)	T (£000)
Incremental revenue from further processing	256 (768 − 512)	88 (232 − 144)	60 (240 − 180)
Additional processing costs	160	128	8
Incremental net revenue	96	(40)	52

Product R should be sold at split-off point, since the additional further processing costs exceed the incremental revenues. The overall profit will therefore rise from £244 000 to £284 000.

Solution IM 6.6 (a)

Process 1 account

	Litres	CPU (£)	(£)		Litres	CPU (£)	(£)
Direct materials	80 000	1.25	100 000	Normal loss	8 000	0.50	4 000
Direct wages			48 000	Output A	22 000	2.50	55 000
Production overhead			36 000	B	20 000	2.50	50 000
(75% of direct				C	10 000	2.50	25 000
wages)				D	18 000	2.50	45 000
				Abnormal			
				loss	2 000	2.50	5 000
	80 000		184 000		80 000		184 000

$$\text{Cost per unit} = \frac{£184\,000 - £4000}{72\,000 \text{ litres}} = £2.50 \text{ per litre}$$

Profit and loss statement

	A	B	C	D	Total
Sales (litres)	22 000	20 000	10 000	18 000	
Selling price per litre (£)	4	3	2	5	
Sales (£000)	88	60	20	90	
Joint cost apportionment from Process A (£000)	(55)	(50)	(25)	(45)	
Post separation costs: direct wages + overhead (£000)	(21)	(14)	(7)	(28)	
Profit/(loss)	12	(4)	(12)	17	13

Note that the profit will be reduced by the £5000 abnormal loss.

(b) Profit from the present output can be maximized by further processing only those products whose incremental revenues exceed the incremental costs.

	A	B	C	D	Total
Incremental revenue per litre (£)	1.50	0.20	0.80	2.00	
Output (litres)	22 000	20 000	10 000	18 000	
Incremental revenue (£000)	33	4	8	36	
Incremental costs of further processing (£000)	(21)	(14)	(7)	(28)	
Contribution to joint costs	12	(10)	1	8	11

Product B should not be subject to further processing, since it yields £10 000 negative contribution. It is assumed that overheads and direct labour are avoidable costs. If the overheads are fixed costs (i.e. not avoidable costs) and the direct wages are avoidable costs, it is still not worthwhile further processing product B.

Revised profit statement

	A	B	C	D	Total
Sales (£000)	88	56	20	90	
Post separation costs (£000)	21	—	7	28	
Contribution to joint costs (£000)	67	56	13	62	198
Less joint costs (£000)					175
Revised profit (£000)					23

Note the above profit will be reduced by the £5000 abnormal loss.

(c) Product B should not be processed beyond process 1, and the abnormal loss should be investigated. Product C makes a loss, but an alternative apportionment method (e.g. the sales value method) might indicate that it makes a profit. The important point to note is that the process as a whole yields a profit. If product C were abandoned, the common and unavoidable joint costs would still continue, but the company would lose the sales revenue of £20 000.

(a) The diagram shown in Figure Q6.7 illustrates the production process. The relevant costs and revenues over the two-year period are:

Solution IM 6.7

	Without further processing (£000)	With further processing (£000)
Sales	1200	3720
Transport costs	(148)	—
Variable costs		(1200)
Annual fixed costs		(74)
Transport and vats		(200)
Excess of relevant revenues over relevant costs	1052	2246

Further processing increases profits by £1 194 000, or £597 000 per annum.

(b) (i)

	D (£000)	C (£000)	Total (£000)
Sales	10 400	600	
Variable costs	(1 560)	—	
Fixed costs	(177)	(74)	
Net realizable value	8 663	526	9189
Less joint costs[a]	(8 155)	(495)	(8650)
Plant administration costs[a]	(89)	(6)	(95)
	419	25	444

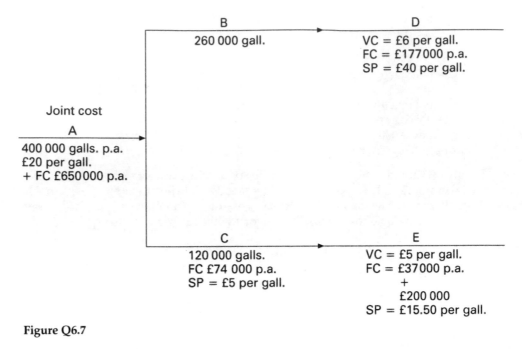

Figure Q6.7

(ii)		D (£000)	E (£000)	Total (£000)
	Sales	10 400	1860	
	Variable costs	(1 560)	(600)	
	Fixed production costs	(177)	(37)	
	Depreciation[b]		(100)	
	Net realizable value	8 663	1123	9786
	Less joint costs[a]	(7 657)	(993)	(8650)
	Plant administration costs[a]	(84)	(11)	(95)
		922	119	1041

Notes
[a] Several alternatives may be used to apportion joint costs. In this answer joint costs are apportioned in proportion to net realizable values. (See 'Sales value method' in Chapter 6 for an explanation of why this method is preferred.)
[b] Transport and vats are written off on a straight-line basis over a period of two years.

The layout of the above statements emphasizes the benefit each joint product contributes to joint costs. The joint product contributions (i.e. net realizable values) can be used for performance evaluation because they do not include unavoidable non-controllable joint costs.

(c) Assuming that the projected costs for 2001 and 2002 are appropriate for 2000 and joint costs are apportioned on the basis of net realizable values, the stock valuations are:
  (i) Stock of C = (10/120) × (£495 000 + £6000) = £41 750
     Note that the £74 000 transport costs are non-manufacturing costs, and therefore are not included in the stock valuation.
  (ii) Stock of E = (10/120) × (£737 000 + £1 004 000) = £145 083
(d) It is necessary to adjust the joint costs and the apportionment of joint costs in order to calculate the revised stock valuation. The revised calculation is:

	(£000)
Original joint cost calculation	8 650
Add replacement cost adjustment for material A (0.25 × £8000)	2 000
Plant administration costs	95
	10 745
Costs apportioned to E [(£1123/£9786) × £10 745]	1 233
Add further processing costs of E	737
Total cost of E	1 970

Stock valuation = (10/120) × £1 970 000 = £164 167

Replacement cost stock valuation is preferred because it provides a better approximation of the value of the stock to the business than historic cost valuations.

(a) *Preliminary calculations*

Solution IM 6.8

	A	B	Z	Total
Production of separable products (tonnes)	3600	4000	380	
Evaporation beyond split-off point (%)	10	20	5	
Yield after evaporation (%)	90	80	95	
Yield from joint process (tonnes)	4000	5000	400	9 400
Input to joint process (tonnes)				10 000

Therefore the yield from joint distillation is 94%
The cost of the joint distillation process is as follows:

		(£)	(£)
10 000 tonnes at £5 variable cost		50 000	
Fixed cost		5 000	
			55 000
Less by-product Z sales: 380 tonnes at £5		1 900	
Less variable cost 400 tonnes at £1	400		
Fixed cost	500		
		900	
			1 000
			54 000

We now apportion the above costs to joint products using an acceptable basis of apportionment. Either units produced or net realizable value at split-off point can be used. In order to simplify the calculations, the joint costs are apportioned on a units-produced basis. The calculations of the unit costs for products A and B and the profit for the year are:

	A	B	Total
	(£)	(£)	(£)
Joint costs	24 000 [(4000/9000) × £54 000]	30 000 [(5000/9000) × £54 000]	
Added variable cost	44 000 (4000 × £11)	10 000 (5000 × £2)	
Fixed cost	4 000	8 000	
	72 000	48 000	
Sales	86 400 (3600 × £24)	58 000 (4000 × £14.50)	
Profit	14 400	10 000	24 400
Cost per unit	£20 (£72 000/3600)	£12 (£48 000/4000)	
	(a) (i)	(a) (i)	(a) (ii)

(b)

	A	B	Z	Total
Revised yield from joint process (tonnes) (previous yield less 10%)	3600 (0.9 × 4000)	4500 (0.9 × 5000)	360 (0.9 × 4000)	8460
Input to joint process [(100/94) × 8460]				9000

The calculation of the revised joint costs is as follows:

		(£)
Cost of joint process:		
Variable costs (9000 × £5)		45 000
Fixed cost		5 000
Plant overhead		17 000
		67 000
Less income from by-product Z:		
Variable cost (360 × £1)	360	
Fixed cost	500	
Sales (342 × £5)	(1710)	850
		66 150

The joint cost of £66 150 is now apportioned to products A and B:

	A (£)		B (£)	
Joint costs	29 400	(£66 150 × 3600/8100)	36 750	(£66 150 × 4500/8100)
Added variable costs	39 600	(3600 × £11)	9 000	(4500 × £2)
Added fixed cost	4 000		8 000	
	73 000		53 750	
Cost per unit	£22.53	(£73 000/3240)	£14.93	(£53 750/3600)

(c)

	A (£)		B (£)	
Production costs per (b)	73 000		53 750	
Imported cost[a]	9 000	(360 tonnes at £25)	6 000	(400 tonnes × £15)
Revised total costs	82 000		59 750	
Sales	86 400	(3600 × £24)	58 000	(4000 × £14.50)
Profit	4 400		(1 750)	

Profit = £2650

Note	A (tonnes)		B (tonnes)	
[a] Revised yield from joint process	3600		4500	
Evaporation beyond split-off point	360	(10%)	900	(20%)
Revised output of final product	3240		3600	
Original production	3600		4000	
Lost output imported	360		400	

(d) (i) Comparing proposal (i) with the answer to (b) and (c), the differential costs are calculated as follows:

	A (tonnes)	B (tonnes)	Z (tonnes)	Total (tonnes)
Yield from joint process	3800 (3600 + 200)	4300 (4500 − 200)	360	8460
Final output	3420 (90% × 3800)	3440 (80% × 4300)		
Sales demand	3600	4000		
Required imports	180	560		

Differential costs

	(£)	(£)
Additional VC in joint process (2% × £45 000)		900
Additional VC after split-off point (A = 200 × £11)	2200	
(B = 200 × £2)	(400)	1800
Savings in imports of A (180 − 360 at £25)	(4500)	
Additional import cost of B (560 − 400 at £15)	2400	(2100)
Additional costs		600

Therefore proposal (i) should be rejected.

(ii) With proposal (ii), the by-product residue is apportioned to A and B in proportion to their output from the joint process (i.e. A = 360 × 3600/8100 = 160, B = 360 × 4500/8100 = 200).

	A (tonnes)	B (tonnes)	Z (tonnes)
Revised yield from joint process	3760 (3600 + 160)	4700 (4500 + 200)	
Final output	3346 (89% × 3760)	3713 (79% × 4700)	
Sales demand	3600	4000	
Required imports	254	287	
Previous imports in (c)	360	400	
Saving in imports	106	113	

Differential costs

	(£)	(£)	(£)
Increase in fixed costs (5% × £4000) + (5% × £8000)		600	
Increase in variable costs (A = 160 × £11)	1760		
(B = 200 × £2)	400	2160	
Loss of contribution from by-product Z (1710 − 360 per part (b))		1350	4110
Savings in import costs (A = 106 × £25)	2650		
(B = 113 × £15)	1695		(4345)
Net gain from the proposal			235

Solution IM 6.9

(a) Figure Q6.9 shows a flow chart based on 100 gallons input (i.e. 50 gallons of L and 50 gallons of M). It appears that this alternative should be chosen. However, before the final decision is made, the following items should be considered, since they cannot be quantified:

  (i) Loss of customer for by-product. (Can this customer be retained or replaced, given that this is a temporary situation only?)

  (ii) The suggestions appear to be experiments. What degree of confidence does management have in these estimates?

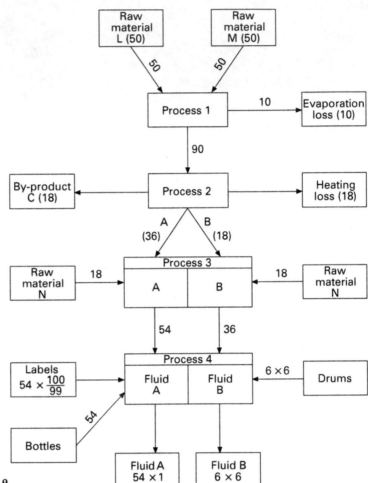

Figure Q6.9

(b) The sales limitation restricts output of B to 54 000 gallons. Figure Q6.9 indicates that for 50 gallons input for each of L and M we obtain an output of 36 gallons of B. Therefore an output of 54 000 gallons of B requires an input of 75 000 gallons of L and M (54 000 × 50/36).

Process 1 account

	Units	CPU	(£)		Units	CPU	(£)
Material L	75 000	0.20	15 000	Evaporation			
M	75 000	0.50	37 500	loss (10%)	15 000	—	—
Direct wages and				Process 2	135 000	0.60	81 000
variable overhead							
(150 000 × £0.15)			22 500				
Fixed overhead			6 000				
			81 000				81 000

Process 2 account

	Units	CPU	(£)		Units	CPU	(£)
From Process 1	135 000	0.60	81 000	Boiling loss (20%)	27 000	—	—
Wages and variable				By-product C	27 000	0.50	13 500
overhead		0.35	47 250	Process 3 (A)	54 000		90 000[a]
Fixed overhead			20 250	Process 3 (B)	27 000		45 000[a]
			148 500				148 500

Note

[a] Joint *net* costs of £135 000 are apportioned on a physical units basis as follows:

$$A = \frac{54\,000}{81\,000} \times £135\,000$$

$$B = \frac{27\,000}{81\,000} \times £135\,000$$

Process 3 account (extract A)

	Units	CPU	(£)		Units	CPU	(£)
Process 2	54 000	1.67	90 000	Process 4 (A)	81 000	2.22	180 000
Material N	27 000	2.0	54 000				
Labour and variable overhead (81 000 × £0.3)			24 300				
Fixed overhead[a]			11 700				
			180 000				180 000

Process 3 account (extract B)

	Units	CPU	(£)		Units	CPU	(£)
Process 2	27 000	1.67	45 000	Process 4 (B)	54 000	2.27	123 000
Material N	27 000	2.0	54 000				
Labour and variable overhead (54 000 × £0.3)			16 200				
Fixed overhead[a]			7 800				
			123 000				123 000

Note

[a] Fixed overheads of Process 3 are apportioned according to the output of this process; e.g. for extract A

$$\frac{81\,000}{135\,000} \times £19\,500$$

Process 4 account (extract A)

	Units	CPU	(£)		Units	CPU	(£)
Process 3	81 000	2.22	180 000	Finished stock	81 000		243 000
Wages and variable overhead (81 000 × £0.4)			32 400				
Fixed overhead[a]			8 550				
Bottles (81 000 × 0.27)			21 870				
Labels[b]			180				
			243 000				243 000

Process 4 account (extract B)

	Units	CPU	(£)		Units	CPU	(£)
Process 3	54 000	2.27	123 000	Finished stock	54 000		202 500
Wages and variable overhead (54 000 × £0.40)			21 600				
Fixed overhead [a]			5 700				
Drums (9000 × £5.80)			52 200				
			202 500				202 500

Notes

[a] Fixed overhead is apportioned according to the output of process 4 (i.e. 60% to A and 40% to B).

[b] 81 000 × (100/99) × (£2.20/1000)

	Manufacturing costs (£)	Production (gallons)	Cost per unit (£)
Fluid A	243 000	81 000	3.00
Fluid B	202 500	54 000	3.75
	(i)		(ii)

(iii) *Selling price structure* (%)

Analysis of net selling price:

	(%)
Selling and distribution cost	12
Administration cost	5
Profit	8
	25
Manufacturing cost	75
Net selling price	100 = $1\frac{1}{3}$ times manufacturing cost

	Fluid A (£)	Fluid B (£)
Manufacturing cost	3.00	3.75
Net selling price (× $1\frac{1}{3}$)	4.00	5.00
List price (× $1\frac{1}{4}$)	5.00	
(× $1\frac{1}{2}$)		7.50

(iv) *Profit for the year*

	(£)
Fluid A: 81 000 gallons at £0.32 [a]	25 920
Fluid B: 54 000 gallons at £0.40 [a]	21 600
	47 520

Note

[a] Profit margins are 8% of net selling prices.

(c) The answer is based on the following assumptions:

   (i) That the incidental production of fluid A ($1\frac{1}{2}$ gallons per gallon of fluid B) as well as the by-product C would be saleable at usual prices.

   (ii) That no additional fixed manufacturing overhead would be incurred.

   (iii) That fluid A would incur marketing and administrative costs at the normal rate of £0.68 per gallon (17% of net selling price). One would expect such costs to include a 'fixed' element, but since no breakdown is given and since they are stated in the question as percentages of net selling price, it is assumed that they are intended to be treated as 'variable'.

   (iv) That the exported fluid B would incur marketing and administrative costs of £1260 only, i.e. £0.42 per gallon.

The fixed overhead included in the manufacturing costs must be removed in order to calculate the incremental cost of production. The calculations are as follows:

	Total (£)	Fluid A (£)		Fluid B (£)	
Processes 1 and 2	26 250	17 500	$(\frac{2}{3})$	8 750	$(\frac{1}{3})$
Processes 3 and 4	33 750	20 250	(60%)	13 500	(40%)
	60 000	37 750		22 250	
Output (gallons)		81 000		54 000	
Per gallon		£0.47		£0.41	

The incremental costs per gallon and required selling price are:

	Fluid A (£)	Fluid B (£)
Total cost of manufacture	3.00	3.75
Less fixed overhead	0.47	0.41
Marginal cost of manufacture	2.53	3.34
Marketing and administration cost:		
(normal)	0.68	
(special)		0.42
	3.21	3.76
Net selling price (fluid A)	4.00	
Contribution:		
1 gallon fluid A	0.79	
$1\frac{1}{2}$ gallons fluid A	1.19	(1.19)
Break-even selling price of fluid B		2.57

(d) It is not possible to quote a price based on cost factors alone. We need information on the state of market demand, competitors' prices, quality differences etc. If the prices in the overseas market are low and this chemical company wishes to establish a market to unload its spare capacity of B then any price above £2.57 would increase company profits. However, the company should not undercut competitors too much, since this may result in a price war with a resulting long-term reduction in profits for the chemical company. A price of £3 may be appropriate if the company merely wishes to unload its spare capacity [profit increase = 3000 × (£3 − £2.57)].

However, if the chemical company wishes to sell B overseas and to pay for itself (not being subsidized by A in the UK market) then any selling price in excess of £3.76 would be acceptable. If the market is tight or the company wishes to develop a market in the long term then a price of £4 may be appropriate.

Alternatively, if the company wishes merely to dispose of the spare capacity and the prices in the export country are similar to the UK then the normal selling price of £5 may be appropriate.

The cost information merely indicates the minimum prices for certain policies, and the final price depends on the interaction of cost with a number of other important variables which are not given in the question.

Income effects of alternative cost accumulation systems

Solutions to Chapter 7 questions

Solution IM 7.1 See Chapter 7 for the answer to this question.

Solution IM 7.2 See Chapter 7 for the answer to this question.

Solution IM 7.3

Fixed cost per unit (£6000/500)	£12
Variable cost per unit	30
Total cost	42

(a) *Operating statement for periods 1–4 (marginal costing)*

	Total (£)	Period 1 (£)	Period 2 (£)	Period 3 (£)	Period 4 (£)
Sales	104 500	27 500	22 000	30 250	24 750
Opening stock	0	0	0	3 000	0
Production at £30 per unit	58 500	15 000	15 000	13 500	15 000
Closing stock	(1 500)	0	(3 000)	0	(1 500)
Marginal cost of sales	57 000	15 000	12 000	16 500	13 500
Contribution	47 500	12 500	10 000	13 750	11 250
Fixed costs	(24 000)	(6 000)	(6 000)	(6 000)	(6 000)
	23 500	6 500	4 000	7 750	5 250

(b) *Operating statement for periods 1–4 (absorption costing)*

	Total (£)	Period 1 (£)	Period 2 (£)	Period 3 (£)	Period 4 (£)
Sales	104 500	27 500	22 000	30 250	24 750
Opening stock	0	0	0	4 200	0
Production (at £42 per unit)	81 900	21 000	21 000	18 900	21 000
Closing stock	(2 100)	0	(4 200)	0	(2 100)
Total cost of sales	79 800	21 000	16 800	23 100	18 900
Sub-total	24 700	6 500	5 200	7 150	5 850
Over/(under) absorbed Overheads	(600)	0	0	(600)	0
Net profit	24 100	6 500	5 200	6 550	5 850

(c) In period 1 production equals sales and there are no stock movements so that profits are the same with both systems. When production exceeds sales (periods 2 and 4) absorption costing reports the greater profits because fixed costs are deferred in the stock valuations. For example, in period 2 stocks increase by 100 units thus resulting in fixed costs of £1200 (100 × £12) being deferred as an expense with the absorption costing system. Therefore absorption costing profits exceed marginal costing profits by £1200. When sales exceed production the opposite situation occurs and marginal costing reports the higher profits. For a more detailed explanation of these issues see 'Variable costing and absorption costing: a comparison of their impact on profit' in Chapter 7.

(a) *Calculation of unit costs and selling price*   **Solution IM 7.4**

	(£)
Variable production cost	16
Fixed production cost (£800 000/160 000)	5
Total production cost	21
Variable selling, distribution and administration costs	8
Fixed selling, distribution and administration costs	7.50
Total cost	36.50
Selling price	40

(i)   *Marginal costing statement*

	(£000)
Variable production cost (55 000 × £16)	880
Less closing stock (15 000 × £16)	240
Variable cost of goods sold	640
Fixed manufacturing cost (£800 000/4 quarters)	200
Total production cost	840
Variable non-manufacturing costs (40 000 × £8)	320
Fixed non-manufacturing costs (£1200/4 quarters)	300
Total cost	1460
Sales (40 000 × £40)	1600
Profit	140

(ii)   *Absorption costing statement*

	(£000)
Full production cost (55 000 × £21)	1155
Less closing stock (15 000 × £21)	315
Cost of goods sold	840
Less over absorption of fixed overheads (15 000 × £5)	75
Total production cost	765
Variable non-manufacturing costs	320
Fixed non-manufacturing costs	300
Total cost	1385
Sales	1600
Profit	215

(b) For the answer to this question see 'Variable costing and absorption costing: a comparison of their impact on profit' in Chapter 7. In particular, the answer should draw attention to the 15 000 units increase in stocks in part (a). With an absorption costing system, £75 000 fixed overhead (15 000 units × £5) is included in the closing stock valuation and deferred as an expense until the next accounting period. In contrast, with the marginal costing system the full amount of production fixed overheads is charged as an expense in the current accounting period. Therefore profits are £75 000 higher with the absorption costing system. SSAP9 requires that all non-manufacturing costs are treated as period costs. Hence both systems treat non-manufacturing costs as period costs.

(c) Budgeted contribution per unit   £50
     Budgeted total contribution (profit plus fixed costs)   £1 200 000
     Budgeted sales volume   £24 000 (£1 200 000/£50)

   Strategy 1
             24 000 (1.10) sales volume × unit contribution (£50 − [0.05 × £80])
                            = £1 214 400 total contribution

   Strategy 2
             24 000 (1.20) sales volume × unit contribution (£50 − [0.075 × £80])
                            = £1 267 200 total contribution

   Strategy 3
             24 000 (1.25) sales volume × unit contribution (£50 − [0.10 × £80])
                            = £1 260 000 total contribution

   The above information suggests that strategy 2 should be chosen since it yields a
   contribution of £67 200 in excess of the budgeted contribution.

Solution IM 7.5

(a) (i) *Absorption costing*

	September (£000)		October (£000)	
Opening stock	—		730.24	(28 000 × £26.08)
Production cost	2999.20	(115 000 × £26.08)	2034.24	(78 000 × £26.08)
Less closing stock	730.24	(28 000 × £26.08)	130.40	(5000 × £26.08)
	2268.96		2634.08	
Under/(over) absorption (W1)	(208.80)		45.44	
	2060.16		2679.52	
Non-manufacturing overheads	200.00		200.00	
Total cost	2260.16		2879.52	
Sales	2784.00	(87 000 × £32)	3232.00	(101 000 × £32)
Net profit	523.84		352.48	

   Working
   (W1) 100% capacity production = 1 008 000/0.7 = 1 444 000 gross per annum
                                                  = 120 000 gross per month

	September	October
Production (units)	115 000	78 000
Capacity	96%	65%
Fixed costs (£)	656 000	632 000
Fixed overhead absorbed (£):		
115 000 × £7.52	864 800	—
78 000 × £7.52	—	586 560
Under/(over) absorption (£)	(208 800)	45 440

(a) (ii) *Marginal costing*

	September (£000)		October (£000)	
Opening stock	—		519.68	(28 000 × £18.56)
Production cost	2134.40	(115 000 × £18.56)	1447.68	(78 000 × £18.56)
Less closing stock	519.68	(28 000 × £18.56)	92.80	(5000 × £18.56)
	1614.72		1874.56	
Fixed production costs	656.00		632.00	

Non-manufacturing overheads	200.00		200.00
	2470.72		2706.56
Sales	2784.00 (87 000 × £32)		3232.00 (101 000 × £32)
Net profit	313.28		525.44

(b) For cost control purposes flexible budgets should be used and costs should be separated into their fixed and flexible elements. Using absorption costing for stock valuation and profit measurement purposes therefore does not preclude the analysis of fixed and variable costs for cost control purposes.

Marginal costing does not eliminate any distortion of interim profits where seasonal fluctuations in sales occur and production is at a fairly constant level. Marginal costing exerts a smoothing effect only when sales are relatively stable and production fluctuates from period to period.

The adoption of a relevant costing/variable costing approach for decision-making is not dependent upon stocks being valued on an absorption costing basis. The statement is confusing decision-making applications with cost information required for stock valuation and profit measurement purposes. However, break-even analysis is based on the assumption that profits are measured on a marginal costing basis, and consequently marginal costing is preferable for profit planning purposes.

(a) *Calculation of fixed manufacturing overhead rate (£000)*

Solution IM 7.6

	Prodn dept 1	Prodn dept 2	Service dept	General factory	Total
Allocated	380.0	465.0	265	230	1340
Allocation of general factory	92.0 (40%)	115.0 (50%)	23 (10%)	(230)	
Share of service department:			288		
Labour related costs (60%)	76.8 (8/18)	96.0 (10/18)	(172.8)		
Machine related costs (40%)	57.6	57.6	(115.2)		
	606.4	733.6			1340
Units of output (000)	120	120			
Overhead rate per unit (£)	5.0533	6.1133			

Calculation of total manufacturing cost per unit

	(£)
Direct materials	7.00
Direct labour	5.50
Variable overhead	2.00
Fixed overhead: department 1	5.0533
department 2	6.1133
Manufacturing cost	25.6666

Absorption costing profit statement

	(£000)
Production cost (116 000 × £25.666)	2977.33
Less closing stocks (2000 × £25.6666)	51.33
Cost of sales	2926.00
Under absorption of overhead:	
Department 1 (£20 000 + (4000 × £5.0533))	40.21
Department 2 (4000 units × £6.1133)	24.45
Non-manufacturing costs	875.00
Total cost	3865.66
Sales (114 000 × £36)	4104.00
Net profit	238.34

Note that the under recovery of fixed overheads consists of £20 000 arising from actual overheads exceeding estimated overheads plus 4000 times the fixed overhead rate because actual volume was 4000 units less than estimated volume.

(b)

Marginal costing profit statement

	(£000)
Variable production cost (116 000 × £14.50)	1682
Less closing stocks (2000 × £14.50)	29
	1653
Fixed manufacturing overhead (1340 + 20)	1360
Non-manufacturing overhead	875
	3888
Sales	4104
Net profit	216

(c) See 'Variable costing and absorption costing: A comparison of their impact on profit' in Chapter 7 for the answer to this question. The answer should also explain why the profits calculated on an absorption costing basis in (a) exceed the variable costing profit computation in (b) by £22 340 (£238 340 − £216 000). This is because stocks have increased by 2000 units and with the absorption costing profit computation fixed manufacturing overheads of approximately £22 340 (2000 units × £11.166 fixed overhead rate) are included in the closing stock valuation. Therefore £22 340 of the fixed overheads is incurred as an expense in the following period. The total fixed manufacturing overhead charged as an expense against the current period is £1 337 660 ((116 000 × £11.166) − (2000 × £11.166) + £64 660 under absorption). With the variable costing system all of the fixed overheads incurred during the period of £1 360 000 is charged as an expense against the current accounting period. The difference between the fixed overheads charged as an expense (£1 337 660 − £1 360 000) accounts for the difference in the profit computation.

Solution IM 7.7

(a) Calculation of fixed overhead rates per unit:

$$\text{Product 1} = £6 \ (£180\ 000/30\ 000)$$
$$\text{Product 2} = £8 \ (£480\ 000/60\ 000)$$

Therefore the unit overhead costs can be analysed as follows:

	Product 1 (£)	Product 2 (£)
Fixed	6	8
Variable (balance)	1	1
Total	7	9

The total overheads included in the income statement presented in the question are as follows:

	Product 1 (£)	Product 2 (£)
Variable overheads	24 000 (24 000 × £1)	60 000 (60 000 × £1)
Fixed overheads	180 000	480 000
	204 000	540 000

Therefore the under/over recovery of fixed overheads is not shown separately in the profit statement in the question, but is included within the total overhead charge. In order to be consistent, this approach is adopted in the answer to part (a).

To construct the profit statement for the quarter commencing January, it is necessary to determine the budgeted opening stocks. The calculation is as follows:

	Product 1 (units)	Product 2 (units)
Budgeted opening stock	?	?
Budgeted production	30 000	52 500
Budgeted closing stock	(8 000)	(3 000)
Budgeted units available for sale (as April quarter)	30 000	57 000
Opening stock (difference)	8 000	7 500

Budgeted income statement for January, February and March

	Product 1	Product 2
Budgeted sales quantity (units)	30 000	57 000
Budgeted production quantity (units)	30 000	52 500
Budgeted sales revenue (£)	450 000	1 026 000
Budgeted production costs	(£)	(£)
Direct material	60 000	157 500
Direct labour	30 000	105 000
Factory overhead [a]	210 000	532 500
	300 000	795 000
Add budgeted finished goods stock at 1 January	(8000) units 80 000	(7500 units) 105 000
	380 000	900 000
Less budgeted finished goods stock at 31 March	(8000 units) 80 000	(3000 units) 42 000
Budgeted manufacturing cost of budgeted sales	300 000	858 000
Budgeted manufacturing profit	150 000	168 000
Budgeted administrative and selling costs (fixed)	30 000	48 000
Budgeted profit	120 000	120 000

Note
[a] Product 1 = £180 000 fixed + £30 000 variable (30 000 units at £1)
Product 2 = £480 000 fixed + £52 500 variable (52 500 units at £1)

(b)   *Budgeted income statements for the two quarters to the 30 June*

	January/February/March		April/May/June	
	Product 1	Product 2	Product 1	Product 2
Budgeted sales quantity (units)	30 000	57 000	30 000	57 000
Budgeted production quantity (units)	30 000	52 500	24 000	60 000
	(£)	(£)	(£)	(£)
Budgeted sales revenue	450 000	1 026 000	450 000	1 026 000
Budgeted production costs				
Direct material	60 000	157 500	48 000	180 000
Direct labour	30 000	105 000	24 000	120 000
Factory overhead (variable)	30 000	52 500	24 000	60 000
	120 000	315 000	96 000	360 000

	Product 1	Product 2	Product 1	Product 2
Add budgeted opening finished goods stock	32 000	45 000	32 000	18 000
	152 000	360 000	128 000	378 000
Less budgeted closing finished goods stock	32 000	18 000	8 000	36 000
Budgeted manufacturing cost of budgeted sales (variable)	120 000	342 000	120 000	342 000

	Product 1 (£)	Product 2 (£)	Product 1 (£)	Product 2 (£)
Budgeted manufacturing contribution	330 000	684 000	330 000	684 000
Budgeted fixed manufacturing overheads	(180 000)	(480 000)	(180 000)	(480 000)
Budgeted administrative and selling costs (fixed)	(30 000)	(48 000)	(30 000)	(48 000)
Budgeted profit	120 000	156 000	120 000	156 000

(c) The profits in the budgeted profit statements have been calculated on the basis of absorption costing. With a system of absorption costing, fixed manufacturing overheads are included in the stock valuations. The effect of this is that the fixed overheads charged against profits for a period may not be the same as the fixed overheads incurred during a period. When stocks are decreasing, fixed overheads charged will be greater than the fixed overheads incurred. This occurs in the second quarter for product 2.

With an absorption costing system, profits are a function of sales and production. This can result in a distortion in the profit calculations, thus causing the situation which has occurred in the question. This situation can be avoided by adopting a marginal (variable) costing system. From the answer to part (b) we can see that profits are identical for both periods when a marginal costing system is adopted.

The following differences between absorption and marginal costing statements can arise:

(i) *Production = sales*: absorption and marginal costing profit calculations will be identical. This situation occurs with product 1 in the first quarter.
(ii) *Production > sales (second quarter for product 2)*: profits will be greater with an absorption costing system.
(iii) *Production < sales*: profits will be lower with an absorption costing system. This situation occurs with product 1 in the second quarter.

For a detailed explanation of the above differences see 'Variable costing and absorption costing: a comparison of their impact on profit' in Chapter 7.

Solution IM 7.8

(a)

	(£000)
Actual variable cost profit	60
Less adjustment for stock reduction using absorption costing method [a]	12
Actual absorption cost profit	48
Add adjustment for apportionment of cost variances to closing stocks [b]	9
Actual costing profit	57

Notes
[a] Stocks are reduced by 2000 units and fixed production overheads are absorbed at the rate of £6 per unit. Therefore an additional £12 000 fixed production overhead

is charged as an expense with the absorption cost method. Variable costing charges £66 000 fixed production overhead as an expense for the period (£80 000 fixed production overhead – £14 000 fixed production overhead expenditure variance), whereas the absorption cost method charges £78 000 fixed production overhead as an expense for the period (£140 000 absorption cost of sales – £80 000 variable cost of sales – £14 000 expenditure variance + £32 000 volume variance).

[b] The total of the production cost variances is £14 000 adverse. With the standard absorption costing method, £14 000 is written off as a period cost. Consequently the production costs charged as an expense for the period are £154 000 (£140 000 cost of sales + £14 000 production cost variances). The production costs charged as an expense with the actual cost system are £145 000 cost of sales. The £9000 difference is because 18 000/28 000 of the cost variance of £14 000 is apportioned to the closing stock valuation. Therefore the actual costing profit is £9000 higher.

(b) The answer should include a discussion of the relative merits of absorption costing and variable costing. For a discussion of the relative merits see 'Some arguments in support of variable costing and absorption costing' and 'The variable costing versus absorption costing debate' in Chapter 7. In addition the answer should indicate that a change to a standard costing system will provide better information for decision-making and cost control purposes.

(c) The report should emphasize that for decision-making and cost control purposes the standard variable costing system is recommended. However, to meet the requirements of external reporting, it will be necessary to adjust the variable cost accounts to an absorption costing basis.

Projected profit and loss accounts for November and December 2000
(variable costing basis)

	November		December	
	(£000)	(£000)	(£000)	(£000)
Sales (10 000 units at £25)		250		
Sales (12 000 units at £25)				300
Opening stock	160		144	
Production costs	64		112 (W1)	
	224		256	
Closing stock	144	80	160 (W2)	96
		170		204
Variable selling costs		10		12
Contribution		160		192
Other expenses				
Production: fixed	80		80	
Administration: fixed	28		28	
Selling: fixed	16	124	16 124	
Standard variable cost profit		36		68
Variance:				
Production:				
Variable: expenditure	(4)		4 (W3)	
Fixed: expenditure	(14)		10 (W4)	
Administration: expenditure	(5)		(3.5) (W5)	
Selling:				
Variable: expenditure	1		– (W6)	
Fixed: expenditure	(2)	(24)	(1) (W7)	9.5
Actual variable cost profit		60		58.5

Workings
(W1) 14 000 units × £8.
(W2) 18 000 units opening stock + 14 000 units production − 12 000 units sales
= 20 000 units closing stock valued at £8 per unit.

(W3) Variable production cost variance: $(14\,000 \times £8) - £116\,000 = £4000$.

(W4) Fixed production expenditure variance: $£80\,000 - £90\,000 = £10\,000$.

(W5) Administration expenditure variance: $£28\,000 - £24\,500 = £3500$ (F).

(W6) Variable selling cost variance: $(12\,000 \times £1) - £12\,000 = $ nil.

(W7) Fixed selling cost variance: $£16\,000 - £15\,000 = £1000$ (F).

The budgeted fixed production overheads calculation is: $(160\,000 \text{ units} \times £6)/12$ months.

Cost–volume–profit analysis

Solutions to Chapter 8 questions

Solution IM 8.1

(a) The selling price is in excess of the variable cost per unit, thus providing a contribution towards fixed costs and profit. At point (A) sales are insufficient to generate a contribution to cover the fixed costs (difference between total cost and variable cost lines in the diagram). Consequently a loss occurs. Beyond the break-even point sales volume is sufficient to provide a contribution to cover fixed costs, and a profit is earned. At point (B) the increase in volume is sufficient to generate a contribution to cover fixed costs and provide a profit equal to the difference (represented by the dashed line) between the total revenue and cost line.

(b) See Chapter 8 for the answer to this question.

Solution IM 8.2

The comparisons of CVP models represented in management accounting and economic theory are presented in the first half of Chapter 8. Additional points include the following:

 (i) Both models are concerned with explaining the relationship between changes in costs and revenues and changes in output. Both are simplifications of cost and revenue functions because variables other than output affect costs and revenues.

 (ii) The value of both models is reduced when arbitrary cost allocation methods are used to apportion joint costs to products or divisions.

(iii) The economic model indicates two break-even points whereas the management accounting model indicates one break-even point.

(iv) Both models are based on single value estimates of total costs and revenues. It is possible to incorporate uncertainty into the analysis using the methods outlined in 'CVP analysis under conditions of uncertainty' in the appendix to Chapter 12.

 (v) The model based on economic theory provides a theoretical presentation of the relationship between costs, revenues and output. The model is intended to provide an insight into complex inter-relationships. The management accounting model should be seen as a practical decision-making tool which provides a useful approximation for decision-making purposes if certain conditions apply (e.g. relevant range assumption).

Solution IM 8.3

(a) See 'Cost–volume–profit analysis assumptions' in Chapter 8 for the answer to this question.

(b) Examples of the circumstances where the underlying assumptions are violated include:

 (i) *Variable cost per unit remaining constant over the entire range*: This assumption is violated where quantity discounts can be obtained from the purchase of larger quantities. Consequently the variable cost per unit will not be constant for all output levels. However, over a restricted range, or several restricted ranges, a linear relationship or a series of linear relationships may provide a reasonable approximation of the true cost function.

 (ii) *Selling price is constant per unit*: In order to increase sales volume, the selling price might be reduced. Therefore selling price will not be a linear function of volume. A series of linear relationships may provide a reasonable approximation of the true revenue function.

(iii) *The sales mix is known*: It is unlikely that the planned sales mix will be equal to the actual sales mix. To incorporate the possibility that the actual sales mix may differ from the planned sales mix, a range of total cost and revenue curves should be prepared corresponding to each possible sales mix. This will give a range of break-even points and profit/losses for possible mixes of sales.

Solution IM 8.4   See 'Cost–volume–profit analysis assumptions' in Chapter 8 and 'Cost–volume–profit analysis under conditions of uncertainty' in Appendix 12.1 to Chapter 12 for the answer to this question.

Solution IM 8.5   (a)

Product	Unit contribution	Sales volume (units)	Total contribution (£000)	Total sales revenue (£000)
J	6	10 000	60	200
K	32	10 000	320	400
L	(0.20)	50 000	(10)	200
M	3	20 000	60	200
		90 000	430	1000

Average contribution = 43% of sales revenue

(b) and (c)   The profit arising from the most profitable product (Product K) is drawn first on the profit-volume graph (see Fig. Q8.5). At £400 000 sales revenue a profit of £80 000 (£320 000 contribution – £240 000 fixed costs) is plotted on

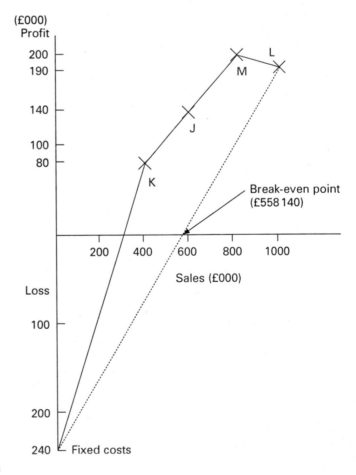

Figure Q8.5

COST–VOLUME–PROFIT ANALYSIS

the graph. The profits arising from the remaining products are then entered on the graph. Since fixed costs have already been covered by Product K, the next product (Product J) will increase profits by £60 000 (i.e. total contribution of £60 000). The second point to be plotted is therefore cumulative sales of £600 000 and profits of £140 000. The addition of Product M results in cumulative profits of £200 000 (£140 000 + £60 000) and cumulative sales revenue of £800 000. Finally, the addition of product L reduces total profits to £190 000.

The dashed line on the graph represents the average contribution per £1 of sales (43%) arising from the planned sales mix. The break-even point in sales value is £558 140 [fixed costs (£240 000)/contribution ratio (0.43)]. This is the point where the dashed line cuts the horizontal axis. At zero sales level a loss equal to the fixed costs will be incurred and at the maximum sales level profits will be £190 000 [(£1m × 0.43) – £240 000].

Product K yields the largest contribution/sales ratio (80%) and Products J and M yield identical ratios. Product L has a negative contribution and discontinuation will result in profits increasing by £10 000.

(d) The contribution/sales ratio can be improved by:
   (i) increasing selling price;
   (ii) reducing unit variable costs by improving labour efficiency or obtaining cheaper materials from different suppliers;
   (iii) automating production and substituting variable costs with fixed costs.

(a) See 'Cost–volume–profit analysis assumptions' in Chapter 8 for the answer to this question.

Solution IM 8.6

(b) (i)

Holiday resort cost and income statement

Guests in residence	Income p.a. (£)	Variable costs (£)	Contribution (£)	Fixed costs (£)	Surplus (deficit) (£)
6	18 000	7 740	10 260	16 000	(5740)
7	21 000	9 030	11 970	16 000	(4030)
8	24 000	10 320	13 680	16 000	(2320)
9	27 000	11 610	15 390	16 000	(610)
10	30 000	12 900	17 100	16 000	1100
11	33 000	14 190	18 810	22 000	(3190)
12	36 000	15 480	20 520	22 000	(1480)
13	39 000	16 770	22 230	22 000	230
14	42 000	18 060	23 940	22 000	1940
15	45 000	19 350	25 650	22 000	3650

There are two break-even points. If provision is made for between 6 and 10 guests, the first break-even point occurs just in excess of 9 guests per week (or 270 guests per annum). If provision is made for 11 or more guests per week, the break-even point changes to 13 guests per week.

(ii) The total costs for various activity levels are as follows:

Guests	Total costs (£)
6	23 740
10	28 900
11	36 190
15	41 350

The above costs are plotted on the break-even chart shown in Figure Q8.6.

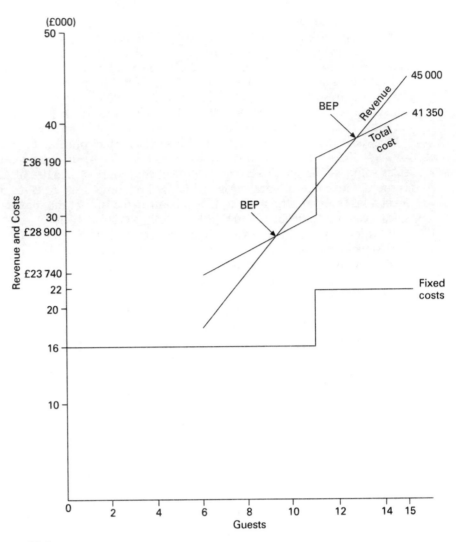

Figure Q8.6

Solution IM 8.7   (a) For the answer to this question you should refer to 'cost behaviour' in Chapter 2.

(b)

	Output (units)	Total cost (£)
Lowest activity	11 500	102 476
Highest activity	14 000	113 201
	2 500	10 725

$$\text{Variable cost per unit of output} = \frac{\text{Difference in cost (£10 725)}}{\text{Difference in output (2500 units)}}$$

$$= £4.29 \text{ per unit}$$

The fixed cost can be estimated at any level of activity by subtracting the variable cost portion from the total cost. At an activity level of 11 500 units the total cost is £102 476 and the total variable cost is £49 335 (11 500 units × £4.29). The balance of £53 141 is assumed to represent the fixed costs.

(c) Break-even point = $\dfrac{\text{Fixed costs (£53 141)}}{\text{Contribution per unit (£10.60 − £4.29)}}$ = 8422 units

Because the break-even point is outside the range of observations that were used to estimate the variable and fixed costs it is possible that estimates of cost behaviour may not be accurate. However, given that the lowest observed level of activity is significantly above the break-even point output level there is a very high probability that profits will be generated at all likely levels of activity.

Task 1 – Preliminary workings

Planned sales volume for draft budget = 0.75 × 3.2m = 2.4m units
Draft budget = 2/3 of maximum capacity
Therefore maximum capacity = 2.4m × 3/2 = 3.6m units

The following is an analysis of the draft budget:

	(£m)	(£ per unit)
Sales revenues	960.0	400
Less variable costs	777.6	324
Contribution	182.4	76
Less fixed costs	171.0	
Net profit	11.4	
Break-even point in units (£171m/£76)	2.25m	
Break-even point in sales revenues (2.25m × £400 selling price)	£900m	

(a) (i) and (a)(ii)

Proposal A

Commission per unit in the draft budget (£38.4m/2.4m units)	= £16
Revised commission per unit	= £18
Revised unit contribution	= £74
Revised sales volume (units)	2.64m
Projected total contribution (2.64m × £74)	£195.36m
Less fixed costs (£171m + £14m)	185.00m
Projected profit	10.36m
Break-even point in units (£185m/£74)	2.5m
Break-even point in sales revenues (2.5m × £400)	£1 000m
Change in profit	−£1.04m

Proposal B

Reduction in selling price (5% × £400)	£20
Projected sales volume	3.2m
Reduction in cost of materials per unit	£4
Revised unit contribution (£76 – £20 + £4)	£60
Projected total contribution (3.2m × £60)	£192m
Less fixed costs	171m
Projected profit	21m
Break-even point in units (£171m/£60)	2.85m
Break-even point in sales revenues (2.85m × £380)	£1 083m
Change in profit	+£9.60m

Proposal C

Reduction in selling price (10% × £400)	£40
Projected unit sales volume (restricted to maximum capacity)	3.6m
Reduction in cost of materials per unit	£4
Revised unit contribution (£76 – £40 + £4)	£40
Projected total contribution (3.6m × £40)	£144m
Less fixed costs (£171m – £45m)	126m
Projected profit	18m
Break-even point in units (£126m/£40)	3.15m
Break-even point in sales revenues (3.15m × £360)	£1.134m
Change in profit	+£6.6m

(b) Proposal B would appear to be the best strategy in terms of profitability. All three proposals increase the break-even point although proposal A shows the smallest increase. However, provided that management is confident that the predicted sales can be achieved proposal B should be chosen.

(c) Before making a final decision the following issues should be considered:
  (i) the promotion campaign might generate increased sales beyond the current year;
  (ii) the price reduction for proposals B and C may cause competitors to react thus provoking a price war;
  (iii) the price reduction for proposals B and C may not result in the predicted sales volume if customers perceive the product to be of low quality;
  (iv) proposal C will result in the company operating at full capacity. This may result in changes in cost structure if the company is operating outside the relevant output range.

Task 2

(a)

	(£m)	(£m)
Proposed selling price		3.0
Less relevant costs:		
Material A (replacement cost)	0.8	
Material B (0.1 NRV + 0.3 replacement cost)	0.4	
Direct labour [a] (1.0 – 0.2)	0.8	
Variable factory overhead	0.9	
Fixed factory overhead	nil	2.9
Contribution to fixed costs and profit		0.1

Note:
[a] It is assumed that the direct labour of £0.8m charged to the order includes the opportunity cost of the direct labour since the question implies that this labour will be utilized elsewhere if the order is not accepted.

(b) The relevant cost approach described in Chapter 9 has been used in part (a). It is assumed that it is a one time short-term special order and that no other costs can be avoided if the order is accepted.

(a) (i)

Product	P	E
Unit contribution	£5	£2
Weightings	4	3
Total contribution	£20	£6

Average contribution per unit based on above weightings = (£20 + £6)/7
$$= £3.714$$

Break-even point = fixed costs (£561 600)/unit contribution (£3.714)
$$= 151\ 212 \text{ units [consisting of 86 407 units of P(4/7) and}$$
64 805 units of E]

Break-even point (sales value):
P: 86 407 units × £10 =   £864 070
E: 64 805 units × £12 =   £777 660
                          £1 641 730

(ii)

Product	P	E
Unit contribution	£5	£2
Weightings	4	4
Total contribution	£20	£8

Average contribution = (£20 + £8)/8 = £3.50
Break-even point = £561 600/£3.50
$$= 160\ 457 \text{ units [consisting of 80 228 units of each product]}$$
Break-even point (sales value) = (80 228 × £10) + (80 228 × £12)
$$= £1\ 765\ 016$$

(iii) The product mix in (a) (i) above is preferable because it yields the higher average contribution per unit.

(iv) Machine hours are the limiting factor and the company should concentrate on the product which maximizes the contribution per machine hour.

Product	P	E
Contribution	£5	£2
Contribution per machine hour	£12.50 (£5/0.40 hrs)	£20 (£2/0.10 hrs)

The company should therefore concentrate on Product E. If all the 32 000 machine hours are allocated to Product E the profit will be as follows:

Contribution (32 000 hrs at £20 per hour) £640 000
Less fixed costs   £561 600
Profit   £78 400

(b) See Fig. 8.7 and Fig. 8.8 in Chapter 8 for illustrations of both break-even charts. The answer should stress that the contribution graph enables the contribution at any activity level to be determined and so provides more information than a conventional graph.

Solution IM 8.10

Task 1

(1) Production volume (packs)	40 000	50 000	60 000	70 000
(2) Average cost	£430	£388	£360	£340
(3) Total cost (1 × 2)	£17 200 000	£19 400 000	£21 600 000	£23 800 000
(4) Cost per extra 10 000 packs		£2 200 000	£2 200 000	£2 200 000
(5) Unit variable cost ((4)/10 000)		£220	£220	£220

(a)

	(£)
Total cost for 40 000 packs	17 200 000
less Variable costs (40 000 × £220)	8 800 000
Fixed costs	8 400 000

(b)

Unit contribution (£420 − £220)	200
Total contribution (£200 × 65 000 packs)	13 000 000
less Fixed costs	8 400 000
Profit	4 600 000

(c) Break-even point (packs) = Fixed costs/Unit contribution = £8 400 000/£200 = 42 000

(d) Margin of safety = (65 000 − 42 000)/65 000 = 35.4%

Task 2

(a) Additional contribution = 5000 × (£330 − £220) = £550 000
Fixed costs are assumed to remain unchanged. Therefore profits should increase by £550 000.

(b)

Additional contribution from the order =	
15 000 × (£340 − £220) =	£1 800 000
Lost contribution from current sales =	
10 000 × (£420 − £220) =	£2 000 000
Loss from the order	£200 000

(c) The order for 5000 units at £330 should be accepted since this yields an additional contribution of £550 000. Fixed costs are assumed to remain unchanged for both orders. However, accepting an order for 15 000 units can only be met by reducing current sales by 10 000 units (planned existing sales are 65 000 units and capacity is restricted to 70 000 units). The order can only be justified if the lost sales can be recouped in future periods with no loss in customer goodwill.

(d) Non-financial factors that should be considered include:
  (i) The effect on existing customers if they become aware that the company is selling at a lower price to other customers.
  (ii) The long-term potential of the new order. If the order is likely to result in repeat sales it might be financially viable to increase capacity and obtain the increased contribution without the loss of contribution from existing sales. The financial appraisal should compare the present value of the increase in contribution with the additional costs associated with increasing capacity.

Solution IM 8.11

(a) Absorption costing unitizes fixed production overheads and includes them in the stock valuation whereas marginal costing does not include fixed overheads in the stock valuation. Instead, total fixed production overheads incurred are treated as period costs. Therefore, the total fixed overheads of £385 000 (250 000 units of A plus 100 000 units of B valued at £1.10 per unit) are charged as an expense with a marginal costing system.
  Total production is 350 000 units (250 000 of A plus 100 000 units of B) and total sales volume is 335 000 units (225 000 units of A plus 110 000 units of B).

Production exceeds sales by 15 000 units resulting in an equivalent increase in stocks. With an absorption costing £16 500 (15 000 units × £1.10) out of a total fixed overheads incurred of £385 000 will be included in the stock valuation and not recorded as an expense for the current period. Therefore the cost of sales with an absorption costing system will be £16 500 lower than marginal costing cost of sales thus resulting in absorption costing showing an extra £16 500 profits for the period.

(b) Total fixed overheads for the period is calculated as follows:

	(£)
Production fixed overhead	
(350 000 units normal production × £1.10)	385 000
Other fixed overheads (335 000 units sales × £0.50)	167 500
	552 500

It is assumed that other fixed overheads are absorbed on the basis of sales volume rather than production volume.

The cost–volume–profit analysis should be based on the assumption that sales will be in accordance with the planned sales mix of 225 000 units of A and 110 000 units of B. This sales mix will yield the following total contribution:

	Product A	Product B	Total
(1) Selling price	5.70	6.90	
(2) Variable cost	3.45	4.80	
(3) Unit contribution	2.25	2.10	
(4) Sales volume (units)	225 000	110 000	
(5) Total contribution (3 × 4)	£506 250	£231 000	£737 250
(6) Total sales revenue (1 × 4)	£1 282 500	£759 000	£2 041 500

Average contribution per unit = £737 250/335 000 units total sales
= £2.2007

Average selling price per unit = Total sales revenue (£2 041 500)/Total sales
volume (335 0000) = £6.094

Break-even point (units) = Total fixed costs/Average contribution per unit
= £552 500/£2.2007
= 251 056 units

Break-even point (sales value) = 251 056 units × average selling price
(£6.094) = £1 529 935

Alternatively, the break-even point in sales value can be computed using the following formula:

$$\frac{\text{Total fixed costs (£552 500)}}{\text{Total contribution (£737 250)}} \times \text{Total sales (£2 041 500)}$$

$$= £1\ 529\ 913.$$

Solution IM 8.12

(a) The capacity usage in single-room days is as follows:

		Days
Single rooms:		
Peak period:		
60 rooms × 6 weeks × 7 days		2 520
Non-peak period:		
60 rooms × 14 weeks × 7 days × 80%		4 704
		7 224
Double rooms		
35 rooms × 7 days × 20 weeks = 4900 days		
Double rooms expressed as		
equivalent single-room days		7 840 (4900 × 160%)
Total equivalent single-room days		15 064

Required contribution = fixed costs (£29 900) + target profit (£10 000) = £39 900
Required contribution per single-room day = £2.65 (£39 900/15 064)
Required charge per single room = £6.65 (£2.65 + £4 variable cost)
Required charge per double room = £10.64 (£2.65 × 160%) + £6.40 variable cost

The following calculations can be used to check that the above charges will yield £10 000 profit.

	(£)
Single-rooms contribution	
[7224 days × (£6.65 − £4 variable cost)]	19 144
Double-rooms contribution	
[4900 days × (£10.64 − £6.40 variable cost)]	20 776
Total contribution	39 920
Fixed costs	29 900
Profit	10 020

(b)

	(£)	(£)
Accommodation		10 020
Sports centre:		
Residential guests: Single rooms (7224 × £2)	14 448	
Double rooms (4900 × 2 × £2)	19 600	
Casual visitors: (30 × 20 weeks × 7 days = 4200 × £3)	12 600	
	46 648	
Fixed costs	15 500	31 148
Sports shop (7224 + 9800 + 4200 = 21 224 persons × £1)	21 224	
Fixed costs	8 250	12 974
Cafeteria (21 224 persons × £1.50)	31 836	
Fixed costs	12 750	19 086
Total profit		73 228

(c) It is assumed that the fixed costs do not include any depreciation and that the profit calculated in (b) is equivalent to cash flow. It is also assumed that the cash flows will remain at £73 228 per annum for the next 5 years.

PV of cash flows (£73 228 × 3.791 10% annuity factor for 5 years) = £277 607

The PV of the cash flows from operating the centre is in excess of the £250 000 offer from the private leisure company. Therefore the decision would be to reject the offer. Note that the annual cash flows (and thus the PV) would be higher if depreciation has been deducted in the calculation of profit in (b).

Measuring relevant costs and revenues for decision-making

Solutions to Chapter 9 questions

(a) See 'Product mix decisions when capacity constraints exist' in Chapter 9 for the answer to this question.

Solution IM 9.1

(b) See 'Product mix decisions when capacity constraints exist' in Chapter 9 and the early part of Chapter 26 for the answer to this question.

(c) See appendix to Chapter 9 for the answer to this question.

(a) The minimum quote is equal to the relevant costs arising from the order. The relevant costs are:

Solution IM 9.2

	(£)
Raw materials:	
X: 960 kg at £3.10 per kg[a]	2 976
Y: 570 kg at £2.30 per kg[b]	1 311
Other materials	3 360
Direct labour[c]:	
2000 hours at £4 per hour	8 000
200 hours at £5.20 per hour	1 040
Variable overhead:	
2200 hours at £2.40 per hour	5 280
Opportunity cost:	
Overtime premium saving forgone as a result of not bringing forward production of future order (2000 hours at £1.20 per hour)	2 400
	24 367

Notes

[a] The original purchase cost of the materials is a sunk cost. The use of materials on this order would result in their replacement and thus represents the future impact of undertaking the order.

[b] Material Y would not be replaced and if the order is not undertaken would yield revenue of £2.30 per kg. Therefore undertaking the order would result in lost sales revenue of £3360.

[c] The question indicates that the labour cost is avoidable if the contract is not undertaken. Thus acceptance of the contract results in additional labour costs of £9040.

(b) See Chapter 2 for an explanation of each of the terms.

Solution IM 9.3

(a) The relevant costs for the production of 400 components are as follows:

	(£)	(£)
Materials:		
M1 (1200 kg at £5.50 replacement cost)	6 600	
P2 (800 kg at £2 per kg)^a	1 600	
Part no. 678 (400 at £50 replacement cost)	20 000	28 200
Labour:		
Skilled (2000 hours at £4 per hour)	8 000	
Semi-skilled (2000 hours at £3 per hour)	6 000	14 000
Overheads:		
Variable (1600 machine hours at £7 per hour)		11 200
Fixed: Incremental fixed costs		3 200
Total relevant cost		56 600
Contract price (400 components at £145 per component)		58 000
Contribution to general fixed costs		1 400

The incremental revenues exceed the incremental costs. Therefore the contract should be accepted subject to the comments in (b) below.

Note
^{a} If materials P2 are not used on the contract, they will be used as a substitute for material P4. Using P2 as a substitute for P4 results in a saving of £2 (£3.60 − £1.60) per kg. Therefore the relevant cost of P2 consists of the opportunity cost of £2 per kg.

(b) Three factors which should be considered are:
  (i) Can a price higher than £145 per component be negotiated? The contract only provides a contribution of £1400 to general fixed costs. If the company generates insufficient contribution from its activities to cover general fixed costs then it will incur losses and will not be able to survive in the long term. It is assumed that acceptance of the contract will not lead to the rejection of other profitable work.
  (ii) Will acceptance of the contract lead to repeat orders which are likely to provide a better contribution to general fixed costs?
  (iii) Acceptance of the contract will provide additional employment for 12 months, and this might have a significant effect on the morale of the workforce.

Solution IM 9.4

(a) *Revised cost estimate:*

	(£)	
Direct materials: paper	2500	(1)
inks	3000	(2)
	5500	
Direct labour (£500 + £625)	1125	(3)
Unskilled labour	—	(4)
Variable overhead	1400	(5)
Printing	600	(6)
Printing press depreciation	—	(7)
Fixed production costs	—	(7)
Estimating department costs	—	(8)
	8625	

Notes:

(1) The alternative use of the paper is to sell it for £2500. Therefore the cashflow impact is £2500.

(2) The incremental cost of undertaking the work is £3000.

(3) Is is assumed that 125 hours not undertaken at weekends is in scarce supply and the decision to undertake the work will result in a lost contribution. The relevant cost is the hourly labour rate plus the lost contribution per hour. The lost contribution is not given in the question and therefore cannot be ascertained. The hourly labour rate consisting of 125 hours at £4 per hour is included in the above answer. It is assumed that the weekend hours represent an incremental cost and do not involve a lost contribution. The incremental cost of weekend work is £625 (125 hours × £5).

(4) At present 200 unskilled hours are recorded as idle time and the work to be undertaken entails 100 plus 50 hours time off in lieu. Therefore idle time will be reduced but no additional expenditure will be incurred.

(5) It is assumed that £1400 is an incremental cost of undertaking the work.

(6) The lost contribution of £600 (200 hours at £3 per hour) is included in the cost estimate. It is assumed that the variable cost of the printing press hours have already been included in the cost estimate.

(7) Fixed overheads and depreciation are fixed costs and therefore do not involve incremental cash flows.

(8) The cost of estimating time has already been incurred and is a sunk cost.

(b) See the section on measuring relevant costs and benefits in Chapter 9 for the answer to this question.

(c) See 'the meaning of relevance' in Chapter 9 and opportunity costs in Chapter 2 for the answer to this question.

(a)

Solution IM 9.5

	(£)	(£)
Direct materials:		
Material A: (30 kg/0.9) × £5.13/kg (W1)	171.00	
Others: £1.34/unit × 100	134.00	305.00
Direct labour:		
Department 1: 40 hours × £4.00/hour	160.00	
Department 2: 15 hours × £4.50/hour	67.50	227.50
Production overhead:		
Department 1: Variable, 40% × £160.00	64.00	
Fixed, 90% × £160.00	144.00	
Department 2: Variable, £0.9 per DLH × 15 hours (W2)	13.50	
Fixed, £2.05 per DLH × 15 hours (W3)	30.75	252.25
Other overhead:		
Variable: £0.70 per unit × 100	70.00	
Fixed: £1.95 per unit × 100	195.00	265.00
Total cost		1049.75

Workings

(W1) 2 400 000 × 30/0.9 per 100 kg = 800 000 purchases p.a.
                = 66 667 per month

(W2) Department 2 overhead:
Variable	£1 980 000
Fixed	£3 444 000 (balance)
	£5 424 000

Variable overhead rate = £1 980 000/2 200 000 hours

= £0.90 per direct labour hour

(W3) Expected usage of direct labour hours:

Expected capacity
(excluding new product) =1.32 million hours (0.6 × 2.2 m)
Capacity required for
new product   =0.36 million hours (2.4 m × 15/100)
Total hours   1.68

Fixed overhead rate = £3 444 000/1 680 000 direct labour hours

= £2.05 per direct labour hour

(b) The total cost per unit of £10.50 (£1049.75/100) is below the expected selling price of £9.95 and it appears that the product is not profitable. However, the new product provides a contribution of £3.15 per unit towards fixed costs. The calculation is as follows:

	(£)
Variable costs:	
Direct materials	3.05
Direct labour	2.275
Variable production overhead	0.775
Other variable overhead	0.70
	6.80
Selling price	9.95
Contribution	3.15

A total annual contribution of £7.56 m (£3.15 × 2.4 m annual sales) towards fixed costs will be obtained if the new product is introduced. If fixed costs will not be affected by the decision to introduce the new product then the new product should be launched because it will provide an annual contribution of £7.5 m which would not otherwise be obtained. The company is currently working at 60% capacity and, with the introduction of the new product, utilization of available capacity will be increased to 76% (1.68 m hours/2.2 m maximum capacity). Therefore sufficient capacity is available to meet the demand for the new product and no opportunity cost is involved resulting from a need to reduce existing output.

With the introduction of the new product, spare capacity would remain, and the company should seek to utilize this capacity with other profitable work. If no other profitable work is likely to be obtained in the long term, then the company should consider reducing capacity to either 60% or 76% of existing capacity. If the annual fixed costs that can be saved from reducing capacity from 76% to 60% exceed the £7.56 m contribution generated by the new product then it is more profitable to reduce capacity to 60% and not introduce the new product.

(c) At a selling price of £9.45 per unit, contribution per unit will be reduced by £0.50, and the annual contribution will be £7.685 (£2.65 × 2.9 m sales). At a selling price of £9.95 the expected contribution is £7.56 m. It is therefore more profitable to reduce selling price if management are confident that the price reduction will increase sales volume by 500 000 units (approximately 20%) and will not affect the selling prices of other products. There is sufficient capacity to meet the additional sales volume and it is assumed that the increase in demand will not result in a change in fixed costs.

(a)

	Product			
	A	B	C	D
Contribution	£16	£17	£23	£22
Unit m/c hours	4	3	4	5
Contribution per m/c hour	£4	£5.67	£5.75	£4.40
Ranking	4	2	1	3

Product	Quantity units	Machine hours	Contribution (£)
C	250	1000	5750
B	180	540	3060
D	92	460	2024
		2000	10 834
	Fixed costs		8000*
	Profit		2834

*1000 labour hours × £8.00 per hour = £8000

(b) (i)

	Sales shortfall units	Unit contribution	Additional cost per unit[a]	Revised unit contribution	Net benefit
		(£)	(£)	(£)	(£)
A	200	16.00	3.50	12.50	2500
D	8	22.00	7.00	15.00	120
					2620

Note:
[a]Labour cost at an overtime premium of £2 per labour hour plus a 50% increase in variable overheads.

(b) (ii)

	(£ per unit)
Variable cost of B	13
Cost of external purchase	20
Increase in cost	7

Reduction in contribution
  = £7 × 180 units = £1260

Hours released	=	540

Allocated as follows:

Product D	8 units (at 5 hours per unit)	40 hours
Product A	125 units (at 4 hours per unit)	500 hours

Additional production		Additional contribution
		(£)
D	8 at £22	176
A	125 at £16	2000
		2176
B	Contribution lost	1260
	Net benefit	916

The report should draw attention to the fact that both options result in an increase in profits. The first option, however, results in the higher profit. Other factors to consider are the extent to which the work force finds overtime to be desirable. The second option involves a loss of control in terms of quality and reliability. Both options have the advantage of satisfying customer demand and increasing customer goodwill.

Solution IM 9.7   (a)

	C (£)	D (£)
Selling price	127	161
Variable costs	66	87
Contribution	61	74

The drilling and grinding hours required to meet the production requirements for the period are calculated as follows:

	A	B	C	D	Total
Hours per unit: Drilling	2	1	3	4	
Grinding	2	4	1	3	
Units of output	50	100	250	500	
Drilling hours required	100	100	750	2000	2950
Grinding hours required	100	400	250	1500	2250

Drilling hours are the limiting factor (1650 hours are available). The contributions per drilling hour are £20.33 for product C (£61/3 hours) and £18.50 (£74/4 hours) for product D. Therefore the maximum demand of product C should be met, resulting in 950 drilling hours being utilized (750 for product C and 200 hours for components A and B). The remaining capacity of 700 hours can be used to produce 175 units of product D. It is assumed that the internal demand for components A and B must have priority over meeting the demand for product D. The estimated profit per week is:

	(£)
Contribution from product C (250 units at £61)	15 250
Contribution from product D (175 units at £74)	12 950
Total contribution	28 200
Allocated fixed overheads (250 × £23) + (175 × £39)	12 575
	15 625

(b) (i) Components A and B are not used to produce either of the finished products but if they are purchased drilling time can be freed up to expand production of product D. The variable costs of components A and B are £32 and £78 respectively and the outside purchasing costs are £50 and £96. Thus variable costs will increase by £18 per unit for both components but the contribution per drilling hour from producing product D is £18.50. Purchase of component A releases 2 drilling hours (yielding £37 additional product D contribution) and purchase of component B releases 1 drilling hour (yielding £18.50 additional contribution). Thus components A and B should be purchased from outside and this will free up 200 drilling hours (50 components × 2 hours for component A plus 100 × 1 hour for component B). This will enable output of product D to be expanded by 50 units (200 hours/4 hours per unit). The increase in contribution is calculated as follows:

	(£)	(£)
Additional contribution from Product D (50 × £74)		3700
Less additional purchasing costs:		
Component A (50 × £18)	900	
Component B (100 × £18)	1800	2700
Additional contribution		1000

(ii) For the answer to this question see 'Single-resource constraints' and 'Two resource constraints' in Chapter 26.

(a) Machine hours are the limiting factor and profits will be maximized by allocating machine hours on the basis of a product's contribution per machine hour. In order to do this it is necessary to compute the output per machine hour for each product.

Calculation of output per machine hour

$$\text{Manufacturing overhead rate} = £427\,500/2250 \text{ hrs}$$
$$= £190 \text{ per machine hour}$$

$$\text{Output per machine hour} = \frac{\text{machine hour rate}}{\text{overhead allocated per unit of output}}$$

Product W = 222.2 (£190/£0.855) units per hour
X = 200 (£190/£0.950) units per hour
Y = 400 (£190/£0.475) units per hour
Z = 250 (£190/£0.76) units per hour

Calculation of contribution per machine hour

	Product			
	W	X	Y	Z
	(£)	(£)	(£)	(£)
Selling price per unit	3.650	3.900	2.250	2.950
Variable costs per unit	1.865	2.110	1.272	1.589
Contribution per unit	1.785	1.790	0.978	1.361
Output per machine hour (units)	222.2	200	400	250
Contribution per machine hour (£)	396.6	358	391.2	340.25
Ranking	1	3	2	4

Required machine hours to meet the maximum demand

Product W = 855 hours (190 000/222.2)
X = 625 hours (125 000/200)
Y = 360 hours (144 000/400)
Z = 568 hours (142 000/250)
2408 hours

Practical capacity is only 2250 machine hours and therefore there is a shortfall of 158 hours. Output of product Z should be reduced by 39 500 units (158 hours × 250 units per hour). The optimum output schedule is to produce 102 500 (142 000 − 39 500) units of product Z and maximum demand as per the sales forecast for products W, X and Z.

(b) *Calculation of profits with overtime*

	Product				Total
	W	X	Y	Z	(£)
Sales volume (units)	190 000	125 000	144 000	142 000	
Contribution per unit (£)	1.785	1.790	0.978	1.361	
Total contribution (excluding overtime premium)	339 150	223 750	140 832	193 262	896 994
Less overtime premium [a]					(10 053)
					886 941
Less fixed costs:					
Manufacturing					(427 500)
Selling and administration					(190 000)
Additional					(24 570)
Net profit					244 871

Note

[a] The production shortfall of 158 machine hours could be made up by working overtime on any of the four products.

The direct labour cost per machine hour for each product is:

$$\text{Product W} = £134.20 \ (222.2 \times £0.604)$$
$$\text{X} = £130.20 \ (200 \times £0.651)$$
$$\text{Y} = £162 \ (400 \times £0.405)$$
$$\text{Z} = £127.25 \ (250 \times £0.509)$$

Therefore it is cheaper to work overtime on product Z.
The overtime premium will be 39 500 × (£0.509 × 0.5)

(c)

	(£)
Additional contribution from working overtime on product Z (39 500 units × £1.361)	53 759
Less:	
Overtime premium	(10 053)
Additional fixed costs	(24 570)
Additional profit	19 136

Prior to making the decision management should ensure that staff are prepared to work overtime and that this will not result in lower productivity due to working longer hours.

Solution IM 9.9

(a) Maximum weekly output requires the following machine hours:

	Machine A hours	Machine B hours
2500 metres of 10″	250 (2500 × 0.1 hrs)	500 (2500 × 0.2 hrs)
2000 metres of 18″	600 (2000 × 0.3 hrs)	400 (2000 × 0.2 hrs)
	850	900
Hours available are:		
Normal time	600 (15 × 40 hrs)	520 (13 × 40 hrs)
Overtime	300 (15 × 20 hrs)	260 (13 × 20 hrs)
	900	780

Therefore some work will have to be contracted in order to meet demand. However, if the cost of subcontracting is less than the relevant manufacturing cost then it will be in the company's interest not to use all of the available machine capacity. It is assumed that the fixed costs cannot be avoided in the short term and are therefore not relevant to the decision. The relevant costs are as follows:

	10″ pipe		18″ pipe	
	Normal	Overtime	Normal	Overtime
	(£)	(£)	(£)	(£)
Materials	10.00	10.00	5.00	5.00
Labour:				
Machine A	1.00	1.50	3.00	4.50
Machine B	2.40	3.60	2.40	3.60
Variable cost	13.40	15.10	10.40	13.10
Subcontract price	18.00	18.00	12.00	12.00
Contribution/cost saving	4.60	2.90	1.60	(1.10)

Hours required (machine A)	0.1	0.1	0.3	0.3
Hours required (machine B)	0.2	0.2	0.2	0.2
Contribution per machine A hour (£)	46.00	29.00	5.33	Loss
Contribution per machine B hour (£)	23.00	14.50	8.00	Loss
Ranking	1	2	3	

From the above analysis it can be seen that the available capacity for each machine should initially be allocated to 10″ pipe. It is more expensive than sub-contracting to produce 18″ pipe if overtime is worked on both machines A and B. However, if normal time is used on machine A and overtime is used on machine B to produce 18″ pipe then the contribution is £0.50. Alternatively, if 18″ pipe is produced using overtime on machine A and normal time on machine B, the contribution will be £0.10. We should therefore allocate capacity in the following order:

(i) Allocate available normal and overtime hours first of all to production of 10″ pipe.
(ii) Use the remaining hours for production of 18″ pipe but do not use overtime for both machines A and B.

	Allocation of hours			
	Machine A		Machine B	
	Normal	Overtime	Normal	Overtime
Hours available	600	300	520	260
2500 metres of 10″	(250)		(500)	
100 metres of 18″	(30)		(20)	
1067 metres of 18″	(320)			(213)

Note that the balance of 320 hours of normal time can produce 1067 metres (320 hours/0.3 hours per metre of 18″ pipe) and this will require 213 machine B hours (1067 metres × 0.2 hours). In addition to the above allocation, 833 metres (2000 − 1167) of 18″ pipe should be subcontracted.

(b)

	Weekly cost	
	(£)	(£)
Labour:		
600 hours of A normal time at £10 per hour	6 000	
520 hours of B normal time at £12 per hour	6 240	
213 hours of B overtime at £18 per hour	3 834	16 074
Materials:		
2500 metres of 10″ pipe at £10 per metre	25 000	
1167 metres of 18″ pipe at £5 per metre	5 835	30 835
Subcontractor: 833 metres at £12 per metre		9 996
Variable cost		56 905
Fixed costs (15 × £450) + (£13 × £160)		8 830
		65 735

(c) Other factors to consider are:
   (i) Is the quality of work and speed of completion of the subcontractor equivalent to the construction company's own standard? If the quality is poor, might the company lose future contracts?
   (ii) The analysis is based on the machines working at maximum capacity. Will this increase the probability that machines will break down? Can the subcontractor cover the lost production from a machine breakdown at short notice?
   (iii) Will the use of a subcontractor cause problems with the public because of insufficient attention to people's property or to keeping the road traffic moving?

(iv) Does the subcontractor maintain adequate safety standards?
(v) Will cooperation of the workers be lost because overtime is not being fully used and yet work is being subcontracted?
(vi) Can the work of two contractors be scheduled and allocated satisfactorily?

Solution IM 9.10

(a) (i)

Hectares suitable for squash, kale, lettuce and beans	680
Hectares suitable for kale and lettuce only	280
	960

Minimum requirement: 10 000 boxes of each } rounded to nearest
Maximum requirement: 227 500 boxes of each } whole hectare.

	Squash	Kale	Lettuce	Beans
Boxes per hectare	350	100	70	180
Minimum requirements (hectares)	29	100	143	56

Cost per hectare:

	(pesos)	(pesos)	(pesos)	(pesos)
Materials	476	216	192	312
Labour: growing	896	608	372	528
harvesting etc.	1260	328	308	936
transport	1820	520	280	1728
Total variable costs	4452	1672	1152	3504

Selling price:

	(pesos)	(pesos)	(pesos)	(pesos)
Per box	15.38	15.87	18.38	22.27
Per hectare	5383.00	1587.00	1286.60	4008.60
Contribution per hectare	931.00	(85.00)	134.60	504.60
Ranking	1	4	3	2

280 hectares are suitable for kale and lettuce only. Given the negative contribution of kale, production should be restricted to the minimum requirements of 10 000 boxes, thus requiring the allocation of 100 hectares. The remaining 180 hectares should be allocated to lettuce. The 680 hectares which are suitable for all four vegetables should be allocated as follows:

Minimum requirements to beans	56 hectares
Balance to squash	624 hectares (680 − 56)

The maximum demand for squash is 227 500 boxes. This output requires 650 hectares (227 500/350). Therefore the maximum requirement will not be exceeded.

(ii) *Largest total profit*

		(pesos)
Squash	624 hectares at a contribution of 931 pesos per hectare	580 944.0
Beans	56 hectares at a contribution of 504.6 pesos per hectare	28 257.6
Lettuce	180 hectares at a contribution of 134.6 pesos per hectare	24 228.0
Kale	100 hectares at a contribution of (85.0) pesos per hectare	(8 500.0)

	624 929.6
Fixed costs	444 000.0
Profit	180 929.6

(iii) The drainage work will make land which is at present only suitable for kale and lettuce suitable for all four vegetables. Therefore 280 hectares could be converted to being suitable for all four vegetables. However, in order to meet minimum production requirements, it is necessary to allocate 100 hectares for kale and 143 hectares for lettuce. This leaves a balance of 37 hectares which should be considered for drainage in order to grow squash and beans. Proposed production of squash in (i) requires 624 hectares yielding 218 400 boxes (624 × 350 boxes). An additional 9100 boxes (227 500 − 218 400) could be grown using 26 hectares (9100/350). The balance of 11 hectares would be allocated to produce 1980 boxes of beans (this is still within the maximum production requirement for beans). Alternatively, the 37 hectares could be used to produce 6660 boxes of beans, and this will still be within the maximum output. The calculation of the change from normal harvesting costs per hectare for these alternatives are as follows:

Squash: (pesos)
First 10 hectares: 350 boxes × 1.2 pesos +420
Second 10 hectares: 350 boxes × 1.3 pesos +455
Third 10 hectares: 350 boxes × 1.4 pesos +490
Fourth 7 hectares: 350 boxes × 1.5 pesos +525

Beans: (pesos)
180 boxes × 1.2 pesos −216
180 boxes × 1.3 pesos −234
180 boxes × 1.4 pesos −252
180 boxes × 1.5 pesos −270

The revised contributions per hectare are:

Squash (pesos)
First 10 hectares: 931 existing less 420 = 511
Second 10 hectares: 931 existing less 455 = 476
Third 10 hectares: 931 existing less 490 = 441
Fourth 7 hectares: 931 existing less 525 = 406

Beans: (pesos)
504.6 existing plus 216 = 720.6
504.6 existing plus 234 = 738.6
504.6 existing plus 252 = 756.6
504.6 existing plus 270 = 774.6

It is therefore more profitable to use all 37 hectares to substitute beans for lettuce. This substitution process will result in the following additional contributions (in pesos):

	Beans	Lettuce	Incremental contribution per hectare	Incremental contribution
First 10 hectares	720.6	134.6	586.0	5860
Second 10 hectares	738.6	134.6	604.0	6040
Third 10 hectares	756.6	134.6	622.0	6220
Fourth 7 hectares	774.6	134.6	640.0	4480

The NPV calculation (in pesos) using a 15% discount rate for a four year period are as follows:

	Cash flow	Present value	Investment	NPV	Cumulative NPV
First 10 hectares	5860	16 730	19 000	(2270)	(2270)
Second 10 hectares	6040	17 244	17 500	(256)	(2536)
Third 10 hectares	6220	17 758	15 000	2758	232
Fourth 7 hectares	4480	12 790	12 950	(160)	72

NPV is maximized if 30 hectares of land are drained to grow beans instead of lettuce.

(b) Financial dangers associated with going ahead with the drainage work include:
   (i) Drainage work may take longer than expected, thus delaying the timing of the cash inflows.
   (ii) Drainage work may cost more than expected.
   (iii) Capital costs or the discount rate might be underestimated. Note that the return is only slightly in excess of the 15% cost of capital.
   (iv) Demand and selling prices of the products might change or the changes in costs might be different from the predictions.

Solution IM 9.11

(a) The relevant costs of the contract are as follows:

	(£)	(£)
Salary of G. Harrison		2 000
Supervision cost[a]		10 000
Cost of craftsmen[a]		16 000
Cost of equipment[b]		3 000
Material costs:[c]		
A $(100 \times £3) + (900 \times £3)$	3000	
B $(1000 \times £0.90)$	900	
C $(100 \times £6)$	600	
D $(100 \times £2) + (100 \times £3)$	500	
E $(5000 \times £0.20)$	1000	
F $(1000 \times £1) + (2000 \times £2)$	5000	11 000
Other direct expenses		6 500
Owner's opportunity cost[d]		3 000
		51 500
Less savings on maintenance work[e]		(1 500)
Minimum contract price		50 000

Notes
[a] The costs given in the question include apportioned fixed overheads which are not a relevant cost. Therefore £1000 has been deducted from the supervision cost (10% × £10 000) and £800 from each of the craftsmen's costs.
[b] The historical cost of the equipment is a sunk cost. It is assumed that the existing equipment would have been sold if the contract were not accepted. Therefore the relevant cost of using the equipment is the reduction in the scrap value over the duration of the contract.
[c] *Material A*: It is assumed that the usage of the 100 units in stock will be replaced in the coming year and be used on property maintenance. This is more profitable than the alternative of selling the materials for £2 and replacing them at a later date at £3. The remaining quantities will be replaced at the current purchase price.
Material B: It is assumed that the 1000 units issued from stock for the contract will be replaced at £0.90 per unit. This material is used regularly in the business.
Material C: This material is purchased specially for the contract.
Materials D and F: The stocks of these materials have no alternative use within the

business and will be sold if not used on the contract. Hence the sale price represents the opportunity cost of using these materials. The remainder of the materials will be purchased at current prices.

Material E: It is assumed that the material taken from stock for this contract will be replaced at the current purchase price. This material is used regularly in the business.

[d] It is assumed that the alternative is for Johnson to pay out £12 000 to maintain the existing business while he earns £15 000 on the one year appointment. If the contract is undertaken then Johnson will lose £3000.

[e] It is assumed that the contract could be completed and maintenance programme carried out during the period in which the supervisor and craftsmen are employed (one year). It is also assumed that the supervision and craftsmen will be employed for one year only. A further assumption is that the lowest quotation will be accepted.

Other assumptions: The lease of the yard would have to be paid even if the contract were not accepted.

(b) (i) What is the likelihood that Johnson will obtain other contract work during the year? If there is a possibility then any lost contribution should be covered in the minimum contract price.

(ii) Given that the profit was £12 000 last year, Johnson should consider closing operations and obtaining a permanent salary of £15 000 per annum.

(iii) Do any alternative uses for the accommodation of the yard exist? If so then appropriate opportunity cost should be added.

(iv) The contract price represents a minimum price. Johnson should aim to earn a surplus on the contract.

(v) Will the loss of one-quarter of Johnson's time to the existing business result in a reduction in profit? If this is the case then the lost profits should be included as an opportunity cost.

Solution IM 9.12

	Discontinue at 30 June (£)	Discontinue at 30 November (£)
Relevant inflows		
Sale of printing material	10 000	
Sale of pallets[a]	380	
Sub-letting income	12 500	
Sale of machines[b]	27 000	25 000
Sale of vehicles[b]	48 000	44 000
	97 880	69 000
Relevant outflows		
Salaries and wages:[c]		
Printing	15 000	90 000
Distribution	—	20 000
Publishing vacancy	7 000	6 500
Materials and supplies:		
Printing [(5 × £31 000) − £18 000]		137 000
Distribution[a]	500	5 500
Cancellation charge[a]	100	
Occupancy costs:[d]		
Apportioned	29 112	34 250
Directly attributable	—	14 250
Printing and distribution fee (£65 000 × 5)	325 000	–
	376 712	307 500
Net cash outflow	278 832	238 500

On the basis of the above information, printing and publishing should be discontinued on 30 November.

Notes

[a] If pallets are taken for July and August and resold to Longplant Ltd, the cash outflow will be £240 (£1000 − 760). If the pallets are taken for July only, the cash outflow will be £220 (£500 + £100 − £380). Therefore the lowest cash outflow option should be chosen and the August delivery should be cancelled.

[b] Only incremental sale proceeds should be included in the analysis. Depreciation and the written-down value of assets represent sunk costs and are not relevant for decision-making purposes.

[c] Two specialist staff (£3000 × 5 months) will continue to be paid if the department is closed in June. If the department is closed in November, it is assumed the publishing vacancy will be filled for five months at a cost of £6500. With a June closure, the publishing vacancy will cost the company £7000 (£1400 × 5). Redundancy payments are not relevant, since the same amount will be paid to all staff irrespective of the date of closure.

[d] The occupancy costs for five months are:

	Printing	Distribution	Total
	(£)	(£)	(£)
Total	42 500	6000	48 500
Directly attributable	12 750 (30%)	1500 (25%)	14 250
Apportioned (balance)	29 750	4500	34 250

It is assumed that company cash flows, in respect of the costs which are apportioned to activities, will be reduced by £5138 (15% × £34 250) if the department is closed in June. In other words, it is assumed cash flows will be reduced and not merely the proportion of costs which are allocated to the department.

Activity-based costing

Solutions to Chapter 10 questions

The answer to this question should describe cost allocation, cost apportionment and absorption within a traditional product costing system. Both traditional and ABC systems use the two-stage allocation procedure. In the first stage costs are assigned to cost centres and in the second stage costs are charged to products passing through the cost centres using appropriate overhead absorption rates.

The terms 'cost allocation' and 'cost apportionment' are often used interchangeably to describe methods that are used in the first stage to arbitrarily share out costs to cost centres on some logical basis (e.g. rent may be apportioned on the basis of floor area of each department and works management on the basis of number of employees in each department). However, some textbooks distinguish between the two terms. Allocations are used to describe those overheads that can be specifically attributed to a cost centre (e.g. depreciation of machinery or the wages of a supervisor located in a specific cost centre). The term 'apportionment' is used where a cost cannot be specifically attributed to a cost centre and the costs have to be apportioned on some logical basis (e.g. rent apportioned to cost centres on the basis of floor area).

The term 'absorption' is normally used to refer to the second stage of the two-stage overheads process by which cost centre overheads are charged to products (i.e. absorbed by products) passing through the cost centre. Direct labour hours or machine hours are the most widely used absorption methods to assign the cost centre overheads to products.

The answer should then go on to describe activity-based-costing systems and also the limitations of traditional product costing systems (see Chapter 10 for a description of ABC).

For the answer to this question see 'A comparison of traditional and ABC systems' and 'volume-based and non-volume based cost drivers' in Chapter 10.

(a) See 'The emergence of ABC systems' and 'Costs versus benefits considerations' in Chapter 10 for the answer to this question.

(b) Organizations may decide not to use or to abandon ABC for the following reasons:

   (i) the high cost cost of operating an ABC system
   (ii) the lack of sufficient employees with the necessary expertise
   (iii) the lack of a 'champion' and top management support to promote ABC
   (iv) the resources required to set up an ABC system may not be available
   (v) difficulty in replacing existing systems that have become embedded in the organization and the resistance to change by employees
   (vi) employee hostility if it is viewed purely as a cost reduction technique that will be accompanied by redundancies
   (vii) a low proportion of costs that can be more effectively controlled and assigned to cost objects using ABC techniques.

(c) The usefulness of distinguishing between value-added and non-value-added activities is discussed in Chapter 22.

Solution IM 10.4   (a) *Production cost per unit (conventional method)*

	Product X (£)	Product Y (£)	Product Z (£)
Direct labour at £6 per hour	3	9	6
Direct materials	20	12	25
Production overhead at £28 per machine hour	42 (1½ hours)	28 (1 hour)	84 (3 hours)
	65	49	115

(b) The total production overhead is derived from the overheads allocated to the product in part (a):

		(£)
Product X	31 500	(750 × £42)
Product Y	35 000	(1250 × £28)
Product Z	588 000	(7000 × £84)
	654 500	

Overhead costs traced to cost pools:

	(£)
Set-up cost	229 075 (35%)
Machining	130 900 (20%)
Materials handling	98 175 (15%)
Inspection	196 350 (30%)
	654 500

Cost driver rates:

	(£)
Cost per set-up	341.903 (£229 075/670)
Cost per machine hour	5.60 (£130 900/23 375[a])
Cost per material movement	818.125 (£98 175/120)
Cost per inspection	196.35 (£196 350/1 000)

Note
[a] Machine hours = (750 × 1½) + (1250 × 1) + (7000 × 3) = 23 375

Overhead cost assigned to each product:

	Product X (£)	Product Y (£)	Product Z (£)
Set-up costs at £341.903	25 643 (75)	39 319 (115)	164 113 (480)
Machining at £5.60 per machine hour	6 300 (1125)	7 000 (1250)	117 600 (21 000)
Materials handling at £818.125 per movement	9 817 (12)	17 181 (21)	71 177 (87)
Inspection at £196.35 per inspection	29 453 (150)	35 343 (180)	131 554 (670)
	71 213	98 843	484 444
Number of units	750	1250	7000
Overhead cost per unit	£95	£79	£69

Production cost per unit (ABC principles)

	Product X (£)	Product Y (£)	Product Z (£)
Direct labour	3	9	6
Materials	20	12	25
Production overhead	95	79	69
	118	100	100
Change (compared with traditional method)	+82%	+104%	−13%

(c) The traditional method allocates overheads in proportion to machine hours to products (4.8% to X, 5.3% to Y and 89.9% to Z). However, when overheads are assigned on the basis of number of set-ups, movements of materials and inspections the proportion of overheads assigned to product Z are 72% (480/670) for set-up costs, 72% (87/120) for materials handling costs and 67% (670/1000) for inspection costs. In contrast, the traditional method allocates approximately 90% of all costs to product Z. Therefore the unit cost for product is higher with the traditional method. The opposite situation applies with products X and Y and, as a result, unit costs are lower with the traditional method.

(i) *Tradition volume-based system*

The first stage of the two-stage overhead allocation procedure requires that the service department overheads are reallocated to the production departments (Machinery and Fittings). Typical allocation bases are:

Materials handling	– Direct material cost
Material procurement	– Direct material cost
Set-up	– Direct labour hours
Maintenance	– Machine cost or maintenance hours
Quality control	– Direct labour hours

It is assumed that the £10 500 service department costs will be apportioned as follows:

	(£000)
Machinery	6500
Fittings	4000

(Note that students will require details of the above allocation since the details are not given in the question.)

The computation of the departmental overhead rates is as follows:

	Machinery department (£)	Fitting department (£)
Original overhead allocation	2 500 000	2 000 000
Service department reallocations	6 500 000	4 000 000
Total production overhead cost (£)	9 000 000	6 000 000
Total direct labour hours	1 100 000	350 000
Overhead rate	£8.182 per DLH	£17.143 per DLH

Product costs

	Product A (£)	Product B (£)
Machinery department:		
500 000 DLH × £8.182	4 091 000	
600 000 DLH × £8.182		4 909 200
Fitting department:		
150 000 DLH × £17.143	2 571 500	
200 000 DLH × £17.143		3 428 600
Total production overhead cost (£)	6 662 500	8 337 800
Production volume (£)	300 000	300 000
Unit product overhead cost (£)	22.21	27.79

(ii) *Activity-based costing system*

Computation of cost driver rates:

Overhead	Annual cost (£000)	Annual cost driver volume	Cost driver rate
Material handling	1500	2540 material movements	£590.55 per material movement
Material procurement	2000	6500 orders	£307.69 per order
Set-up	1500	624 set-ups	£2403.85 per set-up
Maintenance	2500	30 000 maintenance hours	£83.33 per maintenance per hour
Quality control	3000	4120 inspections	£728.16 per inspection
Machinery	2500	1 100 000 direct labour hours	£2.27 per DLH
Fitting	2000	350 000 direct labour hours	£5.71 per DLH

Overheads assigned to part numbers

	Material handling	Material procurement	Set-up	Maintenance	Quality control	Machinery	Fitting	Total (£000)
Part 1:								
Cost driver consumption	180	200	12	7000	360	150 000	50 000	
Cost driver rate (£)	590.55	307.69	2 403.85	83.33	728.16	2.27	5.71	
Total cost (£000)	106.30	61.54	28.85	583.31	262.14	340.50	285.50	1 668
Part 2:								
Cost driver consumption	160	300	12	5000	360	350 000	100 000	
Cost driver rate (£)	590.55	307.69	2 403.85	83.33	728.16	2.27	5.71	
Total cost (£000)	94.49	92.31	28.85	416.65	262.14	794.50	571.00	2 260
Part 3:								
Cost driver consumption	1000	2000	300	10 000	2400	200 000	60 000	
Cost driver rate (£)	590.55	307.69	2 403.85	83.33	728.16	2.27	5.71	
Total cost (£000)	590.55	615.38	721.16	833.30	1 747.58	454.00	342.60	5 305
Part 4:								
Cost driver consumption	1200	4000	300	8000	1000	400 000	140 000	
Cost driver rate (£)	590.55	307.69	2 403.85	83.33	728.16	2.27	5.71	
Total cost (£000)	708.66	1 203.76	721.16	666.64	728.16	908.00	799.40	5 763

Product costs

	Product A (£)	Product B (£)
Part 1	1 668 000	
Part 2	2 260 000	
Part 3		5 305 000
Part 4		5 763 000
Production overhead cost (£)	3 928 000	11 068 000
Production volume	300 000 units	300 000 units
Unit cost (£)	13.09	36.89

This answer is adapted from Innes, J. and Mitchell, F. (1990) *Activity Based Costing: A review with case studies*, Chartered Institute of Management Accountants, London.

(a) (i) *Budgeted analysis of net profit based on the sales value allocation base*

Operating profit	840 000	370 000	290 000
Central cost allocation in ratio 5000: 4000: 3000	416 667	333 333	250 000
Net profit	423 333	36 667	40 000

The report should draw attention to the following:

- Traditional costing systems allocate costs on the basis of volume measures such as direct labour hours, machine hours and sales values or volumes.
- Using sales values assumes that central costs are caused by sales values thus departments with the higher sales values are allocated with higher proportions of central costs. The result is that the high sales value stores will be overcosted and low sales values stores will be undercosted if central costs are caused by factors unrelated to sales volumes or values.
- Central costs should be traced to stores on the basis of cost drivers that are the cause of the costs being incurred. Cost drivers are the events or forces that are significant determinants of the warehousing activities and the activities undertaken at head office.
- In many cases it is the complexity of dealing with different products, customers or stores locations that are the cause of overhead costs, rather than volume. Activity-based-costing systems attempt to capture complexity by using cost drivers such as the number of dispatches. For example, some warehousing costs will be caused by the number of dispatches. Thus, if a low sales volume store dispatches many small orders and a high sales volume store dispatches a small number of high volume orders using the number of dispatches as the cost driver will capture the greater complexity and the warehouse resources consumed by the low sales volume store. In contrast, using sales values as the cost driver will not capture the complexity and high sales value stores will be overcosted and low sales values stores will be undercosted.

(a) (ii) *Budgeted analysis of net profit based on the revised allocation bases*

Warehouse operations

	Total (£)	(£)	A (£)	B (£)	C (£)
Head Office					
Salary[a]	200 000	20 000	60 000	60 000	60 000
Advertising[b]	80 000	—	33 333	26 667	20 000
Establishment[c]	120 000	12 000	36 000	36 000	36 000
		32 000			
Warehouse					
Depreciation[d]	100 000	—	40 000	30 000	30 000
Storage[e]	80 000		32 000	24 000	24 000
Operating and despatch[f]	152 000		55 000	45 000	52 000
Delivery[g]	300 000		100 000	71 429	128 571
			356 333	293 096	350 571
Operating profit			840 000	370 000	290 000
Net profit/(loss)			483 667	76 904	(60 571)

Notes
[a] Allocated on the basis of note 1 in the question
[b] Allocated on the basis of note 2 in the question
[c] Allocated on the basis of note 1 in the question
[d] Allocated on the basis of storage space occupied
[e] Allocated on the basis of storage space occupied

f £120 000 given in the question plus £32 000 allocated to warehousing operations in the above analysis
g Allocated on the basis of delivery distances

The revised allocations show that the costs identified to store C exceed the current level of operating profit and an overall loss is disclosed. Stores B and C show improved results based on the revised allocations. The allocation bases selected bear a closer cause-and-effect relationship than the current method of cost allocation. However, for some costs (e.g., advertising and depreciation) it is difficult to establish meaningful cause-and-effect relationships. Nevertheless, the revised basis provides more meaningful profitability analysis attention directing information. It shows that the viability of maintaining store C should be subject to a more detailed special study. Some of the costs, such as depreciation, may represent facility or business-sustaining costs that are unavoidable and that would still continue if C were closed. Such factors should be taken into account when the special study is undertaken. If the special study still suggests that C is unprofitable steps should be taken to reduce costs by reducing the demand for activities, such as by reducing the number of low volume dispatches so that resource consumption is reduced without reducing sales revenues. In addition, direct deliveries from some suppliers and the more efficient routing of deliveries should be considered. The important point to note is that the revised profitability analysis has highlighted issues for investigation which were not highlighted by the previous allocation method.

(b) Regression analysis and tests of reliability can be used to examine the relationship between some of the costs and the allocation bases (cost drivers) proposed. Details of the costs of activities and the potential cost drivers should be accumulated at frequent intervals (e.g. monthly) and a regression equation established and reliability tests undertaken. For a more detailed explanation of these issues you should refer to Chapter 24.

Solution IM 10.7

(a) (i) *Preliminary workings*

Making

Estimated minutes for the making activity	
$(5000 \times 5.25) + (3000 \times 5.25)$	42 000
Variable conversion costs absorption rate	
(£350 000/42 000 minutes) per minute	£8.333
Fixed conversion costs absorption rate	
(£210 000/42 000 minutes) per minute	£5
Variable conversion costs charged to both products	
(5.25 minutes × £8.333)	£43.75
Fixed conversion costs charged to both products	
(5.25 minutes × £5)	£26.25
Product specific fixed conversion costs charged to both products	
(40% × £26.25)	£10.50

Packing

Estimated minutes for the packing activity (5000 × 6) + (3000 × 4)	42 000
Variable conversion costs absorption rate	
(£280 000/42 000 minutes) per minute	£6.666
Fixed conversion costs absorption rate	
(£140 000/42 000 minutes) per minute	3.333
Variable conversion costs charged to product VG4U	
(6 minutes × £6.666)	£40
Variable conversion costs charged to product VG2	
(4 minutes × £6.666)	£26.67

Fixed conversion costs charged to product VG4U
   (6 minutes × £3.333)   £20
Fixed conversion costs charged to product VG2
   (4 minutes × £3.333)   £13.33
Product specific fixed costs are 40% of £20 for VGU4 and
   40% of £13.33 for VG2

The unit cost calculations are as follows:

	VG4U (£)	VG2 (£)
Direct material	30	30
variable conversion cost – Making	43.75	43.75
– Packing	40.00	26.67
	113.75	100.42
Product specific fixed costs:		
Making	10.50	10.50
Packing	8.00	5.33
Total product specific (relevant) cost	132.25	116.25
Company fixed cost:		
Making	15.75	15.75
Packing	12.00	8.00
Total cost	160.00	140.00

(a) (ii) The management suggestion is presumably based on the fact that the reported cost for VG4U exceeds the selling price. However, the relevant or avoidable costs for the product are £132.25 and if the company fixed costs remain unchanged if the product is discontinued then the company will lose a contribution of £17.75 (£150 – £132.25) on sales of 5000 units. This will result in profits for the period being reduced by £88 750 (5000 × £17.75) unless there is an alternative opportunity for the production capacity.

(b) Costs are charged to each activity in the estimated proportions and then to each product using the cost driver proportions given in the question.

		Total	VG4U	VG2
Product units			5000	3000
	(%)	(£)	(£)	(£)
Variable conversion cost:				
Moulding (temperature)	(60)	210 000	140 000	70 000
Trimming (consistency)	(40)	140 000	40 000	100 000
Packing (time)	(70)	196 000	117 600	78 400
Packing material (complexity)	(30)	84 000	21 000	63 000
			318 600	311 400
Cost per product unit			63.72	103.80
Product specific fixed costs:				
Moulding (60% × (40% of £210 000))		50 400	33 600	16 800
Trimming (40% × (40% of £210 000))		33 600	9600	24 000
Packing (70% × (40% of £140 000))		39 200	23 520	15 680
Packing material (30% × (40% of £140 000))		16 800	4200	12 600
			70 920	69 080
Cost per product unit			14.18	23.03

Company fixed costs = 60% × £350 000 total fixed costs
                    = £210 000

Overall average cost per unit = £210 000/8000
= £26.25

Hence amended unit costs are as follows:

	VG4U (£)	VG2 (£)
Direct material cost	30.00	30.00
Variable conversion costs	63.72	103.80
	93.72	133.80
Product specific fixed costs	14.18	23.03
Relevant costs	107.90	156.83
Company fixed cost	26.25	26.25
	134.15	183.08

(c) The ABC unit costs should provide a more accurate measure of resource consumption by the products because several different cost drivers are used that are related to the resources consumed by the products for the different activities. A different message emerges from the reported product costs. Product VG2 appears to be a loss making product. A more detailed analysis indicates that the selling price exceeds the relevant costs and VG2 should not be discontinued unless discontinuation enables company fixed costs to be reduced by an amount in excess of the product's current contribution to these fixed costs.

(d) For the answer to this question you should refer to 'Target costing' in Chapters 11 and 22. In particular, the answer should stress that the existing selling prices, costs and volumes results in a net profit margin on sales of approximately 5%. If existing selling prices cannot be changed, or they have been determined by market forces, and volumes are to remain unchanged the focus will be on cost reduction to meet the target profit. This might be achieved by product redesign (such as the use of fewer component parts and eliminating non-standard materials) and the elimination or reduction of activities. For an illustration of the approach you should refer to Chapter 22. Note that *kaizen* costing is applicable here rather than target costing. Target costing is applied to new products whereas *kaizen* costing is applied to existing products.

Pricing decisions and profitability analysis

Solutions to Chapter 11 questions

(a) The ROCE approach would be likely to yield an inadequate return because:
  (i) Prime cost does not include any overheads. Consequently the profit margin may be insufficient to recover overheads and provide sufficient profits to yield an adequate ROCE.
  (ii) The company is working at full capacity, which might suggest underpricing. Consequently limiting factors will apply, and the resources should be costed at their opportunity cost. This approach is not adopted with the current pricing method.
  (iii) Incremental or marginal cost represents the minimum short-run price. Prime cost does not include variable overheads, and therefore provides an underestimate of the minimum short-run price. If the industry is very competitive, there is a danger that the company might tender on the basis of an incorrect short-run price.
  (iv) The profit margin bears no relation to an attempt to earn an adequate ROCE. Tenders involving the use of a large amount of capital equipment do not include a charge for its use – in terms of either depreciation or a target ROCE. It is unlikely that the percentage added to prime cost will be sufficient to cover the depreciation of the equipment or a fair return from the use of the equipment.

(b) The stages are as follows:
  (i) Decide on a target ROCE employed from fixed and current assets and how the ROCE is to be measured (on book value or replacement cost?).
  (ii) Estimate how many working days per year the equipment will be in productive use.
  (iii) For a particular contract estimate the number of days the equipment will be used on the contract.
  (iv) The charge to the contract will be:

$$\frac{\text{estimated number of days on contract per (iii)}}{\text{estimated days in year when in use per (ii)}} \times \text{value of equipment} \times \text{required ROCE}$$

  (v) Estimate the average amount of incremental working capital resulting from the contract and the number of days for which it is required, and calculate the required monetary ROCE following the procedure outlined in (iv).
  (vi) The tender price will be calculated by adding the required ROCE in (iv) and (v) expressed in monetary terms to the total costs of the contract (total cost would consist of prime cost plus manufacturing overhead plus non-manufacturing overheads).
  (vii) It is assumed in (vi) that all assets can be allocated to contracts. The required ROCE on any assets which cannot be directly allocated to contracts (e.g. fixed assets related to administration) should be apportioned to contracts on some acceptable basis.

(c) The problems likely to be encountered in meeting a pre-set profit target on a ROCE basis are:
  (i) The approach ignores demand and the competitive position of the company. If ROCE pricing is strictly applied when competition is keen and

there is surplus capacity in the industry then it is unlikely that tenders will be competitive. Consequently sales will decline and insufficient contribution will be earned to obtain an adequate ROCE.

(ii) Strict application of the pricing method will result in fixed costs and the over-all required monetary ROCE being spread over a smaller number of contracts when demand is declining. Consequently costs and selling prices will be higher per contract when demand is falling. There is a danger that the company will not be competitive, and sales will decline dramatically whereas fixed costs will remain unchanged. Adopting ROCE pricing might therefore lead to reduced profits and ROCE.

(iii) The approach involves circular reasoning because estimates of demand are required to estimate the cost, which in turn is used to estimate the tender price, which in turn determines demand.

(iv) There may be difficulty in estimating which assets will be allocated to contracts and the number of days they will be assigned. If the actual period of the contract is longer than anticipated or if the contract requires more equipment than originally estimated then the return on capital employed included in the tender price will be significantly under estimated.

Solution IM 11.2

(a) See 'Customer profitability analysis' in Chapter 11 for the answer to this question.

(b) The answer should include a discussion of the benefits derived from customer profitability analysis (CPA) that are described in Chapter 11. The question asks for a critical appraisal. Possible criticisms include:

(i) Some organizations have thousands of different customers and it is very expensive, or not feasible, to analyse profits by individual customers. These organizations concentrate on customer segment profitability analysis. However, for some companies it is difficult to identify appropriate customer segments which provide suitable feedback information for decision-making.

(ii) The difficulty in accurately measuring the cost of joint resources consumed by individual customers or customer segments.

(iii) CPA is unlikely to provide useful information in those organizations whose customers do not make repeated purchases.

(iv) The focus is on past profitability and there is a danger that organizations may focus excessively on existing customers rather than creating new customers and developing new markets and products.

Solution IM 11.3

(a) The company could adopt one of the following three approaches for pricing the new car:

(i) A high-price market skimming policy.

(ii) A medium-price policy.

(iii) A low-price market penetration policy.

The new car is expected to have a reputation for high quality, and it appears that the company has a differential advantage over its competitors in terms of quality perceived by its customers. By setting a high price initially, the company can take full advantage of the high demand which is expected. It appears that initial demand will be in excess of supply, and the company should adopt a market skimming policy in order to equate demand with supply. If it does not, some of the potential excess profits may be creamed off by second-hand car dealers. A high price will be consistent with the car's 'quality image' whereas a lower price may create the impression of lower quality. If the launch is supported with a high level of marketing and advertising, a demand will be created which should, at least, be equivalent to its current production capacity. After setting the initial high price, the price can be progressively reduced to stimulate further demand once the initial inelastic demand has been met. One disadvantage of this policy is that it might encourage competitors to enter this market segment.

A medium price would ensure that the company's existing market share for this type of car is maintained or improved. However, this policy might lead to demand initially being in excess of production, and it might be preferable to curtail demand at the launch stage by setting a high price initially and then adopting a medium price at a later stage in the product's life cycle. A medium price at this stage may also be necessary as competitors come along with new models.

The market for luxury cars is likely to be inelastic, and there is little point creating unfulfilled sales demand at a low selling price. At the decline stage of the product's life cycle a low price may be necessary in order to stimulate demand.

(b) In the early stages of the product life cycle a high-price market skimming pricing strategy is likely to be appropriate. Customers will be prepared to pay a premium price for a quality product which is perceived to be superior to the competitors' products. The price should be high enough to limit initial demand to the estimated production output. At a later stage in the product's life cycle, when competitors introduce new models which compete in this market segment, price should be lowered in order to expand the market and maintain market share.

(c) Demand for this type of car is likely to be elastic, and a low market penetration pricing policy is therefore appropriate. A pricing policy should be adopted which maximizes sales volumes at the early stage of the product life cycle, thus ensuring that the high volume of fixed development costs are recovered as quickly as possible.

(a) The minimum selling price should cover incremental costs of meeting the order. It is assumed that labour is an incremental cost and that none of the fixed overheads would be avoidable if a batch of 200 units was not produced. **Solution IM 11.4**

The total cost per unit is £61.92 (£31.65 + £21.82 + £3.05 + £5.40). The fixed cost per unit is £7.84 (£3 + £2.50 +£1.50 + £0.84). Therefore the incremental cost per unit (excluding set-up cost) is £54.08 (£61.92 − £7.84). The incremental cost of a batch of 200 units is £10 816 (£54.08 × 200) plus set-up cost (£20) = £10 836.

The above selling price does not generate a contribution towards fixed costs. In order to make a profit a price should be set that ensures that a contribution is made towards fixed costs.

Adopting a selling price based on a margin above variable cost does not take into account customer demand or competitors' selling prices for similar products. Any attempt to price below competitors should consider their reactions as they may meet the selling price reduction and thus market prices will fall. The overall effect will be the same market share at a lower selling price.

The company also must consider the impact on customer goodwill once its other customers become aware of the special price that is being charged to key customers.

(b) Assuming that all of the fixed costs are unavoidable, and the released capacity has no alternative use if the company sub-contracts the product, the incremental costs of making the product are the variable costs of £6.20 per box. This is lower than the sub-contract price and the company should therefore make the first 7000 units itself. The estimated total contribution for each selling price is as follows:

Selling price (£)	Demand	Unit variable cost (£)	Unit contribution (£)	Total contribution (£)
13	5000	6.20	6.80	34 000
12	6000	6.20	5.80	34 800
11	7000	6.20	4.80	33 600
	200	7.75	3.25	650
				34 250
10	700	6.20	3.80	26 600
	4200	7.75	2.25	9 450
				36 050
9	7000	6.20	2.80	19 600
	6400	7.00	2.00	12 800
				32 400

Profits are maximized at a selling price of £10 per unit.

(c) Management should consider ways of utilizing the limiting factor more efficiently. Examples include:
  (i) improving product design in order to reduce the usage of labour, materials or machinery;
  (ii) improving production methods, plant layout or machine usage in order to avoid bottlenecks so that output can be increased from the existing facilities;
  (iii) introducing overtime where labour is the limiting factor;
  (iv) sub-contracting the manufacturing of components or products in order to 'free up' capacity.

Solution IM 11.5

(a) *Cost per packet for Cohin tender*

	(£)
Raw materials	0.30
Operating wages	0.12
Manufacturing overheads	0.24
Administration overheads	0.12
Packaging and transport	0.10
Full cost	0.88

Normal selling price for 50 000 = £0.88 × 1.15 = £1.012 (say £1.01)
Selling price for 60 000 = £0.88 × 1.145 = £1.0076 (say £1.01)
Selling price for 70 000 = £0.88 × 1.14 = £1.0032 (say £1.00)

(b) *Cohin tender*

	50 000 units (£)	60 000 units (£)	70 000 units (£)
Revenue	50 500	60 600	70 000
Variable costs at £0.52 per unit	(26 000)	(31 200)	(36 400)
Incremental fixed costs	(10 900)	(11 900)	(11 900)
Contribution to general fixed overheads	13 600	17 500	21 700

Stamford tender

	(£)
Contribution [60 000 × (£1.20 − 0.67)]	31 800
Less incremental fixed costs	11 900
Contribution to general fixed overheads	19 900

Recommendation
The Cohin tender is preferable only if sales reach 70 000 units. The decision depends on management's attitude towards risk. The Stamford contract will yield a contribution of £19 900 with certainty, whereas the contribution from the Cohin contract will range from £13 600 to £21 700. Without estimates of probabilities of the likely demand for the Cohin contract, it is not possible to make a specific recommendation.

(c) See 'Limitations of cost-plus pricing' and 'Reasons for cost-plus pricing' in Chapter 11 for the answer to this question.

(d) It is recommended that relevant costs should be used for pricing decisions and these cost estimates should be combined with demand estimates in order to set target selling prices. For a detailed discussion of the approach see 'Pricing non-cutomized products in Chapter 11.

(e) Expected value of Cohin tender = 0.8 (0.3 × £13 600 + 0.5 × £17 500
                                          + 0.2 × £21 700)
                                    = £13 736

Expected value of Stamford tender = 0.7 × £19 900 = £13 930

Based on the expected value decision rule, Stamford should get the greater sales effort.

(f) Any price which just covers the incremental cost per unit should represent the minimum selling price. However, a selling price which just covers incremental cost is unlikely to cover general fixed costs, and can only be recommended in the short term. The incremental cost per unit for an output of 80 000 units is:

(i) Cohin tender = £0.67 [£0.52 variable cost + (£11 900/80 000 units)]
(ii) Stamford tender = £0.82 [£0.67 variable cost + (£11 900/80 000 units)]

The recommended price is the maximum price at which demand for the product is 80 000 units per week. Clearly this is less than £1 for Cohin and £1.20 for Stamford, because neither company is prepared to order 80 000 units at these prices. To determine the recommended price, it is necessary for Josun to negotiate with both companies to ascertain the maximum price at which demand will be 80 000 units.

Solution 11.6

(a) (i) *Second-year demand of 3600 units*

Selling price/unit Year to 31 July 2003 (£)	Cash inflows Year to 31 July 2003 (£000)	Year to 31 July 2004 (£000)	Two-year total (£000)	Cash outflows Year to 31 July 2003 (£000)	Year to 31 July 2004 (£000)	Two-year total (£000)	Net cash inflow to 31 July 2004 Total (£000)
20	40	80[a]	120	32	32[d]	64	56
30	48	96[b]	144	32	32	64	80
40	48	112[c]	160	32	32	64	96
50	55	116	171	32	32	64	107
60	60	120	180	32	32	64	116
70	49	132	181	32	32	64	117
80	32	144	176	32	32	64	112

The initial launch price should be set at £70 per unit in order to maximize the net benefits of the company.

Notes
[a] 2000 units maximum production at £40 per unit. There are no stocks at the end of the first year.
[b] 2400 units at £40 per unit (2000 units maximum production plus 400 units closing stock at the end of the first year).
[c] 2800 units at £40 per unit (2000 units maximum production plus 800 units closing stock at the end of the first year).
[d] For all output levels maximum production of 2000 units is required in year 2 in order to meet demand.

(a) (ii) *Second-year demand of 1000 units*

Selling price/unit Year to 31 July 2003 (£)	Cash inflows Year to 31 July 2003 (£000)	Year to 31 July 2004 (£000)	Two-year total (£000)	Cash outflows Year to 31 July 2003 (£000)	Year to 31 July 2004 (£000)	Two-year total (£000)	Net cash inflow to 31 July 2004 Total (£000)
20	40	40[a]	80	32	16[b]	48	32
30	48	40	88	32	9.6[b]	41.6	46.4
40	48	40	88	32	3.2[d]	35.2	52.8
50	55	40	95	32	1.6	33.6	61.4
60	60	40	100	32	nil[e]	32	68
70	49	40	89	32	nil[e]	32	57
80	32	40	72	32	nil[e]	32	40

The initial launch price should be set at £60 per unit in order to maximize the net benefits to the company.

Notes

[a] In the second year there is sufficient production capacity (irrespective of demand in the first year) to meet sales demand. Therefore second-year sales will be 1000 units.

[b] 1000 units at £16.

[c] 600 units at £16 (1000 units less opening stock of 400 units).

[d] 200 units at £16 (1000 units less opening stock of 800 units).

[e] Opening stocks are sufficient to meet demand in the second year.

(b) In (a) (i) no spare capacity exists, and all production in the year to 31 July 2004 will be sold. In (a) (ii) zero production is required in the second year for initial launch prices of £60, £70 or £80. Stocks at the end of the second year are as follows:

Launch price (£)	60	70	80
Units produced (first year)	2000	2000	2000
Units sold (first year)	1000	700	400
Closing stock	1000	1300	1600
Units sold (second year)	1000	1000	1000
Closing stock (second year)	Nil	300	600

The answer requires the calculation of the selling price of the unsold stock which will result in the overall net benefit to the company being greater than the maximum profit in (a) (ii) of £68 000.

Let x = minimum selling price of unsold stock. Then, at a launch price of £70,

$$300x = £68\ 000 - £57\ 000$$
$$x = £36.67$$

At a launch price of £80,

$$600x = £68\ 000 - £40\ 000$$
$$x = £46.67$$

In other words, at a launch price of £70, unsold stock would have to be sold at a price in excess of £36.67 before this launch price will maximize company profits. At the £80 launch price, the unsold stock would have to be sold at a price in excess of £46.67 before this launch price will maximize total company profits.

(c) At a launch price of £60, £70 or £80, zero production will be required in the second year. Production in the second year is maximized at a launch price of £20. If the company can apply the spare capacity in the second year to alternative uses then the contribution from year 2 unused capacity should be incorporated into the analysis. Also any expected increases in costs in year 2 might lead management to consider selecting a launch price which minimizes production in the second year.

Solution IM 11.7

(a) The report should indicate that there will be no demand for product X at a selling price of £10 each. Demand is estimated to increase by 40 units for each £0.01 decrease in price. Therefore maximum sales are 40 000 units (£10 × £1 × 40) at £0.01 each.

Estimated demand is 20 000 units at half its theoretical maximum. The elasticity of demand of 1 around this level specified in the question is calculated as follows:

$$\frac{\text{proportion by which demand changes } (20\ 000/40\ 000 = 0.5)}{\text{proportional price change } (£5/£10 = 0.5)} = 1.0$$

However, at the current selling price of £6.25 estimated demand is 15 000 units (£3.75 × £1 × 40). The elasticity of demand that would be calculated by the consultants around this level is:

$$\frac{25\ 000/40\ 000 = 0.625}{£3.75/£10 = 0.375} = 1.67$$

Around this level of demand, elasticity of demand is greater than 1 and the observations are in line with the commercial manager's comments, with small changes in price having a significant effect on demand.

(b) At a selling price of £10 demand is zero. To increase demand by one unit, selling price must be reduced by £0.00025 (£0.01/40 units). Thus the maximum selling price for an output of x units is:

$$SP = £10 - £0.00025x$$

Therefore total revenue (TR) for an output of x units is $£10x - £0.00025x^2$.

$$\text{Marginal revenue (MR)} = \frac{d(TR)}{dx} = £10 - 0.00050x$$

Marginal cost is given in the question at £1.50 per unit.

At the optimum output level MR = MC.

Therefore the optimum output level is where

$$£1.50 = £10 - 0.0005x$$
$$x = 17\ 000 \text{ units}$$

The selling price at the optimum output level is £10 − 0.00025(17 000) = £5.75.

At a selling price of £5.75 the elasticity of demand is:

$$\frac{(40\ 000 - 17\ 000)/40\ 000}{(10 - £5.75)/10} = 1.35$$

(a) (i) *Calculation of cost per unit*

	Labour hours recovery method		Machine hours recovery method	
	X	Y	X	Y
	(£)	(£)	(£)	(£)
Direct labour	5	28	5	28
Direct materials	6	16	6	16
Directly attributable overhead[a]	3	28	3	28
General factory overhead[b]	6 (1 × £6)	48 (8 × £6)	16 (4 × £4)	8 (2 × £4)
Cost per unit	20	120	30	80
Selling price at cost plus 20%	24	144	36	96

Notes
[a] Fixed overheads directly attributable to the product divided by maximum production (X = 40 000 units, Y = 10 000 units).
[b] The calculations of the general fixed overhead rates are as follows:

	Labour hours (000)	Machine hours (000)
X	40 (40 000 × 1)	160 (40 000 × 4)
Y	80 (10 000 × 8)	20 (10 000 × 2)
Total hours	120	180
General fixed overhead (£000)	720	720
Hourly overhead rate (£)	6	4

The hourly overheads are based on maximum production.

(ii) and (iii) *Calculation of disclosed profits and stock values*

	Labour hours recovery method		Machine hours recovery method	
	X	Y	X	Y
1. Cost per unit (£)	20	120	30	80
2. Selling price per unit (£)	24	144	36	96
3. Sales quantity (000)[a]	36	7	18	10[b]
4. Production (000)	40	10	40	10[b]
5. Closing stock (4) − (3)	4	3	22	0
	(£000)	(£000)	(£000)	(£000)
Sales revenues, (2) × (3)	864	1008	648	960
Manufacturing costs, (1) × (4)	800	1200	1200	800
Less closing stock, (1) × (5)	80	360	660	0
Cost of goods sold	720	840	540	800
Disclosed profit	144	168	108	160
	Total = 312		Total = 268	

Notes

[a] Sales demand based on estimated demand for different selling prices as given in the question.

[b] Sales limited to maximum production of 10 000 units for product Y.

(b) The cost allocation methods result in different unit costs and selling prices. Price/demand relationships result in significant changes in sales quantities for different output levels. Units sold vary because of changes in accounting methods when cost-plus pricing is used. It is most unlikely that such an approach will produce optimal selling prices. Selling prices should be determined on the basis of an analysis of price/demand relationships and cost structure for different activity levels and selling prices. They should not be influenced by arbitrary cost apportionments. See 'Limitations of cost-plus pricing' and 'Relevant costs for pricing decisions' in Chapter 11 for a more detailed discussion of a possible answer to this question.

(c) Where year 2 demand is below productive capacity (case 1) then French Ltd should concentrate on maximizing year 1 profits. Year 1 sales will not result in any lost sales in year 2 because demand can be met from year 2 production.

Where year 2 demand is in excess of productive capacity then sales in year 1 will reduce the units available for sale in year 2. Any unsold stocks at the end of year 1 can be sold at the year 2 prices in year 2. In other words, the presence of stocks in year 1 will enable greater sales revenue to be earned in year 2. The question is whether it is more profitable to sell more in year 1 (thus reducing closing stocks which can be sold in year 2) or to reduce the sales in year 1 and sell more in year 2.

With case 1, our analysis is for year 1 only; but with case 2, it is necessary to analyse the output of year 1 production over 2 years. Fixed costs are not included in the analysis because they remain unchanged for all activity levels. The following information enables the optimal selling price to be established:

Case 1 (product X)			Case 2 (product Y)	
Contribution per unit[a] (£)	Sales quantity (000)	Total contribution (£000)	Contribution from closing stock sold in year 2[b] (£000)	Total contribution from year 1 production[c] (£000)
13 (24 − 11)	36	468	76	544
19 (30 − 11)	32	608[d]	152	760
25 (36 − 11)	18	450	418	868[d]
31 (42 − 11)	8	244	608	852

Notes

[a] Maximum selling price per price/demand estimates given in the question less unit variable cost.

[b] Maximum production in year 1 is 40 000. Unsold production can be sold in year 2 at a selling price of £30 per unit. Contribution is calculated on the basis of a £30 selling price less £11 per unit variable cost.

[c] Case 1 total contribution + contribution from closing stock sold in year 2.

[d] For case 1 a selling price of £30 maximizes total contribution, whereas for case 2 a selling price of £36 maximizes total contribution. The calculations for product Y are as follows:

	Case 1 (product Y)		Case 2	
			Contribution from	Total contribution
Contribution	Sales	Total	closing stock	from year 1
per unit	quantity	contribution	sold in year 2[a]	production[b]
(£)	(000)	(£000)	(£000)	(£000)
52 (96 − 44)	10	520	0	520
64 (108 − 44)	10	640	0	640
76 (120 − 44)	9	684	86	770
88 (132 − 44)	8	704[c]	172	876
100 (144 − 44)	7	700	258	958
112 (156 − 44)	5	560	430	990[c]

Notes

[a] Maximum production of year 1 is 10 000 units. Unsold production can be sold in year 2 at a selling price of £130 per unit. Contribution is calculated on the basis of a selling price of £130 less £44 per unit variable cost.

[b] Case 1 total contribution + contribution from closing stock sold in year 2.

[c] For case 1 a selling price of £132 maximizes total contribution, whereas for case 2 a selling price of £156 maximizes total contribution.

(a) Existing capacity = 80 000 machine hours [(20 000 × 2) + (40 000 × 1)]
    Fixed cost per unit = £480 000/80 000 machine hours
             = £6 per machine hour

Solution IM 11.9

	Alpha	Beta
	(£)	(£)
Total cost per unit	20	40
Fixed cost per unit	12 (2 × £6)	6 (1 × £6)
Variable cost per unit	8	34
Selling price per unit	25	50
Contribution per unit	17	16
Contribution per machine hour	8.50 (£17/2)	16

The question states that machine hours are fully utilized at the existing production level. Therefore demand is in excess of current capacity. Profits will be maximized by concentrating on Beta, since this yields the larger contribution per machine hour. In order to meet the maximum demand for Beta, 50 000 machine hours will be required. The remaining capacity of 30 000 hours (80 000 − 50 000) should be allocated to producing 15 000 units of Alpha. The total profit for this output level is as follows:

	(£)
Alpha (15 000 units × £17 contribution per unit)	255 000
Beta (50 000 units × £16 contribution per unit)	800 000
	1 055 000
Less fixed costs	480 000
Profit	575 000

The above profit exceeds the profit arising from the proposed plan given in the question.

(b) The answer to this question should include a discussion of the limitations of cost-plus pricing and an explanation of why it is widely used in practice. For a discussion of these issues see 'Limitations of cost-plus pricing' and 'Reasons for using cost-based pricing formulae' in Chapter 11.

(c) An increase in the selling price of Alpha by £10 reduces demand by 30 000 units. Assuming a linear relationship between price and demand, this price/demand relationship indicates that to increase/decrease demand by 1 unit, the selling price must be decreased/increased by £0.000 333 (£10/30 000 units). Estimated demand is 15 000 units at a selling price of £30. At a selling price of £35 (£30 + (15 000 × £0.000 333)), demand will be zero. To increase demand by one unit, selling price must be reduced by £0.000 333. Thus the maximum selling price (SP) for an output of x units is:

$$
\begin{aligned}
\text{SP} &= £35 - £0.000\,333x \\
\text{Total revenue (TR)} &= x\,(£35 - £0.000\,333x) \\
&= £35x - £0.000\,333x^2 \\
\text{Marginal revenue (MR)} &= \frac{d(\text{TR})}{dx} = £35 - £0.000\,666x \\
\text{Marginal cost} &= £8
\end{aligned}
$$

Optimal output is where MR = MC:

$$
\begin{aligned}
35 - £0.000\,666x &= 8 \\
x &= 40\,540 \text{ units} \\
\text{SP} &= £35 - £0.000\,333 \times 40\,540 \\
&= £21.50
\end{aligned}
$$

An increase in the selling price of Beta by £10 reduces demand by 40 000 units. This implies that an increase/decrease in demand by 1 unit requires a decease/increase in price of £0.000 25 [£55 + (30 000 × £0.000 25)]. To increase demand by one unit, selling price must be reduced by £0.000 25. Thus the maximum selling price (SP) for an output of x units is:

$$
\begin{aligned}
\text{SP} &= £62.50 - £0.000\,25x \\
\text{TR} &= x\,(£62.50 - £0.000\,25x) \\
\text{MR} &= £62.50x - £0.000\,25x^2 \\
&\frac{d(\text{TR})}{dx} = £62.50 - £0.0005x \\
\text{MC} &= £34
\end{aligned}
$$

Optimal output is where:

$$
\begin{aligned}
62.50 - 0.0005x &= 34 \\
x &= 57\,000 \text{ units} \\
\text{SP} &= £62.50 - £0.000\,25 \times 57\,000 \\
&= £48.25
\end{aligned}
$$

It is assumed that capacity is sufficient to meet demand at the above selling prices.

(d) The approach used in (c) was based on a knowledge of price/demand relationships and total cost functions and adopted the theoretical economist's pricing model approach to pricing described in Chapter 11. It is assumed that accurate cost and revenue functions can be obtained at zero incremental cost and that optimal selling prices can be determined.

(a) (i) In order to answer this question, it is necessary to express output in terms of the number of unrefined tonnes processed prior to separation. If the number of tonnes processed is Q then the quantity of crude Alpha (Q_a) and crude Beta (Q_b) processed can be expressed as:

$$Q_a = 0.4Q \text{ and } Q_b = 0.6Q$$

Total revenue from:

$$\begin{aligned} \text{Alpha (TR}_a) &= 1250Q_a - \frac{100Q_a^2}{32} \\ &= 1250\,(0.4Q) - \frac{100\,(0.4Q)^2}{32} \\ &= 500Q - 0.5Q^2 \end{aligned}$$

$$\begin{aligned} \text{Beta (TR}_b) &= 666.67Q_b - \frac{100Q_b^2}{18} \\ &= 666.67\,(0.6Q) - \frac{100\,(0.6Q)^2}{18} \\ &= 400Q - 2Q^2 \end{aligned}$$

The marginal revenue from each product is:

$$\begin{aligned} MR_a &= 500 - Q \\ MR_b &= 400 - 4Q \end{aligned}$$

The marginal revenue from total production is:

$$MR_a + MR_b = 900 - 5Q$$

The marginal cost of processing one tonne is:

$$£170 + £100 + 0.4\,(£125) + 0.6\,(£50) = £350$$

Optimal output is where MR = MC:

$$\begin{aligned} 900 - 5Q &= 350 \\ Q &= 110 \end{aligned}$$

110 tonnes of the raw materials should be processed, with 44 tonnes refined into Alpha and 66 into Beta.

$$\text{Alpha price } (P_a) = 1250 - \frac{100 \times 44}{32} = £1112.50 \text{ per tonne}$$

$$\text{Beta price } (P_b) = 666.67 - \frac{100 \times 66}{18} = £300 \text{ per tonne}$$

(ii) When $Q = 110$,

$$\begin{aligned} MR_a &= 500 - 110 = 390 \\ MR_b &= 400 - 4 \times 110 = -40 \end{aligned}$$

Therefore Alpha is the major product and Beta the minor.

(b) (i) Since Beta is not worth producing at an output level of 110 units, profit is maximized where the marginal cost of producing refined Alpha is equal to its marginal revenue:

$$\begin{aligned} 170 + 100 + (0.4 \times 125) &= 500 - Q \\ Q &= 180 \end{aligned}$$

180 tonnes should be processed and 72 tonnes (0.4×180) of Alpha refined. Alternatively the answer could have been obtained by equating the separation process marginal cost with Alpha's net marginal revenue (NMR):

$$125 = 1250 - 6.25Q$$
$$Q = 180$$

Note that NMR is derived from the price equation given in the question.

(ii) Refining of Beta should be continued until its marginal revenue is equal to its marginal cost of refining:

$$400 - 4Q = 0.6 \times 50$$
$$Q = 92.5$$
$$Q_b = 0.6 \times 92.5$$
$$Q_b = 55.5$$

Alternatively the answer could have been obtained by equating the marginal cost with Beta's net marginal revenue:

$$50 = 666.67 - 11.11Q$$
$$Q = 55.5$$

Beta's NMR is derived from the price equation given in the question.

(c) The answer should consider the following methods:
   (i) Physical measurement methods.
   (ii) Sales value at split-off point.
   (iii) Net-realizable value.
   (iv) Constant gross profit percentage.

You should refer to Chapter 6 for a discussion of these. The answer should stress that there is no 'right way' of allocating joint costs to products and that whichever method is selected will be based on arbitrary apportionments. The answer could also stress that joint costs should not be apportioned to by-products for stock valuation purposes (see 'Accounting for by-products' in Chapter 6).

Solution IM 11.11

(a) (i) *Sales only in the home market*
It is assumed that 'unit variable cost' represents average unit variable cost.
Total variable cost $= 19Q - Q^2$
Therefore marginal cost $= 19 - 2Q$
Total sales revenue $= 68Q - 8Q^2$
Therefore marginal revenue $= 68 - 16Q$
Profit is maximized when MR = MC:

$$68 - 16Q = 19 - 2Q$$
$$14Q = 49$$
$$Q = 3.5$$

Optimum selling price $= 68 - 8 \times 3.5 = £40$
Average variable cost $= 19 - 3.5 = £15.50$
Total contribution $3500 \times (£40 - £15.50) = £85\,750$

(ii) *Sales only in the export market*
Price in £ $= (110 - 10Q)/2$
Total sales revenue $= 55Q - 5Q^2$
Marginal revenue $= 55 - 10Q$
Profit is maximized when MR = MC:

$$55 - 10Q = 19 - 2Q$$
$$8Q = 36$$
$$Q = 4.5$$

Optimum selling price $= 55 - 5 \times 4.5 = £32.50 = \$65$
Average variable cost $= 19 - 4.5 = £14.50$
Total contribution $= 4500 \times (£32.50 - £14.50) = £81\,000$

(iii) *Sales in both markets*
The revised optimum position is established by equating the marginal cost

function with the sum of the marginal revenue functions in the two separate markets:

$$\text{Home:} \quad MR = 68 - 16\,Q_1 \qquad (1)$$
$$\text{Export:} \quad MR = 55 - 10\,Q_2 \qquad (2)$$

Divide equation (1) by 16 and equation (2) by 10:

$$0.0625\,MR = 4.25 - Q_1 \qquad (3)$$
$$0.1\,MR = 5.5 - Q_2 \qquad (4)$$

Adding these:

$$0.1625\,MR = 9.75 - Q_1 - Q_2$$

Let Q represent the total of Q_1 and Q_2:

$$MR = \frac{9.75 - Q}{0.1625} \qquad (5)$$

The profit-maximizing output is where MR = MC:

$$\frac{9.75 - Q}{0.1625} = 19 - 2Q$$

$$9.75 - Q = 0.1625\,(19 - 2Q)$$

$$9.75 - Q = 3.0875 - 0.325Q$$

$$0.675Q = 6.6625$$

$$Q = 9.870$$

Substituting for Q in the combined marginal revenue function [equation (5)]:

$$MR = \frac{9.75 - 9.87}{0.1625} = -0.738$$

The allocation of the total quantity (Q) between the two markets will be determined by the need to keep MR equal to -0.738.

In the home market

$$Q_1 = 4.25 - 0.0625 \times (-0.738) \text{ [equation (3)]}$$
$$Q_1 = 4.296$$

and

$$P = 68 - 8 \times 4.296$$
$$P = £33.63$$

In the export market

$$Q_2 = 5.5 - 0.1 \times (-0.738) \text{ [equation (4)]}$$
$$Q_2 = 5.574$$

and

$$P = 55 - 5 \times 5.574 = £27.13 = \$54.26$$

Average variable cost $= 19 - 9.87 = £9.13$
Total contribution $= [4296 \times (£33.63 - £9.13)] + [5574 \times (£27.13 - £9.13)]$
$= £205\,584$

(b) For every two units produced, one must be sold in the home market and one in the export market. The marginal revenue from the sale of these two units will be:

$$MR = (68 - 16Q) + (55 - 10Q) = 123 - 26Q$$

Note that the above expression refers to the sale of two units (one in each market).

If Q is expressed in pairs of output (represented by q for the sale of 1 unit in each market) then

$2q = Q$ or $q = \frac{1}{2}Q$

Total variable cost $= 19Q - Q^2$
$$= 38q - 4q^2$$

Marginal cost per pair $= 38 - 8q$

Profit is maximized where MR = MC:

$$123 - 26q = 38 - 8q$$
$$q = 4.722$$

Total production should be 9444 units (4722 units in each market).
In the home market $P = 68 - 8 \times 4.722 = £30.22$
In the export market $P = 55 - 5 \times 4.722 = £31.39 = \$62.78$
Average variable cost $= 19 - 9.444 = £9.556$
Total contribution $= (4722 \times £30.22) + (4722 \times £31.39) - (9444 \times £9.556)$
$$= £200\,676$$

Sensitivity analysis

	$\$1 = £0.25$	$\$1 = £1$
Exchange rate		
Price (£)	$(110 - 10Q)/4$	$110 - 10Q$
	$= 27.5 - 2.5Q$	
Total revenue (£)	$27.5Q - 2.5Q^2$	$110Q - 10Q^2$
Marginal revenue (£)	$27.5 - 5Q$	$110 - 20Q$
MR for one unit sold in each market £	$(68 - 16Q) + (27.5 - 5Q)$ $= 95.5 - 21Q$	$(68 - 16Q) + (110 - 20Q)$ $= 178 - 36Q$
MR = MC where	$95.5 - 21Q = 38 - 8Q$ $Q = 4.423$	$178 - 36Q = 38 - 8Q$ $Q = 5$
Home market P (£)	$68 - 8 \times 4.423 = 32.62$	$68 - 8 \times 5 = 28$
Export market P (£)	$27.5 - 2.5 \times 4.423$ $= 16.44$	$110 - 10 \times 5 = 60$
P ($)	$16.44 \times 4 = 65.76$	60
Average variable cost	$19 - 8.846 = £10.154$	$19 - 10 = £9$
Total contribution	$4423 \times (£32.62 + £16.44)$ $- 8846 \times £10.154$ $= £127\,170$	$5000 \times (£60 + £28)$ $- 10\,000 \times £9$ $- £350\,000$

Summary

$\$1 = £0.25$		
	Home market price: $\dfrac{32.62 - 30.22}{30.22}$	7.9% increase
	Export market price: $\dfrac{65.76 - 62.78}{62.78}$	4.75% increase in dollar terms
	Contribution: $\dfrac{200\,676 - 127\,170}{200\,676}$	36.6% decrease
$\$1 = £1$	Home market price: $\dfrac{30.22 - 28}{30.22}$	7.3% decrease
	Export market price: $\dfrac{62.78 - 60}{62.78}$	4.4% increase in dollar terms
	Contribution: $\dfrac{350\,000 - 200\,676}{200\,676}$	74.4% decrease

It can be seen that, while the changes in exchange rates have relatively little impact on either the quantities sold in the two markets or the prices charged within each market, the overall effect of such changes on the total sterling contribution is significant.

(c) The answer should draw attention to the need to take steps to reduce the risk of currency exposure when foreign exchange rates are volatile. In particular the following points should be included:

    (i) Exporters should consider invoicing in foreign currency so that the currency can be converted at the spot rate applicable on the date of payment.

    (ii) During the period between invoicing and the date of payment, firms can cover their position in the foreign exchange market by selling foreign currency forward at the appropriate foreign exchange rate.

    (iii) There is a greater need to continuously review selling prices and monitor competitors' prices charged in the exporting country.

    (iv) The period between the invoice date and the payment date should be shorter than for home sales so that exposure to changes in exchange rates is minimized.

Decision-making under conditions of risk and uncertainty

Solutions to Chapter 12 questions

Solution IM 12.1

(a) *Tabulation of cost and profit – colour printed catalogues*

	80%		100%		120%	
Capacity utilization						
Quantities	40 000		50 000		60 000	
	Total (£)	Unit (£)	Total (£)	Unit (£)	Total (£)	Unit (£)
Variable costs						
Direct materials	180 000	4.50	225 000	4.50	270 000	4.50
Direct wages	120 000	3.00	150 000	3.00	180 000	3.00
Direct expenses	52 000	1.30	65 000	1.30	78 000	1.30
	352 000	8.80	440 000	8.80	528 000	8.80
Semi-variable costs						
Indirect materials	46 800	1.17	47 000	0.94	74 400	1.24
Indirect wages	51 200	1.28	55 000	1.10	72 000	1.20
Indirect expenses	6 000	0.15	8 000	0.16	9 600	0.16
	456 000	11.40	550 000	11.00	684 000	11.40
Fixed costs	60 000	1.50	60 000	1.20	60 000	1.00
Total costs	516 000	12.90	610 000	12.20	744 000	12.40
Sales price of £16.00 per unit	640 000	16.00	800 000	16.00	960 000	16.00
Profit	124 000	3.10	190 000	3.80	216 000	3.60

Comments

(i) Only at an activity level of 40 000 units is the contract not worth undertaking. At activity levels of 50 000 and 60 000 units, profits are in excess of £132 000 annual profits from other customers.

(ii) Profits are maximized at an activity level of 60 000 units per annum.

(b) The expected direct material cost is £4.85 [(£4.50 × 0.5) + (£5 × 0.3) + (£5.50 × 0.2)]. The revised profits based on the expected direct material cost of £4.85 are as follows:

	40 000 units (£)	50 000 units (£)	60 000 units (£)
Profit calculation in (a) using a material cost of £4.50 per unit	124 000	190 000	216 000
Adjustment to reflect expected material cost	(14 000)	(17 500)	(21 000)
Revised profit	110 000	172 500	195 000

Expected profit (0.4 × £110 000) + (0.5 × £172 500) + (0.1 × £195 000) = £149 750

(c) The expected profit of £149 750 is in excess of the estimated profit from the 'other customers'. However, the £149 750 represents an average profit based on the weighted average of the possible outcomes. If the worst possible outcome occurs (an order for 40 000 catalogues and a direct material cost of £5.50), the profit from the order will be £84 000. The probability of this event occurring is 0.08 (0.4 × 0.2). It would be preferable to construct a probability distribution of the range of possible outcomes in order that management can decide whether or not the risk of undertaking the order which has an uncertain outcome is justified.

The long-term impact of accepting the order should also be considered. Will the contract be renewed after one year? Will the company become dependent on one major customer? Will the company still be able to earn £132 000 per annum profits after the contract has been completed? It is important that qualitative information which cannot be quantified should be taken into account when choosing between the alternatives.

(a)

Demand	Inflation (%)	Contribution[a] (£)	Fixed costs[b] (£)	Profit/ (loss) (£)	Joint probability
Pessimistic	10	33 000	40 600	(7 600)	0.12
Pessimistic	5	31 500	40 300	(8 800)	0.15
Pessimistic	1	30 300	40 060	(9 760)	0.03
Most likely	10	49 500	40 600	8 900	0.24
Most likely	5	47 250	40 300	6 950	0.30
Most likely	1	45 450	40 060	5 390	0.06
Optimistic	10	66 000	40 600	25 400	0.04
Optimistic	5	63 000	40 300	22 700	0.05
Optimistic	1	60 600	40 060	20 540	0.01

Notes
[a] Demand at current selling prices × (1 + inflation rate) × contribution percentage. For example, with £50 000 demand at current prices, sales revenue will increase to £55 000 if the inflation rate is 10%. The contribution margin percentage remains constant at 60%, and therefore contribution will be £33 000.
[b] £40 000 fixed costs + (inflation rate × 0.15 fixed costs)

Summary of probability distribution
Probability of loss = 0.30
Probability of at least breaking even = 0.70
Probability of at least a profit of £20 000 = 0.10

Alternatively the entire probability distribution could be presented:

Probability of a loss of more than £9000 = 0.03
Probability of a loss of more than £8000 = 0.18
Probability of a loss of more than £7000 = 0.30
Probability of a profit of at least £5000 = 0.70
Probability of a profit of at least £6000 = 0.64
Probability of a profit of at least £7000 = 0.34
Probability of a profit of at least £8000 = 0.34
Probability of a profit of at least £20 000 = 0.10
Probability of a profit of at least £22 000 = 0.09
Probability of a profit of at least £25 000 = 0.04

It should be noted that it is inappropriate to assume that all costs and selling prices will alter in line with each other. Also the existence of stocks will introduce a lag in the system.

(b) A continuous probability distribution should be prepared for each variable which is subject to uncertainty; for example, sales demand, costs and inflation rate. Probabilities would be assigned to ranges of sales demand, costs and the inflation rate. For example, sales demand might be presented with probabilities attached for the following ranges:

£25 000–£49 999
£50 000–£74 999
£75 000–£99 999
£100 000–£124 999
£125 000 or more

The answer should next describe the Monte Carlo simulation approach (see 'Simulation' in Chapter 14 for a description).

Solution IM 12.3

Part A

(a) *Scenario 1*

Expected value = average long-run demand of 350 tickets

Scenario 2

(1) Type of artiste	(2) Ticket sales	(3) Probability	(4) Weighted average, (2) × (3)
Popular	500	0.45	225
Lesser known	350	0.30	105
Unknown	200	0.25	50
		Expected value	380 tickets

(b) *Purchase 200 tickets*

Type of artiste	Revenue (£)	Purchase costs (£)	Sale by box office (£)	Profit/ (loss) (£)	Probability	Expected value (£)
Popular	600	480[a]	0	120	0.45	54
Lesser known	600	480	0	120	0.30	36
Unknown	600	480	0	120	0.25	30
						120

Purchase 300 tickets

Type of artiste	Revenue	Purchase costs	Sale by box office	Profit/ (loss)	Probability	Expected value
Popular	900	675[b]	0	225	0.45	101.25
Lesser known	900	675	0	225	0.30	67.50
Unknown	600	675	18[c]	(57)	0.25	(14.25)
						154.50

Purchase 400 tickets

Type of artiste	Revenue	Purchase costs	Sale by box office	Profit/ (loss)	Probability	Expected value
Popular	1200	840[d]	0	360	0.45	162.0
Lesser known	1050	840	9[e]	219	0.30	65.7
Unknown	600	840	36[f]	(204)	0.25	(51.0)
						176.7

Purchase 500 tickets

Type of artiste	Revenue	Purchase costs	Sale by box office	Profit/ (loss)	Probability	Expected value
Popular	1500	900[g]	0	600	0.45	270.0
Lesser known	1050	900	27[h]	177	0.30	53.1
Unknown	600	900	54[i]	(246)	0.25	(61.5)
						261.6

Notes

[a] Purchase price = £2.40.
[b] Purchase price = £2.25.
[c] 10% of 100 unsold tickets at £1.80.
[d] Purchase price = £2.10.
[e] 10% of 50 unsold tickets at £1.80.
[f] 10% of 200 unsold tickets at £1.80.
[g] Purchase price = £1.80.
[h] 10% of 150 unsold tickets at £1.80.
[i] 10% of 300 unsold tickets at £1.80.

DECISION-MAKING UNDER CONDITIONS OF RISK AND UNCERTAINTY

Scenario 1
The schedule of expected values indicates that for lesser known artistes the highest profit is £225 when 300 tickets are purchased.

Scenario 2
The purchase of 500 tickets yields the highest expected profit (£261.60)

Part B: Specialist prediction

Type of artiste	No. of tickets purchased to yield maximum profit
Popular	500
Lesser known	300
Unknown	200

The expected value if the specialist is employed is equal to the sum of the maximum profit for each possible outcome times the probability of the outcome occurring:

Outcome	Profit (£)	Probability	Expected value (£)
Popular	600	0.45	270.0
Lesser known	225	0.30	67.5
Unknown	120	0.25	30.0
			367.5

The maximum sum payable per concert is equal to the expected value of certain information (£367.50) prior to appointing the specialist less the maximum expected value under uncertainty (£261.60). Therefore the maximum sum payable is £105.90 per concert. With 60 concerts per year, the maximum sum payable per annum is £6354 (£105.90 × 60).

(a) Maximum monthly capacity = 2400 nights (80 × 30 days)

Solution IM 12.4

Contribution per normal guest = £21 (£20 − £4 + £5)
Contribution per air-travel guest = £11 [(0.6 × £20) − £4 + £3]
Monthly fixed costs = £28 000
The number of nights to be considered for the contract are:
  (i) 960 (2400 − 1440)
  (ii) 720 (2400 − 1680)
  (iii) 480 (2400 − 1920)
  (iv) 2400 (assuming air travel takes all the available capacity)

  (i) *Contract 960 nights*: If 960 nights are contracted, the remaining capacity of 1440 nights will be used whatever the weather conditions.

  Expected contribution = (960 × £11) + (1440 × £21) = £40 800

  (ii) *Contract 720 nights*: If 720 nights are contracted, the remaining capacity will be 1680 nights. There is a 0.3 probability that weather condition A will apply and demand will be 1440 nights, resulting in the hotel being partly empty. There is a 0.7 probability that weather conditions B or C will apply, thus resulting in the remaining capacity of 1680 nights being fully used.

  Expected contribution = (720 × £11) + (0.3 × 1440 + 0.7 × 1680) × £21
    = £41 688

  (iii) *Contract 480 nights*: The remaining capacity is now 1920 nights. There is a 0.3 probability that demand will be for 1440 nights, 0.4 that demand will be for 1680 nights, and 0.3 that demand will be for 1920 nights.

$$\text{Expected contribution} = (480 \times £11)$$
$$+ (0.3 \times 1440 + 0.4 \times 1680 + 0.3 \times 1920)$$
$$\times £21 = £40\,560$$

(iv) *Contract 2400 nights*: Expected contribution $= 2400 \times £11 = £26\,400$

Using the expected value decision rule, 720 nights should be contracted. It would be possible to use other approaches, such as a comparison of the probability distributions or a maximin approach, but these are likely to be too time-consuming given that only six marks are allocated to this part of the question.

(b) The relevant cost of hotel accommodation is £4 variable cost, but a contribution of £3 is obtained from the restaurant. Hence the net marginal cost is £1 per night. Therefore the minimum price per guest night for accommodation (and assuming each guest takes a meal in the restaurant) is £1. If meals are not taken, the minimum price is £4 per night. A price in excess of these amounts will result in a contribution towards fixed costs which would otherwise not be obtained. It is assumed that there will be no effect on occupancy from normal business. The maximum number of guest nights that it would be worthwhile contracting for (assuming a charge slightly in excess of £1 per night for accommodation) would be 480 (2400 − 1920).

(c) The monthly fixed costs for each alternative are:

	Close (£)	Stay open (£)
Staff wages and general overheads	3 500	20 500
Other fixed costs	7 500	7 500
	11 000	28 000

The increase in monthly fixed costs from staying open is £17 000.

(i) *Contribution from basic winter trade and conferences*

	Total guest nights for three months	Contribution per night (£)	Total contribution (£)
Basic winter trade	1080 (12 × 90 days)	15 (19 − 4)	16 200
Conferences	2700 (30 × 90 days)	13 (17 − 4)	35 100
			51 300
Less additional fixed costs (£17 000 × 3)			51 000
Profit			300

(ii) *Contribution from language courses*

Occupancy	Contribution (£21 per night) (£)	Fixed costs (W1) (£)	Profit/ (loss) (£)	Probability	EV (£)
2160	45 360	67 500	(22 140)	0.3	(6 642)
4320	90 720	67 500	23 220	0.4	9 288
6480	136 080	67 500	68 580	0.3	20 574
					23 220

Working
(W1) Additional fixed costs in (i) of £51 000 + £15 000 tutor fees + £1500 advertising.

On the basis of the above information, language courses should be offered.

The reservations include:
1. The owner's attitude to risk. There is a 0.3 probability that a loss of £22 140 will occur.
2. The reliability of the estimates used in terms of occupancy levels and the probabilities attached to them.
3. The validity of the assumption that monthly general overheads (which include electricity) will be £8000 in the winter.
4. The effect on wear and tear and summer sales from the hotel being used as a language school in winter.

(d) The criterion for identifying costs in (a)–(c) is whether or not costs will change for the alternative under consideration. In other words, a relevant cost approach has been used, and sunk costs (i.e. committed fixed costs) have been ignored. Only incremental fixed costs are included in the analysis. Alternatives have been compared using the expected value method. Expected values represent long-run average costs and suffer from the disadvantage that they ignore the decision-maker's attitude to risk.

(a) There are two possible selling prices and three possible direct material costs for **Solution IM 12.5** each selling price. The contributions per unit before deducting direct material costs are £12 (£15 − £3) for a £15 selling price and £17 for a £20 selling price. The purchase costs per unit of output are £9 (3 kg × £3), £8.25 (3 kg × £2.75) and £7.50. Where the firm contracts to purchase a minimum quantity any surplus materials are sold at £1 per kg.

Statement of outcomes

Sales quantities (000)	Gross contribution (£000)	Net purchase cost (£000)	Fixed costs (£000)	Profit/ (loss) (£000)	Probability	Expected value (£000)
£15 selling price (£3 purchase price)						
36	432	324	65	43	0.3	12.9
28	336	252	65	19	0.5	9.5
18	216	162	65	(11)	0.2	(2.2)
						20.2
£15 selling price (£2.75 purchase price)						
36	432	297	65	70	0.3	21.0
28	336	231	65	40	0.5	20.0
18	216	148.5	65	2.5	0.2	0.5
						41.5
£15 selling price (£2.50 purchase price)						
36	432	270	65	97	0.3	29.1
28	336	210	65	61	0.5	30.5
18	216	159[a]	65	(8)	0.2	(1.6)
						58.0
£20 selling price (£3 purchase price)						
28	476	252	136	88	0.3	26.4
23	391	207	136	48	0.5	24.0
13	221	117	136	(32)	0.2	(6.4)
						44.0

£20 selling price (£2.75 purchase price)

28	476	231	136	109	0.3	32.7
23	391	189.75	136	65.25	0.5	32.625
13	221	126.5[b]	136	(41.5)	0.2	(8.3)
						57.025

£20 selling price (£2.50 purchase price)

28	476	210	136	130	0.3	39.0
23	391	174[c]	136	81	0.5	40.5
13	221	144[d]	136	(59)	(0.2)	(11.8)
						67.7

Notes

[a] 170 000 kg minimum purchases at £2.50 per kg less 16 000 kg [70 000 − (3 kg × 18 000) at £1 per kg].

[b] 50 000 kg minimum purchases at £2.75 per kg less 11 000 kg [50 000 − (3 kg × 13 000) at £1 per kg].

[c] 70 000 kg minimum purchases at £2.50 per kg less 1000 kg [70 000 − (3 kg × 23 000) at £1 per kg].

[d] 70 000 kg minimum purchases at £2.50 per kg less 31 000 kg [70 000 − (3 kg × 13 000) at £1 per kg].

If the objective is to maximize expected profits then the £20 selling price combined with purchasing option (iii) is recommended. On the other hand, if the maximin criterion is adopted then the £15 selling price combined with purchasing option (ii) is recommended. An alternative approach is to examine the probability distributions (final column of the statement) and adopt a combination which best satisfies the decision-maker's risk/return preferences.

(b) If demand is predicted to be optimistic, the highest payoff of £130 000 (£20 selling price and £2.50 purchase price) for the most optimistic demand level would be chosen. If the most likely demand is predicted, the highest payoff is £81 000 (£20 selling price and £2.50 purchase price). If the pessimistic demand level is predicted, the highest payoff is £2500. The expected value of profits assuming it is possible to obtain perfect information is:

$$
\begin{array}{rl}
 & (£) \\
£130\,000 \times 0.3 = & 39\,000 \\
£81\,000 \times 0.5 = & 40\,500 \\
£2\,500 \times 0.2 = & 500 \\
\hline
 & 80\,000
\end{array}
$$

The highest expected profit without perfect information in (a) is £67 700. Therefore the maximum price payable for perfect information is £12 300 (£80 000 − £67 700).

(a) The relevant costs per unit are as follows:

	1–2000 units (£)	2001–4000 units (£)	4001–8000 units (£)	Over 8000 units (£)
Labour:				
Grade 1[a]	—	4	4	4
Grade 2[a]	—	—	3	3
Material:				
X[b]	9	9	9	9
Y[c]	(4)	(4)	(4)	8
Variable overhead[d]	6	6	6	6
Total relevant cost per unit	11	15	18	30

Notes

[a] Labour costs are only relevant when idle time has been exhausted. This occurs at 2000 units for grade 1 labour (2000 units × 2 hours) and 4000 units for grade 2 labour (4000 units × 1 hour). It is assumed that beyond these output levels incremental labour costs of £2 per hour for grade 1 and £3 per hour for grade 2 will be incurred.

[b] Replacement cost of £9 per unit.

[c] Each unit of Y used saves the company £2 disposal costs. The product requires 2 units of Y, thus saving £4 disposal costs. When the stock of 16 000 units has been used (8000 units produced) additional supplies will be purchased at £4 per unit.

[d] Variable overheads are assumed to vary with hours of input.

The relevant production costs for various output levels are as follows:

Output (000 units)	Total cost (£000)
2	22
3	37 (£22 + 1 × £15)
4	52 (£37 + 1 × £15)
5	70 (£52 + 1 × £18)
6	88 (£70 + 1 × £18)
8	124 (£88 + 2 × £18)
10	184 (£124 + 2 × £30)
15	334 (£184 + 5 × £30)

The outcomes and expected values for each selling price are presented in the following schedule:

Outcomes and expected values

Volume (£000)	Sales revenues (£000)	Production costs (£000)	Advertising costs (£000)	Profit (£000)	Probability	Expected value (£000)
Selling price £20						
4	80	52	20	8	0.1	0.8
6	120	88	20	12	0.4	4.8
8	160	124	20	16	0.5	8.0
						13.6
Selling price £25						
2	50	22	50	(22)	0.1	(2.2)
5	125	70	50	5	0.2	1.0
6	150	88	50	12	0.2	23.4
8	200	124	50	26	0.5	13.0
						14.2

Selling price £40

0	0	0	100	(100)	0.2	(20.0)
3	120	37	100	(17)	0.5	(8.5)
10	400	184	100	116	0.2	23.2
15	600	334	100	166	0.1	16.6
						11.3

(b) On the basis of the expected value decision rule, a selling price of £25 should be selected. Management might use criteria other than maximizing expected value. For example the decision might be based on the minimization of risk. The above probability distributions indicate that £20 is the only selling price at which a loss will not arise. The final decision should be based on an examination of each of the above probability distributions and management's attitude towards risk.

(c) Assuming that management is proposing a selling price of £40, if the information indicated that demand would be zero or 3000 units then Warren should cancel the advertising at a cost of £10 000. This would give the following expected value:

Volume demanded (000)	Action	Gross profit (£000)	Cost of information (£000)	Net profit	Probability	Expected value (£000)
0	Cancel advertising	(10)	5	(15)	0.2	(3.0)
3	Cancel advertising	(10)	5	(15)	0.5	(7.5)
10	Continue	116	5	111	0.2	22.2
15	Continue	166	5	161	0.1	16.1
						27.8

It is worthwhile obtaining the information, since the expected value increases from £11 300 to £27 800. The £40 selling price now yields the highest expected value, and this selling price should be selected if decisions are based on maximizing expected values. Nevertheless, management might select another selling price, since the £40 selling price still has a 0.7 probability of making a loss.

Solution IM 12.7

(a)

Possible demand (000)	Sales at £40 per unit (£000)	Total costs[a] (£000)	Profit (£000)	Probability	Expected value (£000)
Machine A					
10	400	435	(35)	0.5	(17.5)
14	560	571	(11)	0.3	(3.3)
16	640	649	(9)	0.2	(1.8)
					(22.6)
Machine B					
10	400	460	(60)	0.5	(30.0)
14	560	548	12	0.3	3.6
16	640	616	24	0.2	4.8
					(21.6)
Machine C					
10	400	500	(100)	0.5	(50.0)
14	560	536	24	0.3	7.2
16	640	554	86	0.2	17.2
					(25.6)

Note
[a] The calculations of total costs are as follows:

	Demand		
	10 000 units (£000)	14 000 units (£000)	16 000 units (£000)
Machine A (maximum capacity of 10 000 units)			
Variable costs at £6.50 per unit[a]	65	65	65
Fixed costs	320	320	320
Material costs[b]	50	66	74
Subcontracting costs[c]	—	120	190
Total costs	435	571	649
Machine B (maximum capacity of 12 000 units)			
Variable costs at £6 per unit[a]	60	72	72
Fixed costs	350	350	350
Material costs[b]	50	66	74
Subcontracting costs[c]	—	60	120
Total costs	460	548	616
Machine C (maximum capacity of 16 000 units)			
Variable costs at £5 per unit[a]	50	70	80
Fixed costs	400	400	400
Material costs[b]	50	66	74
Subcontracting costs[c]	—	—	—
Total costs	500	536	554

Notes
[a] Variable cost per unit demanded up to maximum capacity level for each machine.
[b] £5 per unit for first 10 000 units plus £4 per unit for demand in excess of 10 000 units.
[c] Demand in excess of machine capacity × £30 per unit (up to 4000 units subcontracted) plus £35 per unit for any subcontracting in excess of 4000 units.

Recommendation
Machine B yields the lowest expected loss, and should be chosen if decisions are made on the basis of expected values. With machine C, there is a probability of 0.2 of obtaining a profit of £86 000, but there is also a possibility of a large loss. A risk-taker might prefer machine C to machine B.

(b) (i) With certain information, the following decisions will be made:

Certain demand of 10 000 units:
Purchase machine A which yields a minimum loss of £35 000.
Certain demand of 14 000 units:
Purchase machine C which yields a maximum profit of £24 000.
Certain demand of 16 000 units:
Purchase machine C which yields a maximum profit of £86 000.

Prior to purchasing the information, the probability that the market researchers will predict each demand level is as follows:

0.5 for a demand level of 10 000 units
0.3 for a demand level of 14 000 units
0.2 for a demand level of 16 000 units

With perfect information, the revised expected value will be as follows:

Demand units (000)	Machine	Profit (£000)	Probability	Expected value (£000)
10	A	(35)	0.5	(17.5)
14	C	24	0.3	7.2
16	C	86	0.2	17.2
				6.9
Value of best decision using imperfect information				(21.6)
Difference				28.5

Therefore the maximum which it is worthwhile to pay for perfect information is £28 500. For an explanation of this see 'Buying perfect and imperfect information' in Chapter 12.

(ii) The expected value of perfect information gives an approximation of the upper limit on the value of information. Any information which costs more than this upper limit is not worth obtaining. The model can be adapted to indicate the expected value of imperfect information.

Solution IM 12.8

(a)

(1) Contribution (£)	(2) Probability	(3) Weighted amount, (1) × (2) (£)
1 000 000	0.75	750 000
(400 000)	0.25	(100 000)
	Expected value	650 000

The expected contribution is £650 000. Using the expected value criteria, BEM should be given further consideration.

(b) *Expected reduction on contribution of LOG*
(i) *BEM's sales = £3 200 000*

Decline in sales (£)	Contribution (£)	Probability	Weighted average (£)
1 600 000	400 000	0.5	200 000
800 000	200 000	0.25	50 000
2 400 000	600 000	0.25	150 000
	Expected reduction in contribution		400 000

(ii) *BEM's sales = £800 000*

400 000	100 000	0.5	50 000
200 000	50 000	0.25	12 500
600 000	150 000	0.25	37 500
	Expected reduction in contribution		100 000

Expected reduction in total contribution = £325 000 [(0.75 × 400 000) + (0.25 × 100 000)]

Revised expected contribution if BEM is launched = £325 000 (£650 000 − £325 000)

Using the expected value criteria, BEM should still be given further consideration.

(c) The expected value if the survey is commissioned is calculated as follows:

	Contribution (£)	Probability	Weighted amount (£)
Survey predicts BEM's acceptance	600 000 (£1 000 000 − £400 000)	0.75	450 000
Survey does not predict BEM's acceptance	0	0.25	0
Expected value			450 000

If the survey is commissioned, expected value increases by £125 000 (£450 000 − £325 000). Since this is in excess of the survey cost of £100 000, the survey is justified.

(d) The expected value if the report indicates that BEM will gain acceptance is calculated as follows:

	Contribution (£)	Probability	Weighted amount (£)
Report correct	600 000 (£1 000 000 − £400 000)	0.9	540 000
Report incorrect[a]	(500 000)	0.1	(50 000)
Expected value			490 000

Note
[a] If the report is incorrect and the product is not accepted, there will be a negative contribution from BEM's sales of £400 000 [see part (a)]. In addition the reduction in the contribution from LOG is expected to be £100 000 [see part (b)]. Therefore the expected negative contribution if the product is not accepted is £500 000.

If the report indicates that BEM will not gain acceptance, BEM will not be launched and the expected value will be zero. There is a 75% chance that Delphi will indicate acceptance. Therefore the expected value of the report is as follows:

	Contribution (£)	Probability	Weighted amount (£)
Report indicates acceptance	490 000	0.75	367 500
Report indicates non-acceptance	0	0.25	0
Expected value			367 500

Without the report the expected value is £325 000. Therefore the maximum sum payable is £42 500 (£367 500 − £325 000).

(e) The strengths of the expected value (EV) approach are as follows:
   (i) EV forces management to recognize different possible outcomes and quantify them.
   (ii) EV attempts to measure expectations systematically.
   (iii) EV forces management to consider probabilities of possible outcomes and to quantify them.

The weakness of the EV approach are as follows:
   (i) The method of assigning probabilities is subjective.
   (ii) EV ignores risk since it fails to consider the dispersion of the possible outcomes.
   (iii) Only a few discrete estimates are used. The actual estimate represents the midpoint of a range of possible outcomes rather than a single estimate.
   (iv) The expected value is an average outcome. Therefore it is best suited to repetitive decisions. This is not the case in this question.
   (v) EV is best suited to situations where the risk of negative outcomes will not have a dramatic effect on the ability of a firm to survive.

Capital investment decisions: 1

Solutions to Chapter 13 questions

Solution IM 13.1

(a) The answer should include a discussion of the following points:
  (i) In theory, the acceptance of projects with positive NPVs (when discounted at the required rate of return, which is related to the project's risk) should result in an increase in the share price.
  (ii) The NPV method is superior to non-discounting methods because it takes into account the time value of money. Also, by adding a risk premium, it is possible to relate the project to the opportunity cost of investors in terms of the returns forgone from an investment of equivalent risk.
  (iii) The NPV method is superior to IRR method because:
    1. The reinvestment assumptions of NPV;
    2. IRR is unsatisfactory because it focuses on the return itself rather than the magnitude of the earnings;
    3. IRR method can give more than one IRR calculation when unconventional cash flows occur, and this might lead to decisions which do not maximize NPV;
    4. IRR can incorrectly rank mutually exclusive projects.

(b) The answer should include a discussion of the following points:
  (i) An awareness of the surveys by Pike (1996) and Drury *et al.* (1993). (See Bibliography in main text for details.)
  (ii) Reasons why the payback method is widely used (avoids long-term forecasts of future cash flows, reduces risk, etc.)
  (iii) A discussion of why the accounting rate of return is widely used. It may be that managers select those projects which will have the greatest impact on profitability when the annual accounts are published. For a discussion of this point see 'The effect of performance measurement on capital investment decisions' in Chapter 13.
  (iv) A discussion as to why managers might prefer IRR to NPV methods:
    1. It is claimed that with the IRR method it is unnecessary to explicitly formulate the cost of capital.
    2. Managers prefer to evaluate projects in percentage terms.

Solution IM 13.2

(a) *Cumulative cash flows*

	A (£)	B (£)	C (£)
Year 1	80 000	100 000	55 000
2	150 000	170 000	120 000
3	215 000	220 000	215 000
4		270 000	

Payback periods
Project A = 2 years + (200 − 150)/65 = 2.77 years
Project B = 3 years + (230 − 220)/50 = 3.2 years
Project C = 2 years + (180 − 120)/95 = 2.63 years

(b) Accounting rate of return = $\dfrac{\text{average profits}}{\text{average investment}}$

Average profits = total net annual cash inflows/asset life

$$A: (330 + 10 - 200)/5 = £28\,000$$
$$B: (320 + 15 - 230)/5 = £21\,000$$
$$C: (315 + 8 - 180)/4 = £35\,750$$

Assuming that depreciation is charged on the straight line basis:

Average investment = (initial investment + scrap value)/2

$$A: 210/2 = £105\,000$$
$$B: 245/2 = £122\,500$$
$$C: 188/2 = £94\,000$$

Accounting rate of return:

$$A: £28\,000/£105\,000 = 26.67\%$$
$$B: £21\,000/£122\,500 = 17.14\%$$
$$C: £35\,750/£94\,000 = 38.03\%$$

(c)

	Outflow (£)	Inflows (£)	Discount factor	Present value (£)
Project A				
Year 0	−200 000	—	1.00	−200 000
1		+80 000	0.8475	+67 800
2		+70 000	0.7182	+50 274
3		+65 000	0.6086	+39 559
4		+60 000	0.5158	+30 948
5		+65 000	0.4371	+28 411
				+16 992
Project B				
Year 0	−230 000		1.00	−230 000
1		+100 000	0.8475	+84 750
2		+70 000	0.7182	+50 274
3		+50 000	0.6086	+30 430
4		+50 000	0.5158	+25 790
5		+65 000	0.4371	+28 411
				−10 345
Project C				
Year 0	−180 000		1.00	−180 000
1		+55 000	0.8475	+46 613
2		+65 000	0.7182	+46 683
3		+95 000	0.6086	+57 817
4		+108 000	0.5158	+55 706
				+26 819

(d) The NPV method of evaluation is superior to the other methods, and the project with the largest NPV ought to be selected: project C. It should be noted that project C is also preferred to A and B when the payback and accounting rate of return methods are used.

(e) Other factors which should be considered are qualitative factors such as the impact on existing sales, the effect on employees and the effect on the environment from each of the three projects. In addition the risk and reliability of the cash flows for each project should be considered.

Solution IM 13.3 (a) *Cash flow*

	Year				
	1	2	3	4	5
	(£)	(£)	(£)	(£)	(£)
Saving in fleet costs	250 000	275 000	302 500	332 750	366 025
Less driver's costs	33 000	35 000	36 000	38 000	40 000
Repairs and maintenance	8 000	13 000	15 000	16 000	18 000
Other costs	10 000	15 000	20 000	16 000	22 000
	51 000	63 000	71 000	70 000	80 000
Net savings	199 000	212 000	231 500	262 750	286 025

Depreciation of £120 000 per annum (£750 000 less £150 000 scrap value depreciated over 5 years) has been deducted from other costs since it is not a cash expense.

(b) (i) Payback $= 3 + (£750\,000 - £642\,500)/£262\,750$ years
$= 3.41$ years

(ii) Accounting rate of return $= \dfrac{\text{average profit } (£118\,255)}{\text{average investment } (£450\,000)}$
$= 26.3\%$

Average profit $= \dfrac{\text{savings over 5 years} - \text{depreciation}}{5 \text{ years}}$

$= (£1\,191\,275 - £600\,000)/5$ years

$= £118\,255$ per year

Average investment $= \tfrac{1}{2} \times$ initial outlay $+ \tfrac{1}{2} \times$ scrap value
$= \tfrac{1}{2}(£750\,00) + \tfrac{1}{2}(£150\,000)$
$= £450\,000$

(iii) *Net present value*

			Cost	Discount factor	
			(£)		(£)
Year 0					(750 000)
	1	Saving	199 000	0.893	177 707
	2	Saving	212 000	0.797	168 964
	3	Saving	231 500	0.712	164 828
	4	Saving	262 750	0.636	167 109
	5	Saving	286 025	0.567	162 176
	5	Sale of proceeds	150 000	0.567	85 050
Net present value					175 834

(c) The answer should draw attention to the fact that the transport fleet investment has a higher NPV but a longer payback and lower accounting rate of return than the alternative. The decision should be based on the NPV rule and it is recommended that the company invests in the new transport fleet. The answer should also explain the superiority of the NPV technique over the accounting rate of return and payback methods (see 'The concept of NPV', 'Payback method' and 'Accounting rate of return' in Chapter 13).

Task 1:

(a)

Year	Cash flow (£)	Discount factor	Present value (£)
1	18 000	0.926	16 668
2	29 000	0.857	24 853
3	31 000	0.794	24 614
			66 135
Less investment outlay			55 000
			11 135

(b) Payback occurs during the third year. Assuming even cash flows throughout the year the payback period is:

$$2 \text{ years} + \frac{(£55\ 000 - £47\ 000)}{£31\ 000} = \text{Approximately 2.3 years}$$

Task 2:

(a) The proposal should be accepted because it has a positive net present value.

(b) See the sections on the concept of net present value and payback method in Chapter 11 for the answer to this question.

(c) The answer should draw attention to the following points:

(i) Incremental profits arising from a project are taxable. The tax is normally payable approximately 12 months after the receipt of the associated inflows and taxation should therefore be recorded as a cashflow in the appraisal with a time lag of 12 months.

(ii) Depreciation is not an allowable expense for taxation purposes. Instead, the Inland Revenue specifies depreciation schedules (known as capital allowances or writing down allowances) that must be used to compute taxable profits. Incremental taxation on project cash flows are therefore normally determined by multiplying the incremental profits arising from a project (cash inflows less cash outflows (excluding depreciation) less capital allowances) by the company's taxation rate.

(a) Machine A

End of year	Volume	Variable costs (£)	Fixed costs (£)	Cash flow (£)	Discount factors	Present value(£)
1	145 200(1)	726 000	20 000	746 000	0.870	649 020
2	159 720	798 600	20 000	818 600	0.756	618 862
3	175 692	878 460	20 000	898 460	0.658	591 187
						1 859 069
Capital cost						60 000
						1 919 069

Machine B

End of year	Volume	Variable cost (£)	Fixed cost (£)	Cash flow (£)	Discount factors	Present value (£)
1	145 200	755 040	38 000	793 040	0.870	689 945
2	159 720	830 544	38 000	868 544	0.756	656 619
3	170 000	884 000	38 000	922 000	0.658	606 676
3	5 692	56 920		56 920	0.658	37 453
						1 990 693

Note:

(1) Annual growth rate = 12 000/120 000 = 10%.

(b) Machine A should be purchased because it has the lowest present value of cash outflows. Sales revenues are irrelevant because the cash inflows are indentical for both machines. A benefit that has not been quantified in the above analysis is Machine A's surplus capacity which provides a safeguard should demand be under-estimated.

(c) Because the machine must be replaced the £10 000 sale proceeds will occur whichever alternative the company chooses. Therefore the sale proceeds are not relevant for decision-making.

(d) See the sections on compounding and discounting and the concept of net present value in Chapter 13 for the answer to this question.

Solution IM 13.6

The present values (discounted at 10%) for each of the projects are as follows:

	Project A (£)	Project B (£)	Project B − A (£)
Year 0	−1000	−10 000	−9000
1	240	2 300	2060
2	288	2 640	2352
3	346	3 040	2694
4	414	3 500	3086
5	498	4 020	3522
NPV	309	1 441	1132
IRR	20%	15%	14%

The IRR method ranks project A in preference to project B, whereas the NPV method ranks B in preference to A. The IRR method is misleading because it expresses the result as a percentage rather than in monetary terms. This can result in incorrect decisions when projects with differing investments are compared. If projects A and B were mutually exclusive then project A would be selected using the IRR method and NPV would not be maximized.

In order to compare projects with unequal investments, it is necessary to consider what use will be made of the funds as represented by the difference between the investment costs between the two projects. A correct comparison between projects A and B requires that we ascertain how the £9000 (difference between the investments) will be invested. If the company is not in a capital rationing situation then other investment opportunities will not be available which will yield positive NPVs. Therefore the £9000 will be invested at the cost of capital and NPV will be zero. Hence the total NPV for an investment of £10 000 when project A is selected will be £309 compared with £1441 when project B is selected.

If a capital rationing situation exists then the acceptance of project A will enable £9000 to be invested in other profitable projects. Project A should be selected if the £9000 will yield an NPV in excess of £1132 (project B − project A) or an IRR of 14%. If this is not possible then project B should be selected. The objective is to maximize NPV; but when projects are ranked in terms of IRR, there is no guarantee that NPV will be maximized. When capital rationing applies, NPV is maximized by ranking projects in terms of the NPV per £1 of investment (i.e. the profitability index). For a discussion of the superiority of the NPV method over the IRR method see 'Comparison of the NPV and IRR' in Chapter 13.

(a) *Preliminary workings*

The cash flow savings are calculated as follows:

	Year 2 (£)	Year 3 (£)	Years 4–8 (£)
Maintenance cost (75 per house):			
Contractor A	6 750 (90 × £75)	13 500 (180 × £75)	22 500 (300 × £75)
Contractor B	11 250 (150 × £75)	18 000 (240 × £75)	22 500 (300 × £75)
Heating cost (£150 per house):			
Contractor A	13 500 (90 × £150)	27 000 (180 × £150)	45 000 (300 × £150)
Contractor B	22 500 (150 × £150)	36 000 (240 × £150)	45 000 (300 × £150)
Rental income increase (£315 per house):			
Contractor A	28 350 (90 × £315)	56 700 (180 × £315)	94 500 (300 × £315)
Contractor B	47 250 (150 × £315)	75 600 (240 × £315)	94 500 (300 × £315)

The payments to the contractors would be £600 000 (300 × £2000), allocated as follows:

	Contractor A (£)	Contractor B (£)
Year 0	100 000	300 000
1	150 000 (90/300 × £500 000)	150 000 (150/300 × £300 000)
2	150 000 (90/300 × £500 000)	90 000 (90/300 × £300 000)
3	200 000 (120/300 × £500 000)	60 000 (60/300 × £300 000)
	600 000	600 000

The cash flow schedules (in £000) and DCF calculations are as follows:

Year	0	1	2	3	4	5	6	7	8	Total
Contractor A										
Maintenance cost reduction			6.75	13.5	22.5	22.5	22.5	22.5	22.5	132.75
Heating cost reduction			13.50	27.0	45.0	45.0	45.0	45.0	45.0	265.50
Rental income increase			28.35	56.7	94.5	94.5	94.5	94.5	94.5	557.55
Payments to contractor	(100)	(150)	(150)	(200)						(600)
Net cash flow	(100)	(150)	(101.4)	(102.8)	162.0	162.0	162.0	162.0	162.0	355.8
Discount factor at 14%	1.000	0.877	0.769	0.675	0.592	0.519	0.456	0.400	0.351	
Net present value	(100)	(131.6)	(78.0)	(69.4)	95.9	84.1	73.9	64.8	56.9	(3.4)
Contractor B										
Maintenance cost reduction			11.25	18.0	22.5	22.5	22.5	22.5	22.5	141.75
Heating cost reduction			22.50	36.0	45.0	45.0	45.0	45.0	45.0	283.50
Rental income increase			47.25	75.6	94.5	94.5	94.5	94.5	94.5	595.35
Payments to contractor	(300)	(150)	(90)	(60)						(600)
Net cash flow	(300)	(150)	(9.0)	69.6	162.0	162.0	162.0	162.0	162.0	420.6
Discount factor at 14%	1.000	0.877	0.769	0.675	0.592	0.519	0.456	0.400	0.351	
Net present value	(300)	(131.6)	(6.9)	47.0	95.9	84.1	73.9	64.8	56.9	(15.9)

The proposal for Contractor B gives the greater net cash inflow of £420 600 where the time value of money is ignored. The NPV calculations indicate that both projects yield a negative NPV. If non-financial factors demand that one of the quotations must be accepted then the above analysis suggests that on purely financial grounds the quotation from Contractor A should be accepted.

(b) Let x = additional annual cash inflow required to yield a zero NPV. Then x can be found by solving the following equation:[a]

$$0.3x\,(0.877) + 0.3x\,(0.769) + 0.4x\,(0.675) + 3400 = 0$$
$$0.7638x = 3400$$
$$x = £4451$$

In other words, additional annual cash inflows of £4451 per annum are required in order to yield a zero NPV. Therefore a reduction in cash outflow per house of £14.84 (£4451/300 houses) is required. Hence the maximum refurbishment price per house is £1985.16 (£2000 − £14.84).

Note
[a] The figure of 0.3 refers to the proportions paid in years 1 and 2 (90 houses completed out of a total of 300), and 0.4 refers to the proportion paid in year 3 (120/300). The figures in parentheses refer to the discount factors for years 1, 2 and 3, and £3400 represents the negative NPV in (a) which must be recovered for NPV to be zero.

(c) The maintenance and heating cost savings have not been adjusted for inflation. A discount rate of 14% suggests that a nominal discount rate has been applied. The payments to the contractor are fixed and not subject to inflation. If the cash flows are adjusted for inflation, it is possible that the project will yield a positive NPV.

   If the cash flows are uncertain, there might be a case for presenting a range of possible outcomes and applying probabilities. Expected values of NPVs or probability distributions could then be presented.

Solution IM 13.8

(a) *Evaluation of machine, ignoring the time value of money*

	(£)
Labour savings ($\frac{3}{5}$ × 200 000 × £0.25 for 3 years)	90 000
Extra labour cost for transferred workers (20% × $\frac{3}{5}$ × £50 000 × 3 years)	(18 000)
Material saving[a]	2 000
Power saving 0.4 × 200 000 kW × £0.05 for 3 years	12 000
Scrap value of new machine	10 000
Sale of old machine	40 000
Savings in supervision costs ($\frac{3}{5}$ × £10 000 × 3 years)	18 000
Total savings over 3 years	154 000
Cost of new machine	130 000
Net savings	24 000

Note
[a] If the new machine is purchased, the material costs will be

	(£)
(200 000 × 2 kg × £70/1000 × 3 years)	84 000
Less sale of old material (40 000 × 2 × £25/1000)	(2 000)
Net cost	82 000

If the new machine is not purchased, the stock of 80 000 kg can be used.
Total purchases over 3 years will be

(200 000 × 2 kg × 3 years − 80 000 kg) × £75/1000	84 000
Cash flow savings if the new machine is purchased	2 000

(b) *Departmental profit and loss accounts (old machine)*

	1989 (£000)	1990 (£000)	1991 (£000)
Sale of brushes	200	200	200
Variable production costs (200 000 × £0.45[a])	(90)	(90)	(90)
Overheads	(60)	(60)	(60)
Depreciation (£210 000/7)	(30)	(30)	(30)
Profit	20	20	20

Note

[a] Variable cost per unit = labour (£0.25) + materials (2 × £75/1000) + electricity (£0.05).

Departmental profit and loss accounts (new machine)

	1989 (£000)	1990 (£000)	1991 (£000)
Sale of brushes	200	200	200
Variable production costs (200 000 × £0.27[a])	(54)	(54)	(54)
Overhead:			
Supervision	(4)	(4)	(4)
Other	(50)	(50)	(50)
Depreciation (130 − 10)/3 years	(40)	(40)	(40)
Loss on sale of old machine[b]	(50)		
Loss on sale of stocks[c]	(4)		
	(2)	52	52

Notes

[a] Variable cost per unit = labour ($\frac{2}{5}$ × £0.25) + materials (2 × £70/1000)
                                 + electricity (0.6 × £0.05)
                             = £0.27

[b] ($\frac{3}{7}$ × £210 000) − sale proceeds (£40 000).
[c] 80 000 × (£75 − £25)/1000.

In 2001 there will be a loss of £2000 if the new machine is purchased. If the old machine is retained, the profit in 2001 will be £20 000. The manager may choose not to replace the machine if he or she focuses mainly on the impact of the decision on short-term performance. There is a conflict between the decision-making model and the performance evaluation model. For a more detailed discussion of this topic see 'The effect of performance measurement on capital investment decisions' in Chapter 13.

(c) When the time value of money is incorporated into the analysis, the cash flow savings in the later years have a lower present value, and this will make the project less attractive. If the machine's life is extended, the benefits will accrue for a longer period and any replacement will be delayed. Consequently the machine will yield a higher NPV.

Details of the cost of capital are not given in the question. The effect of incorporating the time value of money can be illustrated by selecting any discount rate and showing that the present value of the net savings will be less than £24 000. The higher the discount, the lower the benefit. At very high discount rates, the project will have a negative NPV. The discounting process can also be used to illustrate that NPV is increased if project life is extended and cash flow savings are maintained.

Note that where machines are being compared which have different economic lives, it would be appropriate to use the equivalent annual cost method illustrated in Chapter 14.

Solution IM 13.9

(a) *Present value of costs*

	(£)	Discount factor	Present value (£)
Raw material	7 000	21.243[a]	148 701
Labour	5 000	21.243[a]	106 215
Rental:			
Instalment 1	15 000	1.000	15 000
Instalment 2	15 000	0.942[b]	14 130
Plant cost	32 400	1.000	32 400
Plant realizable value	(14 000)	0.7876[c]	(11 026)
			305 420

Notes

[a] £7000 and £5000 are received each month from months 1 to 24. The discount factor is obtained from the cumulative discount tables for the 24-period row.
[b] One instalment in month 6 obtained from Appendix A of the main text.
[c] £14 000 is received in month 24.

Present value of receipts

Month	Receipt (£)	Discount factor	Present value (£)
6	92 500	0.942	87 135
12	92 500	0.8874	82 084
18	92 500	0.836	77 330
24	92 500	0.7876	72 853
			319 402

NPV = £13 982 (£319 402 − £305 420)

(b) The PV of the receipts must be £319 402.
Let X = each instalment. Then

$$X + 0.942X + 0.8874X + 0.836X = £319\ 402$$
$$3.6654X = £319\ 402$$
$$X = £87\ 140$$

Contract price = £348 560 (£87 140 × 4)
The total mark-up is £12 160 (£348 560 − £336 400)

Percentage mark-up = (£12 160/£336 400) × 100 = 3.61%

(c) The cash outflows in (a) and (b) are identical. However, there is a difference in the contract price and the timing of the instalments. Consequently the interest resulting from the costs is identical for both alternatives. The analysis will therefore concentrate on the interest difference between the cash receipts.

	Interest on original cash receipts (£)	Interest on revised cash receipts (£)
t_0		23 502 (£87 140 for 24 months)
t_1	18 139 (£92 500 for 18 months)	17 088 (£87 140 for 18 months)
t_2	11 729 (£92 500 for 12 months)	11 049 (£87 140 for 12 months)
t_3	5 689 (£92 599 for 6 months)	5 359 (£87 140 for 6 months)
t_4	0	
	35 557	56 998

Note that the above interest calculations are done using the future value tables, which can be found in Appendix E of the main text. For example, £23 502 is calculated as follows:

$$£87\ 140 \times 1.2697 \text{ (obtained for period 24)} - £87\ 140 = £23\ 502$$

The cash surpluses for each alternative (but ignoring interest on costs) are:

	Original (£)	Proposed (£)
Revenues	370 000	348 560
Interest on receipts	35 557	56 998
Materials	(168 000)	(168 000)
Labour	(120 000)	(120 000)
Plant (cost – sale proceeds)	(18 400)	(18 400)
Rental	(30 000)	(30 000)
	69 157	69 158

(d) Several factors will influence the tender price. The relevant cost (avoidable cost plus opportunity cost) will determine the minimum price below which it is not worth undertaking the contract. However, the question refers to long-term contracts, and there is a strong argument for incorporating a provision for the recovery of a contribution to general fixed overheads when determining the relevant costs of the contract.

The optimum price is the highest figure above the relevant cost (i.e. the minimum price) that the market will bear. It is unlikely that optimal prices can be determined, but a knowledge of the market, competitors' prices, the existing state of their order books and other potential orders is necessary for management to be able to make a sensible guess at a suitable selling price.

It can be difficult accurately to predict future costs for long-term contracts. Once the contract price has been agreed, it will be fixed. If the cost estimates prove to be inaccurate, it is possible that the costs of the contract will exceed the tender price. The accuracy of the estimates will depend on the extent to which the company has undertaken similar contracts in the past, the length of the contract and the rate of inflation. The greater the uncertainty in the cost estimates, the greater will be the need to increase the tender price to compensate for the extra risk. It might be possible to mitigate the effects of inflation by agreeing to fix the tender price to some agreed price index and thus pass the risk of inflation on to the customer.

It is also important to consider the timing of the cash inflows and outflows when setting the tender price. The present value of the future outflows should represent the minimum price. The final tender price will be influenced by the timing of the cash inflows. If the majority of the cash inflows are received towards the end of the contract, it will be necessary to tender a higher price in order to compensate for the time value of money.

Capital investment decisions: 2

Solutions to Chapter 14 questions

Solution IM 14.1

(a) A positive net present value indicates the potential increase in consumption which the project makes available after any funds have been repaid with interest. For a more detailed description see 'The concept of NPV' and 'Calculating NPV' in Chapter 13.

(b) It is incorrect to use the borrowing rate as the discount rate. Presumably the firm is using up borrowing capacity by financing the project with 100% debt capital. The implication of this is that it will be necessary to use less debt capital in the future in order for the firm to maintain its target capital structure. For example, if the firm has a target 50% debt/equity ratio then it will be necessary to raise more equity capital in the future in order to maintain the target debt/equity ratio. For projects which are equivalent to the average risk of the firm's existing assets the financing aspects should be incorporated into the analysis by discounting a project at the weighted average cost of capital based on the company's target debt/equity ratio. See 'Weighted average cost of capital' in Chapter 14 for a more detailed description of the appropriate discount rate.

(c) For the answer to this question see 'The effect of inflation on capital investment appraisal' in Chapter 14.

(d) See 'The opportunity cost of an investment' in Chapter 13 and 'Calculating risk-adjusted discount rates' in Chapter 14 for the answer to this question.

Solution IM 14.2

(a) See 'Calculating risk-adjusted discount rates' in Chapter 14 for an explanation of beta.

(b) The answer should consist of a description of the capital asset pricing model formula. See 'Calculating risk-adjusted discount rates' in Chapter 14 for an explanation of the capital asset pricing model formula.

(c) The observed beta for a company represents the beta of the company's shares. In other words, the observed beta represents the beta for the company as a whole. This represents the average beta for the company's assets based on the company's existing capital structure. If a new capital project is not typical of the company's existing average risk then the observed equity beta will be the incorrect risk measure. In this situation it will be necessary to use as a proxy the beta of a similar company which specializes in the projects being considered (or preferably the industry beta). It will also be necessary to adjust this proxy beta to reflect any difference between the gearing of the proxy company/industry and the gearing of the company investing in the project.

(d) The major limitation of the capital asset pricing model is that it is a single-period model whereas most capital projects are for longer than one year. If the model is extended beyond one period, it is assumed that beta is constant from period to period and this will result in using a constant discount rate. This implies that risk will increase over time at a constant rate.

Solution IM 14.3

See 'The capital investment process' in Chapter 13 for the answer to this question.

(a)   *Computation of tax payable and capital allowances*

Year	1	2	3	4
	(£000)	(£000)	(£000)	(£000)
Capital Allowances				
Opening WDV	10 000	7 500	5 625	4 219
Writing down allowances (25%)	2 500	1 875	1 406	4 219
				(Balancing
				Allowance)
Corporation Tax payable				
Sales	8 750	12 250	13 300	14 350
Less:				
Materials	1 340	1 875	2 250	2 625
Labour	2 675	3 750	4 500	5 250
Overheads	185	250	250	250
Profit before depreciation	4 550	6 375	6 300	6 225
Capital allowance	2 500	1 875	1 406	4 219
Taxable profit	2 050	4 500	4 894	2 006
Tax payable at 30%	615	1 350	1 468	602
Payable one year later (year)	2	3	4	5

Computation of NPV

Year	1	2	3	4	5
	(£000)	(£000)	(£000)	(£000)	(£000)
Sales	8 750	12 250	13 300	14 350	
Outflows:					
Materials	1 340	1 875	2 250	2 625	
Labour	2 675	3 750	4 500	5 250	
Overheads	185	250	250	250	
Working Capital Recovered				(1000)	
Corporation Tax	0	615	1 350	1 468	602
Net Cash Flow	4 550	5 760	4 950	5 757	(602)
Discount Factors at 17%	0.855	0.731	0.624	0.534	0.456
DCF	3 890	4 211	3 089	3 074	(275)

	(£000)
Cumulative DCF	13 989
Capital expenditure and working capital	11 000
NPV	2 989

(b) The project should be accepted because it has a positive NPV.

(c) The report should include the following points:
  (i) The taxable profits are based on operating cash flows before depreciation. Capital allowances of 25% per annum on a reducing balance basis are available instead of depreciation for taxation purposes.
  (ii) At the end of the project's life a balancing allowance is available to ensure that the net cost of the asset has been allowed as a taxable expense over the life of the project.
  (iii) Tax is assumed to be payable one year after the year end.

(d) The report should include the following points:
  (i) The NPV appraisal has been based on cash flows whereas the analysis in the question is based on profits using the accruals basis. This approach results in timing differences in the analyses relating to the payment of corporation tax and the incorporation of the capital cost of the asset.
  (ii) The analysis in the question ignores the time value of money whereas it is incorporated in the NPV appraisal.

(iii) Interest payments are included in the analysis in the question whereas interest payments are not included in the NPV appraisal. This is because interest payments are incorporated into the NPV appraisal within the discounting process which takes into account the cost of capital. Including interest payments in the NPV appraisal will lead to double counting.

Solution IM 14.5

(a) If the Reclo machine is purchased there will be no incremental cash flows (or opportunity costs) for operating space since the company has adequate spare space that has no alternative use. The feasibility survey is a sunk cost and the allocated overheads do not represent incremental cash flows. The charge from the marketing department is an internal charge and is not an incremental cash flow to the company. Only the cost of the salesmen is a relevant incremental cash flow.

Reclo cash flows

Year	0	1	2	3	4	5
	(£000)	(£000)	(£000)	(£000)	(£000)	(£000)
Sales at £3.50 per unit		455	478	502	527	
Materials at £0.80 per unit		104	109	115	120	
Labour at £1.30 per unit		169	177	186	196	
Supervisor		20	21	22	23	
Maintenance		20	42	44	46	
Salesmen		45	47	50	52	
		358	396	417	437	
Net taxable operating cash flows		97	82	85	90	
Tax at 25% with a one-year delay			(24)	(21)	(21)	(23)
Investment outlay	(175)					
Scrap value[a]					10	
Tax saved on WDAs[b]			11	8	6	16
Working capital[c]	(40)	(2)	(2)	(2)	(3)	49
Net cash flow	(215)	95	67	70	82	42

$$\text{NPV at } 15\% = +\pounds 32.1$$
$$\text{NPV at } 25\% = -\pounds 12.8$$

Using the interpolation formula shown in Chapter 13:

$$\text{IRR} = 15\% + \frac{32.1}{32.1 + (12.8)} \times (35\% - 25\%) = 22.2\%$$

Notes

[a] It is assumed that the scrap value has already been expressed in year 5 purchasing power.

[b]

Year	WDV	Writing down allowance (WDA)	Tax saving (25%)
			(£000)
1	175	44	11
2	131	33	8
3	98	25	6
4	73	18	5
5	55	45 (55 − 10)	11

In year 4 the balancing allowance is the WDV less the sale proceeds.

[c] It is assumed that the working capital in year 4 is released in year 5.

Bunger cash flows

	Year					
	0 (£000)	1 (£000)	2 (£000)	3 (£000)	4 (£000)	5 (£000)
Taxable operating cash flows		50	53	55	59	
Taxation at 25%			(13)	(13)	(14)	(15)
Investment outlay	(90)					
Scrap value					9	
Tax savings on WDAs[a]			6	4	3	7
Working capital	(40)	(2)	(2)	(2)	(3)	49
	(130)	48	44	44	54	41

NPV at 15% = +£25.2
NPV at 25% = –£5.3

$$IRR = 15\% + \frac{25.2}{25.2 + (5.3)} \times (35\% - 25\%) = 23.3\%$$

Notes

[a]
Year	WDV	Writing down allowance (WDA)	Tax saving (25%) (£000)
1	90	23	6
2	67	17	4
3	50	13	3
4	37	9	2
5	28	19 (28 – 9)	5

In year 4 the balancing allowance is the WDV less the sale proceeds.

(b) The incremental yield is calculated by considering the increments of cash flows of Reclo less Bunger. For an explanation of this method you should refer to 'Mutually exclusive projects' in Chapter 13. The incremental cash flows are:

	Year					
	0 (£000)	1 (£000)	2 (£000)	3 (£000)	4 (£000)	5 (£000)
Cash flows:						
Reclo	(215)	95	67	70	82	42
Bunger	(130)	48	44	44	54	41
Incremental	(85)	47	23	26	28	1

The IRR on the incremental project is approximately 19.7%. The incremental project should be accepted only if the cost of capital is less than 19.7%. Acceptance of the incremental project means that having initially chosen the project with the higher IRR (Bunger) we should move from Bunger to Reclo. This implies that Reclo should be purchased as long as the cost of capital is less than 19.7%. If the cost of capital exceeds 19.7% Bunger should be purchased but neither machine should be purchased if the cost of capital exceeds 23.3% (i.e. Bunger's IRR). The above comments are consistent with the NPVs that have been calculated with Reclo having a higher NPV at 15%.

(c) For a discussion of the limitations of the IRR method see 'Comparison of net present value and internal rate of return' in Chapter 13.

Solution IM 14.6 (a)

	t_0	t_1 2001	t_2 2002	t_3 2003	t_4 2004	t_5 2005
Year ending		2001	2002	2003	2004	2005
Initial outlay	(256)					
Tax on WDAs[a]			22.40	16.80	12.60	
Savings		60	66.00	72.60	79.86	
Tax on savings			(21.10)	(23.10)	(25.41)	(27.95)
Sale of new machine					108.00	
Sale of old machine	40					
Balancing charge			(14.00)			
Net cash flow	(216)	60	53.30	66.30	175.05	(27.95)

(£000)

NPV at 15% = £6334

Note

[a] Calculation of tax on writing down allowances (WDAs):

(£000)

	2001	2002	2003	2004
Opening WDV	256	192	144	108
Sale proceeds				(108)
WDA (25%)	(64)	(48)	(36)	
Closing WDV	192	144	108	Nil
Tax on WDAs (35%)	22.40	16.80	12.60	
Timing	t_2	t_3	t_4	

(b) The answer to this question requires a calculation of the incremental profits and the incremental investment from replacing the machine for 2001 and 2002.

Incremental profits (2001)

	(£000)
Cost savings	60.00
Depreciation on new machine (256 − 108)/4	(37.00)
Savings in depreciation of old machine (50/4)	12.50
Loss on sale of old machine	(10.00)
Additional taxes[a]	(12.60)
	12.90

Incremental profits (2002)

	(£000)
Cost savings	66.00
Depreciation on new machine	(37.00)
Savings in depreciation of old machine	12.50
Additional taxes[a]	(6.30)
	35.20

Incremental capital employed (2001)

	(£000)
Closing WDV of new machine (256 − 37)	219.00
Closing WDV of old machine retained (50 − 12.5)	37.50
	181.50

Incremental capital employed (2002)

	(£000)
Closing WDV of new machine (256 − 74)	182
Closing WDV of old machine retained (50 − 25)	25
	157

Return on incremental investment
2001 = 7.1% (12.90/181.50)
2002 = 22.4% (35.20/157)

In both years replacing the equipment will result in a decline in ROI.

Note
[a] Additional taxes arising from the investment are calculated as follows:

	2001 (£000)	2002 (£000)
Cost savings	60	66
WDA	(64)	(48)
Balancing charge	40	
Increase in taxable profits	36	18
Tax at 35%	12.6	6.3

(c) The report should include the following points:
  (i) A recommendation that the project should be accepted is justified on the basis of the NPV rule.
 (ii) An explanation that NPV is based on the assumption that the share price is the discounted present value of the future dividend stream and the market is aware of the effect on future cash flows arising from an investment decision. NPV takes no account of the effects of investment decisions on short-run reported profits. It is assumed that share price is based on future cash flows arising from an investment.
 (iii) Acceptance of the project will lead to a decline in ROI in 2001 and 2002, but ROI is likely to increase in later years. It is assumed that the lower ROI in the early years will not adversely affect the share price.
 (iv) The NPV calculation was based on the company's overall cost of capital of 15%. This rate would be appropriate only if the project's risk is equivalent to the average risk of the firm's existing assets.
  (v) The conflict between the performance measurement system and the NPV decision-making model (see 'The effect of performance measurement on capital investment decisions' in Chapter 13 for a detailed discussion of this point). The report should draw attention to the conflict arising with the replacement decision faced by the Towelling division (the project has a positive NPV, but ROI declines in the short run). Managers will tend to select the alternatives which have the most beneficial effect on the performance measure against which they are judged. It is therefore important that a performance measurement system is implemented which encourages managers to take decisions which are in the best interests of the company as a whole (in other words, to achieve goal congruence). If top management places too much emphasis on short-term performance then managers will tend to select those projects which have the most favourable impact in the short-term even if such decisions are at the expense of projects which are more beneficial in the long term. It is therefore important that performance is measured in accordance with criteria which will encourage managers to pursue a company's long-term objectives.

Solution IM 14.7

(a) The present values for the various replacement periods are as follows:

Present value of cash outflows if the fleet is replaced at the end of year

	1 (£)	2 (£)	3 (£)	4 (£)	5 (£)
Cash flows					
1. Costs 29 800 × 0.885	26 373	26 373	26 373	26 373	26 373
Resale (35 000) × 0.885	(30 975)				
Purchase 55 000 × 0.885	48 675				
2. Costs 33 700 × 0.783		26 387	26 387	26 387	26 387
Resale (24 000) × 0.783		(18 792)			
Purchase 55 000 × 0.783		43 065			
3. Costs 39 000 × 0.693			27 027	27 027	27 027
Resale (12 000) × 0.693			(8 316)		
Purchase 55 000 × 0.693			38 115		
4. Costs 45 100 × 0.613				27 646	27 646
Resale (2000) × 0.613				(1 226)	
Purchase 55 000 × 0.613				33 715	
5. Costs 72 000 × 0.543					39 096
Resale (200) × 0.543					(109)
Purchase 55 000 × 0.543					29 865
Present values	44 073	77 033	109 586	139 922	176 285

Note that if a replacement period of one year is selected, the cash flows will be repeated in years 2, 3, 4 and so on. If the two-year period is selected, purchases and resale will take place at the end of year 2, year 4 and so on. With a three-year replacement chain, purchase and resale will take place in years 3, 6, 9 and so on. In order to recognize these differences in cash flows, the present values should be calculated over a common time horizon for the various replacement periods (1, 2, 3, 4 and 5 years). Therefore the lowest common multiple will result in a common time horizon of 60 years.

An alternative approach, which is equivalent to establishing the lowest common time horizon and which recognizes the potential replacement chains, is to use the equivalent annual cost method. In this approach, the annual equivalent annuity is estimated. The calculations are as follows:

Replacement period (years)	1 (£)	2 (£)	3 (£)	4 (£)	5 (£)
Present value	44 073	77 033	109 586	139 922	176 285
Annual equivalent factor at 13%	0.885	1.668	2.361	2.974	3.517
Annual equivalent annuity	49 300	46 183	46 415	47 017	50 114

The minimum equivalent annual cost is for a two-year replacement cycle. Therefore a two-year replacement cycle period should be selected.

(b) The main problem with this type of analysis is that it is assumed that the replacements will be identical taxis with the same cash flows as the old taxi fleet until the lowest common time horizon is reached. It is unlikely that costs, capital allowances and taxation rates will remain unchanged over this time horizon. In addition, the cash flows have not been adjusted for inflation. Because of these difficulties, there might be a case for evaluating the alternatives over a selected time horizon which is sufficiently short to enable reasonable estimates to be made and estimate the terminal values for each alternative at the end of the time horizon. This approach is illustrated in Chapter 14.

(a) The calculation of the incremental cash flows and NPVs for projects 1 and 2 are shown below: **Solution IM 14.8**

Estimate of tax liability, Project 1

	Year		
	1	2	3
	(£000)	(£000)	(£000)
Incremental sales	840	1840	2176
Incremental operating costs	569	970	1315
Incremental operating profits	271	870	861
Tax (35%)	95	304	301
Tax benefit from incremental depreciation	175	131	98
Tax payable	(80)	173	203

Note that interest is not included in the above calculations because the tax effect is already reflected within the discount rate.

Cash flows, Project 1

	Year			
	1	2	3	4
	(£000)	(£000)	(£000)	(£000)
Sales	840	1840	2176	
Operating costs	569	970	1315	
	271	870	861	
Taxation (payable) recoverable	0	80	(173)	(203)
Salvage value			750	
Tax effect of balancing allowance[a]				33
Net cash flow	271	950	1438	(170)
Discount factor at 8%	0.926	0.857	0.794	0.735
Present value	251	814	1142	(125)
Present value at 8%	2082			
Investment outlay	2000			
NPV	82			

Note
[a] Balancing allowance = $[750 - (2000 - 1156)] \times 0.35$.

Estimate of tax liability, Project 2

	Year		
	1	2	3
	(£000)	(£000)	(£000)
Incremental sales	1930	2876	3854
Incremental operating costs	1380	1820	2160
Incremental taxable profit	550	1056	1694
Tax (35%)	192	370	593
Tax benefit from incremental depreciation	306	230	172
Tax payable (recoverable)	(114)	140	421

Cash flows, Project 2

	Year			
	1	2	3	4
	(£000)	(£000)	(£000)	(£000)
Sales	1930	2876	3854	
Operating costs	1380	1820	2160	
	550	1056	1694	
Taxation		114	(140)	(421)
Salvage value			1500	
Tax effect of balancing charge[a]				(8)
	550	1170	3054	(429)
Discount factor at 8%	0.926	0.857	0.794	0.735
Present value	509	1003	2425	(315)

	(£000)
Present value at 8% =	3622
Investment outlay =	3500
NPV =	122

Note

[a] Balancing charge = $[1500 - (3500 - 2023)] \times 0.35$

Project 2 should be accepted, since it has the higher NPV.

(b) Additional factors to be considered include:
   (i) Have all alternative projects been considered?
   (ii) Are the projects of similar risk? Is the riskiness of the projects similar to the average risk of the current projects? If the projects are not of risk equal or similar to the risk of the existing assets then it is inappropriate to use the company's existing weighted average cost of capital as the discount rate.
   (iii) Are there any important qualitative factors which have not been considered in the analysis in (a)?

(c) The projects will now have unequal lives. In order to take this into account, the equivalent annual value method can be used. The calculations are as follows:

Project 1

	Year				
	1	2	3	4	5
	(£000)	(£000)	(£000)	(£000)	(£000)
Cash flow	271	950	1438	77	(188)
Discount factor at 8%	0.926	0.857	0.794	0.735	0.681
Present value	251	814	1142	57	(128)

NPV = £136 000 (2136 − 2000)

Annual equivalent values: Project 1 = £34 060 (£136 000/3.993)
                          Project 2 = £36 836 (£122 000/3.312)

Note that 3.993 and 3.312 represent the annuity factors for four and five years respectively.

Project 2 should still be undertaken, since it has the highest equivalent value. It is assumed that the cash flow patterns will be repeated until a common time horizon is reached.

(d) For the answer to this question see 'Comparison of net present value and internal rate of return' and 'Payback method' in Chapter 13.

(a) *Calculation of return on average investment*

	Year				
	1	2	3	4	5
	($000)	($000)	($000)	($000)	($000)
Sales: Parcels[a]	682	1075	1129	1185	1244
Letters[b]	2048	2867	3010	3160	3318
	2730	3942	4139	4345	4562
Wages[c]	2457	2580	2709	2844	2986
Premises[d]	158	165	174	182	191
Running and maintenance:					
Vans[e]	210	265	333	420	529
Trucks[e]	84	106	133	168	212
Advertising	525	276			
Cash expenses	3434	3392	3349	3614	3918
Depreciation[f]	232	232	232	232	232
	3666	3624	3581	3846	4150
Taxable profit	(936)	318	558	499	412
Taxation[g]	(374)	127	223	200	165
Profit after tax	(562)	191	335	299	247

$$\text{Average investment is } \frac{\$1\,160\,000^{h}}{2} = \$580\,000$$

$$\text{Average annual after tax return is } \frac{[(-562) + 191 + 335 + 299 + 347]}{5} = \$102\,000$$

$$\text{Annual after tax return on investment} = \frac{102\,000}{580\,000} = 17.6\%$$

Net present value calculation

	Year						
	0	1	2	3	4	5	6
	($000)	($000)	($000)	($000)	($000)	($000)	($000)
Sales		2730	3942	4139	4345	4562	
Cash expenses		3434	3392	3349	3614	3918	
Taxation			(374)	127	223	200	165
Initial investment[h]	1160						
	(1160)	(704)	924	663	508	444	(165)
Discount factor (14%)		0.877	0.769	0.675	0.592	0.519	0.456
Present value	(1160)	(617)	711	448	301	230	(75)

Net present value = ($162 000)

Notes and assumptions

[a] Year 1 = 500 parcels × $5.25 × 5 days × 52 weeks, year 2 = 750 parcels × $5.25 (1.05) × 5 days × 52 weeks, year 3 = year 2 × 1.05, year 4 = year 3 × 1.05, year 5 = year 4 × 1.05.

[b] Year 1 = 15 000 × $0.525 × 5 days × 52 weeks, year 2 = 20 000 × $0.525 (1.05) × 5 days × 52 weeks. From year 3 onwards, prices are assumed to increase at 5% per annum.

[c] Year 1 = 180 × $13 000 (1.05). It is assumed that the salaries of the five managers are payable whether or not the new service is introduced, and are not relevant cash flows. Other assumptions could be made. For example, if it is planned to make the managers redundant, the salaries would be relevant from the planned date of redundancy. Outflows from year 2 onwards have been increased by 5% for inflation.

^d Year 1 = $150 000 (1.05). Cash flows are assumed to increase at 5% per annum from year 2 to year 5.

^e Vans: 100 × $2000 × 1.05 (year 1), year 2 = 100 × $2000 (1.20) (1.05)². Trucks: 20 × $4000 × 1.05 (year 1), year 2 = 20 × $4000 (1.20) (1.05)², year 3 = year 2 × 1.20 × 1.05, year 4 = year 3 × 1.20 × 1.05, year 5 = year 4 × 1.20 × 1.05.

^f $1 160 000/5 years.

^g It is assumed that the estimated annual profits of the postal service are in excess of $500 000 per annum and that incremental income will be subject to taxation at a rate of 40%.

^h Initial investment = (100 × $8000) + (20 × $18 000).

Note that market research is a sunk cost.

The report should include the following comments:
  (i) The proposed new investment satisfies the return on investment criterion of 5% per annum (excluding financing costs), but has a negative expected NPV.
  (ii) The government criteria relate to the overall performance of the service as a whole and not individual projects. It might be possible that the service as a whole satisfies the criteria, even though the proposed new service does not.
  (iii) Qualitative factors have not been taken into account. There might be additional financial advantages to the economy, arising from the introduction of a postal service, which have not been included in the financial appraisal.
  (iv) The discount rate used in the NPV calculation assumes that the risk of the new service is the same as the postal service as a whole. If this is not the case, the cash flows should be discounted at the revised risk adjusted discount rate.
  (v) The estimates are based on constant demand after the first year. Is this correct? The possibility of demand increasing after the first year should be investigated. Other possibilities for increasing net cash flows should also be investigated. For example, can vehicle costs and wages be reduced?
  (vi) Consideration should be given to evaluating the project over a longer time horizon than five years. The vehicles would need replacing after five years, but it is unlikely that the advertising costs (which are significantly in excess of the negative NPV) will be repeated.
  (vii) Conclusion: the project has a negative NPV and the financial evaluation suggests that it should not be accepted. However, attention should be directed to the factors specified above and the project should be re-evaluated over a 10-year time horizon. If the cash flows are repeated over a 10-year horizon (without the advertising costs) it is likely that it will yield a positive NPV.
 (b) See 'Simulation' in Chapter 14 for the answer to this question.

Solution IM 14.10 (a) Average profits do not incorporate the time value of money or incremental cash flows. Profits represent a periodic performance measure. Capital investment decisions should be based on cash flows and not accounting profits.

Payback is a widely used appraisal method. It is a particularly useful method where a firm faces liquidity constraints and requires a fast repayment of investments. The payback method may also be appropriate in situations where risky investments are made in uncertain markets that are subject to fast design and product changes or where future cash flows are extremely difficult to predict. Its major weakness is that it ignores the time value of money and cash flows after the payback period is complete.

Discounted payback does take into account the time value of money but it ignores cash flows after the payback period. It may also lead to the rejection of positive NPV projects if they do not recoup the investment within the payback period set by management. Alternatively, because the cash flows are discounted projects will not be accepted that have negative NPVs.

Director C is focusing on profits rather than NPVs. Cost of capital has been ignored. If the risk-adjusted cost of capital is also 10% then the project will have a zero NPV. It is extremely unlikely that the risk-adjusted cost of capital will be less than the returns available from investing in financial markets.

(b) *Investment 1: cash flows*

				Year			
	0	1	2	3	4	5	6
	(£000)	(£000)	(£000)	(£000)	(£000)	(£000)	(£000)
Initial cost	500						
Sales^a		400	491	594	712	847	
Production costs^b		260	327	416	583	706	
Taxable cash flow		140	164	178	129	141	
Tax at 25%^{b}			(35)	(41)	(45)	(32)	(35)
Taxed saved by depreciation			31	24	18	13	10
Balancing allowance saving^c							30
Net cash flow	(500)	140	160	161	102	122	5
Discount factor^d	1	0.865	0.749	0.648	0.561	0.485	0.420
Present value^e	(500)	121	120	104	57	59	2

Payback period: none
Expected NPV = (£37 000)

Investment 2: cash flows

				Year			
	0	1	2	3	4	5	6
	(£000)	(£000)	(£000)	(£000)	(£000)	(£000)	(£000)
Initial cost	(175)						
Sales^a		500	654	760	829	988	
Production costs^b	—	460	567	653	764	889	
Taxable cash flow		40	87	107	65	99	
Tax at 25%			(10)	(22)	(27)	(16)	(25)
Tax saved by depreciation			11	8	6	5	4
Balancing allowance saving^c	—	—	—				10
Net cash flow	(175)	40	88	93	44	88	(11)
Discount factor^d	1	0.865	0.749	0.648	0.561	0.485	0.420
Present value^e	(175)	35	66	60	25	43	(5)

Discount payback period: approximately 3–5 years
Expected NPV = £49 000

Notes
^{a} The cash flows have been expressed as nominal/money cash flows. It is assumed that cash flows have been expressed in year 1 purchasing power. Therefore year 2 cash flows have been increased by 9%, year 3 by $(1.09)^2$, year 4 by $(1.09)^3$ and so on. Alternatively, cash flows can be expressed in real terms and discounted at the real discount rate. If this approach is used the depreciation tax shields must be deflated by the inflation rate because they do not rise in line with the general rate of inflation.
$^b (T - 1)$ cash flows $\times$ 25%.
^{c} The WDV of investment 1 at the end of year 5 is £118 000. Therefore the balancing allowance at the end of the project's life is £118 000 $\times$ 25% tax rate = £29 500. Investment 2 has a WDV at the end of year 5 of £41 000 resulting in a balancing allowance of £10 250 (£41 000 $\times$ 25%).
^{d} The cash flows have been expressed in nominal/money terms. Therefore the nominal/money discount rate has been used. It is calculated by multiplying the real discount rate (1.07) by [1 + the expected general rate of inflation (8%)] giving

a discount rate of 15.56%. The discount factors are 1/1.1556 for year 1, $1/(1.1556)^2$ for year 2, and so on.

[e] The financing costs of the investment have not been included in the cash flows because the financing cost is already incorporated in the discount rate. Internal funds do not represent a zero cost of financing since they have an opportunity cost in terms of the returns that could have been earned from investing the funds elsewhere.

(c) Non-financial factors that might influence the investment include the following.
   (i) Investment 2 is more labour-intensive and creates more jobs.
   (ii) Investment 2 is dependent on the availability of appropriate skilled labour.
   (iii) The impact of any environmental factors should be taken into account.
   (iv) The reliability of both items of equipment should be considered.

Solution IM 14.11

(a) The annual net savings are:

	(£)
Data processing costs saved	46 000
Less: Maintenance costs	(2 000)
Staff costs	(15 000)
Stationery and related costs	(4 000)
	25 000

$$(\text{annual saving} \times \text{discount factor}) - \text{investment cost} = \text{NPV}$$

The discount factor at which NPV is zero is:

$$(£25\,000 \times \text{DF}) - £161\,500 = 0$$

$$\text{DF} = \frac{£161\,500}{£25\,000} = 6.46$$

By inspecting the discount tables for the 5% column, it can be seen that 5% and eight years yields a discount factor of 6.46. Therefore the life which produces a zero NPV is eight years.

(b) (i) Six-year life: NPV at 5% = $(£25\,000 \times 5.0757) - £161\,500$
   $= -£34\,607$
   NPV at 0% = $(£25\,000 \times 1.00 \times 6 \text{ years}) - £161\,500$
   $= -£11\,500$
   The IRR is negative, and a precise calculation is unlikely to provide any meaningful information.

   (ii) Indefinite life: $£25\,000 \times \text{DF} - £161\,500 = 0$
   $$\text{DF} = 6.46$$
   An indefinite life implies infinity. However, the discount factors for 50 years will provide a close approximation to the discount factor when discounting to infinity. The discount rate for 50 years with a discount factor of 6.46 is between 15 and 16%. Therefore IRR is appropriately 15.5%. Alternatively the perpetuity formula can be used:

   $$\frac{£25\,000}{\text{discount rate}} = £161\,500$$

   Discount rate = 15.5%

(c) Let X = annual running costs. Then

$$(£46\,000 \times 7.722) - 7.722X - £161\,500 = 0$$
$$7.722X = £193\,712$$
$$X = £25\,086$$

(d) The first stage should be to calculate the NPV using the expected value of the relevant variables. A risk-adjusted discount rate should be used to discount the cash flows. The viability of the project can then be examined by testing its sensitivity to changes in the values of the crucial variables. Sensitivity analysis takes each variable in turn and calculates the critical value which will result in the project having a zero NPV, assuming that the estimated values of all the other variables are correct.

The critical life of the project is eight years, and, assuming an indefinite life, the project will have a positive NPV as long as the cost of capital is less than 15.5%. Alternatively if the life of the computer is only six years, the project is only acceptable if the company has a negative cost of capital in real terms (i.e. the cost of capital is lower than the level of inflation). In part (c) it was shown that if an optimistic estimate of project life is taken, annual running costs can increase to £25 086 before the NPV becomes negative.

The accountant should present the estimated NPV and provide details of the values of the relevant variables on which the NPV calculations are based. The critical values of these variables based on varying assumptions should then be tabulated to give the decision-maker an indication of the risk associated with the project.

(e) Sensitivity analysis is a crude method of analysing risk, because the critical variable which is calculated is based on the assumption that the estimates of the other variables are correct. Risk analysis could be improved by establishing probability distributions for each variable. Simulation techniques can then be used to estimate a probability distribution of the possible net present values from the project.

Better estimates of the uncertain variables might be obtained by discussing with users of similar systems their experiences from implementing and running the new system.

The question does not provide any information on how the 5% cost of capital is determined. Is it a risk-adjusted rate or the company's overall cost of capital? The overall cost of capital should be used only to evaluate projects of similar risk to existing projects. It is quite likely that the computer project is not of similar risk to existing projects. The project should therefore be discounted at a lower rate if it is below-average risk and at a higher rate if it is above-average risk. The precise rate is difficult to specify and this is the one variable where it might be appropriate to ascertain how sensitive the NPV is when different discount rates are used.

Inflation can be dealt with by discounting real cash flows at the real discount rate or discounting cash flows which are adjusted for inflation at a discount rate which incorporates a premium for inflation. The accountant has used cash flows which are expressed in current prices and discounted at a real rate. Estimating cash flows expressed in terms of current prices is only appropriate when all cash flows increase at the average rate of inflation. If the cash flows are subject to different rates of inflation then it is preferable to adjust each component by the specific rate of inflation and discount the inflation-adjusted cash flows at a money rate cost of capital (i.e. a rate which incorporates inflation).

(a) *Workings*

Solution IM 14.12

	Year 1 (£)	Year 2 (£)	Year 3 (£)
Contribution (internal manufacture)	10.50 (£10 × 1.05)	11.03 (£10 × 1.05²)	11.58
External purchases:			
Selling price	52.50 (£50 × 1.05)	55.13	57.88
Internal costs	26.25 (£25 × 1.05)	27.56	28.94
Contribution before purchase cost	26.25	27.57	28.94
Purchase cost	20.00	20.00	20.00

Note that external purchase costs are paid in advance. Therefore payments occur at t_0, t_1 and t_2.

Present value of fixed costs:

$$£10\,000/1.15 + £12\,500/(1.15)^2 + £15\,000/(1.15)^3 = £28\,021$$

Economic condition A

	Year 1	Year 2	Year 3
Contribution per unit (£)	10.50	11.03	11.58
Demand	10 000	12 000	14 400
Total contribution (£)	105 000	132 360	166 752

	(£)
PV of contribution	301 129
PV of fixed costs	(28 021)
Investment cost (375 + 25)	(400 000)
NPV	(126 892)

Economic condition B

	Year 1	Year 2	Year 3
Contribution per unit (£)	10.50	11.03	11.58
Internal output	15 000	18 000	20 000[a]
Total contribution (£)	157 500	198 540	231 600

	(£)	(£)
PV of contribution		439 362
PV of units bought in [1600[a] × £28.94 = £46 300/(1.15)³]	30 446	
Less PV of purchase costs 1200[a] × 20 = £40 000/(1.15)²]	30 245	201
PV of fixed costs		(28 021)
Investment cost		(400 000)
NPV		11 542

Note

[a] Demand in year 3 is 21 600 units. Therefore 1600 units demand must be met from external purchases. However, the contract requires that purchases must be in batches of 2000 units. It is assumed that the surplus purchases have no realizable value.

Economic condition C

	Year 1	Year 2	Year 3
Contribution per unit (£)	10.50	11.03	11.58
Internal demand	20 000	20 000	20 000
Total contribution (£)	210 000	220 600	231 600
Sale of external production:			
Year 2: 4000 × £27.57		110 280	
Year 3: 8000[a] × £28.94			231 520
External purchase:			
Year 2: 4000 × £20)	(80 000)		
Year 3: 8000 × £20)		(160 000)	
Total contribution	130 000	170 880	463 120

	(£)
PV of total contribution	546 762
PV of fixed costs	(28 021)
Investment cost	(400 000)
NPV	(118 741)

Note

[a] Total demand in year 3 is 28 800 units, but external purchases can only be obtained in batches of 2000 units. It is therefore economic to purchase 8000 units. The purchase of a final batch of 2000 units to meet the unfulfilled demand of 800 units cannot be justified.

$$\text{Expected NPV} = (-£126\,892 \times 0.25) + (£11\,542 \times 0.45) + (£118\,741 \times 0.30)$$
$$= £9093$$

On the basis of the expected NPV decision rule, the refurbishment is justified.

(b) The expected value represents the weighted average of the possible outcomes. However, the expected value calculation will be flawed if biased estimates of the range of outcomes are presented. It should also be noted that the expected value represents the average long-run outcome if a project were undertaken many times. It is most unlikely that the actual outcome will equal the expected value for 'one off' decisions. Care must therefore be taken when interpreting expected values.

Expected values focus on averages and ignore the range of variations around the mean. Risk is therefore ignored when decisions are based on expected values. In part (a) the project has an expected NPV of £9093, but this does not draw attention to the fact that the NPVs can range from −£126 892 to + £119 741.

In order to incorporate risk into the analysis, finance theory advocates that cash flows expressed in expected values should be discounted at a risk-adjusted cost of capital. The risk-adjusted cost of capital can be determined by using the capital asset pricing model. The NPV calculation in (a) is based on a cost of capital of 15%. It is assumed that this rate is the company's risk-adjusted discount rate. This rate would only reflect the risk-adjusted cost of capital for the refurbishment project if its risk is equivalent to average firm risk. A higher cost of capital should be used if the project's risk is greater than the average risk for the firm's existing assets.

To summarize, expected values ignore risk. The latter is incorporated into the analysis by discounting cash flows expressed in expected values at the risk-adjusted cost of capital. The resulting risk-adjusted expected NPV represents the average outcome. To assess how sensitive the expected NPV calculation is to the changes in the variables which are used to calculate it, sensitivity analysis should be employed. For a discussion of sensitivity analysis and the use of standard deviations as a measure of dispersion about the expected value see 'Traditional methods of measuring risk' in Chapter 14.

(a) *Cash flows*

Solution IM 14.13

	0 (£000)	1 (£000)	2 (£000)	3 (£000)	4 (£000)	5 (£000)
Sales			4500	5300	6000	
Outflows						
Materials		200	850	1200	1320	
Wages		180	960	1200	1360	
Salaries[a]		75	136	158	179	
Head office overhead[b]		40	45	50	55	
Other fixed costs[b]		20	400	420	440	
Warehouse rent[c]		60	60	60	60	
Lost exports[c]		110	110	110	110	
		685	2561	3198	3524	
Taxable cash flow		(685)	1939	2102	2476	
Taxation[e]		—	226	(640)	(694)	(817)
Tax saved by allowances[e]		2	60	47	36	
After-tax flow		(683)	2225	1509	1818	(817)

Other relevant cash flows

Redundancy saving[a]	40					
Skilled labour[c]		(80)	(80)			
Land[f]	(300)				365	
Buildings[f]	(240)	(510)			882	
Machinery[f]		(650)			80	
Taxation impact[f]						(21)
Working capital[g]		(400)	(40)	(20)	(20)	480
Net cash flow	(500)	(2323)	2105	1489	3125	(358)
Discount factor[h] (16.43%)	1	0.859	0.738	0.634	0.544	0.467
Present value (£000)	(500)	(1995)	1553	944	1700	(167)

Expected net present value is £1 535 000. On the basis of this information the investment should be undertaken.

Notes

[a] The £25 000 paid to the manager transferred from another division represents an incremental cash flow to the company and should be included in the analysis. However, if the investment is accepted the company will avoid *after-tax* redundancy payments of £40 000.

[b] Only incremental head office overhead should be included in the analysis. It is assumed that the cash flows quoted in the question have already been adjusted for inflation. It is also assumed that other fixed costs represent incremental cash flows.

[c] The warehouse rental payment does not represent an incremental cash flow but the opportunity cost represents a differential *before-tax* cash flow that must be incorporated into the appraisal. The opportunity costs for lost exports and salaries are also differential cash flows which are incorporated respectively into the appraisal as before-tax and after-tax cash flows.

[d] The interest cost represents the cost of financing which is already incorporated in the discount rate. Financing costs should not be included in the DCF appraisal as this represents double counting of the cost of capital.

[e] Tax allowable depreciation (capital allowances) is 4% straight line on buildings and 25% reducing balance on machinery. The working notes have applied 25% on all assets. The correct calculation is as follows:

	Year				Total
	1	2	3	4	5
	(£000)	(£000)	(£000)	(£000)	(£000)
Building ($2\frac{1}{2}$% straight line)	6	19	19	19	63
Machinery (25% reducing balance)		163	122	91	376
Total	6	182	141	110	
Tax savings (33%)	2	60	47	36	

Note that it is also assumed that the taxation on year 1 losses may be offset against other profits of the company, thus reducing the company's overall tax payment in year 2.

[f] Because the company has a time horizon of three years of sales for evaluating the investment, rather than the whole life of the investment, an estimate of the realizable value of the investment at the end of the third year of sales must be incorporated into the analysis. Estimated disposal values are as follows:

Land: $£300(1.05)^4 = £365$
Buildings: $£240(1.05)^4 + £510(1.05)^3 = £882.1$
Machinery: £80 (given)

The taxation impact also must be taken into account. It is assumed that the gain on the land is taxable at 33%. The taxation liability is calculated as follows:

Gain on the land [33% × (£365 − £300)] = £21
Buildings WDV = £750 − £63 = £687
Tax on gains = 33% × (£882 − £687) = £64
Machinery WDV = £650 − £376 = £274
Balancing allowance = 33% × (£80 − £274) = −£64

Therefore the net tax liability in year 5 is (£21 + £64 − £64) = £21.

g Only incremental working capital should be included in the analysis. It is assumed that working capital will be released at the end of year 5.

h Although the project has been financed by a specific fixed rate term loan, the specific cost of finance should not be used as the discount rate since it will involve a departure from the target capital structure. To maintain the target capital structure less fixed interest finance will have to be used in the future. To reflect the target capital structure the weighted average cost of capital should be used. The betas for the companies in the same industry as the new project differ from the company's betas. This implies that the risk for the new project differs from the average risk of the firm's assets. Therefore the cost of capital should be based on the average beta of companies in the same industry as the new project. The average asset beta (i.e. a beta assuming all equity financing) for the industry is 1.2. This beta must be adjusted to reflect the capital of the company (76% equity and 24% debt) by calculating the equity beta. The equity beta is calculated as follows:

$$\text{Equity beta} = \text{asset beta} \times \frac{\text{market value of equity} + \text{value of debt} (1 - \text{tax rate})}{\text{market value of equity}}$$

$$= 1.2 \times \frac{76 + 24\,(1 - 0.33)}{76} = 1.454$$

The above beta can now be used to calculate the cost of equity using the capital asset pricing model:

Cost of equity = Risk-free rate + (return on market − risk-free rate) beta
= 6% + (15% − 6%) × 1.454
= 19.08%

The weighted average cost of capital based on the company's debt and equity ratios in market values is:

$$(19.08 \times 76/100) + 12(1 - 0.33) \times 24/100 = 16.43\%$$

Note that 12% is the current before-tax borrowing rate.

i Market research is a sunk cost and is not relevant.

(b) Most of the limitations relate to the difficulty in obtaining accurate estimates that are required to calculate NPV. They include:

(i) Accuracy of the estimated cash flows.

(ii) Difficulty in accurately estimating a project's cost of capital, particularly when the project has a risk different from the average risk of the company as a whole. In this situation it is necessary to use the beta of a proxy company that operates solely in similar activities to the project that is being evaluated. In practice it is extremely difficult to identify proxy companies.

The budgeting process

Solutions to Chapter 15 questions

Solution IM 15.1   (a) See 'The multiple functions of budgets?' in Chapter 15 for the answer to this question.
(b) See 'Administration of the budget process' and 'Stages in the budget process' in Chapter 15 for the answer to this question.

Solution IM 15.2   (a) See 'Stages in the budget process' in Chapter 15 for the answer to this question.
(b) See 'Computerized budgeting' in Chapter 15 for the answer to this question.

Solution IM 15.3   See 'Zero-base budgeting' in Chapter 15 for a description of zero-base budgeting and an explanation of how it differs from other more traditional forms of budgeting. In profit-orientated organizations those costs which are of a discretionary nature such as service and support activities are appropriate candidates for zero-base budgeting. Examples of departments which fall into this category include personnel, research and development, accounts, and data processing.

Solution IM 15.4   (a/b) See 'Zero-base budgeting' in Chapter 15 for the answer to these questions.
(c) It is preferable to introduce zero-base budgeting selectively rather than 'across the board'. The approach should initially be applied to those activities where immediate benefits are likely. This might lead to a greater acceptance by its users. Care should be taken in selecting the activities to which zero-base budgeting is to be applied. In Chapter 15 it will have been noted that it is best suited to non-manufacturing activities and non-profit making organizations. When the system is introduced, meetings and seminars should be arranged explaining the principles of zero-base budgeting. Because zero-base budgeting is costly and time-consuming, there are strong arguments for selective *ad hoc* applications which are likely to yield benefits. It is unlikely that a universal application of zero-base budgeting in an organization can be justified.

Solution IM 15.5   (a/b) See 'Zero-base budgeting' in Chapter 15 for the answer to this question.
(c) The problems that might be met in introducing zero-base budgeting include:
  (i) The implementation of zero-base budgeting might be resisted by staff. Traditional incremental budgeting tends to protect the empire that a manager has built. Zero-base budgeting challenges this empire, and so there is a strong possibility that managers might resist the introduction of such a system.
  (ii) There is a need to combat a feeling that current operations are efficient.
  (iii) The introduction of zero-base budgeting is time-consuming.
  (iv) Top-management support may be lacking.
(d) See 'Zero-base budgeting' in Chapter 15 for the answer to this question.

For the steps in the preparation of master budgets see 'Stages in the budgeting process' in Chapter 15. **Solution IM 15.6**

The main budgets that should normally be prepared are:
  (i) sales budget;
  (ii) production budget;
  (iii) direct material usage budget;
  (iv) direct materials purchase budget;
  (v) direct labour budget;
  (vi) factory overhead budget;
  (vii) selling expenses budget;
  (viii) administration budget;
  (ix) cash budget;
  (x) budgeted balance sheet and profit and loss account.

For comments and illustrations of the above budgets see the detailed illustration presented in Chapter 15.

(a/b) See 'The budget period' in Chapter 15 for a description of rolling budgets and an explanation of how a rolling budget system works. The 'CIMA Terminology' defines a rolling budget as 'The continuous updating of a short-term budget by adding, say, a further month or quarter and deducting the earliest month or quarter so that the budget can reflect current conditions.' **Solution IM 15.7**

(c)   The following are some advantages of rolling budgets:
  (i) Actual performance is likely to be compared with a more realistic target because budgets are being constantly reviewed and updated.
  (ii) Planning is not something that takes place once per year when the budget is being formulated. With rolling budgets, budgeting is a continuous process, and managers are encouraged constantly to look ahead and review future plans.
  (iii) The work load of the budget staff is spread throughout the year rather than the whole budget process being concentrated into a few months.

(d)   Problems that may be encountered include:
  (i) The work load is increased in comparison with preparing annual budgets once per year.
  (ii) Because budgets are reviewed and changed at the end of each quarter, there may be a danger when a new quarter's budget is added that staff will not give sufficient attention to preparing this budget because they know it is likely to be changed in the revision process.
  (iii) Too much attention might be given to the continuous short-term aspects of budgets at the expense of long-term planning.

See 'The multiple functions of budgets' and 'Conflicting roles of budgets' in Chapter 15 for the answer to this question. **Solution IM 15.8**

(a) (i) *Sales budget in quantity and value* **Solution IM 15.9**

	July	August	September	Total
Sales units	400	300	600	1 300
Sales value (£)	100 000	75 000	150 000	325 000

  (ii) *Production budget in units*

Sales	1300
Closing stock	225
	1525
Opening stock	(200)
Good output required	1325
Normal loss (1325 × 1/9)	147
Production required	1472

(iii) *Raw material usage budget*

Production (units)	1472
	(kg)
Material A (at 3 kg per unit)	4416
Material B (at 2 kg per unit)	2944
Material C (at 4 kg per unit)	5888

(iv) *Raw material purchases budget*

	A (kgs)	B (kgs)	C (kgs)	Total
Kgs used	4 416	2 944	5 888	
Stock increase (20%)	200	80	120	
Purchases in kgs	4 616	3 024	6 008	
Unit cost	£3.50	£5.00	£4.50	
Purchases cost	£16 156	£15 120	£27 036	£58 312

(v) *Labour requirements budget*

Production in units	1 472
Unit labour hours	10
Total hours	14 720
Cost per hour	£8.00
Total cost	£117 760

(b) The principal budget factor (also known as the limiting factor) is the factor that constrains or limits the activities of the organization during a budget period. During the budget process, the principal budget factor is the foundation upon which all of the budgets must be based and which constrains activity from being expanded. For example, if machine hours are the principal budget factor, the production budget, sales budget and all of the remaining budgets will be restricted to the maximum output from the available machine hours. Prior to the preparation of the budgets it is necessary for management to identify the principal budget factor, since this factor will determine the point at which the annual budgeting process should begin.

(c) *Labour requirements budget*

Product	Z
Production in units	= D15
Labour hours per unit	= A5
Total hours	= D15*A5
Cost per hour	= D5
Total cost	= D5*E30

The labour requirements budget would be drawn from a spreadsheet containing the basic input information (such as cells A5, D6, etc) and a working area from which information is derived and which then cascades throughout the spreadsheet. A change in input information, or any relationships within the model, is immediately reflected in the output information.

(a)

(i) *Sales budget*

	Quarter 1	Quarter 2	Quarter 3	Quarter 4	Total
Sales units	40 000	50 000	30 000	45 000	165 000
Unit price (£)	150	150	160	160	
Revenue (£000)	6 000	7 500	4 800	7 200	25 500

(ii) *Production budget (units)*

Opening stock	9 000	5 000	3 000	4 500	
Production (difference)	36 000	48 000	31 500	44 500	160 000
	45 000	53 000	34 500	49 000	
Closing stock[a]	5 000	3 000	4 500	4 000	
Sales	40 000	50 000	30 000	45 000	

Note
[a] 10% of next quarter's sales.

(iii) *Material usage budget (units)*

					Total
	(000)	(000)	(000)	(000)	(000)
Component R	144 (36 000 × 4)	192	126	178	640
Component T	108 (36 000 × 3)	144	94.5	133.5	480
Shell S	36 (36 000 × 1)	48	31.5	44.5	160

(iv) *Production cost budget*

					Total
	(000)	(000)	(000)	(000)	(000)
Materials:					
Component R	1 152	1 689.60	1 108.80	1 566.40	5 516.80
Component T	540	792.00	519.75	734.25	2 586.00
Shell S	1 080	1 440.00	945.00	1 335.00	4 800.00
	2 772	3 921.60	2 573.55	3 635.65	12 902.80
Labour (at £30 per unit)	1 080	1 440.00	945.00	1 388.40	4 853.40
Variable overhead	360	480.00	315.00	445.00	1 600.00
Fixed overhead[a]	54	72.00	47.25	66.75	240.00
Total production cost	4 266	5 913.60	3 880.80	5 535.80	19 596.20

Note
[a] Charged out at £1.50 per unit of output (£240 000/160 000 units).

(b) The principal budget factor is the factor which limits the organization's ability to achieve increasing profits. In most organizations the principal budget factor is sales. For a brief discussion of how sales may be forecast see 'Sales budget' in Chapter 15.

(a)

	June	July	August
	(£)	(£)	(£)
Closing stock	3 500	6 000	4 000
Material usage	8 000	9 000	10 000
	11 500	15 000	14 000
Less: Opening stock	5 000	3 500	6 000
Direct material purchases	6 500	11 500	8 000

(b) *Cash budgets for June, July and August:*

	June (£)	July (£)	August (£)
Receipts			
Sales cash (10%)	4 500	5 000	6 000
Credit	29 500	40 500	45 000
	34 000	45 500	51 000
Payments			
Wages	12 000	13 000	14 500
Overheads (less depreciation)	6 500	7 000	8 000
Direct materials	6 500	11 500	8 000
Taxation	—	25 000	—
	25 000	56 500	30 500
Opening balance	11 750	20 750	9 750
Receipts	34 000	45 500	51 000
Payments	25 000	56 500	30 500
Closing balance	20 750	9 750	30 250

(c) See the section on cash budgets in Chapter 15 for the answer to this question.

Solution IM 15.12

(a) *Cash budget*

	Week					
	1 (£000)	2 (£000)	3 (£000)	4 (£000)	5 (£000)	6 (£000)
Cash receipts from sales[a]	80	80	75	70	70	80
Cash payments:						
Materials[b]	27	46	12	–	–	–
Direct labour and variable overhead[c]	41	41	16	16	16	16
Fixed overhead[d]	16	16	12	12	12	12
	84	103	40	28	28	28
Weekly surplus/(deficit)	(4)	(23)	35	42	42	52
Opening cash balance	(39)	(43)	(66)	(31)	11	53
Closing cash balance	(43)	(66)	(31)	11	53	105

Notes

a

	Week					
	1 (£000)	2 (£000)	3 (£000)	4 (£000)	5 (£000)	6 (£000)
Opening debtors	80	40				
Week 1 sales		40	40			
2			35	35		
3				35	35	
4					35	35
5						45
	80	80	75	70	70	80

The above sales can be achieved because opening stocks of finished goods (2800 units) + production in weeks 1 and 2 (2400 units) are greater than sales in weeks 1–5 (3800 units) by 1400 units.

^{b} Purchase of materials:

	Week 1 (£)	Week 2 (£)
Closing stock	40 000	10 000
+ Production	42 000	42 000
(1200 × £35)		
– Opening stock	(36 000)	(40 000)
= Purchases	46 000	12 000 (paid for 1 week later)

^{c}

$$\text{Weeks 1 and 2} = 1200 \times £30 = 36\,000$$
$$+ \quad 5\,000 \text{ (overtime premium)}$$
$$41\,000$$
$$\text{Weeks 3–6} = 800 \times £20 \quad = 16\,000$$
$$^d\text{Weeks 1 and 2} = 800 \times £25 \quad = 20\,000$$
$$- \quad 4\,000 \text{ (depreciation)}$$
$$16\,000$$
$$\text{Weeks 3–6} = £16\,000 - £4000 = 12\,000$$

(b) The matters which should be drawn to the attention of the management are:
   (i) The overdraft limit will be exceeded in week 2, and arrangements should be made to increase this limit.
   (ii) Excess funds will be available from weeks 4 to 6 and plans should be made to invest these funds on a short-term basis.
   (iii) Funds will be required as soon as production recommences in order to re-establish stocks of raw materials and finished goods.

(a) The costs incurred over the three-year period are as follows:

Solution IM 15.13

	2001 (£)	2002 (£)	2003 (£)
Direct material			
(270 houses p.a.)^a	20 250 (270 × £75)	21 263 (£20 250 × 1.05)	22 326 (£21 263 × 1.05)
Direct labour	72 900 (270 × £270)	78 003 (£72 900 × 1.07)	83 463 (£78 003 × 1.07)
Variable overheads^b	25 515 (270 × £94.50)	27 046 (£25 515 × 1.06)	28 669 (£27 046 × 1.06)
Fixed overheads:^{c}			
Avoidable	15 430	16 356 (£15 430 × 1.06)	17 337 (£16 356 × 1.06)
Depreciation	10 287	10 287	10 287
Head office	25 718	27 261 (£25 718 × 1.06)	28 897 (£27 261 × 1.06)

Notes

^{a} Number of houses maintained each year = (500 × 30%) + (600 × 20%) = 270

^{b} Overhead cost per house: (£)
          Material related   15 (20% × £75)
          Labour related   270 (100% × £270)
                            285

Variable overhead per house   = £4.50 (30% × £15) + £90 ($\frac{1}{3}$ × £270) = £94.50

^{c} Fixed overhead per house   = £190.50 (£285 − £94.50)
Total fixed overheads for 2001   = £51 435 (£190.50 × 270 houses)
Avoidable fixed overheads   = £15 431 (30% × £51 435)
Depreciation   = £10 287 (20% × £51 435)
Head office   = £25 718 (50% × £51 435)

Painting and decorating cash budget

	2001 (£)	2002 (£)	2003 (£)
Direct materials payments:[a]			
Previous year creditors	2 100	1 823	1 914
Current year	16 402	17 223	18 084
Cash purchases	2 025	2 126	2 233
Direct labour payments:[b]			
Previous year accruals	2 800	2 916	3 120
Current year	69 984	74 883	80 124
Variable overhead:[c]			
Previous year	600	851	902
Current year	24 664	26 144	27 713
Fixed overhead:[d]			
Avoidable	15 430	16 356	17 337
Head office	25 718	27 261	28 897
	159 723	169 583	180 324

Notes

[a] Current year purchases = 90% × (90% × direct material cost)
  Cash purchases = 10% × direct material cost
  Previous year creditors = 10% × (90% × direct material cost)
[b] Current year labour cost = 96% × direct labour cost
  Previous year accrual = 4% × direct labour cost
[c] (Variable overhead incurred/12 months) × 40%.
[d] Depreciation is a non-cash flow expense.

(b) (i) The relevant cash flows (see part (a)) are:

	2001 (£)	2002 (£)	2003 (£)	Total (£)
Direct materials	20 250	21 263	22 326	
Direct labour	72 900	78 003	83 463	
Variable overhead	25 515	27 046	28 669	
Avoidable fixed overhead	15 430	16 356	17 337	
	134 095	142 668	151 795	428 558

The quotation from the outside company is £405 000 (3 × £135 000). On the basis of the information given in the question, it would be cheaper if the work were undertaken by the outside company.

(ii) Other factors which have not been taken into account in the financial analysis and which support the work being undertaken by the outside company include:

1. There may be additional savings/cash inflows arising from closing down the painting and decorating department, such as the sale of stocks of paint, subletting the premises or benefits arising from the use of the premises for other activities.
2. The payments to the outside company may be payable quarterly in arrears. Thus when the time value of money is taken into account the benefits will be greater than indicated in the analysis in (a).

Other factors not considered in (b) which do not support closing the department down include:

1. The housing association has less control over the quality of work and this could cause dissatisfaction amongst the tenants.
2. The closure of the department could lead to redundancy payments which are in excess of the savings made by the change.

3. What will happen when the contract is completed? If the market is not very competitive, the outside company will be in a dominant bargaining position when the contract is re-negotiated if the housing association cannot easily set up a painting and decorating function. This could lead to the housing association being 'ripped off' when the contract is re-negotiated.

(a)

		Product 1	Product 2	Product 3
(i)	Sales	850 000	1 500 000	510 000
(ii)	Stock change	100 000	45 000	(35 000)
(iii)	Units packed	950 000	1 545 000	475 000
(iv)	Rejects [5/95 × (iii)]	50 000	—	25 000
(v)	Units filled	1 000 000	1 545 000	500 000
(vi)	Units filled per hour	125	300	250
(vii)	Units packed per hour	95	100	95
(viii)	DLHs required:			
	Filling [(v)/(vi)]	8 000	5 150	2 000
	Packing [(iii)/(vii)]	10 000	15 450	5 000
	Total DLHs	18 000	20 600	7 000

Total hours required for direct labour personnel = (18 000 + 20 600 + 7000)/0.8 = 57 000 hours
Hours per employee per annum = 38 hours × 50 weeks = 1900 hours
Direct labour personnel required = 30 (57 000 hours/1900 hours)

(b)
$$\text{(£)}$$
Payroll cost: Basic pay (30 × 35 hours × 52 weeks × £4) = 218 400
Overtime (30 × 3 hours × 52 weeks × £5) = 23 400
241 800

Direct labour hour rate = £5.30 (£241 800/45 600 DLHs)

(c)

	Product 1	Product 2	Product 3
Filling	4.46 p [£5.30/(0.95 × 125)]	1.77 p (£5.30/300)	2.23 p [£5.30/(0.95 × 250)]
Packing	5.58 p (£5.30/95)	5.30 p (£5.30/100)	5.58 p (£5.30/95)
	10.04 p	7.07 p	7.81 p

Management control systems

Solutions to Chapter 16 questions

Solution IM 16.1   See Chapter 16 for the answer to this question.

Solution IM 16.2   See 'Responsibility accounting' in Chapter 16 for the answer to this question.

Solution IM 16.3   See Chapter 16 for an explanation of budgetary slack and fixed budgets and Chapter 15 for incremental budgets.

In particular, the answer should stress that slack budgets lead to an understatement of revenues and an overstatement of costs. This may result in the generation of misleading budgets and inappropriate decisions and may not reflect actual outcomes. See answer to Questions IM 16.14 and IM 16.15 for a discussion of how budget slack might be eliminated.

With regard to incremental budgets, past inefficiencies are unlikely to be eliminated and this will tend to increase budgeted cash outflows and expenses. The deficiencies of incremental budgeting might be eliminated by implementing zero-base budgets.

Fixed budgets will result in inaccurate cash and profit budgets if actual activity is significantly different from the fixed budget level of activity. The problem can be reduced by generating budgets for a range of activity levels using sensitivity analysis to ascertain how sensitive the plans are to changes in activity levels. If outcomes are particularly sensitive to changes in activity levels, consideration should be given to including a monetary provision for volume changes at the planning stage.

Solution IM 16.4   (a) See 'Rolling budgets' in Chapter 15, 'Flexible budgets' in Chapter 16 and 'Planning and operational variances' in Chapter 19 for the answer to this question.

(b) The continuous nature of rolling budgets and the fact that the budget will be reviewed at frequent intervals may reduce the need for budgetees to protect themselves against the uncertainties inherent in the annual budgeting process. Alternatively, if rolling budgets seek to incorporate a continuous improvement, or if a good performance in the previous period is reflected by a more demanding budget, then rolling budgets might be seen as an additional short-term threat and thus encourage the need to build in slack.

Without flexible budgets managers might restrict activity in order to ensure that actual expenditure will be lower than budget (purely because of the lower level of activity). At the budget setting stage flexible budgets are unlikely to have much impact on budget slack.

Planning and operational variances should reduce the incidence of budget slack at the budget setting stage if the targets are likely to be adjusted to reflect the changing conditions that have occurred during the budget period.

Solution IM 16.5   A large proportion of non-manufacturing costs are of a discretionary nature. In respect of such costs, management has some significant range of discretion as to the amount it will budget for the particular activity in question. Examples of *discretionary* costs (sometimes called managed or programmed costs) include advertising, research and development and training costs. There is not optimum relationship between inputs (as measured by the costs) and outputs (as measured by revenues of some other objective function) for these costs. Furthermore, they are not predetermined by some previous commitment. In effect, management can determine what quantity of service it wishes to purchase. For example, it can choose to spend small or large amounts on research and development or advertising. The great difficulty in controlling such costs is that there is no established method for determining the appropriate amount to be spent in particular periods.

One approach to this problem is to compare amounts spent on the various discretionary items with those of similar organizations or with past periods. However, past periods may represent excessive or deficient budget allocations, and therefore are a weak base for comparison purposes. Another approach is to allow the spending of an amount that management believes it can afford. For example, some firms budget discretionary expenses as a percentage of sales. The weakness of this approach is that future sales may be determined by such items as research and development and advertising expenditure, but when the sales revenue declines, the budgeted expenditure on research and development and advertising will be similarly reduced. This may be an incorrect approach, since it may be more appropriate in the circumstances to increase expenditure on research and development and advertising to stimulate future sales.

The major argument for selecting sales as a basis for determining the amount of budgeted expenditure in discretionary items is not because there is any presumed causal relationship with sales, but because sales represents a useful indication of how much the company can afford to spend.

It is essential that fixed budgets be used for the control of discretionary expenses. At the budget stage management will have determined the amount to be spent. This will normally be a policy decision to be implemented, and the costs will then be regarded as fixed for the appropriate budget period. Flexible budgets based on the adjustment of expenditure because of changes in activity are therefore inappropriate for the control of discretionary expenses. Note also that any underspending may not necessarily be a good thing, since this may result in a lower level of service than that originally planned by management. For example, underspending on research and development may indicate that the policy on the amount to be spent on research and development has not been followed.

(a) For an explanation of how financial control systems work in the same way as machine control systems see 'Cybernetic control systems' and 'Results or output controls' in Chapter 16.

Solution IM 16.6

The role that performance evaluation plays in a management information system is explained within the sections headed 'Results or output controls' and 'Harmful side-effects of controls' in Chapter 16.

Output and input controls are discussed in 'The budgeting process in non-profit-making organizations' in Chapter 15 and 'Results or output controls' in Chapter 16. Line-item budgets described in Chapter 15 are a form of input control.

(b) See 'Harmful side-effects of controls' in Chapter 16 for the answer to the first part of the question. For the actions that might be taken to avoid the distortions see 'Dealing with the distorting effects of uncontrollable factors before (and after) the measurement period'. In addition, the different styles of using accounting information described at the end of Chapter 16 are relevant to answering this question.

(c) The answer should describe the more sophisticated systems, such as ABC, that can be implemented as a result of the developments in information technology, particularly the declining costs of information processing. The answer could discuss the cost–benefit issues of cost system design described in Chapter 3 and indicate that the sophistication of the costing system should be increased up to the point where the additional benefits cease to exceed the additional costs. The declining information processing costs should therefore result in the implementation of more sophisticated systems.

Solution IM 16.7   (a) A description of each of the terms is presented in the text. See the index for the relevant pages.

(b) See 'Aspiration levels' and 'Setting financial performance targets' in Chapter 16 for the answer to this question.

Solution IM 16.8   *Feedback control* consists of a comparison of actual outcome with budgeted outcomes. This comparison should be used to initiate remedial action. Such action might include a change in operating methods or a change in the budget.

Feedforward controls arise where predictions are made regarding future costs, revenues or outputs and these predictions are compared with objectives and plans set previously. If the comparison indicates a significant deviation between forecast and the plan then action is taken to minimize the difference. Thus feedback is concerned with corrective action by reference to *past* deviations from budget, whereas feedforward control is concerned with corrective action on *anticipated* future deviations.

Budget slack: see answers to questions IM 16.3, 16.14 and 16.15.

Aspiration levels: see 'Aspiration levels' in Chapter 16.

Control limits represent limits which are set for investigating variances from budget or standard. Variances may be due to random uncontrollable factors or they may be so insignificant that the benefits from investigation do *not* exceed the costs of investigation. Alternatively variances might be due to assignable causes, and the benefits *may* exceed the costs of investigation. Variances which fall within the control limits are assumed to be due to non-assignable causes. Only variances which fall outside the control limits should be investigated.

Noise: An example of noise would be the presentation of performance reports containing too much information. This information overload might result in important variance information being ignored because it is buried in a mass of other information.

Solutions IM 16.9–16.12   These are open-ended questions that are intended to test independent thought and initiative in relating the literature to the questions asked. Therefore anwers are not provided for these questions.

Solution IM 16.13   (a) Budgets may be imposed upon managers who are responsible for their implementation. Alternatively managers may participate in determining the budget for which they are responsible. For a discussion of the advantages and disadvantages of allowing managers to participate in the budget process see 'Participation in the budget and target setting process' in Chapter 16. In particular, the answer should stress the following advantages which have been claimed to have resulted from a participative budgeting process:

(i) Participation increases the aspiration levels and motivation of the budgetees and increases the probability that the budget will be accepted as a legitimate target for which to aim.

(ii) Participation may lead to an increased level of efficiency.

(iii) Participation improves communication between the budgetees and their superiors.

The disadvantages of participative budgeting include:

(i) It may lead to creation of budget slack. Where managers are able to influence their budget standard, there is a possibility that they will bias the information in order to gain the greatest possible benefit. This will apply particularly where the reward system places great stress on achieving the budget.

(ii) The personality traits of the budgetees may limit the benefits of participation. Individuals with certain personality traits may perform better when budgets are imposed by a higher authority.

(iii) Participation may encourage managers to adopt a departmental self-centred approach and concentrate solely on maximizing the benefits of their own departments at the expense of the benefits of the organization as a whole.

Some of the disadvantages which result from imposed budgets include:

(i) Non-acceptance of the budget as a target may result in the budgetees not attempting to achieve the target set.

(ii) The budget is likely to be viewed as a punitive device which management uses in a recriminatory manner to evaluate subordinates. There is a danger that this might create hostility towards the budget system and a failure to use the system as a planning and control device.

(iii) Pressure to achieve an imposed budget might result in the falsification of data or under performance in order to influence the setting of future budget targets so that they are set at easily attainable levels.

Problems are likely to apply whichever approach is used.

(b) The answer to this question should focus on describing incremental and zero-base budgeting. In particular the answer should stress that, with incremental budgeting, past inefficiencies and slack can perpetuate and be built into future budgets. It is claimed that zero-base budgeting can overcome the problems of incremental budgeting. For a more detailed explanation see 'Zero-base budgeting' in Chapter 15.

(a) Managers may attempt to create budget slack in the following ways:

Solution IM 16.14

(i) Overestimating expenses, particularly with regard to discretionary costs. Senior managers might identify this by comparing expense categories with those in other similar areas of the business (possibly expressed as a percentage of sales) or with previous-year figures, or by using zero-based budgeting approaches.

(ii) Under estimating sales revenue. Again senior managers might identify this by comparing the trend in sales revenue with other areas of the business, previous-year figures and similar companies. Ideally, the trend in sales ought to take account of projected market growth and market share.

(iii) Unnecessary spending in the current budget period in order to spend up to budget so as to preserve the current budget allocation for the next budget period. Senior managers might identify such behaviour by examining the content and amount of spending towards the end of the budget period.

(b) Managerial behaviour may be quite different from that specified in (a) where they participate in budget setting and senior managers adopt a profit-conscious style of budget evaluation. In addition, the answer should draw attention to those situations where aspiration levels exceed budget (see 'Aspiration levels' and 'The effect of budget difficulty on motivation and performance' in Chapter 16).

(c) See 'Contingency factors' in Chapter 17 for the answer to this question. Waterhouse and Tiessen (1978) postulate that firms operating routine technologies in a predictable environment prefer to centralize decision-making. Line managers have limited power and formalized, standardized rules predominate. In contrast, firms operating in unpredictable environments with non-routine technologies decentralize decision-making and authority, thus giving middle managers a great deal of discretion and power. Little emphasis is given to rules or standardized and formalized procedures. Management accounting systems present more generalized information with the focus on output measurements. In addition, the environment needs to be monitored more frequently, and there is a greater reliance on external data and shorter budgeting horizons.

Reference
Waterhouse, J. H. and Tiessen, P. A. (1978) A contingency framework for management accounting systems research, *Accounting, Organisations and Society*, **3**(1), 65–76.

Solution IM 16.15 (a) The report should include the following items:
  (i) An indication that the budget holder will have a greater knowledge of his, or her, activities than the management accountant or senior management and thus may be in a position to obtain more resources (or an easier sales target) than is justifiable.
  (ii) To reduce slack both the management accountants and senior management should seek to thoroughly understand the budget holder's activities, past budget performance and any future changes in circumstances that might apply.
  (iii) Past trends should be reviewed in order to establish whether current budget requests appear to be realistic.
  (iv) Wherever possible budgets should be compared with external reference points, such as similar departments within the group or with data obtained from trade associations. Quotations might be obtained from potential suppliers relating to outsourcing the activity to compare the cost of outsourcing with the proposed budget.
  (v) Budget holders should be required to make a presentation to senior managers to justify the reasonableness of their budgets.

(b) The answer could include the following points:
  (i) The financial markets expect profit forecasts to be achieved. Non-achievement can have an adverse effect on share prices. The budget is set sometime before the start of the budget year and the outcomes are subject to much uncertainty. The incorporation of some slack may therefore be justifiable to cope with the uncertainty and to increase the probability that the budget, and profit forecasts, for the organization as a whole will be achieved.
  (ii) Failure to achieve the budget is de-motivating and can result in a loss of rewards. Achieving the budget creates the feeling of achievement and success and avoids the dysfunctional consequences of failure. Budgets are more likely to be achieved if some budget slack is accepted. Budget slack may reduce the negative consequences of budgets described in Chapter 16 by reducing the short-term pressure on managers. Budget slack also allows some flexibility since an overspend in one area might be compensated by reducing expenditure in another area. This may only be possible if the budget holder has some slack within his, or her, overall budget.
  (iii) All of the activities of the organization are based on the budgets being achieved. For example, liquidity requirements are determined from the outcomes of the budget process. Failure to achieve the budget can have serious consequences if costs exceed budget and revenues are less than budget. By accepting some form of budget slack there is a greater guarantee that the plans reflected in the budget will be achieved and all activities within the organization will be co-ordinated. Also by having some slack managers may be less tightly constrained and be more innovative. In addition, panic budget reductions may be avoided when it becomes apparent that the budget may not be achieved.
  (iv) It is questionable whether the acceptance of budget slack should formally be incorporated into the budget process. This would diminish the role that budgets play in ensuring that resources are wisely managed and may result in excessive slack. Budget slack might be recognized unofficially, possibly by adopting a flexible approach to budget approval within the budget setting process and ensuring that budgeting is accompanied by a profit-conscious style of budget evaluation.

(a) The report should include the following points:
  (i) Actuals are compared with a fixed budget which results in a comparison of actual and budgeted expenses for different output levels. Flexible budgeting should be adopted for performance reporting.
  (ii) Variances should be analysed into their price and quantity elements since different managers are likely to be accountable for different categories of variances.
  (iii) The report is confusing with both physical volumes and values being presented for each budgeted items. They should be reported separately to avoid confusion.
  (iv) The report should be split into two separate sections – a section for controllable expenses and another for uncontrollable expenses. It is possible that all the expenses are controllable but if this is the case it should be clearly indicated in the report. No controllable fixed costs are included in the report. If such expenses do exist they should be reported separately.
  (v) No indication is given of the output which should have been attained from the actual level of activity.

Revised monthly variance report:

Original budget : Sales volume
: Production volume

Actuals : Sales volume
: Production volume

	Flexed budget (£)	Actuals (£)	Quantity variance (£)	Price variance (£)	Total variance (£)	Cumulative variances for the year (£)
Sales (based on original budget)						
Less controllable expenses:						
Direct materials						
Direct labour						
Controllable contribution						
Less controllable fixed costs						
Controllable profit						

(b) Standard costing is most suited to controlling those activities that involve repetitive operations. Standard costing procedures cannot easily be applied to non-manufacturing activities where the operations are of a non-repetitive nature, since there is no basis for observing repetitive operations and consequently standards cannot easily be set.

Where standards cannot easily be applied budgets are used to control costs. A budget relates to an entire activity or operations where standards can be applied to the units of output and thus provide a basis for the detailed analysis of variances.

A single organization might use standard costing to control the costs relating to manufacturing activities and budgetary control to control the costs of support departments and non-manufacturing activities.

Solution IM 16.17

(a) Actual volume exceeds the budgeted volume by 12½% [(720 – 640)/640]. Therefore all of the variable costs are increased by 12½% and the fixed costs remain unchanged in the flexed operating statement reproduced below.

Flexed operating statement based on actual sales volume of 720 000 units:

	Budget (£000)	Actual (£000)	Variance (£000)
Sales	1024	1071	47
Cost of sales			
Materials	189	144	45
Labour	270	288	(18)
Overheads (Variable)	36	36	Nil
Labour (Fixed)	100	94	6
	595	562	33
Selling and distribution costs			
Fixed	72	83	(11)
Variable	162	153	9
	234	236	(2)
Administration			
Fixed	184	176	8
Variable	54	54	Nil
	238	230	8
Net profit	(43)	43	86

Possible reasons for variances:

Actual sales volume exceeds budgeted sales volume thus generating revenues in excess of budgets. However, actual selling price was less than budgeted selling price but the overall effect has been favourable in terms of sales revenues.

The favourable material variance may be due to negotiating more favourable prices and/or more efficient usage of the materials.

The adverse labour variance may have arisen because of the purchase of poor quality materials or more overtime being worked to meet the increased sales volume. The decline in the fixed labour cost may have been caused by employees leaving and not being replaced immediately.

The adverse fixed selling and distribution cost variance may be due to an increase in the cost of advertising or extra advertising. The variable element may be due to more efficient distribution methods resulting in a reduction in delivery costs.

The favourable fixed administration cost variance may be due to reduction in rentals of office machinery or office staff leaving and not being replaced immediately.

(b) See 'Flexible budgeting' in Chapter 16 for the answer to this question.

(c) The answer should focus on the following points:
   (i) Difficulty in accurately dividing costs into fixed and variable elements. Past cost and activity information is used to provide an estimate to predict future cost behaviour. Inaccurate estimates will result in the prediction of inaccurate costs.
   (ii) Past information is used to predict future costs. Past trends are normally used to predict price behaviour but what has happened in the past does not always provide a reliable guide for the future.
   (iii) Step fixed costs may occur but it is difficult to predict the exact point where the step increases will occur.

(iv) Flexible budgeting normally assumes that variable costs are constant per unit but this may be inappropriate if curvilinear cost–volume relationships exist.

Task 1(a)

The existing statement suffers from the following weaknesses:

(i) There are no actual or budgeted figures or variances for the most recent month.

(ii) The actual expenditure is based on cash payments and does not show committed expenditure. Cash expenditure can provide misleading information on the expenditure that will be incurred and it is preferable if expenditure is recorded on an accruals basis.

(iii) There is no attempt to distinguish between controllable and non-controllable expenses or break down the statement into meaningful sub-headings.

(iv) It is not very user-friendly. The term 'Cr' in the under/over spend is likely to be confusing to non-accountants.

(v) No attempt is made to forecast the year end result. It is useful to add expenses to date to estimated expenses to the end of the year so that the likely year end outcome can be compared with the budget.

(vi) Capital expenditure is included rather than it being included in the capital expenditure budget and then depreciated over time.

Task 1(b)

Proposed statement format

	Monthly data for current period			Cumulative variances to data	Year and forecast		
	Budget	actual	variance		Original budget	revised	variance forecast
Direct teaching							
Teachers – full-time							
Teachers – part-time							
Other employee expenses							
Resources							
Administration							
Administration staff							
Stationery, postage and phone							
Property services							
Caretaker and cleaners							
Lighting and heating							
Repairs and maintenance							
Rates							
Other							
Miscellaneous expenses							
Total revenue expenditure							
Fixed assets							
Total capital expenditure							

Task 1(c)

Advantages of the proposed format include:

(i) Identification of budget, actual and variance for the current month. This allows for speedy remedial action and provides early warning of potential problems.

(ii) The introdution of a forecast of the position at the end of the period which can provide an indication of the likely outcomes and used for feedforward control.

(iii) The grouping of expenditure by similar items which will enable managers to focus on major areas of expenses and identify those areas that need attention.

(iv) The cumulative variances to date which will enable management to examine current variances within the context of the performance throughout the whole budget year.

Task 2(a)

Calculation of number of year 1 pupils

Junior School	Number in final year	Proportion choosing Mayfield School	Number choosing Mayfield School
Ranmoor	60	0.9	54
Hallamshire	120	0.8	96
Broomhill	140	0.9	126
Endcliffe	80	0.5	40
Total choosing Mayfield School			316

Forecast of pupil numbers

Year	Age range	Numbers as at 31 May	Year commencing August
1	11–12	300	316
2	12–13	350	300
3	13–14	325	350
4	14–15	360	325
5	15–16	380	360
6	16–17	240	304 (80% × 380)
7	17–18	220	228 (95% × 240)
		2175	2183

Note:
Current years 1–4 pupils become years 2–5 pupils next year.
80% of current year 5 pupils become year 6 pupils next year.
95% of current year 6 pupils become year 7 pupils next year.

Forecasted income

Years	Pupil numbers	Annual fee	Total income
1–5	1651	£1200	£1 981 200
6–7	532	£1500	£798 000
Totals	2183		£2 779 200

Task 2 (b)

Budgeted surplus

Income	£2 779 200
Expenditure £2 581 296 × 1.05	£2 710 361
Budgeted surplus	£68 839

Solution IM 16.19 *General comments*

The plants have no control over raw coffee costs, which are over 60% of total costs. This can be dealt with in two ways: (a) eliminate raw coffee costs from the operating statement or (b) transfer coffee at a standard price. The disadvantage with (a) is that plant managers may not be careful about coffee wastage if raw coffee costs are not included in the performance report. On the other hand, setting a transfer price for (b) is not straightforward, given the rapidly fluctuating prices for coffee. One possibility is to set a yearly standard cost for coffee, using this in the budgets for both plants and purchasing operations.

The next issue is whether the plant should be made an expense centre (with a flexible budget) or kept as a profit centre. Because the plant manager cannot influence sales volume, expense centres are preferable. Alternatively, if quality influences sales volume then a profit centre may be appropriate. There appears to be an absence of formal controls in the purchasing department.

Current problems
Purchasing: Purchasing is evaluated on the trading profit produced and the success in having the required coffee at the plants when needed. Coffee purchase costs are recorded on a contract-by-contract basis, but profit on an open market sale consists of the selling price minus contract price. This results in a situation which allows the purchasing department to make extra trading profits at the expense of plants. For example, if four lots have been purchased at different prices and the plants only need two lots then it is in the purchasing department's best interest to trade the two lots at the lowest costs and transfer the two highest price lots to the plants.

Plants: Bonus is based on gross margin, but plant managers have little influence over sales volume, sales revenue and purchasing cost, and there is also a possibility that the purchasing department discriminates against the plants. Therefore the current control system promotes dissatisfaction and adverse motivational effects with the plant managers.

Proposed control system
Purchasing: The objective is to encourage purchasing to pay the lowest possible prices for coffee purchased. If coffee is to be used in May then the price paid for a May futures contract should be less than the May spot price. Because purchasing can make a profit on outside trading, the objective should be to maximize profit while tying up as little money as possible in coffee inventories and supplying plants with the coffee they need.

The purchasing department could be operated as an investment centre, with operating expenses monitored on an expense budget basis. Therefore the amount of investment would consist of the amount of money the department has tied up in inventories and purchase commitments. Profit would be based on the sale price realized from trading minus the purchase price of the coffee and the interest tied up in inventories. Sales to company plants should be credited at the spot price for that variety of coffee on that date. The system should motivate the purchasing department to do the following:

(a) Watch the market closely to determine when to make the purchases commitments.
(b) Keep inventories as low as practical.
(c) Maximize trading revenue with no unfair advantage in trading to the company plants.

Plants: Plants are responsible for producing output at the lowest cost consistent with a satisfactory quality. They should be evaluated on the basis of a comparison of actual cost with standard cost for each item of expense (except purchase of coffee, which should be based on a usage variance only).

Flexible budgeting should be used with variances appropriately analysed. Bonuses could be based on a comparison of actual and budgeted costs, but this could result in dysfunctional behavioural effects if too much stress is placed on meeting the budget. The proposed system should motivate managers to do what they can to help company profits by concentrating on meeting standards. Note that if price and usage are controllable then managers should be responsible for both. If only usage is controllable then managers should be charged with a predetermined cost, and any resulting variance would be for usage only. If the manager cannot control price or usage, the expense should be included in the uncontrollable section. Such a system should not have the same adverse behavioural implications as the present system where managers are held responsible for factors over which they have little influence.

Solution IM 16.20

(a) *Budgeted outcomes for 2001*

	Strategic plan prepared Aug. 2000	Budget prepared Oct. 2000	Estimate prepared Apr. 2001	Ex-post budget DGM's view	Ex-post budget GMD's view
Market size[a]	150 000	150 000	165 000	165 000	165 000
Sales volume[a]	35 000	36 000	35 800	38 500	38 500
Market share (%)	23.3	24	21.7	23.3	23.3
	(£000)	(£000)	(£000)	(£000)	(£000)
Sales revenue[b]	28 000	28 800	28 100	29 834	30 800
Marginal cost[c]	14 350	15 300	14 900	16 024	15 785
Contribution	13 650	13 500	13 200	13 810	15 015
Fixed cost	6 500	6 800	7 200	7 200	6 500
Product development[d]	2 000	2 000	1 400	1 400	2 240
Marketing[d]	3 500	3 200	2 600	3 800	3 920
Profit	1 650	1 500	2 000	1 410	2 355

Notes

[a] Ex-post budget = strategic plan + 10%.

[b] 35 000 × £800; 36 000 × £800; 35 800 × £784.92; 38 500 × £774.92; 38 500 × £800.

[c] Strategic plan = 35 000 × £410; April 2001 estimate = 35 800 × £416.20; DGM ex-post budget = 38 500 × £416.20; GMD ex-post budget = 38 500 × £410.

[d] DGM ex-post budget = strategic plan + £300 000 for marketing; April 2001 estimate for product development.

GMD ex-post budget = sales revenue (£30 800) × 20% = £6160, which is allocated between product development and marketing using the strategic plan ratio of 20/55 for product development and 35/55 for marketing.

Comments

(i) The projected profit is £500 000 in excess of budget and the estimated bonus is 46.7% (20% + [100% × 20% × £0.5 m/£1.5 m]).

(ii) Projected product development costs have declined by approximately one-third and this suggests that the manager is seeking to improve short-term profits by actions that will reduce long-term profits.

(iii) Projected marketing costs have also declined by approximately 25% and this may have contributed to the decline in market share and the failure to achieve the ex-post budgeted sales based on the group managing director's view. The reduced marketing expenditure may also have a detrimental impact beyond the current year.

(iv) The divisional general manager (DGM)'s proposal to reduce selling prices and not maintain marketing expenditure specified in the strategic plan has resulted in a reduced profit when compared with the group managing director (GMD)'s ex-post budget.

(v) Fixed costs have increased significantly over budget and strategic plan whereas average unit variable cost is less than budget but above strategic plan. Further investigation is required to ascertain the reasons for these changes.

(vi) It seems that the manager has attempted to obtain the bonus by making short-term savings that may produce significant reductions in long-term profit.

(b) The existing bonus scheme focuses entirely on profit as the single performance measure. The main advantage of the current bonus scheme is that it is easy to understand and encourages managers to focus on the same measure that is used by the external financial markets to evaluate the performance of the company as a whole.

The current system encourages the DGM to try to negotiate a budget that understates potential profit by overstating costs and understating sales. This may have a detrimental impact on group planning.

The profit calculation includes a large proportion of discretionary expenses. The current scheme encourages managers to spend less than budget on those items that are unlikely to have a short-term impact, e.g. product development expenditure. However, the short-term reduction in costs may result in a much higher reduction in long-term profits.

The bonus scheme gives no bonus for a failure to meet budgeted profit by only a small amount whereas a 20% bonus is given if the budget is just achieved. Also, if profit is greater than the maximum there is no incentive to increase profits any further. There is also no attempt to distinguish between controllable and non-controllable profit or provide an incentive to achieve other important goals, e.g. quality, market share, flexibility, innovation etc.

(c) The revised bonus scheme should be based on controllable profit defined as follows:

Contribution
Less: Controllable fixed costs
     Planned product development costs
     Planned advertising costs

Note that the use of planned discretionary costs will reduce the incentive for the manager to undertake unnecessary cost cutting. Using planned discretionary spending motivates DGMs to spend the amount agreed in the strategic plan.

Ideally, additional qualitative and non-financial performance measures should be included in the bonus scheme. However, this would involve some form of weighting system to determine the contribution of each measure to the overall bonus. Without additional information it is difficult to make specific recommendations and there is always the danger that the proposed solution will be too complex. Alternatively, the bonus might be reduced by specific amounts because of a failure to achieve other important group goals.

Finally, attention should be given to removing the fixed bonus of 20% and the maximum of 100%. If the bonus continues to be based on profits then it would be preferable to fix it at a specific percentage of the amounts by which they exceed the targets.

(d) Extending the bonus scheme throughout the organization ought to increase motivation. However, bonuses based on total company profits are less suited to lower management levels because individuals are likely to consider that they cannot significantly influence total company profits. A further disadvantage is that those who contribute little are awarded the same bonus as those that contribute a great deal. A possible solution is to introduce differential bonuses but such schemes are more complex and may cause conflict as some individuals will be perceived as receiving more favourable treatment.

Solution IM 16.21

(a) The answer should highlight the following factors in terms of budget preparation and form and content of the performance report.
  (i) There was a lack of participation in the preparation of the budget.
  (ii) There was failure to distinguish between controllable and non-controllable costs. For example, the manager is presently accountable for allocated administration costs.
  (iii) There was failure to flex the budget.
  (iv) The memorandum has been written in a very authoritarian style.
  (v) The investigation of variances with a variation in excess of a fixed percentage is questionable.

The above factors might have the following effects on the behaviour of the supervisor.
  (i) The lack of participation might result in the budgetees not accepting the budget as being a legitimate target. Consequently the budget will fail to motivate the budgetees to keep within the budgeted expenditure.

(ii) There might be creation of negative attitudes, resulting in low morale, increased tension and the creation of anti-management groups.

(iii) Management is adopting a budget-constrained style of evaluation.

(iv) The budgetees might reduce performance and put more effort into ensuring that the budget is just achieved rather than attempting to minimize costs.

(v) There may be over emphasis on just meeting the budget (possibly through the falsification of data) and a failure to consider other important organizational objectives (such as a speedy turnround period and production of clean linen) because they are not included in the performance evaluation.

The answer could also incorporate published research findings which relate to the above comments. For example, participation (Coch and French), styles of performance evaluation (Hopwood), imposed standards compared with acceptance of budgets (Stedry), budget pressure (Argyris). A detailed description of some of the published research findings is presented in Chapter 16.

(b) The re-drafted report should include an introductory section explaining the purpose of the new system and emphasizing that the present report is a trial run. In other words, the report should be written in more personal terms and encourage the cooperation of the budgetees in running the new system. In addition, it should indicate that a meeting will be held in a few days' time to explain the purpose of the performance reporting system. The administrator should also stress that he or she will be pleased to arrange appointments to discuss individual problems.

The performance report should be re-drafted, distinguishing between controllable and non-controllable costs (allocated administration costs and equipment depreciation). The re-drafted budget should be flexed using either weight-processed or patient days, but from the information given it is difficult to estimate cost behaviour. Consequently the answer should illustrate the flexible budget approach rather than concentrating on accurate calculations. The report should conclude by congratulating the manager on exceeding budgeted activity. In addition, it should highlight the need to incorporate non-financial measures such as average turnround period, number of days' absenteeism, and quantity of linen returned because of inferior cleaning quality.

Solution IM 16.22

In Table 1 performance was measured against four different targets, one of which was an implicit target that was not disclosed. It is assumed that the aspiration level (measured in units) and the actual performance are identical. The actual achievement was measured where the aspiration level of the individual was set before and after knowing the target. The average actual achievement is the sum of the two aspiration levels divided by 2. The table indicates that:

(i) Where the aspiration levels are set after knowing the target the individual tends to aspire to achieve them.

(ii) Where an implicit target exists and no specific goal is set the best average results of 55 are obtained.

(iii) Where an explicit low target is set actual achievement is low but higher than the low target. Presumably the low target is perceived as being easily attained and the individual expects to exceed it.

(iv) Where a medium target is set it is achieved irrespective of the timing of the setting of the aspiration level. This suggests that the medium target approximates the target level that the individual expects to achieve.

(v) Where a high target is set it has a strong motivational effect where the individual has not already set his, or her, aspiration level and the highest performance level is achieved. Where the individual has set an aspiration level in advance of knowledge of the high target, performance is lowest suggesting that it conflicts with the individual's own aspiration level. It thus ceases to have a motivational effect.

In Table 2 the aspiration level and the actual performance differ. The table indicates that:

(i) The higher the target the higher the aspiration level of the individual up to a certain level after which the aspiration level declines slightly and then ceases to exist. It would appear at this point that the target is considered impossible to achieve and the individual ceases to set an aspiration level.

(ii) At the lowest target level the aspiration level and performance exceeds the target and at a target level of 90 the target, aspiration level and performance are identical.

(iii) Performance is maximized at a high target level (130) but at this level actual performance is below the aspiration level.

(iv) Performance is increased and maximized at levels where the target is not achieved up to a target of 130 units.

(v) Up to 130 units increasing the target increases the aspiration level and performance.

(a) See 'Participation in the budget and target setting process' in Chapter 16 for a discussion of the advantages and disadvantages of allowing managers to participate in budget setting. With regard to the changes in the current system, the answer should include a discussion of the following factors.

Solution IM 16.23

(i) Head office does not appear to provide any guidelines or policy to those who are responsible for preparing the budgets. Steps should be taken by senior management at head office to communicate the policy effects of the long-term plans and objectives of the company and provide appropriate guidelines which should govern the preparation of the budgets.

(ii) The present system is based on pseudoparticipation, and there is a lack of negotiation in the budget setting process. Area managers should work with branch managers at the budget setting stage and negotiate a challenging budget which the branch managers perceive that they have influenced. The area managers should combine the agreed branch budgets into an area budget and negotiate this budget with head office. There should be a formal opportunity for the area managers to justify their budgets at head office level, and head office senior management should justify to area managers any changes which are made to the budgets. Head office should consider setting up a budget committee which provides the formal mechanism for negotiating and approving area budgets. For a discussion of a procedure for negotiating and approving budgets see 'Negotiation of budgets' and 'Coordination and review of budgets' in Chapter 15. Where budget changes are made, reasons for the changes should be explained to all parties involved in the preparation of budgets. At present there appears to be a lack of budget communication from head office to area managers and from area managers to branch managers.

(iii) The bonus system is currently directly linked to the budgetary control system. This can lead to dysfunctional behaviour and encourage managers to bias the budget estimates. Consideration should be given to developing an alternative to the present bonus system where rewards are linked to wider quantitative and qualitative targets rather than the ability to 'meet the budget'.

(b) The main advantage of using the net margin target as a single performance measure is simplicity. Where multi-performance measures are used, the problem arises as to how much emphasis should be placed on the individual performance measures and how to respond when one measure can be improved at the expense of another. The net margin figure is easy to understand and interpret, and represents the overall measure upon which the survival of the business depends.

The use of net margin as the only target has a number of limitations. Managers may be encouraged to focus on improving this measure in the short term, even when their actions have adverse long-term consequences. For example, short-term net margins may be pursued at the expense of product quality and developing long-term customer goodwill and future growth.

A performance evaluation based on net margin would result in managers being evaluated on a measure which is based on items which are beyond their control. A controllable profit measure which excluded items beyond a manager's control would be more appropriate.

Evaluation of managerial performance is a complex area, and one summary financial measure cannot capture all of the variables which influence managerial performance. The net margin target is a short-run measure which deals only with the past period, whereas performance measures should attempt to assess *future* results that can be expected because of present actions. Multi-performance measures are better than a single-performance measure in assessing likely future results from current actions, and they also reduce the potential dysfunctional consequences arising from concentration on a single performance measure. Appropriate multi-performance measures should be developed. Possible measures include the value of new loans, margin percentages, percentage of bad debts, development of new products, time taken to process applications, ability of clients to meet repayment schedules, and customer quality analysed by credit risk.

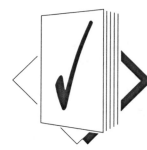

Standard costing and variance analysis: 1

Solutions to Chapter 18 questions

(a) (i) *Flexed budget for month 6*

	Original budget	Flexed budget	Actual cost	Total variance
Units of J	20 000	18 500	18 500	
	(£)	(£)	(£)	(£)
Direct materials	480 000	444 000	442 650	1 350F
Direct labour	140 000	129 500	129 940	440A
Variable overhead	60 000	55 500	58 800	3 300A
Fixed overhead	100 000	100 000	104 000	4 000A
	780 000	729 000	735 390	6 390A

(ii) Material price variance = (standard price − actual price) × actual quantity
= (AQ × SP) − (AQ × AP)
= (113 500 × £4) − £442 650 actual cost = £11 350F

Material usage variance = (standard quantity − actual quantity) × standard price
= ((18 500 × 6) − 113 500) × £4 = £10 000A

Wage rate variance = (standard rate − actual rate) × actual hours
= (SR × AH) − (AR × AH)
= (£7 × 17 800) − £129 940 = £5340A

Labour efficiency variance = (standard hours − actual hours) × standard rate
= (18 500 × 1 hr − 17 800) × £7 = £4900F

(b) See 'The budget period' in Chapter 15 for a description of rolling budgeting (i.e. rolling forecasts).

Task 1(a)

Preliminary workings:

	Standard		Actual	
Metres per Alpha	36 000/12 000=	3	32 000/10 000=	3.2
Cost per metre	£432 000/36 000=	£12.00	£377 600/32 000=	£11.80
Labour hours per Alpha	72 000/12 000=	6	70 000/10 000=	7
Cost per hour	£450 000/72 000=	£6.25	£422 800/70 000=	£6.04

The standard marginal cost per unit of Alpha is:

	(£)
Materials (3 metres at £12 per metre)	36.00
Labour (6 hours at £6.25 per hour)	37.50
	73.50

	(£)
The standard cost of the actual production is:	
Materials and labour (10 000 units at £73.50)	735 000
Fixed overheads	396 000
	1 131 000

Task 1(b)

		(£)
Price variances	= (Standard price – Actual price) Actual Quantity	
	= (Standard price × Actual Quantity) – Actual cost	
Materials price	= (£12 × 32 000 metres) – £377 600	6 400F
Labour rate	= (£6.25 × 70 000 hours) – £422 800	14 700F
Quantity variances	= ((Standard quantity for actual production) – Actual Quantity) Standard rate	
Material usage	= (10 000 × 3 = 30 000 – 32 000) £12	24 000A
Labour efficiency	= (10 000 × 6 = 60 000 – 70 000) £6.25	62 500A

Fixed overhead expenditure variance = Budgeted fixed overhead – Actual cost

	= £396 000 – £405 000	9 000A

Task 1(c)(i)

Reconciliation statement for 3 months ending 31 May

Standard cost of actual production	1 131 000
Materials price variance	6 400F
Material usage variance	24 000A
Labour rate variance	14 700F
Labour efficiency variance	62 500A
Fixed overhead expenditure variance	9 000A
Actual cost of production	1 205 400

Task 1(c) (ii)

The report should indicate that:

(i) The original variances were based on a comparison of the costs of 12 000 units actual output with the costs for a fixed budget output of 10 000 units. Therefore like has not been compared with like. The revised analysis has been based on a flexible budget comparison with the actual costs being compared with the standard cost for an output of 12 000 units.

(ii) The revised statement analyses variances by price and quantity whereas the original statement only reports total variances.

Task 1(c) (iii)

The revised statement provides more meaningful information because:

(i) It provides a different message. The original statement implied an overall favourable situation in terms of the variances whereas the revised statement indicates that overall the variances are adverse.

(ii) It highlights the major areas where investigations are required based on a management by exception approach.

(iii) It reports only an expenditure variance for fixed overheads rather than unitising fixed overheads (see 'Standard absorption costing' in Chapter 18 for an explanation of this point).

Task 2

A separate idle time variance of £75 000 adverse (12 000 hours at £6.25) arising from the machine breakdown of 12 000 hours should be reported. Note that the standard wage rate should be used to calculate the variance. The following revised labour efficiency variance should be reported that recognizes that the actual labour hours engaged on production were 58 000 and not 70 000 as originally reported. The revised variance is:

(10 000 × 6 hours = 60 000 – (70 000 – 12 000)) £6.25 = £12 500F

The material price variance should be divided into a material price purchasing efficiency variance and a material price planning variance as described in Chapter 19.

The change in the price index is −10% (420.03/466.70 − 1) so the revised standard price is 90% of £12 = £10.80. The price variance is divided as follows:

Material price planning variance = (£12 − £10.80) 32 000 metres
= £38 400F
Material price purchasing efficiency variance = (£10.80 × 32 000 metres) − £377 600
= £32 000A

Revised Reconciliation Statement

	(£)		(£)	
Standard cost of production			1 131 000	
Variances arising from normal production				
Material price variance	£32 000	(A)		
Material usage variance	£24 000	(A)		
Labour rate variance	14 700	(F)		
Labour efficiency variance	£12 500	(F)		
Fixed overhead expenditure variance	£9000	(A)	37 800	(A)
Variance arising from the machine breakdown				
Labour efficiency variance	£75 000	(A)	£75 000	(A)
Variance arising from the change in material prices				
Material price variance			£38 400	(F)
Actual cost of production			1 205 400	

Tasks 3 (a) and 3(b)

See 'Cost of quality report' in Chapter 22 for the answer to this question.

Task 3(c) (i)

In the new production environment there are fixed price contracts with guaranteed levels of quality. This suggests that there will be few material price variances. Also the cost of labour has now become a short-term fixed cost so labour efficiency variances are unlikely to reflect the cost of either the resources saved or the extra costs that will be incurred in the short-term. Wage rate variances are also likely to be uncontrollable. It is therefore questionable whether a standard marginal costing system will continue to provide meaningful information for cost control. For a more detailed discussion of these issues see 'Criticisms of standard costing' in Chapter 19.

Task 3(c) (ii)

With flexible working practices it can become extremely difficult to capture actual labour costs by individual jobs. If most of the overhead costs are common and unavoidable to all alternatives (i.e. facility or business-sustaining) only material costs will be easily traceable to jobs. If overhead costs are only a small proportion of total costs then accumulating the full marginal cost of individual jobs will become questionable.

Task 3(d)

With the introduction of just-in-time techniques inventory levels will be substantially reduced, thus resulting in a saving in the interest cost of money tied up in inventories. This information will not be recorded in the costing system.

Solution IM 18.3

(a) The standard cost details are as follows:

		(£)
Selling price		10
Materials (10 000kgs/5 000 units = 2kgs per unit at £0.50)	1	
Labour (0.5 hours at £4)	2	
Fixed production overhead (£10 000/5000 units	2	5
Standard profit		5

The price variances are calculated as follows:

(Standard price – Actual price)Actual quantity

		(£)
Material price	= (£0.50 – £0.60)10 600kgs	1 060A
Wage rate	= (£4 – £3.80)2970	594F
Sales price	= (£10 – £11)4900	4 900F

Note that actual hours worked are 5400 units × 0.55 = 2970

The usage variances are calculated as follows:

((Standard quantity for actual production) – Actual quantity)Standard rate

Material usage	= (5400 × 2kgs = 10 800 – 10 600)£0.50	100A
Labour efficiency	= (5400 × 0.5 hours = 2700 – 2970)£4	1 080A

Fixed production overhead expenditure:

(Budgeted cost) – (Actual cost)
£10 000 – £10 300 — 300A

Administration overhead expenditure:

(Budgeted cost) – (Actual cost)
£3000 – £3100 — 100A

Fixed production volume

(Actual production – Budgeted production)Fixed overhead rate
(5400 – 5000)£2 — 800F

Sales volume:

(Actual sales volume – Budgeted sales volume)Standard profit margin
(4900 – 5000) £5 — 500A

Budget/actual reconciliation statement – April

	(£)	
Budgeted profit (5000 × £5 – £3000 administration cost)	22 000	
Sales price variance	4 900	(F)
Sales volume profit variance (100 × £5)	500	(A)
Budgeted profit on actual sales	26 400	

Variances:	(£)(F)	(£)(A)		
Direct material:				
Price		1060		
Usage	100			
Direct labour:				
Rate	594			
Efficiency		1080		
Fixed production overhead:				
Expenditure		300		
Volume	800			
Administrative cost expenditure variance		100		
	1494	2540	1 046	(A)
Actual profit			25 354	

Calculation of actual profit:

	(£)	(£)
Actual sales revenue		53 900
Actual costs:		
Material	6 360	
Labour (2970 × £3.80)	11 286	
Production overhead	10 300	
	27 946	
Stock c/fwd	2 500	
		25 446
		28 454
Fixed administration		3 100
		25 354

(b) See relevant variances in Chapter 18 for the answer to this.

(c) Interdependence occurs when an event has a favourable impact on one variance but an adverse impact on another variance. For example, the purchase of inferior quality materials may account for a favourable material price variance but it may also have a negative impact on the material usage and labour efficiency variances due to the poorer quality causing an increase in usage.

Solution IM 18.4

(a) Budgeted fixed overhead rate = $\dfrac{\text{Fixed overheads (£22 260)}}{\text{Direct labour hours (8400)}}$ = £2.65

Standard hours per unit of output = 8400 hours/1200 units = 7 hours
Actual production in standard hours = 1100 × 7 hours = 7700 hours

Fixed overhead variance	= Standard cost for actual production – Actual cost
	= 7700 × £2.65 = £20 405 – £25 536
	= £5131 Adverse
Fixed overhead expenditure variance	= Budgeted cost – Actual cost
	= £22 260 – £25 536 = £3276A
Fixed overhead efficiency	= (Standard hours – Actual hours) Standard rate
	= (7700 – 7980) × £2.65
	= 742A
Fixed overhead capacity	= (Actual hours – Budgeted hours) Standard rate
	= (7980 – 8400) × £2.65
	= £1113A

Variance summary:

		(£)
Fixed overhead expenditure variance	=	3276A
Fixed overhead efficiency variance	=	742A
Fixed overhead capacity variance	=	1113A
Total fixed overhead variance		5131A

(b) See the section on fixed overhead expenditure variance, volume efficiency variance and volume capacity variance in Chapter 18 for the answer to this question.

(c) The purchase of cheaper, poor quality materials may result in a favourable material price variance but may also result in adverse material usage, labour efficiency and overhead efficiency variances.

Replacing skilled labour with unskilled labour will tend to result in a favourable wage rate variance and also adverse labour efficiency, material usage and overhead efficiency variances.

Solution IM 18.5

Task 1(a)

                                                                                            (£)

Labour rate = (Standard price – Actual price)Actual Quantity
         = (Standard price × Actual Quantity) – Actual cost
         = £5.25 × 11 440 = £60 060 – £59 488   572F

Labour efficiency = ((Standard quantity for actual production) – Actual
                   Quantity) Standard rate
         = (1040 × 10 hours = 10 400 hours – 11 440)£5.25   5 460A

Fixed overhead expenditure = (Budgeted cost) – (Actual cost)
         = (1200 × £157.50 = £189 000) – (£207 000)   18 000A

Fixed overhead volume = (Actual production – Budgeted production)
                  Fixed overhead rate
         = (1040 × 10 hours = 10 400 stand. hours –
           (1200 × 10 hours)) £15.75   25 200A
        or (1040 units – 1200 units)£157.50 per unit
           giving £25 200A

Fixed overhead capacity = (Actual hours – Budgeted hours) Fixed
                 overhead hourly rate
         = (11 440 – (1200 × 10)) £15.75   8 820A

Fixed overhead efficiency = ((Standard hours for actual production) –
                 Actual hours)
                 × Fixed overhead hourly rate
         = (1040 × 10 = 10 400 – 11 440) £15.75   16 380A

Task 1 (b)   *Reconciliation of standard and actual cost*

	£
Standard cost of production (1040 × £570)	592 800
Labour rate variance	572F
Labour efficiency variance	5 460A
Fixed overhead expenditure variance	18 000A
Fixed overhead capacity variance	8 820A
Fixed overhead efficiency variance	16 380A
Actual cost of production	640 888

Task 2

(a) The original labour rate before allowing for the 5% increase was £5 (£5.25/1.05)

(b) Revised labour rate = £5 × (104.04/102.00) = £5.10

(c) The labour rate can be analysed as follows:
Planning variance due to error in estimating wage rates:
(Original standard rate – Revised standard rate) × Actual hours
(£5.25 – £5.10) × 11 440 hours   £1 716F

Operational wage rate variance
(Revised standard rate – Actual rate) × Actual hours
= (Revised standard rate × Actual hours) × Actual wages cost
(£5.10 × 11 440 hours = £58 344 – £59 488   1 144A

Original wage rate variance   572F

(d) The initial analysis suggests a favourable variance but the revised analysis indicates that this was due to an incorrect estimate of the wage rate. After allowing for an ex-post adjustment of the standard an adverse variance of £1144 is reported. This provides a different message from the initial analysis and the reasons for the adverse variance should be investigated. The revised analysis provides useful feedback information that will help management to improve the future estimates of wage rates.

(e) The index may not be valid because of the following reasons:
   (i) The rate is an average and may incorporate many different skill levels. The average may not be applicable to Eastern Division.
   (ii) The index applies to the whole country but regional variations may apply.
   (iii) The company may have a policy of offering higher wage rates to attract high calibre personnel. Alternatively, there may be a shortage of labour in the area resulting in the need to offer higher wage rates to attract the requisite amount of labour.

(f) See relevant variances within Chapter 18 for the answer to this question.

(a) The answer should include a description and explanation of the following **Solution IM 18.6** variances:
   (i) variable overhead expenditure;
   (ii) variable overhead efficiency;
   (iii) fixed overhead expenditure;
   (iv) fixed overhead efficiency;
   (v) fixed overhead capacity;
   (vi) fixed overhead volume.
See Chapter 18 for a description of each of the above variances.

(b) Actual output = 680 000 (completed units) + 25 000 (closing WIP equivalent
                      production) − 21 000 (opening WIP equivalent production)
                  = 684 000 units
Fixed overhead rate = £2 per DLH (£246 000/123 000 DLHs)
Standard labour hours per unit = 0.2 hours (123 000 DLHs/615 000 units)
Standard FOAR = £0.40 (0.2 hours × £2 per hour)
Standard hours produced = 136 800 (684 000 × 0.2 hours)

Variance analysis
Expenditure = budgeted cost (£246 000) − actual cost (£259 000)
          = £13 000A

Volume = [budgeted production (615 000) − actual production (684 000)]
       × FOAR (£0.40)
    = £27 600F
      or
      (123 000 budgeted SHP − 136 800 SHP) × FOAR (£2)
    = £27 600F

Efficiency = [standard hours produced (136 800) − actual hours (141 000)]
       × FOAR (£2)
     = £8400A

Capacity = [actual DLHs (141 000) − budgeted DLHs (123 000)] × FOAR (£2)
    = £36 000F

Solution IM 18.7

(a) (i) Sales margin (profit) volume variance:

(Actual volume – Budgeted volume) × Standard margin (£3) =
£5250 Adverse
(Actual volume × Standard margin) – (Budgeted volume × Standard margin)
= £5250A
(Actual volume × Standard margin) – £30 000 = –£5250
(Actual volume × Standard margin) = £24 750
Actual volume = £24 750/£3 = 8250 units

(ii) Labour efficiency variance:

(Standard hours – Actual hours) × Standard rate = £4000 Adverse
(Standard hours × Standard rate) – (Actual hours × Standard rate) = –£4000
(8250 units × 4 hours =33 000 × £4) – (Actual hours × £4) = –£4000
£132 000 – (Actual hours × £4) = –£4000
Actual hours × £4 = £136 000
Actual hours = £136 000/£4 = 34 000 hours

(iii) Material usage variance:

(Standard quantity – Actual quantity) × Standard rate = £400F
(Standard quantity × Standard rate) – (Actual quantity × Standard rate) =
£400
(8250 × 5 litres = 41 250 litres × £0.20) – (Actual quantity × £0.20) = £400
£8250 – (Actual quantity × £0.20 = £400
Actual quantity × £0.20 = £7850
Actual quantity used = 39 250 litres
Actual quantity purchased = 39 250 – stock decrease (800) = 38 450 litres

(iv) Total variable overhead variance:

Standard variable overhead cost – Actual cost = £500 Adverse
(8250 × £6 = £49 500) – Actual cost = –£500
Actual cost = £50 000

(v) Fixed overhead expenditure variance:

Budgeted cost – Actual cost = £500 Favourable
10 000 units × £14 = £140 000 – Actual cost = £500
Actual cost = £139 500

Note that budgeted output = $\dfrac{\text{Budgeted profit (£30 000)}}{\text{Standard profit margin (£3)}}$

(b) The answer should draw attention to the fact that standard costing is
most suited to an organization whose activities consists of a series of common or
repetitive operations. Standard costing procedures cannot easily be applied to
non-manufacturing activities where the operations are of a non-repetitive nature,
since there is no basis for observing repetitive operations and consequently
standards cannot be set.

In those non-manufacturing organizations where routine operations do not
exist, standard costing cannot easily be applied. Instead, budgetary control is used
to control costs. A budget relates to an entire activity or operation whereas
standards can be applied to the units of output and thus provide a basis for the
detailed analysis of variances. Therefore budgeting focuses on controlling costs at
the aggregate level and does not analyse the difference between actual and
budgeted expenditure by price and quantity variances.

(a) *Statement of total standard costs for product EM*

Solution IM 18.8

	Actual cost (£)	Total variance (£)	Standard cost (£)
Direct material: E	6 270	270A	6 000
M	650	50A	600
Direct labour	23 200	2 200A	21 000
Variable overhead	6 720	720A	6 000
Fixed overhead	27 000	3 000F	30 000

(b) *Standard product cost*

	(£)
Direct material E (1 metre at £10 per metre)	10.00[a]
Direct material M (0.333 metres at £3)	1.00[b]
Direct labour (5 hours at £7)	35.00[c]
Variable overhead (5 hours at £2)	10.00[d]
Fixed overhead (5 hours at £10)	50.00[e]
	106.00

Notes

[a] Standard direct material cost per unit = £6000/600 units = £10
Actual quantity × standard price = £6600 (£6270 + £330)
Standard price per metre = £10 (£6600/660 metres)
Standard quantity = 1 metre (£10 standard cost/£10 per metre standard price)

[b] Standard direct material cost per unit = £1 (£600/600 units)
Actual quantity × standard price = £600 (£650 − £50)
Standard price = £3 (£600/200 metres)
Standard quantity = 0.333 metres (£1/£3 metres)

[c] Standard direct labour cost per unit = £35 (£21 000/600 units)
Actual hours × standard price = £22 400 (£23 200 − £800)
Standard rate = £7 (£22 400/3200 hours)
Standard quantity = 5 hours (£35/£7 per hour)

[d] Standard variable overhead rate per unit = £10 (£6000/600 units)
Standard hours calculated in note c = 5 hours
Standard rate = £2 (£10/5 hours)

[e] Standard fixed overhead rate per unit = £50 (£30 000/600 units)
Standard hours calculated in note c = 5 hours
Standard fixed overhead rate = £10 (£50/5 hours)

(c) Actual fixed overheads + expenditure variance = budgeted fixed overheads
Budgeted fixed overheads = £27 000 + £500 = £27 500
Budgeted production = budgeted fixed overheads/standard cost
= £27 500/£50
= 550 units

(d) See 'Establishing cost standards' in Chapter 18 for the answer to this question.

Solution IM 18.9　　(a)　*Operating control statement*

Budgeted sales and production (units)			8000
Sales orders received (units)			8200
Actual sales and production (units)			7500
Productivity (efficiency ratio) (%)			95.7

	Original budget (£)	Flexed budget (£)	Actual (£)	Variance (£)
Direct material	48 000	45 000	43 400	1600F
Direct labour	24 000	22 500	24 675	2175A
Variable overhead	2 400	2 250	2 150	100F
Fixed overhead	47 600	47 600	46 850	750F
Total costs	122 000	117 350	117 075	275F
Sales	132 000	123 750	123 750	—
Profit	10 000	6 400	6 675	275F

Volume variance against original budget (6400 − 10 000)	3600A
Cost variances against flexible budget	275F
Total variances	3325A

Analysis of variances

	(£)	(£)
Efficiency variances		
Direct material usage	3150F	
Direct labour	1000A	
Variable overhead	100A	
		2050F
Overhead spending variances		
Variable overhead	200F	
Fixed overhead	750F	
		950F
Price variances		
Direct materials	1550A	
Wage rate	1175A	
		2725A
Volume variance		3600A
Total variances		3325A

A variable costing approach has been adopted to calculate the above variances. The volume variance is therefore calculated by multiplying the difference between budgeted and actual sales volume (500 units) by the contribution per unit of £7.20. The above presentation categorizes the variances according to operating efficiency, price/spending and volume. The volume variance can be due to either a failure to generate sufficient sales to meet the budgeted sales volume or a failure by production to produce sufficient to meet sales demand.

(b)　For the answer to this question see 'Responsibility accounting' in Chapter 16. In particular, the answer should focus on:
　(i)　The problem of dual responsibility.
　(ii)　Interdependencies where the action of one manager can have an impact on other managers.
　(iii)　Distinguishing between variances that are due to changes in the environment and those that are controllable by managers.
In addition it should be noted that control is based on comparisons against a flexible budget that takes account of changes in activity. Producing flexible budgets

requires good approximations of cost estimates for various activity levels. In practice it is extremely difficult to estimate accurately costs for a range of activity levels. Caution is therefore necessary when making managers accountable for variations from flexible budgets.

(a) *Standard product cost*

	(£)	(£)
Direct materials: WALS (15 × £60)	900	
LOPS (8 × £75)	600	
		1500
Direct labour (60 hours at £10.50 per hour)		630
Production overheads (£504 000/2400 units)		210
Standard product cost		2340

(b)

	(£)
Direct material usage variance	
= (standard quantity — actual quantity) × standard price	
WALS = [(180 × 15 − 2850[a]) × £60]	9 000A
LOPS = [(180 × 8 − 1470[a]) × £75]	2 250A
Direct material price variance	
= (standard price − actual price) × actual quantity	
WALS = [(£60 − £57) × 3000[b]]	9 000F
LOPS = [(£75 − £81) × 1000[b]]	6 000A
Labour efficiency variance	
= (standard hours − actual hours) × standard rate	
[(180 × 60 hours – 11 700 hours) × £10.50]	9 450A
Wage rate variance	
= (standard rate − actual rate) × actual hours	
[(£10.50 − £112 320/11 700) × 11 700]	10 530F
Fixed production overhead expenditure	
= budgeted fixed overhead − actual fixed overhead	
(£504 000/12 − £42 600)	600A
Fixed production volume	
= (actual production – budgeted production) × fixed overhead rate	
[(180 − 2400/12) × £210]	4 200A

Notes

[a]Actual usage of components is calculated as follows:

	WALS		LOPS
Opening stock	600		920
Purchases	3000	(£171 000/£57)	1000
	3600		1920
Less closing stock	750		450
Components used	2850		1470

[b] Material usage variances can be calculated by defining actual quantity as either 'material purchases' or 'material usage'. In the above answer the variances have been calculated on the basis of material purchases. For cost control purposes it is preferable to report price variances in the period in which they arise rather than delaying the reporting of the variances until the period when the materials are used.

(c) *Reconciliation of standard and actual gross profit*

	(£)
Sales	504 000
Standard cost of sales (180 × £2340)	421 200
Standard gross profit	82 800

	Favourable (£)	Adverse (£)	
Material usage: WALS		9 000	
LOPS		2 250	
Material price:[a] WALS	8 550		
LOPS		8 820	
Direct wage rate	10 530		
Labour efficiency		9 450	
Fixed expenditure		600	
Fixed volume		4 200	
	19 080	34 320	15 240A
Actual gross profit			67 560

Note

[a] The direct materials consumed of £281 520 given in the question has been calculated on the basis that raw material stocks are valued at actual cost and not standard cost. This implies that price variances are included in the stock valuations and not written off as an expense until the period in which they are used. In order to reconcile the profits, it is necessary to calculate material price variances on the basis of 'quantity used' rather than quantity purchased. The revised calculations are as follows:

$$\text{WALS: } (£60 - £57) \times 2850 = £8550F$$
$$\text{LOPS: } (£75 - £81) \times 1470 = £8820A$$

(d) The report should emphasize that the statement in (c) above provides management with an explanation of why actual profit differs from budget profit. It is important that the report be used to assist in ascertaining the reasons for the variances and taking appropriate remedial action to eliminate future inefficiencies, or altering future plans to reflect changing circumstances. Preferably the report ought to be supplemented with an explanation of the causes of the variances of significant amounts. It is possible that the price variances reflect price changes which are beyond the control of management. However, usage variances are likely to be controllable, and it is important that these variances be investigated and appropriate remedial action taken to eliminate any inefficiencies.

Solution IM 18.11 (a) *Budgeted profit and loss account*

	(£)
Income from fares (40 000 × £1)	40 000
Variable costs: Fuel (40 000 × 2.5 × £0.08)	(8 000)
Overheads (40 000 × 2.5 × £0.05)	(5 000)
Fixed costs: Employment (10 drivers)	(10 000)
Other	(9 000)
Profit	8 000

Actual profit and loss account

	(£)
Income from fares (38 000 × £0.95)	36 100
Variable costs: Fuel (105 000 × £0.084)	(8 820)
Overheads (105 000 × £0.048)	(5 040)
Fixed costs: Employment	(9 600)
Other	(9 300)
Profit	3 340
Profit variance	4 660A

(b) *Variance analysis*

Sales margin volume {2000 × [£1 – 2.5 × (£0.08 + £0.05)]}	1 350A
Sales margin price [38 000 × (£0.95 – £1)]	1 900A
Variable cost efficiency variances:	
Fuel {[(38 000 × 2.5) – 105 000] × £0.08}	800A
Overheads {[(38 000 × 2.5) – 105 000] × £0.05}	500A
Variable cost spending variances:	
Fuel [(£0.08 – £0.084) × 105 000]	420A
Overhead [(£0.05 – £0.048) × 105 000]	210F
Fixed cost variances:	
Employment	400F
Other	300A
	4 660A

The report should contain an explanation of the major variances. There was a 5% reduction in fare-paying miles (2000 miles) and a 5% increase in driven miles (5000 miles). The reduction in fare-paying miles resulted in a decline in profits of £1350, and the increase in driven miles caused variable costs to increase by £1300. The average fare income per mile was 5p less than budget, and this resulted in actual revenue being less than budgeted revenue by £1900.

Fuel costs per mile exceeded the budgeted rate by £0.04, causing an adverse spending variance of £420. This was compensated by variable overhead spending being £210 less than budget. Employment costs were £400 less than budget.

The failure to immediately replace the driver had a significant impact on the profit variance. The unavailability of taxis at peak times may account for the adverse sales volume variance. With one car fewer operating during the period, it may have been more difficult to minimize mileage. Consequently adverse mileage efficiency variances are reported. The adverse sales margin price variance may have resulted from 'off-peak' business increasing at the expense of peak business because of the unavailability of taxis at peak times. The saving in fuel costs may be due to a reduction in the price of petrol or a greater proportion of off-peak longer-journey business which requires less petrol consumption per mile.

The savings in employment costs are likely to result directly from the driver leaving during the month. Alternatively the driver may have left early in the month, and the variance is a combination of savings in three weeks' wages and the extra cost of overtime paid.

(c) The following additional information and variances would be useful:
   (i) Efficiency variances analysed by cars to pinpoint where the variances occur.
   (ii) Analysis of sales variances by business segments (e.g. late evening peak or daytime off-peak).
   (iii) Separate planning and operating variances to ascertain how much of the petrol price variance is due to price changes and how much is due to efficient driving.
   (iv) An analysis of variable and fixed overheads by categories and employment costs by fixed salaries, overtime etc.
   The above recommendations can only be justified if the additional costs of operating the control system do not exceed the benefits from the recommended changes.

(a) The reconciliation statement in the question shows standard sales revenue. This indicates that the sales volume variance has been expressed in standard sales revenue. Budgeted sales volume is 5000 units (£450 000/£90) and the sales volume variance indicates that actual sales volume is 980 units (£88 200/£90) less than budget. Therefore actual sales volume is 4020 units. The standard margins per unit are:

Solution IM 18.12

Standard contribution margin = £35.55 (£90 – £54.45)
Standard profit margin = £18.55 (£90 – £71.45)

The sales volume variances are:

$$980 \times £35.55 = £34\,839A \text{ (on a standard contribution basis)}$$
$$980 \times £18.55 = £18\,179A \text{ (on a standard profit margin basis)}$$

The sales volume variance on a standard contribution basis, combined with the sales price variance, provides a measure of the net cash effect from actual sales volume and selling price differing from budgeted sales volume and selling price. The standard profit margin includes unitized fixed costs in the variance calculation but total fixed costs are unavoidable whatever sales volume is achieved. Thus the resulting variance does not measure the change in cash flows. The sales volume variance measured in sales revenues ignores the variable costs associated with the sales and therefore is not a measure of net cash flow.

(b) Actual sales volume for the period was 4020 units (see answer to part (a) and stocks have increased by 300 units. Therefore actual production was 4320 units. Raw material stocks are valued at standard prices and this implies that the material price variance is calculated on purchases rather than usage. The material price and usage variances are:

Material price = [standard price (£5.40) − actual price (£5.60)] × actual
purchases (42 000)
= £8 400A

Material usage = [standard quantity (4320 × 8 kg) − actual usage (36 000 kg)]
× £5.40
= £7776A

For a discussion on whether the material usage variance should be calculated on material purchases or material issues see 'Calculation on quantity purchased or quantity used' in Chapter 19.

(c) It is assumed that fixed overheads are recovered on the basis of direct labour hours. The fixed overhead rate per direct labour hour is £6.80 (£17/2.5 hrs).

Volume efficiency variance = [standard hours (4320 × 2.5 hrs)
− actual hours (12 000 hrs)] × £6.80
= £8160A

Volume capacity variance = [actual hours (12 000)
− budgeted hours (5000 × 2.5 hrs)] × £6.80
= £3400A

For a discussion of the relevance of the above variances see 'Volume Efficiency Variance' and 'Volume Capacity Variance' in Chapter 18.

(d)

			(£)
Budgeted profit (5000 units × £18.55 budgeted profit per unit)			92 750
Sales variances: Volume	£34 839A		
Price	£30 150F		
			4 689A
			88 061
Cost variances:			
Direct materials price	£8 400A		
Direct materials usage	£7 776A		
			16 176A
Fixed overhead expenditure variance			1 500F
Actual profit			73 385

Note that the actual profit shown in the question has been calculated on an absorption costing basis. The marginal costing actual profit can be calculated by deducting the fixed overhead included in the increase in finished goods stock (300 × £17 = £5100) from the absorption costing profit (£78 485).

In the above statement the sales variance has been valued at the unit contribution margin whereas the absorption costing statement values the variance at the standard net profit margin. The second difference is that, because fixed overheads are unitized with absorption costing, a volume variance is reported. Fixed overheads are recorded as a period cost with marginal costing and therefore no under/over absorption of fixed overhead (i.e. the volume variance) will arise.

Standard costing and variance analysis: 2

Solutions to Chapter 19 questions

Solution IM 19.1

(a) See the section on 'Standard absorption costing' in Chapter 18 for the answer to this question.

(b) See the section on 'Direct materials mix and yield variances' in Chapter 19 for the answer to this question.

(c) See ' Ex-post variance analysis' in Chapter 19 for the answer to this question. In particular, the answer should point out that the labour rate variance is likely to be uncontrollable and an analysis of this variance into its planning and operational elements may not provide any meaningful information for control purposes.

Solution IM 19.2

(a) For the answer to this question you should refer to 'The future role of standard costing' in Chapter 19.

(b) See 'Target costing' in Chapter 22 for the answer to this question. In addition, the answer should stress that the target cost should be analysed by the different elements of cost for cost management. Actual costs for each cost element should be reported on a regular basis and the variances represent feedback information in the quest to drive actual costs down to target costs. Target costs are viewed as a tool for cost management and reduction rather than short-term operational cost control. They represent a strategic and marketing approach rather than an internal focus.

(c) Standard costs are derived from a study of internal operations whereas target costs are market-driven, based on market information and target profit margins. Standard costs are internally focused and established after production has begun with the emphasis being on cost control. In contrast, target costs are externally focused and are established before production commences. The emphasis is on cost reduction rather than seeking to ensure that costs adhere to some predetermined standard.

Solution IM 19.3

(a) The cost of investigating and correcting a variance is £1 800 and the probability of this event occurring is 0.25. The cost of investigating a variance where a correctable cause is not found is £1400. The probability of this event is 0.75.

Therefore the expected value of the cost of investigation is (£1800 × 0.25) + (£1400 × 0.75) = £1500.

The expected value of the benefits from investigation is 75% of the size of the variance and the probability of a correctable cause is 25%. Therefore the expected value of the benefits is 0.1875 of the amount of the variance (0.75 × 0.25 × the amount of the variance).

The indifference point is where 0.1875 × Benefit = £1500 expected cost of investigation so that the benefit (i.e. the amount of the variance) = £1500/0.1875 = £8000

Thus variances in excess of £8 000 should be investigated.

(b) (i) For the answer to this question see 'The investigation of variances' in Chapter 19. In particular, the answer should point out the difficulty in estimating the cost and benefits of investigation and the fact that past observations of when the operation is under control should be observable. This information may not be available for new operations.

(ii) See 'The investigation of variances' in Chapter 19 for the answer to this question.

Solution IM 19.4

(a) See answer to Question 19.28 in the *Students' Manual*.

(b) See 'Accounting disposition of variances' in Chapter 19 for the answer to this question.

(a) *Calculation of variances*

Solution IM 19.5

$$\text{Material price} = (SP - AP)\,AQ = (AQ \times SP) - (AQ \times AP)$$
$$= (34\,900 \times £7) - £245\,900$$
$$= £1600A$$

$$\text{Material usage} = (SQ - AQ) \times SP$$
$$= [(230\,000 \text{ units}/100 \times 15 \text{ kg}) - 34\,300] \times £7$$
$$= £1400F$$

$$\text{Wage rate} = (SR - AR)\,AH = (AH \times SR) - (AH \times AR)$$
$$= (22\,900 \times £6) - £138\,545$$
$$= £1145A$$

$$\text{Labour efficiency} = (SH - AH) \times SR$$
$$= [(228\,000/100 \times 10) - 22\,900] \times £6$$
$$= £600A$$

$$\text{Variable overhead efficiency} = (SH - AH) \times SR$$
$$= [(228\,000/100 \times 10) - 22\,900] \times £5$$
$$= £500A$$

$$\text{Variable overhead expenditure} = (AH \times SR) - \text{actual cost}$$
$$= (22\,900 \times £5) - £113\,800$$
$$= £700F$$

Note that actual production for the period is calculated as follows:

	Materials	Labour and overheads
Transferred to finished goods stock	226 000 units	226 000 units
WIP equivalent production	4 000 units	2 000 units
	230 000 units	228 000 units

Raw materials

	(£)		(£)
Opening balance[c]	113 400		
Financial ledger control		Work in progress	
(AQ × SP)	244 300	(SQ × SP)	241 500
Material usage variance	1 400	Closing balance	117 600
	359 100		359 100

Wages

	(£)		(£)
Financial ledger control	138 545	Labour efficiency variance	600
		Labour rate variance	1 145
		Work in progress	
		(SQ × SP)	136 800
	138 545		138 545

Variable production overheads

	(£)		(£)
Financial ledger control	113 800	Work in progress (SQ × SP)	114 000
Variable overhead expenditure variance	700	Variable overhead efficiency variance	500
	114 500		114 500

Fixed production overheads

	(£)		(£)
Financial ledger control	196 800	Profit and loss	196 800

Work in progress

	(£)		(£)
Raw materials (SQ × SP)	241 500	Finished goods[a]	485 900
Wages (SQ × SP)	136 800		
Variable production overhead	114 000	Closing balance[b]	6 400
	492 300		492 300

Finished goods

	(£)		(£)
Opening balance[c]	597 700	Profit and loss[a]	468 700
Work in progress[a]	485 900	Closing balance[b]	614 900
	1 083 600		1 083 600

Variances

	(£)		(£)
Financial ledger control (material price)	1600	Raw materials (materials usage)	1400
Wages (labour rate)	1145	Variable production overheads (variable production overhead expenditure)	700
Wages (labour efficiency)	600		
Variable overhead (variable production overhead efficiency)	500	Profit and loss	1745
	3845		3845

Profit and loss

	(£)
Finished goods	468 700
Fixed product overhead	196 800
Variances	1 745

Financial ledger control

			(£)
		Opening balance	711 100
		Raw materials	244 300
		Variance a/c (raw materials)	1 600
		Wages	138 545
		Variable overhead	113 800
		Fixed overhead	196 800

Notes

		(£)
[a] Completed units transferred:		
To finished goods, 226 000 units at £2.15/unit		485 900
From finished goods, 218 000 units at £2.15/unit		468 700
[b] Closing stocks:		
Raw materials, 16 800 kg at £7/kg		117 600
Work in progress:		
Raw materials, 4000 units at £1.05 unit		4 200
Labour and variable overhead, 2000		
equivalent units at £1.10/unit		2 200
		6 400
Finished goods, 286 000 units at £2.15/unit		614 900
[c] Opening stocks:		
Raw materials, 16 200 kg at £7/kg		113 400
Finished goods, 278 000 units at £2.15/unit		597 700

(b) See 'Types of cost standards' in Chapter 18 for the answer to this question.

Workings

Parts (a) and (b) require a detailed analysis of the variances. The variance calculations are as follows.

	(£)
Material price: (standard price − actual price) × actual quantity purchased	
Plaster of Paris [£8 − (£43 200/5400)] × 5400	0
Paint [£30 − (£5800/173)] × 173	610A
Material usage: (standard quantity − actual quantity[a]) × standard price	
Plaster of Paris (286[b] × 20 − 5420) × £8	2400F
Paint (286 × ½ − 143) × £30	0
Wage rate: (standard rate − actual rate) × actual hours	
(£10 − £11) × 730	730A
Labour efficiency: (standard hours − actual hours) × standard rate	
(286 × 2.5 − 730) × £10	150A
Fixed overhead expenditure (budgeted fixed overheads − actual fixed overheads)	
(300 × £100 − £34 120)	4120A
Volume efficiency: (standard hours − actual hours) × fixed overhead rate[c]	
(715 − 730) × £40	600A
Volume capacity: (actual hours − budgeted hours) × fixed overhead rate[c]	
(730 − 300 × 2.5) × £40	800A
Sales margin price: (actual selling price − budgeted selling price) × actual sales volume	
(£380 − £380) × 284	0
Sales margin volume: (actual sales quantity[d] − budgeted sales quantity) × standard margin	
(284 − 300) × £80	1280A

(a) *Stores ledger control account (plaster of Paris)*

	(kg)	(£)		(kg)	(£)
Balance b/f	2800	22 400	WIP (SQ × SP)	5720	45 760
Creditors	5400	43 200	Balance c/f		
Material usage variance	300	2 400	(closing stock)	2780	22 240
	8500	68 000		8500	68 000

Stores ledger control account (paint)

	(litres)	(£)		(litres)	(£)
Balance c/f	140	4200	WIP a/c (SQ × SP)	143	4290
Creditors	173	5190	Balance c/f		
			(closing stock)	170	5100
	313	9390		313	9390

WIP account

	(£)		(£)
Stores ledger control account:		Finished goods stock a/c	85 800
Plaster	45 760		
Paint	4 290		
Wages control account			
(SQ × SP)	7 150		
Fixed overhead account	28 600		
	85 800		85 800

Finished goods stock account

	(£)		(£)
Opening balance (9 × £300)	2 700	Cost of sales (284 × £300)	85 200
WIP a/c	85 800	Closing stock c/f	3 300
	88 500		88 500

The entries in the creditors, wages and fixed overhead control accounts are shown below:

Creditors

	(£)
Stores ledger (plaster)	43 200
Stores ledger (paint)	5 190
Material price variance a/c	610

Wages control

	(£)		(£)
Wages accrued a/c	8030	WIP	7150
		Wage rate variance a/c	730
		Labour efficiency variance a/c	150
	8030		8030

Fixed overhead control

	(£)		(£)
Expense creditors	34 120	Overhead expenditure variance	4 120
		Volume efficiency	600
		Volume capacity	800
		WIP a/c	28 600
	34 120		34 120

(b) It is assumed that (ii) refers to a statement showing standard profit on actual sales and (iii) refers to a statement showing actual profit.

   (i) *Budget trading statement*

	(£)	(£)
Sales revenue (300 × £380)[d]		114 000
Cost of sales: Materials − plaster (300 × £160)	48 000	
− paint (300 × £15)	4 500	
Direct wages (300 × £25)	7 500	
Fixed production overheads (300 × £100)	30 000	
	90 000	
Budgeted profit		24 000

   (ii) *Standard cost trading statement*

	(£)
Actual sales (284 × £380)	107 920
Standard cost of sales (284 × £300)	85 200
Standard profit on actual sales	22 720

   (iii) *Financial trading statement*

	(£)	(£)
Actual sales		107 920
Opening stock[e] (£22 400 + £4200 + £2700)	29 300	
Materials (£43 200 + £5800)	49 000	
Labour	8 030	
Fixed overhead	34 120	
	20 450	
Less closing stock[e] (£22 240 + £5100 + £3300)	30 640	89 810
Actual profit		18 110

   (iv) *Reconciliation*

	(£)
Budgeted profit (i)	24 000
Less sales margin volume variance	1 280
Standard profit on actual sales (ii)	22 720

Cost variances

	Favourable (£)	Adverse (£)	
Paint price		610	
Plaster usage	2400		
Wage rate		730	
Labour efficiency		150	
Fixed overhead expenditure		4120	
Volume efficiency		600	
Volume capacity		800	
	2400	7010	4 610A
Actual profit (iii)			18 110

Notes

[a] Note that actual material usage is calculated as follows:

       opening stock + purchases − closing stock

[b] Throughout the answer, actual production and sales are expressed in 100 sets.

^{c} The fixed overhead rate is expressed as a rate per standard hour (i.e. 1 hour $\times £10 \times 400\%$).

^{d} Note that budgeted production and sales are expressed in 100 sets.

^{e} Note that opening and closing stocks are valued at standard cost. The variances are written off as period costs.

Solution IM 19.7

(a) Total revenue $= Q (76 - 0.002Q)$
$= 76Q - 0.002Q^2$
Marginal revenue $= 76 - 0.004Q$
Total cost $= 100\,000 + 20Q + 0.005Q^2$
Marginal cost $= 20 + 0.01Q$
Optimal output is where MR = MC:

$$76 - 0.004Q = 20 + 0.01Q$$
$$0.014Q = 56$$
$$Q = 4000 \text{ barrels}$$

(b) *Preliminary workings*

	Barrels
Opening WIP	600
Input	3700
	4300
Production (calculated in (a))	4000
Closing WIP	300

A standard costing system is used. The process WIP account will be credited with the standard cost of completed production and closing WIP equivalent units. The debit entry in the process WIP account will consist of the standard cost of the opening WIP equivalent production and the standard cost of the production input for process 2 during the period. The calculations are as follows:

Opening WIP = £13 500 (this valuation is given in the question and is determined by multiplying opening WIP equivalent production by the standard costs)

Completed production = £200 000
Closing WIP (300 barrels):

	(£)		
Input material	300 equivalent units $\times £5$	=	1500
Process 2 material	150 equivalent units $\times £20$	=	3000
Process 2 labour	120 equivalent units $\times £10$	=	1200
Process 2 overhead	120 equivalent units $\times £15$	=	1800
			7500

The production input for the period will consist of the completed production of 4000 units less opening WIP equivalent units completed in the previous period plus closing WIP which will have been completed during this period. The calculation of the production input for each element of cost is therefore:

	Completed production less opening WIP equivalent units	Closing WIP equivalent units	Total equivalent units
Process 2 material	3700 (4000 − 300)	150	3850
Process 2 labour	3820 (4000 − 180)	120	3940
Process 2 overhead	3820 (4000 − 180)	120	3940

Therefore the standard cost of the input for process 2 is calculated as follows:

		(£)
Process 2 material	3850 × £20 =	77 000
Process 2 labour	3940 × £10 =	39 400
Process 2 overhead	3940 × £15 =	59 100
		175 500

Process 2 account

	Barrels	(£)		Barrels	(£)
Opening			Transfer to finished		
work in progress	600	13 500	goods	4000	200 000
Transfer from			Closing		
process 1 at £5	3700	18 500	work in progress	300	7 500
Materials introduced		77 000			
Labour		39 400			
Overhead		59 100			
	4300	207 500		4300	207 500

(c) *Process 2 materials account*

		(£)		(£)
Stores		79 500	Process 2	77 000
			Material variance account	2 500
		79 500		79 500

Process 2 labour account

	(£)		(£)
Wages	39 150	Process 2	39 400
Labour variance account	250		
	39 400		39 400

Process 2 overhead account

	(£)		(£)
Overheads	60 200	Process 2	59 100
		Overhead variance account	1 100
	60 200		60 200

(a) *Sales mix variance*

Solution IM 19.8

Actual sales volume	Actual sales volume in budgeted proportions	Difference	Standard contribution margin	Sales margin mix variance
Male 2000	3200 (80%)	− 1200	£4.50	− £5400
Female 2000	800 (20%)	+ 1200	£8.00	+ £9600
				+ £4200F

Sales quantity variance

Actual sales volume in budgeted proportions	Budgeted sales quantity	Difference	Standard contribution margin	Sales margin quantity variance
Male 3200 (80%)	4000	− 800	£4.50	− £3600
Female 800 (20%)	1000	− 200	£8.00	− £1600
				− £5200

Comparison of budgeted and actual performance

	£ Budget	£ Actual
Sales – Male	30 000	16 000
Female	18 000	40 000
Commissions – Male	12 000	7 000
Female	10 000	22 000
Fixed costs	20 000	24 000
Profit	6 000	3 000

Analysis of profit variance

Sales price variances – Male (£8 – £7.50)2000	1 000F
Female (£20 – £18)2000	4 000F
Sales mix variance	4 200F
Sales quantity variance	5 200A
Fixed overhead expenditure variance (£20 000 – £24 000)	4 000A
Labour rate variances – Male (£3 – £3.50)2000	1 000A
Female (£10 – £11)2000	2 000A
Profit variance	3 000A

(b) The report should include the following points:
  (i) The favourable sales price variances suggests that selling prices may have increased or that the clients may have required different treatments.
  (ii) Compared with the budget the sales volume has declined resulting in an overall sales volume variance of £1000A (£4200 – £5200). This has been offset by the favourable mix variance with sales consisting of a greater proportion of the higher margin female clients. Overall the sales variances for the period were £4000 favourable.
  (iii) The decline in profit, compared to budget, was due to an increase in fixed overhead expenditure and higher than planned commission rates. The latter may be due to commission rates being linked to selling prices. To ascertain the reasons for the adverse fixed overhead expenditure variance the individual fixed overhead expense categories should be examined.

(c) For the answer to this question see 'Difficulties in interpreting sales margin variances' in Chapter 18 and 'criticisms of sales margin variances' in Chapter 19. In addition, the answer should stress the benefits from adopting an *ex post* variance analysis approach as described in Chapter 19.

Solution IM 19.9

(a) *Material usage revision variance*
(Original standard usage − *ex post* usage) × original standard price
[(4000 × 1.5 kg = 6000) − (4000 × 1.8 kg = 7200)] × £8 = £9600A

Material price revision variance
(Original standard price − *ex post* standard price) × *ex post* budgeted quantity
(£8 − £7.50) × 7200 = £3600F

Wage rate revision variance
(Original standard price − *ex post* standard price) × *ex post* budgeted quantity
(£4.50 − £4.30) × 8000 hours = £1600F

Other variances
Material usage = (standard quantity − actual quantity) × standard price
  = [(4400 × 1.8 kg) − 7800 kg] × £7.50 = £900F
Material price = (standard price − actual price) × actual quantity
  = (£7.50 − £7.90) × 7800 = £3120A

Labour efficiency = (standard quantity − actual quantity) × standard price
= [(4400 × 2 hrs = 8800) − (9200 − 150)] × £4.30 = £1075A
Labour idle time = 150 hours at £4.30 = £645A
Wage rate = (standard rate − actual rate) × actual hours
(£4.30 − £4.60) × 9200 = £2760A

(b) *Revised standard contribution per unit*

	(£)	(£)
Selling price		30.00
Direct materials (1.8 kg × £7.50)	13.50	
Direct labour (2 kg × £4.30)	8.60	22.10
Contribution		7.90

The sales volume variance has been calculated as follows:

(Budgeted sales volume − actual sales volume) × standard contribution per unit
(4000 − 4100) × £7.90 = £790F

The calculations for the breakdown of the sales volume variance are as follows:

Extra capacity = ((9200 labour hours/2) − 4000 units) × £7.90 = £4740F
Productivity drop = lost production arising from labour efficiency of 125 units
(250 hours/2 hours) at £7.90 = £987.50A
Idle time = 75 lost units (150 hours/2) at £7.90 = £592.50A
Stock increase = 300 units at £7.90 = £2370A

The net effect of adding the above variances is 100 units with a value of £790.

(c) The report should indicate that the original budgeted contribution of £36 000 has been adjusted in order to reflect the permanent changes which have arisen since the original budgets and standards were set. The revised budgeted contribution of £31 600 represents the revised target against which performance will be evaluated.

A favourable sales volume variance of £790 has been reported, and the operating statement analyses this variance by the following causal factors:

(i) *Extra capacity*: The 1200 extra labour hours which have been made available have created the potential for 600 units additional sales generating an extra contribution of £4740. Given that the additional sales did not materialize, it is questionable with hindsight whether it was appropriate to increase capacity. This decision can only be justified if demand in future periods is likely to exceed productive capacity.

(ii) *Productivity drop*: The decline in labour efficiency of 250 hours has resulted in a lost output of 125 units with a potential additional contribution of £987.50. If this will (say in the next period) result in future lost sales demand then the variance represents lost contribution arising from labour efficiency. On the other hand, if the decline in production will not lead to reduced future sales volume then the monetary value of this variance has little economic significance.

(iii) *Idle time*: An idle time of 150 hours has resulted in a lost output of 75 units with a potential contribution of £592.50. Comments similar to those outlined in (ii) apply. The causes of the idle time should be established and appropriate remedial action taken.

(iv) *Stock increase*: The variance relating to the stock increase of 300 units is intended to represent the potential loss in contribution of £2370 if the stocks deteriorate and cannot be sold in the future. The reasons for the stock increase should be established. If the stocks on hand were a result of a failure by sales management to dispose of them then sales management should be held accountable for the variance. On the other hand, if the stock increase was a result of over production by the production staff then production should be held accountable for the variance.

The remaining variances relate to production operating variances and require explanations relating to possible causes.

Material usage: The favourable variance suggests efficient usage in materials, although the 20% increase in the standard might have been an over estimate of the target material usage.

Material price: The adverse variance indicates that the company is paying in excess of the current target market price of £7.50. This might reflect a failure to change the sources of supply or contracts entered into when the standard price was £8. It could also be due to the purchase of higher-quality materials as reflected in the previous standard. This might also explain the favourable usage variance. It is important that the variance be investigated and appropriate remedial action taken to avoid future adverse variances.

Solution IM 19.10 (a) *Variance report for quarter ending 30 November*

		(£000)
Budgeted profit		111
Sales volume planning variance[a]		168A
Revised *ex post* budget		(57)
Sales variances: Operating volume (market share)[b]	126F	
Mix[c]	10F	
Price[d]	5F	141F
		84F
Material cost[e]	6.25F	
Sales commission price[f]	0.25A	6F
Fixed overhead[g]		6A
Selling and administration		5A
Actual net profit		79A

A contribution approach has been adopted since it is considered that this approach will provide more meaningful information. The budgeted contributions per square metre for each product are:

	Plastic	Mahogany
	(£)	(£)
Selling price	220	340
Materials	(49)	(131)
Commissions	(11)	(17)
	160	192

Note that labour is a fixed cost.
The average contribution per unit sold is:

$$\frac{£1\,000\,000 - (£278\,000 + £50\,000)}{4000\ units} = £168$$

Notes

Variance analysis	(£)
[a] Sales planning volume variance (market volume variance)	
$(3000 - 4000) \times £168$	168 000A
[b] Sales operating volume variance (market share)	
$(3750 - 3000) \times £168$	126 000F
[c] Sales mix variance:	
(actual sales volume − actual sales in standard mix)	
× standard margin	

Plastic $(2500 - \frac{3}{4} \times 3750) \times £160 = -50\,000$

Mahogany $(1250 - \frac{1}{4} \times 3750) \times £192 = +60\,000$ 10 000F

^{d} Sales price variances: (actual price − standard price) × AQ

Plastic $(£208 - £220) \times 2500 = 30\,000A$

Mahogany $(£368 - £340) \times 1250 = \underline{35\,000F}$ 5 000F

^{e} Material cost variances:

Plastic $2500 \times £49 - £120\,000 = 2500F$

Mahogany $1250 \times £131 - £160\,000 = \underline{3750F}$ 6 250F

^{f} Sales commissions price:

Plastic $(2500 \times £11) - £26\,000 = £1500F$

Mahogany $(1250 \times £17) - £23\,000 = \underline{£1750A}$ 250A

^{g} Fixed overhead variances:

	Mahogany	Plastic	
Labour	108 − 105 = £3000F	84 − 85 = £1000A	2 000F
Production overheads	162 − 166 = £4000A	79 − 83 = £4000A	8 000A
			6 000A

(b) The answer should emphasize the favourable performance by the firm during a period in which the regional market has declined by 25%. The difference between the actual profit and the original budget has arisen because of the change in the market conditions with an adverse planning variance of £168 000. Given the benefit of hindsight, the firm would have budgeted for a £57 000 loss. The favourable performance was due to a favourable sales mix variance of £126 000. The planned market share was 12% whereas the actual market share was 15%. Attention should also be drawn to the favourable sales mix and price variances. Overall, there was a net adverse selling cost variance of £5000.

(c) The answer should include a discussion of the following points:

   (i) The shop-floor employees may consider that there is little relationship between their efforts and net profit. Therefore it may not motivate the employees to improve their productivity.

  (ii) The sales force is currently provided with an incentive via sales commission. They are likely to be more motivated by a direct incentive scheme rather than an indirect scheme where the rewards are shared equally amongst all the staff.

 (iii) The guarantee of 90% of earnings and a possible loss of earnings may cause suspicion and create hostility to the new scheme.

 (iv) There is a danger that a reward system based on net profits may encourage dysfunctional behaviour which focuses entirely on short-term profits and ignores long-run profits.

  (v) Production managers may feel that they have 'lost out' at the expense of the factory employees and no longer have a status symbol.

Solution IM 19.11

(a) You should refer to Chapter 16 for a description of feedforward and feedback controls and Chapter 19 for a description of operating and planning vacancies.

(b) The original standard cost is £1600 (1000 units × 0.4 hour × £4) and the actual cost is £1890 (420 hours × £4.50). The adverse total wage variance of £290 can be broken down into planning and operational price and quantity variances using the following information:

(1) Original (*ex ante*) standard	(2) Revised (*ex post*) standard	(3) Actual results
400 hours at £4 = £1600	440 hours at £4.25 = £1870	420 hours at £4.50 = £1890

The operational variances are derived from a comparison of the actual results with the *ex post* standard:

	(£)
Labour efficiency variance (20 hours at £4.25)	85F
Wage rate variance (420 hours × £0.25)	105A
Planning variance = difference between columns (1) and (2)	270A
	290A

It is questionable whether any benefit can be derived from analysing the variance into planning and operational variances. However, the planning variance can be analysed as follows:

	(£)
Planning labour efficiency variance (40 hours × £4)	160A
Planning wage rate variance (£0.25 × 400 hours)	100A
Joint price/quantity planning variance (40 hours × £0.25)	10A
	270A

The operational price and quantity variances provide more meaningful feedback information than traditional variances on the efficiency and the acquisition cost of labour. The adverse wage rate variance suggests the need to investigate why the actual wage rate exceeded the *ex post* standard. This may be due to the use of a different grade of labour from that specified in the standard. The operational variances can provide useful information for feedforward controls by ensuring that any controllable variances are eliminated in future periods. Planning variances provide useful feedback information to management on how successful they are in forecasting and thus helping them to improve their future forecasts. The reporting of planning variances can help to improve the accuracy of future plans and thus provide more meaningful estimates for feedforward control.

Solution IM 19.12

(a) *Preliminary calculations*
Fixed overhead rate per hour = £8 (£19 200/2400 hours)
Variable overhead rate per hour = £16 (£38 400/2400 hours)
Contribution per unit of sales = £128 (£268 selling price − £140 variable cost)
Contribution per unit of materials = £8 (£128/16 units)
Contribution per labour hour = £32 (£128/4 hours)

Reconciliation at budgeted and actual profit

	(i)	(ii)	(iii)	(iv)
			Scarce	
	Traditional	Materials	labour	Sales =
	method	scarce	hours	limiting factor
	(£)	(£)	(£)	(£)
Budgeted profit	57 600	57 600	57 600	57 600
Direct material usage variance	6 400A^a	19 200A^b	6 400A	6 400A
Direct material price variance	0	0	0	0
Wage rate variance	0	0	0	0
Labour efficiency variance	900A^c	900A	10 500A^d	900A
Variable overhead efficiency variance	4 800A^e	4 800A	4 800A	4 800A
Variable overhead expenditure variance	3 600A^f	3 600A	3 600A	3 600A
Volume efficiency variance	2 400A^g	0	0	0
Volume capacity variance	800A^h	0	3 200A^i	0
Fixed overhead expenditure variance	800A	800A	800A	800A

Sales margin price variance	0	0	0	0
Sales margin volume variance	9 600A[j]	0	0	12 800A[k]
Actual profit	28 300	28 300	28 300	28 300

Notes

[a] 1600 units at £4 per unit.

[b] Acquisition cost of £6400 plus lost contribution (1600 units at £8).

[c] 300 hours at £3 per hour.

[d] Acquisition cost of £900 plus lost contribution (300 hours at £32).

[e] 300 hours at £16 per hour.

[f] Flexed budget allowance (2300 hours at £16) less actual variable overheads (£40 400).

[g] 300 hours at £8 per hour.

[h] 100 unused hours at £8 per hour.

[i] 100 hours at a lost contribution of £32 per hour.

[j] 100 units at a profit margin of £96 per unit.

[k] 100 units at a contribution of £128 per unit.

(b) See 'Variance analysis and the opportunity cost of scarce resources' in Chapter 19 for the answer to this question.

The question does not indicate whether a standard variable costing or a standard absorption costing system should be used. It is considered that a standard variable costing system provides more useful information. Sales variances are therefore expressed in the terms of contribution margins, and a fixed overhead volume variance will not arise. The calculations are as follows.

1. *Contribution per unit*

	Quicut (£)	Powacut (£)
Selling price	120 (£28 800/240)	200 (£24 000/120)
Variable cost	40 (£9600/240)	60 (£7200/120)
Contribution	80	140

2. *Analysis of sales volume variances*

	(1) Budgeted sales volume in standard mix (000)	(2) Revised sales target in standard mix[a] (000)	(3) Actual sales volume in standard mix (000)	(4) Actual sales volume in actual mix (000)
Q	240	312	260	280
P	120	156	130	110

Note

[a] Revised forecast increased by 30% because the total market sales volume was 30% greater than the original forecast.

Sales volume variance, (1)–(4):

		(£000)
Q	40 × £80 unit contribution	3200F
P	10 × £140 unit contribution	1400A
		1800F

Volume variance can be analysed as follows.

Planning variance, (1)–(2):

		(£000)
Q	72 × £80 unit contribution	5 760F
P	36 × £140 unit contribution	5 040F
		10 800F

Marketing share variance (controllable sales volume variance, (2)–(4))

		(£000)
Q	32 × £80 unit contribution	2560A
P	46 × £140 unit contribution	6440A
		9000A

It is possible to extract a sales mix variance to ascertain how much of the £9000 controllable sales volume variance is accounted for by a change in the sales mix. The sales mix variance is the difference between columns (3) and (4):

		(£000)
Q	20 × £80 unit contributions	1600F
P	20 × £140 unit contributions	2800A
		1200A

In other words, if the actual sales mix had been in accordance with the budgeted sales mix, the controllable sales volume variance would have been £7.8m.

3. *Sales price variances*
(Actual selling price − budgeted selling price) × actual quantity:

		(£000)
Q	[(£32 200/280) − £120] × 280	1400A
P	[(£24 200/110) − £200] × 110	2200F
		800F

4. *Variable cost variances*
Flexed budget − actual cost:

		(£000)
Q	(280 × 40 = £11 200) − £11 480	280A
P	(110 × 60 = £6600) − £6820	220A
		500A

5. *Fixed costs*

	(1) Original budget (350 000 units) (£000)	(2) Revised budget (360 000 units) (£000)	(3) Actual (£000)
Traceable manufacturing: Q	8200	9200[a]	7600
P	6800	6800[a]	6800
Manufacturing period costs	5700	6000	6000
Administration and selling period costs	4300	4500	4500

Note
[a] The question does not indicate how changes of output levels affect the fixed costs of individual departments. It is assumed that the increase in fixed costs is attributable purely to Quicut, where the output has increased.

Traceable fixed costs:	Activity/planning variances, (1)–(2)		(£000)
		Q	1000A
		P	0
	Expenditure, (2)–(3)	Q	1600F
		P	0
Manufacturing period costs:	Activity/planning variances, (1)–(2)		300A
	Expenditure, (2)–(3)		0
Administration and selling costs:	Activity/planning variances, (1)–(2)		200A
	Expenditure, (2)–(3)		0

(a) (i) *Analysis for sales director*

	Q (£000)	P (£000)	Total (£000)
Budgeted contribution (W1)	19 200	16 800	36 000
Planning/forecasting volume variance (uncontrollable)	5 760F	5 040F	10 800F
Controllable market share variance (of which £1200 is accounted for by a change in sales mix)	2 560A	6 440A	9 000A
Sales price variance	1 400A	2 200F	800F
Increase in contribution due to sales performance	1 800F	800F	2 600F
Administration and selling cost variances:			
Period costs planning/activity variance			200A
Period costs expenditure			—
Increase in profit due to sales performance			2 400A

(ii) *Analysis for product managers*

	Quicut (£000)	(£000)	Powacut (£000)	(£000)
Budgeted departmental profit		11 000		10 000
Planning/forecasting sales volume variance	5760F		5040F	
Market share variance	2560A		6440A	
Sales price variance	1400A	1 800F	2200F	800F
Variable cost variance		280A		220A
Actual departmental contribution		12 520		10 580
Less traceable fixed manufacturing costs:				
Planning/activity variance	1000A		—	—
Expenditure variance	1600F	600F	—	—
Actual departmental profit		13 120		10 580

Working

(W1) Budgeted contribution:

	(£000)	
	Q	19 200 (£28 800 − £9600)
	P	16 800 (£24 000 − £7200)
		36 000

(b) The initial impression is that the company has done well, with actual profits in excess of budgeted profits. The selling price of Powacut has been increased and sales volume has declined, whereas the selling price of Quicut has decreased and sales volume has increased. The net result has been an overall improvement over budget in sales performance for both products. The adverse sales mix variance, however, indicates that it might have been better to increase the sales volume of Powacut since this is the most profitable product. Cost variances are small, but they do require further investigation.

The variances are less impressive when the increase in the total sales volume for the industry is considered. The comparison with the original budget indicates a favourable volume variance of £1.8 m, but in view of the increase in the market one would have expected a volume variance of £10.8 m. Consequently the favourable volume variance can be attributed to an increase in the total market rather than an improvement by the company. The company has not performed as well as it should have done considering the change in the environment.

The variances resulting from a change in the total market represents the planning variances. The planning variances consist of the following:

	(£000)
Sales volume planning	10 800F
Traceable fixed costs	1 000A
Manufacturing fixed costs	300A
Administration and selling	200A
	9 300F

The remaining variances of £7.1 m represent adverse operating variances. The company should take steps to improve sales forecasts and consider fully the consequences of adjusting selling prices to influence sales volume. The reduction in Quicut's selling price might have had an adverse effect in view of the £1.5 m increase in fixed costs.

Solution IM 19.14

(a) See 'Statistical control charts' in Chapter 19 for the answer to this question.

(b) The costs incurred for each decision for each potential state of nature will be as follows:

	Potential states of nature	
	Process in control	Process out of control
	(£)	(£)
Decision:		
Investigate the variance	1000	1000 + 2000
Do not investigate the variance	Nil	10 000

The total variance is £7000 and the question indicates that there is a 0.80 probability that the process is in control. The probability that the process is out of control is 0.20 $(1 - 0.80)$. The expected value of the costs for each alternative are:

	(£)
Investigate the variance $[(0.8 \times £1000) + (0.2 \times £3000)]$	1400
Do not investigate the variance $(0.20 \times £10\ 000)$	2000

The variance should be investigated since the expected cost of investigating the variance is lower than not investigating.

(c) The indifference point will occur when the expected cost of investigating and correcting the variance is equal to the benefits arising from investigating and correcting the variance (i.e. the cost of allowing the variance to continue).

Let x = probability that the variance is out of control.

The indifference point will occur where:

$$1000 + 2000x = 10\ 000x$$
$$8000x = 1000$$
$$x = 0.125$$

Thus the variance should be investigated if the probability that the process is out of control exceeds 0.125 or if the probability that the process is in control is less than 0.875 $(1 - 0.125)$.

(d) The answer should draw attention to the difficulty in determining the costs and benefits of investigation (see 'Decision models with costs and benefits of investigation' in Chapter 19 for an explanation). In addition the answer should include a discussion of the following points.

    (i) Developing a model provides a conceptual understanding of the factors influencing the variance investigation decision.

   (ii) The model identifies the most important elements influencing the decision and specifies them in a predetermined mathematical form.

  (iii) Because the model is specified in mathematical terms there is a danger that it may oversimplify the variance investigation decision.

  (iv) There is a danger that decisions may become too mechanistic. It may be preferable to rely on human judgement.

Divisional financial performance measures

Solutions to Chapter 20 questions

Solution IM 20.1

(a) See 'Profit centres and investment centres' in Chapter 20 for the answer to this question.

(b) See 'Pre-requisites for successful divisionalization' in Chapter 20 for the answer to this question.

(c) The main behavioural and control consequences which may arise if profit or investment centres are introduced relate to designing performance measures that encourage goal congruence and avoid dysfunctional behaviour. This situation may occur when divisional managers make decisions to increase their performance at the expense of the company as a whole. Friction may also arise with transfer pricing where this leads to incorrect decisions or fails to provide a reasonable measure of divisional performance.

(d) See 'Return on investment', 'Residual income' and 'Economic value added' in Chapter 20 for the answer to this question.

Solution IM 20.2

See 'Responsibility centres' in Chapter 16 for an explanation of a cost centre, a profit centre and an investment centre. For a discussion of the strengths and weaknesses of each organizational unit see Chapters 16 and 20.

Solution IM 20.3–20.5

See Chapter 20 for possible answers to these questions.

Solution IM 20.6

(a) See the introduction and 'Advantages of divisionalization' in Chapter 20 for the answer to this question.

(b) See 'Disadvantages of divisionalization' and 'Pre-requisites for successful divisionalization' for the answer to this question. In addition, the answer should discuss the difficulty of establishing performance measures that encourage goal congruence and avoid the dysfunctional consequences described in Chapters 16 and 20.

(c) See the answer to Question IM 20.16 (part 2c) for the answer to this question. In addition the answer should point out that group management will need to place greater emphasis on co-ordinating the activities of the divisions, including managing the transfer pricing system, and implementing and controlling the divisional reward structures.

Solution IM 20.7

(a) The answer should stress the need for divisional measures to focus on performance measures that are more directly related to the strategic objectives and the strategies of the organization. At the operational level these are cascaded down into operational measures that are more related to specific operational activities. In particular at the divisional level a balanced scorecard approach should be adopted. The answer should draw off 'The balanced scorecard as a strategic management system' in Chapter 23 whereas for operational measures the discussion should draw off 'Operational measures' in Chapter 23.

(b) The answer could draw off the section titled 'Results or output controls' in Chapter 16. In addition, the answer should point out the difficulties of measuring performance in non-profit organizations because output is often difficult to measure. The following issues should also be discussed:

  (i) goal congruence;

  (ii) establishing measurable objectives;

 (iii) cultural factors.

It is important that the employees identify with the goals and objectives that are set and accept their performance being measured on the basis of these factors. Participation has a significant role to play in ensuring that the goals and objectives and the resulting performance measures are accepted and will act as a motivating force (see Chapter 16 for a discussion of the role of participation in performance evaluation). Particular care must be taken in developing performance measures so that they will encourage goal congruence and minimize the dysfunctional consequences. Here the answer could draw off the discussion in Chapter 16 relating to the harmful side-effects of controls.

Control in non-profit organizations is particularly difficult, because it is not always possible to state the objectives in quantitative terms or to measure the output of services. If it is not possible to produce a statement of a particular objective in measurable terms, the objective should be stated with sufficient clarity for there to be some way of judging whether or not it has been achieved.

In a non-profit organization performance measures should attempt to measure both the *quantity* and the *quality* of outputs. It is usually much easier to measure quantity than quality. For example, in an educational establishment the quantity measure of the number of students who graduated in the previous year is much easier to measure than the quality measure of how well the students were educated. Nevertheless, the quality measure should not be overlooked. In some cases the quantity indicator may provide an approximate measure of quality. For example, the number of students who have graduated in the previous year, analysed according to degree classification, may provide an approximation of the quality of the education.

Frequently in non-profit organizations input measures are used as proxy measures for output. If no satisfactory output measures can be formulated, input measures are a better measure of output than no measure at all. For example, it may not be feasible to construct output measures reflecting the quality of health care. In the absence of such measures, the amount spent on salaries and medicines may provide a useful clue to output. If, in the extreme, nothing was spent, we can conclude that nothing was accomplished. When inputs are used as proxy output measures, care must be exercised to avoid undue reliance on them. For example, the amount spent on wages and medicines may not represent an improved service to the users because the resources may not have been used effectively. Attempts should be made to develop useful measures of output so that efficiency and effectiveness can be measured. It is important that financial measures are not overemphasized and that a balanced scorecard approach (see Chapter 23) is adopted using realistic targets that relate the performance measures to the objectives of the organization.

It is important that management are aware of cultural issues in designing a performance measurement and evaluation system. Any changes should be handled carefully and thoroughly explained. Staff should be fully involved in order to secure their support. If staff are alienated the system will not be successful.

(a) (i) *Investment in new equipment*

Solution IM 20.8

It is unlikely that the new equipment could be installed until 2001. Assuming that the new equipment is installed at the start of 2001 profits would be increased by £11 333 p.a. (£18 000 cost savings less £6667 straight line depreciation over 15 years). If the ROCE is calculated on the basis of the year end WDV (£90 000) then the return in 2001 will be 12.6%. This is less than the target return of 15% and the existing return and the proposal will thus have a negative effect on the overall ROCE calculation for 2001. However, ROCE will increase over future years as the WDV declines.

From the group's point of view the proposal should be accepted because it has a positive NPV of £5246 (£18 000 × 5.847 annuity factor for 15 years less £100 000 investment). There are no ethical issues involved. Goal congruence does not exist if the divisional manager focuses on the impact the investment has on the performance measure for 2001.

(ii) *Deferred payment*
Cash is not included in the net assets and the deferring of a trade creditor until 2001 will thus have a beneficial effect in 2001. The impact on the ROCE will be as follows:

$$\text{ROCE} = \frac{\text{profit } (£190\,000 - £1000)}{\text{net assets } (820\,000 - £42\,000)} = 15.3\%$$

Therefore the 15% target will be achieved.

There would be no commercial merit in the proposal since the additional interest received on deferring the payment for 2 weeks assuming a 10% return would be £161 (£42 000 × 10% for 2 weeks) whereas the penalty cost is £1000. Furthermore, this would harm the relationship between the company and the supplier. It is also unethical to cause the company a loss of £1000 in order to obtain a salary bonus.

(iii) *Earlier completion of an order*
Profit would be improved by £4500 (£6000 − £1500) and the increase in debtors would cause net assets to increase by £6000. If this proposal is adopted ROCE will increase to 15.1% [(£124 500/£826 000) × 100] and the 15% target will be achieved.

There is no commercial benefit from this proposal as £1500 additional costs will be incurred. It is unethical to cause the company a loss of £1500 in order to obtain a salary bonus.

(iv) *Sale of plant*
The ROCE target is based on trading profit and therefore the profit on the sale of the asset and redundancy payments would be excluded. Assuming that all of the profit has been earned in the current year and that the plant can be sold in 2000 the net assets will decline by £90 000 and ROCE will increase to 16.4% [(£120 000/£730 000) × 100]. If the asset is fully depreciated profits will decline in 2001 by £12 600 and net assets will reduce by £90 000. This is equivalent to eliminating an asset with a return of 14% [(£12 600/£90 000) × 100] and the existing ROCE will improve if it is currently above 14%.

If the plant is retained there will be a loss of net sale proceeds of £70 000 (£120 000 less £50 000) (less £50 000 redundancy pay) to maintain £12 600 cash inflows for 15 years. Assuming a cost of capital of 15% the NPV is £3672 (£12 600 × 5.847 annuity factor less £70 000). The plant should be retained and goal congruence will not occur. It is unethical to close the plant when it is profitable in order to obtain a bonus, particularly when this will also lead to redundancies.

(b) The Finance Director should point out to the Divisional Manager, Chief Accountant and the Head of Internal Audit the unethical nature of the proposals. As the Chief Accountant and the Head of Internal Audit are likely to be accountable to the Finance Director they should be reprimanded and it should be emphasized that they should ensure that financial integrity is maintained. In particular, they should report situations where divisional managers engage in unethical behaviour in order to manipulate the profitability measures. Attention should also be given to modifying the bonus scheme so that performance just below target does not result in the loss of a large bonus. Ideally, the bonus should be based on long-run average profitability rather than short-term performance. If evidence is found to suggest that the existing bonus scheme encourages dysfunctional and unethical behaviour then consideration should be given to abandoning it in favour of higher salaries.

(a) The economic evaluation of the three projects using the NPV decision rule is as follows:

$$\text{Project A: } (£21\,000 \times 2.855) - £60\,000 = -£45$$
$$\text{Project B: } [£25\,000/1.15 + £20\,000/(1.15)^2 + £20\,000/(1.15)^3$$
$$+ £15\,000/(1.15)^4] - £60\,000 = -£1412$$
$$\text{Project C: } [£10\,000/1.15 + £20\,000/(1.15)^2 + £30\,000/(1.15)^3$$
$$+ £40\,000/(1.15)^4] - £60\,000 = + £6414$$

Consequently, from the company's point of view, project C should be accepted, project A is marginal and project B should be rejected. The following ROI and residual income (RI) measures in respect of each project over the four-year period would be reported:

	Year			
	1	2	3	4
	(£)	(£)	(£)	(£)
Project A				
Net asset value at beginning of year	60	45	30	15
Net cash flow	21	21	21	21
Depreciation	15	15	15	15
Net profit	6	6	6	6
Cost of capital (15% of NAV)	9	6.75	4.5	2.25
Residual income	(3)	(0.75)	1.5	3.75
ROI	10%	13.33%	20%	40%
Project B				
Net asset value at beginning of year	60	45	30	15
Net cash flow	25	20	20	15
Depreciation	15	15	15	15
Net profit	10	5	5	0
Cost of capital (15% of NAV)	9	6.75	4.5	2.25
RI	1	(1.75)	0.5	(2.25)
ROI	16.67%	11.1%	16.67%	–
Project C				
Net asset value at beginning of year	60	45	30	15
Net cash flow	10	20	30	40
Depreciation	15	15	15	15
Net profit	(5)	5	15	25
Cost of capital (15% of NAV)	9	6.75	4.5	2.25
RI	(14)	(1.75)	10.5	22.75
ROI	(8.3%)	11.1%	50%	166.7%

Divisional managers are rewarded and evaluated on the basis of ROI. If the divisional manager places a great emphasis on the short-term performance measure, it is unlikely that he or she would consider project C, since this yields a negative ROI in years 1 and 2. It is likely that the manager would opt for project B, since this yields the highest ROI in the first year. If the divisional manager adopts a longer-term perspective, he or she may opt for project C, since this yields the highest average yearly ROI over the four-year period. If divisional managers were evaluated on the basis of RI, it is likely that the manager would again choose project B if a short-term perspective is adopted and project C if a long-term perspective is adopted. Note that project C has the largest average annual RI.

From the company's point of view, decisions ought to be made based on the NPV rule. This would lead to the acceptance of project C and the rejection of projects A and B. Thus there is a possibility that there will be a divergence of views between the company and the division regarding which project should be accepted.

(b) For the answer to this question see 'The effect of performance measurement on capital investment decisions' and 'Reconciling short- and long-term residual income measures' (Appendix 20.1) in Chapter 20.

Solution IM 20.10

(a)

	Grain	Bakery
Return on capital employed	$23.34\% \left(\dfrac{£44\,000 - £40\,300}{£15\,850} \right)$	$21\% \left(\dfrac{£25\,900 - £23\,800}{£10\,000} \right)$
Residual income (£000)	$£1322.5 \; [£3700 - (15\% \times £15\,850)]$	$£600 \; [£2100 - (15\% \times £10\,000)]$
Controllable profit (£000)	$£4400 \; (£3700 + £700)$	$£3200 \; (£2100 + £1100)$

The gain on the sale of plant of the Bakery division has been excluded from the above figures, since this is assumed to refer to a decision taken by central management. The objective is to measure managerial performance. Therefore allocated head office costs are excluded from the above calculations. With the ROCE and residual income (RI) calculations, depreciation has been deducted to calculate the divisional profits. However, for the purpose of measuring managerial performance the majority of the depreciation charge will be non-controllable because central management controls the majority of investment decisions. Consequently the ROCE and RI calculations should only include depreciation on controllable investment. The calculation of controllable profit excludes all of the depreciation charges, but in practice should include a charge for depreciation on controllable investment.

The ROCE and RI calculations are based on written down values for the year ended 30 November. It would be preferable to base the calculations on the average value for the year rather than the year-end value. When written down values are used, the asset valuation declines each year, and this can cause ROCE and RI to increase even though profits have not increased. An alternative is to use gross book values, but this can also distort the performance measure. Preferably assets should be valued at market values or replacement cost when calculating RI and ROCE (see 'Impact of depreciation' in Chapter 20).

The overall company cost of capital has been used to calculate RI. An overall cost of capital charge is appropriate only when divisional projects are equal to the average risk of the company as a whole. In other words, the cost of capital charge should depend on the risk of divisional investments (see 'Determining the divisional cost of capital charge' in Chapter 20 for a more detailed discussion).

Finally, only controllable divisional overheads should be included in divisional profit calculations. If divisions cannot acquire supplies from outside the group then they should be charged for actual quantities at an agreed standard price or market price. Care must be taken to ensure that the profit calculations are not distorted by using transfer prices which are inappropriate for performance evaluation.

(b) See 'Distinguishing between the managerial and economic performance of the division', 'Return on investment', 'Residual income' and 'Economic value added' in Chapter 20 for the answer to this question. In particular, answers should indicate that the managers have minimal control over investment decisions and are being incorrectly treated as investment centres. Controllable profit attempts to exclude items which are beyond the control of divisional managers, and is therefore preferable to methods which do not distinguish between controllable and noncontrollable items. The weakness of controllable profit is that it fails to motivate managers to control the investment in working capital. It is also an absolute measure, thus making interdivisional or company comparisons inappropriate when capital employed differs significantly. The determination of performance levels would have to be based on a comparison of actual and budgeted divisional profits supplemented by a standard costing and budgetary control system.

RI is appropriate where managers have a significant influence over their investment decisions. Managers are thus encouraged to improve their performance rating by seeking investment opportunities which earn a return in excess of cost of capital. Divisional independence is maximized and goal congruence is encouraged. Managers are not motivated to accept only projects which are in excess of their current ROCE. RI is consistent with maximizing the present value of future cash flows in the long run if assets are valued at their economic values and annuity depreciation is used. If these conditions do not hold, there is no guarantee that the short-run RI will be consistent with maximizing the present value of future cash flows. If Sliced Bread were to adopt the RI measure, it would be essential that depreciation and interest charges be based on controllable assets valued at replacement cost or market values. The resulting RI calculation should be compared with a budget based on previous years' performance and anticipated future changes. In addition, the performance measures should be supplemented by a system of standard costing and budgetary control.

ROCE is widely used for measuring divisional performance. This is because it is a relative measure which is widely understood by managers and which is capable of being analysed in a pyramid of sub-ratios. The weakness of ROCE is that it does not motivate managers of investment centres to invest in projects which are less than the existing ROCE but above the cost of capital. Consequently it may not encourage goal congruence and is not consistent with a DCF appraisal. If ROCE is used, it is preferable to value the investment at replacement cost or market values. Care should be taken when comparing divisional ROCE with other divisions and companies, because different accounting policies and asset valuations might be used. ROCE is most suited to measuring the performance of profit centres.

(c) See 'Addressing the dysfunctional consequences of short-term financial performance measures' in Chapter 20 for the answer to this question. In particular, the answer should stress that information on market share, product diversification and product quality should be included as further measures of divisional performance.

(a) *Return on investment*

Solution IM 20.11

	A	B	C	D
Profit (£m)	4.0	1.1	1.2	0.5
Net assets (£m)	23.5	9.5	4.0	1.8
Return on investment	17.02%	11.58%	30%	27.78%

Residual income

	A	B	C	D
Profit (£m)	4.0	1.1	1.2	0.5
Interest charge (16% on net assets) (£m)	3.76	1.52	0.64	0.29
Residual income (£m)	0.24	(0.42)	0.56	0.21

Assumptions

The divisions are investment centres, and it is therefore appropriate to charge managers an imputed interest charge on divisional assets. The interest/cost of capital charge is based on the average cost of capital for the company $(0.4 \times 10\% + 0.6 \times 20\% = 16\%)$. It is assumed that the risk attaching to the activities of each division is equivalent to the average overall risk on the company's assets. If risk varies from division to division, a different percentage cost of capital/interest charge should be applied to each division. The higher the risk, the higher should be the interest charge. The group interest charge has been ignored, since it is a purely notional charge which bears no relation to the company's cost of capital.

The above calculations are after taking into account the exchange gain by division A. It is assumed that managers are accountable for foreign exchange management where overseas transactions occur. However, the exceptional charge to division C has not been included in the above calculations, since it is assumed to be an exceptional item and results from a decision taken at head office level. The profits are after charging depreciation, since this reflects a charge for the use of divisional assets. It would be preferable to base the depreciation charge on replacement cost rather than historical cost.

For a detailed discussion of the usefulness of residual income (RI) and return of investment (ROI) see Chapter 20. The answer should stress that ROI is a relative measure which gives an approximate indication of the return on a division's investment. This can be compared with an appropriate cost of capital and thus signify whether or not divisional investments are obtaining adequate returns. The measure highlights those divisions where economic viability may need to be reviewed using appropriate relevant economic cost and revenue estimates. ROI can also be used for comparing the returns between divisions of different sizes. It is also widely used by financial analysts for making intercompany comparisons. RI is an absolute measure which in the long-run takes into account the opportunity cost of an investment and is equivalent to NPV. By making a risk-adjusted cost of capital charge, risk is incorporated into the performance measure.

RI also encourages managers to invest in projects whose returns are in excess of the cost of capital.

Possible standards for comparison include budgeted/target ROI or RI, comparisons with other divisions within the group, comparisons with previous periods and comparisons with similar companies operating outside the group. However, care must be taken to ensure that one is 'comparing like with like' and that the measurements are consistent and based on the same asset valuation and profit measurement principles.

(b) It is unclear whether the question relates to the evaluation of the division as an economic entity or the evaluation of the performance of the divisional managers. Where the economic performance of a division is being evaluated, all head office costs should be allocated to divisions. Allocations should be based on benefits received (e.g. sales values for the credit control department) using appropriate cost allocation bases. Alternatively a transfer pricing system can be established for those head office services where divisional usage can be measured. Head office costs are joint costs, and it is inevitable that arbitrary allocations will be used to trace some costs to divisions. Care should therefore be taken when interpreting the economic performance of a division, and the performance measures should be seen as a monitoring system which can be used to trigger off an economic investigation of the viability of a division.

For evaluating managerial performance, only controllable head office expenses should be charged to divisional managers. For the answer to this part of the question see 'Alternative divisional profit measures' in Chapter 20. Arbitrary allocations should be avoided. It is preferable to use transfer prices based on divisional usage when charging head office costs to divisional managers.

(c) The main problems are:
   (i) The initial high investment together with long paybacks may result in a low ROI or negative RI in the early years of a project's life.

(ii) The cash flows are more uncertain in high-tech industries, and it is therefore difficult to set budgets against which to monitor actual performance.

(iii) Many of the benefits are of a qualitative nature and not easy to quantify.

(iv) It is difficult to establish an appropriate cost of capital which takes into account risk when calculating RI. If ROI is used, the ROI should be higher to compensate for the increased risk. However, it is extremely difficult to determine the additional return which is required to justify the additional risk.

(v) The RI and ROI measures are overstated if written down values are used in the calculations. Managers will be reluctant to replace old assets with new assets, because this will lead to a large increase in the investment base and an accompanying decline in ROI and RI.

The following actions should be taken to improve these measures:

(i) Value assets at replacement cost instead of historical cost. Depreciation charges should also be based on replacement costs (see 'The impact of depreciation' in Chapter 20).

(ii) Use other performance measures in addition to ROI and RI so that some of the dysfunctional consequences which arise from placing too much emphasis on single financial measures can be avoided (see 'Addressing the dysfunctional consequences of short-term financial measures' in Chapter 20).

(iii) Set realistic budgets and accept that cash flows may decline in the short term. Compare actual results with realistic budgets and avoid placing too much emphasis on short-term results.

(iv) Use risk-adjusted imputed interest charges using the capital asset pricing model (see Chapter 14). For a more detailed discussion of the conflict between short-run and long-run performance measures and alternative depreciation methods see Appendix 20.1 to Chapter 20.

(a) Performance statements similar to that illustrated in Exhibit 20.1 in the text should be presented in the answer to this question. In addition, the statements should contain columns for budgeted, actual and variances. If the statements are produced at frequent intervals, a column for the cumulative variances for the year to date should be included. Alternatively it might be preferable to show comparisons with previous period or year figures.

Solution IM 20.12

Managers should be held responsible for the *controllable* residual income. Where managers have no control over the investment in fixed assets or working capital, it is inappropriate to evaluate them on the basis of residual income. Instead, managers could be evaluated on the basis of budget and actual controllable contribution or controllable contribution as a percentage of assets invested in the division. Where the divisions (e.g. coal mines) sell mainly to other divisions within the group and have little influence over the level of total sales revenue, it might be preferable to regard them as service cost centres. Performance should be evaluated based on a comparison of budget (target) and actual costs.

In addition, the reports should be supplemented by appropriate non-financial measures such as physical output measures, output per employee, stock levels and labour turnover.

(b) Key measurement issues to resolve include:

(i) The basis for determining appropriate transfer prices based on the objectives of a transfer pricing system specified in Chapter 21. Where possible, market-based transfer prices ought to be used. Otherwise a choice must be made between using negotiated or centrally determined transfer prices.

(ii) The basis for determining asset valuations for the purpose of calculating the residual income interest charge or return on capital employed. For these calculations a choice must be made between valuing assets at historical cost (gross or net book value) or some departure from historical cost. See 'The impact of depreciation' in Chapter 20 for a discussion of asset valuation for a responsibility accounting system.

(iii) Where residual income or EVA is used, the basis for determining the percentage interest charge should be determined. Should this percentage be constant or vary from division to division? See 'Determining the divisional cost of capital' in Chapter 20 for a discussion of this point.

(iv) The extent to which non-financial measures should be included in the performance measurement system and the weighting to be given to specific measures when multi-performance measures are used.

(c) For tariff-setting purposes, all costs incurred will be allocated to the various products/tariffs in order to calculate unit full costs. In addition, unit costs will be categorized into their fixed and variable elements in order to provide information for determining short- and long-run minimum prices and cost−volume−profit relationships. Estimates of demand functions will be required for the various tariffs if optimal prices are to be set.

For performance evaluation, costs are allocated to responsibility centres (instead of products), based on the principles outlined in Chapter 16. It is important that the performance reporting system distinguish between controllable and non-controllable costs. Consequently the problem of allocating joint costs to cost objects may not arise. Actual performance should be compared with an appropriate target such as a flexed budget, past results or other profit/investment centres. Responsibility accounting places more emphasis on the use of non-financial measures.

Solution IM 20.13

(a) The depreciation charges on a current cost basis are likely to be greater than the charges on a historical cost basis. This is because the replacement cost of similar assets is likely to be greater than their historical cost. The impact of a change from historical cost to current cost is likely to have a much greater proportional impact on class B investment centres because the assets are older. Consequently the assets in class B are likely to be considerably understated if they were acquired many years ago, whereas assets in class A investment centres are likely to approximate more closely their replacement cost.

The question also indicates that technology is likely to change for class B investment centre assets. This will reduce the economic life of the assets and thus produce higher depreciation charges.

The change to a current cost basis of asset valuation will eliminate the advantage which class B companies currently obtain from historical cost asset valuations.

Current cost accounting is likely to reduce profits because of the increase in depreciation charges. In addition, the recorded value of the fixed assets is likely to increase because of the higher replacement cost of such assets. Consequently the numerator (profits) is decreased and the denominator (assets employed) is increased. Therefore ROCE will be lower than under historical costing. Because of the difference discussed in (a), class B investment centres will tend to have their ROCEs reduced to a much greater extent than class A investment centres. However, comparisons between investment centres will be more realistic than the current system.

(b) The steps required to revalue plant and equipment are as follows:

(i) Revalue each asset using manufacturer's current prices for similar equipment or published indices of price changes for specialized equipment.

(ii) Adjust the value to reflect for any differences (e.g. more advanced features) between new assets and the assets currently used.

(iii) Estimate the backlog depreciation using the current replacement as the asset base.

(iv) Estimate the remaining life for each asset.

(v) Estimate the current depreciation charge based on the current replacement cost and the estimated remaining life of the asset.

(vi) Show the revised asset value at its replacement cost less accumulated revised depreciation based on the revalued figure.

(a) (i) Exhibit 20.1 in the text provides an illustration of the calculation of alternative divisional profit measures. Controllable divisional profit before taxes is calculated as follows:

	(£)
Sales to outside customers	××
Transfers to other divisions	×××
	×××
Less: Variable costs (including goods purchased from other divisions)	×××
Variable Contribution margin	×××
Less: Controllable divisional fixed costs	×××
Controllable profit before tax	×××

(ii) The degree of divisional autonomy can influence controllable profits. Where central headquarters imposes a transfer pricing system, reported controllable profit may be significantly influenced by the input and output prices set by central headquarters. Alternatively, where a competitive external market exists market prices can be used for inter-divisional sales and purchases and divisional profit is more likely to represent the real economic contribution of the division to total company profits. In these circumstances divisional controllable profit is mainly subject to those factors that can be influenced by divisional management.

In some situations divisional managers are not allowed to purchase and sell goods outside the group. Therefore divisional managers do not have full control over input and output decisions. Where divisional managers have full autonomy they can seek cheaper sources of supply and are thus able to increase controllable profits. Divisional managers can also determine the mix of internal and external sales and purchases. Thus the degree of divisional autonomy determines the extent to which divisions can influence controllable profit.

If divisions are not investment centres they cannot influence divisional investment, and depreciation on divisional assets will be beyond the control of divisional managers. However, where divisions are regarded as investment centres the accounting policy for depreciation may be determined at group level. Group depreciation policy will therefore have a significant influence on reported controllable divisional profit.

(b) The investment should be undertaken because it has a positive NPV of £45 060 [(£380 000 × 2.487) − £900 000)]. However, divisional management is likely to make the decision on the basis of the impact that acceptance of the investment will have on the divisional performance measure. The residual income calculations are as follows:

(i) *Residual income using straight line depreciation*

	Year 1 (£000)	Year 2 (£000)	Year 3 (£000)
WDV at start of year	900	600	300
Net cash inflow	380	380	380
Less depreciation	300	300	300
Net profit	80	80	80
Less interest on capital (10%)	90	60	30
Residual income	(10)	20	50

(ii) *Residual income using annuity depreciation*

	Year 1 (£000)	Year 2 (£000)	Year 3 (£000)
WDV at start of year[a]	900	628.1	329
Net cash inflow	380	380	380
Less: Depreciation[a]	(271.9)	(299.1)	(329)
Interest on capital	(90.0)	(62.8)	(32.9)
Residual income	18.1	18.1	18.1

Note
[a] *Calculation of annuity depreciation:*

Year	(1) Annual repayment (£000)	(2) 10% interest on capital outstanding (£000)	(3) = (1) – (2) Capital repayment (£000)	Capital outstanding (£000)
0				900
1	361.9	90	271.9	628.1
2	361.9	62.8	299.1	329.0
3	361.9	32.9	329.0	

The annual repayment is calculated by dividing the investment outlay of £900 000 by the present value of an annuity for 3 years at 10% (2.487). Alternatively, the annual repayment can be determined by referring to the capital recovery table in Appendix D on page 1089 of the text for 3 years at 10%. The capital recovery factor is 0.4021 and this is multiplied by the capital outlay to give an annual repayment of £361 900 (rounded to the nearest £100).

If straight line depreciation is used general management may reject the investment if they adopt a short-term perspective because the residual income is negative in the first year. With annuity depreciation residual income is positive and constant each year and management is motivated to accept the investment. The annuity method of depreciation will not necessarily be constant and positive in all years for positive NPV projects where cash flows vary from year to year. For a discussion of the impact of depreciation methods on residual income where unequal cash flows occur see Appendix to Chapter 20.

Solution IM 20.15

(a) (i) In a decentralized organization top management no longer has detailed knowledge of the activities of the decentralized units. Divisionalized managers are allowed to exercise greater autonomy and make decisions without the approval of top management. Decentralization frees top management from the detailed involvement in day-to-day operations and enables them to devote more effort to strategic planning and coordinating the activities of the divisions.

The divisional managers will only have access to information relating to their own divisions. There is a danger that the planning and control activities of divisions will not be coordinated, since they do not have access to information for all the activities within the group. It is therefore important that top management provides guidelines and implements control and planning procedures to ensure that divisional activities are coordinated. This can be achieved by setting transfer prices for inter-company trading, and approving budgets and major capital expenditure commitments.

It is argued that top management loses some control by delegating decision-making to divisional managers. However, a good system of performance evaluation together with appropriate control information can enable top management to control divisional operations effectively.

(ii) Because top management delegates divisional decision-making to divisional managers, it is important that performance measures be developed for the purpose of indicating how successful divisional managers are in planning and controlling the activities of their divisions. In addition, top management should ensure that potential profitable activities are expanded and non-profitable activities contracted. It is therefore important that steps be taken to evaluate at periodic intervals the economic performance of divisions. Where performance measures such as profitability and sales trends suggest that activities are not sufficiently profitable, special investigations should be made to ascertain the viability of the division's activities.

Performance measures comparing trends and actual against target thus provide a means by which top management can exercise control and compensate for delegating decision-making to divisional managers. Divisional managers can also be encouraged to achieve company objectives by being evaluated on the performance measures applied to them.

(b) (i) The ROI calculations using the different valuation bases are as follows:

	Hotel		
	X	Y	Z
	(%)	(%)	(%)
ROI			
Historic cost basis	40	17.4	14.3
Replacement cost basis	17.8	11.4	10.9
Disposal value basis	11.1	10.5	11.1

Hotel X produces the best results on a historic cost basis. However, the historic cost returns are misleading, since they fail to take into account changing asset values arising from price level changes. The ROI (on a historic cost basis) for hotel X is particularly misleading. This is because the asset valuations will tend to be based on price levels at the time the hotels were opened. Division X assets will be recorded in 1987 pounds and, assuming rising prices, will tend to have lower asset valuation relative to Y and Z. Consequently X is likely to have the highest ROI.

On a replacement cost basis, X is the most successful division and is the only division which earns a return in excess of the cost of capital. When the returns are expressed in terms of disposal values, all the divisions earn a return below the minimum required rate of return. This would suggest a need for a special investigation with a view to examining the feasibility of increasing the profitability of the assets, or alternatively disposing of the assets. However, a comparison of the historic cost with the disposal values suggests an appreciation in values in excess of 10% per annum compound.

Assuming that the assets have earned operating incomes throughout their lives similar to the current levels, this would suggest that the initial investments have yielded a return in excess of 12%.

The modernization proposals do not give any indication of the time period of the investments. By dividing the investment cost by the annual operating income, we can ascertain the number of years the cash flows will be required to continue in order to yield an internal rate of return of 12%. For example, the investment by hotel X would require annual cash flows of £67 000 for a minimum of 20 years in order to yield a return in excess of 12% (£500/£67 = 7.46 annuity factor, which is approximately 20 years at a 12% interest rate). Hotels Y and Z would require the annual cash flows specified to continue for 32 and 8 years respectively. It would therefore appear that only the investment by hotel Z is justified.

(ii) In addition to the rate of return measures, residual income can be used. However, it is virtually impossible to capture in summary financial measures such as return investment or residual income all the variables which measure the success of the hotels. Therefore it is important that non-financial measures also be used to support the financial measures and also to indicate the future potential of the hotels. Examples of additional measures which could be used by the group include:

1. costs per guest;
2. value added per employee;
3. occupancy rates;
4. market shares;
5. predictions on a regional basis of future growth rates and likely future competition;
6. predictions of future growth rates in property prices;
7. statements on expected environmental changes which might have an impact on the future values of the hotels (e.g. decisions by major companies to re-locate in the region and potential of the area as a future tourist attraction).

Solution IM 20.16

Part One

(a) The reported performance for 2000 and 2001 without any of the proposals is estimated to be as follows:

ROCE: £450 000/£4 800 000 = 9.4%

Average daily purchases: (£2 920 000/365) = £8 000

Average daily sales: (£6 900 000/365) = £18 904.10

Average daily cost of sales: (£6 900 000 − £450 000)/365 = £17 671

Cash conversion period: Number of days debtors (£1 035 000/£18 904) = +55 days
Number of days stocks (£530 000/£17 671) = +30 days
Number of days creditors (£320 000/£8000) = − 40 days
_____
45 days

Number of innovations = 4

On the basis of the above information none of the divisional managers would receive an annual salary bonus.

The office manager's proposal

This will cause stocks to be £160 000 lower for both years and creditors will be £180 000 more than predicted for 2000 and revert to the predicted level for 2001.

ROCE for 2000: (£450 000 − £2000) / (£4 800 000 − £160 000 − £180 000) = 10.04%

ROCE for 2001: (£450 000 − £16 500) / (£4 800 000 − £160 000) = 9.3%

Revised average sales per day: (£6 900 000 + £160 000)/365 = £19 342

Revised cash conversion period: Number of days debtors
(2000) (£1 035 000/£19 342) = +54 days
Number of days stocks
(£530 000 − £160 000)/£17 671) = +21 days
Number of days creditors
(£320 000 + £180 000)/£8000) = − 63 days
_____
12 days

Revised cash conversion period: Number of days debtors
(2001) (£1 035 000/£18 904) = +55 days
Number of days stocks
(£530 000 − £160 000)/£17 671) = +21 days
Number of days creditors
(£320 000)/£8000) = − 40 days
_____
36 days

The number of innovations remain unchanged at 4.

For 2000 all of the divisional managers, with the exception of the chief executive and the design manager, will receive their bonuses. In 2001 only the accountant and office manager will receive their bonuses.

Production manager's proposal
It is assumed that the increase in operating profit is after charging annual depreciation on the new equipment of £45 000. In the first year of purchase the ROCE would be:

(£450 000 + £25 000) / (£4 800 000 + £400 000 − £45 000) = 9.2%

This will result in a decline in the ROCE, and since the other measures will remain unchanged, the proposal is unlikely to be accepted. Also in the second year of purchase the ROCE will still be less than the existing return of 9.4% so it is unlikely to be accepted if a longer time horizon is adopted.

Design manager's proposal
In the first year of implementation profit will increase from £450 000 to £470 000. The change in net assets will be as follows:

Original estimate	4 800 000
Net cost of investment in the first year (£100 000 – £10 000 depreciation)	+90 000
Increase in stocks less creditors (£530 000 – £320 000) × £20 000/£450 000	+9 333
Increase in debtors from goods on sale or return (£6 900 000 × £20 000/£450 000 × 0.5)	+153 333
Estimated net assets	5 052 666

Revised ROCE (£470 000 / £5 052 666)	9.3%

The cash conversion period without considering the proposal is 45 days which is in excess of the target of 40 days. The proposal will increase the conversion period and a detailed calculation is unnecessary since it will be in excess of the 40 days target required for the bonus.

Presumably the proposal will be classed as being successfully brought to the market after it has overcome the initial market resistance. This will not occur until 2001. The proposal would therefore generate bonuses for the chief executive and design manager in 2001 but not for any of the remaining members of DE management.

(b) *Office manager's proposal*

It is assumed that the £16 500 per annum represents cash flows. The NPV of the proposal is as follows:

	£
Annual 10 year cash flows (£16 500 × discount factor for 10 years of 6.710)	−110 715
Assumed replacement of stock after 10 year time horizon (£160 000 × 0.4632)	−74 112
Immediate penalty cost	−2 000
Proceeds from disposal of stock	+160 000
NPV	−26 827

Production manager's proposal

Annual cash flows (£25 000 + £45 000 depreciation) discounted for 8 years (£70 000 × 5.747)	402 290
Residual value (£40 000 × 0.5403 discount factor)	21 612
Initial outlay	−400 000
NPV	23 902

Design managers's proposal

Investment outlay	−100 000
Increase in working capital (£9 333 + £153 333 see part (a))	−162 666
Annual incremental cash flows (£20 000 + £10 000 depreciation discounted for 10 years = £30 000 × 6.710)	+201 300
Assumed residual value of incremental working capital in year 10 = £162 666 × 0.4632	+75 347
NPV	+13 981

The design manager and the production manager's proposal should be accepted and the office manager's proposal should be rejected.

Part Two

(a) The advantages are:
  (i) The consultants are likely to have greater experience of designing and implementing new management accounting systems.
  (ii) The consultants are likely to have a greater knowledge of new innovations.
  (iii) The consultants have the resources to implement new systems whereas FPE's staff are likely to be too busy with day to day activities and therefore unable to devote sufficient time to implementing new systems.
  (iv) They can draw off staff who specialize in different areas or who have the experience across a wide range of business functions.

  The disadvantages are:

  (i) Lack of detailed knowledge of existing systems.
  (ii) Lack of detailed knowledge of FPE's business.
  (iii) Consultants are costly to employ.
  (iv) Resistance to change by existing staff may be greater if they have not been involved in designing and developing the new systems.

(b) See pages 837–50 in Chapter 20 for the answer to this question.
(c) The answer should explain that cost centres will be replaced by profit or investment centres and how top management will rely more heavily on using results controls, such as ROI or EVA, to monitor divisional performance. In addition the financial measures will be supplemented by non-financial measures using the balanced scorecard approach described in Chapter 23. The answer should include a discussion relating to the move from detailed controls to a delegation of authority and control by means of approval of the master budget (rather than the detailed functional budgets) and long-term plans by central management. Capital expenditure will be controlled by means of an overall ceiling within which divisionalized management can authorize. Beyond a certain limit and for major strategic projects central management approval may be necessary.

Part Three

(a) See 'Return on investment,' 'Residual income' and 'Economic value added' in Chapter 20 for the answer to this question.
(b) The answer should draw attention to the dysfuctional consequences that can arise by placing too much emphasis on performance measures. Such dysfunctional consequences are likely to be exacerbated by linking pay to the performance measures. See 'Harmful side effects of controls' in Chapter 16 for a discussion of why the dysfunctional consequences are likely to arise. For the measures that might be taken to deal with the identified problems see 'Addressing the dysfunctional consequences of short-term financial measures' in Chapter 20.
(c) For an explanation of the JIT philosophy see 'Just-in-time systems' in Chapter 22. The answer should also draw attention to the fact that ROCE includes many

items that the production manager may not be able to influence. The cash conversion period performance measure will support the JIT philosophy by encouraging the reduction in stocks but it also includes debtors and creditors which are not directly related to the activities of the production manager. If top management want to motivate the production manager to follow a JIT philosophy they should adopt performance measures that support the JIT philosophy. Such measures might include a single throughput measure (see 'Operation process measures' in Chapter 23 for an explanation) or a range of measures relating to set-up times, throughput cycle times, percentage defects, stock levels and percentage of deliveries that are on time.

Transfer pricing in divisionalized companies

Solutions to Chapter 21 questions

Solution IM 21.1   See Chapter 21 for the answer to this question.

Solution IM 21.2   (a) For an explanation of why cost-plus transfer prices are unlikely to lead to the maximization of group profits see 'Cost plus a mark up transfer prices' in Chapter 21. If there is an external market for the intermediate product, the cost-plus transfer price would lead to maximization of group profits only if it was equal to the external market price. If the company has no market for the intermediate product and the variable cost per unit of output of the supplying division is constant, the transfer price which would lead to maximization of group profits would be unit variable cost.

If Exel Division transfers the products at actual cost plus 20% mark-up, the division will not be motivated to control its costs. Exel will obtain a greater monetary mark-up if actual costs are higher than they should be. Any inefficiencies will be passed on to the receiving division. Thus actual costs are an inappropriate basis for assessing divisional performance. Transfers should be at *standard* marginal cost and not actual cost. Any difference between the transferred-out costs and actual costs incurred would then result in the supplying division being accountable for adverse or favourable variances. Thus the supplying division is motivated to minimize its costs.

   (b) Where there is a shortage of supply of the raw materials to produce the intermediate product, a linear programming model can be formulated which incorporates all the relevant input, cost, revenue and output information relating to the supplying and receiving divisions. The solution to the model indicates how much of the intermediate products should be produced, the quantity of the intermediate product which should be transferred to the receiving division, and the quantity of the intermediate and final products which should be sold externally in order to maximize group profit. A production programme derived from the output of the linear programming model could be dictated to the divisions by the management at central headquarters. Alternatively transfer prices can be established from the output of a linear programming model which will motivate the managers to produce the optimum output.

   (c) Where the supplying division does not have sufficient capacity to meet the demands placed upon it, the transfer price derived from the linear programming solution will result in the supplying division being credited with all of the contribution arising from the transfers, and the receiving division reporting a zero contribution. Therefore the performance measurement data will not provide an appropriate indication of the receiving division's contribution to total group profit. In addition, imposing a transfer price will result in divisional autonomy being undermined. For a discussion of how this problem might be resolved see 'Proposals for resolving transfer price conflicts' in Chapter 21.

Solution IM 21.3   (a) Figure Q21.3 illustrates the situation faced by the group.

Where there is a perfectly competitive market for the intermediate product the current market price is the most suitable basis for setting the transfer price. The supplying division (Fabri) should supply as much as the receiving division (Gini)

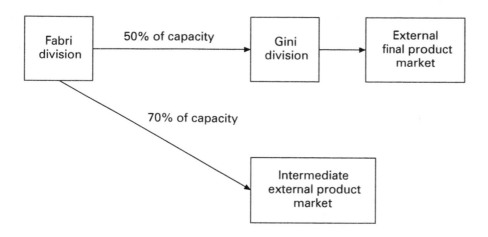

Figure Q21.3

requires at the current market price, so long as the incremental cost is lower than the transfer price. If this supply is insufficient to meet the receiving division's demand, it must obtain additional supplies by purchasing from an outside supplier at the current market price. Alternatively, if the supplying division produces more of the intermediate product than the receiving division requires, the excess can be sold on the outside market at the current market price.

Applying the above principles, 50% of Fabri's output would be transferred to Gini at the current market price and the remaining capacity of 50% sold on the external market. Alternatively, divisional profitability and overall group profitability would remain unchanged if 70% of Fabri's capacity were sold in the external market and 30% transferred to Gini. Gini would then purchase a further 20% in the external market.

Where sales in the external intermediate product market result in selling costs additional to those incurred from internal sales, the market price transfer pricing rule should be modified by deducting the additional selling costs from the external market price.

If the market for the intermediate product is imperfect it is unlikely that market prices will represent the optimal transfer price. With imperfect markets, it is necessary for central headquarters to intervene and examine the marginal cost, marginal revenue and net marginal revenue schedules of the supplying and receiving division and set the transfer price at the point where the marginal cost of the supplying division is equal to the sum of the marginal revenue and net marginal revenue schedules (i.e. the marginal cost of the supplying division at the optimum output level for the group as a whole).

If Fabri's variable costs are constant and fixed costs remain unchanged throughout the potential output range for the period then variable cost per unit of output is the optimal transfer price. In addition Gini division could pay Fabri division a fixed payment for the period for the privilege of obtaining the intermediate product at marginal cost. For example, if 70% of Fabri's output is allocated to the intermediate external market and the remaining 30% for transfers to Gini then Gini should negotiate a fixed payment equivalent to approximately 30% of Fabri's fixed costs for the period. The aim should be to motivate Gini to reject any external supplier quotes in excess of the marginal cost of Fabri division.

(b) If the market for the intermediate product is imperfect and divisional autonomy is limited then it is likely that central headquarters will intervene and set an imposed transfer price as described in part (a) of the question. However, if the divisions have full independence then the divisions are likely to negotiate a mutually acceptable transfer price. Negotiated transfer prices may not maximize group profits but this may be offset by the motivational advantages that arise from granting full independence.

Divisional profitability measures will be affected by the transfer price used, since the transfer price represents revenue to the supplying division and an expense to the receiving division. Where a perfectly competitive market price exists, the divisional profitability measures are more likely to represent the real economic contribution of the divisions to total company profits. However, where an imperfect external market exists, or is non-existent, there is a danger that the transfer price will not reflect a division's real contribution to group profits. Distortions are likely to be greater when internal purchases/sales represent a significant percentage of total divisional purchases/sales and where the percentage fluctuates from period to period. Thus the impact of the transfer price on the divisional performance measure is a factor that must be considered when setting transfer prices.

Solution IM 21.4

(a) (i) See Exhibit 20.1 in Chapter 20 for the answer to this question.

(ii) It is assumed that the question relates to transfer pricing issues only. Where there is a perfect competitive market for the intermediate product, and full autonomy is granted, it is likely that divisional managers will choose to trade at the external market price. This should result in optimal decisions in most circumstances. However, if the supplying division cannot sell all of its output externally, to ensure that group profits are maximized, the receiving division must be instructed to purchase from the supplying division the quantity it is prepared to supply at the market price. If full autonomy is given to divisions they might not follow this rule and overall optimality may not ensue.

Where the market for the intermediate product is imperfect corporate headquarters must gather data from the divisions to set the optimal transfer price at the marginal cost of the supplying division at the optimal output for the company as a whole. To achieve this objective divisions cannot have full autonomy. If divisions are given full autonomy it is unlikely that optimality will be achieved where the market for the intermediate product is imperfect. The motivational advantages of corporate headquarters not interfering excessively must also be taken into account and the benefits arising from this may outweigh any loss of profits.

In addition to the above points the answer could also discuss negotiated transfer pricing where divisions are allowed to establish transfer prices by negotiation rather than using prices set by corporate headquarters. See 'Negotiated transfer prices' in Chapter 21 for a discussion of the issues involved.

(b) See 'Domestic transfer pricing recommendations' in Chapter 21 for the answer to this question.

Solution IM 21.5

(a) The major disadvantage of the transfer price is that it will not motivate the receiving division to operate at the optimal output level for the company as a whole (see 'Cost-plus a mark-up transfer prices' in Chapter 21). The main advantage is that it will enable the supplying division to earn a profit on inter-group transfers. Also using standard cost, rather than actual cost, ensures that inefficiencies cannot be passed on to the receiving division by the supplying division. Distinguishing between planning and operating variances enables only planning variances, that are due to environmental changes, to be included in any changes in the transfer price. Any increase in costs due to inefficiencies will result in operating variances. Separately identifying operational variances ensures that any inefficiencies will not be incorporated into the transfer price.

(b) This situation would apply when external selling expenses are significant but such costs would be either avoided or lower on inter-group transfers. See Appendix to Chapter 21 for a more detailed explanation of this situation. The question does not limit the answer to domestic transfer pricing. Therefore issues relating to multinational transfer pricing could be included in the answer. For an explanation of these issues see 'International transfer pricing' in Chapter 21.

(c) To maximize group profits a linear programming model must be formulated centrally which incorporates all relevant information relating to the divisions involved. The solution to the model will provide information on the opportunity costs (shadow prices) of the scarce resources. The transfer price that will motivate the optimal output for the group as a whole is incremental cost plus the opportunity cost of any scarce resources. This will result in a transfer price where all of the profits are allocated to the supplying division that has the scarce resources.

The report should include an estimate of divisional profits and return on investment (ROI) based on current demand:

Solution IM 21.6

	Division A (£000)	Division B (£000)
Contribution from outside sales	1500	250
Contribution from internal transfers	375	
Total contribution	1875	250
Fixed costs	500	225
Profit	1375	25
Investment	6625	1250
ROI	20.8%	2%

Assuming there is a single market price of £30, the current system is motivating correct decisions since both managers are encouraged to expand output. However, the current transfer pricing system is causing motivational problems because it under estimates the contribution which division B makes to overall company profits. In other words, the current system results in an inadequate measure of divisional performance.

Division A has 30 000 units capacity available to meet the demand of Division B. Therefore Division A can meet the demand of Division B without forgoing any sales to outside customers. Consequently the relevant cost of the transfers is £15 per unit variable cost. A transfer price of £15 per unit would be unfair to Division A, since internal transfers would not provide any contribution to fixed costs.

A possible solution is to set the transfer price at £15 per unit, and Division B should also pay Division A an annual lump sum contribution to cover the fixed costs of Division A. Total output of Division A is 125 000 units, consisting of 100 000 units outside sales and 25 000 units internal transfers. Therefore 20% of Division A's capacity is devoted to Division B, and thus the lump sum payment should be £100 000 (20% of £500 000 fixed costs). If in any year it is anticipated that demand in the external market will be in excess of Division A's capacity, the transfer price should be set at the prevailing market price.

It is assumed that additional sales of 5000 units of product J can only be obtained if a new branch is opened. The incremental costs to the company are £175 000 (£125 000 variable cost + £50 000 establishment costs) and the incremental revenues are £250 000. Therefore total company profits will increase by £75 000 if the new branch is opened. However, with the present transfer pricing system Division B will regard the transfer price as an incremental cost. Consequently contribution will be £10 per unit and the annual establishment costs of £50 000 will equal Division B's total contribution of £50 000. Therefore Division B profits will remain unchanged and the manager will not be motivated to open the new branch. If the new branch is opened then, with the present transfer pricing system, the £75 000 additional profit will be allocated to Division A.

A transfer price system consisting of £15 variable cost plus a lump sum payment is recommended. The revised transfer pricing system will motivate the manager of Division B to open the new branch. The divisional profit calculations (without the new branch) based on the proposed transfer pricing system are as follows:

	Division A (£000)	Division B (£000)
Contribution from outside sales	1500	625
Contribution from internal transfers	—	—
Lump sum payment	100	(100)
Fixed costs	(500)	(225)
Profit	1100	300
Investment	6625	1250
ROI	16.6%	24%

Solution IM 21.7

(a) Figure Q21.7 illustrates the inter-group trading:

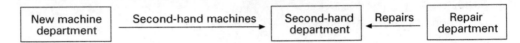

Figure 21.7

A market price exists for the transfers between the departments. Therefore the transfer price for the repair department work is assumed to be the market price of £8 per hour plus the cost of materials. The transfer of the second-hand machine should be at the market price. The second-hand machine quoted in the question has a market price of £3700 (without any repairs being necessary). In order to repair the machine on the outside market, a cost of £850 (100 × £8 + material cost) would be incurred. Therefore the current market value of the machine in its current state is assumed to be £2850 (£3700 − £850).

New machine department	(£)
Net sales value of new machine (£16 000 − £5000)	11 000
Transfer price of second-hand machine	2 850
	13 850
Cost of new machine	12 000
Profit contribution	1 850

Second-hand machine department

	(£)	(£)
Sale to ST Ltd		4200
Less: Transfer price paid to new machines department	2850	
Transfer price paid for repairs to repairs department	850	3700
Profit contribution		500

Repairs department

	(£)	(£)
Transfer price received from second-hand machine department		850
Less: Variable costs		
Materials	50	
Variable costs (100 × £4.50)	450	500
Contribution to fixed costs and profit		350

(b) (i) The repairs department will charge an additional £400 for repairs to the second-hand machine department. The repairs department should earn the normal revenue on the extra work, since Walker was not responsible for the repair cost estimate error. The question is to whom should £400 be charged?

Because both Newman and Handley were responsible for the repairs estimate, there is a case for apportioning the £400 between them. An alternative view is that Handley could obtain £500 profit by buying the similar machine from another dealer for £3700. However, he chose to support Newman in selling the new machine. Therefore there is a case for Handley being allowed to maintain the £500 profit. Assuming that the £400 is charged to the new machine department, the revised profit contributions will be as follows:

	(£)
New machine department	1450
Second-hand machine department	500
Repairs department	525 [£350 + (50 × £3.50 contribution)]

(ii) In this situation Walker is responsible for the error, and should bear the cost of repairs. Consequently, the contribution of the repairs department will be reduced from £350 to £125 (£350 original contribution less £225 variable cost of repairs).

(c) (i) Because the new machines department will make additional profit margins on the sale of the new machines in the form of a reduced purchase price, the cost of the warranty repairs (including profit margins) should be charged to the new machines department. Because the warranty decision was presumably taken by Newman, the warranty excess repairs should be charged to the new machines department.

(ii) If the normal charge of £8 is made, the repairs department will gain because it will obtain an additional contribution to fixed costs and profits. Also, the repairs department will maintain its budgeted contribution from outside customers. If the profit centres were individual firms then the new and second-hand machine departments would pay £8 per hour and the repairs department would receive £8 per hour. Therefore there are strong arguments for maintaining the normal charge and thus enabling the repairs department to obtain an additional contribution to fixed costs and profits. However, if the second-hand department can obtain cheaper repairs from outside the group, the £8 charge should be reviewed.

(a) (i) *Normal selling price less variable selling and distribution costs*

Solution IM 21.8

	(£)
Normal selling price	12.00
Less variable selling cost (£20 000/100 000)	0.20
Transfer price proposed by EMD	11.80

(ii) *Standard variable manufacturing cost plus 20% profit margin*

	(£)
Direct manufacturing costs (£630 000/100 000)	6.30
Variable overheads (£10 000/100 000)	0.10
Variable manufacturing cost	6.40
20% profit margin	1.28
Transfer price proposed by OPD	7.68

(iii) *Standard full manufacturing cost plus 15%*

	(£)
Full manufacturing cost per unit (£880 000/100 000)	8.80
15% margin	1.32
Proposed transfer price	10.12

It could be argued that since the company will be operating at 100% capacity if the transfers take place, the unit fixed costs ought to be determined on the basis of 120 000 units instead of 100 000 units. This will result in the following revised calculations:

	(£)
Unit variable manufacturing cost	6.40
Fixed overhead unit cost [(30 + 150 + 60)/120]	2.00
Full manufacturing cost per unit	8.40
15% profit margin	1.26
Transfer price	9.66

Comments

In 2001 EMD has 20 000 units surplus capacity. Therefore any price in excess of its variable manufacturing cost of £6.40 per unit will be acceptable to the manager of EMD. Orders in excess of 20 000 units will result in lost sales on the external market. The minimum transfer price acceptable for internal transfers in excess of 20 000 units is £11.80 (lost sales revenue less savings on variable selling costs). With a transfer price of £11.80, OPD would purchase externally at a price of £9 per unit. This is the correct decision for the group as a whole.

A transfer price of £7.68 would be acceptable to both EMD and OPD for the first 20 000 units. This transfer price will not be acceptable to EMD for demand in excess of 20 000 units and OPD would buy externally.

A transfer price of £9.66 or £11.80 would encourage OPD to purchase 30 000 units from the external market. However, only 10 000 units are available externally, and OPD will seek to purchase 20 000 units internally. At a transfer price of £9.66, EMD would be willing to allocate only its unused capacity to meet internal demand. With the £11.80 transfer price, EMD would be prepared to transfer 120 000 units to OPD.

In 2001 EMD's external sales will utilize all its available capacity. EMD will only be prepared to transfer goods to OPD at a transfer price of £11.80. At any of the other prices suggested, the lost external sales revenue will exceed the revenue generated by inter-divisional transfers.

(b) The transfer pricing system should be based on the opportunity cost approach. This is derived from the sum of the incremental cost of the supplying division from meeting the internal demand plus any lost contribution. Where EMD has spare capacity (the first 20 000 units), the resulting transfer price will be £6.40 (£6.40 + zero lost contribution). For demand in excess of 20 000 units the resulting transfer price will be £11.80 (£6.40 incremental cost + £5.40 lost contribution). Note that the lost contribution is £11.80 net selling price less £6.40 variable cost.

With the £6.40 transfer price, OPD would purchase from EMD, but EMD would be indifferent about transferring goods to OPD. Any negotiation ought to lead to a transfer price between £6.40 and £9 for the first 20 000 units capacity. With the £11.80 transfer price, OPD would buy 10 000 units from the foreign supplier. This is the correct decision if EMD is operating at full capacity.

(a) To answer this question, it is necessary to adopt an approach similar to that
illustrated in Exhibits 21.6 and 21.7 in Chapter 21. The following schedule
provides details of the marginal cost of the supplying division Engcorp (denoted
by MC), the marginal revenue from the sale of the intermediate product by
Engcorp (MR) and the net marginal revenue from the transfer of the intermediate
product and the sale as a final product by Flotilla (NMR).

Output	MC (£000)	MR (£000)	NMR (£000)	Total net revenue (£000)
100	115	204 (1)	133 (3)	133 (703 − 570)
200	70	158 (2)	122 (5)	255 (1375 − 1120)
300	76	124 (4)	111 (7)	366 (2036 − 1670)
400	83	112 (6)	90	456 (2676 − 2220)
500	91	105 (8)	79	535 (3305 − 2770)
600	100	100	68	603 (3923 − 3320)
700	110	95	57	660 (4530 − 3870)
800	121	90	46	706 (5126 − 4420)

The numbers in parentheses in columns 3 and 4 refer to the order of ranking for
the allocation of the intermediate product on the basis of MR and NMR. The optimal output is 700 units. At this output level, MC is £110 000 and NMR is
£111 000. At an output level of 800 units, MC is £121 000, and the most beneficial
use of this output is to sell it in the intermediate market where MR is £105 000.
Therefore output should not be expanded from 700 to 800 units.

At the optimal output level 400 units should be sold on the intermediate market
and 300 units should be transferred to Flotilla and sold as a final product.

(b) Where the market for the intermediate product is imperfect, it is unlikely that
market prices will represent the optimal transfer price. With imperfect markets,
it is necessary for central headquarters to intervene and examine the MC, MR
and NMR schedules of the supplying and receiving divisions and set the
transfer price at the point where MCs is equal to the sum of MRs and NMR of
the supplying and receiving divisions (i.e. MCs of the supplying division at the
optimum output level of the group). Applying this rule will result in an optimal
transfer price which is greater than £1100) (£110 000/100) per unit but less than
£1110 per unit (£111 000/100). At a transfer price of, say, £1105, the supplying
division will choose to sell 400 units on the external market (the supplying
division's MR is above £1105 per unit for the first 400 units) and transfer 300
units to the receiving division (MC per unit is less than the transfer price at
output levels up to 700 units). At a transfer price of £1105 per unit, the receiving
division will purchase 300 units internally (at output levels above 300 units, NMR
is less than the transfer price).

Both divisions will therefore select the optimal output levels at a transfer price
of £1105. Total group profit will be £319 000 (£598 000 total revenue from the
intermediate market plus £366 000 total net revenue from the final product
market less £645 000 total cost of the supplying division). With the transfer price
set at £1105, divisional profits will be:

(£)

Engcorp 284 500 (£598 000 external sales + 300 × £1105 internal sales − £645 000
production cost)

Flotilla 34 500 (£2 036 000 sales − £1 670 000 conversion costs − 300 × £1105
internal purchases)

If central headquarters do nor intervene, Engcorp would examine its cost and revenue schedules and choose to produce 600 units, which is the level at which it
maximizes profits. At this output level, profits are £268 000 (£803 000 −£535 000)
and the selling price per unit of output is £1338 (£803 000/600 units). Note that the

question states that the current market price is £1350. The manager of Engcorp is not prepared to transfer engines to Flotilla at a price of £1300, since this is less than the current market price. The manager of Engcorp could improve divisional profits by transferring the remaining capacity of 200 units at £1300 each, since this is in excess of the marginal cost (£231 000).

At a market price of £1350 (or £1338), the manager of Flotilla will purchase 100 units externally to be converted into the final product. The group and divisional profits, assuming that Engcorp sells 600 units on the intermediate market, will be:

$$(\pounds)$$

Engcorp	268 000	(£803 000 − £535 000)
Flotilla	3 000	(£133 000 − (100 × £1300))
Group	271 000	

At the optimum transfer price of £1105, both divisions increase their profits, and group profit is increased by £48 000 (£319 000 − £271 000).

From the above discussion the following points emerge:
  (i) Transfer prices set at the prevailing or planned market price when markets are imperfect are not optimal.
  (ii) Central intervention is necessary in order to ensure that optimal output levels are set but this process may undermine divisional autonomy.
  (iii) To induce optimal output levels, transfer price is not equal to market price where markets are imperfect.
  (iv) If both managers had been provided with all the information and were educated to use the information correctly, it is likely that a negotiated solution would have emerged which would have been acceptable to both the divisions and the group.

The major issue is therefore whether to intervene and impose an optimal transfer price. The advantage is that short-term profits will be increased by £48 000, but the disadvantage of this policy is that divisional autonomy will be undermined.

(c) The major considerations are:
  (i) Taxation.
  (ii) Import duties.
  (iii) Restrictions on dividend repatriations.
  (iv) Legislation: situations may arise where multinationals can transfer goods at low prices, which would result in the transferred product being sold at prices significantly below the prices charged by local firms. Legislation may be introduced in the importing country which protects local firms and affects the transfer prices of imported goods.
  (v) Exchange rates: reported profits may be severely affected by adverse changes in the exchange rates. Transfer pricing can be used to influence the location and level of profits so that group reported profits are maximized.

For a discussion of items (i)–(iii) above see 'International transfer pricing' in Chapter 21.

Solution IM 21.10 (a) At a selling price of £2200 estimated demand is 1000 beasts. Each increase or decrease in price of £100 results in a corresponding decrease or increase of 125 beasts. Therefore if the selling price were increased to £3000 demand would be zero. To increase demand by one unit the selling price must be reduced by £0.80 (£100/125). Thus the maximum selling price for an output of x units is:

$$SP = \pounds3000 - \pounds0.80x$$

Total revenue for an output of x units $= \pounds3000x - \pounds0.80x^2$

$$\text{Marginal revenue} = \frac{d\text{TR}}{dx} = \pounds3000 - 1.60x$$

Marginal cost = variable cost = £1050 (£700 + £350)

At the optimum output level where MR = MC:

$$£3000 - 1.60x = £1050$$
$$x = 1218.75 \text{ units (say 1219 units)}$$

The highest selling price at which this output can be sold is:

$$SP = £3000 - 0.80(1219) = £2025$$

(b) At a selling price of £700 estimated demand is 9000 engines. Each increase or decrease in selling price of £1 results in a corresponding decrease or increase of 10 engines. Therefore if the selling price were increased to £1600 demand would be zero. To increase demand by one unit the selling price must be reduced by £0.10. Thus the maximum selling price for an output of x units is:

$$SP = £1600 - £0.10x$$

Total revenue for an output of x units = $£1600x - £0.10x^2$

$$\text{Marginal revenue} = \frac{dTR}{dx} = £1600 - 0.20x$$

Marginal cost = variable cost = £350

At the optimum output level:

$$£1600 - 0.20x = £350$$
$$x = 6250 \text{ units}$$

The highest selling price at which this output can be sold is:

$$SP = £1600 - 0.10(6250) = £975$$

If the transfer price is set at the profit maximizing market price for the sale of engines the marginal cost of the motorcycle division will be £1675 (£975 transfer price plus £700 variable conversion cost). The motorcycle division's revised optimum output level will be where:

$$£3000 - 1.60x = £1675$$
$$x = 828 \text{ units}$$

At the optimum output level of 828 units:

$$SP = £3000 - £0.80(828) = £2337.60$$

(c) The engineering division produces an intermediate product that is sold in an imperfect final product market with a declining marginal revenue schedule. In this situation it is necessary for central headquarters to intervene and gather cost and revenue schedules for each division in order to determine the selling prices that will maximize the profits for the group as a whole. This process will undermine divisional autonomy but if the divisions are allowed to set their own selling prices they may seek to maximize their own profits at the expense of the group as a whole. For a more detailed discussion of the issues arising in this part of the question see 'Economic theory of transfer pricing' in Chapter 21.

Solution IM 21.11　*Part One*

(a) *Engines division*

At a selling price of £1000 demand is 5000 units. Each increase or decrease in price of £1 results in a corresponding increased or decrease in demand of 5 units. Therefore if selling price were increased to £2000, demand would be zero. To increase demand by one unit, selling price must be reduced by £0.2 (£1/5 units). The maximum selling price for an output of x units is:

$$SP = £2000 - £0.2x$$

Total revenue (TR) for an output of x units $= £2000x - 0.2x^2$
Marginal cost $= £600$
$MR = dTR/dx = £2000 - 0.4x$

The optimal output level is where MR = MC.

That is, where $£2000 - 0.4x = £600$
so that $x = 3500$ units
and $SP = £2000 - £0.2(3500) = £1300$

giving a total revenue from external sales of £4 550 000 (3500 units at £1300)

Transmissions division

At a selling price of £1200 demand is 2500 units. Each increase or decrease in price of £2 results in a corresponding increase or decrease in demand of 5 units. Therefore if selling price were increased to £2200, demand would be zero. To increase demand by one unit, selling price must be reduced by £0.40 (£2/5 units). The maximum selling price for an output of x units is:

$$SP = £2200 - £0.4x$$

Total revenue (TR) for an output of x units $= £2200x - 0.4x^2$
Marginal cost $= £350$
$MR = dTR/dx = £2200 - 0.8x$

The optimal output level is where MR = MC.

That is, where $£2200 - 0.8x = £350$
so that $x = 2312$ units
and $SP = £2200 - £0.4(2312) = £1275$

giving a total revenue of £2 947 800 (2312 units at £1275)

Assembly division

At a selling price of £6000 demand is 4000 units. Each increase or decrease in price of £1 results in a corresponding increase or decrease in demand of 2 units. Therefore if selling price were increased to £8000, demand would be zero. To increase demand by one unit, selling price must be reduced by £0.50 (£1/2 units). The maximum selling price for an output of x units is:

$$SP = £8000 - £0.5x$$

Total revenue (TR) for an output of x units $= £8000x - 0.5x^2$
Marginal cost $= £1500 + £1300 + £1275 = 4075$
$MR = dTR/dx = £8000 - 1x$

The optimal output level is where MR = MC.

That is, where $£8000 - 1x = £4075$
so that $x = 3925$ units
and $SP = £8000 - £0.5(3925) = £6037.50$

giving a total revenue of £23 697 188 (3925 units at £6037.50)

Summary of outcomes

	Units sold	Revenues (£)	Total cost (£)	Profit (£)	ROCE (%)
Engines	7425[a]	9 652 500	9 455 000	197 500	3.8
Transmission	6237[a]	7 952 175	7 382 950	569 225	7.0
Assembly	3925	23 697 188	21 794 375	1 902 813	18.7
				2 669 538	

Note

[a] Units demanded by the assembly division plus the demand calculated above for outside sales.

(b) *Assembly division*

The question indicates that the marginal cost of engines and transmissions is used to arrive at the optimum selling price for the company as a whole, but that market prices will be used to determine divisional performance. The marginal cost for the assembly division will be £2450 (£1500 + £350 + £600). Repacing this marginal cost in the computation in (a) gives:

$$£8000 - 1x = £2450 = 5550 \text{ units}$$

and SP = £8000 − £0.5(5550) = £5225 so that:

Total revenues = £28 998 750 (5550 units at £5225)
Total costs = £28 416 250 (using market based transfer prices)
Profit = £582 500
ROCE = 5.7%

Engines division

Total demand = 9050 units (5550 units transferred plus 3500 external sales)
Total revenues = £11 765 000 (9050 units at £1300)
Total costs = £10 430 000
Profit = £1 335 000
ROCE = 25.7%

Transmissions division

Total demand = 7862 units (5550 units transferred plus 2312 external sales)
Total revenues = £10 024 050 (7862 units at £1275)
Total costs = £7 951 700
Profit = £2 072 350
ROCE = 25.6%

The profit for the company as a whole is £3 989 850 when the marginal cost transfer price rule is applied for the assembly division. This represents a significant increase compared with (a) where market prices are used to set the optimal output level for the assembly division.

(c) *Transmissions division*

The revised optimum output and selling price will be where:

$$£2200 - 0.8x = £320$$
so that $x = 2350$ units
and SP = £2200 − £0.4(2350) = £1260

Assembly division

The revised marginal cost is £4060 (£1260 + £1500 + £1300)

£8000 − 1x = £4060 = 3940 units

and SP = £8000 − £0.5(3940) = £6030 so that:

Total revenues   = £223 758 200 (3940 units at £6030)
Total costs   = £21 796 400 (using market based transfer prices)
Profit   = £1 961 800
ROCE   = 19.2%

The total demand of the transmissions division becomes 6290 units giving:

Total revenues   = £7 925 400 (6290 units at £1260)
Total costs   = £7 382 800
Profit   = £542 600
ROCE   = 6.1% (£542 600/£8 950 000)

Engines division

Total demand   = 7440 units (3940 + 3500)
Total revenues   = £9 672 000 (7440 units at £1300)
Total cost   = £9 464 000
Profit   = £208 000
ROCE   = 4%

The total profit for the company as a whole is £2 712 400, an increase of £42 862. However, given that the ROCE for the transmissions division declines from 7% to 6.1% it is unlikely that the divisional manager will recommend acceptance.

(d) Adding back depreciation on the new investment of £170 000 per annum to the incremental total profits of £42 682 gives annual cash flows of £212 682. The NPV is:

£212 862 × a cumulative discount factor of 4.100   =   £872 374
Less investment outlay   =   £850 000
NPV   =   22 374

The investment should be undertaken but the performance measurement system does not encourage goal congruence.

Part Two

(a) See 'Advantages of divisionalization' in Chapter 20 for the answer to this question. In addition, the answer should stress the benefits of decentralization and point out that the creation of profit or investment centres is dependent on establishing a sound transfer pricing system.
(b) See 'Return on investment', 'Residual income' and 'Economic value added' for the answer to this question.
(c) See sections entitled 'Functional and divisionalized organizational structures' and 'Pre-requisites for successful divisionalization' in Chapter 20 for the answer to this question. The principles discussed in these sections should be applied to government/public service organizations. In addition, the answer should discuss that such structures will be dependent on the ability to measure output and implement an internal trading/transfer pricing system. Divisionalized structures are most suited to situations where market prices exist for the internal services thus enabling an internal market to be established.
(d) Increased work is likely to result from establishing and maintaining a satisfactory performance measurement and transfer pricing system and implementing sound control systems. There is a need to tailor-make these systems to the different circumstances faced by the different divisions. This is likely to be very time-consuming. In addition the management accountant is likely to be involved in dealing with transfer pricing conflicts and setting annual divisional targets.

Part Three

(a) See 'Purposes of transfer pricing' and 'Conflict of objectives' in Chapter 21 for the answer to this question.

(b) An imperfect market exists for the intermediate product and therefore the present transfer price based on market prices does not motivate sound decisions. A comparison of parts (a) and (b) for the answer to part one of the question indicates that the present system will not lead to the selection of the optimum output for the company as a whole. However, the current system does have the advantage of ensuring that divisional autonomy is not undermined and it is probably perceived as representing a fair basis for performance evaluation by the divisional managers. Imposing a system of transfer price at the marginal cost of the intermediate products would ensure that sound decisions are made. However, this would undermine divisional autonomy and would not represent a sound basis for measuring divisional performance.

The company should modify its transfer pricing system by implementing either a dual rate transfer pricing system or a marginal cost plus a fixed lump-sum fee. See Chapter 21 for a more detailed explanation of these methods.

(c) See 'Marginal cost transfer prices' and 'Cost-plus a mark-up transfer prices' in Chapter 21 for the answer to parts (i) and (iii) to the question. Opportunity cost represents the marginal cost of producing the intermediate product plus any lost contribution (opportunity cost) on the resources used in making the intermediate product. If spare capacity exists then the opportunity cost will be zero and the opportunity cost method would result in a transfer price that is equal to marginal cost. Where a perfect market for the intermediate product exists marginal cost plus the lost contribution will be equal to market price. If an imperfect market exists, applying economic theory, the optimal transfer price is the marginal cost of producing the intermediate product for the optimal output for the company as a whole. At this output level the opportunity cost of the resources required for the intermediate product would be zero and the opportunity cost method would result in a transfer price equivalent to marginal cost; the same as economic theory. The opportunity cost method thus represents a re-expression of economic theory as described in Chapter 21.

Cost management

Solutions to Chapter 22 questions

Solution IM 22.1

(a) Overtime premiums and shift-work premiums should normally be classified as indirect costs. If they are treated as direct costs then work undertaken during the overtime or night shift period will bear higher costs than those undertaken during the regular working week. Overtime and shift work is usually necessitated by a generally high work load and not by the specific job or customer. It is therefore inappropriate to record work done during overtime or night hours as being more costly than their counterparts undertaken during, say, a regular 8 hour day. The cost of overtime and shift premiums should be collected and analysed by responsibility centres for control purposes.

If, however, the overtime or shift premiums are a direct result of a customer's urgent request for completion of an order and not due to the general pressure of work then it may be appropriate to charge the overtime or shift premiums directly to the customer.

(b) The answer to this question should include a description of JIT manufacturing, the benefits of JIT and the impact of JIT on a firm's costing system. For a discussion of these items see Chapter 22, and 'Criticism of standard costing' in Chapter 19.

In particular, the answer should stress the following effects of JIT on the costing system:

(i) There will be a move towards process costing techniques, since there will be less need to track the flow of costs through the production process.

(ii) Much less emphasis will be placed on detailed inventory product costing techniques, and a backflushing system may be used to derive the production cost of sales for the period.

(iii) Greater emphasis will be placed on non-financial measures and the measurement of quality, delivery times, set-up times etc., rather than inefficiencies.

(iv) There will be less emphasis on labour efficiency and material price variances.

Solution IM 22.2

(a) See Chapter 22 for a description of life-cycle costing. At the planning stage, before a decision is made to introduce a new product, it is necessary to estimate revenues and costs incurred over the whole life of the product. Periodically it is appropriate to undertake a post-audit by comparing revenues and costs incurred plus predictions of costs and revenues to the end of the product's life. These costs and revenues should be compared with the original estimates that were made to justify the launch of the product. Therefore the answer should focus on the difficulty in estimating costs and revenues from the design stage to the abandonment of the product. Difficulties are encountered with determining how joint costs should be assigned to the product and learning rates. Where unit costs are computed, volume estimates significantly influence the accuracy of unit cost calculations.

(b) See 'Product life cycle' in Chapter 11 for an explanation of the terms. At the start-up (introductory) stage accurate costs will be difficult to determine because production volumes are extremely difficult to predict and learning effects may also exist. The emphasis at this stage is likely to be on actual costs rather than standard costs. Planned costs are extremely difficult to estimate but close monitoring of costs is essential so that continuous improvements in terms of cost reduction are encouraged.

At the growth stage uncertainties will still remain relating to volume and possibly learning effects. If a high-margin product is involved then accurate cost estimates may not be critical but for low-margin products inaccurate estimates may lead to incorrect volume and pricing decisions. Target costing is likely to be particularly appropriate at this stage

At the maturity and harvest stages learning effects are unlikely to apply and volume will be easier to predict. Thus standard costing may be appropriate and more accurate product costs are likely to be reported. At the harvest stage the focus will be on the short-term and maximizing short-term cash flows. Greater emphasis will be given to using short-term marginal costs for pricing and output decisions. For a discussion of the impact of product life cycles on pricing decisions see 'Product life cycle' in Chapter 11.

It is claimed that in today's competitive markets product life cycles have shortened considerably for many products.

Solution IM 22.3

(a) The main requirements for effective operational control are described in Chapter 16. In particular, see 'Results or output controls'. The answer should also stress the importance of incorporating non-financial measures.

The aim of a product costing system is to accurately trace the resources consumed by products. For a more detailed answer to this question see Chapter 10, and 'Backflush costing' in Chapter 4.

(b) The answer should discuss the limitations of traditional product costing systems which are based on arbitrary overhead allocations (see Chapters 3 and 10). For a discussion of the deficiencies of traditional operational control and performance measurement systems see 'Side-effects from using accounting information for performance evaluation' in Chapter 16 and 'Criticisms of standard costing' in Chapter 19.

(c) The answer to this question should incorporate 'The future role of standard costing' in Chapter 19 and aspects of the balanced scorecard in Chapter 23. In addition, the answer should also focus on the methods of tracing more accurately the resources consumed by cost objects using an ABC system.

Solution IM 22.4

(a) See 'A comparison of ABC with traditional costing systems' and 'The emergence of ABC systems' for the answer to this question.

(b) See 'Activity-based budgeting' in Chapter 15 for the answer to (b)(i), 'Activity-based management' in Chapter 22 for the answer to (b)(ii) and Example 11.2, relating to a pricing decision, for the answer to (b)(iii). Alternatively, the answer could draw off the content in the sections in Chapter 11 entitled 'A price-taker firm facing a long-run product-mix decision' and 'Customer profitability analysis' if you wish to focus on product or customer discontinuation decisions.

Solution IM 22.5

(a) The benefits of JIT are gained by rearranging the factory layout from a batch production layout towards a product layout using flow lines. In addition, work practices are changed with the aim of achieving zero defects and batch sizes of one and adopting JIT purchasing techniques. For a description of these items you should refer to 'Just-in-time systems' in Chapter 22. The answer should also draw attention to the fact that the JIT approach involves a change in company culture, commitment to the pursuit of excellence and continuous improvement in all phases of manufacturing systems design and operations. The full benefits of JIT are not obtained overnight.

(b) For a discussion of how management information systems should be developed in order to facilitate and make the best use of JIT see 'Just-in-time systems' in Chapter 22 and 'The future role of standard costing' in Chapter 19. In particular, the answer should indicate the need to place greater emphasis upon developing fast feedback performance measures which are congruent with the JIT philosophy. Such performance measures are more likely to be of a non-financial nature.

Solution IM 22.6

(a) (i) See 'Cybernetic control systems' in Chapter 16 for the answer to this question.

 (ii) See 'Feedback and feedforward controls' in Chapter 16 for the answer to this question.

(b) (i) For the answer to this question see 'Cost of quality' in Chapter 22. In particular, the answer should indicate that quality costs should be classified as follows:
1. Prevention costs.
2. Appraisal costs.
3. Internal failure costs.
4. External failure costs.

 (ii) The two philosophies appear to be directly opposed. The first accepts the fact that 100% quality cannot be maintained, and seeks to monitor and measure the cost of inferior quality output. The second philosophy aims to achieve zero defects. Thus standards and budgets should be based on zero defects, and any deviation from this goal should be regarded as unacceptable. The emphasis is on doing the job correctly the first time rather than accepting and monitoring the costs of inferior quality. The cost of reporting inferior quality output is regarded as a non-value-added activity.

 The two approaches adopt different philosophies to achieve the same objective (i.e. reducing waste and defective work). The cost of quality report can be used as an attention-directing device to make top management aware of how much is being spent on quality-related costs. This information can provide the justification for the need to adopt a 'zero-defects' philosophy. Furthermore, once such a philosophy has been introduced, cost of quality reports can be used to monitor the reduction in costs arising from implementing such a policy. It is therefore possible to reconcile the two philosophies.

Solution IM 22.7

(a)

Evaluation of quality management programme

	(£)
Synthetic slabs cost reduction	
Elimination of synthetic slabs stores losses	
68 711 units × (£40 − 1)/100	26 797
specification check	14 000
Savings on purchase quantity of synthetic slabs:	
(2 748 450 − 2 090 651) × £40/100	263 120
Less: increase price: 2 090 651 × £4/100	(83 626)
Curing/moulding process costs:	
variable cost reduction	
(2 679 739 − 2 090 651) × £20/100	117 818
scrap sales foregone of sub-components	
(267 974 − 20 907) × £5/100	(12 353)
Finishing process cost reduction:	
variable cost reduction (see note 1)	158 656
scrap sales foregone (361 765 − 51 744) × £10/100	(31 002)
Finished goods stock:	
holding costs (45 000 − 1500) × £15/1000	653
	454 063
Less: cost of quality management programme	250 000
Net (cost)/benefit of proposed changes	204 063

Note 1: Variable cost of reduction for curing/moulding process

	(£)
Existing cost	
Type AX 964 706 × £15/100 =	144 706
Type BX 1 447 059 × £25/100 =	361 765
	506 471
Amended cost	
Type AX 826 667 × £12/100	(99 200)
Type BX 1 243 077 × £20/100	(248 615)
Net reduction in cost	158 656

(b) See 'Cost of quality' in Chapter 22 for the answer to this question.

Strategic management accounting

Solutions to Chapter 23 questions

Solution IM 23.1   See 'Strategic management accounting' and 'The balanced scorecard as a strategic management system' for the answer to this question. In addition the answer should describe the role of strategic management accounting in the selection of strategy (see 'Stages in the planning process' in Chapter 15) and the evaluation of strategic options. There is also a need for the organization to be aware of its own cost structure and any significant differences between its cost structure and those of its main competitors in order for that area of competitive advantage to be identified.

Solution IM 23.2   (a) See 'Criticisms of standard costing' in Chapter 19, 'Harmful side-effects of controls' in Chapter 16 and 'JIT and management accounting' in Chapter 22 for the answer to this question.

(b) See 'Future role of standard costing' in Chapter 19 and the content relating to incorporating a wider range of performance measures within the balanced score-card perspective described in Chapter 23.

Solution IM 23.3   (a) See a description of the customer, internal business and learning and growth perspectives within the balanced scorecard in Chapter 23 and also 'Performance measurement in service organizations' in Chapter 23 for the answer to this question.

(b) The answer should incorporate some of the content relating to 'The future role of standard costing' in Chapter 19, 'Addressing the dysfunctional consequences of short-term financial performance measures' in Chapter 20, 'Dealing with the distorting effects of uncontrollable factors' in Chapter 16 and issues relating to the balanced scorecard perspective and performance measurement in service organizations in Chapter 23.

Solution IM 23.4   (i) See 'The balanced scorecard' in Chapter 23 for the answer to this question.
(ii) For service organizations in general see 'Performance measurement in service organizations' in Chapter 23. For a firm of consultants the answer could be related to Question IM 23.6 which adopts a balanced scorecard perspective for measuring the performance of a consulting organization.

Solution IM 23.5   (a) See Chapters 16 and 20 for a description of cost centres, profit centres and investment centres. Note that because investment centres are accountable for investment decisions, performance should be evaluated over longer periods than for profit and cost centres. The benefits from using different types of responsibility centres are to enable the accounting system to stress the authority, responsibility and specialization within the organization and to tailor the internal reporting system to the elements of an organization's structure. Besides identifying management responsibilities, establishing responsibility centres can have an important motivational influence. The main problems are:
(i) distinguishing between controllable and uncontrollable costs;
(ii) dual responsibility;
(iii) determining the lowest level of responsibility for reporting purposes;

(iv) determining which information should be reported and the frequency of reports;

(v) avoiding dysfunctional behaviour and a lack of goal congruence.

For a more detailed discussion of the above items you should refer to Chapter 16.

(b) The regional companies are investment centres, and therefore broader performance measures should be used. Examples include:

    (i) return on capital employed;

    (ii) residual income;

    (iii) gross profit and net profit percentages;

    (iv) market share percentages;

    (v) sales growth rates;

    (vi) profit per square metre;

    (vii) average debtors credit period;

    (viii) capital expenditure (actual, planned and committed expenditure).

The outlets are profit centres, and the following measures should be used:

    (i) total sales value;

    (ii) controllable net profit;

    (iii) controllable net profit as a percentage of sales;

    (iv) gross profit as a percentage of sales;

    (v) each category of expense expressed as a percentage of sales;

    (vi) controllable and non-controllable cost variances;

    (vii) stock turnover;

    (viii) gross profit per square metre (by departments and overall);

    (ix) sales per trade sales representative.

(c) Because the regional company can take capital investment on expenditure below £100 000, an assessment of performance should relate to the amount of capital tied up as a result of investment decisions. ROCE provides a *relative* measure of performance, and this measure can be further divided into two subcomponents – net profit as a percentage of sales and the ratio of sales to capital employed. Residual income and economic value added (see Chapter 20) can also be used as an absolute profit measure after deducting the opportunity cost of funds invested by the regional company. Gross and net profit percentages should be compared with other regional companies and similar companies outside the group. This comparison should indicate whether costs are being efficiently controlled. Sales growth and market share statistics provide an indication of the sales function relative to the external environment. Profit per square metre can be used as an inter-company performance comparison in relation to space. Debtors are controlled at regional offices, and therefore average credit periods should be monitored. It is also necessary to monitor capital expenditure.

The outlets should be regarded as profit centres and evaluated on controllable net profit (i.e. sales less controllable expenses such as bad debts). Outlet managers will be evaluated in terms of sales performance and their ability to control costs. Total sales revenue, gross profit per square metre and sales per trade representative provide an indication of sales performance (e.g. pricing and marketing mix decisions). Outlet managers are responsible for the performance of the trade sales representatives, and their performance should be monitored using measures such as number of calls made, number of new customers, increase in customers' orders and invoice value per trade call. Costs should be controlled by comparing actual costs against budgets, with expense items segregated into controllable and uncontrollable categories. Flexible budgets should be used to control costs. Various expense categories as a percentage of sales should be compared between outlets. Outlet managers are responsible for stock control, and therefore stock turnover ratios should be used to monitor stock levels.

(d) *Monthly report*

	Timber		Kitchen		Building supplies		Sawmill		Total	
	(B)[a] (£)	(A)[a] (£)	(B) (£)	(A) (£)	(B) (£)	(A) (£)	(B) (£)	(A) (£)	(B) (£)	(A) (£)
Sales:										
Retail	×	×	×	×	×	×	×	×	×	×
Trade	×	×	×	×	×	×	×	×	×	×
	×	×	×	×	×	×	×	×	×	×
Less cost of sales	×	×	×	×	×	×	×	×	×	×
Gross profit	×	×	×	×	×	×	×	×	×	×
Less other department costs	×	×	×	×	×	×	×	×	×	×
Departmental profit	×	×	×	×	×	×	×	×	×	×
Less other controllable overhead									×	×
Controllable profit									×	×
Less non-controllable expenses									×	×
Outlet net profit									×	×

Notes

[a] B = budget, A = actual.

Comments

(i) The statement should also show expenses and profits as a percentage of sales.

(ii) Some form of cumulative comparisons should be included or percentages under/over budget to date, but care should be taken to avoid information overload. One possibility is to report only those cumulative variances or percentages under/over budget which significantly deviate from the budget.

(iii) An additional supplementary statement should be given for cost control purposes. This statement should provide a detailed analysis by individual expenses for the 'other controllable overheads' in the above statement (e.g. vehicle running expenses and energy costs).

(iv) An additional statement should be presented giving details of key performance efficiency ratios. It might take the following format:

	Timber		Kitchen		Building supplies		Sawmill		Total	
	(B)	(A)	(B)	(A)	(B)	(A)	(B)	(A)	(B)	(A)
Gross profit per square metre										
Sales per square metre										
Stock turnover ratio										

(a)   *Financial statement for the year ended 31 May*   **Solution IM 23.6**

	Medical (£000)	Dietary (£000)	Fitness (£000)	Total (£000)
Budget				
Client fees	450.0	600.0	450.0	1500.0
Healthfood mark-up (cost × 110%)		120.0		120.0
Salaries	(240.0)	(336.0)	(225.0)	(801.0)
Budget gross margin	210.0	384.0	225.0	819.0
Variances:				
Fee income – favourable/(adverse)	(37.5)	(100.0)	275.0	137.5
Healthfood mark-up loss		(30.0)		(30.0)
Salaries increase	(15.0)		(75.0)	(90.0)
Extra fitness equipment			(80.0)	(80.0)
Actual gross margin	157.5	254.0	345.0	756.5
Less: company costs:				
Enquiry costs – budget				(240.0)
– variance				(60.0)
General fixed costs				(300.0)
Software systems cost				(50.0)
Actual net profit				106.5
Budget margin per consultation (£)	35.00	32.00	25.00	
Actual margin per consultation (£)	28.64	25.40	23.79	

(b) *Competitiveness*
- Compared with the budget new business enquiries have increased by 60% and the existing business enquiries have declined by 33%.
- The uptake from enquiries was : New business – Budget (30%) and Actual (25%) Repeat business – Budget (40%) and Actual (50%)
Repeat business represents a measure of customer loyalty and the figures are encouraging whereas there has been a decline in the take up rate for new business.
- Even though there has been a decline in the uptake from new enquiries the increased number of enquiries has resulted in new business exceeding budget by 5000 consultations in absolute terms. However, repeat business consultations are 2000 below budget arising from a decline in the number of client enquiries.
- Medical and dietary consultations are below budget by approximately 8% and 16% respectively and fitness has exceeded budget by approximately 60%.
- Ideally, competitiveness should also be measured against external benchmarks rather than the budget.

Flexibility

Flexibility relates to the responsiveness to customer enquiries. For example, the ability to cope with changes in volume, delivery speed and the employment of staff who are able to meet changing customer demands.

Outside medical specialists have been employed thus providing greater flexibility on the type of advice offered and additional fitness staff have been appointed to cope with the increasing volume. The measure of the uptake of new enquiries (see competitiveness above) can also provide an indication of the responsiveness to customer enquiries. It could be argued that the organization has failed to respond to a change in demand, given that dietary consultations have declined by 16%, but staff numbers have remained unchanged. The organization may, however, be anticipating an upsurge in future demand.

Resource consultation

The average consultations per consultant are budgeted at 1000 for each type of consultant. The actual figures and utilization percentages are:

full-time medical (900 – a 10% decline)
dietary (833 – a 16.7% decline)
fitness (1208 – a 21% increase)

The fact that full-time medical consultants appear to be under-utilized raises the question as to whether too many clients are being referred to outside specialists. This may be a consequence of pursuing the flexibility objective in the use of outside specialists to provide greater flexibility on the type of advice offered. It is also apparent from the above figures that dietary consultants are under-utilized whereas fitness consultants are over-utilized. Staffing levels should be investigated taking into account the long-term needs of the business.

Quality of service

The number of complaints has risen from 1% to 2% of all clients and should be investigated. The purchase of new equipment may be indicative of the provision of a better quality service. Quality may also have been improved by the better management of client appointments and records resulting from the introduction of new software systems.

Innovation

Innovation relates to the ability of the organization to provide new and better quality services. Here there is a need to ascertain whether the appointment of outside consultants has provided a wider range of medical services. Also the new computer software may have provided a better quality of service relating to scheduling appointments.

Cost estimation and cost behaviour

Solutions to Chapter 24 questions

See Chapter 24, in particular pages 1046–51 for the answer to the question.

Solution IM 24.1

See Chapter 24 for the answer to this question.

Solution IM 24.2

See 'Cost estimation when the learning effect is present' in Chapter 24 for an explanation of the learning curve. If the learning effect is ignored and standards are set when cumulative output is low then the resulting standards will ignore the cost reductions resulting from the learning curve. Consequently the standards will represent easily attainable standards, and favourable variances which are not due to improved efficiency will occur. Alternatively standards might be set at the steady-state level, and this will result in adverse variances throughout the 'start-up' phase. In order that meaningful targets can be set, it is essential that the learning-curve principles be applied when setting standards.

Solution IM 24.3

(a) For a detailed answer to this question see Chapter 24 (pages 1046–51). In particular, the answer should stress the following points:

    (i) The answer should describe the different techniques used to analyse fixed and variable costs, and illustrate the weaknesses of specific methods. For example, the high–low method only uses two extreme observations to derive the cost estimate equation.

    (ii) The presence of fixed cost step functions makes it difficult to derive a simple cost regression equation which will accurately predict the changes in costs arising from changes in volume.

    (iii) Changes in production technology and product mix will mean that equations derived from past cost observations will be inaccurate when predicting future cost–volume relationships.

    (iv) Costs may be influenced by other variables besides activity/volume. Therefore simple regression equations will yield inaccurate cost–volume relationships. Under these circumstances, multiple regression analysis should be used.

    (v) Choice of the wrong activity base – for example, different measures such as direct labour hours, machine hours or units of output can be used to measure activity. Inaccurate cost estimation equations will be derived if activity bases are used which are not highly correlated with total cost.

    (vi) An insufficient number of observations is used to derive the cost estimation equation.

(b) Analysis of costs into their fixed and variable elements is used by the management accountant in the following areas:

    (i) *Planning*: An analysis of costs into fixed and variable costs is necessary to predict costs for a range of output levels in order to determine the target activity level at which the budget should be set.

    (ii) *Control*: Flexible budgets are needed for cost control purposes.

    (iii) *Decision-making*: Analysis of fixed and variable costs is necessary in order to determine the incremental costs for various short-term decisions. For example, the incremental costs of making a component would be assessed where a company has spare capacity and wishes to evaluate a make or buy decision.

Solution IM 24.4

Solution IM 24.5

(a) The number of employees (X_2) is likely to be the least good estimator of total costs. There is a large decline in total costs in month 8 and a large increase in month 9. The number of employees remains unchanged whereas the other two independent variables decrease in month 8 and increase in month 9. Consequently changes in the number of employees will not predict changes in total costs. For example, the number of employees will remain unchanged when output and total costs decline because of sickness, idle time or holiday periods.

(b) (i) X_1 and Y

$$\beta = \frac{(373.5374 \times 10^6) - [12 \times (6300/12) \times 637\,200/12]}{(3.8582 \times 10^6) - [12(6300/12)^2]}$$

$$= 70.83$$

$$\alpha = (637\,200/12) - [70.83 \times (6300/12)]$$
$$= 15\,912.99$$

$$R^2 = \frac{(15\,912.99 \times 637\,200) + (70.83 \times 373.5374 \times 10^6) - [12(637\,200/12)^2]}{(36\,614.05 \times 10^6) - [12(637\,200/12)^2]}$$

$$= 0.994$$

(ii) X_3 and Y

$$\beta = \frac{(3692.2774 \times 10^6) - [12 \times (65\,220/12) \times 637\,200/12]}{(374.423 \times 10^6) - [12(65\,220/12)^2]}$$

$$= 11.48$$

$$\alpha = (637\,200/12) - [11.48 \times (65\,220/12)]$$
$$= -9305.51$$

$$R^2 = \frac{(-9305.51 \times 637\,200) + (11.48 \times 3692.2774 \times 10^6) - [12(637\,200/12)^2]}{(36\,614.05 \times 10^6) - [12(637\,200/12)^2]}$$

$$= 0.9467$$

(c) X_1 should be used, because this variable has the largest coefficient of determination. A coefficient of determination of 0.994 implies that 99.4% of the variation in total cost is explained by X_1 and 0.6% by other variables. Another reason for favouring X_1 is that X_3 is difficult to interpret and is of little practical significance because it implies that fixed costs are negative.

(d) (i) X_1

	X_1	Y
		(£)
Lowest activity	250	32 720
Highest activity	820	75 800
Difference	570	43 080

Unit variable cost = £75.58 (= £43 080/£570)
Fixed costs = £32 720 − (250 × £75.58) = £13 825
Therefore the equation is

$$Y = 13\,825 + 75.58X_1$$

(d) (ii) X_3

	X_3	Y
		(£)
Lowest activity	3200	32 720
Highest activity	7300	75 800
Difference	4100	43 080

Unit variable cost = £10.51 (= £43 080/4100)
Fixed costs = £32 720 − (3200 × £10.51) = −£912
Therefore the equation is

$$Y = -912 + 10.51X_3$$

The differences arise because the regression technique used in (b) makes use of all the data, whereas the high–low method uses only the extreme values, which might not be typical of normal operating conditions (e.g. economies or diseconomies of scale).

(e) See 'High–low method' and pages 1046–51 for criticisms of the high–low and least-squares regression methods. For a discussion of the advantages and problems of multiple regression see 'Multiple regression analysis' in Chapter 24. In view of the large coefficient of determination of variable X_1, there is a strong justification for relying on the least-squares method and not using multiple regression analysis.

Coefficient of determination

Solution IM 24.6

$$r^2 = \frac{(n\Sigma xy - \Sigma x \Sigma y)^2}{[n\Sigma x^2 - (\Sigma x)^2[n\Sigma y^2 - (\Sigma y)^2]}$$

Applying to x_1:

$$r^2 = \frac{[(10 \times 58\,040) - (113 \times 4550)]^2}{(10 \times 1533 - 12\,769)(10 \times 2\,451\,300 - 20\,702\,500)}$$

$$= \frac{66\,250^2}{2561 \times 3\,810\,500}$$

$$= \frac{4\,389\,062\,500}{9\,758\,690\,500}$$

$$= 0.4498$$

Applying to x^2:

$$r^2 = \frac{[(10 \times 121\,100) - (212 \times 4550)]^2}{(10 \times 6120 - 44\,944)(10 \times 2\,451\,300 - 20\,702\,500)}$$

$$= \frac{246\,400^2}{16\,256 \times 3\,810\,500}$$

$$= \frac{60\,712\,960\,000}{61\,943\,488\,000}$$

$$= 0.9801$$

Regional advertising has the higher coefficient of determination, and this implies that the level of sales varies more with regional advertising than local advertising. A coefficient of 0.9801 implies that 98.01% of the variation in total sales is explained by regional advertising.

Solution IM 24.7 (a)

	Units (packets)	Costs[a] (£)
Lowest activity	10 000	3 600
Highest activity	50 000	11 600
Increase	40 000	8 000

Variable cost per unit = £8000/40 000 = £0.20 per packet

Note
[a] £0.36 × 10 000 = £3600, £0.232 × 50 000 = £11 600.

Note that factory overhead costs are fixed for the factory as a whole, and are not included in the analysis.

(b) Price is assumed to be the dependent variable (y) and sales volume the independent variable (x). The price received by CBC is 50% of the retail price. Sales volume for each price level is calculated by dividing the revenue received by the price received by CBC:

(1) Retail price (£)	(2) Price received by CBC (£)	(3) Total revenue (£)	(4) Sales volume, (3)/(2) (£)
0.62	0.31	15 190	49 000
0.68	0.34	14 960	44 000
0.78	0.39	11 310	29 000
0.84	0.42	10 500	25 000
0.90	0.45	10 350	23 000
0.98	0.49	4 900	10 000

The regression equation can be derived from the following two equations (see (24.1) and (24.2) in Chapter 24) and solving for a and b:

$$\Sigma y = Na + b\Sigma x$$
$$\Sigma xy = a\Sigma x + b\Sigma x^2$$

x (000)	y (price in pence)	x^2	xy
49	31	2401	1519
44	34	1936	1496
29	39	841	1131
25	42	625	1050
23	45	529	1035
10	49	100	490
180	240	6432	6721

Inserting the above computations into the formulae:

$$240 = 6a + 180b \tag{1}$$

$$6721 = 180a + 6432b \tag{2}$$

Multiplying equation (1) by 30 gives:

$$7200 = 180a + 5400b \tag{3}$$

Subtracting equation (3) from equation (2) gives:

$$-479 = 1032b$$
$$b = -0.4641$$

Substituting the value for b in one of the above equations gives a value of 53.9244 for a.

Alternatively the formula outlined in the question could have been used:

$$b = \frac{n\Sigma xy - \Sigma x\Sigma y}{n\Sigma x^2 - (\Sigma x)^2}$$

$$= \frac{6(6721) - 180(240)}{6(6432) - (180)^2} = -0.4641$$

$$y = a + bx$$
$$a = \bar{y} - b\bar{x}$$
$$a = (240/6) - [-0.4641 \times (180/6)] = 53.923$$

Therefore $y = 54 - 0.46x$ (i.e. p(price) $= 54 - 0.46Q$)
Note that Q = quantity demanded, in thousands.

(c) *Optimum price*
Optimum output is where MC = MR:

$$p = 54 - 0.46Q$$
$$TR = 54Q - 0.46Q^2$$
$$MR = 54 - 0.92Q$$
$$MC = 20$$

Optimal output is where $20 = 54 - 0.92Q$
$$Q = 36.96$$
Optimum price $(p) = 54 - 0.46(36.96) = 37$ pence per packet

Sensitivity of solution of changes in price
It is assumed that this part of the question refers to how sensitive profit is to changes in prices with other factors (e.g. variable costs and demand function held constant).

$$\text{Contribution } (c) = \text{total revenue} - \text{total variable cost}$$
$$TR = \text{price } (p) \times \text{quantity } (Q) = Qp$$
$$p = 54 - 0.46Q$$

$$Q = \frac{54 - p}{0.46} = 117.39 - 2.174p$$

$$Qp = 117.39p - 2.174p^2$$
$$\text{Total VC} = 20Q = 20(117.39 - 2.174p) = 2348 - 43.48p$$
$$\text{Contribution } (TR - TC) = 117.39p - 2.174p^2 - (2348 - 43.48p)$$
$$= 160.87p - 2.174p^2 - 2348$$

The relationship between the variation in contribution (c) with variations in selling price is:

$$\frac{dc}{dp} = 160.87 - 4.348p$$

(d) The answer should stress that direct costs can be obtained without too much difficulty using engineering methods outlined in Chapter 24. It is important that appropriate activity bases (cost drivers) be selected which adequately explain variations in costs when establishing variable overhead rates. Unit product costs can then be calculated by multiplying cost drivers by the appropriate variable overhead rates. For a discussion of the problems involved in determining variable overhead rates see pages 1046–51 in Chapter 24. The major problems faced in deriving appropriate unit costs relate to tracing *fixed* overheads to products. Determining appropriate cost drivers for some fixed overhead costs can be difficult and time-consuming. Assumptions must also be made concerning the level of future volume in order to determine fixed overhead rates. Consequently it is necessary to predict demand prior to selling the new product. Other problems include predicting future inflation rates, learning effects as the workforce become more familiar with producing the product, and the effect on the economies of scale if more intensive use is made of existing resources. For a more detailed explanation of some of the above items see 'Limitations of cost-plus pricing' in Chapter 11.

Solution IM 24.8 (b)

(1) Units produced	(2) Total production time (hours)	(3) Average production time per unit in successive lots (hours)	(4) Cumulative average production time per unit (hours)	(5) Percentage decline in (4) (%)
1	1 000	1000	1000	0
2	1 800	800	900	10
4	3 240	720	810	10
8	5 832	648	729	10
16	10 498	583	656	10

Solution IM 24.9 (a)

	6 months (£)	12 months (£)
Direct materials[a]	271 000	514 000
Direct labour[b]	191 340	315 423
Variable overhead[c]	76 536	126 169
Directly attributable fixed costs	90 000	180 000
Total costs	628 876	1 135 592
Sales revenues	720 000	1 260 000
Net cash inflow[d]	91 124	124 408
Required return (£75 000 + 33.33%)	100 000	
(£75 000 + 50%)		112 500
Shortfall	8 876	

The target return is achieved over the 12 month life cycle but not over the 6 month life cycle

Notes

[a] (200 batches at £500) + (200 batches at £450) + (200 batches at £405) = £271 000 for 6 months, £271 000 + (600 × £405) = £514 000 for 12 months

[b] For the first 6 months: $y = ax^b = £2500 \times 600^{-0.3219} = £318.90$
  Total cost = £318.90 × 600 batches = £191 340

For the first 7 months: $y = ax^b = £2500 \times 700^{-0.3219} = £303.461$
  Total costs = £303.461 × 700 batches = £212 423
All batches after the first 700 have the same labour cost of the 700th batch

For 699 batches: $y = ax^b = £2500 \times 699^{-0.3219} = £303.601$
  Total cost = £303.601 × 699 batches = £212 217
Therefore the cost of the 700th batch = £212 423 – £212 217 = £206
Total costs for 12 months = £212 423 + (£206 × 500) = £315 423

[c] Variable overheads vary with direct labour hours at £2 per direct labour which is equivalent to 40% of the direct labour cost.

[d] For 6 months: 100 batches per month = 600 batches at £1200 per batch
  For 12 months: 100 batches per month = 1200 batches at £1050 per batch

(b) The maximum labour and variable overhead cost of £259 000 given in the question can also be derived from part (a):
Direct labour cost (£191 340) + variable overheads (£76 536) – shortfall (£8876) = £259 000
Maximum direct labour costs = £259 000/1.4 = £185 000 (Variable overhead costs are 40% of direct labour costs)
Required average direct labour cost for a cumulative output of 600 batches = £308.333 (£185 000/600)

$$y = ax^b$$
so that, £308.333 = a × 600$^{-0.3219}$
£308.333 = 0.1276a
a = £2416 giving initial labour hours of 483.2 (£2416/£5)

(c)(i) Product X could be viewed as an example of target costing because of the following:
  (i) The market has been identified in terms of a target selling price and demand.
  (ii) A required profit margin over the whole life of the project has been established.
  (iii) A target cost to achieve the required six month profit has been established.

(c)(ii) The following actions could be considered:
  (i) Investigate how the learning rate can be improved. For example, changes in production methods or additional training could be considered.
  (ii) Investigate ways of reducing the material losses that occur in the batches prior to the steady state being reached.
  (iii) Ascertain the content of the directly attributable fixed costs and investigate ways of eliminating any non-value-added elements;
  (iv) Investigate whether direct materials can be sourced more cheaply.

(c)(iii) All of the items included in the evaluation are subject to uncertainty. In particular, sales demand may be less than anticipated or the learning rate might not be achieved.

(a) The first batch was completed in 120 hours (£600/£5). Applying a 90% learning curve the average time per batch is calculated as follows.

Number of batches	Average time per batch (hours)	Total time per batch (hours)
1	120	120
2	108 (0.9 × 120)	216
4	97.2 (0.9 × 108)	388.8

Hours required for batch 2 = 96 hours (216 − 120).
Hours required for batches 3 and 4 = 172.8 hours (388.8 − 216).

(b) The data given in the question have been derived from the learning-curve formula $Y_x = ax^b$ where Y_x is the cumulative average time required to produce x units, a is the time required to complete the first unit of output and x is the number of units of output under consideration. The exponent b is defined as the ratio of the logarithm of the learning-curve improvement rate (0.9 for a 90% learning curve) divided by the logarithm of 2.

$$\text{Therefore } b = \frac{\log 0.9}{\log 2} = \frac{-0.105}{0.6931} = -0.152$$

The average time taken to produce 15 and 120 batches can be calculated as follows.

$$Y_{15} = 120 \times 15^{-0.152} = 79.51 \text{ hours}$$
$$Y_{120} = 120 \times 120^{-0.152} = 57.96 \text{ hours}$$

The above values are equal to the data given in the question.

Calculation of labour cost
Cumulative production is 30 batches at the end of the fourth quarter, 75 batches at the end of the first quarter and 120 batches at the end of the second quarter.

Time for the first 30 batches = 2146.8 hours (30 × 71.56 hours)
Time for the first 75 batches = 4668.75 hours (75 × 62.25 hours)
Time required for 45 batches   2521.95 hours

Labour cost for quarter 1 = £12 610 (2521.95 hours × £5)

Time for first 75 batches	4668.75 hours (75 × 62.25 hours)
Time for first 120 batches	6955.20 hours (120 × 57.96 hours)
Time required for 45 batches (quarter 2)	2286.45 hours

Labour cost for quarter 2 = £11 432 (2286.45 hours × £5)

Calculation of material costs

Quarter 4:

Units required for first 20 batches (200 × 200)	4000
Units required for next 10 batches (0.98 × 200 × 10)	1960
Total units required	5960

Quarter 1:

Units required for first 10 batches (0.98 × 200 × 10)	1960
Units required for next 20 batches (0.96 × 200 × 20)	3840
Units required for final 15 batches (0.94 × 200 × 15)	2820
Total units required	8620

Quarter 2:

Units required for first 5 batches (0.94 × 200 × 5)	940
Units required for next 20 batches (0.92 × 200 × 20)	3680
Units required for next 20 batches (0.90 × 200 × 20)	3600
Total units required	8220

	(£)
Material costs:	
Quarter 1 (8620 × £1.80)	15 516
Quarter 2 (8220 × £1.80)	14 796
Stockholding costs: Quarter 1 [(8620/2) × £0.30]	1 293
Quarter 2 [(8220/2) × £0.30]	1 233

Average stocks = total usage/2

Budget for Quarters 1 and 2

	Quarter 1 (£)	Quarter 2 (£)
Sales revenue (45 × £1200)	54 000	54 000
Less: Variable costs:		
Direct materials	(15 516)	(14 796)
Stockholding costs	(1 293)	(1 233)
Labour costs	(12 610)	(11 432)
Variable overhead (150% of direct labour)	(18 915)	(17 148)
Contribution	5 666	9 391

(c) (i)

	Quarter 1 (£)	Quarter 2 (£)
Increase in purchase cost	862 (8620 × £0.10)	1644 (8200 × £0.20)
Holding costs avoided	1293	1233
(Increase)/Decrease in costs	431	(411)

On the basis of the above information the just-in-time delivery alternative would be acceptable for quarter 1 but not acceptable for quarter 2.

(ii) Other factors that should be considered are any further benefits arising from eliminating raw material stocks. Examples include cash flow savings or potential revenues from sub-letting released storage space, reduced obsolescence and insurance costs, and reduced materials handling costs. However, the company will be dependent on the reliability of the supplier in terms of the delivery if buffer stocks are not held. Any delays in delivery, changes in demand or process losses may result in stockouts and lost sales. The probability of such events occurring should be carefully checked before adopting the just-in-time delivery alternative.

(d) The first part of the answer to part (b), which describes the learning-curve formula, can be used to answer this question. In addition, the answer should explain, or illustrate, the application of the formula for producing 12 batches in quarter 3.

$Y_{132} = 120 \times 132^{-0.152} = 57.13$ average hours per batch
$Y_{120} = 120 \times 120^{-0.152} = 57.92$ average hours per batch

Total hours required for 132 batches = 7541 hours (132×57.13 hours)
Total hours required for 120 batches = 6950 hours (120×57.92 hours)
Incremental hours for 12 batches   591 hours

Labour cost = £2955 (591 hours $\times$ £5)

Quantitative models for the planning and control of inventories

Solutions to Chapter 25 questions

Solution IM 25.1

EOQ = $\sqrt{2DO/H}$
Demand (D) = 90 800 units
Ordering cost (O) = £5910/30 × 1.02 = £200.94 per order
Holding cost (H) = £20 per unit × 15% = £3 per unit

$$EOQ = \sqrt{\frac{2 \times 200.94 \times 90\,800}{3}} = 3448 \text{ units (349 boxes)}$$

$$\text{Orders per year} = \frac{9080 \text{ boxes annual demand}}{349 \text{ boxes per order}} = 26 \text{ orders}$$

Order frequency = Every 2 weeks (52 weeks/26 orders per year)

Solution IM 25.2

(a) (i) Total cost of ordering:

$$\frac{D}{Q} \times C_o$$

(ii) Total cost of storage:

$$\frac{Q}{2} \times p \times C_h$$

(iii) Total cost of ordering and storage:

$$\frac{D}{Q} \times C_o + \frac{Q}{2} \times p \times C_h$$

(iv) Optimal re-order quantity (RoQ)

$$\sqrt{\frac{2 \times C_o \times D}{C_h}}$$

(b) For a discussion of the practical limitations you should refer to 'Assumptions of the EOQ formula' in Chapter 25. The answer should also draw attention to the fact that significant changes in any of the variables will have little effect on the EOQ (see 'Effect of approximations' in Chapter 25).

(c)

$$EOQ = \sqrt{\frac{2 \times 2000 \times £30}{20\% \times £70}} = 93 \text{ units}$$

(d) The answer to this question should describe how a JIT purchasing philosophy can reduce the need to carry stocks. For an explanation of this see 'Just-in-time purchasing' in Chapter 25.

(a)

$$EOQ = \sqrt{\left(\frac{2DO}{H}\right)}$$

where D = total demand for period = 12 500 (3125 × 4)
O = ordering cost per batch = £10
H = holding cost per unit in stock for one year = £1

Therefore

$$EOQ = \sqrt{\left(\frac{(2 \times 12\,500 \times 10)}{1}\right)} = 500$$

Annual ordering cost = number of orders × £10

$$= \frac{12\,500}{500} \times £10$$

$$= \underline{\underline{£250}}$$

Annual cost of holding stock = average stock × £1

$$= \frac{500}{2} \times £1$$

$$= \underline{\underline{£250}}$$

Therefore minimum annual cost = £500 (£250 + £250)

(b) *Quarterly sales of 781 units*
Total demand for period = 3124 (781 × 4)

Therefore

$$EOQ = \sqrt{\left(\frac{2 \times 3124 \times 10}{1}\right)} = 250$$

Quarterly sales of 6250 units
Total demand for period = 25 000 (6250 × 4)

Therefore

$$EOQ = \sqrt{\left(\frac{2 \times 25\,000 \times 10}{1}\right)} = 707$$

The EOQ formula shows that the optimum batch size varies in proportion to the square root of total demand (sales volume). Therefore when quarterly sales are 781 units, sales volume changes by a factor of $\frac{1}{4}$ compared with (i). Consequently the optimal batch size changes by a factor of $\frac{1}{2}$ ($\frac{1}{2} = \sqrt{\frac{1}{4}}$)

When quarterly sales are 6250 units, sales volume increases by a factor of 2. Therefore the optimal batch size increases by a factor of $\sqrt{2} = 1.414$ approximately.

(c) For an explanation of the economic batch size $\sqrt{(2DO/H)}$ see 'Determining the economic order quantity' in Chapter 25.

Solution IM 25.4

The cost of placing an order when the component is purchased is not given. This can be obtained from the EOQ formula:

$$Q = \sqrt{\left(\frac{2DO}{H}\right)}$$

$$Q^2 = \frac{2DO}{H}$$

$$HQ^2 = 2DO$$

$$O = \frac{HQ^2}{2D}$$

$$= \frac{0.25(2000)^2}{2(20\,000)}$$

$$= £25 \text{ (cost of placing an order).}$$

Average stock level $= $ Minimum stock level $+ \frac{1}{2}$ EOQ
$= 400 + \frac{1}{2}(2000) = 1400$ units

Comparison of annual costs

	Make		Buy	
		(£)		(£)
Purchase cost			20 000 × £9 =	£180 000
Storage	1400 × £0.25 =	350		
Ordering costs	10 × £25 =	250		
Direct labour	20 000 × £6	= 120 000		
Direct material	20 000 × £2	= 40 000		
Leasing		= 2 400		
		163 000		180 000

It is cheaper to make the component unless the released facilities have some alternative use. If this opportunity cost is greater than £17 000 per annum then it will be cheaper to buy the component. Note that direct labour is assumed to be a variable cost. The qualitative factors arising from the direct labour force being made redundant should be considered if the component is not made by the company.

Solution IM 25.5

(a) For a definition of variable, semi-variable and fixed costs see Chapter 2. Examples of each cost are as follows.
Variable: The purchase price of raw materials, the cost of placing an order at £50 per order and the cost of holding stocks at £0.40 per unit per annum are all variable.
Semi-variable: Ordering costs and stock holding costs are both semi-variable since they consist of a variable and fixed portion.
Fixed: The £40 element of placing an order is a fixed cost. These costs will consist of staff involved in placing and handling orders, and their salaries will be unaffected by the number of orders placed.

(b) Annual usage is 6000 kg (12 000 × 0.4 × 10/8). It is assumed that the apportioned order costs and the £0.50 long-term holding costs are not relevant costs in the short term for establishing the economic order quantity. Because purchase costs are not constant per unit, it is not possible to use the EOQ formula.

QUANTITATIVE MODELS FOR THE PLANNING AND CONTROL OF INVENTORIES

Annual costs

Order quantity	Purchase cost of 6000 kg p.a. (£)	Order costs at £50 (£)	Holding costs at £0.40 per unit (W1) (£)	Total costs (£)
1000	6000	300 (6 × £50)	200	6500
1500	5880	200 (4 × £50)	300	6380
2000	5790	150 (3 × £50)	400	6340
2500	5700	120 (2.4 × £50)	500	6320
3000	5640	100 (2 × £50)	600	6340
3500	5640	86 (1.71 × £50)	700	6426

Working

(W1) Assuming constant usage, the relevant average stock is one half of the order quantity. The safety stock of 250 units will be the same for all order quantities, and is therefore not included in the analysis. The order quantity which minimizes the costs in the short term is 2500 kg.

(a) EOQ = $\sqrt{2DO/H}$

where D = Demand for the period (20 000 units)

O = Ordering cost (£31.25 actual and £120 proposed)

H = Holding cost per unit (20% of £6.25 = £1.25 actual and 20% of £6 = £1.20 proposed)

The current EOQ is $\sqrt{\dfrac{2 \times 20\,000 \times £31.25}{£1.25}}$ = 1000 units per order

The EOQ after the change will be $\sqrt{\dfrac{2 \times 20\,000 \times £120}{£1.20}}$ = 2000 units

The EOQ will thus increase by 1000 units and the number of orders required will be reduced from 20 to 10.

(b) The present ordering and holding costs are:

	£
Ordering costs (20 orders at £31.25)	625
Holding costs (1000/2 × £1.25)	625
	1250

The ordering costs for the proposed method are:

Ordering costs (10 orders at £120)	1200
Holding costs (2000/2 × £1.20)	1200
	2400

The additional holding and ordering costs are £1150 (£2400 – £1250) but this is offset by the quantity discounts of 20 000 units £0.25 = £5000. Hence the overall annual savings are £3850 (5000 – £1250). The annual after tax cash flows are:

Year	0 (£)	1 (£)	2 (£)	3 onwards (£)
Outlay	(10 000)			
Tax saving		3300		
Annual cost savings		3850	3850	3850
Tax on cost savings			(1271)	(1271)
Net cash flow	(10 000)	7150	2579	2579

The net cash inflows after 2 years amount to £9729 and so the payback period is just over 2 years. If the cash flows were to accrue evenly throughout the years the precise payback period would be:

2 years + (£10 000 – £9729)/£2579 = 2.11 years. A payback period of 2 years would suggest the new policy is likely to be beneficial but ideally the discounted payback period should be calculated to ascertain how long the savings should continue for the new policy to be justifiable.

(c) See 'Payback method' in Chapter 13 for the answer to this question.

Solution IM 25.7

(a) The hourly opportunity cost of checking an order is £9 (£5 labour cost plus £4 contribution). Note that the employees are paid irrespective of output or the activities on which they are engaged, and opportunity cost is thus represented by lost cash inflows before the labour cost is deducted. The relevant ordering cost for the EOQ model is therefore £75 [£30 + (£5 × 9)].

$$EOQ = \sqrt{\left(\frac{2 \times £75 \times 4000}{£15}\right)} = 200 \text{ units}$$

(b) The savings available if the firm purchases in batches of 400 units are:

	(£)
Saving in purchase price (4000 × £0.24)	960
Saving in ordering cost {[(4000/200) − (4000/400)] × £75}	750
Total savings	1710

The additional holding cost if the larger order is purchased is:

$$[(400 - 200)/2] \times £15 = £1500$$

The savings exceed the additional costs by £210. Therefore the company should accept the discount.

(c) See 'Uncertainty and safety stocks' and 'The use of probability theory for determining safety stocks' in Chapter 25 for the answer to this question.

Solution IM 25.8

(a) *Preliminary calculations*

D (total demand for period) = 24 000 units
O (ordering cost per order) = (£1000 fixed shipment charge per order
 + £500 administration costs)
H (holding cost per unit) = £18 [£10 + warehouse space
 opportunity cost (2 × £4)]

Note that the acquisition cost and delivery charge per unit remain unchanged irrespective of the order quantity. Therefore they are not relevant to the EOQ model.

Calculation of EOQ

$$EOQ = \sqrt{\left(\frac{2DO}{H}\right)}$$

$$= \sqrt{\left(\frac{2 \times 24\,000 \times 1500}{18}\right)}$$

$$= \underline{\underline{2000}}$$

The annual cost of purchasing, ordering and holding Lakers based on an EOQ of 2000 units is:

holding cost	+ ordering cost	+ purchase cost	+ base stock cost
$\frac{2000}{2}$(£18)	+ $\frac{24\,000}{2000}$(£1500)	+ 24 000(£15.50)	+ 1000(£18)
= £18 000	+ £18 000	+ £372 000	+ £18 000
= £426 000			

	(£)
Annual revenue	480 000 (24 000 × £20)
Annual costs	426 000
Profit from purchase and sale of Lakers	54 000

(b) *Purchase price of £15.25 + £0. 50 delivery cost*: This purchase price should not be considered, since the EOQ would still be 2000 units and for this order quantity the purchase price will be in excess of that of May Ltd.

Purchase price of £14.50 + £0.50 delivery cost: The annual cost if the firm purchases the minimum batch size of 3000 units necessary to obtain the cheaper purchase price is as follows:

$$\text{holding cost} + \text{ordering cost} + \text{purchase cost} + \text{base stock cost}$$
$$\frac{3000}{2}(\pounds18) \quad + \frac{24\,000}{3000}(\pounds1500) \qquad + 24\,000(\pounds15) \ + 1000(\pounds18)$$
$$= \ \pounds27\,000 \qquad + \pounds12\,000 \qquad\qquad + \pounds360\,000 \qquad + \pounds18\,000$$
$$= \ \pounds417\,000$$

Purchase price of £14.25 + £0.50 delivery cost: The annual cost if the firm purchases the minimum batch size to obtain the £14.25 purchase price is as follows:

$$\text{holding cost} + \text{ordering cost} + \text{purchase cost} + \text{base stock cost}$$
$$\frac{5000}{2}(\pounds18) \quad + \frac{24\,000}{5000}(\pounds1500) + 24\,000(\pounds14.75) + 1000(\pounds18)$$
$$= \ \pounds45\,000 \qquad + \pounds7200 \qquad\quad + \pounds354\,000 \qquad + \pounds18\,000$$
$$= \ \pounds424\,200$$

The annual costs are:

	(£)
Purchase at £15 from May Ltd	426 000
Purchase at £14.50 from Richardson Ltd	417 000
Purchase at £14.25 from Richardson Ltd	424 200

Therefore batches of 3000 units at £14.50 per unit should be obtained from Richardson Ltd.

(c) The limitations of the above analysis are as follows.
  (i) The model assumes that annual demand can be predicted and constant usage applies throughout the year.
  (ii) The relevant order cost (incremental cost) per unit is extremely difficult to estimate. In practice most of the order costs are likely to be semi-fixed.
  (iii) The costs of placing an order are assumed to be constant and not to vary with the size of the order.
  (iv) Some of the holding costs are extremely difficult to estimate. Examples include materials handling and obsolescence.

For a discussion of the above points see 'Assumptions of the EOQ formula' in Chapter 25. It should be noted that the EOQ model is very insensitive to errors in predictions.

Solution IM 25.9

(a)

(i) $\text{EOQ} = \sqrt{\left(\dfrac{2 \times £48.46 \times 4095}{4}\right)} = 315$

(ii) Order frequency $= \dfrac{4095}{315} = 13$ times per annum

(iii) Total annual procurement costs $= \dfrac{C_s d}{Q}$

$$= \frac{£48.46 \times 4095}{315} = £630$$

Total annual holding costs $= \frac{1}{2} \times \text{EOQ} \times C_h$

$$= \frac{315}{2} \times £4 = £630$$

(b) (i) The EOQ model is based on an annual demand of 4095 units. Demand per four-week period is assumed to be constant at 315 units. If demand is less than 315 units in a four-week period, there will always be sufficient stock in hand to meet demand. However, if demand is in excess of 315 units, stockouts will occur. Possible corrective actions would be:
1. To maintain a level of safety stocks in excess of the expected use during the lead time in order to provide a cushion against running out of stocks.
2. To continue to order the EOQ, but vary the re-order point based on the latest estimate of the trend in sales demand.
3. To adjust the EOQ according to the latest estimate in sales demand.

(ii) If the lead time is certain at three weeks, the order should be placed when stocks fall to 237 units [(315/4) × 3]. With an EOQ of 315 units and an annual demand of 4095 units, 13 orders will be placed at four-weekly intervals. However, with a lead time of three weeks, an order will be placed one week after the first delivery, when stocks will have fallen to 237 units (315 units EOQ less one week's usage). The order will then be repeated at three-weekly intervals. Should the lead time turn out to be five weeks instead of three then an order will be placed when stock reaches the re-order level of 237 units, but demand during the lead time will be 394 units [(315 units/4) × 5 weeks]. Therefore two weeks' sales demand of 157 units will not be met. The normal way of overcoming uncertain lead times is to maintain a level of safety stocks to cover sales demand during the delivery delay.

(c) For the answer to this question see 'Uncertainty and safety stocks' and 'The use of probability theory for determining safety stocks' in Chapter 25. In particular, the answer should stress that re-order level is determined by adding safety stocks to the expected usage during normal delivery time. If normal lead time is three weeks then the re-order point will be 237 units (three weeks' normal usage) plus a safety stock. If the objective is to reduce the probability of a stockout to zero then two weeks' safety stock consisting of 157 units should be maintained [(315 units/4) × 2 weeks]. Therefore the re-order point will be 394 units (237 units + 157 units). At this point a purchase order will be placed for the EOQ of 315 units and, under normal conditions, this order will be delivered when the stock has fallen to the safety level of 157 units. At this point in time, stocks will be at a maximum level of 472 units (315 + 157 units). If there was a delay in the lead time from three to five weeks then usage during this period would be 394 units, and therefore a stockout would be avoided. For an illustration of a graph see the lower section of Figure 25.3 in Chapter 25. A re-order point of 394 units and safety stock of 157 should be entered on the horizontal axis. Demands of 237, 315 and 394 units for lead times of 3, 4 and 5 weeks should then be plotted.

(a) Annual purchases are £6 m divided equally between three suppliers. Therefore £2 m is purchased from each supplier consisting of 100 000 units at £20 each.

$$EOQ = \sqrt{\left(\frac{2DO}{H}\right)}$$

$$= \left(\frac{2 \times 100\,000 \times 100}{2}\right) = 3162 \text{ units from each supplier}$$

Note that the variable cost per unit of £0.10 is the same irrespective of the number of orders placed and is not relevant in determining the EOQ.

(b) The expected value of demand per month is 25 000 units (i.e. the sum of each potential outcome multiplied by the probability factor). Assuming no safety stocks and a lead time of 1 month the re-order level will be 25 000 units (25 000 units × 1 month). Safety stocks are required to cover monthly demands of 27 000 or 30 000 units as all other levels of demand can be satisfied from a re-order point of 25 000 units.

The expected costs for various levels of safety stock are as follows.

Safety stock (units)	Re-order point (units)	Stockout per order (units)	Stockout per year[a] (units)	Probability of stockout	Expected stockout cost[b] (£)	Holding cost[c] (£)	Total expected cost (£)
5000	30 000	0	0	0	0	10 000	10 000
2000	27 000	3000	94 860	0.12	4553	4 000	8 553
0	25 000	2000	63 240	0.20	(5059)	0	
		5000	158 100	0.12	(7589)		12 648

Notes
[a] During the year 31.62 orders will be made from each supplier (100 000 units annual demand/EOQ of 3162 units). Stockout per year in units is calculated by multiplying the stockout per order by 31.62 orders.

[b] Expected stockout costs = annual stockout in units × probability of stockout × £0.40

[c] Holding cost = safety stock × £2

Expected costs are minimized when 2000 units of safety stock are held.

(c) Total relevant costs for three suppliers are:

	(£)
Holding costs (£2 × EOQ/2 = £2 × 3162/2)	3 162
Fixed ordering costs (100 000/3162 × £100)	3 162
Relevant costs per supplier	6 324
Relevant costs for three suppliers	18 972

Total relevant costs for one supplier:

$$EOQ = \sqrt{\left(\frac{2 \times 100 \times 300\,000}{2}\right)} = 5477 \text{ units}$$

	(£)
Holding costs (£2 × 5477/2)	5 477
Fixed ordering costs (300 000/5477 × £100)	5 477
	10 954

Annual relevant costs are £8018 lower when only one supplier is used. Note that the above analysis ignores variable ordering costs since they are common to both alternatives.

(d) Advantages of JIT include:
  (i) large reduction in stockholding costs;
  (ii) quicker response to customer demand via closer liaison with suppliers;
  (iii) risk of obsolete stocks being passed on to suppliers;
  (iv) benefits arising from increased storage space that is no longer required.
  Disadvantages of JIT include:
  (i) possible occurrence of major production stoppages or stockouts if suppliers do not meet the scheduled delivery dates;
  (ii) possible increase in suppliers' prices to recoup the increased stockholding and ordering costs. The net effect is that stock management costs are merely transferred to suppliers with no overall reduction in costs.

The company should implement JIT if the incremental benefits (reduced stock management costs plus other qualitative benefits) exceed the increased purchase costs. However, a crucial factor in the decision will be the reliability of Mexet's suppliers.

Solution IM 25.11

(a) (i) *Annual cost if plant is retained*
Variable cost per 1000 litres (£840 000/3 m × 1000) = £280

		(£)
Holding costs per 1000 litres:	Storage cost	20
	Evaporation cost (5% × £280)	14
	Cost of capital (15% × £280)	42
		76

		(£)
Total annual cost:	Production costs (£840 000 + £330 000)	1 170 000
	Storage costs (60 000/1000 × £76)	4 560
		1 174 560

The opportunity cost on the lost sale proceeds should be added to the above cost. This item is considered in more detail in (iii) below.

(ii) *Annual cost if plant is sold and materials purchased externally*
Purchase price per litre (£370 + £30)/1000 = £0.40

		(£)
Holding cost per 1000 litres:	Storage cost	20
	Evaporation cost (5% × £0.40 × 1000)	20
	Cost of capital (15% × £0.40 × 1000)	60
		100

Holding cost per litre (£100/1000) = £0.10

In order to calculate total annual cost, it is necessary to establish the EOQ:

$$EOQ = \sqrt{(2DO/H)} = \sqrt{[(2 \times 3\,m \times £60)/0.10]} = 60\,000$$

		(£)
Total annual cost:	Purchase price (3 m × £0.40)	1 200 000
	Storage cost ($\frac{1}{2}$ × 60 000 × £0.10)	3 000
	Ordering costs [(3 m/60 000) × £60]	3 000
	Cost of holding safety stocks	
	(100 000 × £0.10)	10 000
	Administration costs	15 000
		1 231 000

(iii) *Comments and interpretation*

The above figures show that the annual cost of purchasing externally is £56 440 greater than the cost of manufacturing the materials. However, this analysis ignores the opportunity cost from the alternative use of the plant. The question states that the site would have to be sold for £400 000 or retained 'for the time being'. This implies that the alternative is to sell the plant now or at some future point in time. The analysis requires details of the point in time when the plant would be sold. If the alternative is to sell the plant in one year's time, the present value of the sale proceeds will be £347 826 compared with £400 000 if the materials were purchased and the plant closed down immediately. The opportunity cost of operating the plant for one more year would be £52 174. If this opportunity cost is incorporated into the analysis, there is a saving of £4266 (£56 440 − £52 174). Given the small value of the savings, the decision is likely to depend on qualitative factors such as the reliability of the supplier, future purchasing costs and the competitiveness of the market for the materials. If the market is not competitive, Rainbow Ltd will have little bargaining power when negotiating a new purchasing contract.

(b) (i) It is assumed that demand during the lead time can only be 10 000 or 14 000 units per day. The possible demand levels during the lead time are:

Lead time demand (litres)	Probability	Expected value
50 000	$0.5 \times 0.8 = 0.4$	20 000
70 000	$0.5 \times 0.8 = 0.4$	28 000
100 000	$0.5 \times 0.2 = 0.1$	10 000
140 000	$0.5 \times 0.2 = 0.1$	14 000
		72 000

This would suggest a re-order point of 172 000 litres (expected usage + safety stock). Maximum demand would be 140 000 units and the probability of a stockout would be zero. It is assumed that the 100 000 safety stock is intended to represent the re-order point (consisting of 72 000 expected usage and 28 000 safety stocks). The probability of a stockout (i.e. demand being greater than 100 000 units) is 0.1. During the period, 50 orders would be placed (3 m demand/60 000 EOQ), and this would result in the expected value of annual stockouts in litres being:

$$0.1 \times (140\,000 - 100\,000) \times 50 \text{ orders} = 200\,000 \text{ litres}$$

(ii) In order to determine whether it is worthwhile increasing the re-order level, it is necessary to compare the annual cost of holding the safety stocks plus the stockout costs for the re-order points prescribed in the question.

Re-order level of 100 000 litres (28 000 litres safety stock)
Let S = stockout cost per litre

Cost of holding safety stocks (28 000 × £0.10)	£2 800
Expected cost of stockout	200 000S

Re-order level of 120 000 litres (48 000 litres safety stock)

Cost of holding safety stocks (48 000 × £0.10)	£4 800
Expected value of annual stockouts in litres:	
$0.1 \times (140\,000 - 120\,000) \times 50$ orders	100 000 litres
Expected stockout cost	100 000S

It would be appropriate to increase the re-order level to 120 000 litres, where:

$$£4800 + 100\,000S < £2800 + 200\,000S$$
$$S < £0.02 \text{ per litre}$$

(c) The requirements for the successful adoption of a JIT inventory policy are:
  (i) Production of a small range of stable and high-volume products.
  (ii) Rearrangement of factory floor away from batch production.
  (iii) Close co-operation with suppliers.
  (iv) Reduction in the number of suppliers.
  (v) Negotiation of purchasing contracts with suppliers who are in close proximity.
  (vi) More frequent deliveries and smaller re-order quantities.
  (vii) A strong emphasis on training so that the employees fully understand the JIT philosophy and are committed to operating JIT techniques.
      The benefits of JIT are:
  (i) Substantial savings in stockholding costs.
  (ii) Elimination of waste.
  (iii) Savings in factory and warehouse space.
  (iv) Reduction in obsolete stocks.
  (v) Reduction in paperwork arising from the issue of blanket purchase orders.
      The costs of operating a JIT policy include:
  (i) Investment costs in rearranging plant layout and goods inwards facilities.
  (ii) Increased risk due to greater probability of stockout costs arising from strikes or other unforeseen circumstances which restrict production or supplies.

For a more detailed answer to this question see 'JIT purchasing and manufacturing' in Chapters 22–5.

The application of linear programming to management accounting

Solutions to Chapter 26 questions

(a)

	Pixie (£)	Elf (£)	Queen (£)	King (£)
Selling price	111	98	122	326
Direct material	(25)	(35)	(22)	(25)
Variable overhead	(17)	(18)	(15)	(16)
Direct labour	(40)	(30)	(75)	(175)
Contribution	29	15	10	110
Type 1 labour hours	8	6		
Contribution per Type 1 labour hour	£3.63	£2.50		
Ranking	1	2		

In order to maximize the contribution from Type 1 labour the company should maximize the output of Pixie by producing 1000 units (8000 hours/8 units per hour). There are two production constraints applying to Queen and King and it is therefore necessary to use linear programming to determine the optimum production mix. The LP model is:

Maximize $10Q + 110K$ subject to:

$10Q + 10K \leqslant 20\,000$	(Type 2 labour)
$5Q + 25K \leqslant 25\,000$	(Type 3 labour)
$Q \qquad\quad \leqslant 1\,500$	(Demand)
$K \leqslant 1\,500$	(Demand)

The above constraints are plotted on the graph (Figure Q26.1) as follows:

Type 2 labour: line from $Q = 2000, K = 0$ to $K = 2000, Q = 0$

Type 3 labour: line from $Q = 5000, K = 0$ to $K = 1000, Q = 0$

The optimum solution is where the lines intersect on the graph. The optimum output can be determined exactly by solving the simultaneous equations for the constraints that intersect:

$$5Q + 25K = 25\,000 \qquad\qquad (1)$$

$$10Q + 10K = 20\,000 \qquad\qquad (2)$$

Multiplying equation (1) by 2 and equation (2) by 1 gives:

$$10Q + 50K = 50\,000 \qquad\qquad (3)$$

$$10Q + 10K = 20\,000 \qquad\qquad (4)$$

Subtracting equation (4) from equation (3) gives:

$$40K = 30\,000$$

$$K = 750$$

Substituting this value for K in equation (4) gives:

$$10Q + 10\,(750) = 20\,000$$
$$Q = 1250$$

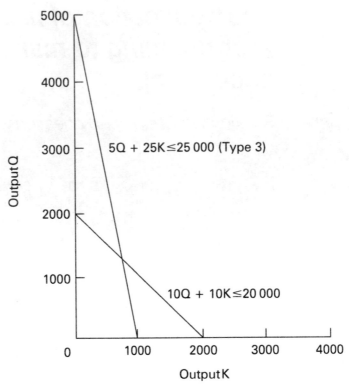

$5Q + 25K \leq 25\,000$ (Type 3)

$10Q + 10K \leq 20\,000$

Figure Q26.1

Therefore the production mix and contribution which maximizes profits is:

	(£)
1000 units of Pixie at £29 unit contribution	29 000
1250 units of Queen at £10 unit contribution	12 500
750 units of King at £110 unit contribution	82 500
Total contribution	124 000
Less: Fixed costs	15 000
Profit	109 000

(b) Pixie yields the largest contribution per scarce labour hour and therefore the additional hours should be allocated to producing pixies. The revised contribution per labour hour is £1.13 (£3.63 − £2.50 overtime premium). Hence profits will increase by £1130 (1000 hours × £1.13).

(c) The principles used were:
  (i) maximization of an objective function subject to constraints;
  (ii) assumption of linear relationships. In practice it is questionable whether linearity applies throughout the entire output range.

(d) Software linear programming packages are available which enable the model to be formulated and solved using the Simplex method. The output from the model will generate details of the optimum output level, binding constraints and shadow prices based on the principles outlined in Chapter 26.

(a) Maximize $124X + 80Y$ subject to

$$2.5X + 1.5Y \leqslant 225 \text{ (department 1)}$$
$$1.67X + 2Y \leqslant 200 \text{ (department 2)}$$
$$Y \leqslant 75 \text{ (sales demand)}$$
$$X, Y \geqslant 0$$

The above constraints are plotted on the graph shown in Figure Q26.2 as follows:

Department 1: line from $X = 90$, $Y = 0$ to $Y = 150$, $X = 0$
Department 2: line from $X = 120$, $Y = 0$ to $Y = 100$, $X = 0$

The feasible region is area OABCD on the graph and the optimum output is at point C, where $X = 60$ and $Y = 50$. The revised contribution is:

$$
\begin{array}{rcl}
 & & (\pounds) \\
X \,(60 \times \pounds124) & = & 7\,440 \\
Y \,(50 \times \pounds80) & = & \underline{4\,000} \\
 & & \underline{11\,440}
\end{array}
$$

At the optimum output level, contribution will increase by £1720 (£11 440 − £9720 current contribution).

(b) It is assumed that the capacity of both departments cannot be increased at the same time. In other words, the decision is to increase capacity in one department only. If the department 1 capacity constraint is removed, line DG will no longer be a constraint and the optimal output level will be 120 units of X. This will yield a total contribution of £14 880 (120 × £124).

   If the department 2 capacity constraint is removed, line EF will no longer be a constraint and the optimal output level will be at point H (75 units of Y and 45 units of X). This output level will yield a total contribution of £11 580. It is therefore preferable to increase capacity in department 1. The total hours required in department 1 in order to achieve the optimal output level of 120 units are 300 (120 × 2.5 hours). Therefore 75 additional hours (300 − 225) will be required, and the

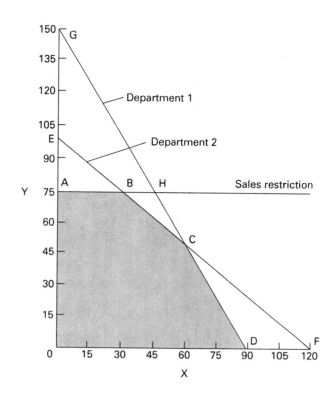

Figure Q26.2

revised contribution will be £14 842.50 [£14 880 − (75 × £0.5)]. This represents an increase in contribution of £3402.50 (£14 842.50 − £11 440).

(c)

	Department 1	Department 2
Total hours	225	200
Hours required for 30 units for Y	45 (30 × 1.5)	60 (30 × 2)
Hours available for X	180	140
Hours per unit of X	2.5	1.67
Production of X	72 units	84 units

Therefore maximum production of X is 72 units

	(£)
Revised contribution [(£124 × £72) + (£80 × 30)]	11 328
Contribution per (a)	11 440
Decrease in contribution	112

The sale of the rights to the quota should yield a minimum total revenue of £112. The minimum price per unit depends on the number of rights purchased. Assuming that the maximum rights of 45 units (75 − 30) are purchased, the minimum price per unit will be £2.49.

Solution IM 26.3

(a) (i) Let R = number of units of Razzle
D = number of units of Dazzle
The model is as follows:

Maximize $C = 12R + 10D$ subject to:

$$5R + 12.5D \leqslant 75 \quad \text{(Raz constraint)}$$
$$8R + 10D \leqslant 80 \quad \text{(Ma constraint)}$$
$$2R \leqslant 15 \quad \text{(Taz constraint)}$$
$$D, R \geqslant 0$$

The constraints are plotted on the graph shown in Figure Q26.3(i) as follows:

Raz   constraint: line from $R = 0, D = 6$ to $D = 0, R = 15$
Ma   constraint: line from $R = 0, D = 8$ to $D = 0, R = 10$
Taz   constraint: line from $R = 7.5$

The optimal production plan is at point X, where the lines $2R \leqslant 15$ and $8R + 10D \leqslant 80$ intersect. The output X is where Razzle = 7.5 sales units.

The output of Dazzle can be read from the graph, but a more accurate calculation can be obtained by solving the equation:

$8R + 10D = 80$ at point X, where $R = 7.5$
Therefore $8 (7.5) + 10D = 80$
$D = 2$

So the optimal production is Dazzle = 2 units and Razzle = 7.5 units. Contribution at this output level:

$$R (7.5 × £12) + D (2 × £10) = £110$$

Profit per day = £110 contribution less fixed costs (£60)
= £50

At the optimal output level, total sales revenue per day is:

$$\text{Razzle} (7.5 × 20) + \text{Dazzle} (2 × £30) = £210$$

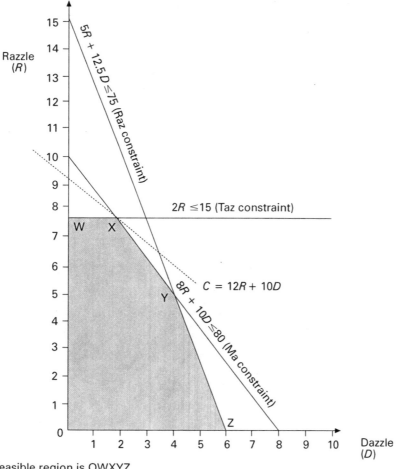

Feasible region is OWXYZ
Optimal sales mix is at point X

Figure Q26.3(i)

(ii) The model is as follows:

Maximize S (sales) = $20R + 30D$ subject to:

$$5R + 12.5D \leq 75 \text{ (Raz constraint)}$$
$$8R + 10D \leq 80 \text{ (Ma constraint)}$$
$$2R \leq 15 \text{ (Taz constraint)}$$
$$12R + 10D \geq 104 \text{ (profit constraint)}$$
$$D, R \geq 0$$

The constraints are plotted on the graph in Figure Q26.3(ii) based on the calculations in (i). The profit constraint is:

line from $R = 8.67, D = 0$ to $D = 10.4, R = 0$

Note that the objective function changes.
The feasible output range is VWX.
The maximum sales mix subject to the profit constraint is at X.
The optimal point can be determined by solving the simultaneous equations for the constraints that intersect at point X:

$$8R + 10D = 80 \tag{1}$$

$$12R + 10D = 104 \tag{2}$$

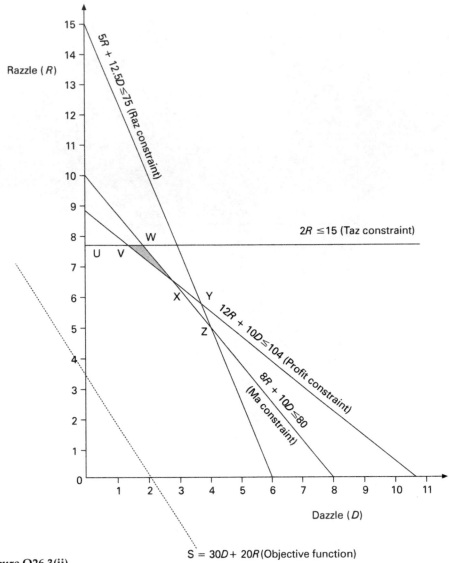

S = 30D + 20R (Objective function)

Figure Q26.3(ii)

Subtracting equation (1) from equation (2):

$$4R = 24$$
$$R = 6$$

Substituting in equation (1):

$$8(6) + 10D = 80$$
$$D = 3.2$$

The optimal solution is Razzle = 6 units and Dazzle = 3.2 units. Contribution at this output level:

$$R (6 \times £12) + D (3.2 \times £10) = £104$$

Profit per day = £104 contribution less fixed costs (£60)
$$= £44$$

At the optimal output level, total revenue per day is:

Razzle (6 × £20) + Dazzle (3.2 × £30) = £216

(b) The objective of maximizing sales revenue subject to a profit constraint is an example of a 'satisfying' model of business behaviour. This model recognizes that single objectives such as profit maximization or revenue maximization may only represent the goal of one of the major interest groups. In practice, a number of different groups seek to achieve goals within the organization.

The objective of maximizing sales revenue subject to a profit constraint can be associated with two interest groups:

(i) The achievement of the minimum profit level represents the interests of existing and potential investors in the firm. It is assumed that managers will be aware that they are relatively free from shareholder interference as long as decisions satisfy dividend expectations and support the share's market value. It is assumed that substantial separation of ownership and control exists.

(ii) The achievement of maximum sales subject to the profit constraint reflects the desire of management to achieve high sales because it is seen as consistent with growth objectives and desire for management power and status. Individual managers might view their personal career progression as being linked to higher output levels and the growth in the size of the organization. Also, securing high market shares in terms of sales might be considered as important in determining what is successful performance.

(a) Assuming that blending hours are the only scarce factor, profits will be maximized by concentrating on the product that yields the largest contribution per blending hour:

Solution IM 26.4

	Gamma	Delta
Contribution per kg	£4000	£8000
Blending hours per kg	100	250
Contribution per blending hour	£40	£32

Since the company can sell all of its output, the scarce resources should be devoted to producing Gamma. There are 1050 blending hours available enabling 10.5 kg (1050/100) of Gamma to be produced. The profit for the period will be:

	(£)
Contribution (10.5 × £4000)	42 000
Fixed costs	36 000
Profit	6 000

(b) The optimal production programme is found using linear programming:

Let x = kg of Gamma produced and sold
y = kg of Delta produced and sold

The linear programming formulation is:

Maximize $4000x + 8000y$ subject to:
$$400x + 120y \leqslant 1200 \quad \text{(heating constraint)}$$
$$100x + 90y \leqslant 450 \quad \text{(refining constraint)}$$
$$100x + 250y \leqslant 1050 \quad \text{(blending constraint)}$$
$$x \geqslant 0$$
$$y \geqslant 0$$

The above constraints are plotted on the graph in Figure Q26.4 as follows:

Heating constraint : line from $x = 3, y = 0$ to $y = 10, x = 0$
Refining constraint: line from $x = 4.5, y = 0$ to $y = 5, x = 0$
Machine time constraint : line from $x = 10.5, y = 0$ to $y = 4.2, x = 0$

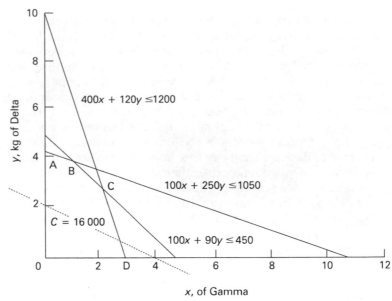

Figure Q26.4

The feasible region is area OABCD. The dashed line on the graph represents an arbitrarily chosen contribution figure of £16 000 giving a maximum output of either 4 kg of Gamma or 2 kg of Delta. By extending the contribution line outwards the optimum production mix can be derived at point B. The optimum point can be determined mathematically by solving the simultaneous equations for the constraints that intersect at point B:

$$100x + 250y = 1050$$
$$100x + 90y = 450$$

The values of x and y when the above equations are solved are 3.75 for y and 1.125 for x. The budgeted loss for the period is:

	(£)
Contribution from Gamma (1.125 × £4000)	4 500
Contribution from Delta (3.75 × £8000)	30 000
	34 500
Fixed costs	36 000
Loss	(1 500)

(c) The optimum production plan results in a loss of £1500. The company must decide whether or not to produce during the period. In the short term this will depend on whether any of the fixed costs can be avoided. If the company ceases production for the period a loss equal to the fixed costs will be incurred. Therefore the company might be worse off if it ceases production.

The company should focus on the long term and ascertain whether future demand is likely to continue to exceed production capacity. If this situation is likely to occur then a financial appraisal should be undertaken to determine whether an expansion of production capacity can be justified after taking into account long-term considerations.

Attention should also be given to the possibility of increasing selling prices or reducing variable costs.

(d) The shadow price can be found by increasing refining time by 1 hour. If one extra hour of refining time is available the optimum solution will still occur at the intersection of the refining and blending contraints where:

THE APPLICATION OF LINEAR PROGRAMMING TO MANAGEMENT ACCOUNTING

$$100x + 90y = 451 \quad \text{(refining)}$$
$$100x + 250y = 1050 \quad \text{(blending)}$$

The revised values when the above simultaneous equations are solved are:

$$x = 1.140625$$
$$y = 3.74375$$

The revised maximum contribution is:

$$(1.140625 \times £4000) + (3.74375 \times £8000) = £34\,512.50$$

Thus contribution is increased by £12.50 and this represents the shadow price for one hour of refining time. Shadow prices are also known as opportunity costs. For an explanation of how shadow price information can be used, see 'Uses of linear programming' in Chapter 26. The limitations inherent in the shadow price calculations relate to those that apply to linear programming in general. For a discussion of these limitations see the answer to question 26.17(f) in the Student's Manual.

(a) Maximize 12.5A + 9.5B + 11C + 8D + 14E (Contribution)

Solution IM 26.5

Subject to A + B + C + D + E ≤ 30 000 (Production capacity)

90A + 75B + 100C + 120D + 200E ≤ 3 000 000 (Funds)

A ≥ 1000

B ≥ 2000

C ≥ 1200

D ≥ 2500

E ≥ 600

A, B, C, D, E ≥ 0

Note that the minimum capacity constraints for each division are 5% of the existing capacity. For example, the capacity constraint for Division A is 1000 hours (5% × 20 000)

(b) (i) The objective function indicates that the maximum contribution from the additional 30 000 hours within the £3 million budget is £359 263.60. The additional hours in each division are as follows:

Division		
A	22 090.9 hours
B	2 000
C	1 200
D	2 500
E	2 209.1
	30 000.0

Divisions A and E have been allocated more hours than the minimum required.

(b) (ii) The shadow prices represent the opportunity cost of the constraints. For divisions B, C and D the shadow prices indicate the cost per hour of providing the minimum capacity to achieve the strategy. For example, allocating a scarce hour to Division B results in a loss of contribution of approximately £2.80 per hour. There is no loss in contribution from allocating scarce hours to divisions A and E.

(b) (iii) The shadow prices indicate the opportunity cost of the constraints. For each extra hour of machine time a contribution of £11.27 can be obtained whereas an additional £1 of investment will yield an extra contribution of £0.0136.

(b) (iv) The table for the sensitivity analysis of objective function constraints indicates that decreases in contribution will have no effect on the planned allocations for divisions B, C and D. For division A the contribution would have to be in excess of £14 per hour or below £10.70 per hour for a change in the planned allocation to occur. The contribution would have to be outside the range of £12.50 to £27.78 per hour in division E for a change in the planned allocation to occur.

(b) (v) The sensitivity analysis of right-hand side values indicates that, if all parameters to the model are to remain unchanged, the capacity hours can increase by 1966.67 hours to 31 966.67 hours. Each additional hour yields a contribution of £11.2727 resulting in an additional contribution of £22 170 (1966.67 hours at £11.2727 per hour).

The additional hours, however, must be obtained within the funds constraint of £3 million. The negative shadow prices for divisions B, C and D mean that additional contribution is obtained from either divisions A or E. Because the investment cost per hour in division E is higher than that for division A, 2.2222 hours in division A can be obtained for each 1 hour of funds invested in division E (£200/£90). In other words, for each hour allocated from division E to division A an extra 1.2222 hours can obtained. Therefore to obtain the extra 1966.67 hours, 1609.1 hours (1966.67 hours/1.2222 hours) of investment cost at £200 hours should be transferred from division E to division A. The investment cost released of £321 820 (£200 × 1609.1 hours) will enable 3575.77 hours (£321 820/£90 per hour) to be utilized in division A consisting of 1609.1 existing hours plus the balance of 1966.67 *additional* hours. This would leave the minimum requirement of 600 hours in division E.

(b) (vi) The sensitivity analysis of right-hand side values indicates for the parameters to remain unchanged the investment funds can decline to £2 823 000, a reduction of £177 000. Contribution will decline by £177 000 × £0.0136 = £2 407. That is, the decline in investment funds multiplied by the shadow price per £1 of investment.

Based on the explanation in (b)(v) this strategy should be implemented by reducing the number of hours in division E to the minimum of 600 and transferring the balance of 1609.1 hours to division A. This will reduce the investment in division E by £321 820 (£200 × 1 609.1 hours) but the investment in division A will cost £144 820 (1 609.1 hours at £90) giving a net reduction in investment of £177 000 (£321 820 – £144 820).

(c) See answer to 26.17(f) in the Students' Manual for the answer to this question.

Solution IM 26.6

(a) In Chapter 26 the approach adopted was to formulate the first tableau with positive contribution signs and negative signs for the slack variable equations. The optimal solution occurs when all the signs in the contribution row are negative. The opposite procedure has been applied with the tableau presented in the question. Therefore if the approach explained in Chapter 26 is adopted it is necessary to reverse all the signs given in the question and ignore the entries of 0 and 1.

(i) *£1 053 671.4*

This is the total contribution obtained from producing the optimal output presented in the linear programming model. This can be checked by multiplying the optimum production by the product contributions:

X_1: 43 287 units at £5.70 contribution 1 ⎫
X_2: 13 333.3 units at £10.10 contribution ⎬ = £1 053 671.4
X_6: 48 019.2 units at £14 contribution ⎭

(ii) *43 287.0 units*

This is the production of X_1 in the optimal solution.

(iii) *15 747.87 hours*

This represents the unused hours of the slack variable X_3 (forming time) in the optimum solution. The forming hours required in the optimal solution are:

$$\frac{43\,287.0}{450} + \frac{13\,333.3}{450} + \frac{48\,019.2}{380} = 252.19 \text{ hours}$$

The total forming hours are 16 000, resulting in 15 747.81 unused hours (16 000 − 252.19 hours).

(iv) *£10*

The optimal solution results in zero output of X_3. If one unit of X_3 is produced, it will be necessary to adjust the optimal programme in order to create the resources to produce X_3. The optimal adjustment if a unit of X_3 is to be produced is:

Contribution (£)

Increase output of X_1 by 1.6 units	+9.12 (1.6 × £5.7)
Decrease output of X_2 by 0.53 units	−5.35 (0.53 × £10.10)
Decrease output of X_6 by 1.9 units	−26.60 (1.9 × £14)
Extra unit of X_3	+12.30
	−10.53

The £10 figure refers to the amount by which total contribution would decrease if the company made one unit of X_3 instead of the optimal mix. The difference between £10 and £10.53 is assumed to be due to rounding errors.

(v) *£16*

This is the shadow price of drilling time (X_9). If an additional hour of drilling time can be obtained, contribution will increase by £16. An additional hour of drilling time should be used to increase output of X_2 by 3.33 units and reduce the output of X_1 by 3.0 units. Contribution will be increased by:

$$(3.33 \times £10.10) - (3.0 \times £5.7) = £16.53$$

The difference between £16.53 and £16 is assumed to be due to rounding errors.

(vi) *18.50*

If X_{10} is increased by one hour then X_1 should be decreased by 18.5 units and X_6 should be increased by 12 units.

(vii) *15 806.72 hours*

This represents unused hours of the slack variable X_{11} (coating time) in the optimum solutions.

(b) (i) If one unit of X_4 is made instead of the optimal mix, total contribution will fall by £4. As long as the contribution from X_4 does not increase by more than £4, the optimal mix will remain unchanged. If the contribution from X_4 increases by more than £4 to over £13.80 the optimal solution will change.

(ii) The optimal solution indicates 15 806.72 spare coating hours. The optimal production programme requires:

$$\frac{43\,287}{500} + \frac{48\,019.2}{450} = 193.28 \text{ coating hours}$$

Hence 15 806.72 coating hours are unused. Consequently coating time could fall to 193.28 hours before the optimal solution changes.

(c) Assuming that contribution per unit remains unchanged, the revised model is:

Maximize $Z = 5.7X_1 + 10.1X_2 + 12.3X_3 + 9.8X_4 + 17.2X_5 + 14.0X_6$ subject to:

$$
\begin{aligned}
700X_1 + 770X_2 + 410X_3 + 500X_4 + 330X_5 + 470X_6 + X_7 &= 12\,000 \\
540X_1 + 540X_2 \quad\quad\quad + 620X_4 + 220X_5 + 460X_6 + X_8 &= 16\,000 \\
200X_2 + 380X_3 \quad\quad\quad + 300X_5 \quad\quad\quad + X_9 &= 4\,000 \\
380X_3 + 670X_4 + 400X_5 + 720X_6 + X_{10} &= 4\,000 \\
500X_1 \quad\quad + 540X_3 + 480X_4 + 600X_5 + 450X_6 + X_{11} &= 16\,000 \\
X_3 \quad\quad\quad\quad\quad\quad\quad + X_{12} &= 150\,000 \\
X_5 \quad\quad + X_{13} &= 20\,000 \\
X_6 + X_{14} &= 70\,000
\end{aligned}
$$

(d) The revised contribution can be obtained by multiplying the binding constraints by the shadow prices:

		(£)
X_7 (cutting):	12 000 hours × £59.30	711 600
X_9 (drilling):	4 000 hours × £14.20	56 800
X_{10} (welding):	4 000 hours × £71.50	286 000
		1 054 400
Cost of change		200
Revised contribution		1 054 200
Original contribution		1 053 671
Increase in contribution		529

The changes will lead to a small increase in profitability.

(e) See 'Uses of linear programming' in Chapter 26 for the answer to this question.

Solution IM 26.7

(a)

Budgeted weekly profit and loss account

Product	X	Y	Z	Total
	(£)	(£)	(£)	
Selling price	70	60	150	
Variable costs:				
Aragons (£5 each)	(5)	(5)	(15)	
Bovons (£8 each)	(16)	(8)	(16)	
Direct labour (£5 per hour)	(30)	(35)	(80)	
Other assembly costs	(4)	(5)	(15)	
Contribution per unit	15	7	24	
Total contribution	1500	700	2400	4600
Fixed costs	(900)	(1050)	(2400)	(4350)
Profit/(loss)	600	(350)	–	250

(i) *No external availability of Aragons and Bovons*

Let X, Y and Z represent the number of Xylos, Yo-yos and Zicons produced each week and C represent the total contribution. The LP model is:

$$\text{Maximize } C = 15X + 7Y + 24Z \text{ subject to:}$$
$$22X + 14Y + 34Z \leq 9600 \quad \text{(process L)}$$
$$15X + 10Y + 25Z \leq 7000 \quad \text{(process M)}$$
$$Z \geq X \quad \text{(process N)}$$

Note that product X requires one Aragon and two Bovons, and these components require a total of 22 minutes in process L [$1 \times 6 + (2 \times 8)$]. Process N must produce at least one Aragon for each Bovon produced. This constraint will not be met if production of X is in excess of Z. Hence the process N constraint is added to meet this production requirement.

(ii) *External availability of Aragons and Bovons*

Let A = number of Aragons bought each week
    B = number of Bovons bought each week

If one Aragon is bought, process L capacity will be increased by 6 minutes and Process M capacity will be increased by 5 minutes. If one Bovon is bought, process L capacity will be increased by 8 minutes and process M capacity will be increased by 5 minutes. Hence the constraints for processes L and M capacity are:

$$22X + 14Y + 34Z \leq 9600 + 6A + 8B \quad \text{(process L)}$$
$$15X + 10Y + 25Z \leq 7000 + 5A + 5B \quad \text{(process M)}$$

Purchasing Aragons and Bovons externally results in an increase in variable costs and a reduction in contribution of £5 for Aragons (£10 − £5) and £4 (£12 − £8) for Bovons. The revised objective function and constraints are:

$$\text{Maximize } C = 15X + 7Y + 24Z - 5A - 4B \text{ subject to:}$$
$$22X + 14Y + 34Z - 6A - 8B \leqslant 9600 \quad \text{(process L)}$$
$$15X + 10Y + 25Z - 5A - 5B \leqslant 7000 \quad \text{(process M)}$$
$$Z - A \geqslant X - B \quad \text{(process N)}$$
$$0 \leqslant A \leqslant 200$$
$$0 \leqslant B \leqslant 300$$

Note that the number of Aragons (A) and Bovons (B) purchased externally is deducted from Z and X in the equation for process N so that the constraint maintains the *internal* production requirement of producing at least one Aragon for each Bovon.

(b) The optimum production plan indicates weekly production of 50 units of X and 250 units of Z. This will result in a production of 800 Aragons and 600 Bovons, and thus satisfy the production requirement of process N. The shadow prices arising in processes L and M indicate that these processes are fully utilized. For every minute of additional production time that can be obtained in processes L and M, contribution will increase by £0.375 and £0.45 respectively. If one more Aragon or Bovon became available, contribution would increase by £9.50 and £13.25 respectively. The optimal plan also indicates that product Y should not be produced. However, if one unit of product Y were produced, it would be necessary to divert resources from X and Z, and this would result in a loss of £2.75 for each unit of product Y produced.

The binding constraints are processes L and M. If process L were increased by one additional minute, the revised constraints would be:

$$22X + 34Z = 9601 \quad \text{(revised process L constraint)}$$
$$15X + 25Z = 7000 \quad \text{(unchanged process M constraint)}$$

The revised optimum output when the above equations are solved is 249.63 units of Z and 50.62 units of X. Therefore if an additional minute of process L is obtained, X should be increased by 0.62 units and Z decreased by 0.37 units.

If an additional minute of process M could be obtained, the revised constraints would be:

$$22X + 34Z = 9600$$
$$15X + 25Z = 7001$$

Solving the above equation results in a revised output of 250.55 units of Z and 49.15 units of X. Therefore production of Z should be increased by 0.55 units and X decreased by 0.85 units.

Assuming that 300 Bovons became available and optimal output requires that only X should be made, the external purchase of Bovons would enable 150 units of X to be made. This output would require 150 Aragons to be produced internally, thus using in processes L and M 900 minutes (150 × 6) and 750 minutes (150 × 5) respectively. The unused capacities would be 8700 minutes for process L and 6250 minutes for process M. Maximum production from this remaining capacity is:

process L: 395 (8700/22)
process M: 416 (6250/15)

Consequently production will be restricted to a further 395 units. Process L will be a binding constraint, but capacity will not be fully utilized in process M. Consequently process M will have a zero shadow price. If capacity of process L can be increased, it will be used to produce product X, thus yielding a contribution of £15. One unit of product X requires 22 minutes in process L. Thus the shadow price for one minute in process L is £0.68 (£15/22).

Solution IM 26.8

(a) If funds are restricted for immediate investment only, the projects should be ranked by the profitability index. The calculations are as follows:

Project	Present value (NPV + investment cost) (£000)	Investment cost (£000)	Profitability index	Ranking
A	557.0	400	1.39	3
B	450.0	300	1.50	2
C	373.5	300	1.24	4
D	159.5	0		1

Therefore the company should undertake projects D, B and half of A. The total NPV (£000) resulting from this strategy is $159.5 + 150 + (0.5 \times 157) = £388\,000$.

(b) Let a, b, c and d represent the proportion of projects A, B, C and D accepted, and X represent surplus funds placed on deposit at t_0 at 7% in £000. Then

$$\text{NPV of £1000 invested in } X = \frac{£1070}{1 + 0.10} - 1000$$

$$= -£27.27$$

Linear programming model

Maximize $157a + 150b + 73.5c + 159.5d - 0.027X^a$ subject to:
$$400a + 300b + 300c + X \leqslant 500 \ (t_0 \text{ constraint in £000})$$
$$200b + 300d \leqslant 300 + 50a + 150c + 1.07X \ (t_1 \text{ constraint in £000})$$
$$a, b, c, d, X \geqslant 0$$
$$a, b, c, d \leqslant 1$$

Note

[a] Note that the model is expressed in £000. Therefore $-£27.27$ expressed in £000 is $-£0.027$. Also note that surplus funds are placed on deposit at t_0 only. After t_1, capital is available without limit. Consequently it is assumed at t_1 that it is unnecessary to maintain funds for future periods by placing funds on deposit to yield a negative NPV. In the above model it is assumed that capital constraints can be eased by project-generated cash flows. If this is not possible and capital constraints are absolute, the formulation is:

Maximize $\quad 157a + 150b + 73.5c + 159.5d - 0.027X$ subject to:
$$400a + 300b + 300c + X \leqslant 500$$
$$200b + 300d \leqslant 300 + 1.07X$$
$$a, b, c, d, X \geqslant 0$$
$$a, b, c, d \leqslant 1$$

(c) The limitations are as follows:

(i) Divisibility of projects may not be realistic, and integer programming may have to be used.

(ii) Constraints are unlikely to be completely fixed and precise as implied in the mathematical models.

(iii) Not all the relevant information can be quantified. For example, market constraints might exist which cannot be quantified.

(iv) All information for the model may not be available. For example, it may not be possible precisely to specify the constraints of future periods.

(v) All the relationships contained within the formulation may not be linear.

(vi) All the potential investment opportunities may not be identified and included in the analysis.

(vii) The linear programming formulation assumes that all the project's cash flows are certain and therefore it cannot incorporate uncertainty. The solution produced can only be considered optimal given this restrictive assumption.

(viii) All investments may not be independent of each other. There may be some unspecified interdependencies.

THE APPLICATION OF LINEAR PROGRAMMING TO MANAGEMENT ACCOUNTING

(d) The answer should distinguish between hard capital rationing (externally imposed) and soft capital rationing (internally imposed). It can be argued with hard capital rationing that if a firm has investment opportunities it will eventually be able to raise the finance even though it might have to pay a high price. If short-term market imperfections exist through lack of information then capital rationing might exist in the short term, but it has no long-term significance. An alternative view is that gaps in the institutional framework for providing finance may result in companies having no access to appropriate financial institutions and therefore no access to investment funds at certain stages in their development. This might occur with small expanding firms. Consequently hard capital rationing might exist in practice.

Soft capital rationing might exist where a firm is obtaining adequate returns and has no wish to expand. Also management expertise might be limited and unable to cope with growth. In addition, some firms may be reluctant to raise additional funds because the shareholders may fear losing control of the business.

(a) The report should recommend investment of £55 000 in project IV and the remaining £35 000 in project I. This decision is based on the following calculation:

Solution IM 26.9

Project	NPV (£000)	Initial investment	Profitability index	Ranking
I	80	50	1.6	2
II	40	40	1.0	4
III	120	90	1.33	3
IV	110	55	2.0	1

The maximum NPV is £166 000, consisting of £110 000 from project IV and £56 000 from project I [i.e. (£35 000 − £50 000) × £80 000]. This recommendation is based on the assumption that the objective is to maximize shareholders' wealth, and this objective will be achieved by maximizing NPV. The NPV decision rule is based on the assumption that the stockmarket values a firm by discounting future dividends at a discount rate which reflects the risk of these dividends. The cash flows from a project will be used eventually to increase dividends, and therefore the value of a firm will increase by the NPV of capital investments provided the market is aware of these cash flows and believes that they will occur. In other words, the efficient market hypothesis is assumed to hold in its strong form.

Risk has been incorporated into the analysis by discounting the cash flows at a risk-adjusted discount rate using the capital asset pricing model (CAPM). The CAPM assumes that all shareholders in the company hold well-diversified portfolios and have eliminated unsystematic risk. If the shareholders do not hold well-diversified portfolios, the adjusted discount rate will not reflect the total risk which the shareholders are exposed to from investing in projects I–IV.

The report should also include a discussion of the issues raised by four directors. Wendling favours investment in project III because it yields the largest NPV. However, Wendling has failed to take into account the high cost of the investment and the fact that projects I and II yield larger NPVs per £1 of investment. In other words, it is necessary to rank projects by the profitability index when the company is faced with a capital rationing situation.

Ramm appears to favour projects with low outlays, so that the number of projects accepted can be maximized. He is also focusing on whole projects and ignoring the fact that all projects are divisible.

Ritter favours risk reduction, and therefore supports acceptance of the project with the lowest beta so as to reduce the company's overall beta. However, he ignores the fact that shareholders can obtain the risk reduction themselves by combining securities with different betas in their portfolio. Consequently there is no point in the company diversifying in this manner. Presumably, in terms of risk, existing shareholders have found the existing beta of the company to be accept-able. Those investors who favour risk reduction will already have sold their shares and invested their funds in low-beta securities. With regard to Ritter's objections to project IV, it should be noted that risk has already been incorporated into the analysis by using risk-adjusted discount rates. The NPV of project IV is high because it is an attractive project even after taking risk into account.

Punto is against project III because the NPV will be much lower when discounted at the company's cost at capital. Punto ignores the fact that project III has the lowest risk, with a beta value of 0.8, whereas the company's present beta is 1.0. The overall company cost of capital will be calculated using a beta of 1.0 (this represents the average of the betas for the firm's existing projects). The cash flows from a project should be discounted at a rate which reflects the risk of a project. The greater the risk the greater the discount rate. It is therefore incorrect to use a discount rate calculated from a beta of 1.0 to discount a project which has a beta of 0.8.

(b) If funds are rationed for a period of longer than one year then a project's profitability index for later years (e.g. NPV/year 2 investment outlay) is likely to differ from the profitability index for year 1. Consequently project rankings will vary from year to year and it will not be possible to use the profitability index to make the optimal decision. The profitability index can only be used when the investment requirements for different projects are always in the same proportion each year. For example, in year 1 the investment in project II is 80% of the investment in project I. If the investment in year 2 for project I is £20 000 then the ratio will be maintained if the outlay for year 2 is £16 000.

(c) The answer to this question should include an explanation of how linear programming can be used to maximize NPV when capital is rationed for more than one period. For a detailed explanation see 'The use of linear programming in capital budgeting' in Chapter 26.

Part III

Case study teaching note

Teaching Note

EVA AT AULT FOODS LIMITED

Professor Sarah C. Mavrinac prepared this teaching note as an aid to instructors in the classroom use of the case EVA at Ault Foods Limited, No. 9A98B001. This teaching note should not be used in any way that would prejudice the future use of the case.

Version: (A) 1998-11-16

This teaching note describes the format and content of a two-session class. The first session is expected to run for 80 minutes and has been designed to focus the students on the practical aspects of EVA calculations. The second session is expected to run for 60 minutes and should focus on such finance-related issues as 1) divisional risk and the cost of capital, 2) market value added, and 3) market signaling.

ASSIGNMENT
Reading: Note on Economic Value Added, Note No. 9-96-B038 (Handout)

Assignment:
1) Skim the technical note.
2) Calculate divisional EVA performance figures for 1996. When calculating NOPAT (Net Operating Profit after Tax) and EBV (Economic Book Value), please use the operating approach. Presume a 10% cost of capital. Note that <u>three</u> EVA adjustments should be made when calculating divisional EVA figures. Specifically, when calculating NOPAT, you should:
   A) use cash v. statutory tax rates,
   B) add back goodwill amortization rates,
   C) add back research and development costs

Refer to the technical note for information on how to make these adjustments.
3) Examine the strengths and weaknesses of each of Ault's divisions. Be sure to consider qualitative and traditional accounting data as well as EVA data when conducting this analysis. What can you conclude about the performance capabilities and value of Ault's divisions?
4) What would you do if you were Graham Freeman?

INTENT
The EVA at Ault Foods Limited case is intended to provide an introduction to the use of EVA in a multi-business setting. Having completed the case, students should
1) have a basic understanding of the EVA concept and its usefulness as a performance indicator
2) have some basic skill in making EVA adjustments and calculating actual EVA measures
3) have a good conceptual grasp of the application of EVA both as an internal control device and as an aid to strategic decision making.

SUMMARY
In the fall of 1996, Graham Freeman, chief executive officer and chairman of Ault Foods Limited (Ault), Canada's largest dairy concern, found himself in the midst of a shareholder revolt. After years of monitoring Ault's troubled earnings and sliding share values, the Ontario Teachers Pension Plan Board, one of Ault's largest shareholders, had sold its 10% stake in the company, expressing disappointment in both the company's earnings potential and senior management.

Freeman was convinced that the company had to be pared down to an essential core if improved performance were to be realized. Most of the company's divisions were seriously underperforming and Freeman was sure that none could be turned around without a dramatic shift in corporate strategy. Rather than trying to tackle all the divisions' problems at once, Freeman hoped that he could sell at least one of the company's divisions to refocus management attention on the company's traditional business in cheese.

The company's board of directors posed the greatest threat to Freeman's plan. This group of individuals saw little value in shrinking the company. Their management philosophy seemed to be, simply, 'Bigger is better.' To help allay their concerns and to convince the board of the value-creating potential inherent in his divestiture plan, Freeman asked John Hamilton, the company's chief financial officer, to build an EVA presentation that Freeman could deliver at the next board meeting. Freeman asked specifically that this presentation highlight: 1) the value of EVA, 2) the results of a divisional EVA analysis, and 3) the pros and cons of a divisional spinoff.

The case material provides ample data for an enthusiastic, detailed debate over the value both of EVA as a strategic measurement tool and of Freeman's divestiture plan.

CLASS SEQUENCE
Below is a brief outline identifying the major topics that might be highlighted during the class period. Detailed notes follow.

Session 1
1. Problem Definition	(10 minutes)
2. Company Overview/Case Size-Up	(10 minutes)
3. The EVA Concept	(15 minutes)
4. Calculating EVA	(20 minutes)
5. Divisional Performance Calculations	(25 minutes)

Session 2
6. Comparing the Alternatives: EVA v. Other Measures	(10 minutes)
7. Evaluating WACC	(10 minutes)
8. EVA and MVA	(10 minutes)
9. Evaluating Divisional Performance	(15 minutes)
10. Debating Divestiture	(10 minutes)
11. EVA as a Management Tool	(5 minutes)

SESSION NOTES

Session 1
Below are notes describing many of the themes and questions that can be explored during the class sessions.

1. *Problem Definition* (10 minutes) The instructor may find it useful to launch the class by encouraging a debate over Freeman's plan for divestiture. One student can be asked to assume the role of Graham Freeman and to argue his/her point of view while another can argue the point of view of the company's board. The students' comments can be focused by asking them to respond to the following questions:

> **Should one of Ault's divisions be sold?**
> **If yes, which one?**
> **What benefits might be realized from sale of a division?**
> **What problems will be solved?**

The students should be encouraged to provide a specific rationale for the decision although the presentation of EVA calculations should be avoided for the moment.

Note that when discussing Ault's 'problems', students should move beyond the obvious earnings and share price difficulties. Freeman also faces a variety of competitive difficulties and regulatory uncertainties. However, one of Freeman's biggest problems is a measurement problem. None of the traditional earnings indicators with which the board is familiar provides much insight into the cause of Ault's performance problems, let alone their solution.

When the students have finished enumerating Ault's difficulties, the question of whether or not a division should be sold should be put to a general vote. The results of the vote should be noted and saved for later reference.

2. *Company Overview/Case Size-Up* (10 minutes) Once the central issues of the case have been aired, the instructor might find it useful to focus the class on a review of the case and the context of this divestiture decision. The instructor can prompt discussion by asking the following questions:

What type of company is this?
According to the case, Ault was one of the largest dairy operations in Canada. The company was created by John Labatt Limited (Labatt) in the spring of 1993 when Labatt merged and spun off a hodge-podge of unrelated acquisitions. Serving customers throughout Ontario and Quebec, Ault manufactured and distributed fluid milk, yogurt, fruit juices, and ice cream as well as its profitable line of cheeses and cheese snackfoods.

What is the company's strategy? What are its key success factors?
Having identified the company's basic businesses, students should spend some time becoming familiar with the company's strategy and its patterns of value creation. Although most of the company's products would appear to be commodities or near-commodities, Freeman had dedicated himself to realizing a premium, value-added niche for the company. As stated in the case, his strategy was to invest heavily in research and development to generate new patented products that would distinguish Ault from its competition.

Is this an appropriate strategy for the dairy industry?
If most of Ault's products are indeed commodities, corporate success can be realized only by increasing volumes to increase manufacturing and distribution efficiencies and, ultimately, to lower cost. We note that most of Ault's competitors, e.g., Natrel and Dairyworld, were following this volume strategy and were working to enlarge the geographic scope and size of their markets. Does this convince us that these products *are* commodities? Was Freeman correct in thinking that Ault's products could be repositioned as value-added consumables. If he were correct, a whole new range of value-oriented strategies would become possible and the 'key success factors' of the industry would shift dramatically.

3. *The EVA Concept* (15 minutes) Having defined the central problem and having discussed the characteristics of the decision context, the class should now consider the EVA topic. Graham Freeman believed firmly that EVA was a tool with which Ault management could solve many of its performance problems. To ensure that students have a reasonable understanding of EVA and its unique capabilities, the class should be prompted to discuss the following questions. Note that all of these questions are addressed both in Exhibit 5 of the case and in the supplementary reading.

What is EVA? Exhibit 5 in the case describes EVA as a simple accounting calculation. Indeed, EVA is nothing other than 'Residual Income' repackaged. Although accounting students have been aware of residual income since the 1950s, Corporate Canada has only recently discovered the concept. But, according to a 1994 study conducted by academics at the University of Waterloo, corporate executives are fast adopting the new tool for a host of uses. For further description of EVA as a performance measurement tool, see the technical note, 'Note on Economic Value Added,' Case No. 9-96-B038, prepared by John Manning and John McCartney under the supervision of Professor James E. Hatch.

4. *Calculating EVA* (20 minutes) EVA is defined simply as net operating profit after tax less a charge for capital employed. The formula for EVA is:

EVA = NET OPERATING PROFIT AFTER TAX − REQUIRED RETURN ON ASSETS   (1)
where

REQUIRED RETURN ON ASSETS = ASSETS EMPLOYED* COST OF CAPITAL   (2)

Although the concept of EVA is relatively simple to grasp and while the formula seems relatively straightforward, EVA calculations can be quite complex if a large number of NOPAT (Net Operating Profit after Tax) or EBV (Economic Book Value) adjustments must be made. According to the Stern, Stewart & Co. text, there are 164 different adjustments that can be made, including adjustments to capital for LIFO reserves, goodwill amortization, and capitalized intangibles, and adjustments to NOPAT for deferred taxes, unusual losses, and increases in reserves, for example. Which adjustments should be made depends largely on the accounting policies of the firm.

In this case, we ask the students to accommodate three adjustments. Specifically, we ask them to:
A) use cash v. statutory tax rates adjustment,
B) add back goodwill amortization values, and
C) capitalize research and development expenses.

To adjust for taxes, changes must be made to both accounting profits and book value figures. Specifically, we adjust profit calculations to include cash taxes only and we define deferred taxes as equity when calculating EBV.

According to the technical note accompanying this case, 'Amortization of goodwill is a non-cash, non-tax deductible amortization and should be accounted for accordingly.' Specifically, one is required to add back accumulated goodwill amortization to capital and to add back the annual accounting charge for goodwill to NOPAT. Research and development adjustments are much like goodwill adjustments. To recognize research and development as a value-creating asset, we add back accumulated research and development costs to capital and add back the annual research and development expense to NOPAT.

To illustrate the process of EVA calculation, the class can collectively walk through the corporate EVA calculations presented in the case.

5. *Divisional Performance Calculations* (25 minutes) The rest of this class session should be spent generating divisional EVA figures. The instructor should refer to TN-1 for illustration of the various calculations.

Session 2

6. *Comparing the Alternatives: EVA v. Other Measures* (10 minutes) To illustrate the value and contribution of EVA analyses, students should spend some time considering the traditional alternatives to EVA. Among those that might be considered are:

- Increases in Sales
- Operating Margins
- ROE
- ROA, and
- Changes in Share Value

7. *Evaluating WACC* (10 minutes) One of the key tasks involved in calculating EVA is the determination of the divisional cost of capital. In this case, we have suggested that students use a simple 10% figure for all divisions. We should ask them now if this is an appropriate assumption.

What are the determinants of WACC?
Note that managers at Ault did not attempt to estimate divisional cost of equity levels. John Hamilton, the company's chief financial officer, informed the casewriter that identifying these figures would have been difficult, it not impossible. Because Ault was a relatively new company and had limited trading history, generating the *corporate* cost of equity figure was difficult enough.

To calculate cost of capital, the firm started by estimating the risk-free rate of return using conventional Canadian bond rates. The equity premium was then inferred using sell-side analysts' best estimates of the company's beta. The company's cost of debt was determined with reference to bank interest charges. Note that all of Ault's debt was negotiated in the form of short-term notes, i.e., none was publicly traded. Interestingly, because Ault used only the contractual cost of debt in its calculation, both pre- and post-tax cost of debt could be lower than the estimated risk-free rate! Hamilton excused this oddity, saying simply that he tried to keep the procedure simple.

On average, Ault's cost of capital, estimated using the procedures described above, was approximately 10.5%. It varied only modestly from year to year, from a high of 11.34% in 1992 to a low of 9.39% in 1994.

While the class should discuss at length the importance of recognizing differences in risk across divisions, the students should also consider Hamilton's concern re simplicity. **What are the pros and cons of calculating divisional WACC?**

8. *EVA and MVA* (10 minutes) The promoters of EVA suggest that one of its key features is its correlation with share value. **How does EVA translate into shareholder value?** At this point, the instructor can discuss with the class the concept of MVA (Market Value Added) and the empirical correlation between EVA and share price. The purpose of this discussion is to encourage continued discussion of the operational improvements suggested above. **Will these truly create shareholder value? Would we expect Ault's stock price to climb upon announcement of these initiatives? Some analysts think the company stock is undervalued? Do you? Why?**

It should be clear to the class that Freeman's problems did not arise over night. Ault's performance problem is visible in a number of continuing performance trends: earnings have dropped, sales are stagnant, and share price is falling. These data, coupled with abysmal share price trends and with information on competitor actions, suggest that Freeman is wrong and that an 'innovator' strategy in the dairy industry is not feasible. However, as the case notes, there are analysts who still have faith in the company and its ability to generate shareholder returns. Some of the factors highlighted by the analysts who favor Ault's stock are:

- Lactantia PurFiltre
- Ault's long history of research and development success,
- the successful launch of the new International division,
- the market share of the company's fluid milk division,
- the dominance of the cheese division, and
- the brand strength of the company's ice cream division.

Others who posted sell and hold recommendations have noted:

- the continuing fluid milk wars that have cut deeply into margins,
- Lactantia PurFiltre's distribution problems,
- the increasing number of fluid milk competitors,
- the entry of Unilever into the Canadian ice cream market, and
- the uncertainty of NAFTA/GATT trade negotiations, for example.

This discussion of the competitive capability of the company overall should provide a nice segue into a discussion of divisional performance.

9. *Critiquing Divisional Performance* (15 minutes) Having calculated EVA values for each division and having assessed the corporate MVA position, the class should now consider the potential for operating improvement and value enhancements. Collectively, the class should consider each individual business, its strengths, its weaknesses, and its patterns of value creation.

To organize the discussion, the instructor might find it useful to create a matrix, identifying each division and offering a description of each division's a) EVA value, b) competitive environment, c) competitive advantage, and d) most significant challenges. See Exhibit TN-2 for an illustration of this matrix. Discussion can be guided by posing the following questions:

1) **Against whom is Ault competing in each division? How strong are these competitors? What are their resources?**
2) **How is value created in each division? What is the most significant feature of each division? What does it do best?**
3) **What are the greatest threats to each division? What are the divisions' greatest weaknesses? Are there opportunities for change and performance improvement?**

During this section of the class, students should be encouraged to consider the various options Ault managers have for improving performance. According to the reading, EVA levels can be enhanced by: 1) improving operating efficiencies, 2) achieving profitable growth, 3) rationalizing and exiting unrewarding businesses, and 4) reducing the cost of capital. The class should discuss the extent to which any of these changes or improvements can be made.

10. *Debating Divestiture* (10 minutes) During these final minutes of class, the students should debate the divestiture decision. **Is divestiture the best solution?** To address this question, the students must look beyond the EVA numbers to consider the mission and strategy of the firm. The students should also be encouraged to think of stakeholders other than shareholders. **How will the company's customers fare if a division is spun off? What will happen to employees? suppliers? and the community at large?** While the students should be aware of all the strengths and uses of EVA, they should also be reminded that every measurement tool is flawed and must be used carefully and with a full understanding of its context and ramification.

11. *EVA as a Management Tool* (5 minutes) The technical note accompanying this case describes three specific uses for EVA, including: 1) goal setting and performance measurement, 2) capital budgeting and restructuring, and 3) incentive compensation. The class should be encouraged to identify and define each of these uses.

While much of the class will be spent debating these applications and comparing EVA to alternative control and measurement systems, it is important that the class focus at this point on the larger messages associated with EVA. One of the most important roles of the EVA tool is to act as a reminder that resources are costly and that firms can generate shareholder returns only when projects and investments generate a return in excess of the cost of capital. The take-away message of the class should be that to be effective firms must continually reinforce the shareholder value message.

THE REST OF THE STORY

The rest of the Ault story is a fascinating case study on hostile takeovers, white knights, and amazing stock price fluctuations. In brief, ...

Summer, 1996 – Saputo Group, a privately held dairy company based in Montreal, began quietly buying Ault shares. Saputo was, at the time, the Canadian market leader in the mozzarella cheese industry, and a significant player in the fluid milk market.

Fall, 1996 – The Ontario Teachers Pension Plan Fund sold its stake in Ault. Graham Freeman launched a reassessment of corporate holdings with an eye towards divesting some divisions.

January 2, 1997 – Ault management convinced its board of the value of divestiture and sold its ice cream division to Nestle Canada for $221 million. Ault communicated its decision to focus on the butter and cheese markets. Share values jumped from a low of approximately $15.00 to $19.00.

March 1, 1997 – Ault sold its fluid milk and yogurt businesses to Agropur, a Quebec competitor for $145 million. Stock price climbed to just over $20.00.

March 12, 1997 – With the proceeds of the sale of the milk and ice cream businesses, Ault repurchased 7.3 million shares at $24.50 each.

April, 1997 – Parmalat Finanziaria SpA (Parmalat) bought Beatrice Foods, Inc. for $290 million, ending the fluid milk price war that waged for years. Parmalat was an Italian food company specializing in dairy products, juices and soups. Annual revenues topped $4 billion U.S.

May 9, 1997 – Saputo launched an unsolicited bid for Ault shares, offering £28 a share. Freeman responded clearly, 'The company's not for sale'. Stock price jumps to $29.75 while analysts post estimates of a $36 buyout offer. Ault's board formally rejected the bid and begins looking for a white knight. Nearly 200 companies were contacted. Saputo complained loudly, pointing out that management repurchased shares on the open market for $24.50 less than a year before and then claimed that $28 per share was inadequate.

June, 1997 – Parmalat considered purchasing Ault and on June 9 bid $412 million or $34 per share. Stock values jumped to $34.30 per share. The board immediately backed Parmalat's friendly bid.

July, 1997 – Parmalat bought Ault Foods for $34 per share. Long-term plans involved a merger of Ault with Beatrice and an expansion of sales to the U.S. and South America. Ian Ferguson, formerly manager of Ault's cheese and butter division, was tapped to take on Parmalat's chief executive role.

Leveraging both Beatrice and Ault's markets, Canadian sales constituted fully one third of Parmalat's global sales in 1998.

TN-Exhibit 1

DIVISIONAL EVA PERFORMANCE CALCULATIONS
(All data in 000s)

1. Divisional Economic Book Value (EBV) Calculations – Operating Approach

	Fluid milk	Cultured	Ice cream	Industrial	International
ASSETS					
CURRENT ASSETS					
Operating cash	$1,045	$174	$364	$1,225	$136
Accounts receivable	12,568	2,095	4,380	14,737	1,637
Inventories	30,988	10,587	52,338	74,198	5,003
Prepaid expenses	4,932	1,822	2,718	6,782	2,642
Income and other taxes receivable	1,267	0	1,236	2,244	647
TOTAL CURRENT ASSETS	$50,800	$14,678	$61,036	$99,186	$10,065
Accounts payable	($46,977)	($7,831)	($16,372)	($55,084)	($6,118)
NET WORKING CAPITAL	$3,823	$6,847	$44,664	$44,102	$3,947
Investments and other	$43,896	$7,316	$15,297	$51,468	$5,719
Net property plant and equipment	88,656	14,776	30,895	103,950	11,551
Research and development (Current)	4,384	133	1,223	3,398	109
Acc. Research and development[1]	8,173	241	2,271	6,315	206
Acc. Goodwill amortization[2]	5,480	913	1,910	6,426	714
EBV capital	$154,412	$30,226	$96,260	$215,659	$22,246

[1] *Allocated on the basis of current R&D expenditure.*

[2] *Allocated on the basis of net property, plant and equipment.*

2. Divisional Net Operating Profit After Tax (NOPAT) Calculations – Operating Approach

	Fluid milk	Cultured	Ice cream	Industrial	International
Earnings before unusual items, interest and taxes	(£2,808)	($47)	$7,739	$22,570	$5,053
R&D addback	4,384	133	1,223	3,398	109
Less: R&D amortization	(3,805)	(115)	(1,062)	(2,950)	(95)
Goodwill amortization addback[3]	1,034	172	360	1,213	135
Corporate overhead addback[4]	6,033	1,005	2,102	7,073	786
Adjusted net operating profit	2,610	258	9,322	27,181	5,297
Cash operating taxes	0	0	1,897	7,832	1,222
Net operating profit after taxes	($1,195)	$143	$6,363	$16,399	$3,980

3. EVA Calculation

	Fluid milk	Cultured	Ice cream	Industrial	International
WACC	10%	10%	10%	10%	10%
EBV capital	$154,412	$30,226	$96,260	$215,659	$22,246
EVA NOPAT	($1,195)	$143	$6,363	$16,399	$3,980
WACC * EBV capital	$15,441	$3,022	$9,626	$21,566	$2,225
EVA	($16,636)	($2,879)	($3,263)	($5,167)	($1,755)

Source: Casewriter calculations.

---

[3] *Allocated on the basis of net property, plant and equipment.*
[4] *Allocated on the basis of sales.*

TN-Exhibit 2

DIVISIONAL PERFORMANCE MATRIX
(All data in 000s)

	Fluid milk	Cultured	Ice cream	Industrial	International
EVA value	($16,636)	($2,879)	($3,263)	($5,167)	($1,755)
Competitive environment	Extremely competitive; cost oriented.	Extremely competitive; cost pressure from private labels.	Extremely competitive; cost pressure from Unilever.	Competitive; cost pressure from private labels.	Competitive; cost pressure from private labels.
Competitive position and sales growth	Limited; need increased geographic market.	Limited without new franchised products.	Limited given Unilever competition.	Good.	Very good with continued international expansion.
Core competence (strengths)	Established distribution; large market share; premium product innovations.	Major brand names.	Major brand names.	Established brand names; R&D capability; innovative snack foods.	First mover advantage; R&D capability; innovative snack foods.
Threats and weaknesses	Increased distribution difficulty; continued price cutting.	Price wars initiated by private labels.	Unilever price war; new competitive offerings.	New competitor with R&D capability; NAFTA/GATT change.	International risk exposure.
Divestiture	Cannot realize efficiencies without acquisition – divest.	Cannot realize efficiencies without new franchise – divest.	Increasing competition; divest unless can focus heavily on this division.	Do not divest.	Do not divest.